ROUTLEDGE HANDBOOK OF THE ECONOMICS OF EUROPEAN INTEGRATION

Routledge Handbook of the Economics of European Integration provides readers with a brief but comprehensive overview of topics related to the process of European integration in the post-Second World War period. Its short chapters reflect the most up-to-date and concise research, written by a collective of experts on their own subjects.

The aim of the *Handbook* is twofold. First, the text illustrates the broad and diverse range of issues associated with European integration, and lastly, the key approaches and findings are summarised. Since institutional integration in Europe is an ongoing process, with possibly frequent and sometimes rapid changes, the chapters are intended to focus on the key features of the economic analyses of these topics.

A wide and diverse set of economic issues is of direct relevance for European integration. These topics cover various fields, ranging from the history of the European Economic and Monetary Union, EU Trade Policy and the stability of international trade, single market issues over fiscal, monetary and other policies, the crisis that faces the Euro area, and institutions such as the EU Council of Ministers. Not surprisingly, many of these issues have also been analysed from a European perspective.

The *Handbook* is designed to provide students, researchers, policy makers and the public with ready and accessible knowledge of issues related to European integration and will provide the definitive overview of research in the area.

Harald Badinger is Full Professor of International Economics, Vienna University of Economics and Business (WU Vienna), Austria.

Volker Nitsch is Full Professor of Economics and Chair of International Economics at the Department of Law and Economics, Darmstadt University of Technology, Germany.

ROUTLEDGE HANDBOOK OF THE ECONOMICS OF EUROPEAN INTEGRATION

Edited by Harald Badinger and Volker Nitsch

LONDON AND NEW YORK

First published 2016 by Routledge

2 Park Square, Milton Park, Abingdon, Oxfordshire OX14 4RN
52 Vanderbilt Avenue, New York, NY 10017

Routledge is an imprint of the Taylor & Francis Group, an informa business

First issued in paperback 2019

British Library Cataloguing in Publication Data
A catalogue record for this book is available from the British Library

Library of Congress Cataloging in Publication Data
Routledge handbook of the economics of European integration / edited by Harald Badinger and Volker Nitsch.
    pages cm
  1. European Union. 2. European Union countries—Economic integration—History. 3. European Union countries—Economic policy—History. 4. Monetary policy—European Union countries—History. 5. Financial services industry—European Union countries—History. I. Badinger, Harald, 1974- editor. II. Nitsch, Volker, editor. III. Title: Handbook of the economics of European integration.
  HC241.R68 2015
  337.1'42—dc23
  2015015193

ISBN: 978-0-415-74770-7 (hbk)
ISBN: 978-0-367-86948-9 (pbk)

Typeset in Bembo
by Keystroke, Station Road, Codsall, Wolverhampton

CONTENTS

List of figures   *ix*
List of tables   *xiii*
List of contributors   *xv*
Preface   *xix*

PART I
History   **1**

1   West European economic integration since 1950   3
    Nicholas Crafts

2   The history of European economic and monetary union   22
    Harold James

3   History of economic thought and policy-making at the European
    Commission   38
    Ivo Maes

PART II
The Single Market and the euro   **53**

4   The economics of the Single Market   55
    Harry Flam

5   Factor movements: FDI   70
    Bent E. Sørensen and Carolina Villegas-Sanchez

6 The euro as an international currency   82
   Agnès Bénassy-Quéré

PART III
Monetary and fiscal policy   **101**

7 The common currency: More complicated than it seems   103
   Charles Wyplosz

8 Design failures in the Euro Area: Can they be fixed?   119
   Paul De Grauwe

9 The credit channel of monetary policy in the Euro Area   132
   Angela Maddaloni and José-Luis Peydró

10 Fiscal policy in the EU: An overview of recent and potential future
    developments   143
    Roel Beetsma

11 The roles of fiscal rules, fiscal councils and fiscal union in EU
    integration   157
    Lars Calmfors

PART IV
Trade issues   **171**

12 European integration and the gains from trade   173
    Gianmarco I.P. Ottaviano

13 The effects of European integration on the stability of international
    trade: A duration perspective   188
    Tibor Besedeš

14 EU trade policy   205
    André Sapir

15 The EU and the US: TTIP   220
    Gabriel Felbermayr

16 The EU and the ACP countries   238
    Ludger Kühnhardt

Contents

PART V

Selected policy areas   **253**

17 Regional policy   255
    Sascha O. Becker, Peter H. Egger and Maximilian von Ehrlich

18 The common agricultural policy   269
    Johan Swinnen

19 Labor and social policy   284
    Giuseppe Bertola

20 Tax competition and tax coordination   295
    Christian Keuschnigg, Simon Loretz and Hannes Winner

21 Financial market integration, regulation and stability   312
    Angel Ubide

PART VI

The crisis   **329**

22 The crisis in retrospect: Causes, effects and policy responses   331
    Fritz Breuss

23 Exceptional policies for exceptional times: The ECB's response to
    the rolling crises of the euro area   351
    Lucrezia Reichlin and Huw Pill

24 Living (dangerously) without a fiscal union   376
    Ashoka Mody

25 Reforming the architecture of EMU: Ensuring stability in Europe   408
    Jakob de Haan, Jeroen Hessel and Niels Gilbert

PART VII

Institutions   **433**

26 The political economy of European integration   435
    Enrico Spolaore

27 Efficiency, proportionality and member states' power in the EU
    Council of Ministers   449
    Nikolaos Antonakakis, Harald Badinger and Wolf Heinrich Reuter

28 Measuring European economic and institutional integration   467
    Helge Berger and Volker Nitsch

29 The dynamics of European economic integration: A legal
    perspective   478
    Erich Vranes

Index   *497*

FIGURES

2.1	Current accounts in Europe 1960–2010	26
4.1	Welfare effects of customs union	57
4.2	Welfare effects of reduction in trade costs	59
4.3	Welfare effects of eliminating quotas	60
4.4	Scale effects of integration	62
4.5	Welfare effects of factor mobility	64
5.1	FDI inflows in EU 27	74
5.2	Main recipients of intra-EU FDI inflows	75
5.3	Main recipients of FDI inflows	76
5.4	EU-27 share of FDI inflows in gross fixed capital formation	76
5.5	GIIPS share of FDI inflows in gross fixed capital formation	77
6.1	Gross cross-border assets and liabilities (excluding own currency area, in USD bn)	84
6.2	Direct and indirect foreign exchange	86
7.1	Budget balances (% of GDP)	107
7.2	Employment rates (% of total population)	109
7.3	Ratio emigrants/immigrants	110
7.4	Trade concentration index (2007)	111
8.1	Inflation and labor costs, 2002–2008	122
8.2	Euro area current accounts	123
8.3	Spreads 10-year government bond rates Eurozone	125
8.4	Relative unit labor costs Eurozone: Debtor nations	126
8.5	Relative unit labor costs Eurozone: Creditor nations	127
9.1	Monetary policy and the credit channel	133
9.2	Lending standards in the euro area, Germany and Italy	136
10.1	Interaction between national and EU level	148
10.2	The European semester	149
12.1	Gains from trade for selected EU countries	182
12.2	Welfare losses from US protectionism for selected EU countries	183
13.1	EU upgrades	196
13.2	The effect of the age of the EU	197

13.3	The first EU expansion	198
13.4	The 1986 expansion with a pre-accession agreement with the EU	198
13.5	Effect of all four expansions	200
14.1	Pyramid of EU trade preferences, as of January 2015 (WTO members only)	214
15.1	Shares of EU and US in world GDP: The past, the present, and the future	221
15.2	EU goods trade with the US over time, volume in bn. current dollars	222
15.3	Shares of EU Member States in EU exports and imports (goods and services) to and from US, 2012, %	223
15.4	Shares of sectors in EU trade with US, 2012, %	224
15.5	Import tariffs, applied MFN, trade weighted, 2007	226
15.6	Bottom-up estimates of non-tariff measures, tariff equivalents	227
17.1	Objective 1 treatment and the 75% threshold	260
17.2	Effectiveness of Objective 1 transfers and human capital	262
17.3	Effectiveness of Objective 1 and human capital	262
17.4	Effectiveness of Objective 1 and quality of government	263
17.5	Dose-response function and treatment function	265
18.1	Government support to agriculture (NRA) in the EU	272
18.2	Agricultural exports and imports of the EU as percent of the world market	273
18.3	CAP budget expenditures (1980–2012)	274
18.4	Direct payments in the EU Member States in 2011 (€/ha)	275
19.1	Social expenditure and income levels in the EU15, 2000	286
19.2	Employment protection and unemployment insurance in the EU15, 1995–2003	287
19.3	Inequality and employment in the EU15, 2000	290
21.1	Stock market capitalization and debt securities (in percent of GDP)	314
21.2	Ten year rates (in percent)	318
21.3	Standard deviation of banks CDS premia (in basis points)	319
21.4	Interest rates on new loans to euro area corporations (in percent)	320
22.1	The evolution of the global financial and economic crises	332
22.2	GDP and world trade during and after the "Great Recession 2009" (real GDP and world trade volume of goods and services; % changes)	333
22.3	Misperception of sovereign default risks in the Euro area (Government bond yields, 10 years, in %)	335
22.4	The "Euro crisis" consisting of multiple crises in the Euro area (vicious circle of debt, macroeconomic imbalances, and banking crises)	336
22.5	Public debts in the Euro area periphery (gross public debt in % of GDP)	337
22.6	New economic governance of EMU since 2010 ("EU economic government")	343
23.1	Spread between secured and unsecured money market rates	354
23.2	Collateral pledged at ECB monetary policy operations	356
23.3	ECB balance sheet	357
23.4	ECB policy rates and EONIA	358
23.5	Euro area real GDP growth and ECB staff forecast of real GDP growth	359
23.6	Euro area HICP inflation and ECB staff forecast of inflation	359
23.7	Bank credit default swaps	361
23.8	Sovereign spreads over 10-year German Bund yields	364
23.9	Warehousing peripheral sovereign debt on official balance sheets	365
23.10	Fragmentation of euro financial markets	366

23.11	TARGET 2 balances	368
23.12	Industrial production and bank loans to non-financial corporations	369
23.13	M3 and bank loans	369
23.14	10-year government bond yields	373
24.1	Fiscal consolidation (annual change in structural balance, % of potential GDP)	377
24.2	Trends in public debt ratios (government gross debt, % of GDP)	378
24.3	Intra-European trade (percentage of country's trade within the European Union, 2013)	379
24.4	Changes in the coefficient on the public debt-to-GDP ratio	383
24.5	Public debt ratio and primary surplus (correlation between debt ratio and surplus, conditional on output gap, 2009–2013)	384
24.6	The changing growth outlook (percentage annual GDP growth, actual outcomes and predictions for different vintages)	386
24.7	Actual consolidation and unexpected growth (2011–2013)	388
24.8	Evolution of debt-to-GDP outlook	389
24.9	Household debt-to-income ratio	390
24.10a–b	Euro area and United States changes in household debt-to-disposable incomes, 2008–2012 (percentage change, 2012 over 2008)	391
24.11	Ireland official credits and risk premia on sovereign bonds	398
24.12	Debt-deflation dynamics: the relationship between unexpected changes in the debt-to-GDP ratio and unexpected changes in inflation	403
25.1	10-year government bond spreads against German bonds	410
25.2	Weighted average Euro-12 budget deficit, plans vs outcome (% of GDP)	412
25.3	Business cycle fluctuations euro area highly synchronized	413
25.4	Financial cycle fluctuations within the euro area highly asymmetric	414
25.5	Net capital flows within the euro area, percentage of GDP	419
27.1	The EU Council of Ministers: efficiency (%) and proportionality (%), 1958–2020	458

TABLES

1.1	A chronology of economic integration of markets	5
1.2	Trade costs	6
1.3	Volume of exports in 2000 (1960 = 100)	7
1.4	Trade effects of European trade agreements (% per year)	9
1.5	Post-accession differences between level of actual and synthetic GDP per person (%)	12
1.6	Unconditional convergence regression Western European regions	12
1.7	Geography and real GDP per person regressions	13
1.8	Balance of payments and static welfare effects of UK entry into EEC: 1970s and 1980s estimates (% GDP)	15
1.9	Modern Ex-Ante estimates of the static welfare effects of UK exit from the EU (% GDP)	17
5.1	Average percent share of FDI stock by source region comparison of OECD/BvD Direct/BvD ultimate FDI data by country	78
6.1	Roles of an international currency	83
6.2	International currencies at end 2013 (market shares in %)	83
6.3	The comparative size of the euro area as of end 2014	90
9.1	The impact of a monetary policy shock through the demand, bank lending and borrower's balance sheet channels	137
12.1	Correlation of welfare losses from a worldwide tariff increase for 20 European countries	184
12.2	The impact of 'Brexit' on UK welfare	185
13.1	Hazard estimates	192
13.2	Average estimated effects on the hazard	193
13.3	Entry estimates	201
14.1	Main trading countries, 1958–2013 (as per cent of world trade)	206
14.2	Product composition of EU trade, 2012 (as per cent of extra-EU27 trade of goods and services)	207
14.3	Main destinations and origins of EU trade, 1958–2012 (as per cent of total extra-EU trade)	207
14.4	Selected trade policy measures by the main trading countries, latest date available	210

15.1	Bilateral trade relative to total trade and GDP	222
15.2	Comparison of welfare effects across studies (comprehensive scenarios)	232
15.3	Welfare effects: selected countries and scenarios	232
17.1	Program periods	257
17.2	Objectives by period	257
17.3	Funds by period	258
17.4	EU funding received across EU regions	264
20.1	VAT rates in EU Member States	298
20.2	Status quo and recent development of direct taxation in EU Member States	301
21.1	A comparison of financial market indicators	313
21.2	Change in cross-border bank holdings during the crisis	316
22.1	Macroeconomic imbalances in the Euro area	338
22.2	The Great Recession of 2009 and its overcoming in Europe and selected countries (real GDP, % change)	340
22.3	Euro area rescue measures, 2010–2013	344
23.1	Timeline of events – Phase 1: The banking crisis	355
23.2	Timeline of events – Phase 2: The sovereign crisis	363
23.3	Timeline of events – Phase 3: The beginning of a new framework?	370
24.1	The intensity of fiscal austerity: eurozone and non-eurozone advanced economies	382
25.1	Budgetary starting situation in 2007 (% GDP)	412
25.2	Verdict EMU-variants	424
27.1	Voting rules in the EU Council of Ministers, 1958–2017 (and beyond)	453
27.2	Evolution of EU Member States' power from 1958–2017, normalized Banzhaf Index (in %)	455
27.3	The EU Council of Ministers: efficiency and proportionality, 1958–2017	457
27.4	Enforcement mechanisms under the revised stability and growth pact	459
27.5	Increasingly complex decision-making	460
27.6	Thresholds and total votes under different QMV regimes	462
27.7	Efficiency and proportionality under different QMV regimes	463
A1	Voting weights under qualified majority voting, 1958–2014	465
28.1	A classification of integration measures	470

CONTRIBUTORS

Nikolaos Antonakakis is Assistant Professor at the Vienna University of Economics and Business (WU Vienna) and Senior Lecturer at the University of Portsmouth.

Harald Badinger is Professor of International Economics at the Vienna University of Economics and Business (WU Vienna).

Sascha O. Becker is Professor of Economics and Deputy Director of the Centre for Competitive Advantage in the Global Economy (CAGE) at the University of Warwick.

Roel Beetsma is MN Professor of Pension Economics at the University of Amsterdam.

Agnès Bénassy-Quéré is a Professor at Paris School of Economics – University of Paris 1 Panthéon Sorbonne and Chairwoman of the French Council of Economic Analysis.

Helge Berger is an Advisor in the International Monetary Fund's European Department and Adjunct Professor of Monetary Economics at Free University Berlin.

Giuseppe Bertola is Professor of Economics at EDHEC Business School, on extended leave as Professore Ordinario, Università di Torino.

Tibor Besedeš is an Associate Professor in the School of Economics at Georgia Institute of Technology.

Fritz Breuss is Jean Monnet Professor and Professor Emeritus at the Vienna University of Economics and Business (WU Vienna).

Lars Calmfors is Professor of International Economics at the Institute for International Economic Studies at Stockholm University, Research Fellow at the Research Institute of Industrial Economics in Stockholm, and Chair of the Swedish Labour Economics Council.

Nicholas Crafts is Professor of Economics and Economic History and Director of the Centre for Competitive Advantage in the Global Economy (CAGE) at the University of Warwick.

Peter H. Egger is Professor of Economics and Head of Division at KOF Swiss Economic Institute at ETH Zürich.

Gabriel Felbermayr is Professor of Economics and Director of the Ifo Center for International Economics at the University of Munich.

Harry Flam is Professor of International Economics at the Institute for International Economic Studies at Stockholm University.

Niels Gilbert is an Economist at De Nederlandsche Bank.

Paul De Grauwe is John Paulson Professor in European Political Economy at the London School of Economics and Political Science as head of the European Institute and Professor Emeritus in International Economics at KU Leuven.

Jakob de Haan is Head of Research of De Nederlandsche Bank and Professor of Political Economy at the University of Groningen.

Jeroen Hessel is a Senior Economist at De Nederlandsche Bank.

Harold James is Professor of History and International Affairs at Princeton University, and Marie Curie Professor at the European University Institute.

Christian Keuschnigg is Professor of Public Economics at the University of St. Gallen.

Ludger Kühnhardt is a Director at the Center for European Integration Studies (ZEI) and professor of Political Science at the University of Bonn.

Simon Loretz is Post-doc Researcher at the Institute for Advanced Studies (IHS) Vienna.

Angela Maddaloni is Adviser in the Research Department of the European Central Bank.

Ivo Maes is Senior Advisor at National Bank of Belgium and a Professor, Robert Triffin Chair, at the Institut d'études européennes of the Université catholique de Louvain.

Ashoka Mody is the Charles and Marie Robertson Visiting Professor in International Economic Policy at Princeton University.

Volker Nitsch is Professor of Economics at Technische Universität Darmstadt.

Gianmarco I.P. Ottaviano is Professor of Economics at the London School of Economics and Political Science and at the University of Bologna.

José-Luis Peydró is Research Professor at the Catalan Institution for Research and Advanced Studies (ICREA) and a Professor of Finance and Economics at Universitat Pompeu Fabra.

Huw Pill is the chief European economist at Goldman Sachs.

Lucrezia Reichlin is Professor of Economics at London Business School and Research Director at the Centre for Economic Policy Research.

Wolf Heinrich Reuter is Assistant Professor at the Vienna University of Economics and Business (WU Vienna) and the Portsmouth Business School.

André Sapir is Professor of Economics at Université Libre de Bruxelles (ULB) and a Senior Fellow at Bruegel.

Bent E. Sørensen is Lay Professor of Economics at the University of Houston.

Enrico Spolaore is Professor of Economics at Tufts University.

Johan Swinnen is Professor of Economics and Director of the LICOS Centre for Institutions and Economic Performance at the University of Leuven (KUL).

Angel Ubide is Senior Fellow at the Peterson Institute for International Economics.

Carolina Villegas-Sanchez is an Assistant Professor in the Department of Economics at ESADE Business School.

Maximilian von Ehrlich is Professor of Public Economics at the University of Bern.

Erich Vranes is Professor of Law at the Vienna University of Economics and Business (WU Vienna).

Hannes Winner is Professor of Economics at the University of Salzburg.

Charles Wyplosz is Professor of International Economics at the Graduate Institute and Director of the International Center of Monetary and Banking Studies.

PREFACE

The economic analysis of the process of European integration has received growing attention in recent years and seems increasingly to have become a separate field in economics, with its own courses, textbooks, symposia, conferences and even journals. For economists, the topic offers, in our view, at least two attractive features. First, the range of issues is extremely broad. Economic aspects of European integration are related to and touch upon many different strands of the literature, from international trade and finance to public economics, from economic geography to industrial economics. Second, the analysis is typically very applied. Often real-world issues are examined, and research findings can be expected to have a direct impact on policies. In recent years, however, also a major disadvantage of the topic has emerged. As the political and economic environment in Europe has become highly dynamic, with policies and institutions being frequently adjusted, many analyses and results turned out to be rather short-lived.

The *Handbook*, which presents an overview of economic research related to the process of European integration in the post-Second World War period, aims to reflect these key features of the field. Facing a trade-off between coherence and diversity, we opted for the latter. As a result, the chapters cover a broad range of issues and apply different styles and techniques. While some chapters summarize a broader literature, others are more specialized, sometimes even dealing with a very specific issue. Also, we hope that the articles are of interest and value for a broad audience. Designed to provide students, the public and policy-makers with ready and accessible up-to-date knowledge of issues related to European integration, the chapters often discuss topics highly relevant for policy-making. For instance, a full section of the *Handbook* is devoted to the latest economic and financial crisis. The chapters are also typically easily accessible to non-specialists. Finally, we put strong emphasis on timeliness at the cost of a selective and therefore not fully comprehensive coverage of the field.

At times of great demand for economic expertise, we are extremely grateful to all authors for their contributions to this *Handbook*. We also wish to thank our publisher Routledge for the efficient and professional handling of the manuscript. We hope the *Handbook* finds the large readership that we believe it deserves.

PART I

History

1

WEST EUROPEAN ECONOMIC INTEGRATION SINCE 1950

Nicholas Crafts

1. Introduction

At the end of the Second World War, it is unlikely that anybody envisaged the extent of European economic integration over the next seventy years. The interwar period was notorious for a backlash against globalization that entailed competitive devaluations, rampant protectionism together with international rivalries that precluded effective economic cooperation. By 2014, the European Union (EU) comprised 28 countries with a combined population of about 500 million people, of which 18 shared a single currency.

This raises a number of obvious questions which this chapter addresses. These include examining the chronology of economic integration and reviewing which countries participated and what the reasons were for their different decisions. Beyond explaining how European economic integration came about, it is also important to explore what were its economic effects both on the growth of international trade and also to evaluate its implications for levels and rates of growth of incomes.

Making such assessments is, of course, difficult. It requires prediction of the counterfactual, i.e., what would have happened in the absence of integration. The economic models and econometric techniques employed to carry out this analysis today are rather different from those which were commonly used at the time. For example, as we shall see, a modern approach to measuring the costs and benefits of EU membership for the United Kingdom is very different from the methods of the 1970s when the economic implications of the UK's accession to the European Economic Community (EEC) were hotly debated by British economists. The important developments in economics include thinking in terms of endogenous growth and gains from trade that go beyond welfare triangles while better procedures to address issues arising from endogenous variables and greater sophistication in the use of gravity models are notable advances in applied econometrics.

The chapter proceeds as follows. In section 2, a brief history of the contours of post-war European economic integration is provided while section 3 looks at the related issues of the implications for trade costs and trade volumes and the reasons for the evolution of the membership of the EU. Section 4 investigates the effects on income levels and growth rates while in section 5 the history of the debate over the UK membership of the EU is reviewed. Section 6 concludes.

2. Economic integration since 1950

The idea of European integration was, of course, not new at the end of the Second World War. The nineteenth century saw important steps towards reductions of policy barriers to trade with the unification of Germany and Italy and a proliferation of commercial treaties (Pahre, 2008). In the interwar period, in the context of the tensions resulting from the First World War and its peace settlement, there was considerable interest in greater political integration of Europe which had its most notable manifestation in the Briand Plan for a 'United States of Europe' put forward by the French government in May 1930 with a view to managing the 'German problem' (Weigall and Stirk, 1992) but which was quickly overwhelmed by events.

A successful approach to European economic integration after the Second World War had to return to the question of how to manage the relationship between (West) Germany and the rest of Western Europe to obtain the benefits of economic cooperation and, linked to this, also to find a politically acceptable form of trade liberalization. The approach that developed was pragmatic and recognized the continuing central role of the nation state, regulation of trade in key areas like agriculture and the pursuit of industrial policies (Milward, 1992). The design of the European Coal and Steel Community which became operational in 1952 provided an institutional blueprint which could be adapted for wider use. American support for integration as a bulwark against the spread of communism was made concrete through the provisions of the Marshall Plan (Crafts, 2013).

Against this background, this section provides a brief descriptive outline of the process of post-war European economic integration. As Sapir (2011) has reminded us, this can usefully be approached using the ideas of Balassa (1961). Balassa distinguished between different degrees of increasingly deep economic integration working up from free trade area to customs union, in which there is also pooling of sovereignty in a common external trade policy, to common market, within which factors of production can move freely, to economic union, in which some economic policies are harmonized, to complete economic integration, where there is political union with a supra-national authority. The last might be thought of as a 'United States of Europe'. A list of key dates is provided in Table 1.1.

The Organization for European Economic Cooperation (OEEC) which was established in April 1948 provided 'conditional aid' of about $1.5 billion to back an intra-Western European multilateral payments agreement: in 1950 recipients of aid under the Marshall Plan were required to become members of the European Payments Union (EPU). The EPU was a mechanism that addressed the problem of the absence of multilateral trade settlements in a world of inconvertible currencies and dollar shortage. In such circumstances, the volume of trade between each pair of countries is constrained to the lower of the amount of imports and exports because a surplus with one country cannot be used to offset a deficit with another. The EPU provided a multilateral clearing system supplemented by a credit line for countries temporarily in overall deficit. This was facilitated by the United States through conditional Marshall Aid acting as the main 'structural creditor' to address the difficulty that would otherwise have arisen from the prospect that some countries were likely to be persistent debtors.[1]

In 1958 the EEC was formed by the original six countries following the signing of the Treaty of Rome in 1957. The signatories pledged to lay the foundations of 'ever closer union' among the peoples of Europe and Article 2 committed members to form a customs union, to establish a common market and to harmonize policies. Article 3 spelt out what this would comprise including a common external tariff, a common agricultural policy, the abolition of barriers to trade and of obstacles to freedom of movement of capital and labour,

Table 1.1 A chronology of economic integration of markets

1950	European Payments Union starts
1952	European Coal and Steel Community established
1958	European Economic Community starts with 6 members (Belgium, France, Italy, Luxembourg, Netherlands, West Germany)
1958	European Payments Union discontinued
1960	European Free Trade Association starts with 7 members (Austria, Denmark, Norway, Portugal, Sweden, Switzerland and the UK)
1962	Common Agricultural Policy begins
1968	EEC Customs Union completed and Common External Tariff established
1970	Iceland joins EFTA
1972	EEC-EFTA free trade agreements signed
1973	1st Enlargement: Denmark, Ireland and UK join EEC; Denmark and UK leave EFTA
1981	2nd Enlargement: Greece joins EEC
1986	3rd Enlargement: Portugal and Spain join EEC; Portugal leaves EFTA; Finland joins EFTA
1987	Single European Act comes into effect
1990	German unification: former East German lands join EEC
1991	Liechtenstein joins EFTA
1992	EEC and EFTA establish European Economic Area
1993	Maastricht Treaty establishing European Union comes into effect
1995	4th Enlargement: Austria, Finland and Sweden join EU and leave EFTA
1999	Eurozone established with 11 member countries (Austria, Belgium, Finland, France, Germany, Ireland, Italy, Luxembourg, Netherlands, Portugal, Spain)
2001	Greece joins Eurozone
2004	5th Enlargement: 10 countries join EU (Czech Republic, Cyprus, Estonia, Hungary, Latvia, Lithuania, Malta, Poland, Slovakia, Slovenia)
2007	6th Enlargement: Bulgaria and Romania join EU
2007	Slovenia joins Eurozone
2008	Cyprus and Malta join Eurozone
2009	Slovakia joins Eurozone
2011	Estonia joins Eurozone
2013	7th Enlargement: Croatia joins EU as 28th member
2014	Latvia joins Eurozone
2015	Lithuania joins Eurozone as 19th member

a competition policy regime, and the coordination of policies to avoid balance of payments disequilibria. In contrast, the European Free Trade Association (EFTA) was set up in 1960 with the much more limited aim of establishing a free trade area. The EEC customs union was achieved in 1968 but the common market took much longer and awaited the Single European Act which addressed non-tariff barriers to trade, liberalized trade in services and ended capital controls and was (less than fully) implemented from 1992. The Maastricht Treaty of 1992 was a significant step towards economic union and paved the way to a single currency which further reduced trade costs as well as eliminating exchange rate instability; the euro started in 1999, initially with 11 countries. Complete economic integration is still out of reach.

Over time, the membership of the EEC/EU expanded considerably through successive enlargements while that of EFTA has shrunk with defections to the EEC/EU. In 1973, the

UK and two of its close trading partners Denmark and Ireland joined the EU. In the 1980s, the newly democratic Greece, Portugal and Spain acceded and in 1995, following the establishment of the European Single Market, Austria, Finland and Sweden left EFTA to join the EU. In 2004, eight former communist-bloc transition economies joined the EU together with Cyprus and Malta followed by further transition economies' accessions by Bulgaria and Romania in 2007 and Croatia in 2013 while a number of these new members were admitted into the Eurozone soon after accession. These southern and eastern enlargements of the EU, especially the latter, considerably increased the range of income levels within the EU.

3. Implications for trade

European economic integration has had significant impacts on the extent and direction of international trade. As these implications became apparent, this information influenced non-members' perceptions of the costs and benefits of membership of EFTA versus the EEC/EU. The integration process involved reductions in trade costs and, of course, this was conducive to increasing the volume of trade. However, regional trade agreements by their very nature discriminate between members and outsiders rather than applying most-favoured-nation principles to trade liberalization. The EEC and EFTA were acceptable under Article XXIV of the GATT but involved both trade creation and trade diversion as barriers to trade were unevenly reduced. In other words, while in most cases economic efficiency was increased through the replacement of higher-cost by lower-cost producers, there would be some instances where the opposite was true. This also implies the possibility that there were external losers as well as internal winners and that the overall economic outcome was a net sum of gains partly offset by losses.

Table 1.2 reports estimates of reductions in trade costs obtained using a gravity model.[2] Trade costs inferred in this way are a composite of all barriers to trade and therefore include the impact of transport costs as well as policy measures. However, the major influence in these decades, and certainly the major difference between these pairs of countries, accrued from

Table 1.2 Trade costs

	Germany-France	Germany-Italy	Spain-France	UK-France	UK-Italy	UK-Norway
1929	0.99	1.10	1.18	1.00	1.22	0.87
1938	1.33	1.12	2.26	1.21	1.54	0.98
1950	1.12	1.27	1.55	1.22	1.36	0.98
1960	0.91	1.01	1.52	1.22	1.25	0.91
1970	0.73	0.79	1.24	1.10	1.21	0.90
1980	0.55	0.61	0.89	0.74	0.86	0.69
1990	0.53	0.56	0.74	0.70	0.84	0.77
2000	0.61	0.66	0.70	0.75	0.90	0.88

Source: Data underlying Jacks et al. (2011) generously provided by Dennis Novy.

Note: Trade costs are inferred using a gravity model and comprise both policy and non-policy barriers to trade; 1929–38 estimates are not strictly comparable with those for 1950–2000; estimates that include Spain are for 1939 not 1938.

Table 1.3 Volume of exports in 2000 (1960 = 100)

	Intra-EU15	Extra-EU15	Total
Austria	1395.6	1273.8	1346.3
Belgium–Luxembourg	1209.4	857.6	1088.3
Denmark	632.8	728.2	665.0
Finland	962.9	1268.2	1079.2
France	1766.1	843.1	1230.5
Germany	1002.2	874.7	942.1
Greece	1586.6	1946.3	1792.5
Ireland	3769.2	12587.6	5356.2
Italy	1820.2	1265.6	1520.0
Netherlands	1585.1	961.7	1389.2
Portugal	1043.2	197.4	555.1
Spain	2690.2	2009.2	2429.7
Sweden	811.2	1142.7	939.2
UK	1099.5	442.1	636.8
EU 15	1320.8	834.2	1075.6
World Trade			987.5

Sources: Badinger and Breuss (2004) and, for world trade, WTO website.

the pace of trade liberalization as the protectionism of the interwar period was reversed. Overall, the picture is one of large reductions in trade costs to levels which were much lower than in 1929. It is also very striking that these reductions start sooner among the original six EEC members, were delayed for UK and Spain, and were quite modest for pairs of EFTA countries pre-1970, as Table 1.2 illustrates. Obviously, not all trade liberalization was under the auspices of the regional trade agreements, as is epitomized by the important Spanish reforms of 1959 (Prados de la Escosura *et al.*, 2010). Finally, it is worth noting that on these estimates trade costs stopped falling during the late 1980s.

The volume of international trade increased very substantially between 1960 and 2000, as is shown in Table 1.3. Overall, the trade of EU15 countries grew faster than world trade and also trade between these countries grew faster than their trade with the rest of the world, although this was not true for all 15 countries where Ireland notably stands out as an exception to this generalization. This raises the question of how far the various components of European economic integration contributed to these trade patterns compared with other factors such as income growth or convergence in income levels.

The most widely-used approach to answering questions of this kind is to rely on some version of a gravity model of trade. As has become well-known, there are a number of serious econometric pitfalls which can lead to seriously biased results from such studies and which were prevalent in papers written before the mid-2000s. In what follows, results are reported from what I think are the most convincing papers available but necessarily some of these are of a relatively old vintage and may perhaps need to be treated with a degree of caution.

An analysis of the data in Table 1.3 using panel estimation of a gravity model by Badinger and Breuss (2004) found that by far the largest reason for the growth of intra-EU trade between 1960 and 2000 was income growth which accounted for about 70 per cent while reduction of tariff barriers accounted for 19 to 26 per cent depending on the specification.

Since trade increased massively overall, this means that the tariff reductions had a major impact. The results appear somewhat different from those in Baier *et al.* (2008) who found that EU membership raises trade between two countries by an average of 100 to 125 per cent after 15 years or an average of 4.8 to 5.6 per cent per year; this implies that the reduction in trade barriers accounted for about 50 to 55 per cent of total intra-EU trade growth.[3] This suggests that EU membership reduces trade costs by more than is captured by tariff reductions per se. Similarly, Baier *et al.* (2008) compare EU membership with being in either EFTA or the European Economic Area (EEA) and find that its effects were considerably larger. The EEA effect is only about 1/5th that of the EU while the EFTA effect is similar to the EEA effect but less robust since in some specifications it is approximately zero.

The first step towards greater integration of European trade was the establishment in 1950 of the European Payments Union (EPU). The design for European trading arrangements was negotiated, notably with regard to British and French concerns, rather than imposed and the EPU did not match the original American plans for a free-trade customs union and early current-account convertibility (Milward, 1984). Nevertheless, the EPU represented an important success as a mechanism for restoring West Germany to its central role in the European economy (Berger and Ritschl, 1995) and for promoting trade growth. The EPU was a second-best way of reviving European trade and multilateral settlements compared with full current-account convertibility but it speeded up the process by solving a coordination problem. It lasted until 1958 by which time intra-European trade was 2.3 times that of 1950 and a gravity-model analysis confirms that the EPU had a large positive effect on trade levels, especially in the early 1950s when it is estimated to have raised intra-EPU exports by about 30 per cent compared with only about 10 per cent in 1958 (Eichengreen, 1993). As might be expected, the EPU increased trade relatively strongly (about 2 or 3 times more) within its boundaries but its effects on trade between EPU and non-EPU countries were nevertheless positive.

Analyses have also been undertaken for further steps along the path of European integration, notably by Bayoumi and Eichengreen (1995) whose results are summarized in Table 1.4. They worked with a gravity equation specified in terms of first differences and they found that each of the episodes which they examined entailed trade creation and trade diversion but that the former typically was the larger effect and quite sizeable. The question of the relative size of trade creation and trade diversion was intensively studied for the early years of the EC6 through a variety of different methods which came to a consensus that trade creation was much bigger with an average estimate of about 20 per cent of EC imports compared with 3.8 per cent of extra-EC exports.[4] Much the same story comes from a long view with an explicit time-varying econometric specification provided by Straathof *et al.* (2008). They find that trade diversion was very small, that EFTA had much smaller (and possibly insignificant) effects on trade, and that trade creation rose appreciably after enlargements and with the Single Market.

Sapir (2001) extended these analyses by considering EC-EFTA trade relationships in more detail. He found that both intra-EFTA and intra-EC trade were boosted initially by fairly similar amounts relative to non-preferential trade. However, by the years 1989–92 intra-EFTA trade was estimated to be 1.6 to 1.7 times smaller than intra-EC trade and EC-EFTA trade 1.4 to 1.5 times smaller than intra-EC trade so that the advent of the Single Market appears to have increased trade diversion to the detriment of EFTA members. At the same time, five EFTA countries applied for EC membership and Sapir (2001) suggested that this reflected a further 'domino effect', as hypothesized by Baldwin (1993).[5] The domino hypothesis is that whereas initial decisions to participate in trade agreements are often motivated by political

Table 1.4 Trade effects of European trade agreements (% per year)

	Intra Trade			*Extra Trade*
1956–73				
EC6	+3.2★★		EC6–EFTA7	−1.5★
EFTA7	+2.3★★		EC6–other OECD	−1.7★
			EFTA–other OECD	
1972–80				
New EC–EC6	+5.9★★		New EC–EFTA5	−1.2
			New EC–other OECD	+2.6★★
			UK–Commonwealth	−6.7★
1975–92				
Greece–EC9	+2.0★★		Greece–other OECD	−1.7
Portugal/Spain–EC10	+2.9★★		Portugal/Spain–other OECD	−0.4

Source: Bayoumi and Eichengreen (1995).

Note: ★ = significant at 5%, ★★ = significant at 1%.

considerations, as was the case with the EC6 spurred on by the aim of securing the peace and, notably, with the UK's refusal to sign the Treaty of Rome prompted by issues of relationships with the Commonwealth and the United States, subsequent pressures to join emerge from the trade diversionary effects. The first domino effect was that the UK quickly changed its mind and its application was followed by countries for which the UK was a main trading partner, namely, Denmark and Ireland.

The final step in the reduction of Western European trade costs came with European Monetary Union (EMU). This is a classic case where more sophisticated estimation procedures have made a huge difference. The currency union effect on trade volumes was initially thought to be very large but better econometrics and the opportunity to examine the actual impact of EMU led to estimates that trade volumes increased by only about 2 per cent (Baldwin *et al.*, 2008) or possibly no effect at all (Berger and Nitsch, 2008; Straathof *et al.*, 2008).

4. Implications for income levels and growth rates

Economic theory suggests various ways in which economic integration might increase prosperity including both static and dynamic effects. Over time, the range of possibilities that theory allows has increased considerably although most, if not all, of these were understood informally even in the early days. The economic historian might also want to distinguish between impacts that were only achieved through the formation of the European Economic Community (or indeed EFTA) and those which would have accrued through alternative routes to integration (Boltho and Eichengreen, 2008).

In terms of short-run static effects, trade liberalization can improve allocative efficiency and/or productive efficiency, i.e., given existing costs, factors of production are deployed more efficiently or production costs are lowered. The former might result from greater specialization along lines of comparative advantage and the latter from a new found ability to realize economies of scale. Insofar as freer trade increases competition in product markets (through actual or potential entry), it may have both effects as market power is reduced and price-cost margins fall while managers of firms are pressured to reduce costs to the minimum feasible (principal agent problems are reduced). If trade integration increases the number of varieties that are available to consumers this may also be a source of welfare gains.

With a medium-term perspective, the capital stock adjusts to a higher level of productivity or perhaps a reduction in the price of capital goods and a further increase in the level of output can be expected. Furthermore, as barriers to capital mobility are reduced, relocation of economic activity may be a consequence, possibly based on matching industrial and regional characteristics on a factor endowments basis (Heckscher-Ohlin) or possibly based on market access considerations (New Economic Geography). Writers in the latter tradition envisage a strong possibility that the process of relocation can lead to divergence of income levels with some regions being disadvantaged, as in core-periphery models.

In terms of long-run dynamic effects, according to endogenous growth models, it is possible that the growth rate will rise as a result of economic integration. In a basic AK model if investment (or more generally the rate of growth of the capital stock) responds positively there is no tendency for diminishing returns to erode this initial effect so there is a 'permanent' impact on growth. Perhaps more plausibly, if a larger market and/or more competition in product markets ensues from economic integration this may raise the rate of innovation and total factor productivity (TFP) growth.

The simplest approach to measuring increases in (equivalent) income from European economic integration is to calculate welfare-triangle gains from improved allocative efficiency in the tradition of Harberger. An approximation is to use the formula $0.5 \star \Delta t \star \Delta TC$ where t is the tariff rate and TC is the volume of trade creation. An early example was Balassa (1975) who estimated that trade creation in manufactures in 1970 for the original EEC6 was \$11.4 billion, that the average tariff reduction was 12 per cent and the welfare gain was \$0.7 billion = 0.15 per cent of GDP.[6] A more recent calculation for the impact of the European Single Market was that the welfare-triangles gain from reduced trade costs would be about 0.5 per cent of EU GDP (Harrison *et al.*, 1994).

Balassa recognized that there would be other probably much more important impacts on income levels from competition, economies of scale and induced capital formation but did not really have any convincing way to estimate these. Owen (1983) provided an estimate of \$8.5 billion for the gains from competition and economies of scale in manufactures for the EEC6 in 1970 based on extrapolating from a small sample of micro-level investigations; together with the welfare triangle gain the total is 1.8 + 0.15 = 1.95 per cent of GDP. A conventional, albeit crude, allowance for capital stock adjustment might raise this to about 2.8 per cent of GDP.[7]

Harrison *et al.* (1994), working with a computable general equilibrium (CGE) model that allows for increasing returns in some sectors, changes in price-cost mark-ups and capital stock adjustment projected that competition and scale effects resulting from the Single Market would raise EU GDP by 0.7 per cent and the total impact on EU GDP of the Single Market would be 2.6 per cent.[8] Ex-post studies have suggested similar effects; for example, Ilzkovitz *et al.* (2007) estimated GDP had been raised by 2.2 per cent by 2006. Establishing a true Single Market in services could probably double this impact by reducing barriers to entry but governments still have considerable discretion to maintain these barriers notwithstanding the Services Directive (Badinger and Maydell, 2009). A recent estimate is that this implementation of this directive has so far raised EU GDP by about 0.8 per cent whereas full implementation would triple this (Monteagudo *et al.*, 2012).[9]

These detailed studies of the impact of the original common market and the later Single Market suggest each had similar useful but not spectacular impacts on the level of income. Clearly, however, they do not encompass all the economic integration that has taken place and they do not necessarily capture all the impact it has had – for example, they are noticeably silent on dynamic effects. Alternative approaches which attempt to capture a wider range of impacts, albeit without identifying these individually, rely on regression techniques to identify the impact of economic integration on income or changes in income. Three variants of this approach that offer useful results are the following.

First, as noted by Boltho and Eichengreen (2008), the well-known paper by Frankel and Romer (1999) can be used to postulate a relationship between the ratio of total trade exposure (exports + imports)/GDP and the level of GDP. A conventional version of this might be to project that an exogenous 1 percentage point increase in trade exposure would raise GDP by 0.5 per cent.[10] Applying this to the EU in 2000 on the basis of the estimate by Baier *et al.* (2008) that the EU 'shock' had raised intra-EU trade by 100 to 125 per cent, from a counterfactual intra-EU trade exposure of 15.6 to 17.3 per cent of GDP to the actual intra-EU trade exposure of 34.6 per cent, the estimated impact on EU GDP is an increase of 8.6 to 9.5 per cent.

Second, growth regressions can be used to estimate the effect of European integration on income growth. Here the most useful paper is Badinger (2005) which made an index of the level of European integration for each EU15 country from 1950 to 2000 and in a panel-regression setting with suitable controls examined its relationship with growth and with investment. The integration index which took account both of GATT liberalization and European trade agreements shows that 55 per cent of the protectionism of 1950 was eliminated between 1958 and 1975, a figure which then rose steadily to 87 per cent by 2000. The results of the regressions were that changes in integration were positive for growth but that the level of integration had no effect and that changes in integration had somewhere between half and three-quarters of their impact through investment with the remainder coming from changes in TFP. Across the EU15 as a whole GDP was estimated to be 26 per cent higher than if there had been no economic integration after 1950 with a narrow range from 21.6 per cent for Sweden to 28.9 per cent for Portugal. The peak effect on the level of income resulting from the rapid liberalization prior to 1975 would have raised the growth rate over the period by about 1 per cent per year – impressive but only about a quarter of the Western European growth rate in a period of rapid catch-up growth (Crafts and Toniolo, 2008). The implication of the results in Badinger (2005) is that European economic integration has had a sizeable impact on the level of income but has not had a permanent effect on the rate of growth. This amounts to rejecting the endogenous growth hypothesis and is line with recent investigations of the impact of trade liberalizations using difference-in-difference approaches (Estevadeordal and Taylor, 2013).

Third, a new approach in the style of 'with-without' comparisons is available in the synthetic counterfactuals method of Campos *et al.* (2014). This compares growth in each post-EU accession country with growth in a weighted combination of other countries which did not accede and which are chosen to match the accession country before its entry to the EU as closely as possible. Results for countries which joined the EU between 1973 and 1995 are reported in Table 1.5. For these countries, the average impact of EU membership after 10 years is estimated to have been a 6.4 per cent income gain but with a wide range between Portugal at +16.5 per cent and Greece at -17.3 per cent.

The different experiences of Greece and Ireland after joining the EU raises the issue of whether European economic integration has been conducive to convergence or divergence of income levels across the EU and whether the common market has encouraged spatial concentration or dispersion of economic activity as firms have a wider choice of locations and capital stock adjustments take place partly across international borders.

Table 1.5 Post-accession differences between level of actual and synthetic GDP per person (%)

	After 5 Years	*After 10 Years*	*Total*
Denmark	10.3	14.3	23.9
Ireland	5.2	9.4	48.9
United Kingdom	4.8	8.6	23.7
Greece	−11.6	−17.3	−19.8
Portugal	11.7	16.5	18.4
Spain	9.3	13.7	19.8
Austria	4.5	6.4	7.2
Finland	2.2	4.0	4.4
Sweden	0.8	2.4	3.2

Source: Campos *et al.* (2014).

Table 1.6 reports the results of convergence regressions for the set of European regions for which data exist for 1950. It provides evidence of unconditional convergence both before and after 1973 but in the latter period this is quite weak. While peripherality per se does not seem to retard growth, population density is an advantage. Table 1.7 reports regressions

Table 1.6 Unconditional convergence regression Western European regions

	1950–73	*1950–73*	*1950–73*	*1973–2005*	*1973–2005*	*1973–2005*
Constant	6.660	5.292	5.633	3.218	2.340	2.419
	(39.755)	(17.567)	(13.926)	(19.608)	(9.731)	(7.913)
Initial Y/P	−0.051	−0.029	−0.035	−0.019	−0.008	−0.011
% Leader	(−14.487)	(−7.521)	(−6.294)	(−7.870)	(−3.396)	(−3.396)
Spain		0.920	0.826		0.793	0.660
		(3.537)	(2.975)		(4.243)	(3.350)
West Germany		1.046	0.917		−0.229	−0.265
		(4.346)	(3.683)		(−1.247)	(−1.514)
UK		−0.833	−0.798		0.195	0.082
		(−3.539)	(−3.198)		(1.088)	(0.469)
France		0.169	0.167		−0.044	−0.028
		(0.766)	(0.765)		(−0.263)	(−0.176)
Italy		0.716	0.645		0.085	0.023
		(3.017)	(2.661)		(0.492)	(0.131)
Density			0.0002			0.0002
			(1.895)			(2.930)
Distance to			−0.0001			0.0001
Luxembourg			(−0.462)			(0.807)
R^2	0.713	0.870	0.873	0.420	0.662	0.696

Sources: Own calculations based on GDP per person relative to national average for France, Italy, Netherlands, Spain, UK and West Germany for set of same 85 regions obtained from Molle (1980), Martinez-Galarraga (2007) and Eurostat, *Regional Statistics*, various issues. These relativities were then applied to national estimates for real GDP per person reported in Maddison (2010). Density (= population/land area) calculated from same sources. Distances to Luxembourg from www.mapcrow. info plus intercept of 100 km.

Table 1.7 Geography and real GDP per person regressions

	1950	1973	2005
Constant	10.032	10.646	10.678
	(19.196)	(24.422)	(23.835)
Log Density	0.206	0.122	0.103
	(4.318)	(3.178)	(2.633)
Log Distance to	−0.407	−0.306	−0.208
Luxembourg	(−5.816)	(−5.231)	(−3.477)
R^2	0.802	0.652	0.327

Sources: Own calculations based on data from sources for Table 1.6.

Note: Dependent variable is the log of real GDP/Person, country dummies included but not reported and density instrumented using land area as in Ciccone (2002).

similar to those performed in Venables (2005) for a common set of regions across three cross-sections. The results show that the level of real GDP per person was always higher in more densely populated regions and was always lower in regions relatively far away from the centre of Europe. Interestingly, however, both the disadvantages of peripherality and the advantages of density were greater in the disintegrated Europe of the 1950s. Reductions in the dispersion of real GDP per person across these European regions have reflected reductions in core-periphery inequality between countries rather than within countries with the Theil index of inequality of real GDP per person between countries falling from 0.055 in 1950 to 0.013 in 1973 and 0.002 in 2005 but the within-country index changing little from 0.036 in 1950 to 0.034 in 1973 and 0.038 in 2005.

New economic geography models suggest that reductions in trade costs may lead industry to move to locations with proximity to markets because they permit realization of economies of scale or because it is advantageous to locate close to either customers or suppliers. Empirical evidence suggests that market access has mattered for industrial location, becoming more important for industries with strong backward and forward linkages, but nevertheless only a subset of industries has become more spatially concentrated (Midelfart-Knarvik et al., 2000). A reason for this may be the very low level of international migration within the EU (Puga, 1999). Overall, EU countries have become slowly more specialized in production over time as economic integration has progressed with the average of the Krugman specialization index across the EU15 rising from 0.409 in 1970–3 to 0.445 in 1994–7, although at the end of the twentieth century industries in the EU remained much less spatially concentrated than in the United States (Midelfart et al., 2003).

European integration has been accompanied by the patterns of spatial disparity highlighted by the new economic geography. Not only are there are agglomeration effects on productivity (Ciccone, 2002) but there is also clear evidence that market access, which, of course, exhibits a strong core-periphery profile, has a strong positive impact on levels of regional GDP per person. Breinlich (2006) found a crude elasticity of about 0.25 or about 0.07 controlling for human and physical capital stocks and density; using the latter estimate implies that moving the Algarve to Cologne would raise its labour productivity by 20 per cent.

It was about 15 years after acceding to the EU that Irish economic growth took off into very rapid (and belated) catch-up growth during its Celtic Tiger phase which lasted until the early twenty-first century. This success clearly was predicated on being within the EU but also was based on the development of appropriate supply-side policies to exploit this opportunity. Strong growth in employment was a key feature of the period as the NAIRU fell dramatically and migration flows reversed. Rapid TFP growth was underpinned by a large ICT production sector based on foreign direct investment (FDI).

A central aspect of the Celtic Tiger economy was the prominence of FDI. 'Export-platform' FDI transformed Ireland's revealed comparative advantage, dominated production in high-skill and knowledge-intensive sectors, and by 2000 accounted for almost half of manufacturing employment and 80 per cent of manufacturing exports (Barry, 2004). In terms of industrial policy, Ireland developed a sophisticated system to select projects for financial support through the Industrial Development Agency and made investments in telecommunications and college education that were conducive to FDI (Buckley and Ruane, 2006).

Nevertheless, the most important factor in Ireland's success in attracting FDI was the combination of its corporate tax regime together with EU membership (Slaughter, 2003). It is clear from the literature that the semi-elasticity of FDI with respect to the corporate tax rate is quite high, perhaps of the order of -2.5 or even -3.5 (OECD, 2007). At the start of the Celtic Tiger period the Irish tax rate for manufacturing FDI was easily the lowest in Europe and a study by Gropp and Kostial (2000) suggested that the stock of American manufacturing investment in Ireland was about 70 per cent higher than if Ireland had had a tax rate equivalent to the next lowest in the EU. As trade costs fell, the impact of low taxes on FDI appears to have been accentuated significantly and their relative importance for location compared with proximity to demand increased (Romalis, 2007).

5. Implications of EU membership for the United Kingdom: Changing perceptions

The UK's membership of the EEC or EU has always been somewhat controversial among British economists and politicians. Within two years of accession, the UK held a referendum in 1975 to decide whether to stay in and, with the Conservatives having won the 2015 general election it is expected that a similar referendum will be held in 2017. This debate, and its evolution through time, deserves some attention. At the same time, it is interesting to compare the analyses made by economists before and after entry. The latter were made with superior information, obviously, but also with more sophisticated economics. The standard approach in recent years to evaluating the impact on trade and growth of the UK withdrawing from the EU or of the UK staying out of the euro is rather different from the 1970s' approaches to measuring benefits and costs of membership.

Ex-Ante analyses of the economic effects of UK entry into the EEC paid a lot of attention to the expected negative impact on the balance of payments, the downsides of the Common Agricultural Policy (CAP) and net UK budget payments which were regarded as definite costs (albeit of somewhat debatable magnitude) to be borne in return for the potential (but unknowable) benefits in the industrial sector of economies of scale and greater competition.[11] The latter were seen as conducive to reductions both in market power and in X-inefficiency. The CAP (and the associated budgetary contributions) was relatively onerous for the UK as a food importer with a small agricultural sector. It was agreed that the welfare triangle gains from trade creation would be quite small. The welfare implications of predicted balance of payments effects were calculated via the terms of trade effects of the exchange rate adjustment required to correct a deficit using the Marshall-Lerner conditions. The findings of some well-known papers of the time are summarized in Table 1.8.

Table 1.8 Balance of payments and static welfare effects of UK entry into EEC: 1970s and 1980s estimates (% GDP)

	Ex-Ante (1)	Ex-Ante (2)	Ex-Post
Balance of Payments			
Manufactures	−0.3	−0.2	−2.6
Import Saving on Food	+1.0	+0.4	+0.7
Excess Food Cost	−0.3	−0.2	−0.1
Official Transfers	−1.0	−0.6	−0.6
Total	−0.6	−0.6	−2.6
Welfare			
Trade Creation	+0.1	+0.1	+0.4
Scale		+0.5	
Competition		+0.5	+1.7
Manufactures Deficit	−0.1	−0.1	−0.9
Import Saving on Food	+0.4	+0.2	+0.1
Excess Food Cost	−0.4	−0.2	−0.1
Official Transfers	−1.2	−0.8	−0.7
Total	−1.2	+0.2	+1.3

Sources: Ex-Ante (1): general equilibrium based on Miller (1971); a later version of these estimates was published as Miller and Spencer (1977). Ex-Ante (2): partial equilibrium based on Josling (1971) for agriculture and on Williamson (1971) for manufactures. Ex-Post: compiled using Morris (1980) and Rollo and Warwick (1979) for agriculture, Gasiorek *et al.* (2002) for trade creation, scale and competition effects in manufacturing, and Winters (1987) for balance of payments effects in manufacturing.

Notes: Welfare effects based on orthodox correction of balance of payments deficits/surpluses, see text. Excess food cost refers to payments to EEC farmers for agricultural commodities purchased at EEC prices, i.e. at greater than world prices. Ex-Post trade creation includes scale effects.

Ex-Post analyses found similar results in terms of the direction of the effects but in some respects quite different magnitudes, notably, with regard to the balance of payments deficit in manufacturing (Winters, 1987) and the welfare gains from competition, even though analysis of these gains was restricted to the static effects of reductions in market power (Gasiorek *et al.*, 2002). Both these papers used considerably more advanced methods to compute their estimates than had the Ex-Ante studies.[12] Adding up all the numbers in the ex-post column seems to give a more optimistic assessment of the net welfare impact of the UK's entry into the EEC – the gamble seems to have paid off with a larger payments' deficit in manufactures being more than offset by greater benefits from competition. In fact, the estimates by Campos *et al.* (2014) reported in Table 1.5 of medium-term growth in the UK compared with a synthetic counterfactual (an 8.6 per cent rise in GDP) suggest that 'dynamic gains' not included in Table 1.8 rewarded this gamble handsomely.

However, in the 1970s a vocal group of economists argued that balance of payments deficits were much more costly to correct than orthodox economics assumed. In a world of relatively immobile international capital which seemed to exclude financing such deficits through the capital account this loomed large. The Cambridge Economic Policy Group (CEPG) model embodied an assumption of real wage rigidity which precluded the use of devaluation and required (permanent) reductions in aggregate demand to hold down imports.

On this analysis, the welfare cost was about three times the balance of payments deficit (Bacon *et al.*, 1978).[13] Thus, the overall impact of entry was seen by these economists as adverse, especially once the manufactured trade deficit had become clear (See Table 1.8).

Indeed, the CEPG argument went further than this since it embraced the need for permanent import controls to allow expansion of aggregate demand and avoid a balance of payments constraint on growth. This was plainly incompatible with the membership of the EEC and implied the need for exit. Analyses of this kind became popular with advocates of an 'alternative economic strategy' on the left of the Labour Party which held considerable sway. In 1981, the Labour Party adopted an official policy of withdrawal from the EEC and this was in its manifesto for the 1983 election. The rationale was to permit greater government intervention in the economy.

In retrospect, however, it seems clear that abandoning protectionism rather than embracing import controls served the British economy well, especially through favourable impacts on productivity performance consequent on stronger competition and entry threats in product markets. The average effective rate of protection fell from 9.3 per cent in 1968 to 4.7 per cent in 1979, and 1.2 per cent in 1986 (Ennew *et al.*, 1990). Trade liberalization in its various guises reduced price-cost margins (Hitiris, 1978; Griffith, 2001). A difference-in-differences analysis found that there was a substantial boost to productivity in sectors which experienced a large reduction in protection (Broadberry and Crafts, 2011).[14]

The welfare gains from the effect of EEC entry on competition were probably considerably bigger than those captured by the Gasiorek *et al.* (2002) model since reductions in market power effectively addressed long-standing impediments to productivity performance from weak management and industrial relations problems in British firms. Nickell *et al.* (1997) estimated that, for firms without a dominant external shareholder (the norm for big British firms at this time), a reduction in supernormal profits from 15 to 5 per cent of value added would raise total factor productivity growth by 1 percentage point. The 1980s saw a surge in productivity growth in unionized firms as organizational change took place under pressure of competition (Machin and Wadhwani, 1989) and de-recognition of unions in the context of increases in foreign competition had a strong effect on productivity growth by the late 1980s (Gregg *et al.*, 1993). This goes a long way to explain the boost to growth found by Campos *et al.* (2014).

The contrast with today's economists' evaluations of the implications of a possible British exit from the EU is striking. This is partly because concern with (and measurement of) balance of payments effects has disappeared. Beyond this, however, the arguments relating to trade are about what future will offer more liberalization rather than whether trade liberalization will have positive effects well in excess of a welfare-triangles gain or whether protectionism could be good for growth. That said, new issues have come to the fore in political debate including issues relating to EU-imposed regulation and to immigration which did not feature 40 years ago.

Table 1.9 displays estimates of static welfare effects of a UK exit from the EU made by Ottaviano *et al.* (2014). These are based on a 'short-cut' method which avoids the need for estimation of a structural model but allows monopolistic competition and scale effects to be accommodated. Likely changes in tariffs and non-tariff barriers (NTBs) to trade are taken into account both in terms of the initial situation and the possibility of being excluded from further reductions in NTBs within the Single Market. This is seen as the biggest downside of exit and would contribute the lion's share of the welfare loss of 3.09 per cent in the pessimistic scenario.[15]

As has become standard in the literature on the impact of trade with the EU on the British economy, these authors also provide a variant of a Frankel and Romer (1999) type estimate

Table 1.9 Modern Ex-Ante estimates of the static welfare effects of UK exit from the EU (% GDP)

	Optimistic	*Pessimistic*
Increased EU/UK Tariffs	0	−0.14
Increased EU/UK NTBs	−0.40	−0.93
Future Falls in EU/UK NTBs	−1.26	−2.55
Fiscal Transfers	+0.53	+0.53
Total	−1.13	−3.09

Source: Ottaviano *et al.* (2014) using a methodology derived from Costinot and Rodriguez-Clare (2013).

which potentially captures a wider array of effects. This is based on the assumption that the reduction in trade associated with exit from the EU would be as predicted by the difference between being in the EU and in EFTA in the gravity model of Baier *et al.* (2008). This is taken to reduce trade with the EU by 25 per cent or overall trade by 12.6 per cent and income by 6.3 to 9.5 per cent.[16]

A case in favour of British exit has been made by Le *et al.* (2011). They note that the EU still imposes barriers against imports through the common external tariff and the CAP and argue that the UK could benefit by leaving the EU and adopting a policy of unilateral free trade.[17] The static welfare gains are put at 2.5 to 3.5 per cent of UK GDP. However, a bigger benefit might accrue through escaping possible future labour-market regulations which would raise unemployment. An illustrative calculation is provided that this could have a levels-effect impact of 6.4 per cent of GDP.

These days, Euro-sceptic voices in the UK frequently raise the issue of excessive EU regulation and the costs that it imposes on the British economy. However, this case has not yet been persuasively made. Gaskell and Persson (2010) reviewed the regulatory impact assessments of this legislation from 1998 onwards and found that overall it averaged a benefit-cost ratio of 1.02. It should also be noted that the UK has persistently been able to maintain very light levels of regulation in terms of key OECD indicators such as PMR (Product Market Regulation) and EPL (Employment Protection Legislation) for which high scores have been shown to have detrimental economic effects (Barnes *et al.*, 2011). In 2013, the UK had a PMR score of 1.09 and an EPL score of 1.12, the second and third lowest in the OECD, respectively.

Unlike the 1970s, immigration from the EU has become a controversial issue in the UK recently. Partly, this may be because difficult economic times generate populist responses but it also reflects a much greater volume of migration and the accession of countries in which wages are much lower to the EU. The stock of EEA immigrants to the UK rose from 0.9 to 2.8 million between 1995 and 2011 of whom 0.4 million were employed in 1995 and 1.5 million in 2011. Despite its bad press, the economic impact of this immigration was most probably positive. Research suggests that the increase in the migrant share of the UK labour force between 1997 and 2007 might have raised labour productivity of domestic workers through spillover effects by between 0.27 and 0.40 percentage points (Rolfe *et al.*, 2013) while a detailed study of the fiscal effects found that, contrary to much political discourse, EEA immigrants made a net fiscal contribution estimated at £28.7 billion (at 2011 prices) between 2001 and 2011 (Dustmann and Fratinni, 2014).

In sum, it seems that the UK has experienced welfare gains from its membership of the EEC/EU in excess of the expectations of even the optimists of 40 years ago. As the analysis of the economic impacts has developed, not only the magnitude but also the scope of the economic benefits of EU membership has become clearer. It is also clear that belonging to the EU has increased trade by much more than belonging to EFTA, originally the preferred form of integration for the UK with its antipathy to 'ever-closer union'.[18] This suggests that the strongest case for a UK exit is political and relates to issues of sovereignty.

6. Conclusions

European economic integration especially through the EEC/EU has had a strong impact on trade flows. The effects of EU membership on trade appear to exceed what would have accrued from tariff reductions alone suggesting that this entails a deeper level of integration than would have accrued through a free trade area. This is also borne out by the evidence of much stronger trade creation from EU compared with EFTA membership. The process of European economic integration gathered momentum in part from 'domino effects' which resulted in EFTA members acceding to the EU to enhance their access to EU markets.

There is very good reason to believe that European economic integration raised income levels significantly but there is little evidence in favour of the hypothesis that growth rates were permanently increased. The income gains are much greater than would be expected on the basis of a narrow welfare triangles approach and entail higher levels of productivity as competition was strengthened and investment adjusted to new opportunities. While it is clear that good market access (a relatively central location) has been favourable for achieving higher income levels, at the same time over the whole post-war experience of integration there has been evidence of catch-up and convergence in income levels between countries and 'peripheral' countries like Ireland which adopted well-designed supply-side policies have been able to take advantage of EU membership to stimulate periods of rapid growth.

The UK has clearly benefited in economic terms from EU membership. Indeed, the welfare gains it has obtained are much bigger than were expected even by optimists at the time of entry in the 1970s. In particular, increased competition in product markets was important for British productivity performance which had suffered under the protectionism of the early post-war decades. The problem for the UK is that, while economic integration under EU auspices has delivered gains which exceed those it would have obtained from staying in EFTA, the price paid in terms of reduced sovereignty is regarded by many British voters as too high.

Notes

1 For a fuller account of the intricate details of the operation of the European Payments Union, see Eichengreen (1993).
2 Strictly speaking, these estimates are reductions in the cost of international trade relative to domestic trade.
3 The EU effect does vary quite a lot depending on the precise specification of the gravity equation; the results quoted here come from the authors' preferred specifications.
4 Badinger and Breuss (2011) report that the average of six studies published in the early 1970s was that trade creation raised imports of the EC6 by $9.52 billion and reduced extra-EC exports by $0.32 billion.
5 Econometric support for the 'domino effect' hypothesis can be found in Baldwin and Jaimovich (2012).
6 Similar results would be obtained given the formula for any reasonable estimate of trade creation; the welfare gain is always small relative to GDP. Insofar as the Common Agricultural Policy entailed trade diversion, there would be a welfare triangle loss to offset the trade creation gain.

7 This calculation assumes a Cobb-Douglas production function with a constant capital to output ratio in equilibrium. Then the total impact on output is $\Delta A/A/(1-\alpha)$ where $\alpha = 0.3$ is the share of capital in income.

8 This is well below the optimistic projections of the Cecchini Report issued by the European Commission which projected 4.8 to 6.4 per cent of GDP before any impact from capital stock adjustment but is in line with other academic ex-ante studies (Badinger and Breuss, 2011, Table 14.3).

9 This does not include any impact from capital stock adjustment.

10 Frankel and Romer (1999) offered a range of estimates of this coefficient with 0.5 at the bottom end. A similar value was used by HM Treasury in its assessment of the effects on the UK economy of joining the euro.

11 The 'estimates' in column (2) of Table 1.8 were admitted by Williamson (1971) to be largely guesswork while the authors of column (1) did not even attempt any such estimates, merely noting how large these effects would have to be to offset the net welfare losses from the other elements of their estimates.

12 Winters (1987) used a fully-articulated AIDS approach to modelling the demand for imports and Gasiorek *et al.* (2002) employed a computable general equilibrium model with imperfect competition and scale economies in some manufacturing sectors.

13 Rather than about 1/3rd, as in Table 1.8; the assumption of real wage rigidity has no empirical validity and was soon rejected by mainstream economists, see, for example, OECD (1989).

14 Sectors which experienced a reduction of 10 percentage points or more in the effective rate of protection saw an additional increase of 1.4 percentage points in the rate of labour productivity growth in 1979–86 over 1968–79.

15 An attempt to model the implications of complete removal of barriers to trade within the EU suggested that this could provide a welfare gain to the UK of 7 per cent of GDP (Aussilloux *et al.*, 2011).

16 This is based on a guess at the elasticity of income to trade of 0.5 or 0.75 following the approach proposed by Feyrer (2009). If this calculation is put on a similar basis to those in section 4 above, there would be a reduction in the trade to GDP ratio of about 8 percentage points with an implied income loss of about 4 per cent of GDP.

17 Both Bradford (2003) based on a price-gap methodology and Fontagne *et al.* (2005) using a gravity model approach found that EU external barriers to trade were quite substantial around the turn of the century.

18 For example, using Baier *et al.* (2008, Table 5, equation 1) both countries being in the EU raises trade by $e^{0.65} - 1 = 92$ per cent whereas both countries being in the EEA raises trade by $e^{0.19} - 1 = 21\%$.

References

Aussilloux, V., Boumellassa, H., Emlinger, C. and Fontagne, L. (2011), The Economic Consequences for the UK and the EU of Completing the Single Market, *BIS Economics Paper*, No. 11.

Bacon, R., Godley, W. and McFarquhar, A. (1978), The Direct Costs of Belonging to the EEC, *Economic Policy Review*, 4, 44–49.

Badinger, H. (2005), Growth Effects of Economic Integration: Evidence from the EU Member States, *Review of World Economics*, 141, 50–78.

Badinger, H. and Breuss, F. (2004), What Has Determined the Rapid Post-War Growth of Intra-EU Trade?, *Review of World Economics*, 140, 31–51.

Badinger, H. and Breuss, F. (2011), The Quantitative Effects of European Post-War Economic Integration, in M. Jovanovic (ed.), *International Handbook on the Economics of Integration*. Cheltenham: Edward Elgar, 285–315.

Badinger, H. and Maydell, N. (2009), Legal and Economic Issues in Completing the EU Internal Market for Services: an Interdisciplinary Perspective, *Journal of Common Market Studies*, 47, 693–717.

Baier, S. L., Bergstrand, J. H., Egger, P. and McLaughlin, P. A. (2008), Do Economic Integration Agreements Actually Work? Issues in Understanding the Causes and Consequences of the Growth of Regionalism, *The World Economy*, 31, 461–497.

Balassa, B. (1961), *The Theory of Economic Integration*. Homewood, Ill.: Irwin.

Balassa, B. (1975), Trade Creation and Diversion in the European Common Market: an Appraisal of the Evidence, in B. Balassa (ed.), *European Economic Integration*. Amsterdam: North Holland, 79–118.

Baldwin, R. E. (1993), A Domino Theory of Regionalism, *NBER Working Paper*, No. 4465.

Baldwin, R. E. and Jaimovich, D. (2012), Are Free Trade Agreements Contagious?, *Journal of International Economics*, 88, 1–16.

Baldwin, R., Di Nino, V., Fontagne, L., De Santis, R. and Taglioni, D. (2008), Study on the Impact of the Euro on Trade and Foreign Direct Investment, *European Economy Economic Papers*, No. 321.

Barnes, S., Bouis, R., Briard, P., Dougherty, S. and Eris, M. (2011), The GDP Impact of Reform: a Simple Simulation Framework, *OECD Economics Department Working Paper*, No. 834.

Barry, F. (2004), Export-Platform Foreign Direct Investment: the Irish Experience, *EIB Papers*, 9, 9–37.

Bayoumi, T. and Eichengreen, B. (1995), Is Regionalism Simply a Diversion? Evidence from the Evolution of the EC and EFTA, *NBER Working Paper*, No. 5283.

Berger, H. and Nitsch, V. (2008), Zooming Out: the Trade Effect of the Euro in Historical Perspective, *Journal of International Money and Finance*, 27, 1244–1260.

Berger, H. and Ritschl, A. (1995), Germany and the Political Economy of the Marshall Plan, 1947–52: a Re-Revisionist View, in B. Eichengreen (ed.), *Europe's Postwar Recovery*. Cambridge: Cambridge University Press, 199–245.

Boltho, A. and Eichengreen, B. (2008), The Economic Impact of European Integration, *CEPR Discussion Paper*, No. 6820.

Bradford, S. (2003), Paying the Price: Final Goods Protection in OECD Countries, *Review of Economics and Statistics*, 85, 24–37.

Breinlich, H. (2006), The Spatial Income Structure in the European Union – What Role for Economic Geography? *Journal of Economic Geography*, 6, 593–617.

Broadberry, S. and Crafts, N. (2011), Openness, Protectionism and Britain's Productivity Performance over the Long Run, in G. Wood, T. C. Mills and N. Crafts (eds.), *Monetary and Banking History: Essays in Honour of Forest Capie*. London: Routledge, 254–286.

Buckley, P. and Ruane, F. (2006), Foreign Direct Investment in Ireland: Policy Implications for Emerging Economies, *The World Economy*, 29, 1611–1628.

Campos, N. F., Coricelli, F. and Moretti, L. (2014), Economic Growth and Political Integration: Estimating the Benefits from Membership of the European Union using the Synthetic Counterfactuals Method, *CEPR Discussion Paper*, No. 9968.

Ciccone, A. (2002), Agglomeration Effects in Europe, *European Economic Review*, 46, 213–227.

Crafts, N. (2013), The Marshall Plan, in R. Parker and R. Whaples (eds.), *Routledge Handbook of Major Events in Economic History*. London: Routledge, 203–213.

Crafts, N. and Toniolo, G. (2008), European Economic Growth, 1950–2005: an Overview, *CEPR Discussion Paper*, No. 6863.

Dustmann, C. and Frattini, T. (2014), The Fiscal Effects of Immigration to the UK, *Economic Journal*, 124, F593-F643.

Eichengreen, B. (1993), *Reconstructing Europe's Trade and Payments*. Manchester: Manchester University Press.

Ennew, C, Greenaway, D. and Reed, G. (1990), Further Evidence on Effective Tariffs and Effective Protection in the UK, *Oxford Bulletin of Economics and Statistics*, 52, 69–78.

Estevadeordal, A. and Taylor, A. (2013), Is the Washington Consensus Dead? Growth, Openness and the Great Liberalization, 1970s-2000s, *Review of Economics and Statistics*, 95, 1669–1690.

Feyrer, J. (2009), Trade and Income: Exploiting Time Series in Geography, *NBER Working Paper*, No. 14910.

Fontagne, L., Mayer, T. and Zignago, S. (2005), Trade in the Triad: How Easy is the Access to Large Markets? *Canadian Journal of Economics*, 38, 1401–1430.

Frankel, J. A. and Romer, D. (1999), Does Trade Cause Growth? *American Economic Review*, 89, 379–399.

Gasiorek, M., Smith, A. and Venables, A. J. (2002), The Accession of the UK to the EC: a Welfare Analysis, *Journal of Common Market Studies*, 40, 425–447.

Gaskell, S. and Persson, M. (2010), *Still Out of Control? Measuring Eleven Years of EU Regulation*. London: Open Europe.

Griffith, R. (2001), Product Market Competition, Efficiency and Agency Costs: an Empirical Analysis, *Institute for Fiscal Studies Working Paper*, No. 01/12.

Gregg, P., Machin, S. and Metcalf, D. (1993), Signals and Cycles: Productivity Growth and Change in Union Status in British Companies, 1984–9, *Economic Journal*, 103, 894–907.

Gropp, R. and Kostial, K. (2000), The Disappearing Tax Base: Is FDI Eroding Corporate Income Taxes? *IMF Working Paper*, No. 00/173.

Harrison, G., Rutherford, T. and Tarr, D. (1994), Product Standards, Imperfect Competition, and Completion of the Market in the European Union, *World Bank Policy Research Working Paper*, No. 1293.

Hitiris, T. (1978), Effective Protection and Economic Performance in UK Manufacturing Industry, 1963 and 1968, *Economic Journal*, 88, 107–120.

Ilzkovitz, F., Dierx, A., Kovacs, V. and Sousa, N. (2007), Steps towards a Deeper Economic Integration: the Internal Market in the 21st Century, *European Economy Economic Papers*, No. 271.

Jacks, D. S., Meissner, C. M. and Novy, D. (2011), Trade Booms, Trade Busts, and Trade Costs, *Journal of International Economics*, 83, 185–201.

Le, V. P. M., Minford, P. and Nowell, E. (2011), Measuring the Extent and Costs of EU Protectionism, in M. Jovanovic (ed.), *International Handbook on the Economics of Integration*. Cheltenham: Edward Elgar, 316–331.

Machin, S. and Wadhwani, S. (1989), The Effects of Unions on Organisational Change, Investment and Employment: Evidence from WIRS Data, *London School of Economics Centre for Labour Economics Discussion Paper*, No. 355.

Maddison, A. (2010), Historical Statistics of the World Economy, 1-2008AD. www.ggdc.net/maddison

Midelfart, K. H., Overman, H. G. and Venables, A. J. (2003), Monetary Union and the Economic Geography of Europe, *Journal of Common Market Studies*, 41, 847–868.

Midelfart-Knarvik, K. H., Overman, H. G., Redding, S. J. and Venables, A. J. (2000), The Location of European Industry, *European Economy Economic Papers*, No. 142.

Milward, A. S. (1984), *The Reconstruction of Western Europe, 1945–1951*. London: Methuen.

Milward, A. S. (1992), *The European Rescue of the Nation State*. London: Routledge.

Molle, W. (1980), *Regional Disparity and Economic Development in the European Community*. Farnborough: Saxon House.

Monteagudo, J., Rutkovski, A. and Lorenzani, D. (2012), The Economic Impact of the Services Directive: a First Assessment Following Implementation, *European Economy Economic Papers*, No. 456.

Nickell, S.J., Nicolitsas, D. and Dryden, N. (1997), What Makes Firms Perform Well?, *European Economic Review*, 41, 783–796.

OECD (1989), *Economies in Transition*. Paris: OECD.

OECD (2007), *Tax Effects on Foreign Direct Investment*. Paris: OECD.

Ottaviano, G., Pessoa, J. P., Sampson, T. and van Reenen, J. (2014), The Costs and Benefits of Leaving the EU, mimeo, London School of Economics.

Owen, N. (1983), Economies of Scale. Competitiveness and Trade Patterns within the European Community. Oxford: Clarendon Press.

Pahre, R. (2008), *Politics and Trade Cooperation in the Nineteenth Century*. Cambridge: Cambridge University Press.

Prados de la Escosura, L., Roses, J. R. and Villaroya, I. S. (2010), Stabilization and Growth under Dictatorship: the Experience of Franco's Spain, *CEPR Discussion Paper*, No. 7731.

Puga, D. (1999), The Rise and Fall of Regional Inequalities, *European Economic Review*, 43, 303–334.

Rolfe, H., Rienzo, C., Lalani, M. and Portes, J. (2013), *Migration and Productivity: Employers' Practices, Public Attitudes and Statistical Evidence*, London, NIESR.

Rollo, J. and Warwick, K. (1979), The CAP and Resource Flows among Member States, Government Economic Service Working Paper No. 27.

Romalis, J. (2007), Capital Taxes, Trade Costs, and the Irish Miracle, *Journal of the European Economic Association*, 5, 459–469.

Sapir, A. (2001), Domino Effects in Western European Regional Trade, 1960–1992, *European Journal of Political Economy*, 17, 377–388.

Sapir, A. (2011), European Integration at the Crossroads: a Review Essay on the 50th Anniversary of Bela Balassa's Theory of Economic Integration, *Journal of Economic Literature*, 49, 1200–1229.

Slaughter, M. J. (2003), Host Country Determinants of US Foreign Direct Investment into Europe, in H. Hermann and R. Lipsey (eds.), *Foreign Direct Investment in the Real and Financial Sector of Industrial Countries*. Berlin: Springer, 7–32.

Straathof, B., Linders, G-J., Lejour, A. and Mohlmann, J. (2008), The Internal Market and the Dutch Economy: Implications for Trade and Growth, *CPB Document*, No. 168.

Venables, A. J. (2005), European Integration: a View from Geographical Economics, *Swedish Economic Policy Review*, 12, 143–169.

Williamson, J. (1971), Trade and Economic Growth, in J. Pinder (ed.), *The Economics of Europe*. London: Charles Knight, 19–45.

Weigall, D. and Stirk, P. (1992), *The Origins and Development of the European Community*. Leicester: Leicester University Press.

Winters, L. A. (1987), Britain in Europe: a Survey of Quantitative Trade Studies, *Journal of Common Market Studies*, 25, 315–335.

2

THE HISTORY OF EUROPEAN ECONOMIC AND MONETARY UNION

Harold James

1. Introduction

Europe's move to monetary integration with a common currency (the euro) is a quite unique process, and is often held up as a model for monetary cooperation in other parts of the world: in the Gulf region, where there are periodic discussions of monetary unification, as well as in Asia and Latin America, where movements towards greater monetary integration also have some support but encounter a plethora of difficulties. Nevertheless, at the latest by the financial crisis of 2007–8, it became clear that there were substantial design flaws in the concept of the Economic and Monetary Union (EMU). As Patrick Honohan put it: "release 1.0 of the euro was under-designed, and robust only to moderate shocks." (Honohan 2012)

There has always been an ambiguity in the story of monetary integration: was it designed primarily to deal with a technical issue – alternatively formulated as exchange rate volatility as a barrier to trade and thus to greater economic integration, or else as a quest for price stability – or was it part of a grand political plan, in which money was used to tie the European knot? Jacques Rueff (1950), France's major mid-century thinker about money, coined a phrase that was subsequently often erroneously linked to Jean Monnet: "L'Europe se fera par la monnaie ou ne se fera pas." In the 1960s, a theory of optimum currency areas was developed by US-based economists (Mundell 1961, McKinnon 1963, Kenen 1969): although they continued to be influential figures in the European debate, their theories were irrelevant to the final push to monetary integration in the 1990s. The states that signed up to economic union had different expectations and hopes: some saw it as a way of building credibility and thus of reducing borrowing costs, while others focused on the constitutionalization of a stable monetary regime. How could the divergent visions of the potential gains from monetary integration be mutually reconciled?

What was the design flaw? It is often claimed – especially but not only by American economists – that the travails of the euro, as well as the history of past monetary unions (Bordo and Jonung 2003), show that it is impossible to have a monetary union in the absence of a political union, which establishes a common political process for determining the distribution of fiscal costs. Tom Sargent used the bully pulpit of the Nobel Prize Acceptance speech to tell Europe to follow the US example in the aftermath of the War of

Independence and assume the debts of the individual states. Assumption for Alexander Hamilton was "the powerful cement of our union." (Sargent 2012) Paul De Grauwe stated the case quite simply: "The euro is a currency without a country. To make it sustainable a European country has to be created" (de Grauwe 2012). The Presidents of the European Central Bank (ECB) (that manages the common currency) seem to endorse this advice. Accepting the Charlemagne Prize in Aachen, Jean-Claude Trichet said: "In a long term historical perspective, Europe – which has invented the concept and the word of democracy – is called to complete the design of what it already calls a 'Union'" (Trichet 2011). Mario Draghi has been even more dramatic, demanding:

> the collective commitment of all governments to reform the governance of the euro area. This means completing economic and monetary union along four key pillars: (i) a financial union with a single supervisor at its heart, to re-unify the banking system; (ii) a fiscal union with enforceable rules to restore fiscal capacity; (iii) an economic union that fosters sustained growth and employment; and (iv) a political union, where the exercise of shared sovereignty is rooted in political legitimacy.
>
> *(Draghi 2012)*

This advice seems appallingly radical to many, since almost every politician denies that there is any real possibility of creating something resembling a European state, and almost every citizen recoils at the prospect. The fact that the discussion to which Draghi contributed to had been going on for decades suggests that there were no very easy solutions.

2. The choice for state or non-state money

In choosing a "pure" money in the 1990s, free of any possibility of political interference and simply designed to meet the objective of price stability, Europeans were taking an obvious risk. They were obviously and deliberately flying in the face of the dominant modern tradition of thinking about money. The creation of money is usually thought to be the domain of the state: this was the widely prevalent doctrine of the nineteenth century, which reached its apogee in Georg Friedrich Knapp's highly influential *State Theory of Money* (Knapp 1905). Money could be issued by the state because of government's ability to define the unit of account in which taxes should be paid. In the *Nicomachean Ethics,* Aristotle explained that money owes its name to its property of not existing by nature but as a product of convention or law. Greek coins usually carried depictions of gods and goddesses, but the Romans changed the practice and put their (presumed divine) emperors on their coins. Christ famously answers a question about obedience to civil authorities by examining a Roman coin and telling the Pharisees, "Render unto Caesar the things which are Caesar's."

The graphical design of the euro currency makes the novelty clear. Unlike most banknotes and coins, there is no picture of the state or its symbols – no Caesar – on the money issued and managed by the ECB. This feature sharply distinguished the new money from the banknotes that had circulated before the common currency and that were carefully designed to depict national symbols. Especially in the nineteenth century, the formation of new nation-states was associated with the establishment of national moneys, which gave the new polities a policy area in which they could exercise themselves. European leaders in the late-twentieth century were self-consciously stepping away from that tradition – in large part because of a widespread sense that national money had been subject to political abuse with inflationary consequences.

There is a long tradition of thinking of currency union as a way of solving a collective action problem. Walter Bagehot and his influential periodical *The Economist* in the mid-nineteenth century pleaded vigorously in favor of what seemed like a common sense solution: "Commerce is anywhere identical: buying and selling, lending and borrowing, are alike all the world over, and all matters concerning them ought universally to be alike too." This obvious appeal was accepted by all the luminaries of the time, including John Stuart Mill and Stanley Jevons. Money, he argued, should not be seen as the creation of the state (Bagehot 1889). He thought it preferable to conceive of money as serving the needs of commerce (and of the people more generally) rather than the interests of the state and its rulers.

There were two major historical eras when cross-border monetary experimentation dominated political discussions. Both of these eras coincide with an intensification of the pace of technical change, and a surge in globalization – interconnectedness through flows of goods, labor, and capital. At the time Bagehot was writing, Napoleon III and his advisers had already pushed through the Latin Monetary Union, by which the coinage systems of France, Belgium, Switzerland and Italy were homogenized, with a standard franc or lira coin of a standard weight and purity of silver that would circulate freely in the member countries of the currency union (Einaudi 2001). The 1867 World Monetary Conference, held in Paris, went substantially further in its ambitions. Only a very slight alteration of parities would be required to bring into line France, Great Britain, as well as the United States, which was just recovering from the massively costly and destructive Civil War. France was on a bimetallic standard, in which its coinage was set both in terms of gold and silver weights; Great Britain was on a pure gold standard; and the United States was considering a return to a stable currency based on metal. The proposals in this form were not realized (the small parity alteration required for Great Britain was too contentious politically); but in a sense the gold standard as a completely credible common standard was a sort of monetary union (Russell 1898).

In the late twentieth century, a new wave of globalization pushed a new interest in monetary unification. A helpful way of thinking about the process of European integration is to present it as an extreme example of a search – driven mostly by Europeans – for rules to manage the process of globalization (Abdelal 2007).

2.1 Myths about the origins

In the wake of the 2007–8 financial crisis, the combination of a bank crisis and a sovereign debt crisis in the Eurozone led to doubts about the economic rationale of integration, primarily political theories about the fundamental drivers of the process. There are two versions of the political story. Both focus obsessively on the politics of the German role in driving the monetary union, so that it again appears as if solving the German question is central to the future of Europe. Both are mirror images of each other: in one Germany appears as uniquely virtuous, in the other as terribly vicious.

In the first view – the virtuous German story – the currency union was a high-minded European political project that ignored economic realities. It was needed to stop the recurrence of war between France and Germany. Both proponents of the euro project such as the veteran German Foreign Minister Hans-Dietrich Genscher but also by opponents such as the economist Martin Feldstein (2012) have touted this theory. But it is implausible. Americans are perfectly aware that they have not had a war with Canada or Mexico recently (although in the long past there were indeed such conflicts), and that they don't need a currency union to improve relations with neighbors. On the other hand, Americans are aware that civil wars can occur in malfunctioning currency unions (in the mid-nineteenth century, at exactly the time Napoleon III was dreaming of world monetary union): and Ireland too also has its own terrible twentieth-century experience of the damage done by civil war.

Then there is the vicious view of the origins of the euro, a conspiracy theory about a deep-seated German masterplan. Some of its earliest proponents were British (like the former British Chancellor of the Exchequer Denis Healey), but now it is circulating widely, above all in southern and peripheral Europe (Healey 1990). Since Germany had lower rates of wage inflation than France and much lower rates than the Mediterranean countries, a locked currency would guarantee increased export surpluses, at the price of misery elsewhere. A German grasp for European economic primacy would succeed at the end of the twentieth century and in the new millennium where a similar German military plan had failed one century earlier.

This view seems as absurd as the first myth about peace and money. If this is what the Germans were aiming at, wouldn't other countries be able to get some whiff of the nefarious plot? And more importantly, if this were really a strategy it is a pretty short-sighted one (not really that much better than the disastrous Schlieffen Plan of 1914 to defeat both France and Russia at the same time). Plunging one's neighbors into national bankruptcy is not a good way of building any kind of stable prosperity.

For the critics, Germany's currency manipulation was a mercantilist strategy of securing permanent trade and current account surpluses that would give Germany a commanding control of resources. In each phase of the negotiation of European monetary integration, Germany's partners in consequence tried to devise an institutional mechanism to control German surpluses.

That is a debate that goes back a long way. Raymond Barre, then Vice-President of the European Commission, for instance argued in 1968 that Germany should take "energetic measures for speedier growth and the stimulation of imports," as well as "special action to inhibit the flow of speculative capital into Germany" (Ungerer 1997).

In the Bretton Woods era of fixed exchange rates and controlled capital markets, even relatively small deficits could not be financed, and produced immediate pressure on the exchange markets. The deficit countries then had to apply fiscal brakes in a stop-go cycle. Germany's partners, notably France, were faced by the prospect of austerity and deflation in order to correct deficits. This alternative was unattractive to the French political elite, because it constrained growth and guaranteed electoral unpopularity. Their preferred policy alternative was thus German expansion, but this course was unpopular with a German public worried about the legacy of inflation and was opposed by the powerful and independent central bank, the Deutsche Bundesbank.

Solving the question of the German current accounts in the European setting at first appeared to require some sophisticated and ingenious political mechanism that would force French politicians to do more austerity than they would have liked, and Germans less price orthodoxy than they thought they needed. A political mechanism however requires continual negotiation and public deliberation that would have been painful given the policy preferences in the two countries (and in those countries that lined up with each one of the Big Two). The increased attraction of monetary union was that it required no such drawn out political process. The operation of an entirely automatic device would constrain political debate, initiative, and policy choice.

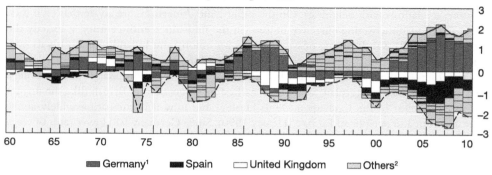

Sum of current account balances of deficit and surplus countries
As a percentage of GDP

Germany[1]　　Spain　　United Kingdom　　Others[2]

Figure 2.1 Current accounts in Europe 1960–2010

Sources: OECD *Economic Outlook*; European commission, Annual Macro Economic database.

Notes:
1 From 1991 the balance of payments statistics also include the external transactions of the former German Democratic Republic.
2 Including Belgium, Denmark, France, Greece, Ireland, Italy, Luxembourg, Netherlands and Portugal.

Monetary union was thus conceptualized as a way of simplifying politics. This had been a feature of European arguments from the beginning. Robert Triffin (1957) had shown how a problem could be reduced to its most basic level: "The significance of monetary unification, like that of exchange stability in a free market, is that both exclude any resort to any other corrective techniques except those of internal fiscal and credit policies."

As evident from Figure 2.1, the problem of current accounts grew bigger, the surpluses and deficits ever larger. The monetary union occurred after a drive to capital market liberalization, and was intended to be the logical completion of that liberalization. Current account imbalances were apparently sustainable for much longer periods – though not for ever. The effects of movements in capital in allowing current account imbalances to build up to a much greater extent, and ensuring that corrections, when they occurred, would be much more dramatic, was already noticeable in the late 1980s and early 1990s, before the move to monetary union. Indeed, those large build-ups in the imbalances were what convinced Europe's policy-makers that a monetary union was the only way of avoiding the risk of periodic crises with currency realignments whose trade policy consequences threatened the survival of an integrated internal European market. The success of the early years of monetary union lies in the effective privatization of current account imbalances, so that the problem disappeared from the radar screen of policy debates. It would only reappear when the freezing up of the banking system after 2008 required the substitution of public sector claims for private claims: with that the old problem of the politicization of current account imbalances immediately reappeared.

The rather more mundane truth about the evolution of Europe's monetary order is that it was in fact the outcome of global debates about currency disorder. European monetary integration appeared urgent in the late 1960s, as the Bretton Woods regime disintegrated, again in the late 1970s, when US monetary policy was subject to big political pressures and the dollar collapsed, and finally – and with an apparently successful outcome in the late 1980s – in the aftermath of a debate about global monetary stabilization at the Plaza and Louvre meetings of the major industrial countries.

3. The Werner Initiative

Global monetary turbulence in the last years of the Bretton Woods system focused on the problematic role of the dollar in the fixed exchange rate regime. From 1968, when the London gold pool stopped operating and the private gold market was disconnected from an official market at which transactions still occurred at the fixed parities, to 1971 when President Nixon finally "closed the gold window," the system was in constant crisis. The dollar was predicted to lose its role in the international system, and France in particular engaged in constant criticism of the dollar order. The older reserve currency, the pound sterling, which still played a significant role (though mostly for countries in the British Commonwealth), was in deeper trouble than the dollar. The aftermath of the British devaluation of 1967 threatened wider monetary instability. There was increased concern about rising inflation. Such concerns raised the question of whether there could be an alternative store of value to the dollar that was at the heart of the Bretton Woods regime. A more stable monetary measure might be desirable, and in the wake of the creation of the IMF's (heavily circumscribed) Special Drawing Rights there was increased interest in the institutional creation of liquidity and also in artificial units of account. In addition, the Europeans wanted a monetary unit that reflected their interests, rather than those of the United States. In consequence, two issues began to be prominent that would remain central to the pursuit of European monetary integration: the possibility of establishing a European unit of account, and the inter-relationship of monetary with more general economic policy. The exchange rate regime of Bretton Woods also posed a specific problem, in that currencies were linked to a par value with the US dollar, from which 1 percent deviations ether side were possible. As a result, if one European currency was at the top of its dollar band and another at the bottom, they would be fluctuating against each other by double the amount that they could move against the dollar. With dollar weakness, it was increasingly common for capital to flee into European safe haven currencies (above all the Deutschemark) putting upward pressure on those currency.

American policy-makers did not see themselves as the source of the world's trouble. On the contrary, they saw the current account surpluses that were building up in West Germany (and also in Japan) as an indication of a currency manipulation in which the surplus countries were forcing exports on the rest of the world. The surpluses of Germany also raised a question about whether there could really be an effectively coordinated European response. Should new exchange rates be negotiated? Or was there a need for a short- or medium-term support mechanism to finance imbalances within Europe?

In the late 1960s, the first of the major sustained political initiatives aiming at the creation of a monetary union was launched by the EEC Commission. The result, usually referred to as the Werner Plan (after the Prime Minister of Luxembourg, Pierre Werner, who chaired the committee that produced the document), is frequently regarded as a damp squib. It was characteristic of many of the phases of European monetary integration in that the approach depended excessively on an unlikely congruence or simultaneity of multifarious aspects of the integration process. But in fact the suggestions made at this time were not dissimilar to those made in more apparently auspicious circumstances at the end of the 1980s and the beginning of the 1990s. Amy Verdun (2001) as a result refers to Werner as being a "remarkably similar blueprint" to that of Jacques Delors and the committee he chaired in 1988–9 that provided a basic draft of the mechanism required for European monetary union. Institutional innovation, in the form of a new institution, the European Monetary Cooperation Fund (EMCF), initially envisaged as a potential Federal Reserve System for Europe, was at the heart of the proposals. The major difficulty lay in the actual implementation, which proved to circumscribe severely the operations of the EMCF (similar considerations would later prevent the emergence of a European Monetary Fund).

The Werner plan originated with a report from European Community Commission Vice-President Raymond Barre, published on February 12, 1969, and focusing on the failure of Community mutual assistance mechanisms in the Italian crisis of 1964 and in the French difficulties of 1968. Barre's initiative was a response to the debacle of the Bonn G-10 meeting in November 1968 and its intense political maneuvring, when the differences between European countries but also their incapacity to coordinate on exchange rate issues had been revealed in a humiliating way. Barre's report analyzed the way in which Community objectives could be frustrated by the action of large member states. It constituted one of the first expressions of the fear that Germany and its anti-inflationary policy priorities might dominate and distort European discussions.

Barre intended to establish a close link between economic policy and monetary co-operation, and also discussed the possibility of coordinating cyclical fiscal policies. Short-term monetary support operations and medium-term financial assistance would be linked with the convergence of medium-term economic objectives and coordination of short-term policies. The short-term assistance would be entirely automatic in the new proposal, and hence would avoid a politicization of the issue of European transfers. The thought ran in parallel lines to John Maynard Keynes's plans for automaticity in IMF lending in the negotiations leading up to the Bretton Woods settlement, an approach which the United States as the largest and most powerful creditor rejected (Skidelsky 1992; Steil 2012).

The veteran Jean Monnet then persuaded the political leaders, German Chancellor Willy Brandt and French President Georges Pompidou, to take up the issues raised by Barre. Monnet presented a paper to Brandt which stated that "Germany could take a peaceful, constructive and generous initiative which would overlay – I might even say efface – the memories of the past." Brandt was aware that a bold European initiative on monetary integration was viewed with great scepticism by his advisers. In particular, the German Foreign Office had been critical of the idea of producing economic convergence through monetary policy. He thought that only a high political initiative could break through the "chicken and egg problem" created by alternate emphases on the primacy of monetary or economic integration (Wilkens 1999, Wilkens 2005, Zimmermann 2001). But there were some exceptions to the German bureaucratic critique, and in the German Economics Ministry the Europe department headed by Hans Tietmeyer, had produced at the end of October a memorandum including a *Stufenplan* (Plan by Stages) for European Economic and Monetary Union. Tietmeyer's document envisaged that coherent economic policy could be achieved by a "codex on cyclical good behavior" (which has resemblances to the discussions of the 1990s of the Stability Pact); and also envisaged a Business Cycle Advisory Council and a European Central Banking council (Tietmeyer 1996).

The outcome of the willingness of Brandt and Pompidou to come together was the appointment in March 1970 of a "Committee of Presidents of Committee," chaired by Werner, in which the Monetary Committee, the EEC Committee of Central Bank Governors, the EEC Committee on Medium Term Economic Policy, the Committee on Business Cycle Policy, and the Budgetary Committee, as well as the Commission were represented. The committee was divided between those who wanted to accelerate monetary integration (France, Luxembourg, Belgium, Italy, and the Commission), and Germany, supported by the Netherlands, which argued the case for greater economic coherence as a prerequisite for closer monetary coordination. From the beginning, the members found that they could only come together around a theme of "parallel" development of economic and monetary integration.

The final version of the Werner Report was presented on October 27, 1970. It came at a moment when the G-10 was debating whether bands of fluctuation in the Bretton Woods system should be *widened*. Such a challenge required some European response.

> The increasing interpenetration of the economies has entailed a weakening of autonomy for national economic policies. The control of economic policy has become all the more difficult because the loss of autonomy at the national level has not been compensated by the inauguration of Community policies. The inadequacies and disequilibrium that have occurred in the process of realization of the Common Market are thus thrown into relief.
>
> *Werner (1970, p. 8)*

The report's most striking feature was the sharp delineation of a final objective, of monetary union.

> Economic and monetary union will make it possible to realize an area within which goods and services, people and capital will circulate freely and without competitive distortions, without thereby giving rise to structural, or regional disequilibrium. [. . .] The implementation of such a union will effect a lasting improvement in welfare in the Community and will reinforce the contribution of the Community to economic and monetary equilibrium in the world.
>
> *Werner (1970, p. 9)*

The report also discussed the principal consequences of economic and monetary union in very broad terms, including the following points:

- the Community currencies will be assured of total and irreversible mutual convertibility free from fluctuations in rates and with immutable parity rates, or preferably they will be replaced by a sole Community currency;
- monetary policy in relation to the outside world will be within the jurisdiction of the Community;
- the essential features of the whole of the public budgets, and in particular variations in their volume, the size of balances and the methods of financing or utilizing them, will be decided at the Community level;
- a systematic and continuous consultation between the social partners will be ensured at the Community level.

In retrospect, the discussions around the Werner Plan seem to have been rapidly overtaken by events. It took over a year just to achieve a consensus on reducing the intra-Community marginal band from 1.50 to 1.20 percent. The date of operation of the new system (June 15, 1971) was agreed on April 19, 1971: but before the system could come into effect, Germany's response to global exchange turbulence (and specifically substantial short-term capital outflows into the Deutschemark) blew up the whole system.

German Economics Minister Karl Schiller tried to persuade other EEC governments of the virtues of a joint float, but failed, and on May 10, 1971, Germany embarked on a unilateral float, even though both the Bundesbank President and the majority of the Central Bank Council were still opposed to such a move. The German float was only the beginning of a process that led to the end of the postwar exchange rate regime (the Bretton Woods system), with President Richard Nixon's announcement on August 15, 1971, that he would close the gold window and impose extraordinary import surcharge.

In the aftermath of exchange rate uncertainty, the Europeans created an exchange rate agreement known as the "Snake." The EEC Commission pressed for a relaunching of the project of economic and monetary union, with proposals on January 12, 1972, for a maximum 2 percent deviation from parity, and for the realization of the monetary fund as a way of administering short- and medium-term support within the EEC. The ECOFIN Council on March 21, 1972, reflecting the consensus that had emerged at the EC Committee of Central Bank Governors, asked the central banks to reduce fluctuation margins to ±2.25 percent, or half the amount allowed under the terms of the Smithsonian, "as a first step towards the creation of [an EEC] monetary zone within the framework of the international system." This new system of a reduced fluctuation band was generally referred to as "the EEC snake in the Smithsonian tunnel." Within this system, the Netherlands and Belgium-Luxembourg continued to have the smaller room for maneuver (1.5 percent), which was sometimes called "the worm". Dutch Treasury Secretary, Conrad Oort, suggested in a speech during the 1974 IMF meeting that:

> The snake has become the favorite animal of the Eurocrats. It resides on an empty floor in Luxembourg, called the European Monetary Fund. So far, its most distinctive virtue is that it has created a whole new serpentine folklore and a Eurolingo exclusively devoted to the life and habits of the snake.
>
> *(Oort 1974)*

But in practice, the Snake proved impossible to operate on an EEC basis, as speculative pressures built of because of mutually incompatible policy regimes. Britain left the snake mechanism less than two months after joining. Ireland, which was in a currency union with the UK, also left at the same time; Denmark, with very extensive trade links with the UK announced its departure on June 27, 1972, but kept the krona within the Snake limits and actually rejoined on October 10. France left the Snake on two occasions; and the Scandinavian countries were forced to abandon their membership too. The result was that the Snake soon looked like a really small currency zone around Germany – with only the Netherlands as a consistently reliable member.

4. The EMS

In 1978, the European monetary regime was remade. The major initiative came from French President Valéry Giscard d'Estaing and German Chancellor Helmut Schmidt. Their high level debates were charged with lofty geo-political thoughts, and the new monetary arrangements were frequently seen as a challenge to the role of the dollar, which they believed was being deliberately depreciated (in a so-called "malign neglect") against other currencies in order to obtain trade advantages.

The eventual outcome of the intense negotiations of 1978, the European Monetary System (EMS) is often regarded as a transformative step on a progressive path to monetary integration (Ludlow 1982). But in practice it amounted to little more than an elegant repackaging of the Snake arrangements, a "swimming trunk" cover up of the bare essentials as Helmut Schmidt contemptuously put it when addressing the German Bundesbank; to soothe French susceptibilities about having been twice ejected ignominiously from that arrangement?

Like the Werner Plan, it began with a suggestion from the EC Commission, whose President, Roy Jenkins, saw the issue of Europe's currency arrangements as primarily a response to the faltering and flawed character of American monetary hegemony, and the strains that were consequently imposed on Europeans (Jenkins 1977).

Members of the new EMS exchange-rate mechanism were obliged to intervene without limits at the 2.25 percent fluctuation margins either side of a central parity calculated bilaterally on the basis of a central rate calculated around a basket currency (European Currency Unit, ECU), which was to be "at the centre of the EMS" (so that there would be no national currency like the Deutschemark as the basis of the peg). Central rates could be adjusted "subject to mutual agreement by a common procedure which will comprise all countries participating in the exchange-rate mechanism and the Commission." A divergence indicator of 75 percent of the maximum spread of each currency would, when attained, allow the identification of the country which was diverging, and then trigger corrective action (Mourlon-Druol 2012).

The most significant feature of the agreement was something that it did not contain: the promise the German Bundesbank extracted from Chancellor Schmidt that the German central bank might be released from the intervention requirements if monetary stability were to be threatened. In a historic appearance before the Bundesbank Council on November 30, 1978, when Chancellor Schmidt tried to persuade the Council to accept the new monetary regime, he explained that the new arrangement was a political necessity, but that it was not completely binding.

> We are doubly vulnerable and will remain so far into the next century. Vulnerable on account of Berlin and also on account of the open flank to the East, on account of the partition of the nation, symbolised by the insular position of Berlin, and secondly we remain vulnerable on account of Auschwitz. The more successful we are in the areas of foreign policy, economic policy, socio-economic matters, and military matters, the longer it will be until Auschwitz sinks into history. So much the more we remain reliant on these two pillars, of which I spoke, one of which is the Common Market.

But Schmidt accepted the critical Bundesbank demand, made in a summary on November 16 of key elements of the EMS agreement, that the Bundesbank should be released from the obligation to unlimited intervention if such a measure would pose a threat to the goal of German price stability. Otmar Emminger had written that the central bank council had agreed "under the precondition that the government and central bank agree on the legal basis and also on the future possibility of opting out in particular circumstances." Schmidt checked the memorandum with the letter "r" for "*richtig*," or "correct," and returned it to the Bundesbank. Germany agreed to a currency mechanism, but only to one that had a readily useable escape hatch.

The Emminger letter and Schmidt's concealed acceptance of the Bundesbank demand leaked out to the public when on December 6, 1978, in the course of a Bundestag debate Economics Minister Otto Graf Lambsdorff explicitly referred to the possibility of suspending the intervention requirement. But the government disliked any reference to it by the Bundesbank, and in the late 1980s as the system became apparently more stable, with fewer realignments (there were none between 1987 and 1992), many people seem not to have been aware that such an exit clause existed. The Governor of the Banca d'Italia, learning of the Emminger letter for the first time in the EMS crisis of September 1992, went deathly pale; and in July 1993 in the final EMS crisis, France was bitterly disillusioned when the Bundesbank stopped its interventions in support of the French franc.

A great deal of the immediate response and analysis was political rather than technical. Especially in France, the new mechanism was heavily criticized from both the left and the nationalist and Gaullist right. *Le Monde* (1978) termed it a German triumph that presaged the "Empire of the Mark", and a brake on European growth. The exchange rate agreement meant in practice in this version a way for Germans to improve their national competitiveness relative to the countries with higher levels of inflation. It also gave Germany the "right to intervene in the policies of its partners." In short, France was replacing an "American master" with a "second master, in practice an accomplice of the former master."

In practice, the EMS was a profoundly truncated system. First, despite the language of the agreement, and as the French critics suspected, the ECU was in reality not at the center of the system: such a role would have required an institution that had the capability of issuing or creating ECUs. Schmidt had told Italy's Prime Minister that "he could not understand Giscard's idea of putting the ECU at the centre of the system but had had to include a reference in the Bremen communiqué to please the French." In the same way as the 1960s vision of an IMF as a world central bank that might create SDRs was doomed to failure, the European monetary mechanism of the late 1970s did not fulfill the aspirations of its most enthusiastic proponents. Second, the divergence indicator was of little practical use, and it did not remove the asymmetric burden of adjustment by deficit countries. By the time it showed a divergence, that divergence would also become clear to speculators, who could mount an attack on the exchange rate. In other words, the indicator sent a signal not as an early warning but when there was already an obvious and imminent crisis – and in the early years, the result was usually a parity adjustment. In this aspect, the mechanism shared a conceptual flaw common in many attempts to establish official early warning systems: that the signals of a potential crisis become self-fulfilling. In addition, in practice countries tended to cluster in groups within the bands, and so it was difficult to single out individual cases. Furthermore, an increased emphasis on convergence and on fighting inflation meant that in reality the pressure to adjust continued to fall on the weaker countries, with deficits. Within a few years, everyone recognized that the divergence indicator had been discarded, or as it was put in officialise turned into "a useful but not a privileged indicator." Third, the agreement provided for a further stage, the establishment of the European Monetary Fund after two years. In practice, there was no attempt to do this.

5. The Delors initiative and the Maastricht Treaty

The most decisive push for a European solution to a global problem occurred in different circumstances. When the dollar was soaring in the mid-1980s, when American manufacturing was threatened and when there appeared to be the possibility of a protectionist backlash, the finance ministers of the major industrial countries pushed for exchange rate agreement. At the G-7 finance ministers' Louvre meeting in 1987 they agreed to lock their exchange rates into a system of target zones.

In practice, nothing came of that global plan, but then Edouard Balladur, the French finance minister who had largely been responsible for the Louvre proposal, came up with a tighter European scheme. When German foreign minister Hans Dietrich Genscher appeared sympathetic, Europe's central bankers were asked by the president of the European Commission, Jacques Delors, to prepare a timetable and a plan for currency union. The Delors Committee met between September 1988 and April 1989, and produced its report at a moment when no one in Western Europe seriously thought that a profound geo-political transformation such as the collapse of the Soviet bloc and of communist ideology could be at all likely.

The positive outcome of the Delors Committee was a surprise in that the most powerful central banker in the Committee, Bundesbank President Karl Otto Pöhl, was generally believed to be opposed to any project for enhanced monetary cooperation, and the Euroskeptic British government tried to keep the British member of the Committee working with Pöhl in order to frustrate such cooperation. Since the report required unanimity in order to be convincing or effective, it thus seemed more or less certain at the outset that the project would not lead to the visionary result intended by Jacques Delors.

The eventual success of his plan invites a comparison of the effectiveness of different Commission presidents and officials: the initiative of Raymond Barre at the end of the 1960s only disappointed and led to bitter disillusion, Jenkins in the late 1970s produced over-bold proposals that in the end were held to be unrealistic and were side-lined by Giscard and Schmidt. Delors produced just the right mixture of vision and practical sense: the vision of a bold move to realize the idea of "Union," and the pragmatic acknowledgment that only the central bankers could really remove the obstacles that lay in the way (especially the political and institutional obstacles that lay in Germany and in the particular position of the Bundesbank). Dismissing the bankers as fundamentally obstructive, as the Commission had done in the late 1970s, would only create an institutional impasse. Binding them in opened the way to a process of innovation.

The Delors Report clearly laid out path to monetary union, defined as "a currency area in which policies are managed jointly with a view to attaining common macroeconomic objectives." But the Committee also added the rider: "The adoption of a single currency, while not strictly necessary for the creation of a monetary union, might be seen for economic as well as psychological and political reasons as a natural and desirable further development of the monetary union. A single currency would clearly demonstrate the irreversibility of the move to monetary union, considerably facilitate the monetary management of the Community and avoid the transactions costs of converting currencies." It provided for a three stage process, in which Stage One simply expanded existing cooperative arrangements.

In Stage Two a new European System of Central Banks (ESCB) would absorb both the EMCF and the EC Committee of Central Bank Governors. It would manage the transition from the combination of monetary policies of national central banks to a common monetary policy. In the third stage, exchange rates would be locked finally and irrevocably. The ESCB would pool reserves and manage interventions with regard to third currencies. "With the establishment of the European System of Central Banks the Community would also have created an institution through which it could participate in all aspects of international monetary coordination" (Section 38). Delors emphasized that the monetary integration would need to be accompanied by a consolidation of the single market and competition policy, as well as by an evaluation and adaptation of regional policies (Section 56).

The central banks continued to play the dominant role in designing the new institutions. It is not surprising that they opted for a strong form of central bank independence, with a primary mandate for the new European central banks in the maintenance of price stability.

The design of the Maastricht Treaty also reflected German preferences for limits on government fiscal activism. Article 104 prohibited overdraft facilities from the central bank to governments (monetary financing): it was later taken over as Article 123 of the 2007 Lisbon Treaty (Treaty on the Functioning of the European Union). Article 104a prohibited privileged access to financial institutions (Article 124 TFEU), and Article 104b (Article 125 TFEU). In practice, however, a consensus soon developed that government bonds would not be subject to a risk of default, and thus were not treated by financial markets as the equivalent of corporate bonds (Prati and Schinasi 1997).

The German character of monetary union became clearer in the aftermath of Maastricht and of the major currency crises that shook the EMS in 1992–3 and almost destroyed the integration project. Frankfurt was chosen as the location of the European Monetary Institute in October 1993, and the name "euro" was agreed in 1995 (as Ecu was thought to be too French). At the same time, German Finance Minister Theo Waigel pushed for a Stability Pact that would enforce the Maastricht deficit and debt levels. It became clear that convergence would not be complete by 1997, the first possible date under the Maastricht Treaty for the final stage of monetary union; but then attention focused on making the alternative date (January 1, 1999) a reality, with the physical introduction of a new money coming some years later (2001). In practice, although the old physical notes continued to circulate after 1999, the Deutschemarks and francs etc. were legally only units of a completely new currency.

It has become fashionable to say that the moves of the early 1990s were undertaken in a mood of carelessness (*sorglosigkeit*), in Otmar Issing's phrase (2012), or that Chancellor Kohl was neglectful (*leichtsinnig*) – according to Hans Peter Schwarz's monumental new biography (2012). Kohl promised a political union: on November 6, 1991, he told an ecstatically applauding German parliament that "one cannot repeat it often enough: political union is the indispensible counterpart of the economic and monetary union." But when the governments negotiated a few weeks later in Maastricht, there were very concrete plans for the monetary union, and for the political union – none at all.

In fact, the planning for monetary union was unbelievably sober and meticulous. In the debates of the central bankers' group that Delors chaired in 1988–9, before the fall of the Berlin Wall, two really critical issues were highlighted: and they were the ones that really mattered.

The first concerned the fiscal discipline needed for currency union. An explicit discussion took place as to whether the capital market by itself was enough to discipline borrowers, and a consensus emerged that market discipline would not be adequate and that a system of rules was needed. The influential Belgian economist from the BIS, Alexandre Lamfalussy, a member of the Delors Committee, brought up cases from the US and Canada as well as from Europe where cities and regions were insufficiently disciplined. Jacques Delors during the meetings of the Committee appropriately raised the prospect of a two-speed Europe, in which one or two countries might need a "different kind of marriage contract" (James 2012). There is a tendency for fiscal policy to be pro-cyclical, particularly when the cycles are driven by property booms, in that enhanced fiscal revenue from real estate exuberance prompts politicians to think that the increase in their resources is permanent. But the pro-cyclical fiscal element may be magnified in a currency union.

The need for fiscal discipline arising from spillover effects of large borrowing requirements is a European issue, but it is clearly not one confined to Europe alone. In emerging markets, this problem was identified after the 1997–8 Asia crisis, and the problem of major fiscal strains became primarily one of the industrial world – and especially of the United States. An appropriate response would involve some democratically legitimated mechanism for limiting the debt build-up, as in the Swiss debt brake (*Schuldenbremse*) which was supported by 85 percent of voters in a referendum.

The debt and deficit criteria built into the Maastricht Treaty in fact proved to be at the center of most the debate of the 1990s. Germany insisted again and again on a strict interpretation of the Treaty, with Finance Minister Theo Waigel repeating that 3.0 meant 3.0, with an insistence that led to the French press dubbing him "Monsieur 3.0." But in practice, some bending of the rules took place. First was the problem of Belgium, with a debt level that looked sustainable but exceeded 60 percent of GDP (it was 130 percent in 1997); but Belgium was in a currency union with Luxembourg, which qualified unambiguously, and Brussels was also the seat of the vital European institutions. Then, since Italy's debt level at 120 percent of GDP was lower than that of Belgium, it was hard to exclude Italy. From the point-of-view of the high debt countries, such as Italy, the great political attraction of membership in the currency union was the added credibility that would reduce interest rates, and thus bring an immediate fiscal saving. The downside was a loss of exchange rate flexibility, but many Italian policy-makers and businessmen recognized that the cycles of inflation and devaluation that had characterized the 1970s and 1980s did nothing to increase productivity or output growth.

The original concept of a Stability Pact to perpetuate the eligibility criteria after the final stage of monetary union was cosmetically watered down to take account of French concerns about growth as a Stability and Growth Pact (SGP). A fatal blow came when France and Germany ignored the SGP and had it suspended in November 2003 as a counter to a – as it proved spurious – threat of recession. European Commission President Romano Prodi called the Pact "stupid." The European Council agreed not to apply the deficit procedure against France and Germany, though later the European Court of Justice ruled that this step contravened EU law. In 2005, the disciplinary mechanism was softened, many processes became merely discretionary, and new procedural provisions made it harder to take action against non-compliant states. Smaller EU countries were outraged by France and Germany's initiative.

The second flaw in the European plans identified by the central bankers as they prepared monetary union was much more serious. In the original version of a plan for a central bank that would run a monetary union, the central bank would have overall supervisory and regulatory powers. That demand met strong resistance, above all from the German Bundesbank, which worried that a role in maintaining financial stability might undermine the future central bank's ability to focus on price stability as the primary goal of monetary policy. There was also bureaucratic resistance from existing regulators. The ECB was thus never given overall supervisory and regulatory powers, and until the outbreak of the financial crisis in 2007–8 no one thought that was a problem.

By 2010, however, it was clear that there was a very big problem. There had previously been a stream of private sector money from north to south in Europe. The flows of capital had important effects on wage rates, differential inflation levels, and hence on the position of competitiveness. In the monetary union, there was no policy tool to limit inflation through a national monetary policy, and hence in the borrowing countries (now often referred to as the periphery), interest rates were lower than they should have been had a Taylor rule been practiced. Indeed Ireland and Spain had negative real rates for substantial periods of the 2000s. After the financial crisis, the sustainability of the flows was threatened by banking crises in the periphery, and the long-developing competiveness positions now looked like an argument that the debt levels (private or public) were unsustainable. Growth prospects that looked brilliant before the crisis no longer existed; so there was a debt servicing problem. That in turn seemed to endanger the banks, including particularly big north European banks that had already taken losses on US sub-prime investments. Funding dried up as US money market funds no longer wished to buy paper issued by European bank borrowers. One of the most obvious lessons of the first phase of the financial crisis was that the failure of big banks would have disastrous consequences. That mantra of the policy technocrats produced its own pushback among many voters and politicians: shouldn't the banks bear some of the burden. At Deauville in October 2010, German Chancellor Angela Merkel and President Nicolas Sarkozy agreed that there should be Private Sector Involvement (PSI).

Far from reassuring markets, the move to make private lenders bear some of the cost of past mistakes made for greater nervousness – much more so, indeed, as Jean-Claude Trichet of the ECB had insistently warned. For a decade, markets had interpreted the no-bailout clause of the Maastricht Treaty as making default impossible. It now seemed to be encouraged by the official sector. After Deauville an unhappy mechanism was created which increased the potential for large bank losses and heightened market nervousness. The official sector put in more money, in effect a substitution for the absent private sector flows of the pre-crisis era; and as that occurred and as the public credit was given seniority, the problems of the private sector debt increased rather than diminished.

Addressing the design flaws may thus not require the politically impossible – a sudden, quick and complete move to political union – but rather the elaboration of a mechanism that prevents or limits the effects of financial sector instability on public finances. The difficulty is that this approach requires a choice between the fundamentally rules-based approach that is at the heart of German economic thinking, and the centralizing and discretionary approach that is more characteristic of the French mindset.

References

Abdelal, R. (2007), *Capital Rules: The Construction of Global Finance*, Cambridge, MA: Harvard University Press.

Bagehot, W. (1889), *A Practical Plan for Assimilating the English and American Money as a Step Towards a Universal Money*, London: Longmans Green, reprint of 1869 edition.

Bordo, M.D. and Jonung. L. (2003), The Future of EMU: What Does the History of Monetary Unions Tell Us? in Capie, F.H. and Wood, G.E. (eds) *Monetary Unions: Theory, History, Public Choice* London, New York: Routledge.

de Grauwe, P. (2012), The Eurozone's Design Failures: Can they be Corrected? LSE lecture, available at www2.lse.ac.uk/publicEvents/pdf/2012_MT/20121128-Prof-Grauwe-PPT.pdf.

Draghi, M. (2012), A European Strategy for Growth and Integration with Solidarity, presented at a conference organised by the Directorate General of the Treasury, Ministry of Economy and Finance – Ministry for Foreign Trade, Paris, November 30, 2012.

Einaudi, L. (2001), *Money and Politics: European Monetary Unification and the International Gold Standard (1865–1873)*, Oxford, New York: Oxford University Press.

Feldstein, M. (2012), The Failure of the Euro: The Little Currency that Couldn't, *Foreign Affairs*, January/February.

Healey, D. (1990), *The Time of My Life*, New York: Norton.

Honohan, P. (2012), A View from Ireland – The Crisis and the Euro, address to the David Hume Institute and the Scottish Institute for Research in Economics, Edinburgh, November 13, 2012.

Issing, O. (2012), Europa in Not – Deutschland in Gefahr, *Frankfurter Allgemeine Zeitung*, June 11.

Jenkins, R. (1977), Europe's Present Challenge and Future Opportunity, lecture delivered in Florence, October 27, 1977, available at http://aei.pitt.edu/4404/.

Kenen, P.B. (1969), The Theory of Optimum Currency Areas: An Eclectic View, in Mundell, R.A. and Swoboda, A.K. (eds) *Monetary Problems in the International Economy*, Chicago: University of Chicago Press.

Knapp, G.F. (1905), *Staatliche Theorie des Geldes*, Leipzig: Duncker & Humblot.

Le Monde. 1978. L'Empire du Mark. December 6, p. 2.

Ludlow, P. (1982), *The Making of the European Monetary System: A Case Study of the Politics of the European Community*, London: Butterworth.

McKinnon, R.I. (1963), Optimum Currency Areas, *American Economic Review*, 53(4): 717–724.

Mourlon-Druol, E. (2012), *A Europe Made of Money: The Emergence of the European Monetary System*, Ithaca: Cornell University Press.

Mundell, R.A. (1961), A Theory of Optimum Currency Areas, *American Economic Review*, 51(4): 657–665.

Oort, C.J. (1974), *Steps to International Monetary Order*, Washington D.C.: Per Jacobsson Foundation.

Prati, A. and Schinasi, G.J. (1997), European Monetary Union and International Capital Markets: Structural Implications and Risks, *IMF Working Paper* WP/97/62.

Rueff, J. (1950), L'Europe se fera par la monnaie ou ne se fera pas, *Synthèses*, 45: 267–271.

Russell, H.B. (1898), *International Monetary Conferences, Their Purposes, Character, and Results, With a Study of the Conditions of Currency and Finance in Europe and America During Intervening Periods, and in Their Relations to International Action*, New York, London: Harper & Brothers.

Sargent, T. (2012), United States Then, Europe Now, Nobel Prize speech, available at www.nobelprize. org/nobel_prizes/economics/laureates/2011/sargent-lecture.html.

Schwarz, H.-P. (2012), *Helmut Kohl: Eine Politische Biographie*, Stuttgart: DVA.

Skidelsky, R. (1992), *John Maynard Keynes: The Economist as Saviour*, London: Macmillan.

Steil, B. (2012), *The Battle of Bretton Woods: John Maynard Keynes, Harry Dexter White, and the Making of a New World Order*, Princeton: Princeton University Press.

Tietmeyer, H. (1996), Währungsstabilität *für Europa: Beiträge, Reden und Dokumente zur Europäischen Währungsunion aus Vier Jahrzehnten*, Baden-Baden: Deutsche Bundesbank.

Trichet, J.-C. (2011), Building Europe, Building Institutions, speech on receiving the Karlspreis 2011 in Aachen, June 2, 2011.

Triffin, R. (1957), *Europe and the Money Muddle*, London: Yale University Press

Ungerer, H. (1997), *A Concise History of European Monetary Integration: From EPU to EMU*, Westport: Quorum.

Verdun, A. (2001), The Political Economy of the Werner and Delors Reports: Continuity amidst Change or Change Amidst Continuity, in Magnusson, L. and Strath, B. (eds) *From the Werner Plan to the EMU: In Search of a Political Economy for Europe*, Bruxelles: Peter Lang.

Werner, P. (1970), Report to the Council and the Commission on the realization by stages of economic and monetary union in the Community, available at http://ec.europa.eu/economy_finance/emu_ history/documentation/chapter5/19701008en72realisationbystage.pdf.

Wilkens, A. (1999), Westpolitik, Ostpolitik and the project of the Economic and Monetary Union. Germany's European policy in the Brandt area, *Journal of European Integration History*, 5(1): 73–102.

Wilkens, A. (2005), Der Werner-Plan: Währung, Politik und Europa 1968–1971, in Knipping, F. and Schönwald, M. (eds) *Aufbruch zum Europa der Zweiten Generation: Die Europäische Einigung 1969–1974*, Trier: Wissenschaftlicher Verlag Trier.

Zimmermann, H. (2001), The Fall of Bretton Woods and the Emergence of the Werner Plan, in Magnusson, L. and Strath, B. (eds) *From the Werner Plan to the EMU: In Search of a Political Economy for Europe*, Bruxelles: Peter Lang.

3

HISTORY OF ECONOMIC THOUGHT AND POLICY-MAKING AT THE EUROPEAN COMMISSION

Ivo Maes[1]

1. Introduction

Economic thought and policy-making at the European Commission are very much a function of two elements: first, the treaties, as they determined the mandate of the Commission and, second, the economic ideas in the different countries of the Community, as economic thought at the Commission was to a large extent a synthesis and compromise of the main schools of thought in the Community.

The basis of the European Community was the Rome Treaty, which transformed economic and legal rules in the countries of the Community. The Treaty comprised the creation of a common market, as well as several accompanying policies. However, the monetary dimension of the Treaty was relatively limited.

According to the Rome Treaty, the Commission has three main functions: (a) guardian of the Treaties; (b) executive arm of the Community; (c) initiator of Community policy, the Commission has the sole right to present proposals and drafts for Community legislation. As the Rome Treaty is a 'framework treaty', the Commission has been active to implement the Treaties.

The main centre for economic thought and policy-making at the European Commission is DG Ecfin (Economic and Financial Affairs – earlier called DG II), which can be considered as the economic department of the Commission. In DG II, most attention is given to macroeconomic and monetary issues, even if also sectoral aspects of Community policy are analysed.

In this chapter, we first focus on the different schools which have been shaping economic thought at the Commission. This is followed by an analysis of the Rome Treaty, especially the monetary dimension. Thereafter we focus on the European Monetary Union (EMU) process and the initiatives of the Commission to further European monetary integration. We will consider three broad periods: the early decades, the Maastricht process and the quest for a 'genuine' EMU.

2. Economic thought at the European Commission

Economic thought at the Commission was to a large extent a synthesis and compromise of the main schools of macroeconomic thought in the European countries, especially the three big ones: Germany, France and the United Kingdom.[2] In the (early) post-war period national traditions were still important in Germany and France, while economics in the United Kingdom was much closer to the mainstream economics profession in the United States. Throughout time, the 'Anglo-Saxon' tradition would more and more dominate the academic economics profession in Europe.

German economic thought was centred around the notion of the social market economy. Two main tendencies can be distinguished. The more free-market-oriented German economists emphasised that economic policy was, in essence, *Ordnungspolitik*, i.e. a policy to create a framework within which markets can operate. The main tasks of economic policy are: (a) monetary policy: assure price stability; (b) fiscal policy: rather limited task for the government; and (c) structural policy: competition policy is emphasised. The other tendency, more Keynesian, emphasised the social dimension of the 'social market economy' and was more influential with the social democrats and the trade unions. It considered a dialogue between the social partners (trade unions and employers) as a crucial element of its strategy to stimulate growth and employment. In general, German economists mostly emphasised that economic policy consisted in the application of certain basic economic principles (especially the respect of market mechanisms and wage moderation) to the actual economic situation.

Initially, French economic ideas were very influential at the Commission. Robert Marjolin, the first commissioner for DG II, had been the deputy to Monnet at the French Planning Office, famous for its five-year plans. The French Planning Office, while being part of the French 'Colbertist' tradition, was also a spearhead of Keynesianism in France, with the national accounts at its heart (Rosanvallon, 1987, 40).

In the post-war period, with the increasing influence of the US academic world, 'Anglo-Saxon' ideas became more influential in the economics profession. These ideas followed different fads: Keynesianism, monetarism and supply-side economics. This was also the case at the Commission. From a methodological point of view, the 'Anglo-Saxons' favoured generally a more analytical approach, whereby economic policy recommendations would be based on more refined economic research. They especially favoured the development of Commission's model building capacity.

Initially, an important transmission channel for Anglo-Saxon ideas was the Organisation for Economic Cooperation and Development. Many Commission officials had worked at the OECD and there were many interactions between the Paris-based international organisation and the Commission. Anglo-Saxon ideas received a big boost with the nomination of Tommaso Padoa-Schioppa as Director-General of DG II in 1979 (Maes, 2013). Also, younger economists had a more Anglo-Saxon education, more of them having studied in the US and having a Ph.D.[3]

During the second half of the 1970s, economic thought at the Commission shifted from a dominance of Keynesian economics towards a more supply-side-oriented approach. While this was a more general tendency in the economics profession, the failure of the very Keynesian Concerted Action Plan of 1978 was an important factor hereby at the Commission.[4] At the beginning of the 1980s, the Commission's analytical framework became basically medium-term oriented, with an important role for supply-side and structural elements and a more cautious approach towards discretionary stabilisation policies (Maes, 1998, 14).

A further push towards integration fitted well into this new conceptual framework. The completion of the internal market, with its elimination of the remaining barriers to a free flow of goods, services, persons and capital, was very much in line with the deregulation strategy being pursued in the various European countries. Macroeconomic policy in the countries of the Community became more stability oriented, as policy-makers realised the illusory nature of the trade-off between inflation and unemployment. This orientation fitted in with a policy of stable exchange rates and a move towards a monetary union.

3. The Rome Treaty

The Rome Treaty would transform economic and legal rules in the countries of the Community. Among its novelties was the creation of a common market, as well as several accompanying policies in areas like agriculture, transport and competition. It also made provision for new institutions: the Parliament, the Council, the Commission and the Court of Justice.

Compared with commercial policy or competition policy, for example, the responsibilities of the Commission were rather limited with respect to macroeconomic and, especially, monetary issues. Triffin (1958, 1) described the limited monetary dimension of the EEC Treaty as 'a Hamlet in which the role of the Prince of Denmark is almost totally ignored'. The Treaty left macroeconomic policy-making mainly at the level of the Member States. The responsibilities of the Commission concerned the orientation and coordination of the national macroeconomic policies.

The most extensive discussion of macroeconomic and monetary issues can be found in the 'Balance of Payments' of the Treaty. It illustrates that macroeconomic and monetary issues were tackled from a 'common market' perspective, as balance of payments disequilibria would threaten the creation and functioning of the common market.

Article 104[5] stated that each Member State should pursue an economic policy 'to ensure the equilibrium of its overall balance of payments and to maintain confidence in its currency, while taking care to ensure a high level of employment and a stable level of prices'. German negotiators emphasised this article, as it implied the commitment of every Member State to adopt economic policies which would ensure balance of payments equilibrium.

Article 105 continued that, in order to attain the objectives of Article 104, 'Member States shall co-ordinate their economic policies'. Furhtermore, the Member States 'shall for this purpose institute a collaboration between the competent services of their departments and between their central banks'. The Commission had a role of initiative herein, as it 'shall submit to the council recommendations for the bringing into effect of such collaboration'.

Article 108 discussed the situation where a Member State has serious balance of payments difficulties which could threaten the functioning of the common market. It stipulated that the Commission should investigate the situation and gave it the right to recommend measures for the Member State to take. Moreover, the article provided for the possibility of granting 'mutual assistance'. Article 109 contained the safeguard clauses that France had insisted on, enabling a Member State to take the 'necessary protective measures' in the event of a sudden balance of payments crisis.

In its Article 105.2, the Treaty also provided for the establishment of the Monetary Committee. It was based on a French Memorandum (Archives NBB, B 436/4). The proposed missions of the Monetary Committee were to provide reciprocal information for the various authorities and to formulate opinions on 'all aspects of monetary policy concerning the functioning of the common market'. The Memorandum explicitly mentioned the mutual assistance procedure.

The EEC Treaty focused strongly on the creation of a common market. Overall, the monetary dimension was limited and macroeconomic policy-making was mainly left to the Member States. The Commission was given certain responsibilities for steering and coordinating national macroeconomic policies. Of special concern here were balance of payments disequilibria, as they could pose a threat to the common market. Moreover, the Commission had a right of initiative to draw up proposals for organising this cooperation. In the following years, the Commission would, on the basis of the Treaty, advocate a strengthening of economic policy coordination and monetary cooperation in the Community.

4. The early decades of the monetary integration project

4.1 The 'European Reserve Fund' project

At the start of the EEC, the French macroeconomic and monetary situation, with galloping inflation and balance of payments deficits, was a matter of significant concern for the Commission, leading it to reflect on how it could fulfil its role in the macroeconomic and monetary area. Marjolin, in collaboration with Triffin, drew up a proposal for the creation of a European Reserve Fund. Triffin reformulated his earlier ideas for a European Reserve Fund in an EEC framework (Maes, 2006). It was discussed at DG II and, in November 1958, Marjolin presented a Memorandum to the Commission.

Marjolin started from the observation that the EEC Treaty provided for the basic principles of the coordination of economic policies, but that the details of this coordination had not been properly worked out. He argued for a common economic policy. This would provide a way of avoiding substantial divergences in inflation and employment, which would lead to balance of payments difficulties and the application of the safeguard clause.

To put the policy coordination into practice, Marjolin proposed to undertake regular surveys of the Member States' economies. Moreover, he proposed that the Community institutions could also formulate policy recommendations. The weight of these recommendations would be stronger if the Community had at its disposal resources to facilitate financial solidarity. Therefore, Marjolin proposed setting up a European Reserve Fund.

This idea of the Community having the resources to facilitate financial solidarity would later become a recurrent theme in Commission proposals. A basic principle behind it was that such mechanisms, by demonstrating a collective stance, were a more efficient way of averting currency speculation than isolated national measures. Also, it made it possible to offer 'carrots' to countries which had to adjust policies, thus increasing the influence of the Commission's own policy recommendations.

The European Reserve Fund could be constituted by pooling a part of the international reserves held by the Member States' central banks, a proposal which was certain to arouse the ire of the central bankers. The Fund would provide for different types of loans, both to assist countries with balance of payments difficulties and also to support economic growth. Marjolin also proposed having the Funds' accounts expressed in a new unit of account.

The proposals gave a key role to the Commission in the macroeconomic and monetary area. It would have a leading role in the coordination of policies and one of its Members would also sit on the Executive Board of the European Reserve Fund.

However, in December 1958, De Gaulle devalued the French franc and introduced orthodox economic policies. Consequently, the proposal for a European Reserve Fund lost its *raison d'être*.

4.2 The Commission's Action Programme of October 1962

The first years of the EEC went well. In October 1962, the Commission submitted a Memorandum with its Action Programme for the second stage of the Community (1962–5).

Walter Hallstein, the then President of the Commission, drafted the political introduction. In the Memorandum, the Commission pushed for the Rome Treaty to be interpreted at most as implying the gradual completion of full EMU and political union (CEC, 1962).

The introduction to the Memorandum strongly emphasised the political character of European economic integration, which was intended to lead to the economies of the six EEC Member States merging in a full economic union. Economic union implied the progressive merger of national economic policies in a common short-term and long-term economic policy. This further implied that the Community would set long-term economic objectives.

In the chapter on monetary policy, it was argued that monetary union could become the objective for the third stage of the common market (1966–9). The Memorandum argued that monetary policy had a 'vital importance' for the Common Market, as exchange rate fluctuations could disrupt trade flows. The Memorandum paid special attention to agriculture in this respect. Monetary union was considered as necessary to protect the customs union and the common agricultural policy from exchange rate fluctuations. The German revaluation in March 1961 had in this respect an important influence on policy-makers at the Commission, as it showed the vulnerability of the international monetary system. For the second stage (1962–5), the Memorandum proposed 'prior consultation' for all important monetary policy decisions, such as changes in the discount rate, minimum reserve ratios, central bank loans to the State, changes in exchange rates, etc.

The Memorandum received a rather mixed welcome. Central bank governors asked for a legal analysis of whether the Council and the Commission had the right to draw-up Regulations and Directives and to take binding decisions for the central banks (*La Politique Monétaire dans le cadre du Marché Commun*, 4/12/62, Archives ECB). Their legal services confirmed this. In their official reaction, the governors argued that monetary coordination could only be efficient if budgetary policy was coordinated as well.

The discussions led to significant adjustments to the Commission proposals. On 24 June 1963, the Commission submitted a Communication on 'Monetary and Financial Cooperation in the European Economic Community' (CEC, 1963), in which it proposed creating two new consultative organs, the Committee of Governors of the Central Banks of the Member States of the European Economic Community and the Budgetary Policy Committee, as well as widening the responsibilities of the Monetary Committee, especially in the area of international monetary matters.

The new Commission proposals received a more favourable welcome. While the decisions of 1964 were a far cry from a monetary union, as proposed in the 1962 Memorandum, they contributed to establishing the Commission as an actor in the monetary area. First, they made it clear that the EEC Treaty gave the Commission a right of initiative in the monetary area. Second, the Commission would be invited, as an observer, to the meetings of the Committee of Governors. This would give the Commission an entrance into the world of the central bankers.

4.3 The Barre Memorandum

In the second half of the 1960s, the Bretton-Woods System came under increasing pressure. In response, the Commission published the so-called 'Barre Memorandum' in February 1969 (Commission of the EEC, 1969). It focused on three main lines of action: (a) convergence of medium-term economic policy. It proposed being more specific about the degree of convergence of the broad orientations of the Member States' medium-term policies and ensuring mutual compatibility; (b) the coordination of short-term economic policies. Here, the emphasis was on sufficiently coherent short-term policies, so that the different economies did not develop in ways which diverged from the medium-term objectives. The Memorandum proposed the reinforcement and more effective application of the consultation procedures and a system of 'early warning' indicators; (c) a Community mechanism for monetary cooperation, to help alleviate pressure on the foreign exchange markets. The proposed Community mechanism for monetary cooperation had two parts: one for short-term monetary support and one for medium-term financial assistance.

Compared with the 1962 Action Programme, the Barre Memorandum was clearly much more modest and pragmatic. This was hardly surprising given the lack of political will, especially – but not only – in de Gaulle's France.

The Barre Memorandum is also characterised by a special mixture of traditional German and French ideas. This is most clear in the first part of the Memorandum, on 'Convergence of medium-term economic policy'. Here, the French-inspired medium-term analysis is applied to the German notion of economic convergence. By doing so, it signalled heightened concern at the Commission concerning the disparities in prices and costs in the Community countries.

The Commission's ideas for closer monetary cooperation between the Community countries initially drew very mixed reactions from the central bank governors. At their meeting of December 1968, Carli (I), while admitting the political nature of the issue, stated that he was 'perplexed' at the possibility of closer monetary cooperation at Community level. He argued that the Community covered rather too small an area. Moreover, the Community constituted only a customs union and not an economic and political union (Minutes of the 27th Meeting of the Committee of Governors, 9/12/68, Archives NBB). Blessing (D) and Zijlstra (N) agreed with him, while Brunet (F) and Ansiaux (B) took more subtle positions. After further discussions, a Community Mechanism for Short-term Monetary Assistance was created in February 1970, in the form of an arrangement between the central banks. Also, in March 1971, a facility for medium-term financial assistance was established. As this last one was based on a Community Decision, it foresaw a role for the Commission in the functioning of the facility.

4.4 The Werner Plan

At the end of the 1960s, doubts about the Bretton Woods system became more and more widespread, especially with the devaluation of the French franc in 1969 and the vulnerable position of the American dollar. The countries of the Community feared that further exchange rate instability would lead to the disintegration of the customs union and the demise of the common agricultural policy. Moreover, new political leaders had come to power. In 1969, de Gaulle resigned and Pompidou was elected in France. In Germany, a new government was formed with Willy Brandt as Chancellor. The Brandt government proposed the EMU project, which also contained a proposal for a European Reserve Fund (drawn up by Triffin).

In a Note for the Commission dated 21 October 1969, Raymond Barre was critical of these proposals:

> For several months now, there has been new talk of a 'European Currency', a 'European Reserve Fund' [...] On several occasions, I have told the Commission that I don't think it is appropriate to support such ideas for the time being.
>
> *(Raymond Barre, Note pour la Commission, 21 October 1969, Archives Snoy)*

At the 1969 Hague Summit, the Heads of State and Government endorsed economic and monetary union as an objective for the Community. A committee was set up, chaired by the Luxembourg Prime Minister, Pierre Werner. It produced a report in October 1970 (Council-Commission of the European Communities, 1970), commonly known as the Werner Report. The Report first presented a general picture of monetary union. On an institutional level, it proposed that two Community organs should be created: a centre of decision for economic policy and a Community system for the central banks. This also implied a revision of the Rome Treaty. It set out a plan to attain EMU in three stages.

Immediately after its publication, the Werner Report was heavily criticised by the orthodox Gaullists in France (Tsoukalis, 1977, 104). Their criticism centred on the supranational elements of the Report. In the ensuing Commission proposals, the creation of new Community institutions was dropped.

The first attempt at monetary unification was not very successful: the new European currency mechanism, the so-called 'snake', was quickly reduced to a Deutsche Mark zone and policy coordination remained limited. This was not only due to the unstable international environment (the collapse of the Bretton Woods system and the oil crisis), but also because national governments were still strongly attached to their sovereignty and the pursuit of national economic objectives, drawing comfort from the then influential theory of the Phillips curve (Maes, 2002). In Germany, priority was given to the fight against inflation, while in France economic growth was considered a more important objective, which contributed to significant differences in inflation.

The failure of the Werner Report stimulated new debates on monetary integration at the Commission. One of the bolder ideas, quite influential among many policy-makers in Brussels, was the creation of a (parallel) common European currency (Bussière and Maes, 2014). However, these ideas provoked a general outcry among central bankers.

Moreover, with the monetary integration process in the doldrums, the Commission also turned to the, much less studied, economic leg of EMU. It asked a group of experts, under the chairmanship of Sir Donald MacDougall, to examine the future role of public finance at the Community level (CEC, 1977). The report provided an overview of public finance in existing federal and unitary states and outlined prospects for public finance functions in the Community.

4.5 The European Monetary System

In the second half of the 1970s, the Commission became increasingly worried about the European integration process stalling and the ensuing risk of the achievements of the past unravelling. Roy Jenkins, the then President of the Commission, tried to revive the monetary union project. The following year, the French President Giscard d'Estaing and the German Chancellor Helmut Schmidt relaunched the monetary integration process with the plan for the European Monetary System (EMS) (Ludlow, 1982).

The key objective of the EMS was to create 'a zone of monetary stability in Europe'. This had a double dimension: internal and external. It represented a compromise and synthesis between the ideas of the 'monetarists', led by France, emphasising the importance of external stability (exchange rate stability) and of the 'economists', led by Germany, advocating internal stability (price stability) and the coordination of economic policy (Maes, 2004).

The EMS was composed of three main elements: the exchange rate mechanism (ERM), credit mechanisms and the European Currency Unit (or ECU). At the core of the EMS was the ERM. A key characteristic was that realignments of the central rates were only possible by common agreement of all the participating countries. This implied that unilateral decisions on devaluations or revaluations, as in the Bretton Woods system, were not allowed. It stressed the Community character of the exchange rates between the participating currencies.

The role of the Commission in the negotiations leading to the EMS was relatively limited. The EMS was very much a Franco-German initiative, with Giscard and Schmidt playing the leading roles. It was only after the Bremen European Council in July 1978 that the EMS negotiations came into the 'normal' Community circuit (Monetary Committee, Committee of Governors, Finance Ministers).

The EMS agreement also foresaw a second 'institutional' phase of the EMS: the creation of a European Monetary Fund. However, this 'second phase' was shelved in December 1980. Therefore, the Commission, very much under the inspiration of Tommaso Padoa-Schioppa, sought other ways of strengthening the EMS. These efforts culminated in the European Commission's March 1982 proposals for a 'non-institutional' development of the EMS. A first element was to strengthen the position of the ECU and the exchange rate mechanism, for instance by increasing the negotiability of the ECU and by expanding the use of Community currencies for intra-marginal interventions. There was also a chapter on encouraging the use of the ECU on the financial markets, for instance, by stepping up the Community institutions' ECU borrowing and lending activity and by keeping restrictions on the use of the EEC's basket currency to a minimum. But there were also proposals with a more political content, especially the participation of all EU currencies in the ERM. The Commission further defended the idea of an ECU coin, which would circulate freely throughout the Community. This should strike public opinion by

> bringing the ECU out of the specialists' circle (central banks, exchange dealers, capital market operators) to which it is now confined, and putting it in the pocket of the man in the street, the ECU's destiny as the monetary symbol of the Community would be fully affirmed.
>
> *(CEC, 1982, 52)*

The Commission moved further towards a 'parallel currency' strategy. The aim was to stimulate the use of the ECU and thus create a 'critical mass' to prepare for the introduction of the ECU as Europe's common currency.

With respect to macroeconomic policy, the 1980 Annual Economic Report marked a break in economic paradigms at the Commission. Most important was the shift in economic policy orientation, away from active demand-management policies and towards a more medium-term orientation, emphasising structural, supply-side-oriented, policies. The new policy orientation was clearly set out in the Introduction:

> While in the past economic policy was often perceived as a problem of demand management, in a world based on the assumption of unlimited supply of energy and raw materials, the importance and critical value of supply constraints and structural adjustment problems are now evident.
>
> *(CEC, 1980, 9)*

The break with the past, along with the medium-term orientation of economic policy, was further illustrated and elaborated:

The *concerted response* to the present general economic situation should be based on the right strategic mix of demand and supply policies and notably the right balance in their application to short- and medium-term problems. Short-term adjustments should be more moderate than at times in the last decade, and a heavier weight has to be given to reducing medium-term inflationary expectations and improving supply conditions in the economy.

(CEC, 1980, 13, original italics)

Behind the new policy orientation was a new view of the functioning of the economy, stressing the limits of demand management. This new view was in the first instance based on an analysis of the failure of the concerted action of the 1978 Bonn Summit. This failure was at the origin of an important discussion on the efficiency and possibilities of economic policy, especially budgetary policy.

The Commission was also influenced by debates in the academic world about the Lucas critique and rational expectations. Commission economists became aware that economic agents were not responding in a mechanical or 'Pavlovian' way to changes in economic policy. Policy-makers had to take into account the fact that markets would anticipate policy measures. This further undermined the belief in the possibility of fine-tuning the economy.

Given the limits of a policy of fine-tuning, a medium-term orientation of budgetary and monetary policy was more appropriate. Moreover, as the macroeconomic policy options were limited, the emphasis had to be on a more microeconomic-oriented policy, with measures to improve the functioning of the different markets, something which was in line with the supply-side economics that was gaining ground at that time. Moreover, this new conceptual framework fitted in perfectly with a further push towards integration.

5. The Maastricht Process

5.1 The Single European Act

In 1985, the process of European integration was relaunched with the Internal Market programme. It would bring a new dynamic to the European Community, leading to an *engrenage*, from one market to one money. An important element was the liberalisation of capital movements, for which also Delors had been pushing. This was having consequences in the monetary field, as the liberalisation of capital movements was a crucial German condition for progress on monetary cooperation. Moreover, central bankers and Finance Ministry officials were being increasingly confronted with the so-called 'impossible triangle', indicating that it is not possible to have free capital movement, fixed exchange rates and an autonomous monetary policy at the same time. During the 1980s and early 1990s, capital mobility increased enormously. Also, the financial markets grew in importance (Abraham, 2004). With stable exchange rates in the EMS, there was no longer much room for an autonomous monetary policy, except in the anchor country. The European Community therefore had to live with the disadvantages of monetary union, while enjoying few of its advantages. So the Internal Market project created pressure for further monetary integration in the Community, a typical example of 'spillover' effects.

The negotiations on the monetary dimension of the Single European Act in 1985 were an important milestone. This was the first major revision of the Rome Treaties. At the end of November, the Commission submitted a draft chapter on economic and monetary union. This codified the practice of the EMS and contained a provision that would allow governments to agree unanimously on the creation of an autonomous European Monetary Fund. This ran into heavy resistance, especially from the UK, but also from other countries as Germany and the Netherlands. For the Commission, it was crucial that the Treaties should mention the *acquis communautaire* in monetary matters (EMU as an aim of the Community, the EMS and the ECU). With the backing of France and Belgium, Delors obtained a small chapter on a '*Monetary capacity*' in the Single European Act. Later, this would become an important stepping stone for further progress on EMU.

5.2 The Delors Report

In early 1988, debates about Europe's monetary future gained momentum. In a January 1988 memorandum, French Finance Minister Edouard Balladur argued that the EMS still had some big defects, notably its asymmetry (Dyson and Featherstone, 1999). Balladur's Memorandum also argued that it was necessary to reflect on further institutional steps in the monetary construction of Europe. It found a perceptive ear in Germany, not at the Bundesbank or the Finance Ministry, but at the Foreign Ministry. The following month, Genscher published a Memorandum in a personal capacity, in which he argued strongly for an EMU and a European Central Bank. At that time, early in 1988, Helmut Kohl was still quite open to the issue of monetary union. On the one hand, he was sensitive to the arguments of Gerhard Stoltenberg that EMU was only possible if a sufficient degree of convergence was achieved (coronation theory). On the other hand, he was also sensitive to the arguments of the advocates of EMU, like Genscher, and also Mitterrand and Delors. Moreover, Kohl gradually realised that EMU was unavoidable if he wanted to attain his vision of a 'United States of Europe'.

In preparation for the June 1988 European Summit in Hanover, DG II prepared a briefing dossier on monetary integration for Delors. The 'Dossier préparatoire au mandat de Hanovre sur la construction monétaire européenne' (23 June 1988, Archives DG ECFIN) was based on three premises: 1) Monetary union and economic union go hand in hand; 2) Monetary union will be set up as part of a gradual process; 3) It is necessary to build on what has been achieved. In the dossier, a parallel currency approach was defended, in line with earlier Commission studies.

The Hanover European Council confirmed the objective of economic and monetary union. Delors, especially through his contacts with Kohl, was very influential in the monetary dossier. The Summit decided to entrust to a committee the task of studying and proposing 'concrete stages leading towards this union', a very shrewd limitation of its future mandate, as it was not asked to analyse whether EMU was desirable or not. According to Delors (2004, 232), Kohl asked him to chair the Committee. Indeed, Delors had the confidence of Kohl and Mitterrand, and, as a former Finance Minister, the technical expertise. The governors of the central banks – in a personal capacity – also sat on the Committee. Delors wanted them to be members, both because of their expertise and because this would bind them to the monetary union project.

The Delors Report (Committee for the Study of Economic and Monetary Union, 1989, hereafter referred to as the Delors Report) would assume a crucial role as a reference and anchor point in further discussions. It basically revolved around two issues: first, what economic arrangements are necessary for a monetary union to be successful; second, which gradual path should be designed to reach economic and monetary union?

Initially, relations between Delors and Pöhl in the Committee were rather tense. However, the crucial aim of Delors was to get a unanimous report. So he took a low profile and focused on seeking out a consensus in the Committee. Pöhl took a 'fundamentalist' position and emphasised the new monetary order which had to be put in place: 'Above all, agreement must exist that stability of the value of money is the indispensable prerequisite for the achievement of other goals.' (Pöhl, 1988, 132). He argued for price stability as the prime objective of monetary policy, which had to be conducted by an independent central bank.

The Delors Committee also rejected a parallel currency strategy as a means of speeding up the pace of the monetary union process (Delors Report, 33). In this way, he agreed to drop an important element of the traditional Commission strategy.[6]

5.3 The Maastricht Treaty

The period 1989–90 was characterised by some of the most dramatic political changes in Europe since the end of the Second World War. With the fall of the Berlin Wall in November 1989, the issue of German unification was suddenly propelled to the forefront. France and other countries were afraid of a strengthened dominance of a unified Germany. They saw EMU as a way to bind in Germany. The German government's policy line could almost be summarised in Thomas Mann's dictum: 'Wir wollen ein Europäisches Deutschland und kein Deutsches Europa' ('We want a European Germany, not a German Europe'). In this context, the EMU process accelerated.

The European Commission nurtured the dynamics of the integration process It strongly emphasised the link between the Single Market process and monetary unification. It made a thorough analysis of the implications of EMU in a very extensive study entitled 'One Market, One Money' (CEC, 1990). The Commission also prepared a draft treaty on EMU.

In the intergovernmental conference on EMU, the debates centred on two main issues: the transition towards 'Stage Three' of EMU and the constitutional structure of EMU. As for the start of Stage Three, two dates are mentioned in the Treaty: 1997 if a majority of countries met the criteria and 1999 as an ultimate date. In order to participate, the Member States had to meet certain conditions, especially central bank independence and the achievement of a high degree of sustainable convergence. These conditions for the start of monetary union, namely a fixed date and compliance with the convergence criteria, were naturally the outcome of much debate. The monetarists, especially France and Italy but also the Commission, insisted on a fixed date to ensure the start of monetary union, while the economists, in particular Germany, insisted on economic criteria so that only countries which were 'fit' could participate in the monetary union. The combination of the convergence criteria with a fixed date proved to be a very powerful stimulus for the convergence process.

There were also major debates on the constitutional structure of EMU. Economic and monetary union became asymmetrical. Monetary policy was centralised. It was the responsibility of the independent European System of Central Banks, with price stability as its primary objective. The coordination of economic policy was the topic of some of the most tense discussions during the intergovernmental conference. France proposed a 'gouvernement économique', whereby the European Council would provide broad orientations for economic policy, including monetary policy. Meanwhile, Delors continued to push for a stronger economic pillar in EMU. However, responsibility for other instruments of economic policy, like budgetary policy and structural policies, remained basically with the national authorities, subject to a coordination and surveillance process. The different conceptions of monetary union and economic union reflected the limits of the Member States' willingness to give up their national sovereignty.

6. The quest for a 'genuine economic and monetary union'

Economic and monetary union was a landmark in the process of European integration. It was the fulfillment of an old aim of the European Commission. But EMU would also change the European institutional landscape, with the creation of a new and strong supranational institution: the European Central Bank. The ECB also set up important economic analysis and research capabilities and developed strong links with the academic world. Furthermore, the institutional landscape changed with the entry into force of the Lisbon Treaty on 1 December 2009: the European Council became an institution of the European Union, with Herman Van Rompuy as its first President.

Initially, EMU seemed to function quite smoothly. Joaquín Almunia, the Member of the Commission responsible for economic and financial affairs, claimed, in his preface to the Commission's study EMU@10:

> A full decade after Europe's leaders took the decision to launch the euro, we have good reason to be proud of our single currency. The Economic and Monetary Union and the euro are a major success. For its member countries, EMU has anchored macroeconomic stability, and increased cross-border trade, financial integration and investment. For the EU as a whole, the euro is a keystone of further economic integration and a potent symbol of our growing political unity.
>
> *(CEC, 2008)*

However, the Commission's study also highlighted significant challenges. It argued for a deepening and, especially, a broadening of macroeconomic surveillance:

> Surveillance should also be broadened beyond a sole focus on fiscal issues. It should include an analysis of developments in the determinants of competitiveness. [...] The objective would be to establish an early warning system to prevent the emergence of macroeconomic imbalances and competitiveness problems.
>
> *(CEC, 2008, 246)*

It thus paid special attention to the financial sector: 'Monitoring developments and trends in the financial sector, e.g. growth in bank credit, the evolution in asset prices, can provide important information on the possible build-up of macroeconomic imbalances and/or incipient threats to financial stability' (CEC, 2008, 260). As Martin Wolf (2008) observed in the Financial Times: the Commission was 'honest' about the challenges facing the euro area.

Europe's sovereign debt crisis revealed the flaws in the structure of EMU. The Commission was active in drafting proposals for a new economic governance framework, not only strengthening the fiscal dimension, but also venturing into new areas like the Macroeconomic Imbalances Procedure and Banking Union. The new blueprint for EMU was drawn up in a report by European Council President Herman van Rompuy, in close collaboration with the Presidents of the European Commission, Eurogroup and the European Central Bank, entitled 'Towards a Genuine Economic and Monetary Union' (European Council, 2012). The report proposed a vision for EMU with not only an economic and monetary union, but also a banking union and moves towards a political union. However, several elements of this 'Genuine' EMU, like the Fiscal Compact or the Single Supervisory Mechanism, were in the form of intergovernmental treaties (with a more limited role for the Commission).

The euro area crisis has further altered the institutional and decision-making structure of the EU. The Commission now has wider responsibilities for the surveillance of national economic policies. However, it is more difficult to assess how its overall influence has evolved. As observed in a UK House of Lords report:

> Some authorities have grown stronger, notably the ECB and the Eurogroup. [...] By contrast, the Commission's power and influence in determining the crisis response has diminished [...] it is noticeable (and perhaps inevitable) that it is euro area authorities, as opposed to those representing the EU 28, that have grown in power and influence.
>
> *(House of Lords, 2014).*

7. Conclusion

Over time, economic thought and policy-making at the European Commission went through some major changes. Initially, economic thought was to a large extent a synthesis of French and German ideas, with a certain predominance of French ideas. Later, Anglo-Saxon ideas would gain ground. At the beginning of the 1980s, the Commission's analytical framework became basically medium-term-oriented, with an important role for supply-side and structural elements and a more cautious approach towards discretionary stabilisation policies. This facilitated the process of European integration, also in the monetary area, as the consensus on stability-oriented policies was a key condition for EMU.

EMU has been a highly political process, with decisions often being taken at the highest level. However, also in the monetary area, the Commission has taken its role as guardian of the Treaties and initiator of Community policies very seriously. In line with its mandate, the Commission always advocated a strengthening of economic policy coordination and monetary cooperation. Although its precise role in the EMU process evolved through time, the Commission usually took the initiative, sometimes with other actors, to drive forward European monetary integration. In the 1960s, the Commission was successful in becoming a member of the newly created Committee of Governors of the Central Banks and in securing the creation of the first mechanisms for monetary cooperation. It was also very influential at several stages in the Maastricht Treaty process, such as getting EMU back on the agenda. More recently, the euro area crisis forced the Commission to deepen its analysis of EMU and draft proposals for strengthening EMU.

Notes

1 National Bank of Belgium and Robert Triffin Chair, Université catholique de Louvain and ICHEC Brussels Management School. The author would like to thank all those who contributed to this project, especially H. Badinger, V. Nitsch, L. Pench and two anonymous referees. The usual caveats apply.

2 For an overview of post-1945 economic thought in Europe, see the contributions in Coats, 2000.

3 In a survey I undertook in 1995, it appeared that DG II economists had a clear preference for studying in a 'foreign' European country rather than in America (Maes, 1996). However, the American share was slightly higher among younger economists. Among the European countries, Belgium was the most popular (13), due to the attraction of the College of Europe in Bruges (8 graduates), followed by the United Kingdom (10) and France (9).

4 The expansionary policies, advocated by the Action Plan, had mainly effects when the economy was already recovering and exacerbated inflationary pressures and payments imbalances. It showed the difficulties of 'steering' the economy with demand management policies.

5 As the references are to the original EEC Treaty, the original numbering of the articles is followed.
6 There was a remnant in the Maastricht Treaty (Article 109j), which specified that the Commission and EMI convergence reports also had to take account of 'the development of the ECU'.

References

Archives: Committee of Governors, ECB, Frankfurt DG ECFIN, Brussels National Bank of Belgium, Brussels Jean-Charles Snoy, Kadoc, Leuven

Abraham, J.-P. (2004), *Monetary and Financial Thinking in Europe, Evidence from Four Decades of SUERF,* SUERF Studies.

Bussière, E. and Maes, I. (2014), Economic and Monetary Affairs: New Challenges and Ambitions. In Bussière, E., Dujardin,V., Dumoulin, M., Ludlow, P., Brouwer, J.W., andTilly, P. (eds), *The European Commission 1973–86: History and Memories of an Institution,* Luxembourg: Publications Office of the European Union.

Coats, A.W. (ed.) (2000), *The Post-1945 Development of Economics in Western Europe,* London: Routledge.

Commission of the EEC (1962), *Mémorandum de la Commission sur le Programme d'Action de la Communauté pendant la 2e Etape,* COM (62) 3000.

Commission of the EEC (1963), Monetary and Financial Co-operation in the European Economic Community, *EEC Bulletin,* 6(7), 33–40.

Commission of the EEC (1969), Mémorandum de la Commission au Conseil sur la Coordination des Politiques Economiques au sein de la Communauté, *EEC Bulletin,* April.

Commission of the European Communities (1977), *Report of the Study Group on the Role of Public Finance in European Integration,* Brussels, April.

Commission of the EEC (1980), Annual Economic Report. *European Economy,* 7(November), 5–29.

Commission des Communautes Européennes (1982), Dossier sur le Système monétaire européen, *Economie Européenne,* 12, Juillet.

Commission of the European Communities (1990), One Market, One Money, *European Economy,* 44, October.

Commission of the European Communities (2009), EMU@10.

Committee for the Study of Economic and Monetary Union (1989), *Report on Economic and Monetary Union in the European Community,* Delors Report, Luxembourg.

Council-Commission of the European Communities (1970), *Report to the Council and the Commission on the Realisation by Stages of Economic and Monetary Union in the Community,* Werner Report, Luxembourg, October.

Delors, J. (2004), *Mémoires,* Paris: Plon.

Dyson, K. and K. Featherstone (1999), *The Road to Maastricht,* Oxford: Oxford University Press.

European Council (2012), *Towards a Genuine Economic and Monetary Union, Report by the President of the European Council, in Collaboration with the Presidents of the Commission, the Eurogroup and the ECB,* December 2012.

House of Lords (2014), *Euro Area Crisis: An Update,* European Union Committee, 4 April 2014.

Ludlow, P. (1982), *The Making of the European Monetary System,* London: Butterworth.

Maes, I. (1996), The Development of Economic Thought at the European Community Institutions, *History of Political Economy,* 28(Supplement), 245–76.

Maes, I. (1998), Macroeconomic Thought at the European Commission in the 1970s: the First Decade of the Annual Economic Reports of the EEC. *Banca Nazionale del Lavoro Quarterly Review,* 207, 387–412.

Maes, I. (2002), *Economic Thought and the Making of European Monetary Union,* Cheltenham: Edward Elgar.

Maes, I. (2004), On the Origins of the Franco-German EMU Controversies, *European Journal of Law and Economics,* 17(1), 21–39.

Maes, I. (2006), The Ascent of the European Commission as an Actor in the Monetary Integration Process in the 1960s, *Scottish Journal of Political Economy,* 53(2), 222–41.

Maes, I. (2013),Tommaso Padoa-Schioppa: Macroeconomic and Monetary Thought, and Policy-making at the European Commission, *History of Economic Thought and Policy,* 2, 21–43.

Pöhl, K.-O. (1988), The Further Development of the European Monetary System, Collection of Papers, *Committee for the Study of Economic and Monetary Union*, Luxembourg, 129-56.

Rosanvallon, P. (1987), Histoire des Idées Keynésiennes en France, *Revue Française de l'Economie*, 4(2), 22–56.

Triffin, R. (1958) La monnaie et le Marché Commun – Politiques nationales et intégration régionale, *Cahiers de l'Institut de Sciences Economiques Appliquées*, 74, December, 1–17.

Tsoukalis, L. (1977), *The Politics and Economics of European Monetary Integration,* London: Allen & Unwin.

Wolf, M. (2008), EMU's Second 10 Years May Be Tougher than its First, *Financial Times*, 28 May.

PART II

The Single Market and the euro

4

THE ECONOMICS OF THE SINGLE MARKET

Harry Flam[1]

1. Background[2]

The Treaty of Rome established the European Economic Community in 1957, and listed measures to be taken to establish a common market. They included the free movement of goods, persons, services and capital between member states, common policies of agriculture, transport and competition, and common trade and commercial policies towards third countries. The Treaty also set a maximum time limit of 15 years to implement the measures.

By the end of the 1960s, a customs union, with free trade in goods and a common external trade policy, plus a common agricultural policy had been created. The rest of the so-called four freedoms – free movement of persons, services and capital in addition to goods – plus common transport and competition policies had to await the Single Market Program, a Commission White Paper adopted in 1986 and listing 279 legislative measures needed to complete the common market by the end of 1992. Nearly all of the measures were adopted and about half were implemented in time. The Single Market Program:

- removed border controls (and the attendant delays) for goods transported on land and water,[3]
- liberalized the provision of services across borders (although the most important measures came later with the so-called Services Directive),
- established the principle of mutual recognition of national product regulations,
- removed controls on financial capital movements,
- removed discriminatory rules on direct investment from other member states,
- established freedom to reside and work in other member states,
- and established a common competition policy.

The Services Directive started to be implemented in 2009. It applies to the case when firms (and also individuals) want to provide services from an establishment in another EU country, either permanently or temporarily, and covers the construction industry, retailing, business services, tourism, real estate services, and private education. Financial services, telecommunication networks, transport and healthcare services are covered by separate regulations.

The Single Market rules and freedoms also apply to Norway, Iceland and Lichtenstein, which make up the European Economic Area (EEA) together with the member states of the EU, and to Switzerland.[4]

Even if the Single Market Program and the subsequently taken measures were quite comprehensive, important obstacles remain to the free movement of goods, services, people and capital. Spurred by the financial and economic crisis, in 2011 and 2012 the Commission presented a package of legislative and other measures to be taken under the heading Single Market Act I and II. They include measures to increase funding of small- and medium-size firms, revise the system for recognition of professional qualifications, establish a uniform patent protection, revise the European standardization system, adopt energy and transport infrastructure legislation, regulate the implementation of the Services Directive, revise public procurement directives, establish more integrated rail, maritime, air and energy transport networks, and facilitate cross-border e-commerce. Apart from proposing new legislation and other measures, the Commission continually reviews and revises directives, monitors the adoption and implementation of Single Market directives at the national level, and takes action against infringements.

Strictly speaking, the Single Market includes the customs union created in the 1960s as well as the measures subsequently taken to establish free movement of goods, services, people and capital within the EU. In the following, emphasis is put on the economics of the later measures.[5] The creation of the customs union undoubtedly had substantial effects at the time, but they have presumably been eroded by subsequent global trade liberalization. However, it should be understood that the removal of tariffs and quotas in principle had the same or similar effects as the Single Market measures on trade, competition, regional development and economic growth.

The structure and contents of this survey of the economics of the Single Market are largely determined by what economic theory has to say about the effects of creating a common market in goods, services, labor, and capital. A common market can both create and divert trade (section 2). It will affect competition, economies of scale, product variety and industrial structure (section 3), and the mobility of labor and capital (section 4). Economic activity may become more or less concentrated (section 5), and economic growth increased temporarily or permanently (section 6), two issues that were much in focus when the Single Market Program was proposed.

2. Trade creation and trade diversion[6]

Traditional analysis of the effects of economic integration is based on Jacob Viner's analysis of customs unions. The creation of a customs union, with free trade between insiders and a common tariff against outsiders, leads to "trade creation" and "trade diversion". Trade creation means that insiders specialize more according to comparative advantage and therefore reap more gains from trade. The elimination of tariffs on internal trade will lower prices to consumers and switch demand from outsiders to insiders. This is commonly labeled trade diversion, but the term should be reserved for the case when the switch involves replacing lower-cost with higher-cost suppliers, which represents a true welfare cost to the customs union. Switching from outside to inside suppliers with the same costs only involves a redistribution of tariff income from the government to consumers. Finally, terms-of-trade may change in favor of the customs union; the decrease in demand for imports from external suppliers may lower the price.[7] Viner's analysis also describes the effects of the Single Market Program in product and service markets. The elimination of trade costs in the form of administrative procedures at the border, or of product regulations, removes distortions

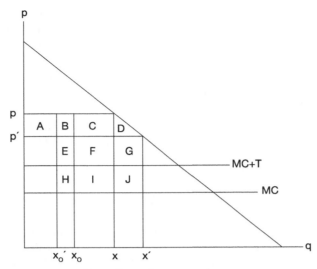

Figure 4.1 Welfare effects of customs union

between domestic and international prices, and gives rise to more trade and gains from specialization according to comparative advantage. The difference is that the elimination of trade costs within the Single Market represents a social economic gain, whereas the elimination of tariffs within the customs union represents redistribution from governments to consumers.

To see the distributional and welfare effects more clearly in partial equilibrium, consider the simplified example in Figure 4.1.[8] Before 1992, the quantity x_O is imported from a future outsider and the quantity $x-x_O$ from a future insider. The two suppliers are Cournot-Nash competitors, they maximize profits by supplying an optimal quantity in the belief that the competitor holds her supply fixed. They are assumed to have an equal constant marginal cost MC and to carry the same constant trade cost T. Their market shares are therefore equal. After 1992, the insider's cost is reduced by the trade cost T. As a result, the insider finds it profitable to expand its supply, while the outsider is induced to contract its supply. Total supply is increased to x'. The increase in supply leads to a fall in price from p to p'. The outsider now supplies x_O' and the insider $x'-x_O'$. More trade has been created between insiders, namely $x'- x$ and $x_O - x_O'$. Note, however, that this is not caused by increased specialization according to comparative advantage, but is caused by more competition. Part of the increase comes at the expense of the outsider. It is a form of trade diversion (although in this case, both supplies have the same marginal cost).

The welfare consequences can also be described with the help of Figure 4.1. Consumer surplus is increased by $A+B+C+D$, the insider loses producer surplus C to consumers, and gains a producer surplus equal to $E+G+H+I+J$. The sum of producer and consumer surplus changes for insider consumers and the insider producer is unambiguously positive. The outsider producer unambiguously loses $A+B$ in consumer surplus to consumers, and E in producer surplus to the insider producer. The overall gain in welfare is equal to the saving of real resources, $H+I$, from reducing trade costs, plus the increase in consumer and producer surplus on the increase in total quantity, $D+G+J$. In general, insider countries are both importers-consumers and producers, and therefore gain in terms of consumer as well as producer surplus.

The theoretical prediction that the Single Market Program would cause more internal and less external trade has, however, not been properly tested by empirical research. If one includes the effects of the trade liberalization in the 1960s, there is empirical support for trade creation. For example, Straathof et al. (2008) estimate an increase of 8 percent (and a resulting increase in GDP of 2 percent). Empirical studies of the trade effects of the euro often control for EU membership. They generally find a significant and sometimes substantial level effect of EU membership, e.g. Micco et al. (2003), Flam and Nordström (2003) and Berger and Nitsch (2008). Straathof et al. (2008) found no evidence of trade diversion. In fact, contrary to the theoretical predictions of customs union theory, empirical research on the effects of a great number of customs unions and other preferential trading areas shows that they tend to promote instead of divert trade with outsiders (Acharya et al., 2011; Freund and Ornelas, 2010; Magee, 2008). Moreover, empirical research on the trade effects of the creation of the European monetary union, where eliminating different currencies within the union can be seen as eliminating trade costs, shows that outsiders have increased their exports to the monetary union as well, see e.g. Micco et al. (2003) and Flam and Nordström (2003). This should come as no surprise; in many ways exporting to EU countries from the outside has become less costly. Before 1992, external suppliers must also bear the costs of different national product standards and other technical barriers to trade, and the administrative costs of crossing national borders. The Single Market Program has made it more profitable to concentrate sales and distribution facilities in one country in order to sell to all EU countries, and has thereby made it more profitable to export to the EU (Ekholm et al., 2007).

Given that the Single Market did create more internal trade, the gains do in part depend on the size of the border costs that were eliminated. The Cecchini report (1988) estimated that the cost saving of eliminating border controls on road transportation amounted to 0.3 percent of GDP with an additional saving of 0.1 percent of GDP from delays in transportation at the border. (No estimates were made for water and rail transportation.) Measured in percent of the value of trade, the cost savings were less than 2 percent for a selection of 40 industries, covering about half of industry value-added (Buiges et al., 1990).

3. Competition, economies of scale, product variety and industrial restructuring

The Single Market Program increased competition in several ways:

- it gave equal access to some markets, such as for public procurement, road transportation and the production of telecommunications equipment and railroad stock, to suppliers from other member states, where access had been severely restricted or denied,
- it eliminated border costs and the need to comply with different national technical standards, and thereby made suppliers from other member states more competitive,
- it removed anti-competitive policies, practices and rules in many member states, in particular against suppliers from other member states,
- all of which presumably made producers more efficient.

We will describe the effects by using simple examples.

3.1 Allowing market access

Increased competition in a market leads to increased output. Consider the extreme case where a monopoly is replaced by a duopoly competing in Cournot-Nash fashion. The sales of the monopoly are divided equally between the duopolists. They would think that their profits could be raised by an increase in sales. More sales would depress the price and thereby offset the positive effect on revenues, but half of the negative effect would be perceived to be borne by the competitor. The new duopoly equilibrium would therefore see a lower price and a larger quantity. There would be a net welfare gain consisting of the consumer and producer surplus on the increase in quantity. Consumers would gain from the lower price, while producers would lose from lower total profits. The case may seem particular but is quite general; a greater number of sellers leads to more competition, gains for consumers and losses for producers, and gains for the economy as a whole.

3.2 Removing trade costs

Removing trade costs in the form of administrative procedures and delays at national borders does not only constitute a saving in terms of real resources, it is also likely to increase competition.

Consider a market for a homogeneous product served by one domestic and one foreign producer which compete in Cournot-Nash fashion, illustrated by Figure 4.2. Both producers have the same constant marginal production cost MC, but the foreign producer also incurs a constant per unit trade cost equal to T before 1992. The domestic producer will have a larger market share due to its lower cost of supply. It sells the quantity x_H and its competitor sells $x - x_H$. Eliminating the trade cost of the foreign seller makes the producers' supply costs equal, induces the foreign seller to expand its sales and the domestic seller to contract its sales to give them equal shares of the market, and makes for a larger total quantity sold, x'. The domestic producer now sells less, x_H', and the foreign producer more, $x' - x_H'$.

Next, consider the welfare effects. Consumers gain equal to the area $A + B$, due to a lower price, plus the area C, since they value the marginal increase in sales higher than the price they have to pay. The domestic producer loses profits equal to the area A from the fall in price, and also the area $D + E$ from the loss in sales to the foreign producer. For the country as a whole, the net effect in the domestic market is a gain in consumer surplus equal to $B + C$ and a loss in producer surplus equal to $D + E$.

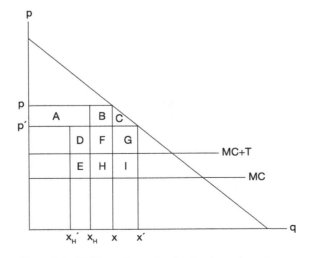

Figure 4.2 Welfare effects of reduction in trade costs

To arrive at the total effect for the country, we must add the producer surplus gained in other countries in the Single Market. For simplicity, assume just one other member state and one market, which is a mirror image of the one described. The domestic country's producer is now the exporter in the market of the other member state. It will lose profits on its exports to the other member state equal to the area B, but also gain profits on its increased exports equal to the area $D + E + G + I$. In addition, it will save on resources in the form of trade costs on its initial exports equal to the area H.

Adding up gains and losses, we have $B + C - D - E$ in the domestic market and $- B + D + E + G + I + H$ in the other member state, making for a total net gain of $C + G + I + H$. Due to the assumed symmetry, the other member state will gain an equal amount.

The results are quite general. A reduction in trade costs lowers the cost of imports and increases competition, leading to more sales, and lower prices (as well as more trade). Consumers and the economy gain, while producers may lose.[9]

3.3 Eliminating implicit and explicit import quotas

Before 1992, trade within the EU in some industries and sectors was subject to quotas. This was the case for agricultural products, steel, cars, and air and road transportation. Lifting a quota on imported goods or services tends to have a stronger pro-competitive effect than the elimination of fiscal or administrative trade barriers. In fact, a pro-competitive effect will emerge even if the quota does not restrict imports below the free trade level.

The effect is illustrated in Figure 4.3 for the simplest possible case, a Single Market for a homogeneous good. The market is supplied by one domestic firm, producing at an increasing marginal cost, and by imports, for which the price is given and constant. Consider first the equilibrium in the absence of a quota. The domestic firm cannot sell at a price above the price of imports, p. To maximize profits, it sells the quantity x_H. The imported quantity is $x - x_H$. Consider now a quota set equal to the level of imports under free trade. Since imports are now restricted, the domestic firm faces residual demand curve D' and marginal revenue MR'. It maximizes profit by restricting sales to x_H' the quantity at which marginal cost equals

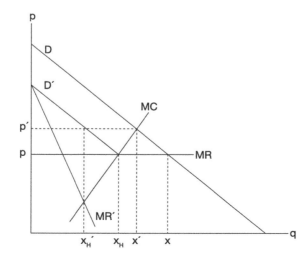

Figure 4.3 Welfare effects of eliminating quotas

marginal revenue, which raises the market price to p'. The level of imports is unchanged, $x' - x_H'$ is equal to $x - x_{H'}$.

The pro-competitive effect of eliminating a quota on imports is quite general. It can be shown to hold in the case of domestic oligopoly and Cournot-Nash competition, and when goods are differentiated (see Bhagwati, 1965, and Helpman and Krugman, 1989). In general, quotas must be assumed to restrict imports to less than the free trade quantity of imports. Lifting a quota should therefore result in increased cross-market penetration and trade.

There is some empirical evidence of the pro-competitive effect of the Single Market Program measured as price-cost margins. One study estimates that the price-cost margin in manufacturing had decreased by nearly 4 percent by 1996 (Allen et al., 1998). Another study, based on a panel of ten EU countries, found that by 1999, the price-cost margin had fallen by 25 percent in manufacturing and by 40 percent in construction, but that it had increased in the service sector.

3.4 Eliminating slack

Economists tend to believe that increased competition will induce more effort and less slack within a firm, although slack – not using the firm's resources efficiently – is assumed away in standard models and is not subject to much empirical research in economics.[10] Slack is presumably economically wasteful; eliminating slack may cost in terms of effort but the cost is assumed to be smaller than the benefit.

The idea that increased openness to international trade can serve to increase the degree of competition in the economy and induce less slack within firms has been modeled by Horn et al. (1995) in a contract-theoretic framework. The marginal cost of making managers exert more effort is shown to be smaller than the marginal revenue. In other words, reducing slack can be shown to be socially beneficial in theory. As mentioned, there exists virtually no research to show that increased competition reduces slack and raises economic welfare in practice, but it is nevertheless reasonable to presume that this is indeed the case and that the effects of increased competition on efficiency within firms might be of the same order of magnitude as the effects on allocative efficiency.

3.5 Increased economies of scale and product variety, and industrial restructuring

The Single Market Program has served to foster competition in product and service markets, which has resulted in lower prices due to lower price-cost margins and higher levels of production and sales. This has, in turn, brought gains in producer and consumer surplus as described. The expansion of production and sales is also likely to result in greater economies of scale, and additional economic gains.

Economies of scale can take different forms. One form arises when the total number of producers and thereby the amount of resources spent on fixed costs of production, such as research and development or production infrastructure, is reduced. For example, the Single Market had the effect of replacing many producers of railroad engines in protected national markets with, in effect, only two producers in a single market. The number of producers was reduced drastically, but competition was increased, there were more economies of scale, and savings were made in research and development and other fixed costs of production. Another form of economies of scale arises when there are decreasing marginal costs. Most production processes benefit from learning-by-doing, so that labor and other

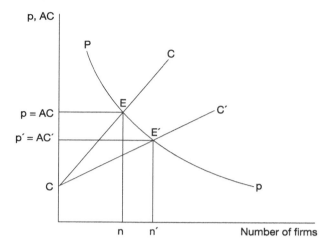

Figure 4.4 Scale effects of integration

resources required to produce an additional unit fall over time. With a larger scale of production in the Single Market, one should expect more so-called dynamic economies of scale. Finally, the agglomeration of firms within an industry in the same geographical location gives rise to economies of scale that are internal to the industry but external to firms. These economies can be due to a larger pool of specialized labor, informal or formal transmission of knowledge between firms, or an increased variety of and more specialized inputs to the industry. One should, in principle, expect that the Single Market Program served to reinforce existing and perhaps create new industrial clusters.

To see the way in which a larger market can result in larger firms and greater economies of scale, consider a closed market with monopolistic competition, where the presence of a fixed cost in combination with constant marginal costs gives rise to decreasing average costs and economies of scale. Firms are assumed to produce differentiated products but have identical costs. The upward-sloping *CC* curve in Figure 4.4 shows the relation between average cost, *AC*, and the number of firms: the average cost increases with the number of firms in a market of given size. The downward-sloping *PP* curve shows the relation between the number of firms and the market price: more firms result in a lower price independent of the size of the market.[11] Next, consider a doubling of the size of the market. At *E*, this shifts the *CC* curve to the right by a distance equal to a doubling of the number of firms at a given price, to *CC'*. There will be a new equilibrium at *E'*, with more firms than before, but not twice as many, a lower price and a lower average cost, that is, larger firms and greater economies of scale.

The example demonstrates how a larger market tends to give rise to more competition, larger firms, and greater economies of scale. It also shows that a larger market yields two additional effects: more product variety and restructuring within industries and sectors, that is, in mergers and closures of existing firms.

Greater product variety means economic gains for both consumers and producers. Consumers may value variety as such (as with so-called Spence-Dixit-Stiglitz preferences), for example by having more beers to choose from, or value the availability of a product with characteristics that are closer to their preferences (as with so-called Lancaster preferences), for example by having access to a beer that they like better than the ones that were available before. By reducing cross-country barriers to trade and entry, the Single Market should benefit consumers both by providing them with greater variety and varieties that come closes to their "ideal" variety. Producers should also gain from an increased variety of inputs and thereby a better fit between their requirements in terms of characteristics and price. The positive effect should be seen as an increase in productivity or as a fall in the price of the finished product.

The example illustrated by Figure 4.4 shows that the Single Market should give rise to restructuring within industries and sectors. What is missing in the example is the fact that firms within a given industry and country are not all alike in terms of costs or size, but exhibit substantial heterogeneity due to a host of factors, such as different vintages of technology. We normally find even greater differences across countries, reflecting additional factors, such as differences in market structure, policies and institutions. The reduction of arbitrage costs and the dismantling of market access restrictions achieved by the Single Market Program have not only reduced costs by achieving greater economies of scale, but have also forced inefficient firms and plants to close down or merge with other firms, leaving room for generally larger and more efficient firms to expand.

It is only relatively recently that theoretical and empirical research in international trade has started to take account of the effects of restructuring and the consequent cost reductions within industries with heterogeneous firms (Bernard et al., 2003; Melitz, 2003). The model by Melitz and Ottaviano (2008) accounts for all the effects of trade liberalization: stronger competition, increased product variety, more exploitation of economies of scale, and – importantly – restructuring within industries, giving the most efficient firms larger market shares by expanding their exports, and forcing the most inefficient firms to close down. Corcos et al. (2012) have used this model to quantify the partial equilibrium effects of undoing the Single Market for a set of 17 manufacturing industries in EU-15. More precisely, the authors interpret their counterfactual experiment as equivalent to re-introducing the previous technical barriers to trade. Moreover, the experiment involves only those industries for which significant effects of the Single Market were estimated; this was not true for all industries. The average country is estimated to make a productivity loss of about 7 percent in manufacturing. This is one order of magnitude greater than the ex-ante estimates that were made of the gains from the Single Market Program. For comparison, the pioneering and influential estimates made by Smith and Venables (1988) for 10 manufacturing industries arrived at gains from greater competition and economies of scale measured in terms of the value of consumption of about 0.5 percent.[12]

4. Free mobility of labor and capital[13]

EU citizens have the right to work and reside in other member states, but relatively few have exercised their right. The number of EU citizens working in another EU country increased from about 6 to nearly 10 million from 2005 to 2012. As a percentage of the total number of EU citizens of working age, the share increased from somewhat more than 2 percent in 2005 to somewhat more than 3 percent in 2012. These numbers make it clear that the share of people who lived and worked in other EU countries was quite low before the accession of ten new members in 2004, and that the enlargements in 2004 and 2007 did little to increase the numbers, despite the relatively large income differences between the old and new member states.[14]

Apart from generic barriers to migration, such as language differences, differences in culture and distance to family and friends, important institutional barriers to the free mobility

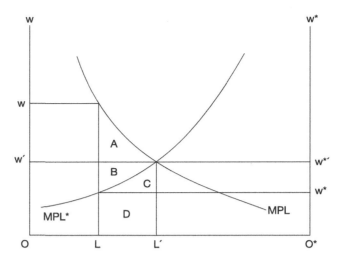

Figure 4.5 Welfare effects of factor mobility

of labor still exist. One such barrier is the limited possibility to receive unemployment benefits while searching for a job in another member state, another is the difference in pension systems across countries. Moving to another member state may mean giving up earned pension rights, especially in private pension schemes, or receiving a low pension in the new country of residence until the minimum age for receiving a pension from the old country of residence has been reached.

The existence of wage differences for similar types of labor across member states makes labor migration in response to such differences economically beneficial for the Single Market as a whole. This is shown in Figure 4.5 in a simple example showing the market for (homogeneous) labor in two countries. The distance $OO^{\star}$ measures the size of the combined labor supply in the two countries, and MPL and $MPL^{\star}$ are the labor demand curves given by the marginal product of labor. Before removing the barrier to labor mobility, the real wage w in one country is higher than the real wage $w^{\star}$ in the other. With free mobility, labor will migrate to the high-wage country, driving down the marginal product of labor in that country and driving up the marginal product of labor in the other, until wages are equalized. The size of the migration is shown by the distance L-L'. The value of the additional output created in the high-wage country is shown by the area $A+B+C+D$ and the value of the output lost in the low-wage country by the area $C+D$, giving a net gain of $A+B$. In this example, the wage is reduced in the receiving country, and increased both for migrants and those remaining in the sending country. In general, with differences in skills and education and depending on what type of labor that migrates, the distributional effects are more ambiguous. What can be said generally is that workers in the receiving country who are complementary to those that immigrate tend to gain, while substitute workers tend to lose.

Free mobility for capital involves real as well as financial capital: foreign direct investment (FDI), loans, credits and transfers via financial institutions, securities, such as stocks and bonds, and real estate investments.

There is no empirical evidence that the Single Market Program has stimulated FDI between EU countries more than FDI from outside countries. If anything, per capita flows into eleven core EU countries in 1990–2010 tend to be lower than into a control group of eight outside countries (Burrage, 2012).

The removal of barriers between national financial markets means that sellers/lenders and buyers/borrowers should have larger and therefore more competitive and efficient markets at their disposal, plus a greater variety of financial services and products. These expectations have been fulfilled on some markets, but many remain fragmented along national borders. The market for lending to small and medium-size firms is an example of this (ECB, 2012). Mortgage rates converged among the initial euro area members in the 1990s, well ahead of 1999, and have not converged since, indicating that the Single Market had an integrating effect, but not the introduction of the euro (Jappelli and Pagano, 2008). In contrast, the market for equities shows clear signs of increased integration due to the Single Market. Equity valuations at the industry level became more equal within the EU in the 1990s, principally due to EU membership and not to the monetary union (Bekaert et al., 2013). Equity market integration has mainly occurred at the global level, but EU membership has been an additional driving force whereas the common currency has had little effect (Everaert and Pozzi, 2014).

5. Differences in regional development

Prior to 1992, there was a great deal of concern about the regional effects of the Single Market Program, in particular that centrally located and larger countries would gain at the expense of peripheral and smaller countries. In an influential paper, Krugman and Venables (1990) demonstrated two opposing tendencies with increased integration. Firms would, on the one hand, have an incentive to locate centrally, in order to save on transportation costs and exploit economies of scale and, on the other hand, have an incentive to locate in the periphery, to take advantage of lower wages. Among policy makers, the concern was that the former tendency would dominate. Their response was to double the budget of the so-called Structural Funds, which mainly subsidize infrastructure, industry and agriculture in poorer regions, and to create the so-called Cohesion Fund, which was initially aimed at co-financing infrastructure projects in Greece, Ireland, Portugal and Spain.

Krugman's (1991) work on economic geography and trade started a great amount of theoretical and empirical research in economics on (differential) regional growth and development. It is fair to conclude that there are no simple explanations for differential rates of regional growth in an integrated market, see for example Breinlich et al. (2013), and no stylized empirical facts. This is not surprising. Theoretically, in industries characterized by imperfect competition, trade costs, and intra- and inter-industry linkages, several forces working for and against agglomeration are present. The precise features of the industry – such as the degree of economies of scale – and the relative strength of the different forces will determine the outcome, as demonstrated by Forslid et al. (2002). In the European context, the low level of labor mobility across borders prevents concentration to the center (Head and Mayer, 2004). The little empirical work that exists on the effect of the Single Market indicates – if anything – less rather than more concentration of industry to the center in the 1990's (Aiginger and Pfaffermayr, 2004).

The experience of Greece, Ireland, Portugal and Spain post-1992 indicates that national policy and institutions may matter much more than the centripetal and centrifugal forces of regional economic models. At the extremes, Ireland has attracted considerable flows of FDI, whereas Greece has received very little. Ireland has a language advantage, but it also offered favorable tax treatment and relatively small regulatory and bureaucratic hurdles to foreign investors.

6. Economic growth

Prior to the official launch of the Single Market, claims were made that the Single Market would bring a higher GDP (Cecchini et al., 1988) and higher economic growth (Baldwin, 1989). An increased ratio of investment to GDP, or greater economies of scale, will serve to raise the level of GDP over a limited number of years, but will not cause a permanent increase in the rate of growth. The total effect on the level of GDP of various static economic effects may amount to several percent of GDP, but is dwarfed in the long run by an increase in the rate of growth of GDP of even a small fraction of one percent.

Economic growth is both the result of an increasing use of productive factors, labor, human and physical capital and natural resources on the one hand, and of an increasing productivity on the other. According to growth accounting research, about half of economic growth is due to the latter (Helpman, 2004). It is the long-term increase in total factor productivity – growth net of the increasing use of productive factors – that has produced the steady increase in real consumption and living standards. Increases in total factor productivity are, in turn, largely dependent on innovation, which yields new and improved products and processes.

The Single Market has made product and service markets more competitive. Should one expect this to have had a positive effect on the rate of innovation and thereby on the rate of growth? Economic theory is ambiguous as to the effect of the degree of competition on the rate of innovation. The Schumpeterian argument is that firms with monopoly power have greater power to appropriate the returns to innovation, which gives them stronger incentives to innovate. In addition, they tend to be larger and may therefore have greater resources to innovate. The Darwinian argument, on the other hand, holds that competitive firms have stronger incentives to innovate in order to escape competition or at least remain in the market. A more competitive market – a greater number of firms – should also result in greater diversity in research and development and in better and faster results. The empirical literature lends some support to the view that more competition induces more innovation, at least for firms that are close to the technology-frontier (Griffith et al., 2006).

To complicate things, it is not certain that a country or region that experiences a relatively high rate of innovation will be able to appropriate the returns sufficiently to also have a relatively high rate of growth. A positive relation exists between the level of total factor productivity and the stock of research and development relative to GDP, measured as cumulative investment in research and development. But it is also clear that much of the research and development that takes place in one developed country spills over to its developed trading partners. Almost all non-military research and development – 95 percent – take place in a handful of countries, but it seems that their developed trading partners profit as much in terms of economic growth. See Helpman (2004) for a survey of the evidence.

Despite the uncertainty about innovation and long-run economic growth, it seems that the level effect registered as higher medium-term growth of becoming a member of the EU – and not only of benefiting from the Single Market Program – is substantial. A recent counter-factual study by Campos et al. (2014) finds that the GDP per capita ten years after accession was increased by 11 percent on average for Denmark, Ireland and the United Kingdom, by 15 percent for Portugal and Spain, and by 15 percent for eight countries in Central and Eastern Europe.

7. Concluding comment

A natural question to ask is if the gains of the Single Market have been exhausted? Cheptea (2012) estimates that trade in manufactures within EU-15 countries is, on average, 11 times higher than trade in manufactures between EU-15 countries that do not share a language and a border, and 5 times higher if they do.[14] Trade within EU-15 countries is 19 times higher than trade between EU-15 countries and Central and Eastern European (CEE) member countries if they do not share a language and a border, and 9 times higher if they do. Manufacturing trade within CEE countries is 23 times higher than manufacturing trade with EU-15 countries if they do not share a language and a border and 10 times higher if they do. It seems that the answer to the question is clearly no for both old and new members of the EU.

Notes

1 Comments by Ian Begg, Rikard Forslid and Anders Åkerman and editing by Christina Lönnblad are gratefully acknowledged.
2 For more on post-war European economic integration, see Part I, Chapter 1.
3 Border controls were made necessary by differences in value-added and excise taxes, by the need to adjust prices on agricultural products to uniform administratively determined prices, by different rules for animal health, by controls of transportation licenses and conformity with national rules for safety in road transportation, and by statistical formalities.
4 It remains to be seen whether and to what extent Switzerland's status as a de facto member of the EEA will be renegotiated as a consequence of its no to free mobility of people in a referendum in 2014.
5 This chapter draws on Flam (1992).
6 For European integration and the gains from trade, see Part IV, Chapter 12.
7 The negative terms-of-trade effect for the rest of the world induces ambiguous second-order terms-of-trade effects in world general equilibrium. The Single Market measures should have had income effects in other ways, as described below, which makes it harder to predict the net effect on the terms-of-trade.
8 For an analysis based on perfect competition and including terms-of-trade effects, see Baldwin and Wyplosz (2012).
9 The example presumes the absence of arbitrage in the more general case where markets are not symmetric and prices may differ across markets, so-called market segmentation.
10 Harvey Leibenstein (1966) introduced the concept of X-inefficiency to differentiate between allocative inefficiency – as when different forms of monopolistic behavior by firms leads to less than a socially optimal level of production, but each firm is on its production possibility frontier – from slack in the sense of producing below the production possibility frontier.
11 See Salop (1979) for a derivation of price as a function of the number of competitors which is also independent of market size in monopolistic competition, and Krugman and Obstfeld (2009) for the use of PP and CC curves.
12 Smith and Venables (1988) modeled the introduction of the Single Market somewhat arbitrarily as a 2.5 percent reduction in trade costs. When they added a change from complete segmentation (producers can set different prices in different markets without being undermined by arbitrage) to complete integration (prices are equalized net of transport costs) the gains became substantially larger. It should be stressed that the model and experiments of Corcos et al. (2012) on the one hand, and of Smith and Venables on the other, differ in many ways, in addition to the absence of firm heterogeneity in the latter.
13 One qualification is in place: most pre-existing member states imposed restrictions on labor migration from the new member states, but these had been lifted by 2011 for the Eastern European countries which joined in 2004, and by 2013 for Bulgaria and Romania.
14 For countries not sharing a language and a border, the ratio fell from 16 in 1994 to 10 in 2007.

References

Aiginger, K. and M. Pfaffermayr (2004), The Single Market and Geographic Concentration in Europe, *Review of International Economics*, 12(1), 1–11.

Allen, C., Gasiorek, M., and A. Smith (1998), European Single Market. How the Programme has Fostered Competition, *Economic Policy*, 13(27), 441–86.

Baldwin, R. (1989), The Growth Effects of 1992, *Economic Policy*, 4(9), 247–282.

Baldwin, R. and Wyplosz, C. (2012), *The Economics of European Integration*, McGraw-Hill Education.

Bekaert, G., Campbell, H., Lundblad, C., and Siegel, S. (2013), The European Union, the Euro, and Equity Market Integration, *Journal of Financial Economics*, 109(3), 583–603.

Berger, H. and Nitsch, V. (2008), Zooming Out: The Trade Effects of the Euro in Historical Perspective, *Journal of International Money and Finance*, 27(8), 1244–1260.

Bernard, A., Eaton, J., Jensen, J.B., and Kortum, S. (2003), Plants and Productivity in International Trade, *American Economic Review*, 93(4), 1268–1290.

Bhagwati, J. (1965), On the Equivalence of Tariffs and Quotas, in Baldwin, R.E. et al. (eds) *Trade, Growth, and the Balance of Payments: Essays in Honor of Gottfried Haberler*, (pp.53–67) Chicago: Rand McNally.

Breinlich, H., Ottaviano, G., and Temple, J. (2013), Regional Growth and Regional Decline, in Aghion, P. and Durlauf, S. (eds) *Handbook of Economic Growth 2*, (pp.683–779) Amsterdam: Elsevier.

Buiges, P., Ilzkovitz, F., and Lebrun, J.-F. (1990), The Impact of the Internal Market by Industrial Sector: The Challenge for the Member States, *European Economy*, special edition.

Burrage, M. (2012), *Does the EU's Single Market Encourage FDI into the UK?*, The Bruges Group.

Campos, N., Coricelli, F., and Moretti, L. (2014), Economic Growth and Political Integration: Estimating the Benefits from Membership in the European Union Using the Synthetic Counterfactuals Method, *IZA Discussion Paper* No. 8162.

Cecchini, P., Catinat, M., and Jacquemin, A. (1988), *The European Challenge 1992 – The Benefits of a Single Market*, Brussels: The Commission of the European Communities.

Cheptea, A. (2012), Border Effects and European Integration, *CESifo Economic Studies*, 59(2), 277–305.

Corcos, G., Del Gatto, M., Mion, G., and Ottaviano, G. (2012), Productivity and Firm Selection: Quantifying the "New" Gains from Trade, *Economic Journal*, 122(561), 754–798.

Ekholm, K., Forslid, R., and Markusen, J. (2007), Export-Platform Foreign Direct Investment, *Journal of the European Economic Association*, 5(4), 776–795.

European Commission, The Economics of 1992, *European Economy*, 35.

Everaert, G. and Pozzi, L. (2014), *The Dynamics of European Financial Market Integration*, Ghent University and Erasmus University Rotterdam.

Flam, H. (1992), Product Markets and 1992: Full Integration, Large Gains?, *Journal of Economic Perspectives*, 6(4), 7–30.

Flam, H. and Nordström, H. (2003), Trade Effects of the Euro: Aggregate and Sector Estimates, *IIES Seminar Paper* No. 746.

Forslid, R., Haaland, J., and Midelfart-Knarvik, K.H. (2002), A U-shaped Europe? A Simulation Study of Industrial Location, *Journal of International Economics*, 57(2), 273–297.

Griffith, R., Harrison, R., and Simpson, H. (2006), The Link Between Product Market Reform, Innovation and EU Macroeconomic Performance, *European Economy – Economic Papers*, 243.

Head, K. and Mayer, T. (2004), The Empirics of Agglomeration and Trade, in Henderson, V. and Thisse, J.-F. (eds) *Handbook of Regional and Urban Economics 4*, (pp.2609–2669) Amsterdam: Elsevier.

Helpman, E. and Krugman, P. (1989), *Trade Policy and Market Structure*, Cambridge, MA: MIT Press.

Helpman, E. (2004), *The Mystery of Economic Growth*, Cambridge, MA: Harvard University Press.

Horn, H., Lang, H., and Lundgren, S. (1995), Managerial Effort Incentives, X-Inefficiency, and International Trade, *European Economic Review*, 39(1), 117–138.

Jappelli, T. and Pagano, M. (2008), Financial Market Integration under EMU, *CEPR Discussion Papers* 7091.

Leibenstein, H. (1966), Allocative Efficiency vs. "X-Inefficiency", *American Economic Review*, 56(3), 392–415.

Krugman, P. and Venables, A.J. (1990), Integration and the Competitiveness of Peripheral Industry, in Bliss, C. and de Macedo, J. (eds) *Unity with Diversity in the European Community*, Cambridge: Cambridge University Press.

Krugman, P. (1991), *Geography and Trade*, Cambridge, MA: MIT Press.

Krugman, P. and Obstfeld, M. (2009), *International Economics. Theory & Policy*, 8th edition, Boston: Pearson.

Melitz, M.J. (2003), The Impact of Trade on Intra-industry Reallocations and Aggregate Industry Productivity, *Econometrica*, 71(6), 1695–1725.

Melitz, M.J. and Ottaviano, G.I.P. (2008), Market Size, Trade, and Productivity, *Review of Economic Studies*, 75(1), 295–316.

Micco, A., Stein, E., and Ordoñez, G. (2003), The Currency Union Effect on Trade: Early Evidence from the EMU, *Economic Policy*, 18, 315–356.

Salop, S. (1979), Monopolistic Competition with Outside Goods, *Bell Journal of Economics*, 10(1), 141–156.

Smith, A. and Venables, A.J. (1988), Completing the Internal Market in the European Community, *European Economic Review*, 32(7), 1501–1525.

Straathof, B., G.-J. Linders, A. Lejour, and J. Möhlmann (2008), The Internal Market and the Dutch Economy, *CPB Document* 168.

5

FACTOR MOVEMENTS: FDI

Bent E. Sørensen and Carolina Villegas-Sanchez

1. Introduction

Financial markets are becoming increasingly more integrated as part of globalization and it is an explicit goal of the European Union (EU) to encourage this. For example, the Financial Services Action Plan (FSAP) is intended to help integrate financial markets in the EU. It was initiated by the EU Council in 1998 and focuses on the removal of regulatory and legislative barriers as well as harmonization of EU laws and regulations across countries. The FSAP includes 27 EU Directives and two EU Regulations as well as technical recommendations. It includes legislation on securities markets, corporate governance, banking, and insurance of varying degrees of importance for Foreign Direct Investment (FDI) – the focus of the present chapter. More recently, Jean-Claude Juncker, on taking over the presidency of the European Commission in the summer of 2014, embraced the idea of creating an EU capital markets union. While the details are still work in progress, the stated goal is to streamline EU institutions and regulations to increase non-bank capital flows to small firms, which at present are almost fully dependent on banks. Encouraging larger flows from non-local sources of capital, i.e. FDI, is likely to be a particularly important focus.

The benefits from financial integration seem obvious to most economists: financial assets allow individuals to disentangle consumption from income. The benefits of this are two-fold and go under the headings of diversification finance and development finance. Regarding the former, diversification increases welfare by allowing consumers to maintain a high level of consumption when negative shocks hit at the cost of less high consumption when good shocks hit. Maintaining a smooth path of consumption in the face of income shocks is usually labeled "risk sharing." (Of course, sharing of risk does not allow for world-wide shocks to be smoothed.) Mainly, two mechanisms are available for the consumers of a country to smooth consumption: i) saving in good time and borrowing (or running down savings) in lean time, thereby separating the timing of consumption from the timing of income and ii) income insurance (diversification), which implies that shocks to aggregate GDP ("output") do not translate fully into shocks to income allowing individuals to maintain most of their usual level of consumption in the face of recessions. At the macro level, countercyclical borrowing and lending can be undertaken by individuals, corporations, and governments with governments doing the lion's share in the EU in recent times (see, Kalemli-Ozcan, Sørensen, and Yosha, 2003). In our view, for which we provide supporting evidence below, income diversification and, especially, FDI, provides a better way of smoothing consumption. The channeling of resources from more developed countries with high savings to developed countries with low savings was labeled development finance by Obstfeld and Taylor (2004). The clearest example of development finance may have been the financing of colonial infrastructure by British savers in the late nineteenth century, but more relevant for the EU is the flow of capital to countries, such as Ireland and Estonia, on the European periphery. Development finance increases the welfare of savers, who according to standard theory get a higher return because the return to capital is higher where it is scarce, and of recipient countries who obtain physical investments faster and without temporary declines in consumption to finance investment. The bulk of intra-EU capital flows in recent years seems better described as diversification finance: the situation where gross capital flows are large while net flows are small.

While in this chapter we focus on the benefits of financial integration, the relationship between financial openness and economic growth remains the subject of heated controversy in the context of emerging markets with underdeveloped financial systems. For example, short-term capital inflows (as opposed to FDI) have been blamed for exacerbating financial crises.[1] This chapter should therefore be interpreted as mainly relevant for The Organisation for Economic Co-operation and Development (OECD) countries.

In light of the world-wide recession which started in 2008, with banks having to be bailed out in many countries due, mainly, to bets on real estate assets, "financial stability" has become a focal point. It is less clear if EU banks were fragile because of too much or too little international integration: most large EU banks had domestic ownership and were regulated by domestic supervisors and while some banks made international bets on US mortgage backed assets, many banks got in trouble by making bets on domestic real estate, notably in Spain.[2] In Section 2, we discuss the theoretical and empirical literature on determinants of net capital flows and growth and the welfare effects from better international allocation of capital. Our survey of this area is very selective and the interested reader will have no trouble locating more comprehensive surveys of this large literature. Section 3 outlines empirical work on the productivity effects that may derive from increased FDI inflows. In Section 4, we discuss international risk sharing and the potential gains from risk sharing, while Section 5 sketches empirical patterns in FDI inflows to EU countries. Section 6 discusses issues regarding measurement of which countries are the ultimate providers of FDI and Section 7 briefly concludes the chapter.

2. Net capital flows: financial integration and the allocation of capital

Financial integration facilitates an efficient global allocation of savings by channeling financial resources to their most productive uses, thereby increasing economic growth and welfare around the world. For example, when two economies integrate, their steady state growth rate will go up since they can exploit scale economies better (Rivera-Batiz and Romer, 1991). In the EU, Eastern European accession countries such as Estonia and Poland have obtained high growth rates partly due to inflows of foreign capital. Savings can be allocated indirectly, via banks which usually provide safe, relatively low, returns, or directly via FDI, which provides volatile, relatively high, returns. Corporate bonds can be seen as being in between, providing relatively safe returns, which can turn volatile in recessions where defaults are more prevalent. However, borrowing at guaranteed rates can be disruptive when borrowers are unable to pay back. Compared to losses associated with direct investment in a floundering firm, bankruptcy comes with potentially large costs in terms of litigation and, in systemic crises, disruption of entire economies. While this survey is not focusing on banks or government lending, it is well known that bank lending to countries such as Greece abruptly reversed in the Sovereign Debt Crises which surfaced in 2010. Kalemli-Ozcan, Luttini, and Sørensen (2014) show that the reversal of the Greek government deficit was sharp and large enough to significantly depress consumption of Greek consumers at a bad time when consumption was already declining. Moral hazard and sovereign risk have long been acknowledged in the developing country literature, see Gertler and Rogoff (1990) and Eaton and Gersovitz (1981), respectively, for early references. Moral hazard and sovereign risk create enforcement problems which can significantly affect international investment and impair the ability of the governments of potentially unstable countries to smooth transitory shocks through borrowing.

According to the neoclassical growth model, financial integration should improve capital allocation and, therefore, growth in capital scarce economics. However, it is surprisingly hard to find direct evidence that FDI increases growth, even for developing countries – see, for example, Carkovic and Levine (2005). Studies finding positive effects stress the importance of various features of the host economies which enable them to utilize capital inflows productively: human capital (Borensztein, De Gregorio, and Lee, 1998), financial development (Alfaro, Chanda, Kalemli-Ozcan, and Sayek, 2004), or institutions (Papaioannou, 2009). Besides the direct capital financing it supplies, MNCs can be a source of valuable technology and know-how that can spur productivity spillovers through linkages with local firms.

3. Productivity benefits of FDI

Do foreign-owned firms become more productive with FDI? It is often assumed that foreign firms bring new knowledge or benefit local firms via increased scales of production. However, while the literature finds a positive correlation between the level of productivity and the level of foreign ownership it is hard to find evidence of productivity effects of increased FDI. Put differently, foreign investors target productive firms but a causal effect of FDI is hard to find, see Aitken and Harrison (1999), Javorcik (2004), and Liu (2008). Only Arnold and Javorcik (2009) and Guadalupe, Kuzmina, and Thomas (2012) find some positive effects of foreign investment on productivity after controlling for selection by comparing acquired firms to similar non-acquired firms, while Fons-Rosen, Kalemli-Ozcan, Sørensen, Villegas-Sanchez, and Volosovych (2013) find small causal effects using a new instrumental variable strategy.

Most of the potential relevance of FDI for the domestic economy relies on the possibility that domestic firms, by being exposed to the new products and production techniques brought in by the MNC, improve their own performance. The literature has explored different channels through which these technology spillovers could take place: competition, imitation, labor mobility, exports and vertical linkages. The literature has found positive "vertical spillovers;" i.e., improved productivity of local suppliers to MNCs, in both developing and emerging countries. In contrast, there has been no evidence of "horizontal spillovers;" i.e., productivity improvements from imitation and learning in firms close to the MNCs, in developing countries – see Javorcik (2004) and the references therein. However, there is firm-level evidence of positive horizontal spillovers in developed countries (see Haskel, Pereira, and Slaughter (2007) for the UK and Keller and Yeaple (2009) for the United States). These studies are done on individual countries, leaving open the external validity of the results. In a recent paper, Fons-Rosen et al. (2013), using data from 15 emerging and 15 developed countries, found that FDI leads to small productivity spillovers on firms in closely related industries while firms in the exact same narrow industry (say, steering wheels for cars) as the recipients of FDI suffer declining productivity.

4. Gross capital flows: risk sharing to insulate consumption from output shocks

The idea that people trade assets in order to hedge themselves against future contingencies has been an important topic of economic research for decades. The simple benchmark models consider risk to be perfectly shared if all countries have similar consumption growth rates, which could be achieved if all EU countries shared equally in EU-wide GDP. For many reasons, this is an unobtainable ideal, although output shocks to the US are more than 50 percent smoothed (Asdrubali, Sørensen, and Yosha, 1996). Van Wincoop (1994) is the first to quantify potential welfare gains from risk sharing and finds for OECD countries that "perfect" risk sharing allocation would improve welfare by the same amount as would a permanent increase in consumption of 3 percent. Demyanyk and Volosovych (2008) evaluate the potential risk sharing benefits that would accrue to the 2005 European Union accession countries and find the estimated gains for the accession countries could be very large. The largest estimate is 18.5 percent for Lithuania, which is very much a result of Lithuania's output being negatively correlated with aggregate output such that output pooling can decrease their volatility steeply.

In the developed world, financial intermediation is typically well developed within countries while cross-border intermediation has lagged behind. "Financial integration," therefore, typically refers to the lowering of barriers (or costs) of cross-border financial intermediation. International financial intermediation poses particular problems. These can be grouped in terms of a) higher costs associated with international assets trade, b) lower information transparency for foreign investors, c) limits to enforcement of international contracts, and d) currency risk. These barriers are relevant for gross as well as net flows.

The portfolio holdings of most countries exhibit "home bias" – the situation where countries hold much less foreign assets than predicted by standard models such as the CAPM. French and Poterba (1991) and Tesar and Werner (1995) were among the first to document such home bias. Other studies include Ahearne, Griever, and Warnock (2004), who study US foreign equity holdings and Buch, Driscoll, and Ostergaard (2010) who show that banks' asset portfolios also are biased towards the home country. Sørensen, Wu, Yosha, and Zhu (2007) study home bias in foreign bond and equity holdings for OECD countries and find that countries with higher level of foreign assets obtain significantly better risk sharing. These authors are not able to separate out the distinct role of FDI versus portfolio investment with statistical precision, because countries that receive large amount of portfolio investment are the same countries that receive large amounts of FDI, so longer time series are needed in order to obtain statistically significant estimates of the relative impact of these investments. However, it is intuitive that FDI, where foreign owners typically are hands-on involved in firms' operations, are associated with the earnings of foreign owners being directly tied to firms' results, which leads to risk sharing between countries.

Potential explanations of home bias center on the role of information. Specifically, lack of information add to the riskiness of foreign investment.[3] Kang and Stulz (1997) demonstrate that Japanese investors overinvest in large firms, consistent with a role for informational costs and Ahearne, Griever, and Warnock (2004) show that patterns of US equity investments in foreign countries are consistent with informational asymmetries. Edison and Warnock (2004) find that equities that are cross-listed on a US exchange do not seem to suffer from home bias in the portfolios of US residents.

A related explanation is one of ethnic identification (which may be due to people feeling they understand the actions of "related" countries better (Guiso, Sapienza, and Zingales, 2009)). Also, individuals do not invest in their own country or in other countries unless they trust the institutions protecting investors, see Ekinci, Kalemli-Ozcan, and Sørensen (2007).

5. FDI flows: EU 2004–2012

Institutions can affect the composition of capital flows. Wei (2000) and Wei and Wu (2002) show that countries with better public institutions and less corruption are likely to attract more FDI relative to bank loans. Albuquerque (2003) finds that countries with low investor protection receive disproportionately large flows of FDI relative to portfolio investments while Kalemli-Ozcan, Korsun, Sørensen, and Villegas-Sanchez (2014) find that, even among the relatively homogenous countries in the OECD, restrictions on FDI hampers inflows of FDI and, maybe less obvious, dissimilarity in product market regulation hampers inflows of FDI. The logic being that it is costly to move production to a country where regulations differ from that of the country of the investor because production processes have to be adjusted to new standards.

In this section, we show the magnitudes of FDI-flows to EU countries with a focus on intra-EU flows. We focus on figures in order to provide the "big picture." In Figure 5.1, the height of each column indicates the overall magnitude of (incoming) FDI for each of the years 2004–12. In the years leading up to the Great Recession, FDI was increasing at a rapid pace, reaching about 1.8 trillion euros in 2007. However, FDI inflows retreated dramatically in 2008 and 2009, falling to about 800 billion euros in each of these years. 2011 saw a strong rebound in FDI but the level fell to 600 billion euros in 2012, so it is too early to discern any secular post-Recession trend. However, it is clear that FDI flows are very large and highly pro-cyclical. The figure shows, in percent, the share of FDI inflows which originated in other EU countries. It is hard to spot a trend in this share, but it is conspicuous how big a share intra-EU FDI constituted in 2008.

Figure 5.2 shows how FDI was allocated across EU countries (except Luxembourg, which is very atypical with very large flows in spite of her tiny size) for the years 2006 and 2010. The columns are sorted according to 2006 flows. All countries, with the exception of Ireland, received positive inflows in 2006 and Malta, Bulgaria, Belgium, and Estonia were the largest

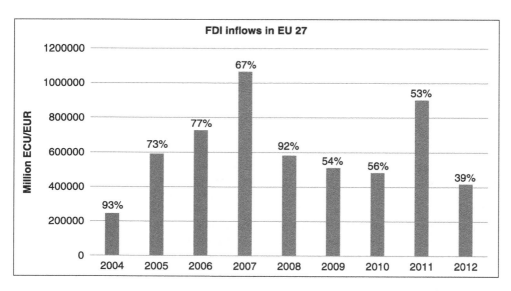

Figure 5.1 FDI inflows in EU 27

Note: The percentage shows the share of intra-EU flows in total flows.

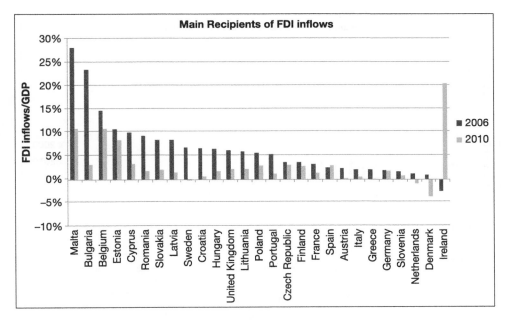

Figure 5.2   Main recipients of intra-EU FDI inflows

recipients. Malta is likely not the final destination of the incoming FDI (an issue we will return to below), Belgium is a mature, very open economy, while Bulgaria and Estonia are emerging economies which, according to the ideas of development finance should be expected to receive large capital inflows. Ireland has been a recipient of FDI before 2006 and this year is a bit atypical. In fact, in 2010 Ireland was the largest FDI recipient while Denmark received a negative amount. Overall, FDI flows in 2010 were less concentrated on certain countries.

Figure 5.3 narrows the scope to intra-EU flows. For those flows Belgium, Spain, and Estonia were, by far, the largest recipients (also indicating that Malta is an EU gateway for out-of-EU countries). Notice, Belgium, Spain, and Ireland are the largest recipients in 2006. For Belgium and Spain the picture was quite different in 2010 where Belgium received little FDI and Spain suffered outflows to intra-EU countries. Portugal saw the largest outflows but large outflows were also visible for Cyprus and Croatia. Did FDI investors feel that investor protection in these countries was too weak in the uncertain environment of 2010? This is likely so, although we are not able to dig deeper in this survey.

Another way of gauging the importance of FDI is to measure the share of FDI in overall capital formation (gross investment). Figure 5.4 displays the share of intra-EU and non-intra-EU FDI in gross fixed capital formation. In total, FDI made up almost 40 percent of investment in 2007 but FDI reverted faster than domestic investment dropping to about 20 percent in 2008 and 2009. Interestingly, intra-EU FDI reverted much slower than FDI from outside the EU in 2008, but the latter rebounded quite rapidly in 2009. However, in spite of a minor peak in 2011, FDI has made up a smaller share of investment since the crisis hit, although FDI from outside the EU seems to exhibit a secular trend, only interrupted by the dip in 2008.

In the development literature, "sudden stops" are important features of capital flows (see Calvo and Reinhart, 2000). Volatile capital flows are referred to as "hot money," which

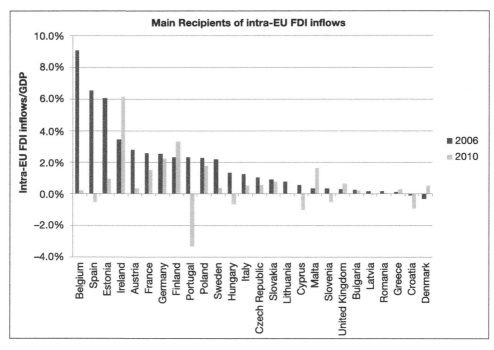

Figure 5.3 Main recipients of FDI inflows

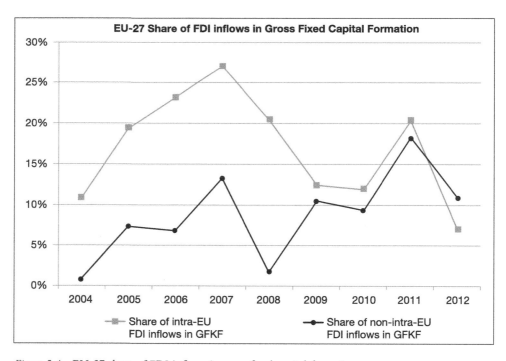

Figure 5.4 EU-27 share of FDI inflows in gross fixed capital formation

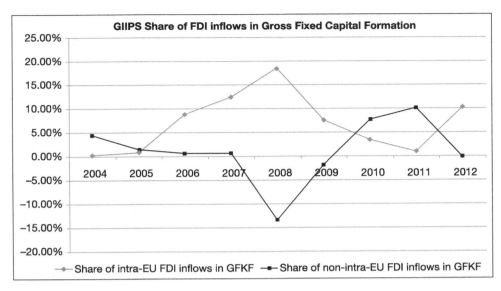

Figure 5.5 GIIPS share of FDI inflows in gross fixed capital formation

reverses direction when a crisis hits. We, therefore, zoom in on the GIIPS (Greece, Ireland, Italy, Portugal, and Spain) countries that were hardest hit in the Great Recession and the subsequent sovereign debt crisis, see Figure 5.5. For these countries, FDI from outside the EU behaved like hot money and turned negative in 2008 and, less so, in 2009 and, after a rebound during 2010–11, was virtually nil in 2012. Interestingly, intra-EU FDI flows are negatively correlated with non-EU FDI flows and increased for the GIIPS countries in 2007 and 2008. We believe that informational barriers are smaller for near-by investors (see Portes and Rey, 2005), as well as more important in uncertain times, which may explain the pattern observed in Figure 5.5.

6. Measurement of FDI

Kalemli-Ozcan et al. (2014) study the origin of FDI using data from the Bureau van Dijk (BvD) dataset AMADEUS which covers 80 million firms in European countries, developed and emerging. Official (OECD or Eurostat) statistics may be improved upon when it comes to measuring the source of foreign equity flows. This is because the official aggregate FDI data are based on the concept of residence which assigns ownership of financial flows to the place of registration of the direct source of FDI. However, the direct owner may often be located in, say, a tax haven even if the ultimate owner resides in a major developed country such as the United States.[4] Typically, therefore, direct ownership overstates exposure to and from (in particular) small financial centers and understates exposure of countries such as the UK, if the object of interest is the nationality of the ultimate owners. Because the ultimate owners bear the risk and control the firms this is typically the case.[5] AMADEUS includes information about both the direct and the ultimate owner. A comparison of OECD and AMADEUS data, when based on direct ownership, gives very similar cross-country and dynamic patterns: both underestimate the share of FDI flows from Asia and the United States to the EU-countries relative to the ultimate owner data. However, there are large differences between these numbers and numbers for ultimate sources of FDI. Table 5.1 shows

Table 5.1 Average percent share of FDI stock by source region comparison of OECD/BvD Direct/ BvD ultimate FDI data by country

Source Region: Country	North America	Western Europe	Eastern Europe	South/Ctrl. America	East/Ctrl. Asia	Total
Austria	10/5/3	80/88/89	2/3/1	1/0/1	3/1/1	95/96/95
Czech Republic	4/8/14	90/87/76	3/4/5	0/0/3	2/0/3	100/99/100
Denmark	10/15/24	82/75/69	1/0/0	5/8/4	1/0/2	99/98/99
Estonia	3/3/3	90/90/87	5/5/7	1/2/2	1/0/0	100/100/100
Finland	3/3/16	96/95/78	1/1/2	0/0/2	0/0/2	100/100/100
France	12/24/41	84/71/53	0/0/0	1/0/0	2/4/5	99/100/99
Germany	13/25/25	82/71/60	1/0/0	1/1/1	3/3/12	99/99/98
Hungary	5/14/21	89/80/72	1/0/1	2/1/2	3/5/2	100/100/99
Ireland	15/38/38	79/52/49	−0/0/1	7/8/9	0/0/1	100/99/98
Italy	6/10/35	90/87/52	1/1/3	1/1/6	1/1/3	99/100/100
Netherlands	20/15/19	69/75/59	0/0/0	7/4/5	3/5/17	99/99/99
Poland	7/10/13	89/87/85	1/2/1	−0/0/0	2/1/1	100/100/100
Portugal	17/2/3	82/91/94	0/0/0	1/6/2	0/1/0	100/99/99
Spain	13/17/33	84/77/59	0/0/0	2/4/4	1/1/5	100/100/100
Sweden	14/12/14	83/84/80	−0/0/0	2/1/1	1/3/5	100/100/100
UK	32/20/28	58/67/45	0/0/1	2/5/9	5/3/12	97/96/94

Notes: Sample of 16 EU OECD members with at least 1000 firms with significant and positive foreign ownership information for each of the years 2005–2008. Each cell shows the average share of foreign investment from origin region o (columns) as a percentage of total foreign investment stock in country d (rows) over 2005–2008 period. The first number is calculated from the OECD International Direst Investment Database, the second from the BvD direct ownership data, and the third from the BvD ultimate ownership data. All the values are rounded to the nearest whole percentage point. Total shows the total share of foreign investment from 5 major origin regions (North America, Western Europe, Eastern Europe, South and Central America, Far East and Central Asia) into country d. It does not include the share of foreign investment from 3 minor origin regions (Africa, Middle East and Oceania) and thus may be less than 100. Prior to constructing the BvD aggregate shares values of shareholder's funds are winsorized at 1% and 99% level.

the average shares of FDI into selected EU countries by source region for 2005–8 according to OECD/BvD direct ownership/BvD ultimate ownership data. The numbers are based on calculations of Kalemli-Ozcan et al. (2014). The focus of the table is the average share of foreign investment for each country by source based on BvD ultimate ownership data in comparison with the source of FDI in official data. According to the direct ownership data, residents of Canada and the United States ultimately own 33 percent of Spanish, 41 percent of French, and 35 percent of Italian foreign investment stocks and residents of the Far East and Central Asia own 12–17 percent of German, British and Dutch foreign investment stocks. From Table 5.1, it is immediately apparent that OECD and BvD direct ownership data greatly underestimate these numbers. This suggests that a significant share of North American and Asian investments are channeled through West European financial centers (e.g., Ireland, the UK, and maybe Malta). While the numbers constructed by Kalemli-Ozcan, Korsun, Sørensen, and Villegas-Sanchez (2014) do not have any official standing, they clearly show that the "intra" in intra-EU FDI has to be taken with a grain of salt because the ultimate owners likely do not reside in the financial centers to which FDI is often credited.

7. Conclusion

It seems by now fairly clear that FDI does not on average lead to large productivity increases in receiving countries. FDI has benefits in terms of risk sharing and, for emerging countries, FDI allows for faster growth compared to the situation where all capital had to be raised domestically, although the magnitude of causal effects of FDI on growth is difficult to pin down. FDI displays some tendency to contract in crises, but this tendency is not so strong, especially for intra-EU investment, as to off-set the benefits of FDI in our opinion. Official data often gives misleading pictures of sources of FDI because it is routed through financial centers which obscure the identity of ultimate owners.

Notes

1 The emerging country crises of the 1990s were accompanied by large reversals in capital inflows (the so-called sudden stops) which were followed by sharply decreasing output, private spending, and credit to the private sector (Calvo, 1998). Critics of financial globalization point out that the global financial system is an intricate network where negative shocks in one region can spread through the system in the presence of market imperfections such as incomplete credit markets (Allen and Gale, 2000) or non-convex production technologies (Stiglitz, 2010). More generally, the recent economic crisis of 2008–9 has restored attention to the financial accelerator mechanism by which imperfect credit markets amplify and propagate shocks to the macroeconomy (Bernanke, Gertler and Gilchrist 1999). Finally, the link between sovereign and financial sector risk can be intensified by large capital inflows. An increase in the riskiness of government debt impairs the financial institutions which have large exposures which then reduce lending to the real sector Reinhart and Rogoff (2011).
2 In particular, Spanish regional semipublic savings banks (cajas) lent heavily to real estate companies subjecting the banks to large losses when the Spanish housing market went into a nose-dive.
3 See for example, Gehrig (1993).
4 See the IMF Balance of Payments manual, 2013.
5 Zucman (2013) shows that official statistics substantially underestimate the net foreign asset positions of rich countries because they fail to capture most of the assets held by households in offshore tax havens.

References

Ahearne, A. G., Griever, W. L. and Warnock, F.E. (2004), Information Costs and Home Bias: an Analysis of US Holdings of Foreign Equities, *Journal of International Economics*, 62(2), 313–36.

Aitken, B., and Harrison, A. (1999), Do Domestic Firms Benefit from Direct Foreign Investment? *American Economic Review*, 89(3), 605–18.

Albuquerque, R. (2003), The Composition of International Capital Flows: Risk Sharing Through Foreign Direct Investment, *Journal of International Economics*, 61(2), 353–83.

Alfaro, L., Chanda, A., Kalemli-Ozcan, S. and Sayek, S. (2004), FDI and Economic Growth: the Role of Local Financial Markets, *Journal of International Economics*, 64(1), 89–112.

Allen, F., and Gale, D. (2000), Financial Contagion, *Journal of Political Economy*, 108(1), 1–33.

Arnold, J., and Javorcik, B. (2009), Gifted Kids or Pushy Parents? Foreign Direct Investment and Plant Productivity in Indonesia, *Journal of International Economics*, 79(1), 42–53.

Asdrubali, P., Sørensen, B.E. and Yosha, O. (1996), Channels of Interstate Risk Sharing: United States 1963–90, *Quarterly Journal of Economics*, 111(4), 1081–110.

Bernanke. B.S., Gertler, M. and Gilchrist, S. (1999), The Financial Accelerator in a Quantitative Business Cycle Framework, in Taylor, J. and Woodford, M. (eds) *Handbook of Macroeconomics*, volume 1C, Handbooks in Economic, vol. 15, 1341–93.

Borensztein, E., De Gregorio, J. and Lee, J.-W. (1998), How Does Foreign Direct Investment Affect Economic Growth? *Journal of International Economics*, 45(1), 115–35.

Buch, C.M., Driscoll, J.C. and Ostergaard, C. (2010), Cross-Border Diversification in Bank Asset Portfolios, *International Finance*, 13(1), 79–108.

Calvo, G. (1998), Capital Flows and Capital-Market Crises: The Simple Economics of Sudden Stops, *Journal of Applied Economics*, 1(1), 35–54.

Calvo, G. A., and Reinhart, C. (2000), When Capital Inflows Come to a Sudden Stop: Consequences and Policy Options, in *Reforming the International Monetary and Financial System*. In Kenen, P., Swoboda, A., Washington, DC: International Monetary Fund.

Carkovic, M., and Levine, R. (2005), Does Foreign Direct Investment Accelerate Economic Growth? in T. Moran, E.M. Graham and M. Blomström (eds), *Does Foreign Direct Investment Promote Development?*, Washington, DC: Institute for International Economics, pp. *195–220*.

Demyanyk, Y., and Volosovych, V. (2008), Gains from Financial Integration in the European Union: Evidence for New and Old Members, *Journal of International Money and Finance*, 27(2), 277–94.

Eaton, J., and Gersovitz, M. (1981), Debt with Potential Repudiation: Theory and Estimation, *Review of Economic Studies*, 48(2), 289–309.

Edison, H. J., and Warnock, F.E. (2004), U.S. Investors' Emerging Market Equity Portfolios: A Security-Level Analysis, *The Review of Economics and Statistics*, 86(3), 691–704.

Ekinci, M. F., Kalemli-Ozcan, S. and Sørensen, B. (2007), Financial Integration within EU Countries: The Role of Institutions, Confidence and Trust, *NBER Working Papers* 13440, National Bureau of Economic Research, Inc.

Fons-Rosen, C., Kalemli-Ozcan, S. Sørensen, B.E., Villegas-Sanchez, C. and Volosovych, V. (2013), Quantifying Productivity Gains from Foreign Investment, *NBER Working Papers* 18920, National Bureau of Economic Research, Inc.

French, K. R., and Poterba, J.M. (1991), Investor Diversification and International Equity Markets, *American Economic Review*, 81(2), 222–26.

Gehrig, T. (1993), An Information Based Explanation of the Domestic Bias in International Equity Investment, *Scandinavian Journal of Economics*, 95(1), 97–109.

Gertler, M., and Rogoff, K. (1990), North-South Lending and Endogeneous Domestic Capital Market Inefficiencies, *Journal of Monetary Economics*, 26(2), 245–66.

Guadalupe, M., Kuzmina, O. and Thomas, C. (2012), Innovation and Foreign Ownership, *American Economic Review*, 102(7), 3594–627.

Guiso, L., Sapienza, P. and Zingales, L. (2009), Cultural Biases in Economic Exchange? *The Quarterly Journal of Economics*, 124(3), 1095–1131.

Haskel, J., Pereira, S. and Slaughter, M. (2007), Does Inward Foreign Direct Investment Boost the Productivity of Domestic Firms? *The Review of Economics and Statistics*, 89(3), 482–96.

Javorcik, B. (2004), Does Foreign Direct Investment Increase the Productivity of Domestic Firms? In Search of Spillovers through Backward Linkages, *American Economic Review*, 94(3), 605–27.

Kalemli-Ozcan, S., Korsun, V., Sørensen, B.E. and Villegas-Sanchez, C. (2014), Who Owns Europe's Firms? Globalization and Foreign Investment in Europe, Discussion paper, *OECD Working Paper*.

Kalemli-Ozcan, S., Luttini, E. and Sørensen, B. E. (2014), Debt Crises and Risk-Sharing: The Role of Markets versus Sovereigns, *The Scandinavian Journal of Economics*, 116(1), 253–76.

Kalemli-Ozcan, S., Sørensen, B.E. and Yosha, O. (2003), Risk Sharing and Industrial Specialization: Regional and International Evidence, *American Economic Review*, 93(3), 903–18.

Kang, J.-K., and Stulz R.M., (1997), Why is there a Home Bias? An Analysis of Foreign Portfolio Equity Ownership in Japan, *Journal of Financial Economics*, 46(1), 3–28.

Keller, W., and Yeaple, S. (2009), Multinational Enterprises, International Trade, and Productivity Growth: Firm-Level Evidence from the United States, *The Review of Economics and Statistics*, 91(4), 821–831.

Liu, Z. (2008), Foreign Direct Investment and Technology Spillovers: Theory and Evidence, *Journal of Development Economics*, 85(1–2), 176–93.

Obstfeld, M., and Taylor, A.M. (2004), *Global Capital Markets: Integration, Crisis, and Growth*, New York, NY: Cambridge University Press.

Papaioannou, E. (2009), What Drives International Financial Flows? Politics, Institutions and Other Determinants, *Journal of Development Economics*, 88(2), 269–81.

Portes, R., and Rey, H. (2005), The Determinants of Cross Border Equity Flows, *Journal of International Economics*, 65(2), 269–96.

Reinhart, C.M., and Rogoff, K.S. (2011), From Financial Crash to Debt Crisis, *American Economic Review*, 101(5), 1676–1706.

Rivera-Batiz, P., and Romer, P. (1991), Economic Integration and Economic Growth, *Quarterly Journal of Economics*, 106(2), 531–55.

Sørensen, B. E., Wu, Y.-T., Yosha, O. and Zhu, Y. (2007), Home Bias and International Risk Sharing: Twin Puzzles Separated at Birth, *Journal of International Money and Finance*, 26(4), 587–605.

Stiglitz, J.E. (2010), Risk and Global Economic Architecture: Why Full Financial Integration May Be Undesirable, *American Economic Review*, 100(2), 388–92.

Tesar, L.L., and Werner, I.M. (1995), Home Bias and High Turnover, *Journal of International Money and Finance*, 14(4), 467–92.

Van Wincoop, E. (1994), Welfare Gains from International Risk Sharing, *Journal of Monetary Economics*, 34(2), 175–200.

Wei, S.-J. (2000), Local Corruption and Global Capital Flows, Discussion Paper 2, Brookings *Papers in Economic Activity*.

Wei, S.-J., and Wu, Y. (2002), Negative Alchemy? Corruption, Composition of Capital Flows, and Currency Crises, in *Preventing Currency Crises in Emerging Markets*, 461–506. National Bureau of Economic Research, Inc.

Zucman, G. (2013), The Missing Wealth of Nations: Are Europe and the U.S. Net Debtors or Net Creditors? *The Quarterly Journal of Economics*, 128(3), 1321–64.

6

THE EURO AS AN INTERNATIONAL CURRENCY

Agnès Bénassy-Quéré[1]

1. Introduction

Launching an international currency has never been the primary objective of European monetary unification.[2] Europeans could still legitimately expect their single currency to reach an international status given its ranking as the currency of the first international trade power, with a population larger than that of the US. Over the first decade of its existence, the euro developed both as a regional and as a diversification currency. While the euro area crisis in 2010 did not put an end to this (limited) movement of internationalization, it has become clear that reaching full internationalization will require further steps in European integration. In this chapter, we first define the concept of an international currency (Section 2). We then rely on the theory (Section 3) and history (Section 4) of international currencies to outline the conditions needed for the euro to become a fully-fledged international currency (Section 5), before analyzing the consequences of such an evolution for the euro area and for international monetary stability (Section 6). Section 7 offers tentative conclusions.

2. What is an international currency?

2.1 The six functions of an international currency

An international currency is a currency that fulfills the three functions of money (medium of exchange, unit-of-account and store-of-value) in an international context. Cohen (1971) and Krugman (1984) go one step further and differentiate between the private and the official sectors. A fully-fledged international currency should thus fulfill six functions (Table 6.1). The private sector uses the international currency as a medium of exchange for trade in goods, services and assets. It also uses it as a way to cheaply exchange two currencies (by carrying out two separate transactions against the international vehicle[3]) and as an invoice currency for goods (e.g. oil)[4] and assets (e.g. emerging countries' debt). In addition, private funds invest in the international currency as a way to limit their risk exposure and safeguard their liquidity. On the official side, central banks and sovereign wealth funds use the international currency for their foreign-exchange interventions, as a reserve currency and as a nominal anchor.

Table 6.1 Roles of an international currency

	Private	*Official*
Medium of exchange	Vehicle	Intervention
Unit of account	Invoice	Peg
Store of value	Banking	Reserve

Source: Krugman (1984).

Although these different functions tend to reinforce each other, a currency may fulfill only some international functions. For example, before 1999, the European Currency Unit (ECU – a basket of European currencies) played only a limited role as a medium of exchange for central banks, and as a store-of-value for both the private and the public sectors; it played a more important role as an anchor currency, but was neither a vehicle nor an invoicing currency. The Special Drawing Rights (SDR) issued by the International Monetary Fund (IMF) are used only by the official sector. As for the yen, sterling and Swiss franc, their international use mainly concerns the store-of-value function, far less the means-of-exchange or unit-of-account ones.

2.2 The limited internationalization of the euro

Since its introduction in 1999, the euro has developed into an international currency, essentially as a store-of-value, for both the official and the private sectors (Table 6.2). However, the share of the euro in international portfolios remains limited, especially for cross-border bank loans. In fact, while the euro may have emerged as an important diversification currency, it has not yet become a liquidity management currency or a vehicle. Although the euro was involved in 33.4 percent of foreign-exchange turnover in April 2013, this figure drops to 9.3 percent of total turnover when excluding euro-dollar trades.

Table 6.2 International currencies at end 2013 (market shares in %)

Function	USD	YEN	EUR	Other
Medium of exchange				
Foreign exchange turnover, April 2013[1]	87.0	23.0	33.4	56.6
Unit of account				
Invoicing/settlement of euro area exports of goods to non–euro area, 2013	na	na	67.2	na
Invoicing/settlement of euro area imports of goods from non–euro area, 2013	na	na	51.7	na
Third countries currency pegs,[2] April 2013	53.8	0.0	25.0	21.2
Store of value				
Allocated official reserves, 2013 Q4	61.2	3.9	24.4	10.5
Outstanding international debt securities, narrow measure,[3] 2013 Q4	54.8	3.5	25.3	16.5

(continued)

Table 6.2 (continued)

Function	USD	YEN	EUR	Other
Outstanding international debt securities, broad measure,[4] 2013 Q4	40.5	2.5	37.8	19.3
Outstanding cross-border bank loans, narrow measure,[5] 2013 Q4	69.2	4.0	14.2	12.5
Outstanding cross-border bank loans, broad measure,[6] 2013 Q4	56.9	3.2	18.3	21.7

Sources: Bank of International Settlements (2013); European Central Bank (2014); International Monetary Fund (2013).

Notes: [1] Out of 200%; [2] out of 104 pegged or semi-pegged currencies; [3] excluding domestic issuance of international debt; [4] including domestic issuance of international debt; [5] loans by banks outside the euro area to borrowers outside the euro area; [6] all cross-border loans.

The cross-border balance sheet of European banks did expand considerably during the 2000s, yet most of this expansion was in dollars (Figure 6.1). This dependence on the dollar proved a major factor of vulnerability during the international financial crisis (Ivashina et al., 2012): private short-term financing suddenly dried up, forcing the European Central Bank (ECB) to request a currency swap line with the Federal Reserve so as to be able to provide both euro and dollar loans to the European banking sector. In order to stabilize the banking sector, these temporary swap arrangements were converted to standing arrangements in 2013 (i.e. arrangements that will remain in place until further notice).

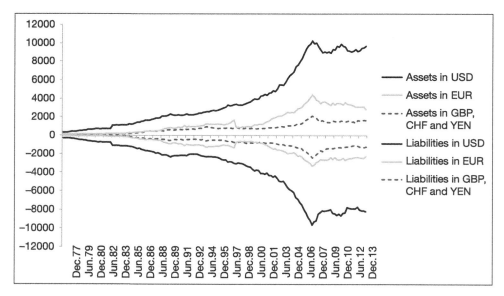

Figure 6.1 Gross cross-border assets and liabilities (excluding own currency area*, in USD bn)

Source: Bank of International Settlements.

Note: * assets in USD excluding assets in USD of banks located in the United States.

Perhaps the euro's rise as a financing currency in the first decade of its existence is to be considered its main international achievement. Using the so-called "broad" definition, the euro's share in outstanding international debt securities overtook that of the dollar as early as 2005–6. Observers ascribed this development to the significant increase in liquidity, triggered by the creation of the single currency, in euro-denominated debt securities markets compared with liquidity in legacy currency markets (Papaioannou and Portes, 2008). This share has somewhat declined since the outbreak of the euro area's debt crisis.

As for the unit-of-account function, the creation of the euro has progressively allowed the invoicing and settling in euro of a large share of trade conducted with non-euro partners. However, there is no evidence of the euro being used to any great extent for invoicing trade between non-euro countries, in contrast with the dollar. Similarly, the euro is being used as an anchor currency mainly by neighboring countries and former African colonies (the CFA franc zone). In short, while the euro has reached a regional status, it has yet to achieve a fully international one.

3. The theory of currency internationalization

According to Helleiner and Kirshner (2009), the literature on currency internationalization can be classified into three strands. The *market-based* approach highlights three major determinants of currency internationalization: confidence, liquidity, and transaction networks. Within this strand of the literature, currency internationalization is mainly the product of decentralized decisions by the private sector. By contrast, the *instrumental* approach stresses the role of public decisions in the internationalization process. For instance, the emergence of a currency is understood to depend on two factors: first, the willingness of central banks to use said currency as an exchange-rate anchor and their foreign-exchange reserves allocation decisions; and second the willingness of the home country to open up its financial system to non-residents and to allow free capital mobility both inwards and outwards. Finally, the *geopolitical* approach relates currency internationalization to the international order in general. Reflecting on the future of the euro as an international currency requires for these three approaches to be combined. Here we will focus mainly on the market-based strand, as it itself covers several approaches to currency internationalization.

3.1 Transaction costs

The role of transaction costs in the currency internationalization process was first stressed by Swoboda (1969). Krugman (1980) sees the emergence of an international vehicle currency as related to the combination of transaction costs and of the structure of international payments. Consider three economies (A, B, C). A and B will exchange directly their currencies if such direct exchange is less costly than using the currency of country C as a vehicle, that is exchanging A for C and then C for B (Figure 6.2). However, multiple equilibria may appear since transaction costs are endogenous to the volume of transactions: if A and B start using the currency of C as a vehicle, liquidity on direct transactions between A and B will dry up, raising the cost of such transactions and convincing new agents to use the vehicle C. Krugman concludes that the structure of the foreign-exchange market may durably depart from that of international payments. A change in the structure of the foreign-exchange market would only be triggered by a large discrepancy (incumbency effect), yet were such a change to happen, it may do so rather abruptly. This approach explains both the hysteresis of the international status of a currency and the possibility of occasional abrupt changes.[5]

Figure 6.2 Direct and indirect foreign exchange

This line of reasoning focuses on the means-of-exchange function of the international currency. However, Portes and Rey (1998) argue that there is a synergy between this function and the store-of-value one: the development of a deep and liquid financial market will lower transaction costs (measured by bid-ask spreads), and enhance the attractiveness of the international currency as a means of exchange. This synergy is magnified by the relative importance of inter-dealer foreign-exchange transactions compared with customer-dealer transactions as a result of chain hedging reactions.

Devereux and Shi (2013) also focus on the interaction between the means-of-exchange and the store-of-value functions, but from another perspective. Using a general equilibrium model with currency "trading posts", they consider the possibility that inflation in country A (home to the vehicle currency) will shift transaction gains away from the rest of the world and towards the residents of country A. At some point, the rest of the world may select another vehicle currency with lower inflation. Reducing the number of currencies (e.g. through monetary unions) may also lower the incentive for countries to use the international vehicle because of lesser savings on transaction costs.

3.2 Search models

Another strand of the literature focuses on network externalities. Matsuyama et al. (1992) consider a random matching model with two countries. Within each period, a resident of the home country has a probability n to meet another resident of the home country and $\beta(1-n)$ to meet a resident of the foreign country, where $n \in [0,1]$ is the relative size of the home population, and $\beta \in [0,1]$ is the degree of economic integration between the two countries. The home agent has a probability $(1-\beta)(1-n)$ of meeting no one. There are at least three types of indivisible commodities in this economy and as many types of specialized agents. Each agent of type i is able to produce one unit of commodity $i+1$ after consuming one unit of his own commodity i. Then, commodity $i+1$ must immediately be sold to an agent of type $i+1$ in exchange of one unit of either the home or the foreign currency, which will then be used to buy a unit of commodity i.[6] At any time, agent of type i can possess one unit of his own production i (the only commodity he can store), the home currency or the foreign currency. The agent of type i derives utility from the consumption of commodity i. To maximize his expected discounted utility, he must meet the right person at the right time. The currency of the larger country then emerges as the international currency; however, unless the degree of integration β is very high, the other currency continues to circulate between the two countries.[7]

As in the model with transaction costs, the central bank can be made to issue the vehicle currency and thus impose an inflation tax. Li and Matsui (2008) explore this possibility by considering the probability that money be confiscated to fund public goods. As in the transaction cost model, the government will find itself forced to implement inflation discipline for fear of its currency losing its international status.

The search model has also been extended to account for the political influence of the country issuing the international currency. For instance, in Pittaluga and Seghezza (2012), the probability that an individual will accept the foreign currency varies depending on the influence capacity of the foreign country. They find that political influence may become the driver of currency internationalization, acting as a substitute for economic integration.

3.3 Market structure and invoicing

The literature on currency invoicing stresses the importance of market structure and macroeconomic volatility. According to Bacchetta and van Wincoop (2005), an exporter will set the price in his foreign customer's currency whenever the price elasticity of foreign demand is high and marginal costs are increasing with output. Failure to do so will induce high volatility of output, with higher marginal costs on average. Under these circumstances, the exporter will also have an incentive to set its price in the same currency as its competitors (strategic externality). In turn, Gopinath et al. (2010) find that firms that adjust their price less frequently will more likely set it in their home currency. An international currency will therefore be more widely used in sectors with frequent price adjustments.

In terms of shocks, Devereux et al. (2004) show that an exporter should set its price in the currency of a country subjected to a limited number of monetary shocks. Goldberg and Tille (2008) suggest that trade invoicing could be explained by hedging strategies, while Goldberg and Tille (2013) argue that it can reflect the outcome of a bargaining game between exporters and importers.

Empirically, Friberg and Wilander (2008) report that Swedish exporters reduce the risk of price deviations across markets by using a limited number of invoice currencies; in particular, they select the currencies of larger markets. Customer negotiation largely determines which currency will be used for each trade, with neither competitors' currency choices, nor expected exchange-rate developments being seen as central issues. The authors also find that differentiated goods are more likely to be invoiced in the home currency (the Swedish Krona). These findings are broadly in line with the theoretical literature, except for the downplaying of externalities across competitors and availability of hedging financial instruments.

3.4 Portfolio choices

The market-based approach to currency internationalization covers the store-of-value function for the private sector. Following the standard portfolio-choice model, the allocation of savings across different types of assets relies on a risk-return trade-off; this leads to currency diversification rather than currency polarization (see e.g. Ben Bassat, 1980; Papaioannou et al., 2006). However, as already mentioned, the country issuing the key currency differs from other countries in its ability to provide liquid assets. In such a case, the assets denominated in the international currency are held not only for their risk-return profile, but also as an insurance policy against liquidity shocks: unlike local assets, international currency assets can be sold at any time and for a relatively predictable price. This generates a large demand for these assets, especially from emerging economies (see e.g. Caballero et al., 2008). Hence, liquidity is as important a characteristic as are stability and confidence in supporting the international status of a currency for the store-of-value function.

3.4 Instrumental approach

The instrumental approach to currency internationalization focuses on the role played by government decisions. For instance, the creation of a central bank in the United States and the implementation of major financial reforms at the beginning of the twentieth century are considered instrumental to the dollar emerging as the key global currency after the First World War (Broz, 1997). The instrumental approach also explains the longevity of the dollar. The US currency kept its key status in spite of the collapse of the Bretton Woods system: this collapse came in the wake of Japan's export-oriented development strategy (and later on that of China and other East Asian countries), which relied on currency undervaluation through continuous reserve accumulation in US dollars (Dooley et al., 2003). Furthermore, the US dollar has been used as a monetary anchor during disinflation periods (McKinnon, 2003) and as a substitute for regional monetary cooperation (Bénassy-Quéré, 1999).

Goldberg et al. (2014) have shown how important financial stability is for a currency's internationalization. The value of the international currency should remain stable in times of global stress. For a currency to exhibit such a trait, a sound institutional and regulatory framework is required, which requires a low probability of seeing a twin sovereign and financial crisis occur. In Maggiori (2013), an international currency will emerge from a country (1) whose financial market is well developed and is able to provide for risk sharing, and (2) whose currency appreciates in case of a global crisis and provides non-residents with profitable hedging opportunities.

3.5 Geopolitical approach

The geopolitical approach concentrates on the store-of-value function of the international currency (i.e. the willingness of foreign residents, especially foreign central banks, to hold the currency). It argues that currency internationalization is part of an international political order. This approach was pioneered by Strange (1971) who opposed "negotiated" and "top" currencies. According to her taxonomy, a "top" currency is a currency that grows internationally due to its inherent market appeal (transaction networks, stability, liquidity). In turn, the international status of a "negotiated" currency relies on either an implicit understanding or else the explicit political deal to preserve or promote the currency's status, with the possibility of sanctions. Kirshner (1995) goes one step further with the concept of "entrapment": the members of a monetary bloc progressively acquire an interest in maintaining the stability of the incumbent order. For instance, exchange-rate stability within the currency bloc tends to divert trade in favor of the bloc's members and to encourage them to hold assets invoiced in the bloc's key currency. They are then "trapped" in the sense that moving away from the currency bloc would involve significant costs.

4. Lessons from History

The conventional historical narrative (Triffin, 1960) states that it was only 30 to 70 years after the United States had overtaken Britain as the leading economic and commercial power that the dollar overtook the sterling as the leading currency of the international monetary system. According to this traditional view, the sterling remained the dominant international currency throughout the interwar years, and even for a brief period after the Second World War. Recent works have challenged this view and contend that the dollar was adopted over a much shorter period of time. Eichengreen and Flandreau (2009, 2012), and Chiţu et al.

(2014) show that, in fact, the US dollar had already overtaken the sterling by the mid-to-late 1920s, be it for official reserve accumulation, international trade, or government bond denomination. They suggest that both inertia and the advantages afforded by incumbency are less potent than previously believed, and find that there may be room for more than one international currency within the global system.[8] Eichengreen et al. (2014a) also argue that several currencies were used simultaneously for the invoicing and payment functions on the oil market, both before and after the Second World War. In fact, Eichengreen et al. (2014b) find that, in the post-Bretton Woods period, the currency allocation of official reserves owes more to inertia, with pure network effects (as proxied by the size of the currency-issuing country) having become less important.

Eichengreen (1998, 2011) highlights how crucial are financial regulations and liquidity for an international currency to develop. Before the First World War, US banks were prohibited from opening overseas branches, to the benefit of British banks trading in finance. US banks were even prohibited from discounting trade acceptances or from accepting bills of exchange. Additionally, Eichengreen argues that, starting from the 1860s, the Bank of England fully played its role of lender of last resort, guaranteeing liquidity of the London market, on the top of already guaranteeing full sterling-gold convertibility. In fact, the starting point of the dollar's internationalization was the creation of the Federal Reserve board in 1913 and, with it, the ability to discount or buy (through open market operations) bills and trade acceptances.

Lessons can also be drawn from Japan's failure to internationalize its currency. Eichengreen and Kawai (2014) argue that Japanese policy was not supportive of the yen's internationalization until the late 1980s. In particular, Japanese authorities restricted capital inflows and outflows which they thought would undermine the effectiveness of their monetary and industrial policies. In the 1990s, international capital flows were liberalized and Tokyo became an international financial center, only for the financial and banking crises and the subsequent "lost decades" (1990s and 2000s) to bring the internationalization of the yen to a halt. Japanese trade was carried out mainly with the United States or with East Asian neighbors that had pegged their currencies to the dollar and had made it their trade currency. Finally, regulatory and tax limitations have hindered the development of Tokyo's market for short-term liquid assets.

Eichengreen et al. (2014b) conclude from these examples that it is easier to discourage rather than to encourage the use of a currency for official reserve accumulation, and that macroeconomic stability and capital account openness are key aspects of currency internationalization.

5. Prospects for euro internationalization

From the above theoretical and historical analysis, we can conclude that the main conditions for a currency to grow internationally are the following: (i) a large country or monetary area; (ii) deep and liquid financial markets; (iii) nominal stability both internally (low inflation) and externally (a stable or at least "not depreciating" exchange-rate); (iv) financial stability and a safe regulatory environment; (vi) some attributes of non-economic power (military force, single voice in international forums). The advantages enjoyed by the incumbent currency should not be overblown, and there is room for more than one international currency.

The euro area fulfills the first criterion. As of 2014, the euro area totaled a larger population and a larger trading power than the United States, although it displayed smaller GDP figures (Table 6.3). Looking ahead, however, the share of the euro area in global GDP

Table 6.3 The comparative size of the euro area as of end 2014

	Euro area19[a]	EU28	United States	Japan	China
Population (million)	337.0	506.9	318.9	127.3	1,368.6
GDP (EUR bn)[b]	10,110.9	13,920.5	16,035.7	3,759.5	6,973.6
Exports of goods and services (EUR bn excluding intra-EU or intra-EZ)[b],[c]	2,380.4	2,233.1	1,717.4	625.4	1,779.5

Sources: World Bank, European Commission, Cepii-Chelem.

Notes: [a]Including Lithuania which joined on Jan. 1st, 2015. [b]at current exchange rates. [c]data for 2013. Share of intra-EU/EZ estimated based on Cepii-Chelem bilateral trade data for goods (year 2012).

is likely to decline. According to Bénassy-Quéré et al. (2013), the share of the EU28 in global GDP could fall from 23 percent in 2010 to 17 percent in 2025, at current relative prices. The share of the United States would also fall from 25 to 17 percent. Conversely, the share of China would rise from 10 to 22 percent over the same period. According to the size criterion, it is China's renminbi, and not the euro, that should be expected to rival the dollar in the future.

The second criterion – deep and liquid financial markets – appears less favorable to the euro for two reasons. First, the financing model of the euro area relies much more heavily on banks than does that of the United States; by construction, this limits the size of the financial market. Second, the monetary union has no fiscal backing: in contrast to the United States, the euro area's "federal" debt continues to be very low.[9] On top of these two weaknesses, the euro area's financial markets remain fragmented due to different regulations and tax treatments across Member States. Eichengreen (1998) also argues that the conduct of monetary policy in the euro area, which relies on regular refinancing operations with fixed or minimum refinancing rates, is less supportive of currency internationaliza-tion than day-to-day liquidity management aiming at stabilizing the short-term interbank interest rate.

The crisis in the euro area undoubtedly dampened the attractiveness of the euro as an international currency, at least in the short term. However, it may also have paradoxically raised the prospects for euro internationalization, thanks to the complete reshuffling of banking supervision (now to be coordinated at the ECB level), the development of the cor-porate bond market (viewed as an alternative to declining bank loans), and the project of a European "capital market union".[10] Additionally, the ECB largely played its role of lender of last resort during the global financial crisis, and closely monitored short-term liquidity. On the fiscal side, a discussion was launched in 2012 regarding the pros and cons of adding a "fiscal capacity" to complete the monetary union.[11] While the euro area started at a disadvantage given the size and liquidity of its financial markets, the situation appears to be changing and it cannot be compared to the low level of development and of openness of China's financial market, however fast-evolving they may be. Uncertainty however remains over the existence of a major financial center for the euro area, especially in the event of a UK exit from the European Union.[12]

The third criterion for euro internationalization (nominal stability) is supportive of the euro. This is due to the central bank being independent and having a clear mandate of price stability, to the monetization of government deficits being prohibited by the Treaties and to national government deficits being limited by fiscal rules, thereby reducing the risk of a "fiscal dominance" over monetary policy. As for the exchange-rate, it has proved unstable like that of every floating currency, but no weakening trend has been observed over the 1999–2014 period.

The fourth criterion (financial stability and a strong legal environment) is becoming more in favor of the euro, notably in view of the progress made toward the establishment of a banking union since the onset of the euro area debt crisis. In contrast, there have been mounting concerns over China and the alleged risks raised by overinvestment, stretched real estate valuations and the shadow banking system. Eichengreen (2013) mentions the lack of a strong, independent legal system as a major impediment to the development of the renminbi as an international currency.[13] In turn, Kirshner (2014) argues that the US-originated global financial crisis of 2008 may have induced a "delegitimization of the American model", especially in Asia.

The final criterion for the emergence of the euro (geopolitical influence) is clearly missing. Europeans have not yet transferred over their national sovereignty over foreign affairs and military forces, and the European External Action Service introduced by the Lisbon treaty has not proved to be game-changing. This is in sharp contrast with the United States (Posen, 2008). Furthermore, no single Eurozone voice is to be heard, be it at the IMF (where euro members are spread over several constituencies) or at G20 meetings (the larger Member States have their own seat at the G20 table while the smaller ones may not feel adequately represented by the EU seat). However, Kirshner (2014) notes that the United States is no longer the first exporting market for its key military allies in Asia, which may reduce these countries' stake in promoting the dollar's continued supremacy.

The dollar's status as incumbent currency has limited the internationalization of the euro. History tells us that several international currencies can coexist over a long period of time, yet the declining weight of the euro area in the world economy, combined with the hysteresis of the international monetary system, is not supportive of the internationalization of the euro. In this respect, the failure of the yen to emerge as an international currency in the 1990s should act as a useful reminder. To take a more positive spin, one could argue that the drop in transaction costs (due to the development of international financial markets and the expansion of the foreign-exchange market) has lowered the weight of the incumbent's advantage (see Eichengreen, 2010).

The next question is that of the transition from a unipolar to a multipolar system. Both theory and history suggest a "tipping point" effect: while the emergence of the euro (or of the renminbi) may be delayed, when it does happens it could do so quite rapidly. When estimating the currency distribution of foreign-exchange reserves as a function of size, nominal stability and financial depth (as proxied by foreign-exchange turnover), Chinn and Frankel (2008) find support for a non-linear form with strong inertia. Under their most conservative scenario, the share of the euro in foreign-exchange reserves would grow to 40 percent by 2020. However, they found mixed results depending on the size, nominal stability and financial depth assumptions; this illustrates the difficulty of making predictions when it comes to currency internationalization.[14]

6. The pros and cons of an international euro

6.1 The euro area viewpoint

Issuing an international currency brings both benefits and costs to the issuing country.

Benefits

The benefits to issuing an international currency are discussed by Papaioannou and Portes (2008). The first benefit is seigniorage, i.e. the benefits from interest-free loans that non-residents extend to the domestic central bank when they hold banknotes or non-remunerated deposits in the international currency. It is estimated that 60 percent of Federal Reserve notes are in circulation outside the United States (approximately 4.1 percent of GDP at end 2013).[15] The volume of seigniorage then depends on the interest rate. With a 1 percent interest rate, the gain for the Federal Reserve is 0.04 percent of GDP. For a 4 percent interest rate, it rises to 0.16 percent of GDP. According to the ECB (2014), the outstanding amount of euro banknotes outside the euro area was EUR 144.5 bn at end 2013, approximately 1.5 percent of GDP. While the euro area has the potential to further benefit from seigniorage, especially in an environment of significant interest rates, the figures will nevertheless remain low.

The second benefit to issuing an international currency are the liquidity discount and efficiency gains related to the intensive use of the domestic financial market. According to Warnock and Warnock (2009), the liquidity premium in the United States could represent as much as 80 basis points, producing an annual saving for US borrowers (especially the Treasury) of around 1.2 percent of GDP; this makes the liquidity discount much more profitable than seigniorage.

The third benefit is the ability to escape the "original sin" problem, i.e. to issue international debt denominated in the home currency (the "exorbitant privilege" mentioned by French Finance Minister Valéry Giscard d'Estaing in the 1960s). Issuing debt in the home currency eases a country's external constraint, as it can go to the printing press to reimburse its creditors. This however is a two-sided advantage given that it could also lead to a higher risk of inflation and hence higher interest rates. In principle, as highlighted by theoretical models, the country issuing the international currency will refrain from resorting to inflation since it would ruin the attractiveness of its currency; this theory has yet to be confirmed empirically.

The fourth benefit of issuing an international currency is reduced uncertainty and transaction costs for domestic firms who can carry out trade in their own currency. This benefit accrues mostly to the tradable sector. The domestic banking sector also benefits from higher activity (compensation, short-term funding), a benefit referred to as "denomination rents" (Swoboda, 1968).

The fifth benefit is partial insulation from foreign shocks. Because most foreign suppliers of the US economy denominate their exports in US dollars, price shocks are not passed onto their US customers. Exchange-rate fluctuations also do not affect US consumer prices to the same extent that they do in other countries, with foreign suppliers absorbing most of the shocks through mark-up adjustments (see Goldberg, 2011).

The final benefit of being the issuer of the international currency is international influence (Cohen, 2012). For instance, the Federal Reserve may extend swap lines in case of a liquidity crisis, yet it will do so at its own discretion. More generally, currency areas and spheres of political influence often run along the same borders. The issuing country can also reap elements of soft power and prestige.

Costs

The main cost traditionally put forward by the literature for issuing an international currency is the loss of control over monetary policy. First, banks outside the issuing country may extend loans in the international currency, triggering possible instability in money creation.

Second, these banks may also run out of liquidity in the international currency, pushing the issuing central bank to play the role of an international lender of last resort, at the risk of contradicting the domestic objectives of its monetary policy. Finally, because the monetary policy of the issuing country is a global, systemic issue, the issuing central bank may find itself forced to take into account the situation abroad when designing its monetary policy, again at the risk of contradicting its domestic mandate.

A second cost sometimes mentioned is the risk of running an overvalued currency. While the international status of a currency should not be confused with its strength (Bénassy-Quéré and Coeuré, 2010), being the main source of international liquidity may trigger a large demand for domestic riskless assets, putting downward pressure on interest rates (see supra) and upward pressure on the exchange-rate.

The third cost of issuing the international currency has to do with risk. Gourinchas et al. (2010) argue that the 'exorbitant privilege' of the United States materializes in the excess return on assets relative to that on liabilities; this is due to the structure of the US balance sheet, akin to that of a 'global banker' with its risky assets and riskless liabilities. Admittedly, this peculiar structure can only be partially attributed to the international role of the US dollar. Yet because one key task of the issuer of the international currency is to provide the rest of the world with safe, liquid assets, the two are strongly correlated. The downside to this 'exorbitant privilege' is an 'exorbitant duty'. It materialized during the 2008 financial crisis with the collapse of the US's net foreign-asset position, which came as a consequence of the collapse in stock prices and the appreciation of the dollar resulting from the safe-haven effect. Gourinchas et al. (2010) hypothesize that only a country with relatively low risk aversion and a high recovery rate on domestic bonds can play this role of a global banker and accrue the associated privileges and duties. This argument raises the question of whether the euro area would be ready for the job.

6.2 The international stability viewpoint[16]

Stabilizing hegemony?

Scholars of international relations often point out that a unipolar system exhibits 'hegemonic stability' properties (see Kindelberger, 1981, or the critical assessment by Eichengreen, 1989). This idea is rooted in the interwar experience, a period when "the international economic system was rendered unstable by British inability and United States unwillingness to assume responsibility for stabilizing it" (Kindleberger, 1973, p. 292). The rationale for hegemonic stability is that the hegemon is supposed to internalize the externalities involved in the provision of a given global public good – here, monetary stability in a broad sense; it can include the provision of liquidity in times of stress, when none of the issuers of competing currencies will have an incentive to behave in this way. For example, the hegemon should refrain from conducting a monetary policy that could destabilize the rest of the world. This discipline results from its global responsibilities and corresponding privileges.

A "leaderless" currency system could theoretically produce the global public good, provided there is effective coordination between the different players. Such coordination was missing during the interwar period (Eichengreen, 1989), and is unlikely to be effective with more than two players; this is all the more so since one player (the euro area) has yet to resolve the issue of its external representation (Cohen, 2009).

According to Cohen (2009), the major risk of monetary power fragmentation is that of "formal leadership aspirations", i.e. a state-driven rather than market-based leadership struggle.

The risk is both economic (e.g. increasingly antagonistic relationships between currency blocs, possibly leading to de-globalization) and geopolitical (e.g. breaking fragile equilibria, such as the one that exists in the Middle East: oil and dollar-support are provided in exchange for military protection).

Although attractive, the "hegemonic stability" theory makes no mention of the possibility that the hegemon will exploit its monetary power rather than internalize global stability in its decision-making process (Walter, 1991). It is unable to account for the actual behavior of past hegemons such as the UK under the gold standard or the US in the post-war period. The US did act as a crisis coordination-leader during the 1997 Asian crisis, and the Federal Reserve supplied partner central banks with US dollars through swap agreements during the 2008 global crisis. However, the loose monetary policy of the Greenspan era may not have fully internalized the worldwide impact of cheap credit; by the same token, the US Federal Reserve's decision to embark on quantitative easing in the aftermath of the crisis, while not deliberately non-cooperative, failed to internalize the impact of the US stance on emerging countries (hot-money inflows).

Under the hegemonic stability approach, the hegemon enjoys undisputed economic predominance and therefore has an unambiguous incentive to preserve and nurture international stability. A straightforward survey of the traditional functions associated with the monetary hegemon immediately suggests however that a country's declining relative size may affect its ability to play that role. When a country's claim to monetary hegemony is no longer backed up by its size, the current unipolar monetary system can no longer be expected to remain stable. By contrast, and as already argued by Kwan (2001) and Eichengreen (2010), a multiple currency system would reduce the scope for large imbalances in the issuer country(ies). Such an argument reminds us of the Triffin dilemma (Triffin, 1960): the internationalization of a currency relies on the overly-dynamic supply of assets in this currency, an unstable situation that could lead up to a crisis. Such was the case in 1971 when the relative scarcity of gold (compared with the dollar liquidity that had been accumulated worldwide) forced the United States to suspend its currency's convertibility into gold. Farhi et al. (2011) argue that the continued dollar supremacy over the international monetary system could give rise to a "new" Triffin dilemma: the rising demand for "safe" US assets, relative to the size of the US economy, is not sustainable, so that the mismatch between dollar supply and gold reserves would be replaced by a mismatch between dollar supply and US fiscal capacity.

The arguments traditionally put forward in favor of the hegemonic system are therefore weaker than may appear at first sight. In post-war Bretton Woods, they may well have provided an initially fair rationale of the monetary order. However, these arguments have since failed to offer any guidance to navigate today's radically different world.

Unstable foreign portfolio choices?

Another argument in favor of a unipolar system, of an entirely different nature, stems from the substitutability of currencies. As long as the international currency is unrivalled in terms of liquidity and risk profile, shocks to expected returns have limited impact on portfolio choices – exchange-rates are relatively stable. But if one (or two) other international currencies were to share the dominant currency's liquidity and risk characteristics, all these currencies would become more substitutable. This would make portfolio allocations more sensitive to shocks to expected returns, and hence exchange-rates would become more volatile (see for example United Nations, 2009).

Although straightforward, this line of reasoning refers only to short-run volatility, not medium-term misalignments. Suppose for instance that US assets are expected to yield lower returns. International investors will switch to the competing key currencies, triggering a fall in the value of the dollar; this fall will in turn lead to a rise in expected returns, increasing the willingness of international investors to hold dollars. In short, enhanced substitutability may increase short-run volatility, but not necessarily long-run deviations of exchange-rates from fundamental equilibria. Short-run volatility is easily hedged, as opposed to long-run deviations: therefore, it could be that higher volatility in the short-run partially off-set the cost of exchange-rate volatility.

Based on a portfolio-choice model with three countries, Bénassy-Quéré and Forouheshfar (2015) show that exchange rates are less volatile when there are more international currencies, i.e. when portfolios are more diversified. The reason is that an external shock will require only small adjustments in exchange-rate variations, while a more diversified system will be less vulnerable to the distortions created by fixed exchange-rates. Common sense, in line with this conclusion, favors an international monetary system that matches the multipolarity of the global economy.

The transition

A number of scholars have pondered whether the international monetary system could switch from unipolar to multipolar. Wouldn't such change trigger a major currency and/or financial crisis? Bergsten (1997) and Mundell (1998) call for closer monitoring by the IMF and/or the G7, while Eichengreen (2010) argues it is in the interest of central banks holding large amounts of dollar to smooth the transition. Angeloni et al. (2011) suggest the transition be prepared by fixing and improving the current unipolar system; to do so, the international safety net and surveillance system should be reinforced, China should move gradually toward more capital openness and exchange-rate flexibility and the euro area should strengthen its sovereign and financial frameworks. They also suggest that a greater use of the SDR could help smooth the transition toward a multipolar system by offering a vehicle for reserve diversification.

7. Conclusion

From the above analysis, we conclude that the euro already has many of the attributes that could give it a status similar to that of the US dollar: it is the single currency of a large area, where governance is strong and in favor of nominal stability; its financial markets are open to inward and outward capital flows; it has considerably strengthened its financial regulations and banking supervision since the onset of the 2008 global financial crisis; and its judicial system is independent from politics.

The euro area does however lack some key features. The most important of which is growth: without growth, the euro will rapidly become a currency of the past. The second element is fiscal backing for the currency, meaning some form of political union. The third one is a large, liquid, resilient, and unified capital market. Finally, the euro area lacks a unified external representation that would enable it to speak with one voice. These four issues are already key questions for the success of the euro area itself. We conclude that there is no such thing as a euro internationalization strategy: making EMU a success will naturally raise the attractiveness of the euro as an international currency. Conversely, delaying the necessary reforms in the euro area will ruin the chances of seeing the euro grow internationally, since the euro may not have much longer than a decade before the renminbi takes over.

Notes

1 I am grateful to Arnaud Mehl and Livia Chiţu for their remarks on a previous draft, and to Alice Keogh for research assistance. All errors remain mine.
2 See ECB (1999): "Since the internationalisation of the euro, as such, is not a policy objective, it will be neither fostered nor hindered by the Eurosystem. [. . .] The Eurosystem therefore adopts a neutral stance, neither hindering nor fostering the international use of its currency." (pp. 31, 45).
3 For instance, it is cheaper to exchange the Korean won for the US dollar, and then the latter for the Mexican peso, rather than to directly exchange the Korean and Mexican currencies on a market that offers limited liquidity.
4 Based on a survey of Swedish companies, Friberg and Wilander (2008) show that the same currency tends to be used for invoice and for settlement.
5 Rey (2001) develops a general equilibrium model in the spirit of Krugman (1980) where transaction costs are endogenously determined by the volume of trade, giving rise to "thick market externalities". Hartmann (1998) rather relates transaction costs to the micro-structure of the foreign-exchange market, where volume and volatility both affect the bid-ask spread.
6 Agent $i+1$ consumes commodity $i+1$ and then produces one unit of commodity $i+2$. The fact that there are at least three commodities eliminates the possibility of "double coincidence of wants": with three types of agents, commodity $i+3$ is the same as commodity i but it cannot be produced by agent $i+1$, so there is no barter between agents of types i and $i+1$.
7 The model goes beyond currency internationalization and covers the case of currency substitution, whereby the international currency is also used for domestic transactions.
8 Eichengreen (1998) also points out that the sterling's position before the First World War was not as strong as generally believed: by 1913, the French franc and the Deutsche mark taken together accounted for the same share of foreign-exchange holdings as did the sterling, whose own share was in fact inflated by large holdings in India and Japan. In Europe, the sterling only ranked third in reserve holdings, after the franc and the mark. According to Schenk (2010), the sterling's decline after the Second World War was cushioned by the collective interest: a number of countries opted to retain a substantial share of their sterling reserve holdings to prevent abrupt changes in the Cold War climate.
9 Claeys et al. (2014) evaluate at EUR 490 bn the total amount of EU-wide public debt denominated in euro at end 2013, covering EFSF/ESM bonds (EUR 230 bn), European Union (EUR 60 bn) and European Investment Bank (EUR 200 bn), and taking into account that the three data sources may not be readily comparable. In any case, the EUR 490 bn hardly compares with the USD 12 600 bn of US federal government debt in 2014.
10 See Véron (2014).
11 See Van Rompuy (2012).
12 See Springford et al. (2014).
13 At the other extreme, the extensive acceptation of extra-territoriality expressed by the US legal system in 2014, both in the Argentina and BNP-Paribas cases, may precipitate the rise of alternative currencies and jurisdictions for future debt issuance and financial transactions.
14 Incorporating the renminbi in the analysis, Liu and Li (2008) project a 22% to 24% share by 2020 for the euro (15% to 21% for the renminbi).
15 According to Federal Reserve data.
16 This section draws on Bénassy-Quéré and Pisani-Ferry (2011).

References

Angeloni, I., Bénassy-Quéré, A., Carton, B., Darvas, Z., Destais, Ch., Pisani-Ferry, J., Sapir, A., and Vallée, S. (2011), Global currencies for tomorrow: a European perspective, CEPII Research report 2011–01/Bruegel Blueprint 13.

Bacchetta, P., and van Wincoop, E. (2005), A theory of the currency denomination of international trade, *Journal of International Economics*, 67 (2), 295–319.

Bank of International Settlements (2013), Triennial Central Bank survey on foreign exchange and derivative market activity in 2013, December 2013.

Bénassy-Quéré, A. (1999), Optimal pegs for East-Asian currencies, *Journal of the Japanese and International Economies*, 13 (1), 44–60.

Bénassy-Quéré, A., and Coeuré, B. (2010), Le rôle international de l'euro: chronique d'une décennie, *Revue d'Economie Politique*, 120, 355–77.

Bénassy-Quéré, A., and Forouheshfar, Y. (2015), The impact of yuan internationalisation on the euro-dollar exchange rate, *Journal of International Money and Finance*, forthcoming.

Bénassy-Quéré, A., Fouré, J., and Fontagné, L. (2013), Modelling the world economy at the 2050 horizon, *Economics of Transition*, 21 (4) 2013, 617–54.

Bénassy-Quéré, A., and Pisani-Ferry, J. (2011), What international monetary system for a fast-changing world economy?, in Boorman, J.T. and A. Icard (eds.), *Reform of the International Monetary System*, The Palais-Royal Initiative, SAGE, 255–98.

Ben Bassat, A. (1980), The optimal composition of foreign exchange reserves", *Journal of International Economics*, 10, 285–95.

Bergsten, C.F. (1997), The dollar and the euro, *Foreign Affairs*, 76 (4), 83–95.

Broz, L.J. (1997), *The International Origins of the Federal Reserve System*, Ithaca: Cornell University Press.

Caballero, R.J. , Farhi, E., and Gourinchas, P.O. (2008), An equilibrium model of global imbalances and low interest rates, *American Economic Review*, 98 (1), 358–93.

Chinn, M., and Frankel, J.A. (2008), Why the euro will rival the dollar, *International Finance*, 11, 49–73.

Chiṭu, L., Eichengreen, B., and Mehl, A. (2014), When did the dollar overtake sterling as the leading international currency? Evidence from bond markets, *Journal of Development Economics*, 111 (November), 225–45.

Claeys, G., Darvas, Z., Merler, S., and Wolff, G. (2014), Addressing weak inflation: the European Central Bank's shopping list, Bruegel Policy Contribution, 2014/05, May.

Cohen, B.J. (1971), *The Future of Sterling as an International Currency*, London: Macmillan.

Cohen, B.J. (2009), Dollar dominance, euro aspirations: recipe for discord? *Journal of Common Market Studies*, 47 (4), 741–66.

Cohen, B.J. (2012), The benefits and costs of an international currency: getting the calculus right, *Open Economies Review*, 23 (1), 13–31.

Devereux, M. Engel, Ch., and Storgaard, P. (2004), Endogenous exchange rate pass-through when nominal prices are set in advance, *Journal of International Economics*, 63 (2), 263–91.

Devereux, M., and Shi, S. (2013), Vehicle currency, *International Economic Review*, 54 (1), 97–133.

Dooley, M., Folkerts-Landau, D., and Garber, P. (2003), An essay on the revived Bretton Woods system, National Bureau of Economic Research working paper No. 9971, Cambridge: NBER.

Eichengreen, B. (1989), Hegemonic Stability Theories of the International Monetary System, NBER Working Paper No. 2193, March.

Eichengreen, B. (1998), The euro as a reserve currency, *Journal of the Japanese and International Economies*, 12 (4), 483–506.

Eichengreen, B. (2010), Managing a multiple reserve currency world, mimeo, April 2010.

Eichengreen, B. (2011), *Exorbitant Priviledge, The Rise and Fall of the Dollar and the Future of the International Monetary System*, Oxford: Oxford University Press.

Eichengreen, B. (2013), Number one country, number one currency?, *The World Economy*, 36 (4), 363–74.

Eichengreen, B., Chiṭu, L., and Mehl, A. (2014a), Network effects, homogeneous goods and international currency choice: new evidence on oil markets from older era", ECB working paper No. 1651.

Eichengreen, B., Chiṭu , L., and Mehl, A. (2014b), Stability or upheaval? The currency composition of international reserves in the long run, ECB working paper No. 1715.

Eichengreen, B., and Flandreau, M. (2009), The rise and fall of the dollar (or when did the dollar replace sterling as the leading reserve currency?), *European Review of Economic History*, 13(3), 377–411.

Eichengreen, B., and Flandreau, M. (2012), The Federal Reserve, the Bank of England and the rise of the dollar as an international currency, 1914–39, *Open Economies Review*, 23, 57–87.

Eichengreen, B., and Kawai, M. (2014), Issues for renminbi internationalization: an overview, Asian Development Bank Institute working paper No. 454, January.

European Central Bank (1999), The international role of the euro, *Monthly Bulletin*, August, 31–24.

European Central Bank (2014), The international role of the Euro, July.

Farhi, E., Gourinchas, P.O., and Rey, H. (2011), *Reforming the International Monetary System*, CEPR e-book.

Friberg, R., and Wilander, F. (2008), The currency denomination of exports – a questionnaire study, *Journal of International Economics*, 75 (1), 54–69.

Gopinath, G., Itskhoki, O., and Rigobon, R. (2010), Currency choice and exchange rate pass-through, *American Economic Review*, 100 (1), 304–36.

Goldberg, L.S. (2011), The international role of the dollar: does it matter if this changes?, Federal Reserve Bank of New York Staff Report No. 522, October.

Goldberg, L.S., and Tille, C. (2008), Vehicle currency use and international trade, *Journal of International Economics*, 76 (2), 177–92.

Goldberg, L.S., and Tille, C. (2013), A bargaining theory for trade invoicing and pricing, *NBER Working Paper*, No. 18985, April 2013.

Goldberg, L.S., Krogstrup, S., Lipsky, J., and Rey, H. (2014), Why is financial stability essential for key currencies in the international monetary system? Vox column, 26 July.

Gourinchas, P.-O., H. Rey, and Govillot, N. (2010), Exorbitant privilege and exorbitant duty, Bank of Japan*, IMES discussion paper* 2010-E-20.

Hartmann, Ph. (1998), *Currency Competition and Foreign Exchange Markets: The Dollar, the Yen and the Euro*, Cambridge University Press.

Helleiner, E., and Kirchner, J. (2009), The future of the dollar: whither the key currency? in Helleiner, E. and J. Kirchner (eds.), *The Future of the Dollar*, Cornell University Press.

International Monetary Fund (2013), *Annual Report on Exchange Arrangements and Exchange Restrictions*, December.

Ivashina, V., Scharfstein, D., and Stein, J. (2012), Dollar funding and the lending behavior of global banks, *NBER Working Paper Series*, No. 18528, November.

Kindleberger, Ch. (1973), *The World in Depression*, Berkeley, University of California Press.

Kindleberger, C. (1981), Dominance and Leadership in the International Economy, *International Studies Quarterly*, 25 (2), 242–54.

Kirshner, J. (1995), *Currency and Coercion: The Political Economy of International Monetary Power*, Princeton NJ: Princeton University Press.

Kirshner, J. (2014), *American Power after the Financial Crisis*, Ithaca and London: Cornell University Press.

Krugman, P. (1980), Vehicle currencies and the structure of international exchange, *Journal of Money, Credit and Banking*, 12 (3), 513–26.

Krugman, P. (1984), The international role of the dollar, in Bilson, J.F.O. and Marston, R.C. (eds.) *Exchange Rate Theory and Practice*, Chicago: University of Chicago Press.

Kwan, C.H. (2001), *Yen Bloc: Towards Economic Integration in Asia*, Washington D.C.: Brookings Institution Press.

Li, Y., and Matsui, A. (2008), A theory of international currency and seigniorage competition, mimeo, November.

Liu, L., and Li, D.D. (2008), RMB internationalisation: an empirical and policy analysis, *Journal of Financial Research*, 2008, 11, 1–16.

Maggiori, M. (2013), Financial intermediation, international risk sharing, and reserve currencies, mimeo.

Matsuyama, K., Kiyotaki, N., and Matsui, A. (1992), Towards a theory of international currency, *Review of Economic Studies*, 60 (2), 283–307.

McKinnon, R. (2003), The world dollar standard and globalization, new rules for the game?, Standford Institute for Economic Policy Research, *SCID Working Paper* 181.

Mundell, R. (1998), What the euro means for the dollar and the international monetary system, *Atlantic Economic Journal*, 36 (3), 227–37.

Papaioannou, E., and Portes, R. (2008), Costs and benefits of running an international currency, *European Economy – Economic Papers* 348, Directorate General Economic and Monetary Affairs (DG ECFIN), European Commission.

Papaioannou, E., Portes, R., and Siourounis, G. (2006), Optimal currency shares in international reserves: The impact of the euro and the prospects for the dollar, *Journal of Japanese and International Economies*, 20 (4), 508–47.

Pittaluga, G.B., and Seghezza, E. (2012), Euro vs dollar: and improbable threat, *Open Economies Review*, 23 (1), 89–108.

Portes, R., and Rey, H. (1998), The emergence of the euro as an international currency, *Economic Policy*, 26 (2) 307–43.

Posen, A. (2008). Why the euro will not rival the dollar, *International Finance,* 11 (1), 75–100.

Rey, H. (2001), International trade and currency exchange, *Review of Economic Studies*, 68 (2), 443–64.

Schenk, C.R. (2010), How have multiple reserve currencies functioned in the past?, Paper presented at the conference of the Reinventing Bretton Woods Committee, Paris, December.

Springford, J., Tilford, S., and Whyte, P. (2014), *The economic consequences of leaving the EU*, Final Report of the CER Commission on the UK and the EU Single Market, Centre for European Reform, June.

Strange, S. (1971), *Sterling and British Policy: A Political Study of an International Currency in Decline*, Oxford: Oxford University Press.

Swoboda, A. (1968), The euro-dollar market: an interpretation, *Essays in International Finance*, 64, International Finance Section, Princeton.

Swoboda, A. (1969), Vehicle currencies and the foreign exchange market: the case of the dollar, in Aliber, R.Z. (ed.) *The International Market for Foreign Exchange*, Praeger Special Studies in International Economics and Development, Frederick A. Praeger Publishers, New York.

Triffin, R. (1960), *Gold and the Dollar Crisis: The Future of Convertibility*, New Haven: Yale University Press.

United Nations (2009), Report of the Commission of Experts of the President of the United Nations General Assembly on Reforms of the International Monetary and Financial System, June.

Van Rompuy, H. (2012), *Towards a genuine economic and monetary union*, Report of the Presidents, 5 December.

Véron, N. (2014), Defining Europe's Capital Markets Union, *Bruegel Policy Brief*, 2014/1, November.

Walter, A. (1991), *World Power and World Money: The Role of Hegemony and International Monetary Order*, New York: St. Martin's Press.

Warnock, F.E., and Warnock, V.C. (2009) International capital flows and US interest rates, *Journal of International Money and Finance* 28 (6), 903–19.

PART III

Monetary and fiscal policy

7

THE COMMON CURRENCY

More complicated than it seems

Charles Wyplosz

1. Introduction

It is painfully banal to observe that the Eurozone crisis has shaken many beliefs about a monetary union. The build-up of public debts, arguably the root cause of the crisis, is neither a surprise nor a specifically Eurozone phenomenon. Public debts also rose in many non-Eurozone countries in the wake of the Global Financial Crisis, but they did not trigger a crisis. In the Eurozone, public debts reached high levels for two seemingly unrelated reasons: fiscal indiscipline in some countries and poor bank supervision in others. Continuing fiscal indiscipline is testimony to the long decried "stupidity" of the Stability and Growth Pact.[1] Poor bank supervision turned into fiscal indiscipline. The socialization of bank losses was unavoidable but the costs were far too large because of a combination of dismal bank resolution procedures, deeply misguided and selfish pressure by other Eurozone countries in the case of Ireland, forbearance in the case of Spain and limits to the mandate of the European Central Bank (ECB).

Thus, the Eurozone was created with two major flaws: an ineffective fiscal discipline framework and the absence of a common approach to the banking sector. Repeated breaches to the Stability and Growth Pact have led to waves of reforms, none of which recognizes the essential fact that member states are sovereign in budgetary matters. Fiscal policy sovereignty is as old as democracy in Europe, which means that collective pressure is bound to fail if it clashes with voter preferences. Of course, fiscal policy measures can be imposed on a country under an IMF-EU program, but this does not mean that the pact, even strengthened, will work when normal conditions return.

While the European Union was engaged in developing a single market for banking services, it failed to recognize its implications, especially within the Eurozone.[2] The need for common supervision and resolution is now recognized – but not fully dealt with – through the creation of the Banking Union. The other implication is that no country with a developed banking (and more generally, financial) system can operate without a central bank ready to act as lender of last resort. Unfortunately, the narrow interpretation of its narrow mandate prevented the ECB from taking on this task until pretty late in the crisis. The Emergency Lending Assistance (ELA) procedure was always part of the ECB framework but it was conducted under considerable opacity until a more open approach was adopted in late 2013. Importantly, ELA is the responsibility of National Central Banks (NCBs), therefore eventual costs are assumed by the respective national Treasuries. Absent a common resolution framework, there is no guarantee that resolution will be adequately structured. In particular, poor resolution, including forbearance, can easily lead to large budgetary costs. This is exactly what happened.

The other surprise has been the fragmentation of banking. The interbank market has been operating at the national level, at best. Because interest rates on sovereign bonds have diverged, private end-users have faced very different credit costs and availability conditions. This was not supposed to happen. Even the rule of thumb that private interest rates are above the sovereign rate makes little sense within a monetary union. The likely explanation is the "redenomination risk", the possibility that some countries could break away from the Eurozone. The ECB has been forced to replace the Eurozone-wide interbank market, which has led to sometimes-misunderstood TARGET imbalances.

Had these flaws been dealt with in good time, the crisis would have been avoided. Once it occurred, four unexpected aspects were revealed. The first one is that the euro is effectively a foreign currency for member countries. De Grauwe (2012) has shown that, because the ECB is not the central bank of any member country, governments cannot expect any direct or indirect support as all other governments do. For three long years, the ECB did not signal any readiness to provide backstops to public debts. It finally did so with the OMT program, but conditionality stands to reduce its effectiveness. The likely reason for the ECB's reluctance is that member governments are unwilling to let it take risks whose possible costs would have to be shared. This is not an unavoidable feature of any monetary union. Rather it is a perfectly understandable issue that has been left simmering rather than faced and treated through appropriate governance.

More generally, the crisis has revealed a surprisingly weak governance arrangement. Decision-making has been haphazard. Summit meetings have been convened at a high frequency, only to make no or inadequate decisions. A totally unpredicted aspect of the decision-making process has been the emergence of a German leadership, the consequence of vetoes on a large number of propositions; some of these vetoes have subsequently been lifted, only after a predictable deterioration of the situation. A related surprise is that policy-makers did not allow their decisions to be challenged, neither *ex ante*, nor *ex post*. Put differently, independent advice was neither sought, nor taken on board. Groupthink has been the defining characteristic of crisis management.

Finally, the surprising strength of the euro, in particular *vis-à-vis* the US dollar, has come as a surprise. How is it possible that the currency of a monetary area subject to panic attacks from financial markets has not been seriously weakened? It has been sometimes asserted that the exchange rate should be the weighted average of what the currencies of member states would have been absent the monetary union. This prediction has not materialized.

This article deals with these issues by picking up a few topics that cut across them. The monetary union was imagined as the last step of a long policy convergence process, which was then called the Coronation Theory. Section 2 explains its logic and describes its failure. To the chagrin of many economists, the Optimum Currency Area (OCA) theory was generally ignored. Section 3 argues that it was a mistake but that the theory, as developed by then, failed to recognize that a monetary union is not just a transfer of monetary policy sovereignty. Section 4 frames this issue within a wider question: is there a fundamental tendency toward ever greater centralization in any inter-national undertaking with federal features? It argues that this is not so, but that other solutions must be found if additional transfers are difficult, or even impossible. The last section concludes.

2. The failure of the Coronation Theory

The Maastricht Treaty sets in great detail the architecture of the Eurozone, both how it would start and then how it would operate. The single most important vision behind the treaty is that the Eurozone should be built in such a way that it would pursue a "stability oriented" strategy, where stability means price stability. The ECB has constantly emphasized this overriding principle. For example, the first President of the ECB, Wim Duisenberg, stated just before the launch of the euro: "At the heart of our approach is the 'stability-oriented monetary policy strategy' recently adopted by the Governing Council."[3] This reflected the idea that the ECB should be seen as continuing the tradition of the Bundesbank. This heritage was duly noted by Issing (2008), the ECB's first Chief Economist and former Chief Economist of the Bundesbank: "The Bundesbank came to be regarded worldwide as an example of a sound institutional framework for conducting a price stability oriented monetary policy."[4]

The stability-oriented strategy was not limited to the mandate of the ECB. In line with the concept of monetary vs. fiscal dominance (Leeper, 1991), the Delors Committee Report duly noted that the common currency would "imply a common monetary policy and require a high degree of compatibility of economic policies and consistency in a number of other policy areas, particularly in the fiscal field. These policies should be geared to price stability, balanced growth, converging standards of living, high employment and external equilibrium. Economic and monetary union would represent the final result of the process of progressive economic integration in Europe." (Delors Committee, 1989). This led to the 'Coronation Theory': the euro would start with countries that had demonstrated their unflinching commitment to that price stability.[5] The theory directly led to the convergence criteria, meant to determine which countries would be allowed to join the monetary union. The five criteria (low inflation, low interest rate, exchange rate stability, low deficits and low debts) were designed to assess both monetary and fiscal policies in the light of this theory.

The Coronation Theory, and the adoption of the convergence criteria, ran against established economic theory (Begg et al., 1998). First, it fully ignored the OCA theory. This theory was developed to determine the desirability of a common currency for a group of economic areas. Its initial "classic" version focused on economic structural considerations (labor mobility, limited specialization and economic integration). It was later extended to policy/institutional considerations (fiscal transfers, homogeneity of collective preferences and a sense of common destiny).[6] The key idea was that the loss of the exchange rate is a source of difficulties when asymmetric shocks occur. The OCA theory asks what features either make such shocks rare or manageable when they occur. The coronation principle simply ignored the possibility of asymmetric shocks; it only wanted to make sure that collective preferences were such that price stability would never be challenged.

The Coronation Theory also contradicted the policy regime switch theory developed by Sargent (1982). This theory asserts that what matters for policy is the policy regime under which it operates, not past history. It implies that the Eurozone can achieve price stability if its central bank has a clear mandate to that effect and the necessary independence to deliver on the mandate. The fiscal/monetary dominance theory adds that the same should apply to fiscal policy. Instead of focusing on past performance, therefore, these theories call for adequate governance.

It is unclear why the proponents of the Coronation Theory ignored the OCA theory altogether. In fact the theory was never developed; it was simply asserted in policymaking circles at Germany's urging.[7] One interpretation is that policymakers simply were not aware of the OCA theory. Alternatively, they suspected that the institutions that they were putting in place were not adequate, but they were awed by the challenges of digging deeper into sovereignty issues. Or else, they rejected the view that past performance is irrelevant when the policy regime is changed.

The history of the Eurozone since 1999 is a resounding confirmation of the relevance of the regime change theory. On the one hand, equipped with a clear mandate toward price stability and adequate independence, the ECB has delivered. On the other hand, poor governance regarding fiscal policy has led to fiscal indiscipline. Member countries struggled to meet the convergence criteria. Most of them passed the hurdle, sometimes through the use of various gimmicks, and then some of them proceeded to ignore the Stability and Growth Pact that was explicitly designed to make the fiscal convergence criteria a permanent requirement, using the same limits to deficits (3 percent of GDP) and debts (60 percent).[8] The failure of the pact is shown in Figure 7.1, which displays the budget balance of the undisciplined and disciplined countries.[9] The 2009 recession, and its aftermath, is an exceptional event that can be ignored for the current discussion. Soon after 1998, when the convergence criteria were observed to decide on admission, the undisciplined countries breached the 3 percent deficit limit and kept doing so. Some of the disciplined countries (Germany and Austria) also relapsed, but only temporarily. Not shown are Luxembourg, a special case, and two disciplined countries, Ireland and Spain, that faced massive deficits after the Global Financial Crisis. Note that the pre-1998 pattern has little predictive power for the following years, in contradiction with the Coronation Theory.

Two lessons are unmistakable. First, the focus on the convergence criteria has been a remarkable failure. This was already obvious by 2004, when the Eurogroup decided to put the Stability and Growth Pact in abeyance, apparently because the two largest – and most powerful – countries were facing the prospect of a fine. The 2005 reform of the pact did not take notice of the deep reasons behind this episode. It dealt with technicalities, correctly shifting the focus to cyclically adjusted budget figures, but missed the essential contradiction between national sovereignty in budgetary matters and the collective need for individual country fiscal discipline.

The more recent reforms (the so called Six Pack and Two Pack directives) seek to tilt the balance toward collectively imposed discipline, but countries remain sovereign. Future failures are all but guaranteed.[10] This illustrates how complex a monetary union can be. The clean solution would be to form a "fiscal union", adopting a federal approach with a large enough central government to provide countercyclical transfers in the presence of asymmetric shocks. However, this would not be just a monetary union anymore. If, in addition, the central government had the power to raise its own taxes, it would in effect be a political union. We know from repeated experience that federal states can work, this is the easy, unimaginative solution. In the absence of popular support, however, the real challenge is to operate a monetary union without establishing a federal state.

The second lesson is related. The crisis has confirmed that a banking union must accompany a monetary union. Common regulation is easy. It was achieved two decades ago in the EU, and the Basel agreements move the whole world in this direction. Common supervision arrived in the Eurozone in 2014, and is not even complete. This is a sensitive element of national sovereignty because governments generally want to protect their banks and to nurture national champions. To that effect, they may be drawn into carrying out lenient supervision on the grounds that it raises bank profitability, credit distribution and growth prospects. However, higher financial profits go hand in hand with higher risk-taking and protected firms rarely develop the skills to grow internationally.

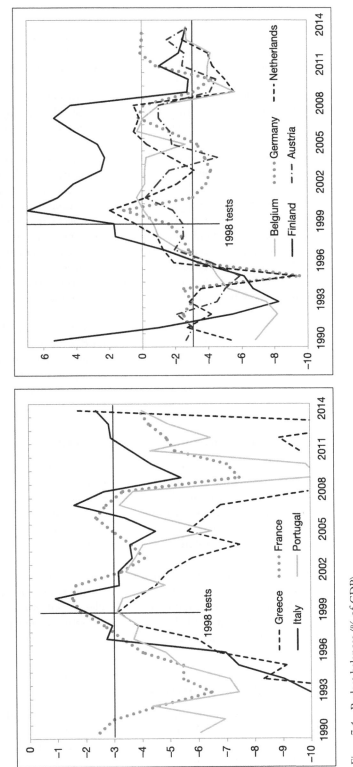

Figure 7.1 Budget balances (% of GDP)

Finally, a common resolution authority is not yet agreed upon. Here again, national sovereignty is at stake. Bank resolution involves transfers between shareholders, creditors, including depositors, and taxpayers. These transfers can be very large, measured in percentage of GDP. Only governments can decide such transfers. A common resolution authority requires, therefore, giving up a bit more sovereignty, which most governments are highly reluctant to do for valid reasons. They fear the political impact of substantial costs imposed on taxpayers by decisions that do not take. They also fear having to bear costs related to foreign bank failures.

This all illustrates the complexity of operating a monetary union. The Eurozone countries thought that they were giving up only monetary policy sovereignty. They have discovered that more is at stake. They are facing a difficult choice between making the euro work and giving up some more sovereignty, or preserving sovereignty and letting the euro experiment end. They hope to find a middle ground, between achieving fiscal discipline and setting up an effective banking union on the one hand, and retaining important components of national sovereignty. Unfortunately, such a middle ground may not exist. The stakes are heightened by the fact that a complete and effective banking union is a necessary condition for fiscal discipline. Cyprus, Ireland and Spain were fiscally disciplined but poor bank supervision led to massive increases in public debts, first to bail banks out, second through excessive borrowing from the IMF and other Eurozone countries.

None of these issues were brought up when the Eurozone was being designed. The monetary union was created with deep flaws and it was only a matter of time until the flaws would be revealed in the midst of a crisis. It is equally clear that a failure to draw the lessons from the current crisis will lead to another crisis. The insistence on keeping with the Stability and Growth Pact and the half-complete banking union is particularly worrisome.[11] Both aim at the impossible middle ground.

3. Limits of the Optimum Currency Area criteria

The sovereign debt crisis represents an unmistakable confirmation of the relevance of the OCA theory. The asymmetric shocks – highly differentiated debt buildups on highly diverse initial debt level positions as well as different inflation and current account evolutions – that occurred are precisely what the OCA theory identifies as the main cost of a monetary union. There was general agreement that the Eurozone is not an OCA. The occurrence of an asymmetric shock was therefore bound to create serious hardship to the adversely affected countries.

The OCA theory further identified where the pain would occur. It would be worse for the less diversified countries. It would hit employment; it would require lower price and wage inflation rates in the affected countries; it would challenge policymakers in calling for transfers; it would exacerbate ingrained divergent beliefs about which policies work and which ones do not; it would also challenge the sense of common destiny. What did we observe, then?

3.1 Labor market mobility

Figure 7.2 displays the average employment rate in the Eurozone countries affected by the crisis and in those that were not. It shows that employment rates in the crisis countries were catching up fast before 1999 and closed the gap in 2007. In 2008, they started to diverge at a fast pace. As expected, the labor markets took the brunt of the crisis.

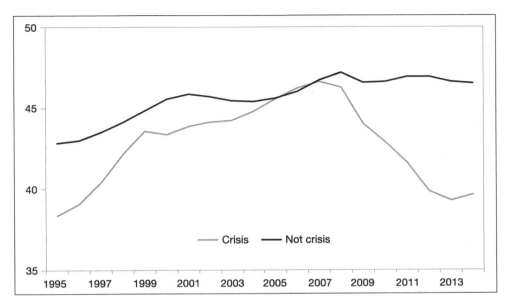

Figure 7.2 Employment rates (% of total population)

According to the OCA theory, following an asymmetric shock, a lack of labor mobility is a key aggravating factor. The surprise has been that labor mobility has considerably increased in the crisis countries. Much informal evidence suggests that migration flows from crisis to non-crisis countries have been important, especially for qualified workers.[12] Figure 7.3 presents the average ratio of emigrants to immigrants in the crisis and non-crisis countries. Before the crisis, the ratio was less than unity and lower in the crisis country group: in all Eurozone countries net migration flows were positive, especially so in Southern Europe. During that period, Germany was the country with the highest emigration/immigration ratio, often close to unity. The situation changed radically with the onset of the crisis. The ratio declined slightly on average in the non-crisis countries, but very strongly in Germany, while it shot up in the crisis countries (reaching 3:55 in Portugal in 2012).[13]

The data presented in Figure 7.3 do not capture migration flows within the Eurozone. This is how it should be. In the simple two-country model used in the OCA literature, following an asymmetric shock, flows should occur from the adversely hit country to the other currency area country. In a multilateral world, the economically desirable adjustment can combine flows from the crisis countries to the rest of the world with flows from the rest of the world to the growing non-crisis countries.

Figures 7.2 and 7.3 together show that employment was not fully protected but that labor mobility has played an important adjustment role, far beyond what previous studies (Fatás, 2000) had suggested would be the case. On that dimension, the Eurozone is less far away from an OCA than hitherto believed, at least in the case of massive shocks.[14]

3.2 Trade specialization and openness

On two OCA criteria, the Eurozone was believed to do generally well: openness to trade and reasonably similar trade specialization. This does not mean that all countries fulfill

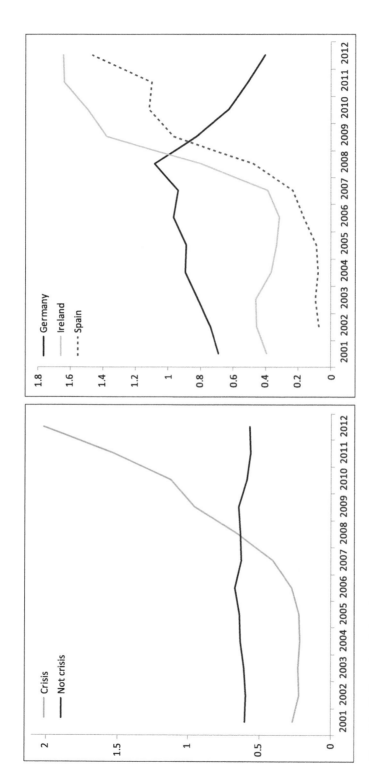

Figure 7.3 Ratio emigrants/immigrants

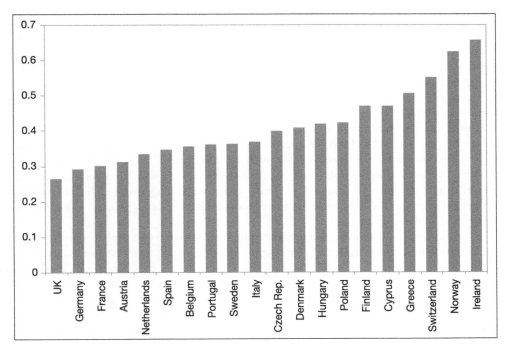

Figure 7.4 Trade concentration index (2007)

the criteria, although nearly all Eurozone countries are very open.[15] Figure 7.4 displays UNCTAD's trade concentration index for European countries in 2007, just before the crisis. This is a measure of the lack of diversification. Three crisis countries, Cyprus, Ireland and Greece are among those with comparatively high trade concentration, but not the two others, Spain and Portugal.

This observation suggests that asymmetric shocks were not the driving factors of the crisis, even though trade imbalances were growing in the run-up. Large and fast growing debts, some of which were the result of banking crises, were the source of the asymmetric shocks. The lesson here is that the OCA criteria miss important aspects.

3.3 Transfers

With an overall "federal" budget capped at about 1 percent of GDP, the EU countries have long been known to fail the transfer criteria. This has been painfully obvious during the crisis. The refusal to allow crisis countries to apply to standard IMF programs has made it necessary for the Eurozone to bail them out, in contradiction with the treaty's no-bailout clause. Anyway, the resources of the IMF would have been insufficient to deal with such costly shocks as bank crises. The result has been the creation of the temporary European Financial Stability Facility (EFSF) and its subsequent replacement with the permanent and better endowed European Stability Mechanism (ESM).[16]

When the EFSF was created, policymakers hoped that it would prevent further contagion. These hopes were defeated. One reason is that even the ESM was too small to impress panicked financial markets. Another reason is that the transfers were not automatic. They required an explicit decision and they came along with drastic conditions. In contrast, the transfers imagined by the OCA theory are automatic and unconditional. In federal states, they operate via cyclical tax revenues and welfare payments. Even so, they would have been too small for the task. Estimates of the size of automatic transfers in the US, for instance, are about 10 percent of the shock. This may be enough for trade shocks, but not for financial shocks. Financial shocks also require central bank interventions as lender of last resort. As noted in Section 1, the ECB has been reluctant to accept this responsibility.

This is another implication of monetary union that has been overlooked by the OCA theory. The creation of the ESM has improved the situation somewhat, but far from enough. Ideally, the Eurozone would equip itself with a "government" large enough to operate automatic transfers. However, this would require transferring very significant tax and spending powers to that government, which is politically ruled out at this juncture. This observation lies behind the view that a monetary union cannot survive without a political union. This is a simplistic view, however.

For real shocks, the amounts are modest enough for a country to replace transfers with public borrowing abroad. External borrowing, on the other hand, requires the capacity to do so, which means low enough public indebtedness. Herein lies another complexity. While the convergence criteria rightfully note the importance of fiscal discipline, this aspect is overlooked by the OCA theory. All of the reasons why fiscal discipline has not been achieved should be included in the OCA criteria. They ultimately hark back to the need for further encroachments of sovereignty. An alternative is the ability to tap on a strong sense of solidarity, to which we now turn.

3.4 Policy preferences and sense of common destiny

It is easy to imagine how the crisis could have been stopped in Greece and prevented from spreading to other countries. The other countries could have provided Greece with unconditional resources to ride through its shock, possibly by absorbing some of its public debt through schemes like Eurobonds. Alternatively, the debt could have been restructured promptly, which would have created significant losses for foreign banks, chiefly French and German. For several reasons, this was never considered.

The first reason is moral hazard. Greece had a long history of fiscal indiscipline, aggravated by "managed" deficit figures. The other crisis countries also suffered from chronic fiscal indiscipline (Portugal) or from inefficient bank supervision (Cyprus, Ireland and Spain). Unconditional support and/or debt restructuring were seen as a reward for past misbehavior. This consideration also put the ECB in an impossible situation should it consider intervening as lender in last resort to governments and banks.

The second reason is that sharp interpretation differences quickly emerged. At the risk of oversimplification, these differences set apart the Northern from the Southern countries. The Northern countries considered that the problem – excessive public debts – had to be dealt with through rapid fiscal consolidation. The Southern countries argued that front-loaded fiscal consolidation would lead to a deep recession, which would further increase the budget deficits. They were right but the tarnished reputation of the crisis countries meant that they could neither win allies among the non-crisis countries nor prevail in negotiations. The ECB aligned itself with the Northern countries, calling for front-loaded fiscal consolidation and for structural reforms that take years to deliver positive effects.

The third reason is that the sense of solidarity that would have alleviated moral hazard concerns quickly vanished. The non-crisis countries quickly determined that they would not pay for the crisis countries. Demonstrators then burnt German flags in the streets of Athens. Southern propositions calling for Eurobonds fell on deaf ears.

OCA theory, once again, was right on the mark. When a powerful asymmetric shock occurs, adversely affected monetary union members cannot benefit from an exchange rate depreciation to absorb the blow. In the event, a strong euro made their situation worse. Absent automatic transfer mechanisms, the preservation of the monetary union requires a coherent view and a sense of common destiny. It took three years for the ECB to create the OMT program that effectively reversed the tide of ever-increasing panic on the financial markets. The justification for the program was precisely the survival of the common currency. Controversies about the program – and about the earlier ECB efforts at bypassing the frozen interbank market through TARGET 2 imbalances – confirm that the sense of common purpose has been sorely missing.

3.5 Limitations of OCA criteria

This review of OCA theory leaves an impression of incompleteness. The trade-related criteria have been largely irrelevant to the Sovereign Debt Crisis. The labor mobility criterion has been less penalizing than previously thought, probably because the crisis has been more disastrous than anticipated. The really binding criteria are the "new" ones, those that concern institutions, either transfers or policy and political divergences. Finally, the OCA theory simply ignores fiscal discipline, the Achilles' heel that has led to the crisis.

The first obvious limitation concerns labor mobility. The changing pattern of migration in response to the crisis can be seen as positive. However, this success ignores the high welfare costs of migration. While migration helps in terms of unemployment, it replaces one hardship with another. In addition, while migration is well adapted to permanent shifts in production specialization, it is especially costly when the shock is macroeconomic in nature; eventually debts will decline and emigrants will want to go home, suffering again from fixed costs. If they do not migrate back, the high public debts will be permanently borne by a reduced population. While it is individually attractive to move from a high to a low public debt jurisdiction, the collective effect is clearly undesirable.

The second limitation of OCA theory concerns the nexus between transfers, fiscal discipline and inherited debt levels. One virtue of the convergence criteria is to have identified fiscal discipline as a key requirement of a monetary union. The OCA theory ignores transfers. Instead, it looks for ways to make them unnecessary. But when a monetary union is not an optimum currency area, which no one fully is, transfers must be part of the criteria. Transfers are meant to be a form of insurance, which benefit all members over time. They cannot be set in place in the midst of a crisis, when the payers and the beneficiaries are clearly identified, unless there is both agreement on accompanying policies and a sense of common destiny. They could have been established *ex ante*, before the launch of the common currency, but they were not. It will be much harder to establish them now that positions have hardened.

An alternative to transfers is borrowing in bad years and paying back in good years. This is the most promising route but the legacy of high public debts may make it impossible for a number of countries to be able to borrow in case of need. The Stability and Growth Pact aims at bringing public debts down over a relatively short period, perhaps over 10 or 20 years. This will be difficult to implement, as shown by Eichengreen and Panizza (2014). The debt legacy is better dealt with through debt restructuring, but there is presently no appetite for such a step.[17] The need for low debts is absent from OCA theory. This is the third limitation.

Finally, borrowing to sail through an adverse shock is possible for goods market shocks. Financial shocks, especially banking crises, involve required amounts of an altogether different order of magnitude. Ireland had to raise its gross debt from 25 percent of GDP in 2007 to 64 percent in 2009, and 91 percent in 2010. Had the central bank advanced a portion of the needs, Ireland probably would not have undergone a full-blown debt crisis on top of its banking crisis.[18] As noted above, the ECB felt paralyzed by Northern governments' vocal hostility to any form of risk sharing. Such considerations have been ignored by both the treaty and OCA theory.

The common thread among all these limitations of the OCA theory is that a monetary union challenges sovereignty in many ways. To deal with large asymmetric shocks, governments can either help each other if there is enough political will, or they need to write down binding contracts – e.g., the conditions imposed by the IMF-EU-ECB Troika – that impinge on sovereignty. Obviously, the lack of political will in favor of solidarity also challenges further restraints on sovereignty.

4. The centralization tendency

Another interpretation of the hard choices faced by the Eurozone is that it is just one instance of a more general phenomenon, sometimes called Bryce's law: the tendency of federal states to become increasingly more centralized. In fact, the evidence is mixed. In mature federal states, there is no such tendency (Vaubel, 1996). Federal states that establish themselves from existing units, on the other hand, see an "early" build-up of the federal entity. For example, in 1902, in the still-growing US, federal tax revenues accounted for 18 percent of total revenues; by 1981 the share had grown to 58 percent. Oates (1993) attributes this evolution to the two World Wars that led the federal government to acquire prerogatives that were not relinquished subsequently in peace time.

Inasmuch as this observation is relevant for the EU – a very young construction that is not even a federation – we should expect more sovereignty transfers in the future. This is indeed what many observers see as the main lesson of the crisis when they call for a greater role of the Commission and/or the pooling of some economic resources. Yet, at the same time, we observe an increasing resistance among voters against such transfers. This goes hand-in-hand with the opinion of Vaubel (1996), who argues that institutional and political arrangements are the reason why Bryce's law has not been operative.

This matters for the questions at hand. It matters for the Stability and Growth Pact, which has failed because the Commission's power has been too limited. The 2012 reforms, including the reverse qualified majority voting procedure, intend to enhance the Commission's formal power to enforce the pact. It will face the very forces that have been successful at keeping centralization tendencies at bay. From an institutional angle, member countries remain sovereign in budgetary matters even if they agree to subject themselves to the pact. Politically, constraints imposed by the pact will only generate popular resistance and resentment.

It matters also for OCA theory. Section 3 argues that the theory's omissions concern issues that imply that a monetary union requires deeper sovereignty transfers than anticipated. If these transfers cannot be achieved, the natural conclusion would seem to be that the Eurozone is not just failing on the thus-extended OCA criteria, but also that its survival is very much in doubt.

However, this could be a misleading conclusion. A different interpretation is that, while broad-brush solutions like a fiscal or political union may be beyond reach at this juncture, more detailed and precise treatments of each failure of the (suitably extended) OCA criteria can be implemented. This however requires that the lessons be fully taken on board and that seemingly simple solutions be replaced by more elaborate ones.

A prime example is the requirement for a fiscal discipline arrangement that cannot be sidestepped. The crisis has shown that the centralized solution inherent in the Stability and Growth Pact has failed. Most of the recent reforms are attempts at transferring power from member states to the center: the combination of the Commission and the Eurogroup. Drawing the lesson requires that the centralized approach be abandoned in favor of a decentralized solution. The Fiscal Compact can achieve this aim if it is made more precise and divorced from the Stability and Growth Pact. The compact aims at making fiscal discipline a national obligation, by including in the constitution of each member state a well-designed fiscal rule. Unfortunately, the compact does not absolutely require that the rule be constitutional and leaves its definition vague. Decentralized fiscal discipline will be achieved when every country follows Germany's example of adopting a mandatory deficit brake rule, written into the constitution and subject to the country's highest court, with possible appeal to the European Court of Justice.

Much of the same concerns the Banking Union, the other major flaw of the Maastricht Treaty, but with different conclusions. The need for single regulation, supervision and resolution authorities is now recognized but it faces resistance because of potentially large income redistribution impacts. One could argue that once European supervisory authorities make decisions, the consequences are naturally borne by European taxpayers. This means a sovereignty transfer. The solution adopted at this stage is a subtle compromise. Regulation is common, the single supervisor only looks at the larger, systemically important banks and resolution is to be coordinated but ultimately remains a sovereign responsibility, with a European resolution fund financed by bank contributions, complemented by national resolution funds. The clean solution would have been that all banks be put under single supervision and that resolution indeed be common. The adopted solution is unwieldy and will probably have to evolve toward a true Banking Union.

Is such centralization unlikely? Opposition will come from banks if they feel that supervision and resolution will be friendlier at the national level. The supervision issue is settled for the large banks and opposition is mainly circumscribed to medium-sized banks that are either state-owned – e.g. the German *Spärkassen* owned by the states – or benefit from a public guarantee. Opposition to a true single resolution authority comes from countries that believe that their banks will never fail and do not want to pay for other countries. For two reasons, opposition should decline. First, the task of the Single Supervision Mechanism (SSM) is to provide a guarantee that all banks under its watch are properly run, irrespective of where they are incorporated. Second, the Banking Union establishes a clear cascade of bail-ins to be imposed in case of resolution. This means that taxpayers are very unlikely to bear the costs of bank resolution (see Huertas, 2014). More opposition comes from member governments that remain attached to protect local champions. Here again the SSM is likely to change the situation. All large banks are now under common regulation and supervision. Favorable treatment is likely to fade away.

The foregoing discussion of the two most important flaws of the Eurozone illustrates the complexity of the construction and the need to move away from simple and standard solutions because of sovereignty concerns. In one case, fiscal discipline, the likely solution is more, not less sovereignty. In the other case – bank supervision and resolution – the likely solution is less sovereignty. In both cases, the contentious sovereignty lens is the easy but misleading way to frame the analysis. The method of economics is to identify the problem and the constraints and to look for the second (or worse) best solution.[19]

5. Conclusions

The single currency was initially seen as the coronation of a gradual process of convergence of macroeconomic policies that would make national monetary policies redundant. In contrast, the classic OCA theory viewed the success of a monetary union as depending on real economic integration (labor and trade markets) while the extended theory focused on institutional and political characteristics. Both approaches saw a monetary union only as a transfer of monetary policy sovereignty. The crisis has shown the undertaking to be far more complex and it also shows that simple solutions are unlikely to deal effectively with complex issues.

It would be equally wrong to see the additional requests as mission creep. Monetary union does not have to be the back door to further sovereignty transfers, even though the Eurozone now challenges national sovereignty in some specific areas. The simple solution, a political union, or just a fiscal union, would indeed make the Eurozone look like a federal state, which could draw on many successful experiments elsewhere. Unfortunately, given the inherent complexity of the European experiment, that solution is too simple to be viable, at least at this point in time. Fortunately, it is not an absolute necessity. The challenge for the current generation of policymakers is to invent solutions that address with surgical precision the shortcomings of the Eurozone architecture. These are less glamorous undertakings than a political union, but they are both necessary and possible.

Some progress has been achieved regarding the long identified necessity of providing a common treatment of banks. Although the Banking Union is still a work in progress, it is an example of how a well-identified flaw can be addressed with punctual transfers of sovereignty. The fiscal discipline requirement, on the other hand, was supposed to be solved with the Stability and Growth Pact. Poorly thought-through, the pact has failed, mainly because it is challenging budgetary sovereignty. The response has been to raise this unwinnable challenge. The Fiscal Compact could provide the solution, a decentralized arrangement.

Another flaw, briefly alluded to in the introduction, concerns the governance of the Eurozone. Admittedly, a financial crisis is an extreme test of the ability of the Eurozone to manage its internal affairs. High frequency summits have delivered poorly prepared decisions, which is a key reason for the depth, width and duration of the crisis. Here too, the situation is complex as the Eurozone is a multi-national arrangement within the EU, another multi-national arrangement not devoid of governance shortcomings.

Pessimists and Euro-skeptics have concluded that the monetary union is bound to fail. Optimists will note that the Eurozone was barely ten-years old when the crisis erupted – very early infancy for such a historical undertaking – and that it has survived, badly bruised but intact.

Notes

1. This refers to the characterization of the pact as the "Stupidity Pact" by Romano Prodi (*Le Monde*, October 17, 2002), then President of the European Commission. Criticism of the pact has been the subject of a large literature, dating back at least to Eichengreen and Wyplosz (1998) and Begg et al. (1998).
2. Here again, see Begg et al. (1998) for an explicit warning that this failure would lead to a crisis.
3. Duisenberg (1998).
4. Issing (2008).
5. On the Coronation Theory, see Dyson and Featherstone (1999), Wyplosz (2006) and Zimmermann (2001).
6. For a complete presentation, see Burda and Wyplosz (2013).

7 According to Nowotny (2014), the Coronation Theory "reflects the experience of the unification of Germany in the nineteenth century and is based on the conviction that there has to be a common political system to guarantee a strict monetary policy".

8 For an analysis of the fundamental weaknesses of the Stability and Growth Pact, see Wyplosz (2013).

9 An even more damming picture emerges from the evolution of public debts.

10 Indeed, at the time of writing, it is already apparent that the reformed pact is losing yet another battle.

11 The "Fiscal Compact" included in the Treaty on Stability, Coordination and Governance (TSCG) represents a breakthrough, as it requires each country to adopt high-level legislation that bans fiscal indiscipline. This could lead to a decentralized approach that eliminates the conflict with sovereignty, see below in Section 4. Unfortunately, the Fiscal Compact is seen as a component of the centralized Stability and Growth Pact and its wording is far too vague.

12 Bräuninger (2014) presents many measures of migration in the Eurozone.

13 The standard informal story is that German pensioners used to settle in Spain before the crisis while Spanish engineers moved en masse to Germany during the crisis.

14 This conforms well to the fixed cost theory of migration, as developed by Burda (1995) and others.

15 With a degree of openness about the same as France and the UK, Greece is relatively less open given its size.

16 In the end, the crisis countries, save Spain, applied to the IMF.

17 Pâris and Wyplosz (2014) develop a seemingly painless solution.

18 A proper resolution process would have cut the financial needs.

19 Both the Fiscal Compact and the Banking Union were first proposed by the Chairman of the ECB, Mario Draghi, in December 2011 and May 2012, respectively.

References

Begg, D., de Grauwe, P., Giavazzi, P. and Uhlig, H. (1998), The ECB: Safe at Any Speed? *Monitoring the European Central Bank* 1, CEPR.

Bräuninger, D. (2014), The Dynamics of Migration in the Euro Area, Deutsche Bank Research.

Burda, M. (1995), Migration and the Option Value of Waiting, *Economic and Social Review* 27(1): 1–19.

Burda, M. and Wyplosz, C. (2013), *Macroeconomics, a European Text*, Oxford: Oxford University Press.

De Grauwe, P. (2012), The Governance of a Fragile Eurozone, *Australian Economic Review* 45(3): 255–68.

Delors Committee (1989), Report on Economic and Monetary Union in the European Community, Office for Official Publications of the European Communities, Luxembourg.

Duisenberg, W.F. (1998), The ESCB's Stability-Oriented Monetary Policy Strategy, Institute of European Affairs, Dublin, 10 November. www.ecb.europa.eu/press/key/date/1998/html/sp981110.en.html

Dyson, K. and Featherstone, K. (1999), *The Road to Maastricht, Negotiating Economic and Monetary Union*, Oxford: Oxford University Press.

Eichengreen, B. and Panizza, U. (2014), A Surplus of Ambition: Can Europe Rely on Large Primary Surpluses to Solve its Debt Problem?, *CEPR Discussion Paper*, No. 10069.

Eichengreen, B. and Wyplosz, C. (1998), The Stability Pact: Minor Nuisance, Major Diversion? *Economic Policy* 13(26): 67–113.

Fatás, A. (2000), Intranational migration: business cycles and growth, in: van Wincoop, E. and Hess, G. (eds), *Intranational Macroeconomics*, Cambridge: Cambridge University Press.

Huertas, T. (2014), *Safe to Fail*, Basingstoke: Palgrave Macmillan.

Issing, O. (2008), In Search of Monetary Stability: The Evolution of Monetary Policy Some Reflections, Experience – Lessons – Open Issues, Seventh BIS Annual Conference 26–27 June 2008.

Leeper, E.M. (1991), Equilibria under 'Active' and 'Passive' Monetary and Fiscal Policies, *Journal of Monetary Economics* 27(1): 129–47.

Mongelli, F.P. and Wyplosz, C. (2009), The Euro at Ten: Unfulfilled Threats and Unexpected Challenges, in: Bartosz Mackowiak, Francesco Paolo Mongelli, Gilles Noblet and Frank Smets (eds), *The Euro at Ten – Lessons and Challenges*, (pp.24–57) European Central Bank.

Oates, W.E. (1993), Fiscal Decentralization and Economic Development, *National Tax Journal* 46(2): 237–43.

Nowotny, E. (2014), European Monetary Union – past, present and future, in honor of Alexandre Lamfalussy, Lamfalussy Lectures Conference, Budapest.

Pâris, P. and Wyplosz, C. (2014), Politically Acceptable Debt Restructuring in Europe, PADRE 2.0, The Graduate Institute of International Studies, Geneva.

Rosen, H. (1988), Introduction, in: H. Rosen (ed.), *Fiscal Federalism: Quantitative Studies*, Chicago: University of Chicago Press.

Sargent, T. (1982), The Ends of Four Big Inflations, in: Hall, R.E. (ed.), *Inflation: Causes and Effects*, Cambridge (Mass.): NBER.

Vaubel, R. (1996), Constitutional Safeguards Against Centralization in Federal States: An International Cross-Section Analysis, *Constitutional Political Economy* 7(2): 79–102.

Wyplosz, C. (2006), European Monetary Union: the Dark Sides of a Major Success, *Economic Policy* 21(46): 207–62.

Wyplosz, C. (2013), Europe's Quest for Fiscal Discipline, *European Economy Economic Papers* 498.

Zimmermann, H. (2001), The Euro under Scrutiny: Histories and Theories of European Monetary Integration, *Contemporary Economic History* 10(2): 333–41.

8

DESIGN FAILURES IN THE EURO AREA

Can they be fixed?

Paul De Grauwe[1]

1. Introduction

The Eurozone looked like a wonderful construction at the time it was built. Yet it appeared to be loaded with design failures. In 1999 I compared the Eurozone to a beautiful villa in which Europeans were ready to enter. Yet it was a villa that did not have a roof. As long as the weather was fine, we would like to have settled in the villa. We would regret it when the weather turned ugly (De Grauwe, 1999). With the benefit of hindsight, the design failures have become even more manifest as the ones that were perceived before the start. In this chapter I analyze these design failures, and I ask the question of whether they can be fixed.

2. Booms and busts in capitalism

Capitalism is a wonderful human invention that manages to steer individual initiative and creativity towards capital accumulation and ever more material progress. However, it is also inherently unstable. Periods of optimism and pessimism alternate, creating booms and busts in economic activity. The booms are wonderful; the busts create great hardship for many people.

Booms and busts are endemic in capitalism because many economic decisions are forward-looking. Investors and consumers look into the future to decide to invest or to consume. But the future is dark. Nobody knows it. As a result, when making forecasts, consumers and investors look at each other. This makes it possible for the optimism of one individual to be transmitted to others creating a self-fulfilling movement in optimism. Optimism induces consumers to consume more and investors to invest more, thereby validating their optimism. The reverse is also true. When pessimism sets in, the same herding mechanism leads to a self-fulfilling decline in economic activity. Animal spirits prevail (Keynes, 1936; Akerlof and Shiller, 2009).

The role of banks and financial markets is key to understanding the unstable nature of booms and busts. When, during a boom optimism, even euphoria, prevails, households and firms cheerfully take on more debt so as to profit from high perceived rates of return. Bankers, who are equally gripped by euphoria are happy to oblige. As a result, a boom in consumption and investment is set in motion fueled by debt and excessive bank credit (Minsky, 1986).

119

When it becomes obvious that optimism was excessive and that debt is unsustainable, the inevitable crash occurs. Firms and households have to reduce their debts, banks with bloated balance sheets have to deleverage. The economy turns into a downward spiral.

This dynamics of booms and busts has been repeated so many times in history. Yet so many people are surprised when the crash occurs. This may have something to do with the fact that during the boom and the bubble, many people think "this time is different" as Reinhart and Rogoff (2009) argued (see also the wonderful classic of Kindleberger, 2005).

3. Stabilizers in the system: only at national level

Since the Great Depression of the 1930s many countries have introduced stabilizing features in their economies. I will discuss two of these, i.e. the role of the central bank as a lender of last resort and the automatic stabilizers in the government budgets. These will also play a central role when I discuss the fragility of the Eurozone.

Central banks were originally created to deal with the inherent instability of capitalism. They were not primarily set up to maintain price stability. The concern for price stability came only much later. As argued earlier, the instability of capitalism arises because of the involvement of financial institution in the booms and busts. Thus, the central bank was given the role of lender of last resort, i.e. a backstop needed to inject liquidity in financial markets when panic after a crash leads everybody to sell assets and to scramble for liquidity (Goodhart and Illing, 2002).

Right from the start the role of lender of last resort was not restricted to injecting liquidity in the banking sector. It also extended to the government bond markets. The reason is very simple and quite fundamental. It has to do with the existence of a "deadly embrace" between the sovereign and the banks. When the sovereign gets into problems the falling government bond prices threaten the banks, which are the main holders of government debt. When the banks collapse, governments that do not want to let down the banks are threatened with insolvency. If one of the two falls off the cliff the other one is also pulled down. As a result, when central banks took on the responsibility of lenders of last resort it was understood that restricting this responsibility to the banks would be unworkable and would not stabilize the financial system. I will return to this issue when I discuss the European Central Bank (ECB) as this idea was totally disregarded when that institution was created.

There is another reason why the lender of last resort commitment of the central bank was given to both the banks and the sovereign. This has to do with the fact that both suffer from a similar fragility. Their balance sheets have a similar unbalanced maturity structure. Banks borrow short and lend long, i.e. their liabilities (demand and saving deposits) are highly liquid while their assets (mortgages, long-term loans) are illiquid. As a result, in the absence of a lender of last resort, distrust in banks can trigger a run on the bank. Such a collective movement of distrust will bring down the banks, even those that are solvent.

The government balance sheet has a similar unbalanced maturity structure. The liabilities of the government consist mainly of bonds that are highly liquid and can be sold almost instantaneously. The assets consist of infrastructure and more importantly of tax claims. The latter however are illiquid, i.e. the government has to go through a democratic decision process to increase tax revenues; a process that can take a lot of time. As a result, in the absence of a lender of last resort, a collective movement of distrust can lead to a liquidity crisis that can push the government into default.

The second stabilizing feature of the dynamics of booms and busts in capitalism was gradually introduced through the government budget that increasingly built in stabilizing features. These stabilizing features were essential to stabilize an otherwise unstable system for the following reason. When, after the crash, the private sector is in need to deleverage there is high potential for deflationary dynamics. This was first recognized by Fisher (1933) and by Keynes (1936).

When the private sector needs to reduce its debt it will try to do two things. First it will attempt to save more. But as Keynes stressed this will lead to the savings paradox. By saving more (and consuming less) output declines and so does national income. In the end less can be saved by the private sector, increasing the desire to save more. This can only be solved if the government sector is willing to save less, i.e. to increase its borrowing. Put differently if some (the private sector) wishes to save more, others (the government sector) must be willing to borrow more. If the latter does not want to do this, it prevents the former from saving more and from unwinding its debt.

The second way to reduce the debt is by selling assets. Thus if the private sector as a whole sells assets so as to reduce its debt, asset prices decline, thereby creating solvency problems of agents that were in no need to deleverage. These will now have to do the same and sell assets. In order to stop this downward spiral, somebody (the government) has to be willing to take over the debt of private agents. In doing so, it helps the private sector to deleverage and puts a floor on the downward deflationary forces that follow a crash.

These two stabilizers, the lender of last resort and the automatic budget stabilizers, were introduced in the system at the national level. They are now relatively well organized at the level of nation states. They were not organized at the international level, nor at the level of a monetary union such as the Eurozone. This has led to the major design failures of the Eurozone, to which we now turn our attention. These design failures were only recognized after the financial crisis, also because mainstream theory about how to organize a monetary union (the optimal currency area theory) was preoccupied with exogenous shocks, not with the endogenous dynamics that is embedded in capitalism. And even then in many countries, especially in Northern Europe, these design failures are still not recognized mainly because of a dramatic diagnostic failure that focuses on government profligacy as the sole source of the euro-crisis. (I will have more to say about this diagnostic failure in section 4.)

4. The Eurozone's design failures

The design failures of the Eurozone find their origin in the two factors discussed in the previous section. In this section I will argue first that the endogenous dynamics of booms and busts continued to work at the national level and that the monetary union in no way disciplined these into a union-wide dynamics. On the contrary, the monetary union probably exacerbated these national booms and busts. Second, the existing stabilizers that existed at the national level prior to the start of the union were stripped away from the member-states without being transposed at the monetary union level. This left the member-states "naked" and fragile, unable to deal with the coming national disturbances. Let us expand on these two points.

4.1 Booms and busts dynamics

In the Eurozone money and monetary policy are fully centralized. However, the rest of macroeconomic policies has remained firmly in the hands of national governments, producing idiosyncratic movements unconstrained by the existence of a common currency. As a result, there is very little in the monetary union that can make the booms and busts converge at the Eurozone level. The effect of all this is that booms and busts originate at the national level and have a life of their own at the national level without becoming a common boom-and-bust dynamics at the Eurozone level.

In fact it is even worse. The existence of the monetary union can exacerbate booms and busts at the national level. The reason is that the single interest rate that the ECB imposes on all the member countries is too low for the booming countries and too high for the countries in recession. Thus, when in Spain, Ireland, and Greece the economy started to boom, inflation also picked up in these countries. As a result, the single nominal interest rate led to a low real interest rate in the booming countries, thereby aggravating the boom. The opposite occurred in the countries experiencing low growth or a recession.

Thus, the fact that only one interest rate exists for the union exacerbates these differences, i.e. it leads to a stronger boom in the booming countries and a stronger recession in the recession countries than if there had been no monetary union.

The effects of these divergent macroeconomic movements have by now been well documented. In Figures 8.1 and 8.2 I show how these led to divergences in inflation and relative unit labor costs and to current account imbalances. Figure 8.1 shows how the booming Southern European countries (including Ireland) experienced systematically higher inflation rates and increases in unit labor costs than in the rest of the Eurozone. Figure 8.2 shows how these booms led to large current account deficits in the South and surpluses in the North. It is important to stress here that the booms in the South allowed the Northern European countries to accumulate large current account surpluses. These were financed by credit that the Northern European countries granted to the South. Thus in a way it can be said that Northern Europe behaved like the automobile salesman who sells cars to his customers by providing them with cheap credit. It is important to recognize this because in the North of Europe the irresponsibility of Southern countries to take on too much debt is often stressed. The truth is that for every foolish debtor there must be a foolish creditor.

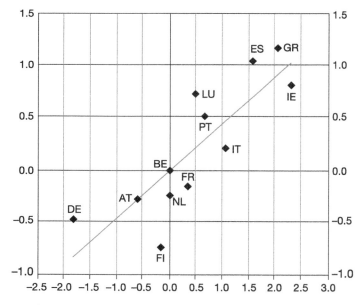

Figure 8.1 Inflation and labor costs, 2002–2008

Source: ECB, Monthly Bulletin, November 2012.

Notes: Average yearly inflation differential (y-axis) and average change in relative unit labor costs (x-axis).

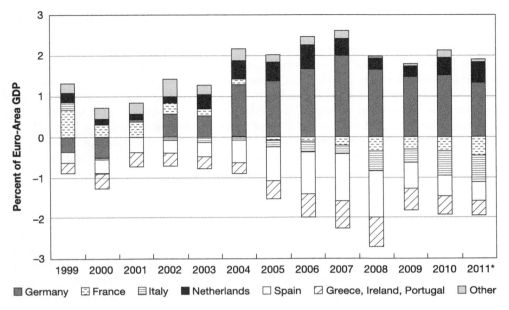

Figure 8.2 Euro area current accounts

Source: Citigroup, Empirical and Thematic Perspectives, 27 January 2012.

4.2 No stabilizers left in place

When the Eurozone was started a fundamental stabilizing force that existed at the level of the member-states was taken away from these countries. This is the lender of last resort function of the central bank. Suddenly, member countries of the monetary union had to issue debt in a currency they had no control over. As a result, the governments of these countries could no longer guarantee that the cash would always be available to roll over the government debt. Prior to entry in the monetary union, these countries could, like all stand-alone countries, issue debt in their own currencies thereby giving an implicit guarantee that the cash would always be there to pay out bondholders at maturity. The reason is that as stand-alone countries they had the power to force the central bank to provide liquidity in times of crisis.

What was not understood when the Eurozone was designed is that this lack of guarantee provided by Eurozone governments in turn could trigger self-fulfilling liquidity crises (a sudden stop) that would degenerate into solvency problems. This is exactly what happened in countries like Ireland, Spain and Portugal.[2] When investors lost confidence in these countries, they massively sold the government bonds of these countries, pushing interest rates to unsustainably high levels. In addition, the euros obtained from these sales were invested in "safe countries" like Germany. As a result, there was a massive outflow of liquidity from the problem countries, making it impossible for the governments of these countries to fund the rollover of their debt at a reasonable interest rate.

This liquidity crisis in turn triggered another important phenomenon. It forced countries to switch off the automatic stabilizers in the budget. The governments of the problem countries had to scramble for cash and were forced into quick austerity programs, by cutting spending and raising taxes. A deep recession was the result. The recession in turn reduced government revenues even further, forcing these countries to intensify the austerity programs.

Under pressure from the financial markets, fiscal policies became pro-cyclical pushing countries further into a deflationary cycle. As a result, what started as a liquidity crisis in a self-fulfilling way degenerated into a solvency crisis (De Grauwe and Ji, 2013).

The Eurozone crisis that we now witness is the result of a combination of the two design failures identified here. On the one hand, booms and busts continued to occur at the national level. In fact these were probably intensified by the very existence of a monetary union. On the other hand, the stripping away of the lender of last resort support of the member-state countries allowed liquidity crises to emerge when the booms turned into busts. These liquidity crises then forced countries to eliminate another stabilizing feature that had emerged after the Great Depression, i.e. the automatic stabilizers in the government budgets. As a result, some countries were forced into bad equilibria (De Grauwe, 2011 provides a theoretical model that generates multiple equilibria. See also Gros, 2011.).

The latter then exposed a third important design failure. Countries pushed into bad equilibria were immediately confronted with banking crises. This had to do with the "deadly embrace" between the sovereign and the banks that we identified earlier. The collapse of the government bond prices in the countries pushed into a bad equilibrium also deteriorated the balance sheets of many banks which were holding these bonds. They were threatened by insolvency. Remarkably, only when the banks were at risk (not when the sovereigns were) did the ECB start acting and provided massive liquidity support to the banking systems of the troubled countries.

What are the policy implications of these insights? We analyze three of them. The first one relates to the role of the ECB; the second one has to do with macroeconomic policies in the Eurozone; the third one relates to the long-run need to move into a fiscal union

5. The ECB as a lender of last resort in the government bond markets

The ECB is the only institution that can prevent market sentiments of fear and panic in the sovereign bond markets from pushing countries into a bad equilibrium. As a money creating institution it has an infinite capacity to buy government bonds. The European Stability Mechanism (ESM) that became operational in October 2012 has limited resources and cannot credibly commit to such an outcome. The fact that resources are infinite is key to be able to stabilize bond rates. It is the only way to gain credibility in the market.

On September 6, 2012 the ECB finally recognized this point and announced its "Outright Monetary Transactions" (OMT) program, which promises to buy unlimited amounts of sovereign bonds during crises. The ECB made the right decision to become a lender of last resort, not only for banks but also for sovereigns, thereby re-establishing a stabilizing force needed to protect the system from the booms and busts dynamics. In Figure 8.3 we show the evolution of the spreads before and after the OMT announcement of 2012. It can be seen that since that announcement the spreads declined dramatically. By taking away the intense existential fears that the collapse of the Eurozone was imminent the ECB's lender of last resort commitment pacified government bond markets and led to a strong decline in the spreads of the Eurozone countries.

However, the credibility of the program suffers because of continuing vehement criticism. This criticism reached its climax in early 2014 when the German Constitutional Court declared OMT illegal and referred the case to the European Court of Justice with the demand that conditions be imposed on the OMT program that would make it ineffective and useless. The main argument made by the German judges is that the spreads reflect underlying economic fundamentals. Attempts by the ECB to reduce these spreads are attempts to counter

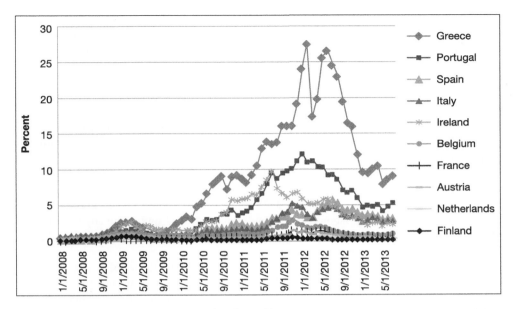

Figure 8.3 Spreads 10-year government bond rates Eurozone

Source: Datastream.

the view of market participants. In doing so, the ECB is in fact pursuing economic policy, which is outside its mandate.

Implicit in this argument is the view that markets are efficient (see De Grauwe, 2014, and Winkler, 2014). The surging spreads observed from 2010 to the middle of 2012 were the result of deteriorating fundamentals (e.g. domestic government debt, external debt, competitiveness, etc.). Thus, the market was just a messenger of bad news. Its judgment should then be respected, also by the ECB. The implication of the efficient market theory is that the only way these spreads can go down is by improving the fundamentals, mainly by austerity programs aimed at reducing government budget deficits and debts. With its OMT program the ECB is in fact reducing the need to improve these fundamentals.

Another theory, while accepting that fundamentals matter, recognizes that collective movements of fear and panic can have dramatic effects on spreads. These movements can drive the spreads away from underlying fundamentals, very much like how stock market prices can be gripped by a bubble pushing them far away from underlying fundamentals. The implication of that theory is that while fundamentals cannot be ignored, there is a special role for the central bank that has to provide liquidity in times of market panic. This is the view we have defended in the previous sections.

6. Towards symmetric macroeconomic policies in the Eurozone

Financial markets have split the Eurozone in two, forcing some (the Southern European countries, the "periphery") into bad equilibria and others (mainly Northern European countries, the "core") into good equilibria. The Southern European countries (including Ireland) are also the countries that have accumulated current account deficits, while the Northern European countries have built up current account surpluses.

The first best policy would have been for the debtor countries to reduce and for the creditor countries to increase spending. Thus, the necessary austerity imposed on the Southern European countries could have been offset by demand stimulus in the Northern European countries. Instead, under the leadership of the European Commission, tight austerity was imposed on the debtor countries while the creditor countries continued to follow policies aimed at balancing the budget. This has led to an asymmetric adjustment process where most of the adjustment has been done by the debtor nations. The latter countries have been forced to reduce wages and prices relative to the creditor countries (an "internal devaluation") without compensating wage and price increases in the creditor countries ("internal revaluations"). We show the evidence in Figures 8.4 and 8.5.

Figure 8.4 shows the evolution of the relative unit labor costs of the peripheral debtor countries (where we use the average over the 1970–2010 period as the base period). Two features stand out. First, from 1999 until 2008/09, one observes the strong deterioration of these countries' relative unit labor costs. Second, since 2008/09 quite dramatic turnarounds of the relative unit labor costs have occurred (internal devaluations) in Ireland, Spain and Greece, and to a lesser extent in Portugal.

These internal devaluations have come at a great cost in terms of lost output and employment in the debtor countries. As these internal devaluations are not yet completed (except possibly in Ireland), more losses in output and employment are to be expected.

Is there evidence that such a process of internal revaluations was going on in the surplus countries? The answer is given in Figure 8.5 which presents the evolution of the relative unit labor costs in the creditor countries. We observe that since 2008/09 there is very little movement in these relative unit labor costs in these countries. The position of Germany

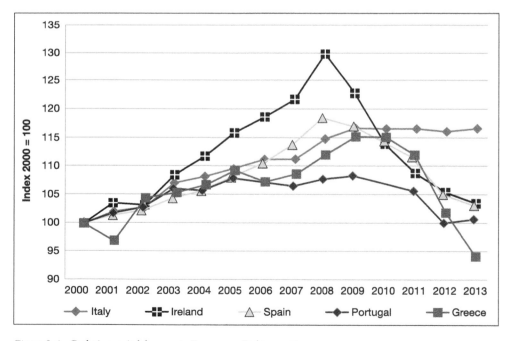

Figure 8.4 Relative unit labor costs Eurozone: Debtor nations

Source: European Commission, Ameco.

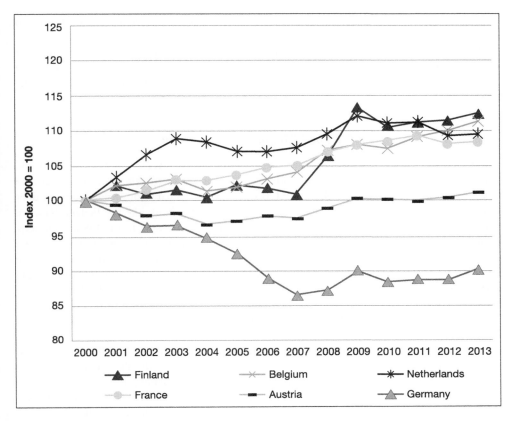

Figure 8.5 Relative unit labor costs Eurozone: Creditor nations

Source: European Commission, Ameco.

stands out. During 1999–2007 Germany engineered a significant internal devaluation that contributed to its economic recovery and the buildup of external surpluses. This internal devaluation stopped in 2007/08. Since then no significant internal revaluation has taken place in Germany. We also observe from Figure 8.5 that the other countries remain close to the long-run equilibrium (the average over 1970–2010) and that no significant changes have taken place since 2008/09.

Thus, one can conclude that at the insistence of the creditor nations, the burden of the adjustments to the imbalances in the Eurozone has been borne almost exclusively by the debtor countries in the periphery. This has created a deflationary bias that explains why the Eurozone has been pulled into a double-dip recession in 2011–12, and why it continues to be subject to deflationary forces as testified by the sharp decline in inflation, which at the end of 2014 became negative.

7. Completing the monetary union with political union

Even if the OMT program set up by the ECB can be salvaged from the onslaught of the German Constitutional Court, the institutional setup that has been created in the Eurozone is not sustainable and will have to be completed with steps towards a fiscal union. The latter implies a degree of political union that goes much farther than what has been achieved so far. Let us develop these points further.

The present institutional setup of the Eurozone is characterized by the fact that a number of bureaucratic institutions have acquired significant responsibilities without political accountability. Thus there has been a transfer of sovereignty without a concomitant democratic legitimacy.

7.1 The ECB and political union

The ECB's power has increased significantly as a result of the sovereign debt crisis. With the announcement of the OMT program and given the success of this program it has become clear (at least outside Germany) that the ECB is the ultimate guarantor of the sovereign debt in the Eurozone. In this sense the ECB has become a central bank like the Federal Reserve and the Bank of England. There is one important difference though. In the US and the UK there is a primacy of the government over the central bank, i.e. in times of crisis it is the government that will force the central bank to provide liquidity. When the sovereign in these countries is threatened it will prevail over the central bank. This is not the case in the Eurozone. In the latter, the governments depend on the goodwill of the ECB to provide liquidity. They have no power over the ECB and cannot force that institution, even in times of crisis, to provide liquidity. Thus, in the Eurozone today there is a primacy of the central bank over the sovereigns.

This is a model that cannot be sustained in democratic societies. The ECB consists of unelected officials, while governments are populated by elected officials. It is inconceivable that these governments (especially if they are large) will accept being pushed into insolvency while unelected officials in Frankfurt have the power to prevent this but refuse to use this power. When tested such a model of the governance of the Eurozone will collapse and rightly so.

Thus we arrive at the following conundrum. The role of the ECB as a lender of last resort is essential to keep the Eurozone afloat. Yet at the same time the present governance of this crucial lender of last resort function is unsustainable because its use depends on the goodwill of the ECB, thereby making democratically legitimate governments' fate depend on the judgment of unelected officials. In order to sustain this role of the central bank as a lender of last resort it has to be made subordinate to the political power of elected officials, as it is in modern democracies such as the US, Sweden, the UK, etc. This can only be achieved by creating a Eurozone government that is backed by a European Parliament and that has primacy over the central bank.

7.2 The European Commission and political union

We face a similar problem with the European Commission. The latter has seen its responsibilities increase. This has been motivated by the desire of the creditor nations to impose budgetary and macroeconomic discipline on the debtor nations. As a result, the Stability and Growth Pact has been strengthened, and the European Commission has been entrusted with the responsibility of monitoring macroeconomic imbalances and to force debtor nations to change their macroeconomic policies.[3]

The idea that macroeconomic imbalances should be monitored and controlled is a good one. As we have argued the emergence of such imbalances is at the heart of the emergence of the euro-crisis. Yet the way this idea has been implemented is unsustainable in the long run. The new responsibilities of the European Commission create a similar problem of democratic legitimacy as the one observed with the ECB. The European Commission can now force countries to raise taxes and reduce spending without, however, having to bear the political cost of these decisions. These costs are borne by national governments. This is a model that cannot work. Governments that face the political costs of spending and taxation will not continue to accept the decisions of unelected officials who do not face the cost of the decisions they try to impose on these governments. Sooner or later governments will go on strike, like the German and French governments did in 2003–4. Only the small countries (Portugal, Belgium, Ireland, etc.) will have to live with this governance. Larger countries will not.

7.3 Bureaucratic versus political integration

Increasingly, European integration has taken the form of bureaucratic integration as a substitute for political integration. This process started as soon as the European political elite became aware that further political integration would be very difficult. This process has become even stronger since the start of the sovereign debt crisis in the Eurozone. The outcome of this crisis has been that the European Commission and the ECB have seen their powers increase significantly, without any increase in their accountability. More and more these two institutions impose decisions that affect millions of people's welfare, but the people who are affected by these decisions do not have the democratic means to express their disagreements.

Political scientists make a distinction between output and input legitimacy. Output legitimacy means that a particular decision is seen to be legitimate if it leads to an increase in general welfare. In this view a government that is technocratic can still be legitimate if it is perceived to improve welfare. This view is very much influenced by the Platonic view of the perfect State. This is a State that is run by benevolent philosophers who know better than the population what is good for them and act to increase the country's welfare.

Input legitimacy means that political decisions, whatever their outcome, must be based on a process that involves the population, through elections that allow people to sack those who have made bad decisions.

Much of the integration process in Europe has been based on the idea of output legitimacy. The weak part of that kind of legitimacy becomes visible when the population is not convinced that what the philosophers at the top have decided, has improved welfare. That is the situation today in Europe. In many countries there is a perception that the decisions taken in Brussels and Frankfurt have harmed their welfare.

7.4 Towards a fiscal union?

The only governance that can be sustained in the Eurozone is one where a Eurozone government backed by a European parliament acquires the power to tax and to spend. This will then also be a government that will prevail over the central bank in times of crisis and not the other way around. This will also be a government that has the political legitimacy to impose macroeconomic and budgetary policies aimed at avoiding imbalances. Put differently, the Eurozone can only be sustained if it is embedded in a fiscal and political union.

A fiscal union involves two dimensions. First, it involves a (partial) consolidation of national government debts. Such a consolidation creates a common fiscal authority that can issue debt in a currency under the control of that authority. This protects the member-states from being forced into default by financial markets. It also protects the monetary union from the centrifugal forces that financial markets can exert on the union. Finally, by creating a common fiscal authority (a government) we can create a governance structure in which the (European) sovereign prevails over the central bank and European bureaucracies rather than the other way around.

Second, by (partially) centralizing national government budgets into one central budget a mechanism of automatic transfers can be organized. Such a mechanism works as an insurance transferring resources to the country hit by a negative economic shock. Although there are limits to such an insurance that arise from moral hazard risk, it remains true that such a mechanism is essential for the survival of a monetary union, like it is for the survival of a nation state. Without a minimum of solidarity (that's what insurance is) no union can survive.

8. Conclusion

While the need for a political union to sustain a monetary union is well known, it is equally clear that the willingness to move in the direction of a political union in Europe today is non-existent. This fact will continue to make the Eurozone a fragile institution, the future of which remains in doubt. The euro-crisis is not over.

The unwillingness to create a political union has also led to a continuing temptation to resort to technical solutions to the problem. Thus there has been a proliferation of technical schemes to introduce Eurobonds (see Delpla and von Weizsäcker, 2010; De Grauwe and Moesen, 2009 and insurance mechanisms against asymmetric shocks; Von Hagen and Diamond, 1998; Drèze, 2012; Enderlein et al., 2013). These are interesting intellectual exercises to which the present author has also contributed. They do not solve the essential problem, however, which is that there is no future for the euro except in a political union. In fact they generate a fiction that technical solutions (and therefore also bureaucratic integration) can be a substitute for political unification. As a result, they comfort policymakers in their decision to set aside all further attempts towards a political union.

Notes

1 The research reported in this chapter has been made possible by an ECFIN Fellowship grant of the European Commission. I am grateful for comments made by Marco Buti, Shanin Vallee, Frank Vandenbroucke and members of seminars given at the European Commission and the University of Leuven.

2 Elsewhere I have argued that Greece does not fit this diagnosis. Greece was clearly insolvent way before the crisis started, but this was hidden to the outside world by a fraudulent policy of the Greek government of hiding the true nature of the Greek economic situation (see De Grauwe, 2011).

3 In principle the macroeconomic imbalance procedure should work symmetrically. It is, however, very unlikely to work that way. In fact we see already today that the European Commission exerts more pressure on deficit countries than on surplus countries that are handled with a lot of care.

References

Aizenman, J. and Hutchison, M. (2012), What is the Risk of European Sovereign Debt Defaults? Fiscal Space, CDS Spreads and Market Pricing of Risk, presented at the Danmarks Nationalbank/JIMF Conference, 13–14 April 2012.

Akerlof, G. and Shiller, R. (2009), *Animal Spirits: How Human Psychology Drives the Economy and Why It Matters for Global Capitalism*, Princeton: Princeton University Press.

Arghyrou, M. and Kontonikas, A. (2010), The EMU Sovereign-Debt Crisis: Fundamentals, Expectations and Contagion, Cardiff Economics Working Papers E2010/9.

Attinasi, M., Checcherita, C. and Nickel, C. (2009), What Explains the Surge in Euro Area Sovereign Spreads During the Financial Crisis of 2007–09?, ECB Working Paper 1131.

Beirne, J. and Fratzscher, M. (2012), Pricing and Mispricing of Sovereign Debt in the Euro Area During the Crisis, presented at the Danmarks Nationalbank/JIMF Conference, 13–14 April 2012.

Caceres, C., Guzzo, V. and Segoviano, M. (2010), Sovereign Spreads: Global Risk Aversion, Contagion or Fundamentals?, IMF Working Paper 10/120.

Calvo, G. (1988), Servicing the Public Debt: The Role of Expectations, *American Economic Review*, 78(4), 647–61.

Corsetti, G.C. and Dedola, L. (2011), Fiscal Crises, Confidence and Default. A Bare-Bones Model with Lessons for the Euro Area, Cambridge University.

De Grauwe, P. (1999), Risks of a Roofless Euroland, *Time Magazine*, 11 January.

De Grauwe, P. and Moesen, W. (2009), Gains for All: A Proposal for a Common Eurobond, *Intereconomics*, 44(3), 132–35.

De Grauwe, P. (2011), The Governance of a Fragile Eurozone, CEPS Working Documents, available at www.ceps.eu/book/governance-fragile-eurozone.

De Grauwe, P. and Ji, Y. (2013), Panic-Driven Austerity and Its Implication for the Eurozone, www.voxeu.org, 21 February.

De Grauwe, P. (2014), Economic Theories That Influenced the Judges of Karlsruhe, www.voxeu.org, 13 March.

Delpla, J. and von Weizsäcker, J. (2010), The Blue Bond Proposal, *Bruegel Policy Brief* 2010/03.

Dreze, J.H. and Durre, A. (2013), Fiscal Integration and Growth Stimulation in Europe, *CORE Discussion Paper* 2013/13.

EC Commission (1977), Report of the Study Group on the Role of Public Finance in European Integration (MacDougall Report), Brussels: Commission of the European Communities.

Enderlein, H., Guttenberg, L. and Spiess, J. (2013), Making One Size Fit All: Designing a Cyclical Adjustment Insurance Fund for the Eurozone, *Notre Europe Policy Paper* 61.

Fisher, I. (1933), The Debt-Deflation Theory of Great Depressions, *Econometrica*, 1(4), 337–57.

Goodhart, C. and Illing, G. (eds) 2002 *Financial Crises, Contagion, and the Lender of Last Resort, a Reader,* Oxford: Oxford University Press.

Gros, D. (2011), *A Simple Model of Multiple Equilibria and Default*, Centre for European Policy Studies.

Gros, D. (2012), Banking Union: Ireland versus Nevada, www.voxeu.org, 27 November.

Keynes, J. (1936), *The General Theory of Employment, Interest and Money*, London: Macmillan.

Kindleberger, C.P. (2005), *Manias, Panics, and Crashes: A History of Financial Crises*, Houndmills, Basingstoke: Palgrave Macmillan, 5th edition.

Minsky, H. (1986), *Stabilizing an Unstable Economy*, New York: McGraw-Hill.

Reinhart, C. and Rogoff, K. (2009), *This Time is Different*, Princeton: Princeton University Press.

Tommaso Padoa-Schioppa Group, (2012), Completing the Euro: A Road Map towards Fiscal Union in Europe, Notre Europe.

Winkler, A. (2014), The Federal German Constitutional Court Decides Which Theory of Finance is Correct, Frankfurt School of Finance and Management.

9

THE CREDIT CHANNEL OF MONETARY POLICY IN THE EURO AREA

Angela Maddaloni and José-Luis Peydró[1]

1. Introduction

The credit provided by banks is key to fund investment and consumption. In the euro area this is particularly true since bank loans represent the large majority of the credit going to the non-financial sector (corporates and households).[2] How credit provision responds to monetary policy impulses is therefore a crucial question which policy makers are generally confronted with, in particular when a financial crisis strikes.

The theory of the credit channel of monetary policy, as defined by Bernanke and Gertler (1995), states that monetary policy (via monetary rates, reserve requirements but also quantitative easing) affects GDP and prices through credit. Both demand and supply of credit respond to monetary policy impulses, to different degrees, depending on the economic cycle (good or crisis times), on the type of loan and on the identity of the borrower (households, firms and banks).

Figure 9.1 reports a schematic representation of how monetary channels may affect the economy through credit (see ECB, 2011, p. 59, for all the transmission channels of monetary policy). The traditional "cost-of-capital" channel determines the demand for credit from firms and households, by determining the level of market interest rates and borrowing rates. The broad credit channel (as defined by Bernanke and Gertler, 1995) comprises several channels of transmission, through which changes in monetary policy affect the balance sheets of financial intermediaries (banks and other lenders) and of non-financial borrowers (households and firms).

In particular, in the traditional bank lending channel (see Bernanke, 2007; Kashyap and Stein, 2000; Bernanke and Blinder, 1992; Bernanke and Gertler, 1987), changes in policy interest rates affect the external finance premium of lenders, ultimately constraining their ability to extend credit. Therefore, in this case changes of monetary policy affect the supply of credit. Moreover, monetary policy may also affect the risk-taking of banks through the loans (Maddaloni and Peydró, 2011; and Jiménez, Ongena, Peydró and Saurina, 2014). At the same time, though, changes in monetary rates affect the value of the assets held by households and firms that can be posted as loan collateral (housing for mortgage loans and other assets for corporate loans) and, more broadly, the net worth of non-financial borrowers. Since lending conditions depend also on the risk and the net worth of the borrowers, thus monetary rates affect the ability of borrowers to get credit. This is the mechanism of the firm

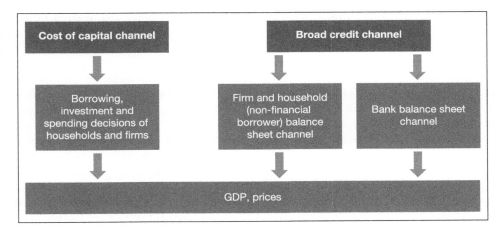

Figure 9.1 Monetary policy and the credit channel

Source: Reproduced from Ciccarelli, Maddaloni and Peydró (forthcoming)

and household (non-financial borrower) balance sheet channel (Bernanke and Gertler, 1989 and 1995).

There are important problems in the identification of the credit channel, as changes to the supply and demand of credit triggered by changes in monetary rates are generally unobserved. Therefore the complete identification of the credit channel and its sub-channels remains a challenging task. The academic literature using both macro and micro data has struggled to address this fundamental identification challenge in a satisfactory manner.

The information about the quantity of granted credit does not convey enough details to identify supply. In fact, credit quantities and prices would suffice to isolate demand and supply only if the quality of actual borrowers did not change. This is not generally the case: for example, it has been shown that after a monetary tightening, a flight to quality of banks to borrowers of better quality occurs (Bernanke, Gertler and Gilchrist, 1996).

Identification using micro data also faces important limitations. The micro identification cannot analyze the total effect of a monetary policy shock on real activity, but only a difference-in-difference effect by comparing banks (see e.g. Kashyap and Stein, 2000) or non-financial borrowers (see e.g. Gertler and Gilchrist, 1994) with different sensitivity to monetary policy. Moreover, financially constrained borrowers may obtain credit from constrained banks, thus it may be difficult to disentangle the firm balance sheet channel from the bank lending channel (Gertler and Gilchrist, 1994). The use of loan applications can partly overcome this problem (see Jiménez, Ongena, Peydró and Saurina, 2012 and 2014), but still only the bank lending (supply) channel can be identified. Furthermore, analyses based on micro data use actual credit granted and thus are forced to make restrictive assumptions on credit demand. Kashyap and Stein (2000), for instance, assume that banks with different liquidity levels face similar changes in loan demand as a response to a monetary policy shock.

A novel approach to tackle this issue is to use the information from the Bank Lending Survey (BLS) for the euro area. This chapter will describe how the responses can be used to analyze the impact of monetary policy on credit provision and to identify the credit channel.[3]

Section 2 describes in detail the questions of the survey. The survey is managed by the national central banks of the euro area. Commercial banks provide quarterly information on the lending standards that they apply to borrowers and on the loan demand that they receive from firms and households. A key feature of this information is that it refers to the actual lending standards that banks apply to the whole pool of borrowers (not only to accepted loans).

Section 3 outlines the results of the analysis for the identification of the credit channel using the survey responses. In the euro area, the credit channel is important for the transmission of monetary policy. In particular, for business loans, monetary policy shocks are amplified more via the bank lending and balance sheet channels than via the demand. The cost of capital (demand) is the most important channel for mortgage loans.

In section 4 the link between monetary policy and risk-taking is addressed. Much has been said about the factors that brought to the financial crisis initiated in 2008. In particular, the question of how monetary policy may have affected banking stability in the previous years has been at the center of an intense academic and policy debate. Nominal rates during the 2002–5 period were the lowest in the last decades, below Taylor-rule implied rates and even real rates were negative in several countries. Therefore, a key issue is whether low monetary policy rates prior to the crisis have spurred risk-taking by banks, and whether appropriate prudential policy, by limiting moral hazard frictions, may have reduced this impact.

Once the risk in the balance sheets of banks realizes and the crisis starts, the information from the BLS can also be used to assess the impact of central bank's actions, based on both standard and non-standards instruments, on the credit supply for firms and households. This is the topic of section 5, where this issue is analyzed also in interaction with banking stability measures and using dynamic models to evaluate the impact of monetary policy over time. Finally, in section 6 we analyze non-standard monetary policies.

2. The Bank Lending Survey for the euro area

The Bank Lending Survey for the euro area (BLS) allows investigating how credit provision in the euro area is related to monetary policy. The survey contains quarterly information on the lending conditions and terms that banks apply to (potential) borrowers and on the loan demand they receive, distinguishing between business, mortgage, and consumer loans. The survey is carried out by the national central banks of the euro area. Senior loan officers typically answer the questions and the response rate has been virtually 100 percent through time.

The survey contains detailed information about credit supply, since there are questions about changes in lending conditions, about the factors responsible for these changes, and about the specific terms applied to customers (i.e., whether, why, and how lending conditions are changed).[4]

The results reported in this chapter are obtained from analysis using a balanced panel of survey responses starting in 2002:Q4 and covering the set of countries comprising the euro area at that time (Austria, Belgium, France, Finland, Germany, Greece, Ireland, Italy, Luxembourg, the Netherlands, Portugal, and Spain). The sample of banks is representative of the banking sector in each country.[5] This implies that the sample generally includes banks of different size, although at the onset of the survey some preference was given to the inclusion of large banks.[6]

The questions imply only qualitative answers and no figures are required: banks indicate softening, tightening or no change of standards. The different answers on standards are quantified by using the net percentage of banks that have tightened their lending standards over the previous quarter: the difference between the percentage of banks reporting a tightening of lending standards and the percentage of banks reporting a softening of standards. Therefore, a positive figure indicates a *net tightening* of lending standards. In the dynamic analysis the net tightening of lending standards identifies the *broad credit channel variable*.

By combining some of the answers related to the bank balance sheet factors affecting the decision to change lending standards, a measure of *credit supply* can be constructed. In particular, the responses on capital and liquidity constraints and difficulty in accessing market funding can be used as a proxy for the *capacity* of banks to extend credit, since these factors are not related directly to borrower's risk. In the dynamic analysis the measure calculated from these responses identifies the *bank lending channel variable*. On the other hand, factors linked to firm (household) balance sheet strength defines borrower's quality and identify the *borrower's balance sheet channel variables*.

The answers related to the demand for loans are a proxy for credit demand. In this case the net percentage is the difference between the percentage of banks reporting an increase in the demand for loans and the percentage of banks reporting a decrease. Therefore, in this case, a positive figure indicates a net increase in the demand for loans.

To give some flavor of the cross-country dimension of the BLS data, Figure 9.2 shows how lending standards have changed over time in the euro area, in Germany and in Italy. The figure shows that there is heterogeneity across the euro area countries. This heterogeneity is present both for credit demand and loan conditions unrelated to borrowers' net worth and risk (for details see Maddaloni and Peydró, 2013). Although factors related to borrower risk (general economic outlook and borrowers specific risks) have played a major role in affecting lending conditions since the start of the crisis, factors related to bank balance sheet factors have been important as well and resurfaced in the last quarters of our sample due to the intensification of the sovereign crisis and the difficulties of banks to access funding. At the same time, during the boom years, lending conditions, especially due to bank balance-sheet factors and competition were softer. There were also notable cross-country differences in the demand for loans.

The use of survey data for economic analysis may spur some discussion about the reliability of the answers. The lack of incentive for respondents to reply truthfully indeed can undermine the reliability of the answers. However, lending surveys are carried out by the central banks which, very often, are also supervisory authorities that can cross-check the data with exhaustive hard bank information. This helps in ensuring the reliability of the information received and the overall credibility of the survey.[7]

3. The credit channel of monetary policy

To study the dynamics of the transmission through the credit channel a vector autoregressive (VAR) model can be used. The rich information from the lending surveys is embedded into an otherwise standard VAR to account for the linkages between the credit and the business cycle. This methodology accounts for the fact that lending standards and loan demand may react to – but also influence – business cycle fluctuations.

The VAR is estimated over the sample 2002:Q4–2013:Q1 for a balanced panel of 10 euro area countries and the euro area aggregate. The overnight rate is the monetary policy instrument and identifies monetary policy shocks, as done in Christiano, Eichenbaum and Evans (1999) and Angeloni, Kashyap and Mojon (2003). The overnight rate in the euro area is a sensible measure of monetary policy, also during the crisis period when credit enhancement actions were introduced (see ECB, 2009, and Lenza et al., 2010).

Policy makers observe current output, prices and the results of the bank lending surveys when deciding the policy rate. Therefore, all these variables do not change at time *t* in response to a time *t* policy shock, and the policy rate is ordered after the macro and the credit variables. This choice is motivated by the fact that policy makers make interest rate decisions

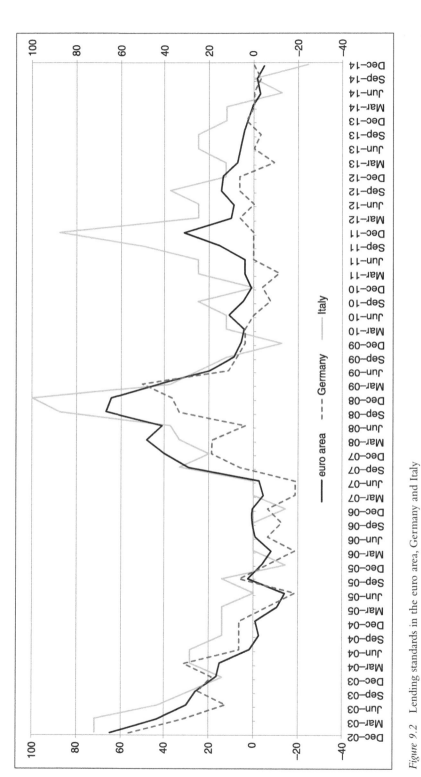

Figure 9.2 Lending standards in the euro area, Germany and Italy

Sources: European Central Bank, Deutsche Bundesbank, Banca d'Italia.

Notes: This figure plots the lending standards in the euro area, Germany and Italy as reported in the Bank Lending Survey. The responses refer to business (non-financial corporations) loans.

based on a strategy that explicitly takes into account developments in credit markets. For instance, as part of the monetary analysis assessment (the so-called second pillar of the monetary policy strategy), the Governing Council of the European Central Bank (ECB) monitor closely the developments of the BLS.

Loan demand and lending standards referring to different borrowers are included in the VAR following an order that broadly reflects the importance of the different loan markets in the euro area, i.e. business loans come first, then mortgage loans and finally consumer loans.[8]

The analysis is run in two steps. First, the effect of a monetary policy shock on macro and credit variables is analyzed. Second, by means of appropriately designed experiments the full dynamics of the credit channel and of its sub-channels is tested, which allows us to quantify how much of the monetary policy innovation is transmitted to output and prices through the credit variables. The impact of heterogeneity of borrowers and lenders on the credit channel of monetary policy is also examined. For details about the analysis, see Ciccarelli et al. (forthcoming), where a similar methodology is also applied to study the credit channel in the US.

Table 9.1 summarizes the results of the analysis, by showing the impact at the peak of a monetary policy shock transmitted through the credit channels.[9] Monetary policy shocks are transmitted to the economy through all credit channels. The results show that the credit channel is operational and amplifies the impact of a monetary policy shock on GDP and price levels through the impact on the balance sheets of households, firms and banks. In the euro area and for business loans, the amplification of monetary policy shocks is higher via the bank lending and the balance sheet channel than via the cost of capital (demand) channel, which is the most important channel for household loans, mortgages in particular. By comparison, in the US the bank lending channel of monetary policy is irrelevant and a monetary policy shock is transmitted to real activity mainly through the firm balance sheet channel. These differences can be explained by relating to the composition of the financial sector in the euro area vis-à-vis the US and on the mechanisms of credit provisions in the two areas. A monetary policy shock transmitted through the bank lending channel may have a higher impact on real activity in the euro area than in the US where firms can, at least partly, diversify their financing needs between banks, other financial intermediaries (not included in the sample of the bank lending surveys) and markets.

Transmission through the bank lending channel may be less important for household loans, especially in the euro area. The bulk of household loan is represented by mortgages. Differently from the US, in most euro area countries mortgage loans are with recourse – the borrower

Table 9.1 The impact of a monetary policy shock through the demand, bank lending and borrower's balance sheet channels

	Impact in the full model	Business loans	Mortgage loans	Consumer loans
		w/out the channel	w/out the channel	w/out the channel
Demand for loans	−0.36	−0.29	−0.24	−0.36
Bank lending channel variable	−0.36	−0.27	−0.32	−0.35
Borrower's balance sheet variable	−0.36	−0.24	−0.25	−0.32

Notes: The table shows the median impact at the peak of the responses of GDP to a 25 basis points monetary policy shock, when the credit channel (bank lending or borrower's balance sheet) and the demand channel are not included in the system. For the full dynamics of impulse responses see Figure 9 of Ciccarelli, Maddaloni and Peydró (forthcoming).

is responsible for any remaining debt after foreclosure (Campbell, 2013) and bankruptcy law does not generally entail protection from creditors. This implies that mortgage loans are highly collateralized (not only with the value of the house but also other assets of the borrower) and agency problems may be less severe. In this case, bank financial constraints are less binding and monetary policy affects the economy significantly more through the demand and the (collateral) household balance sheet channel than through the bank lending channel.

The impact of the credit channel of monetary policy also differs according to the heterogeneity of borrowers and lenders, in particular in firm size and in bank size. The analysis shows that, at least in the euro area, the impact of monetary policy on GDP through the broad credit channel is significant for all firms. While changes in monetary policy affect more significantly credit to small firms, the effect on GDP through large firms is higher, because these firms borrow mainly from banks (Trichet, 2009) and their overall impact on the economy is larger.

Regarding heterogeneity of lenders, small and large banks are also equally important in transmitting a monetary policy shock to the real economy via the bank lending channel. However, in countries that are more financially distressed, the amplification of a monetary policy shock through the non-financial borrower balance sheet channel has operated mainly through small banks (see also Ciccarelli et al., 2013). These results somewhat qualify the findings of Kashyap and Stein (2000) who, over a different sample period (1976–93) and a different country (US), find that the bank lending channel is stronger mainly through small banks.

4. Monetary policy and risk-taking

The analysis in the previous section shows that monetary policy impulses are transmitted through the economy by affecting credit provision. An interesting and related issue is if these effects induce to an accumulation of risk in the financial system which may lead to dramatic consequences, and in particular to financial crises. This issue has been debated especially in the context of the latest financial crisis. Several commentators have argued that key contributing factors to the crisis that started in 2008 were an excessive softening of lending standards due to too low levels of monetary policy interest rates, coupled with very low levels of long-term interest rates, high securitization activity and weak supervision standards.[10]

By linking monetary rates with lending standards, it can be seen that lending conditions are generally relaxed in an environment of low (monetary policy) short-term interest rates, for all (potential) borrowers. Lending conditions are softened relatively more when banks can securitize loans (possibly transferring the risk outside of their balance sheet); when the regulation and supervision concerning bank capital is relatively weak (considering national options and discretions); and when interest rates have been low for a long time, spurring a sort of cumulative effect. Low long-term interest rates do not seem to have the same effect on lending conditions, except for mortgage loans. Lending standards are also pro-cyclical, since higher GDP growth induces softer lending standards.

The analysis can also provide some suggestive evidence on the costs of the softening of lending standards. Countries with softer lending standards related to negative Taylor-rule residuals (low monetary policy rates) prior to the financial crisis had a worse economic performance afterwards, measured by real, fiscal and banking variables.

All in all, according to the findings, low short-term rates – in particular low monetary policy rates for an extended period of time – were a key determinant of the last financial and economic crisis. They led to a softening of lending standards and the consequent accumulation of risk on banks' assets prior to the crisis. High securitization activity and weak supervision for bank capital, moreover, amplified the impact of low monetary policy rates. When the risk materialized and the capacity of bank balance-sheets was impaired, the banks started to reduce lending, thereby inducing a real and fiscal crisis. It is interesting to note that these effects are higher for mortgage loans both before and after the crisis.

These results give some support to policy actions aimed at preventing excessive risk-taking in an environment of very low monetary rates, for example by implementing appropriate macroprudential policies.

5. The credit channel in times of crisis

The occurrence of the financial crisis of course induced some questions on how the transmission through the credit channel could have changed because of impairment arising from the stress in financial markets. A first observation is that the data on credit provision in the euro area clearly showed a decoupling of credit conditions to borrowers residing in countries with a different sovereign risk profile. Using the credit default swap (CDS) spreads as a measure of this risk, the sample of euro area countries can be divided in two groups: the countries under sovereign stress (Greece, Ireland, Italy, Portugal, and Spain) and the other countries (Austria, Belgium, Finland, France, Germany, Luxembourg, and the Netherlands). Starting in 2010 credit conditions in these two groups of countries started to diverge significantly. In particular, changes in lending conditions and standard measured by the BLS diverged significantly, with more tightening in the countries under stress. The tighter lending conditions implied higher loan rates for firms in the distressed countries. At the same time, demand for business loans declined in all countries already at the beginning of the crisis, but only in the very last period the two groups of countries significantly departed from each other.

The standard VAR analysis that was used in the previous section provides a flexible means to analyze the changes that have occurred in the transmission through the credit channel during the crisis years.[11] Estimation of impulse responses suggest that on average the effect of a (single) monetary policy shock on GDP growth has been time-varying during the years of the crisis. In 2008 and 2009 a monetary policy shock had more impact on output and the impulse was transmitted faster. After May 2010 and when looking at the differential impact across groups of countries affected by the sovereign crisis, it can be seen that the impact has been substantially stronger for the sovereign stressed countries.

This suggests that a decrease in the monetary policy interest rate has induced an heterogeneous reaction across countries, with a stronger impact on GDP in countries that have been more in need of stimulus than others. In countries under sovereign distress, financial frictions in the credit markets have increased substantially, implying that higher external finance premia had to be paid by borrowers. In this context, the effect of a standard shock to the overnight interest rate transmitted through the credit channel of monetary transmission should be higher (see Bernanke and Gertler, 1995; Kashyap and Stein, 2000; Bernanke, 2007).

Appropriately designed counterfactual experiments can be used to quantify the amplification effect of a monetary policy (interest rate) shock due to changes in credit conditions and terms, both through the bank and non-financial borrower balance sheet channels. In this way, the effects of monetary policy are linked to the financial fragility of borrowers and lenders via the credit channel of monetary transmission.

The impact of a monetary policy shock on GDP depends significantly on changes in the transmission of the shock through both the broad credit channel and the credit demand channel. This is evident in particular for countries under sovereign stress, where the effects of these channels on GDP growth are economically and statistically significant as of 2008 and for the entire period. Conversely, for the set of other countries results are marginally significant in 2008 and clearly not significant in 2011. Results suggest that the impact of a monetary policy shock on GDP growth is amplified by changes in the credit conditions and standards. In other words, the amplification reflects the underlying problems in credit markets as implied by the credit channel theory. The amplification is stronger in countries under stress and it is significant throughout the crisis period.

To gain further insights on the mechanisms at work, the transmission of a monetary policy shock through the bank lending channel and through the non-financial borrower balance sheet channel is also analyzed. Results show that the bank lending channel of monetary policy has been important only in 2008 and 2009 for stressed countries, but not statistically significant in 2010 and 2011. However, the non-financial borrower (firm and household) channel of monetary policy has been economically and statistically significant throughout the whole period after the Lehman bankruptcy. Instead, for other countries the non-financial borrower channel is not significant and the bank lending channel of monetary policy is only significant in 2008:Q4 but not thereafter.

Overall, it can be concluded that the impact of a monetary policy shock has changed during the crisis in a heterogeneous way across countries and across the different credit channels.

6. Non-standard monetary policy

The malfunctioning of the financial markets and fragmented financial conditions due to the financial crisis had an impact on the transmission of monetary policy. The transmission of the stance of monetary policy to interest rates was particularly impaired in countries with a more constrained fiscal position which translated in a more difficult environment for financial intermediaries of these countries to access funding in the wholesale market (see Praet, 2012). To address these issues and restore the transmission of monetary policy in the euro area, the ECB implemented a series of actions. In particular, in the fall of 2008 it started a policy of full allotment liquidity provision, also stepping up the opportunities to get liquidity at longer maturity (up to 1 year until 2011 and then up to 3 years with a repayment option). Moreover, the central bank enlarged the set of eligible collateral.

The information arising from the BLS and the analysis framework used to study the credit channel of monetary policy can also be directed in investigating the impact of these non-standard measures. As reported in Maddaloni and Peydró (2013), banks that made use of the liquidity provision of the ECB tended to relax credit conditions relatively more as a result of low monetary policy rates. In other words, lower monetary policy rates, in combination with the long-term liquidity provided by the ECB, helped to reduce the liquidity constraints faced by the banks, which in turn tended to soften lending standards. Therefore, the non-standard measures implemented by the ECB have contributed to increasing credit availability to firms and households and helped to restore the transmission of monetary policy.

However, the dynamic analysis also shows that the policies had a heterogeneous impact across countries. In particular, they have been insufficient in increasing credit availability to smaller firms in countries under sovereign financial stress. In these countries, financial frictions for small banks have been significantly reduced, thanks to the actions of the central bank. At the same time, though, the credit frictions faced by their borrowers (mainly small firms) were still present, which increased their riskiness and made lending to these firms relatively unattractive for banks. Therefore, the policies implemented until the autumn of 2011 may not have been comprehensive enough and the analysis would have supported the implementation of more far-reaching policies aimed at increasing credit availability for small firms – especially in countries under stress. The successive decisions of the ECB to buy covered bonds and asset-backed securities indeed seem to follow this path.

7. Conclusions

Transmission of monetary policy through the credit channel is typically unobserved, therefore the identification of this channel and the evaluation of its impact have proven to be particularly challenging for researchers and policy makers. Bank lending surveys provide information that can be used to fill this gap and investigate these issues. A dynamic analysis that makes use of these data shows that the credit channel is operational and amplifies a monetary policy shock on GDP and inflation, by affecting the balance sheets of lenders and borrowers in the credit market. The strength of the amplification depends on the heterogeneity of firms, households and banks, on the differences related to the financial structure of the country and on whether the economy is in a boom or bust. Furthermore, monetary policy affects the risk-taking of financial institutions. Finally, non-standard monetary policies are more powerful in crisis times for weaker countries, as these countries and their economic agents are more financially constrained.

The credit channel of monetary policy and all its sub-channels therefore should be included explicitly when modeling the linkages between monetary policy, credit provision and the real economy, likely amplifying the mechanisms of the financial accelerator. In addition, models should be accurately calibrated to control for heterogeneity of borrowers and lenders and for the different financial structures across countries. Finally, all the results explained in this chapter also have important policy implications for central banks.

Notes

1 The views presented in this chapter are those of the authors and should not be attributed to the European Central Bank or the Eurosystem.
2 See for example Allen et al. (2004).
3 These issues have been analyzed in a set of different papers, some co-authored with Matteo Ciccarelli.
4 The euro area results of the survey – a weighted average of the answers received by commercial banks in each euro area country – are published every quarter on the website of the European Central Bank. In most euro area countries the aggregate answers of the domestic samples are published by the respective national central banks. However, the overall sample including all the answers at the country and bank level is confidential.
5 When foreign banks are part of the sample, the lending standards refer to the credit policy applied in the domestic market.
6 See Berg et al. (2005).
7 Several recent papers support the reliability of the bank lending survey data and their consistency. Del Giovane, Eramo, and Nobili (2011), for instance, cross-check the BLS data using detailed supervisory data on bank lending from Italy and find that the answers from the survey are reliable indicators of actual developments in bank loans. Moreover, lending standards from the surveys are correlated with actual credit spreads and volume (Maddaloni and Peydró, 2011) and are also good predictors of credit and output growth (Lown and Morgan, 2006, and Bassett et al., 2013, for the US, and De Bondt, Maddaloni, Peydró and Scopel, 2010, for the euro area).
8 The results obtained are generally robust to different specifications and ordering of variables (see also Ciccarelli et al., forthcoming).
9 To see the full dynamics of the impulse responses please refer to the paper Ciccarelli et al. (forthcoming).
10 For a detailed analysis of this issues, please refer to Maddaloni and Pedyró (2011).
11 See Ciccarelli et al. (2013) for details of the analysis.

References

Allen, F., Chui, M. and Maddaloni, A. (2004), Financial Systems in Europe, the USA and Asia, *Oxford Review of Economic Policy*, 20(4), 490–508.

Angeloni, I., Kashyap, A. and Mojon, B. (2003), *Monetary Policy Transmission in the Euro Area*, Cambridge University Press.

Bassett, W. F., Chosak, M. B., Driscoll, J. C. and Zakrajsek, E. (2013), Changes in Bank Lending Standards and the Macroeconomy, *Journal of Monetary Economics*, 62, 23–40.

Berg, J., van Rixtel, A., Ferrando, A., de Bondt, G. and Scopel, S. (2005), The Bank Lending Survey for the Euro Area, *ECB Occasional Paper* No. 23, 2005.

Bernanke, B. S. and Blinder, A.S. (1992), The Federal Funds Rate and the Channels of Monetary Transmission, *American Economic Review*, 82(4), 901–21.

Bernanke, B. S. and Gertler, M. (1995), Inside the Black Box: The Credit Channel of Monetary Policy Transmission, *Journal of Economic Perspectives*, 9(4), 27–48.

Bernanke, B. S. and Gertler, M. (1987), Banking in general equilibrium, in: Barnett, W., Singleton, K. (eds), *New Approaches to Monetary Economics*, Cambridge University Press, Cambridge.

Bernanke, B. S. and Gertler, M. (1989), Agency Costs, Net Worth and Business Fluctuations, *American Economic Review*, 79(1), 14–31.

Bernanke, B. S., Gertler, M. and Gilchrist, S. (1996), The Financial Accelerator and the Flight to Quality, *Review of Economics and Statistics*, 78(1), 1–15.

Bernanke, B. S. (2007), *The Financial Accelerator and the Credit Channel, Remarks – Credit Channel of Monetary Policy in the Twenty-first Century*, Board of Governors of the U.S. Federal Reserve System.

Campbell, J. Y. (2013), Mortgage Market Design, *Review of Finance*, European Finance Association 17, 1–33.

Christiano, L. J., Eichenbaum, M. and Evans, C. L. (1999), Monetary policy shocks: What have we learned and to what end? in: J. B. Taylor and M. Woodford (eds), *Handbook of Macroeconomics*, pp. 65–148, Elsevier.

Ciccarelli, M., Maddaloni, A. and Peydró, J.-L. (2013), Heterogeneous Transmission Mechanism: Monetary Policy and Financial Fragility in the Eurozone, *Economic Policy*, July, 459–512.

Ciccarelli, M., Maddaloni, A. and Peydró, J.-L. (forthcoming), Trusting the Bankers: A New Look at the Credit Channel of Monetary Policy, *Review of Economic Dynamics*.

De Bondt, G., Maddaloni, A., Peydró, J.-L. and Scopel, S. (2010), The Euro Area Bank Lending Survey Matters: Empirical Evidence for Credit and Output Growth, *ECB Working Paper* 1160.

Del Giovane, P., Eramo, G. and Nobili, A. (2011), Disentangling Demand and Supply in Credit Developments: A Survey-based Analysis for Italy, *Journal of Banking & Finance*, 35(10), 2719–32.

European Central Bank (2009), Recent Developments in the Balance Sheets of the Eurosystem, the Federal Reserve System and the Bank of Japan, *ECB Monthly Bulletin*, 81–94.

European Central Bank, (2011), *The monetary policy of the ECB*, third edition, May.

Gertler, M. and Gilchrist, S. (1994), Monetary Policy, Business Cycles, and the Behaviour of Small Manufacturing Firms, *Quarterly Journal of Economics*, 109, 309–40.

Jiménez, G., Ongena, S., Peydró, J.-L. and Saurina, J. (2012), Credit Supply and Monetary Policy: Identifying the Bank Balance-Sheet Channel with Loan Applications, *American Economic Review*, 102(5), 2301–26.

Jiménez, G., Ongena, S., Peydró, J.-L. and Saurina, J. (2014), Hazardous Times for Monetary Policy: What do 23 Million Loans Say about the Impact of Monetary Policy on Credit Risk-Taking?, *Econometrica*, 82(2), 463–505.

Kashyap, A. K. and Stein, J. C. (2000), What Do a Million Observations on Banks Say About the Transmission of Monetary Policy? *American Economic Review*, 90(3), 407–28.

Lenza, M., Pill, H. and Reichlin, L. (2010), Monetary Policy in Exceptional Times, *Economic Policy*, 62, 295–339.

Lown, C. and Morgan, D. P. (2006), The Credit Cycle and the Business Cycle: New Findings Using the Loan Officer Opinion Survey, *Journal of Money, Credit and Banking*, 38(6), 1575–97.

Maddaloni, A. and Peydró, J.-L. (2011), Bank Risk-taking, Securitization, Supervision and Low Interest Rates: Evidence from US and Euro Area Lending Standards, *Review of Financial Studies*, 24, 2121–65.

Maddaloni, A. and Peydró, J.-L. (2013), Monetary Policy, Macroprudential Policy and Banking Stability: Evidence from the Euro Area, *International Journal of Cenntral Banking*, 121–69.

Praet, P. (2012), Heterogeneity in a Monetary Union: What Have we Learned? Speech given at the conference 'The ECB and its watchers' in Frankfurt on 15 June.

Trichet, J. C. (2009), The ECB's Enhanced Credit Support, keynote address at the University of Munich, 13 July, ECB speech.

10

FISCAL POLICY IN THE EU

An overview of recent and potential future developments

Roel Beetsma

1. Introduction

The sovereign debt crisis that started with the Greek admission of a substantially-higher-than-expected 2009 budget deficit has shown how important well-designed fiscal institutions are for a proper functioning of the Economic and Monetary Union (EMU) in Europe. The crisis has put a number of EMU Member States under severe budgetary pressure, forcing them to adopt rescue packages, while it brought the Eurozone itself to the brink of collapse. As a result a substantial number of measures have been taken to fortify the fiscal policy framework in the EU. This chapter provides an overview of the main arrangements before the outbreak of the crisis, the changes to the fiscal framework that were adopted in response to the crisis, and the potential paths to further fiscal integration, while embedding this overview within the relevant academic literature. Further fiscal integration will be hard to sell to the general public in the current climate. However, the events in recent years have shown that tighter fiscal integration may be unavoidable to avert future threats to the existence of the euro as a result of new financial crises.

The remainder of this chapter is as follows. In Section 2 we discuss the design of the EU fiscal framework, starting with the original design elements and then moving on to the Stability and Growth Pact's (SGP's) first revision in 2005 and the changes to the fiscal framework in response to the crisis. These changes comprise both emergency measures and measures to guarantee the long-term sustainability of the public finances. Section 3 discusses possible routes for further fiscal integration in the future. Finally, Section 4 concludes this chapter.

2. The design of the EU fiscal framework

2.1 The original elements of the EU fiscal framework

The EU Treaty sets the institutional framework for the operation of the EMU. It requires countries to follow disciplined budgetary policies and, specifically, it forbids other countries or the European Central Bank (ECB) to take over a country's public debt (the so-called "no bail-out clause"). However, in the run-up to the euro some countries were insufficiently convinced that this would provide enough guarantee against profligate fiscal policies. As a result, the so-called Stability and Growth Pact (SGP) was adopted and signed in 1997. The original proposal by the German Finance Minister, Waigel, was to have a pact that would impose automatic sanctions on countries violating its budgetary limits. However, this proposal failed to get accepted. Instead, a long and complicated procedure of semi-automatic sanctions, the so-called Excessive Deficit Procedure (EDP), was adopted to deal with violations of the deficit limit of 3 percent of GDP and the public debt limit of 60 percent of GDP.[1]

What explains the existence of SGP? It is well-known that political distortions, resulting, for example, from government myopia or pressures of powerful interest groups, produce high public deficits and public debt. The SGP can act as an external disciplining device and help to offset this distortion. An alternative explanation for the SGP is that it acts as an alternative to fiscal coordination and helps to offset the potential negative externalities of fiscal expansions. However, these roles of the GDP do not explain why the SGP *only* came into existence together with the EMU. A third explanation is that the SGP helps the ECB in attaining low and stable inflation (Beetsma and Uhlig, 1999). While the ECB enjoys legal independence and an explicit statutory commitment to price stability, a credible monetary policy also needs the support from appropriate fiscal policies. In particular, there is a need to avoid a bad policy mix consisting of a tight monetary policy and a lax fiscal policy, resulting in a game of chicken between the ECB and the fiscal authorities. By constraining fiscal policy, monetary policy is put in a leadership position, so that it can follow a tight policy, with fiscal policy being forced into a follower role.

The SGP consists of two arms. The first arm, based on Regulation 1466/97 "on the Strengthening of Surveillance of Budgetary positions and the Surveillance and Coordination of Economic Policies", aims at the prevention of excessive deficits. To this end, it requires countries to aim at budgetary balance or a surplus in this medium run. Such a situation allows for sufficient leeway to withstand a normal recession without violating the 3 percent deficit limit, while allowing the automatic stabilizers to operate without interruption. The idea is that during a recession public revenues automatically fall, while expenditures on benefits rise, thereby causing a deterioration of the public deficit. If in a cyclically-neutral situation the public budget is sufficiently healthy, then there is enough room for this deterioration not to cause a violation of the deficit constraint. Hence, the government does not need to undertake any discretionary policy measures to raise revenues or reduce spending, while the deterioration of the actual deficit helps to dampen the effect of the recession on the demand side of the economy. The amount of leeway a government needs determines the so-called "minimal balance", i.e. cyclically-adjusted balance that provides sufficient safety margin for the 3 percent actual deficit norm not to be breached in normal circumstances. As part of the preventive arm of the SGP Eurozone governments have to submit so-called Stability Programs in which they set their medium-term budgetary objective and the path towards this objective. Similarly, governments of countries that have not yet entered the Eurozone have to submit Convergence Programs.

Obviously, by letting the automatic stabilizers operate, an economic boom would cause a budget surplus, thereby dampening the rise in the demand for goods and services and thereby also avoiding an upward trend in the debt/GDP-ratio over the course of the business cycle. Unfortunately, however, governments have generally made little use of the opportunities offered by a favorable business cycle situation to bring down public debt ratios, forcing them to resort discretionary interventions to avoid breaching the deficit limit during recessions. Nevertheless, Gali and Perotti (2003) suggest that fiscal policy in the Eurozone had become more countercyclical since the EU Treaty was signed in Maastricht in 1992.

The second arm of the SGP, based on Regulation 1467/97 "on Speeding up and Clarifying the Implementation of the Excessive Deficit Procedure", aims at the correction of a situation in which fiscal limits are violated. This takes place through the EDP, which eventually could lead to sanctions that start with the country in question having to submit a non-interest rate bearing deposit and that end with the imposition heavy financial penalties. Until now, however, no such sanctions have been imposed.

2.2 The first revision of the SGP in 2005

The SGP was revised in March 2005 following the failure to adhere to the formal procedure following the excessive deficits of Germany and France at the end of 2003 (see Beetsma and Oksanen, 2008). The main adjustments to the SGP were intended to discourage pro-cyclical fiscal behavior. In particular, more emphasis was put on public debt and sustainability, while budgetary adjustment would now be judged in terms of the cyclically-adjusted balance, net of one-off items and temporary measures. Also, other adjustments were made. Deadlines for the correction of excessive deficits would be allowed to be revised and extended in the case of unexpected adverse events. Further, more emphasis was put on structural reforms with upfront costs (e.g., pension reforms) and, finally, the medium-term budget objective was made country-specific. Some experts argued that these changes introduced more economic rationale in the operation of the SGP, while others believed that the SGP was relaxed as soon as it was put to its first serious test. In their view, the additional flexibility that was now introduced would further strengthen the incentive of governments to follow profligate policies.

2.3 The crisis and resulting changes to the EU fiscal framework

The crisis made it clear that the existing fiscal architecture in the Eurozone was inadequate on at least three major accounts. First, the SGP had been ineffective in preventing some countries from running high deficits and building up high and even unsustainable debts. Second, monitoring of budgetary behavior was insufficiently tight and critical. After all, how was it possible that Greece could announce in the Fall of 2009 that its deficit for that year would be roughly double the deficit originally announced? Third, even countries that initially had only moderate public debt levels could be cut off or almost cut off from the capital markets. This happened to Spain and Ireland. These countries were forced to inject large amounts of public money into rescuing commercial banks, thereby undermining the financial sustainability of the public sector.

The crisis prompted policymakers to adopt four broad sets of measures. The first set was intended to calm down financial markets, while the second set sought to prevent future budgetary crises, hence to ensure long-run budgetary discipline in the EU. The third set was aimed at addressing the financial inter-linkages between the banking sector and the public budget. The final set of measures aimed at enhancing Europe's growth potential through structural economic reforms. These latter measures will not be discussed here, because they are beyond the scope of a chapter focusing on fiscal policy in a monetary union.

The first set of institutional changes concerned the creation of emergency funds. The first Greek rescue package agreed upon in April 2010 failed to calm down financial markets. Rather, the public debt of other countries threatened to become unsustainable as well. Hence, over the weekend of May 8 and 9, 2010, the European Financial Stability Facility (EFSF) and the European Financial Stabilisation Mechanism (EFSM) were set up. In 2012 these mechanisms were replaced by the permanent European Stability Mechanism (ESM). The basis of the latter is an addition to Article 136 of the Treaty:

> The Member States whose currency is the euro may establish a stability mechanism to be activated if indispensable to safeguard the stability of the euro area as a whole. The granting of any required financial assistance under the mechanism will be made subject to strict conditionality.

The ESM allows for multiple lending instruments. First, it may provide loans in the framework of a macroeconomic adjustment program. Second, it may purchase debt in the primary and secondary debt markets. Third, it can provide precautionary financial assistance through credit lines. Fourth, it may finance recapitalizations of financial institutions through loans to the governments of ESM Member States and, finally, it may provide direct recapitalisation of euro area banks once the single supervisory mechanism has been established. One of the major objectives of the ESM is to break the link between the financial health of banks and that of sovereigns. As argued above this link has proved to be detrimental during the crisis for countries like Spain and Ireland where the financial problems of their weak banking sectors spilled over to the public sector. Hence, this last provision in the ESM will help to break this link.

Financial assistance through the ESM will be provided only under a macroeconomic adjustment program, after a thorough analysis of the sustainability of the public debt. If the adjustment program is expected to be unable to lead the country to a sustainable debt path, then the country needs to negotiate a contribution from its creditors before any financial assistance can be granted. Further, direct recapitalisation of its banks will only take place when banks have a common equity tier-1 ratio of at least 4.5 percent. Otherwise, the government should first inject the necessary resources. In addition, the requesting ESM Member State has to make a capital contribution alongside the ESM (20 percent in the first two years and 10 percent thereafter).

The important question is whether the criterion of "strict conditionality" will be credible. In the end, as was the case with the SGP, it is the Ministers of Finance of the Eurozone who make decisions about financial assistance and the relevant conditions for such assistance. They may find it difficult to deny help to each other. Anticipating this, countries with a culture of weak discipline will not feel sufficiently pressed to fulfil the conditions. This is a standard moral hazard problem on the side of borrowing countries. Similarly, moral hazard may arise on the side of the lenders to these countries, who know that in the end they may get bailed out. This potential for moral hazard is not without precedent, as has been demonstrated in the run-up to the Eurozone crisis. In fact, moral hazard problems may have become even more severe due to fact that a rescue mechanism has now been institutionalised, meaning that any potential uncertainty about a bailout has been reduced.

Besides setting up the emergency institutions, a number of changes have been made to the EU fiscal architecture with the aim of ensuring long-run fiscal sustainability in the EU. The SGP was reformed further in 2011 with the so-called "six pack". The six pack strengthens both the preventive and the corrective arms of the Pact in three major ways (see European Commission, 2014a). First, it defines quantitatively what is a major deviation from the medium-term objective or the adjustment path towards it, thereby allowing for a stricter application of the Pact. Second, it operationalizes the debt criterion allowing the EDP to be launched also on the basis of a violation of the debt criterion. Third, it introduces gradually-increasing financial sanctions going from the preventive arm to the final stages of the corrective arm. In addition, it introduces reverse qualified majority voting, which means that a Commission recommendation or proposal is considered adopted unless a qualified majority of the Members States rejects it. Such a procedure makes it harder to reject a proposal or recommendation in the context of the EDP.

Parallel to the SGP all EU countries, except for the UK, Croatia, and the Czech Republic, have signed the Treaty on Stability, Coordination and Governance (TSCG). The TSCG is an intergovernmental agreement, hence it is not part of the EU law. The so-called Fiscal Compact refers to the fiscal part of the TSCG. The TSCG is binding for all euro-area Member States, while it becomes binding to the other contracting parties once they adopt the euro or earlier if they declare their intention to be bound by it, or part of it, at an earlier date. The Fiscal Compact runs in parallel to the SGP as modified by the six-pack. Some concepts in the six-pack, such as the medium-term objective (MTO), are mirrored in the Fiscal Compact. In fact, some of its provisions are even more stringent than the six-pack.

The Fiscal Compact contains a number of provisions, including a balanced budget rule, a debt brake rule and an automatic correction mechanism in the case of a significant deviation from the MTO or the adjustment path towards it. In addition, to improve the coordination in this area, Member States have to submit their public debt issuance plans in advance to the Commission and the Council of the EU, while Member States subject to the EDP have to submit Economic Partnership Programs that detail the required structural reforms to produce an effective and lasting correction of the excessive deficit. The balanced budget rule and the automatic correction mechanism have to be embedded in the national legal system within one year after the TSCG enters in force for the state. In fact, such legal enshrinement is a condition to be eligible for a bail-out from the ESM.

Member States are subject to country-specific MTOs in which the structural deficit, i.e., the deficit purged of cyclical and one-off effects, is limited to 0.5 percent of GDP, or to 1.0 percent of GDP for countries with debt/GDP ratios significantly below 60 percent. The debt brake rule requires countries with debt ratios exceeding 60 percent of GDP to reduce the excess by one-twentieth per year. The precise formula for the benchmark limit is based on a three-year rolling window of debt ratios. Besides this, there is check on cyclically-adjusted debt ratio. Finally, failure to comply with the MTO, or the adjustment path towards it, should trigger an automatic adjustment mechanism, in which the Member State takes counter measures that correct the situation within a short amount of time, unless there are extraordinary events outside its control or there is a severe economic downturn.

Finally, there is the so-called "two-pack", which is applicable to euro-area Member States only and which aims at strengthening fiscal surveillance. This is done through two regulations. One regulation aims at monitoring and assessing *draft budgetary plans* and ensuring the correction of excessive deficits of euro-area countries. It coordinates the timing of the budgeting process by requiring countries to submit their draft budget before October 15, so that it can be assessed for its compliance with the SGP and earlier recommendations made in the context of the European Semester. This allows for the early detection of the risk that an excessive deficit is not corrected in time. A second regulation deals with euro-area Member States threatened with or experiencing financial problems. These countries will be subject to tighter surveillance. This is in particular the case for countries receiving specific types of precautionary financial assistance.

Figure 10.1, based on d'Elia (2013), visualizes the interaction between the EU fiscal rules and the implementation of fiscal arrangements at the national level. Countries submit their Stability or Convergence Program to the European Commission, which forms an opinion and makes recommendations regarding the adjustment path to the MTO (preventive arm of the SGP) and the correction of an Excessive Deficit (corrective arm of the SGP).

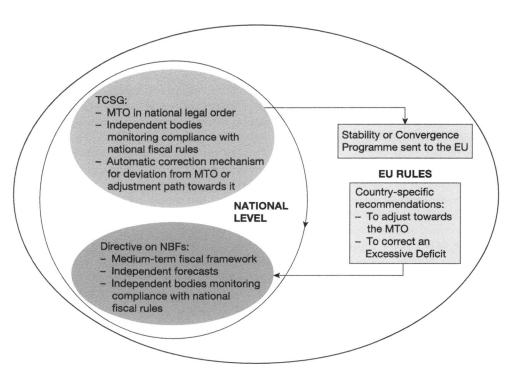

Figure 10.1 Interaction between national and EU level

Further, as the figure shows, all arrangements in connection with the TSCG are set up at the national level.

The national level is also responsible for implementing the directive on national budgetary frameworks with the requirements indicated in the figure (see the *Official Journal of the European Union*, November 23, 2011). The rules established by the Directive are part of the EU budgetary surveillance framework and are intended to have the EU Member States comply with the SGP. While the TSCG only binds the signatories, the Directive on national budgetary frameworks applies to all EU members. The two arrangements feature some overlap in the requirements they impose on countries' budgetary frameworks. The Directive imposes requirements on the systems of budgetary accounting covering in a comprehensive and consistent way all sub-sectors of the general government. Further, forecasts for budgetary planning should be done independently, while planning should be based on the most realistic macroeconomic and budgetary forecasts possible. Moreover, the forecasts as well as the methods and parameters used to produce them should be made public. The Directive also requires budgetary surveillance to be conducted on the basis of country-specific numerical fiscal rules.[2] Finally, it requires Member States to adopt a medium-term budgetary framework (MTBF) that extends fiscal planning to a period of at least three years.

The Netherlands has long operated on an MTBF set at the start of each new government taking office. The analysis in Beetsma et al. (2013b) suggests that in combination with the "trend-based budgeting" fiscal regime, which is characterized by expenditure ceilings, cautious budgeting and a strict separation between the expenditure and revenue side of the budget, it has worked quite well in having governments stick to their budget plans. Moreover, the overview on MTBFs provided by Ljungman (2012) suggests that credit default risk is lower at a given debt level when the MTBF is binding. The analysis in Beetsma et al. (2013a) for EU countries since the start of the euro indicates that improvement in the quality of institutions, whether measured by the tightness of national fiscal rules, the medium-term budgetary framework or budgetary transparency, increases the quality of budgetary reporting at the various stages of the budgeting process. Unfortunately, this study is unable to disentangle which features of the budgetary framework contribute the most to improvement in quality. For example, countries that tend to impose tight numerical fiscal rules, also tend to adopt high-quality medium-term budgetary frameworks, while they are also relatively transparent.

By requiring (legal) adjustments at the national level, the TSCG and the directive on national budgetary frameworks force EU Member States to take ownership of the need to create a stable fiscal environment in the EU in which spill-overs of budgetary irresponsibility are avoided. Such ownership is important, because the particular way in which the aforementioned adjustments take place is the result of democratic choices at the national level, hence the political and public support for these adjustments should be stronger than for the budgetary constraints imposed at the EU level through the SGP.

Figure 10.2, also based on d'Elia (2013), graphically visualizes the European Semester and how it relates to the SGP. By the end of April a country should submit its Stability Program, which will elicit country-specific recommendations as part of the procedures of the SGP. Then, by mid-October the draft budget is made public and sent to the EU. This is where the "two-pack" enters, under which the draft budget is assessed. The opinion formed on the latter forms needs to be taken into account in the budget law to be adopted by the end of the year.

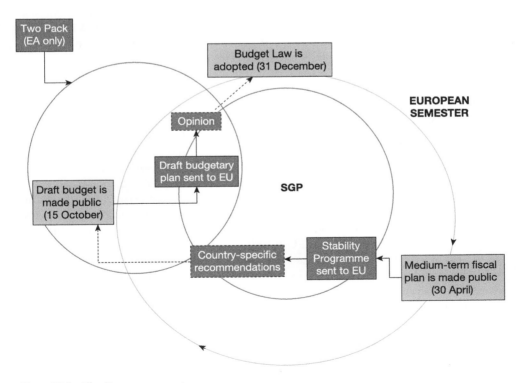

Figure 10.2 The European semester

The financial inter-linkages between the banking sector and sovereigns have proved particularly pernicious during the crisis. These inter-linkages run in both directions. A large bank in financial trouble threatens the stability of the financial system, which forces the government to come to its rescue. It is precisely this channel that forced the rescue of Ireland and provision of emergency funds for Spain. When a government faces financial problems, the market value of its outstanding debt falls. As a large fraction of this debt is usually held by domestic banks, these banks need to write off some of the value of their assets and this produces a reduction in their equity, which may eventually force the bank to go bankrupt. This mechanism has put Greek banks into trouble, as well as foreign banks that had a lot of Greek debt in their portfolios. Because of the financial linkages among banks through the payments system and lending relationships, the bankruptcy of a single bank may have a domino effect throughout the EU.

The interdependency of the financial health of banks and sovereigns has led to the creation of a "banking union" in the Eurozone. The banking union consists of three pillars (see European Commission, 2014b). The first pillar is the Single Supervisory Mechanism of the banking sector by the ECB. It has been in operation since November 2014. Supervision of the systemic banks will be directly conducted at the ECB, while supervision of the other banks will be done by the national supervisors, though according to a common set of rules for all the banks in the Eurozone. The second pillar is the Single Resolution Mechanism that ensures a quick resolution of banks in severe financial trouble. Decisions are taken by the Single Resolution Board (consisting of permanent members and representatives from the ECB, the EC, the European Council and national supervisory authorities) and are binding for all the Member States. To avoid that tax payers have to burdened by the resolution of banks, a Single Resolution Fund will be gradually formed from contributions by all EU banks. Contributions will start in 2016 and by 2024 the Fund should contain approximately 55 billion euros. When a bank needs to be restructured or wound down, a bail-in recapitalization will take place by writing down liabilities or converting liabilities into equity. This way the bank can continue as a going concern still providing its critical services, while the authorities have enough time to restructure the bank or wind it down in an orderly way. Thus, shareholders will be called upon first, followed by instruments like convertible bonds and junior bonds. Deposits under 100,000 euros will never be touched. The question is what will happen when a bank threatens to fall over in the period of the build-up of the Single Resolution Fund. To deal with such a situation, each country will collect bank levies in their so-called "national compartment". Gradually these compartments will combine these resources in the Single Resolution Fund until a full merger has been reached. A final pillar would be a common deposit insurance scheme to prevent bank runs. However, no concrete decisions have been taken regarding this last pillar.

The formation of the banking union has not been an easy process, in particular because of the fear of the financially more solid countries that they would have to pay for the so-called "legacy assets" of weak banks in the EU periphery. For this reason, an asset quality review (AQR) has preceded the entry of large banks into the banking union. Banks that failed the AQR had to find new capital. Overall 130 banks were assessed by the ECB, of which 25 were detected with a capital shortfall amounting to a total of 25 billion euros (ECB, 2014). Hence, the consequences of the AQR were relatively limited.

3. Routes towards further fiscal integration

Many experts would argue that further changes to the EU fiscal framework are necessary for a proper functioning of the Eurozone in the long run. The links between the banking sector and the sovereigns have been severed, although they have not been cut through entirely, especially not as long as the Single Resolution Fund is not at full capacity. How the Eurozone proceeds in terms of the development of its fiscal framework will depend a lot on the economic and political climate and on whether the political elite is able to regain the public's confidence for the European project. Below we sketch a number of potential, though not mutually-exclusive, ways to achieve further fiscal integration. A related discussion can be found in Cottarelli and Guerguil (2014, Ch. 7).

3.1 More intensified monitoring of budgetary policy

Clearly, the lack of budgetary discipline has contributed substantially to the crisis. As a result, the fiscal monitoring powers of the European Commission have been bolstered by strengthening the SGP. Moreover, the countries that received financial help from the emergency funds have been put under additional fiscal scrutiny. However, once these programs have been terminated, monitoring of these countries' budgetary policies will switch back to its standard level. The question is whether this would then be sufficient to prevent a relapse into fiscal profligacy. One possible change could be to impose stricter guidelines on the budgetary policies that may be followed. For example, the European Council, with the help of the European Commission could impose strict limits on the deficit that a country may run or on the amount of debt it can issue. Subject to these restrictions, it would then be allowed to set spending and taxes as it sees fit. However, "Europe" could become even more "intrusive" by imposing strict limits on the level of spending, which would leave governments with even less freedom. Such developments are not particularly likely in the near future, though, as countries have become reluctant to devolve more powers to "Europe". Hence, countries may need to be encouraged to adopt such tight restrictions at the national level and have independent national bodies do the monitoring of these restrictions. In this regard, Germany has set the stage by adopting a debt brake rule in the constitution that imposes strict borrowing limits and requirements for structurally-balanced or close-to-balance budgets of the central and state governments (Deutsche Bundesbank, 2011). There will be a phase-in period until 2016 for the central government and 2020 for the state governments before the limits become binding. The empirical literature reviewed above suggests that tight fiscal rules set at the national level are conducive to the adherence to fiscal plans.

3.2 Insurance mechanisms against idiosyncratic shocks

A second element of further fiscal integration could be a mechanism to insure countries against the consequences of idiosyncratic shocks. Such a mechanism could substitute for the rather well-documented failure of asset markets to provide an efficient sharing of consumption risks (e.g., Sorensen and Yosha, 1998).[3] In fact, such a mechanism could even do without any central budget, because it would merely consist of transfers from lucky to unlucky countries. Hammond and Von Hagen (1995) present a set of criteria that a well-designed insurance mechanism should adhere to. First, it should only insure asymmetric and temporary shocks, because this is the type of shock that a centralized monetary policy cannot handle. Second, for the scheme to be acceptable to the general public, it should be simple and automatic. This property is of particular importance in a multi-country setting when confidence in a proper use by other countries is low. Third, net transfers should on average be zero over time, so as to avoid that some countries systematically become net beneficiaries and others net contributors. Such a situation would be unacceptable for the population in the latter. Fourth, the system should be balanced at the central level to avoid the need for a substantial central budget. Fifth, transfer payments should only be triggered by shocks that are serially uncorrelated. Transfers in response to persistent shocks would undermine the incentive for governments to undertake politically costly structural reforms aimed at eliminating the sources of the persistence of the shocks. Finally, in order to overcome the cost of setting up the system, it should offset a sufficiently large share of the asymmetric shocks.

All in all, setting up a proper insurance mechanism involves a number of substantial design issues. Yet the biggest obstacle may be the identification of the *truly* exogenous shocks on which to condition the transfers. This will prove even more difficult than the identification of exogenous fiscal shocks that so many researchers have been concerned with recently (for example, see Ramey, 2011). The reason is that movements in economic activity are the result of a combination of truly exogenous developments, the institutional setting and current and past government policies. Hence, the role of policy choices needs to be filtered out of the observed developments in economic activity. This requires not only identifying the relevant policy decisions, but also establishing how they interact with the economic and institutional situation to produce the outcomes that are observed. Knowing that these relationships cannot be pinpointed precisely and knowing that there is an insurance mechanism in place, the incentive on the side of governments to embark on politically-costly structural reforms, such as making labor and product markets more flexible, becomes weaker. In other words, a moral hazard problem arises and this problem becomes larger when the size of the scheme is larger.

In the literature a few proposals have been made for international insurance schemes – see, Bartelsman and Beetsma (1998) and Furceri and Zdzienicka (2013). To reduce the moral hazard problem, Bartelsman and Beetsma (1998) propose a scheme in which transfers are based on exogenous sector shocks caused by changes in world market conditions. The scheme is designed in such a way that transfers are absent when all countries have an identical sector structure. To the extent that countries would still exhibit differences in economic performance, these differences would be attributable to domestic conditions and policies, but they would not be a source of cross-border transfers. Hence, the moral hazard issue would be minimized.

The main idea is the following. Assume that there are $j=1,...,s$ sectors trading on the world market and that the Eurozone is composed of n countries. Further, let x_{ijt} be period-t exports by sector j in country i to the rest of the world (RoW), which consists all countries minus the Eurozone. One can write:

$$x_{ijt} = w_{ijt} X_{jt},$$

where X_{jt} is total Eurozone exports of sector j to the RoW, while w_{ijt} is country i's share in this total. Further, one can carry out the following decomposition:

$$x_{ijt} - x_{ij,t-1} = w_{ijt} X_{jt} - w_{ij,t-1} X_{j,t-1} = (\Delta w_{ijt}) X_{j,t-1} + (\Delta w_{ijt})(\Delta X_{jt}) + w_{ij,t-1}(\Delta X_{jt}). \qquad (1)$$

The term $(\Delta w_{ijt}) X_{j,t-1}$ is likely the result of domestically-controlled factors, such as domestic costs and quality, leading to changes in the export share of country i. This component should not form a basis for cross-border transfers. Similarly for the term $(\Delta w_{ijt})(\Delta X_{jt})$, which is likely to be small in any case, because it is of second-order magnitude. Finally, the term $y_{ijt} \equiv w_{ij,t-1}(\Delta X_{jt})$ is largely beyond the short-run control of national policymakers. Of course, $w_{ij,t-1}$ is partly the result of past policies. Hence, cross-border insurance transfers could in principle be based on y_{ijt} for a limited period of time so as to allow the country to restructure activity away from an ailing sector j to other sectors.

3.3 Collective public debt issuance

A third element of further fiscal integration could be formed by the collective issuance of (part of the) public debt, or, in popular language, the issuance of "Eurobonds". Claessens et al. (2012) discuss a number of potential benefits from common debt issues. First, it may promote financial stability by severing the link between the financial health of banks and governments. Banks usually hold a disproportionate amount of national public debt in their asset portfolio. Uncertainty about the repayment of the debt spills over to the health of the banks and may undermine their role as financial intermediaries. The creation of a safe common asset would eliminate this effect. Second, the supply of such a safe asset would also eliminate disruptive flight-to-quality effects. Third, issuance of a common debt instrument would improve market liquidity. Fourth, it could promote the functioning of the monetary transmission mechanism by creating a deep and unified market for such an instrument. Market segmentations would be reduced, while the ECB would find it easier to engage in unconventional monetary policy measures without having to worry about potential losses from holding weak assets on its balance sheet or the danger of giving undue advantage to specific countries by taking their debt on its portfolio.

Several proposals for common debt issuance have been made. Delpla and Von Weizsäcker (2010) suggest the issuance of "blue" and "red" bonds, where the former act as senior debt and are issued under joint and several liability. They make up at most 60 percent of GDP. Any debt above 60 percent of GDP is of the red type and is junior. Hellwig and Philippon (2011) propose the issuance of a maximum of 10 percent of GDP of mutually-guaranteed short-term debt. Related proposals by Bishop et al. (2011) and Boonstra and Bruinshoofd (2012) for the Eurozone foresee a facility for the issuance of jointly-guaranteed short-term debt. The collectively guaranteed Eurobond proposed by De Grauwe and Moesen (2009) envisages a differentiation of the interest rate across the participating countries in line with their market interest rates. Also the European Commission (2011) has explored the complexities involved in the issuance of jointly-guaranteed "stability bonds". In fact, the President of the European Commission installed a commission of experts to explore the desirability and feasibility of introducing Eurobonds.

Claessens et al. (2012) review the different proposals and provide an overview of the various steps needed to set up mechanisms for the joint issuance of public debt. The obvious objection to the issuance of Eurobonds is the potential presence of moral hazard. Knowing that the repayment of debt is collectively guaranteed, governments may have an incentive to issue more debt than they would otherwise do, thereby putting a burden on the collective of countries. The past has shown that this is a realistic danger: with the entry into the Eurozone, public debt interest rates of some countries fell quite substantially. However, the resulting budgetary leeway has been mostly used to increase spending and not to reduce public debt. Beetsma and Mavromatis (2014) argue that by conditioning repayment guarantees on the level of the debt or on structural reform, governments could be induced to actually issue less debt and reform more. However, the question is whether the conditionality is credible once a country's budgetary crisis spills over to panic in the financial markets.

3.4 Centralization of tax-transfer systems

The most far-reaching change in the EU's fiscal architecture would be the centralization of its tax and transfer systems, similar to the US. Hence, taxes will be paid to a central European fiscal authority, in the same way that taxes are now being paid to the central government of a country. These tax revenues will be used to finance transfers, like unemployment transfers. A country that experiences a slowdown in economic activity and an increase in unemployment, will pay less taxes to the center, while it receives more unemployment transfers. Such a centralized tax-transfer system provides an implicit insurance against asymmetric shocks. Empirical work for the US and other countries (e.g., Atkeson and Bayoumi, 1993, Hammond and Von Hagen, 1995, and Mélitz and Zumer, 2002) comes up with widely-differing estimates of this implicit insurance, ranging from 10 to 35 percent of the idiosyncratic shocks.

However, the most important complication of introducing such a system is that it is also likely to introduce systematic redistribution from countries that feature on average stronger economic performance than other countries (e.g., Sachs and Sala-i-Martin, 1991). This, in turn, may discourage the governments of the weaker countries to engage in politically-costly structural reform of their economies. German experience suggests that this is a realistic complication. Germany features an equalization mechanism that redistributes public resources from the richer to the poorer states. It is well known that those resource flows generally go into the same direction over long periods of time. Hence, for the foreseeable future, as long as average incomes and economic efficiency differ considerably across EU countries, it will be difficult introduce more centralization of taxes and transfers.

4. Conclusion

This chapter has discussed the EU fiscal framework and the changes introduced to the framework in response to the recent crisis. The chapter has also described a number of scenarios for further fiscal integration. It has tried to connect these issues to the recent academic literature. Which scenario will unfold in the coming decades will depend a lot on how the EU economies will perform and on whether Europe's politicians will be able to revive the general public's confidence in the EU project. If politicians are not able to do so, then further fiscal integration will become difficult, which, in turn, implies that the existence of the euro may from time to time be threatened by an outbreak of a new financial crisis. The main complication in any step towards further fiscal integration is the danger of moral hazard. This problem should be taken much more seriously than it has been in the past, because it generates distrust among the populations of the more financially disciplined countries, thereby holding back potentially desirable movements towards more fiscal centralization. Redesign of institutions into this direction needs to be robust against moral hazard and accompanied by sufficiently tight monitoring of budgetary policymaking. Another way of limiting moral hazard is to provide more room for financial markets to fulfill their disciplining role of governments, for example, by introducing differences in the risk-weighting of public debt in commercial banks' asset portfolios.

Notes

1 For a description of the original design of the SGP, see Cabral (2001).
2 Wehner (2012) discusses the effectiveness of fiscal rules in medium-term budget planning.
3 Various contributions, such as Sorensen and Yosha (1998), have studied international consumption risk sharing. An analogous analysis of interstate risk sharing in Germany has been conducted by Hepp and Von Hagen (2013).

References

Atkeson, A. and Bayoumi, T. (1993), Do Private Capital Markets Insure Regional Risk? Evidence from the United States and Europe, *Open Economies Review*, 4(3), 303–24.

Bartelsman, E.J. and Beetsma, R.M.W.J. (1998), *Is a Fiscal Insurance Scheme Desirable and How Should It Be Designed?* Dutch Ministry of Economic Affairs.

Beetsma, R.M.W.J., Bluhm, B., Giuliodori, M., and Wierts, P.J. (2013a), From Budgetary Forecasts to Ex-Post Fiscal Data: Exploring the Evolution of Fiscal Forecast Errors in the EU, *Contemporary Economic Policy*, 31(4), 795–813.

Beetsma, R.M.W.J., Giuliodori, M., and Wierts, P.J. (2009), Planning to Cheat: EU Fiscal Policy in Real Time, *Economic Policy*, 24(60), 753–804.

Beetsma, R.M.W.J., Giuliodori, M., Walschots, M., and Wierts, P.J. (2013b), Fifty Years of Fiscal Planning and Implementation in the Netherlands, *European Journal of Political Economy*, 31, 119–38.

Beetsma, R.M.W.J. and Mavromatis, K. (2014), An Analysis of Eurobonds, *Journal of International Money and Finance*, 45, 91–111.

Beetsma, R.M.W.J. and Oksanen, H. (2008), Pensions under Ageing Populations and the EU Stability and Growth Pact, *CESifo Economic Studies*, 54(4), 563–92.

Beetsma, R.M.W.J. and Uhlig, H. (1999), An Analysis of the Stability and Growth Pact, *Economic Journal*, 109(458), 546–71.

Bishop, G. et al. (2011), An "EMU Bond Fund" Proposal, European League for Economic Cooperation, December.

Boonstra, W.W. and Bruinshoofd, W.A. (2012), *Conditional Euro T-Bills as a Transitional Regime*, Rabobank Netherlands.

Cabral, A.J. (2001), Main Aspects of the Working of the SGP, in Brunila, A. et al. (eds), *The Stability and Growth Pact*, Houndmills, Basingstoke: Palgrave.

Claessens, S., Mody, A., and Vallée, S. (2012), Paths to Eurobonds, *IMF Working Paper* 12/172.

Cottarelli, C. and Guerguil, M. (eds) (2015), *Designing a European Fiscal Union: Lessons from the Experience of Fiscal Federations*, London and New York: Routledge.

D'Elia, A. (2013), The Framework for Budgetary Surveillance in the European Union, presentation at the conference Perspectives of the Fiscal Policy in Latvia and the EU, Riga, June 6.

Delpla, J. and von Weizsäcker, J. (2010), The Blue Bond Proposal, *Bruegel Policy Brief* 2010/3.

De Grauwe, P. and Moesen, W. (2009), *Gains for All: A Proposal for a Common Euro Bond*, University of Leuven.

Deutsche Bundesbank (2011), The Debt Brake in Germany – Key Aspects and Implementation, *Monthly Report*, October.

ECB (2014), *Aggregate Report on the Comprehensive Assessment*, November, Frankfurt: ECB.

European Commission (2011), Green Paper on the Feasibility of Introducing Stability Bonds, available at ec.europa.eu/commission_2010–2014/president/news/documents/pdf/green_en.pdf, November 23.

European Commission (2014a), Six-pack? Two-pack? Fiscal Compact? A Short Guide to the New EU Fiscal Governance, available at ec.europa.eu/economy_finance/articles/governance/2012–03–14_six_pack_en.htm.

European Commission (2014b), Banking Union: Restoring Financial Stability in the Eurozone, available at europa.eu/rapid/press-release_MEMO-14–294_en.htm?locale=en.

European Council (2011), *European Council 24/25 March 2011 Conclusions*, available at www.consilium.europa.eu/uedocs/cms_data/docs/pressdata/en/ec/120296.pdf, April 20.

Furceri, D. and Zdzienicka, A. (2013), The Euro Area Crisis: Need for a Supranational Fiscal Risk Sharing Mechanism?, *IMF Working Paper* 13/198.

Gali, J. and Perotti, R. (2003), Fiscal Policy and Monetary Integration in Europe, *Economic Policy*, 18(37), 533–72.

Hammond, G. and von Hagen, J. (1995), Regional Insurance against Asymmetric Shocks: An Empirical Study for the European Community, *Manchester School of Economic & Social Studies*, 66(3), 331–53.

Hellwig, C. and Philippon, T. (2011), Eurobills, Not Eurobonds, www.voxeu.org, December 2.

Hepp, R. and von Hagen, J. (2013), Interstate Risk Sharing in Germany: 1970–2006, *Oxford Economic Papers*, 65(1), 1–24.

Ljungman, G. (2012), A Case for Binding Medium-Term Budget Frameworks, presented at the Joint Conference by the IMF Fiscal Affairs Department and the Swedish Ministry of Finance Medium-Term Budgetary Frameworks and Fiscal Consolidation Programs, Stockholm, May.

Mélitz, J. and Zumer, F. (2002), Regional Redistribution and Stabilization by the Center in Canada, France, the UK and the US: A Reassessment and New Tests, *Journal of Public Economics*, 86(2), 263–86.

Ramey, V.A. (2011), Can Government Purchases Stimulate the Economy? *Journal of Economic Literature*, 49(3), 673–85.

Sachs, J. and Sala-i-Martin, X. (1991), Fiscal Federalism and Optimum Currency Areas: Evidence for Europe from the United States, *NBER Working Paper* No. 3855.

Sorensen, B. and Yosha, O. (1998), International Risk Sharing and European Monetary Unification, *Journal of International Economics*, 45(2), 211–38.

Wehner, J. (2012), The Role of Fiscal Rules in Medium-Term Budget Planning, presented at the Joint Conference by the IMF Fiscal Affairs Department and the Swedish Ministry of Finance Medium-Term Budgetary Frameworks and Fiscal Consolidation Programs, Stockholm, May.

11

THE ROLES OF FISCAL RULES, FISCAL COUNCILS AND FISCAL UNION IN EU INTEGRATION

Lars Calmfors[1]

The right of national parliaments to decide the government budget is usually seen as a key part of national sovereignty. Hence it is natural that the appropriate amount of fiscal integration has all along been a central issue in the debate on European integration. The issue came to the forefront with the introduction of the euro, as it was then necessary to take a stand on whether monetary policy could be centralised without a similar centralisation of fiscal policy (fiscal union). The avenue chosen was to go ahead with the common currency without full-fledged fiscal policy co-ordination. Instead reliance was put on fiscal rules at the European level.

The recent euro crisis with exploding government debt in some countries illustrated vividly the shortcomings of the earlier EU rules. The crisis triggered fundamental reforms of the rules as well as attempts to co-ordinate policy decisions at European and national levels better, including the strengthening of national fiscal frameworks. The latter reforms have included monitoring of fiscal policy by independent fiscal institutions (fiscal councils). At the same time, the discussion on whether a monetary union also requires a fiscal union continues.

This contribution analyses fiscal governance in the eurozone. The focus is on the long-run adequacy of the fiscal institutions, not on the handling of the euro crisis in the short term. Section 1 explains the background for the fiscal rules designed in association with the introduction of the euro and reviews them. Section 2 summarises the main problems with the original rules. Section 3 evaluates the recent reforms of European economic governance. Section 4 analyses the role of fiscal councils. Section 5 discusses fiscal union. Section 6 concludes.

1. The original fiscal rules

The period 1975–95 was characterised by substantial fiscal deficits and increasing government debt in most EU countries. Similar developments occurred in other advanced economies. This led many researchers to the conclusion that unconstrained discretionary fiscal policy in modern democracies may be subject to a *deficit bias*. Different explanations were put forward:[2]

- *General informational problems on the part of both the government and the electorate.* Neither politicians nor voters may realise the long-run consequences of current fiscal deficits. This may be due to 'fiscal illusion', i.e. insufficient understanding of the government's intertemporal budget constraint, i.e. the fact that current debt must be serviced through future primary surpluses (taxes in excess of expenditure). Alternatively there may be over-optimism about future growth and revenue prospects.

- *Informational asymmetries between the government and the electorate.* Voters are imperfectly informed about both fiscal policy and the government's (as well as the political opposition's) competency. An incumbent government may exploit this to boost its re-election chances by trying to signal competency (i.e that it can "deliver") through spending rises or tax cuts in pre-election periods causing deficits the size or long-run consequences of which voters may not realise.

- *Political polarisation and electoral uncertainty.* An incumbent government facing uncertainty over re-election prospects has an incentive to run deficits now, as this allows it to raise expenditure or cut taxes in a way that benefits its own constituency. Such deficits have the strategic advantage that it becomes more difficult for future governments of another political colour to pursue policy according to their preferences, as they must then service the debt incurred by the current government. Put differently, the current government's effective discount rate is raised, so that it cares less about the future than is socially desirable.

- *Common-pool problems.* Various interest groups may be lobbying for specific types of government spending benefitting them without proper regard for the long-run costs of the deficits that may result, since these costs are shared with other groups in society.

- *Time inconsistency of fiscal policy.* There may be a temptation to over-use fiscal deficits as a tool to raise aggregate demand, and therefore output and employment in the short run, because prices and wages are slow to adjust to unanticipated shocks. The mechanism is similar to the one that may cause an inflation bias for monetary policy under unconstrained discretionary policy-making. In equilibrium, when expectations have adjusted to actual government behaviour, such fiscal policy results only in deficits without any output and employment benefits.

- *Exploitation of future generations.* Fiscal deficits could, finally, also reflect a desire of the current generation to shift consumption in its favour (through government spending increases or tax cuts) from future generations either directly in the form of interest payments or indirectly in the form of crowding-out of investment leading to a smaller capital stock in the future.

In the 1980s *fiscal rules* came to be seen as the remedy for the perceived deficit bias of fiscal policy.[3] It was thought that it would be easier to agree on 'constitutional' rules behind a 'veil of ignorance' on how various political parties would be affected by them in the future than on actual policies in a specific situation. One way of viewing the rules that were established with the introduction of the euro is that politicians used this opportunity to introduce constraints at the European level that would have been difficult to do nationally (Calmfors 2005).

But there was also a strong perception that monetary union would reinforce the deficit bias of fiscal policy unless strong safeguards were put in place (see e.g. Keuschnigg 2012). The reason is the negative spillover effects (externalities) of deficits in one euro area member state on other member states, which means that a state running deficits is able to shift part of the cost on to others. First, under 'normal' conditions this could occur because a deficit in one country raises aggregate demand and inflation in the whole union, which may induce the European Central Bank (ECB) to raise the common interest rate. Second, in more extreme situations – as occurred during the euro crisis – the fear of government bankruptcy in one eurozone country could cause investors to demand higher risk premia on government debt both there and in other member countries. This reduces the value of outstanding debt and thus destroys wealth everywhere with negative effects on aggregate demand and on the financial sector. Third, eurozone members threatened by default may in the end – as also happened during the euro crisis – be bailed out by other members (which will in the end hurt their tax payers) in an attempt to avoid financial contagion. Such concerns were another important reason for the fiscal rules established in the euro area. This was done both in the Treaty and in the stability pact, which operationalised the Treaty stipulations. The main *economic contents* of the rules were:

- A prohibition for both EU institutions (including the ECB) and other governments to bail out an individual government that cannot meet its debt obligations (the *no-bail-out clause*).
- A *government deficit ceiling* of 3 per cent of GDP under normal conditions.
- A *ceiling for consolidated general government gross debt* of 60 per cent of GDP: if the debt ratio is larger, it should be 'sufficiently diminishing' and approaching the 60-percent-level 'at a satisfactory pace'.
- Adherence to a *medium-term objective* for the budgetary position, i.e. an objective for the cyclically adjusted budget balance, of 'close-to-balance or surplus'.

Procedural rules were also established. To prevent large deficits from arising in the first place *multilateral surveillance* was introduced: euro area member states were obliged each year to submit economic policy programmes (so called stability programmes) for review by the Commission and the Ecofin Council (the member states' economics and finance ministers). In case of violations of the deficit ceiling an *excessive deficit procedure* should be started against the transgressing country. An excessive deficit that was not corrected would ultimately lead to payment of a non-interest bearing deposit that could be transformed into a fine.

2. The rules in practice before the euro crisis

The fiscal rules were first put to a test in the cyclical downturn of 2001–5 when the deficit ceiling was breached by several eurozone countries. The rules did not stand the test. The most flagrant transgressions occurred when the excessive deficit procedures initiated against France and Germany were halted in clear violation of stability pact stipulations. This was justified ex post by a revision of the pact in 2005 which watered down the rules. The scope for discretionary decisions in the Ecofin Council to extend the deadlines in the excessive deficit procedure was increased. This postponed the maximum time limits for imposing sanctions if excessive deficits were not corrected from the originally envisaged three and five years (for interest-free deposits and fines, respectively) to six–seven and eight–nine years, respectively.[4]

The flouting of the rules in 2001–5 and the subsequent revisions are not surprising. The research literature had early on identified the problem that the same incentives that could make a government make socially undesirable decisions under discretion are also likely to induce such a government to ignore or abandon a policy rule that has been introduced to prevent such decisions. According to this logic, a policy rule only moves the deficit bias problem from one level (discretionary decisions on actual policies) to another (the 'constitutional' level).[5] This implies a *time-inconsistency problem* for fiscal rules. One should expect this incentive to abandon the rules to be weaker when they are embedded in an international agreement, as with the EU rules, than when they are purely national, as the abandonment then might carry additional costs in terms of loss of international prestige and trustworthiness. However, the fact that it was the leading EU powers Germany and France that were involved probably lessened the importance of these considerations.

One can identify several problems with the original deficit rules that made them hard to apply:[6]

- If sanctions were to be used, they could immediately become very harsh. The initial interest-free deposits and fines could amount to as much as 0.5 per cent of GDP. This 'atomic-bomb character' of the sanctions probably was a strong disincentive to use them.
- The pecuniary nature of sanctions may also have been seen as a problem, since the immediate effect of fining a country with an excessive deficit is to add to this deficit.
- Each new step in the excessive deficit procedure (including sanctions) required a discretionary decision in the Ecofin Council with a qualified majority in favour. In a situation where several member states simultaneously had deficits, this facilitated the forming of blocking coalitions.
- Decisions in the excessive deficit procedure form a *repeated game*. Finance ministers therefore have an incentive to act strategically. Since each finance minister may fear also ending up in the future with an excessive deficit that could be sanctioned, lenient treatment of current 'sinners' can be regarded as an investment in lenient treatment of oneself in a similar situation.

The EU rules obviously did not prevent the government debt crises that arose in 2010–12. In Greece and Portugal the crises reflected violations of the deficit ceiling already before the outbreak of the international financial crisis in 2007/2008 (in the Greek case concealed by statistical misreporting). This was not the situation in Ireland and Spain, which had fiscal surpluses before the crisis. They were, however, associated with unsustainable booms involving excessive bank lending, house price bubbles and faster price increases than in the rest of the eurozone. When the booms came to an end, the result was deep recessions and banking crises which triggered large fiscal deficits. The rules were not designed to avoid boom situations that could build up macroeconomic imbalances causing rapid government debt accumulation in a later phase of the business cycle. Nor did the rules put enough emphasis on reducing government debt in good times so as to create more fiscal room in bad times. This would have helped both Greece and Italy, which both had large government debts before the outbreak of the international financial crisis.

During the euro crisis EU leaders chose to ignore the no-bail-out clause. The various government rescue programmes for the crisis countries and the ECB activities (both the actual purchases of those countries' government securities in the beginning of the euro crisis and the commitment from 2012 to buy unlimited amounts of them if that would prove necessary to hold down bond yields) must be regarded as violations of the no-bail-out clause. It remains disputed, however, how this should be judged. On one hand there is the argument that such backstops were necessary to prevent a systemic financial crisis. On the other hand it has been claimed that the bail-outs create moral-hazard problems likely to cause new government debt crises in the future.[7]

3. Reforms triggered by the euro crisis

The euro crisis sparked a number of reforms of the eurozone's governance system.[8] Partly they were motivated by dissatisfaction with the earlier rules. Partly they were seen as a way of counterbalancing the moral-hazard problems arising from the rescue programmes.

The reforms can be grouped in four areas:

- Beefing-up of the deficit and debt rules.
- Broader macroeconomic surveillance.
- More co-ordination between European and national decision levels.
- Stronger national fiscal frameworks.

The sharpening of the *deficit and debt rules*, which reversed the watering down of them in 2005, involves several aspects. As regards *economic contents* the stipulation that government debt exceeding 60 per cent of GDP should be 'sufficiently diminishing and approaching the reference value at a satisfactory pace' has now been operationalised: the differential with respect to that value should decrease over a three-year period at an average rate of 1/20 per year. As to *procedural rules*, new steps in the excessive deficit procedure (as well as in the new macroeconomic imbalance procedure) will not in the future require a qualified majority in favour. Instead a reversed qualified majority stipulation has been introduced: Commission proposals will be adopted by the Ecofin Council unless there is a qualified majority against.[9] Sanctions in the excessive deficit procedure have become more graduated and can now be applied earlier than according to the original rules and also when the debt criterion is violated. In addition, sanctions have been introduced in the preventive part of the fiscal framework to deal with situations when a country 'deviates significantly from its medium-term budget objective or the adjustment path to it'. Finally, common principles regarding the national statistics necessary for EU-level monitoring of public finances have been decided. A member state that misrepresents data can be fined.

A *macroeconomic imbalance procedure* has been introduced with the aim of detecting at an early stage macroeconomic imbalances that can later cause a severe fiscal crisis. The Commission is now annually producing an alert mechanism report in which a number of indicators that could signal such imbalances are monitored. The indicators include variables such as private and public debt, house price developments, credit growth, the current account, the net international investment position and the real exchange rate. If the Commission and the Ecofin Council judge imbalances in a euro area country to be dangerous, an *excessive imbalance procedure* (modelled on the excessive deficit procedure) can be initiated. In this procedure deposits and fines can be imposed if the state fails to comply with recommendations on corrective action.

Better *co-ordination between European and national decision-making* is to be achieved through a *European semester*. It defines an annual 'policy cycle' which starts with the European Council (the heads of state or government) giving member states 'strategic guidance'. It should be taken into account by member states when formulating their economic-policy programmes (stability programmes for eurozone members). The European Council and the Ecofin Council then evaluate the programmes based on recommendations by the Commission. Governments are supposed to take these evaluations into account in their draft budgets. These are assessed by the Commission, which can request changes before the final budget is presented to the national parliaments.

National fiscal frameworks have been strengthened through a number of reforms decided at the EU level. They include a balanced-budget rule (defined as a cyclically adjusted deficit of maximum 0.5 per cent of GDP under normal circumstances) and an 'automatic correction mechanism' which specifies how deviations from budget balance should be corrected. A euro area member state that fails to introduce such rules can be brought before the Court of Justice of the EU. The Court can fine a member state that does not comply with its ruling.

Member states are also obliged to have in place comprehensive public accounting systems covering all subsectors of the government, to base fiscal planning on realistic forecasts (which are to be compared with the Commission's and others' forecasts) and to have a multi-year fiscal planning horizon.

The reforms described address several of the problems with the fiscal rules. The incentives to refrain from statistical misreporting are strengthened, it is harder to form blocking coalitions and the incentive to use sanctions is stronger when they are more graduated. The strengthening of national fiscal frameworks is important, since economic policy-making under normal conditions still is mainly a national issue. The broader macroeconomic surveillance increases the probability of identifying and reacting to macroeconomic imbalances that could later cause fiscal crisis.

But it is an open question how much the reforms will achieve. EU-level decision-making is still a repeated game with strong incentives for a mild stance against problem countries in anticipation of similar lenient treatment of the own country in a similar future contingency. The difficulty of imposing sanctions in the excessive imbalance procedure is particularly obvious, as decisions on whether imbalances are really excessive will always be judgmental. The national budget-balance rules are subject to the great uncertainty surrounding calculations of cyclically adjusted fiscal balances,[10] which could open up for politically motivated manipulations. In addition, there appears to be great leeway in the way that the national automatic correction mechanisms can be constructed: they may not be more 'automatic' than that the parliament should decide in such a situation on a plan to restore budget balance. Most importantly, the violation of the no-bail-out clause implies a severe *credibility problem* for any EU-level fiscal rule. If such a fundamental stipulation could be disregarded, there are likely to be expectations that also the sharpened fiscal rules could be breached in the future if considered politically convenient. The most vulnerable of the new rules is probably the one that an excess of government debt over the 60 per cent ceiling should be reduced at an average pace of 1/20 per year, as this may prove hard for many of the crisis countries to achieve, particularly if a situation with low nominal growth persists.[11] Sanctions against a member state violating this debt criterion also still requires a qualified majority in favour.

In January 2015 the Commission issued new guidelines on 'making the best use of the flexibility within the existing rules' of the stability pact which open up possibilities for a slower adjustment to the fiscal medium-term objectives (for the cyclically adjusted balance) when structural reforms are implemented or some types of public investment are undertaken in recessions.[12] These modifications came after political pressures from especially France and Italy, which have both been struggling to meet the EU's fiscal requirements. These new provisions are quite likely to be used to water down the rules.

At a more theoretical level the basic question is still why one should not expect that a deficit bias under discretionary policy-making should again re-emerge as a tendency to flout the rules. The next section is devoted to this issue. It focuses on the role that can be played by independent monitoring institutions.

4. Fiscal councils

In recent years the idea that a government's fiscal policy should be monitored by a national independent fiscal institution, often labelled a *fiscal council*, has gained traction. Independent institutions with this as one of its tasks have existed for a long time in some countries including in the Netherlands (the Central Planning Bureau from 1945), Denmark (the Economic Council from 1962), Germany (the Council of Economic Experts from 1963) and the US (the Congressional Budget Office from 1974). Belgium and Austria established such institutions in 1989 and 2002, respectively. Recently the establishment of fiscal councils has become a trend. The first councils in this new wave were created in Sweden (2007), Canada (2008), Hungary (2009), Slovenia (2009) and the UK (2010).[13] The current interest in such institutions is reflected, for example, in OECD (2014) work, where common principles for them have been developed.

The idea of independent fiscal institutions first surfaced in the academic discussion in the 1990s.[14] It was initially viewed as a parallel to the delegation of monetary policy to independent central banks with the aim of eliminating inflation bias. Similar delegation of fiscal policy to an independent fiscal authority was seen as a method of counteracting deficit bias. The idea of delegating actual fiscal decisions to independent experts, however, never caught on. The probable reason was the view that fiscal decisions are intrinsically much more redistributive, and hence more political, than monetary-policy decisions since a stand must be taken on exactly which taxes or government expenditures to change.[15] Therefore the academic discussion turned instead to independent fiscal councils without decision-making power but with a role as 'fiscal watchdogs' having the remit to alert politicians and voters to fiscal risks. The aim is then to influence policy either directly through inputs into the decision-making process or indirectly through analysis and participation in the public discussion.

A fiscal watchdog might counteract several of the mechanisms that could cause a deficit bias (see Section 1). It could:

- *Provide better information* to both voters and politicians. This could decrease 'fiscal illusion' and increase general awareness of the government's inter-temporal budget constraint.
- *Reduce informational asymmetries* between the government and the electorate by providing accurate information on actual deficits and their long-run consequences. This would weaken the incentive of an incumbent government to try to signal competency, and thus increase its re-election chances, through deficit-financed expenditure increases or tax cuts.
- *Close the possibility for a government to deliberately use over-optimistic growth forecasts* to justify deficits by either producing the macroeconomic forecast underlying the budget proposal or evaluating the government's own forecast.
- *Mitigate common-pool problems through accurate costing* of various spending and tax cut proposals thus helping to ensure that the full budgetary costs are considered.
- *Raise the reputation cost for a government of deficits* by providing more accurate estimates of them and outlining the future consequences.
- In addition, a fiscal council could help *identify and warn against unsustainable booms* that when bursting can trigger fiscal crises.

Unofficial bodies, such as various think tanks, could in principle do the same thing. But the official mandate of a fiscal council is likely to make it more effective in pursuing these tasks, as this will probably result in much more media interest and less of suspicions of any hidden agenda. The impact can be magnified by stipulations – or by establishing a practice – that the government must respond to the judgments of the council.

Many early academic proposals, such as Wyplosz (2005), saw independent fiscal institutions as a *substitute* for rules, allowing discretionary policy-making with more flexibility than rules. But in practice fiscal councils usually coexist with rules, so it seems more appropriate to regard them as *complements*.[16] This is understandable as a fiscal rule provides a clear benchmark for judging policy. The existence of fiscal councils could also influence how rules are formulated. There is a fundamental trade-off between *simple* rules (such as a ceiling on the actual deficit), which are *easy to verify* but may be *inadequate* in many situations because they are inflexible, and more *complex* rules (referring e.g. to the cyclically adjusted balance), which are more *adequate* because of their flexibility but also more *difficult to verify*. Monitoring by independent and competent experts could permit the rules to be more complex, as this likely reduces the scope for political manipulation.

The recent reforms of EU economic governance include stipulations on independent national fiscal bodies.[17] Several tasks have been outlined. One is to monitor compliance with the agreed national fiscal rules. Another is to advise on the use of the automatic correction mechanism in these rules, described in Section 3, and to assess whether the triggering of possible escape clauses are motivated. The independent body should also provide or endorse the macroeconomic forecast that serves a basis for the government's budget proposal.

A relevant question is whether fiscal councils will be subject to the same time inconsistency problem for institutions as was discussed for rules in Section 3, i.e. that the underlying forces which cause the deficit bias problem under discretion will also make institutions designed to deal with the problem ineffective. More precisely, should one not expect national governments to ignore the recommendations of fiscal councils, to constrain their activities or effectively abolish them because their monitoring activities are likely to come into conflict with short-run government aims?[18]

The answer depends on the causes of the deficit bias in the first place (see Section 1). To the extent that a fiscal council removes these underlying causes time inconsistency problems for the institution itself will not appear. If the deficit bias under discretion is due to general over-optimism or to imperfect understanding of the government's intertemporal budget constraint on the part of both the government and the electorate, the provision of more accurate information may indeed change the incentives of the government (and the voters). With better information there is no reason either to renege on a fiscal rule or to ignore/ dismantle a council. A similar logic holds with respect to the identification of unsustainable booms, which should be in the interest of both voters and governments.

The continued functioning of a fiscal council is also beneficial for both the government and the electorate in the case when asymmetric information induces the government to try to signal competency through expenditure increases or tax cuts leading to pre-election deficits. The reason is that in a rational-expectations equilibrium it is impossible for the government to improve its re-election probability this way as its behaviour will be anticipated by voters, at the same time as it has an incentive to behave like this as long as it cannot directly affect expectations.[19] If a fiscal council can eliminate the informational asymmetry by providing the electorate with true information, there is no point for an incumbent government to try to signal competency through deficits. The re-election probability will be the same as in the asymmetric-information case but without a deficit. Hence a government which cares about both the welfare of citizens and its re-election chances is better-off in this situation. Therefore it has no incentive to dismantle the council.

But with other causes of deficit bias a government may indeed have incentives to ignore or dismantle a fiscal council that makes it harder to renege on a fiscal rule. This is the case if the explanation is political polarisation and electoral uncertainty, time inconsistency of fiscal policy or a desire to exploit future generations (again see Section 1). The only thing that can be said then is that the combination of reneging on a fiscal rule and ignoring/ dismantling a fiscal council likely entails a larger reputation cost than only reneging on a rule when there exists no council. But it is hard to know how great the difference is.

Experience indicates that governments have indeed tried to curtail the activities of fiscal councils. The Hungarian council was effectively abolished in 2010 after having criticised the government. After disagreements with the governments, councils had their budgets cut in Canada and Belgium and in Sweden there were threats of such cuts.[20] To reduce the risk of such interference, strong legal guarantees are important. They could include prohibitions on taking instructions from the government and for the government to give such instructions, a long-term budget providing sufficient resources commensurate with the remit, long and non-renewable periods of office for council members, appointment procedures stressing economic expertise, and guaranteed access to relevant fiscal information (see e.g. OECD 2014). The most important safeguard for a fiscal council is, however, likely to be a strong reputation among the general public for high-quality and politically impartial work. This could be helped by regular reviews of council work made by international experts.

How much difference will fiscal councils in the euro area make? As discussed, this depends on the relative importance of various causes of deficit bias, which we have little knowledge of. The discussion suggests that councils could make a difference. The most favourable case is when deficit bias depends on informational deficiencies. But even in this case it is, of course, implausible that a council could improve the situation so much that all deficit problems vanish.

5. Fiscal union

A recurrent theme in the discussion of the monetary union has been whether it needs to be complemented by *fiscal union*. This debate gained ground again during the euro crisis. There are different interpretations of fiscal union. Here the term is used somewhat vaguely to mean *much closer co-ordination* of fiscal policy at the EU level. According to the most radical proposals this would imply an 'economic government' in the euro area, possibly accountable to the European Parliament, with its own budget and/or powers in certain circumstances to take over decision-making on national budgets or at least to veto them.[21]

The discussion of fiscal union has followed two tracks. The first relates to joint guarantees of the public debt of individual euro area member states and the consequences for decision-making that this implies. The second track is related to fiscal transfer schemes to deal with asymmetric macroeconomic shocks.

When the euro crisis exploded, EU leaders chose to ignore the no-bail-out clause. Bail-outs took the form of both loans from newly constructed rescue funds and various interventions by the ECB (including actual purchases of government bonds, lending against bad collateral and commitments to unlimited further government bond purchases if proven necessary). Both types of support may ultimately result in large costs for tax payers in Germany and other eurozone countries not at the receiving end. The support implies great *moral-hazard risks*. The incentives to avoid large build-ups of government debt are weakened in the eurozone in general, if a borrowing country can expect others to service the debt if it has problems paying itself. The incentives for lenders to be cautious are also weakened, as the risk of not being re-paid is reduced when debt servicing becomes a European, and not only a national, issue.

The moral-hazard problem can be addressed by *centralising* decisions on government debt issuance to the European level or at least allowing it to veto national fiscal decisions that are considered to cause excessive debt levels. The arguments for this are even stronger if the euro area would move to *joint guarantees* of national debt. Many such proposals have been made in recent years, ranging from joint guarantees of all government debt to guarantees for only a portion of the debt, for example up to the 60 per cent of GDP debt ceiling.[22] The proponents have argued that such joint guarantees would rule out the emergence of 'bad' equilibria in situations where multiple equilibria are possible, thus avoiding defaults because expectations of them could be self-fulfilling as they raise government borrowing costs.[23]

The other track in the fiscal-union discussion stresses the need for a *fiscal transfer system* between euro area countries in the case of asymmetric macroeconomic shocks, i.e. diverging cyclical developments. This is an old discussion which started from the observation that within nation states region-specific shocks are counteracted by automatic fiscal transfers (mainly reductions in tax payments to the national level and increases in unemployment benefit payments). Such fiscal insurance could partly substitute for the absence of an own monetary policy in the case of country-specific shocks in the euro area.[24]

Today's EU budget is far too small – around 1 per cent of GDP – to be able to play such a role. The main budget posts are support to agriculture and regional development which are not suitable for this purpose. There are different ways of setting up a fiscal transfer mechanism. It would come about if there were a larger EU budget financed by EU-wide taxes. Another possibility is a system where fiscal transfers between national budgets are triggered based on differences in estimated output gaps.

Several recent proposals have instead focused on unemployment insurance. For instance, Dullien and Fichtner (2013) have advocated the establishment of a European unemployment insurance scheme. Employees would pay contributions to the scheme and receive benefits from it in the event of unemployment. This would result in automatic fiscal transfers that would immediately reach citizens with a high propensity to spend in countries facing a downturn.

There are two key issues in this context. The first concerns the distinction between *insurance* and *redistribution*. For the purpose of stabilisation it is insurance, i.e. transfers when macroeconomic developments in a country deviates from 'normal' that is desirable. Then transfers should rather be linked to deviations of unemployment from a moving average for the country in question rather than be based on the level of unemployment, which will differ among countries for structural reasons. Such an insurance scheme would not imply net transfers between countries over a longer time horizon. In contrast, a scheme based on unemployment levels could mean permanent redistribution.

A second issue is whether a fiscal transfer system should aim at mitigating all shocks (eliminating a certain percentage of them) or if it should instead be activated only in the case of very large shocks. Most proposals are of the first type. However, the need for insurance is much greater with 'catastrophic' shocks to income than with small shocks, as the effects on consumption in the former case can more easily be smoothed by variations in savings or borrowing. This is an argument for high coverage only above a certain threshold (deductible).[25] However, as catastrophic events are rare, such insurance will in all likelihood imply substantial redistribution among countries.

There does not seem to be political support for schemes involving redistribution, at least not *ex ante*. Proposals from both the President of the European Council (van Rompuy 2012) and the Commission (2012b) on a 'fiscal capacity' for the eurozone and joint guarantees for borrowing have been shelved by the heads of state and government in the Council on the initiative of Germany and other critical states around it.[26] With the strong support that anti-EU parties received in the elections to the European Parliament in 2014 it is indeed very difficult to see that any moves to more centralised fiscal decisions will be politically feasible within the foreseeable future.

This raises the question of whether the present trajectory of the eurozone is sustainable. An alternative would be to try to restore the no-bail-out clause. A credible such clause would mean that there would be earlier interest rate reactions to rising government debt in a member state, which would impose much stronger market discipline on national fiscal policy. This would reduce the need for centralisation of fiscal decisions. The main reason for ignoring the no-bail-out clause was fear of a systemic financial crisis if government defaults had been allowed. But the banking union could change that. With stricter supervision, better capitalised banks and bail-in provisions (implying that some liabilities of a bank in distress can be used for covering losses and recapitalisation) as well as sufficient resources for handling a banking crisis at the European level, individual governments could be left to take care of their own debts, and possibly to default, as originally envisaged in the no-bail out clause. The banking union in its present form does not, however, permit that. Resources in the resolution fund for banks will, also when the fund has reached the agreed size, be too small to handle a major bank crisis in Europe. A backstop with much larger resources than the earlier established rescue fund (ESM) – and with a changed focus to recapitalise banks instead of bailing out governments – would have to be created.

A full-fledged fiscal union does not seem politically feasible for a very long time to come – perhaps never – because citizens in the euro area are not prepared to relinquish national sovereignty regarding fiscal policy. However, a fiscal union – in the form of bail-outs – has already partly been established but without the logical counterparts in the form of common decision-making. This could make the eurozone dysfunctional in the long run. It remains to be seen whether EU leaders can revert to another politically more feasible track.

6. Conclusions

My main conclusions are:

- It is not surprising that the fiscal rules established with the start of the monetary union did not work as planned. This reflects several shortcomings of the original rules: too harsh sanctions to begin with which made politicians reluctant to use them; too much discretion on whether they should be used or not; too little emphasis on government debt and insufficient focus on preventing macroeconomic imbalances from arising in good times. At a more theoretical level, one should have expected the factors that explain deficit bias under discretionary decisions to lead to the flouting of rules once they had been adopted, i.e. to a time-inconsistency problem for the rules.

- Recent reforms of the economic governance in the eurozone have addressed several of the earlier shortcomings: sanctions can now be applied earlier and are more graduated, EU interventions against misbehaving countries have become more automatic, focus has increased on government debt and a procedure to identify macroeconomic imbalances in good times has been established. In addition, national fiscal frameworks have been strengthened according to common principles. Still, it is an open question whether this will be enough. The repeated-game character of EU supervision continues to provide incentives for finance ministers to be lenient against 'sinners', as this can be seen as an investment in lenient treatment of oneself in case of a similar contingency.

- Fiscal policy monitoring by independent national fiscal watchdogs, fiscal councils, has been introduced through EU-level agreements. This should strengthen the reputation costs for governments of violating the rules. To the extent that deficit bias depends on informational problems (fiscal illusion or over-optimism of both governments and electorates, asymmetric information between governments and electorates resulting in pre-election fiscal profligacy, or failures to recognise unsustainable boom situations), the activities of a fiscal council may serve to mitigate the underlying causes of the problem. If so, governments may be more time-consistent about fiscal councils than about rules. But experience suggests that governments are sometimes inclined to interfere with the activities of fiscal councils. They should therefore be given strong legal protection. They could likely make a contribution to better economic governance, but one should probably not expect too much from improved information.

- The moral-hazard problems created by the bail-outs of crisis countries could be overcome by more centralised fiscal decisions in the eurozone. Such fiscal union does not, however, seem politically feasible. There are sound arguments for a fiscal insurance system implying temporary transfers among eurozone states when cyclical developments differ, perhaps through a common unemployment insurance system. But such constructs also appear politically unfeasible because of fears that they would imply permanent redistribution among member states.

- It is an open question whether a monetary union where bail-outs of governments are part of the system is viable in the long run without centralised fiscal decision-making. Hence the political infeasibility of such centralisation is a threat to the long-run sustainability of the euro. This suggests that it might be better to try to restore the no-bail-out clause and rely more on the market to discipline fiscal policy. This would require that financial repercussions could arise from allowing government bankruptcies.

Notes

1 I am grateful for helpful comments from Niklas Frank, Erik Höglin and Hans Tson Söderström.
2 See e.g. Calmfors (2005), Morris *et al.* (2006), Debrun *et al.* (2009) and Calmfors and Wren-Lewis (2011) for brief reviews of the various explanations.
3 The academic starting point for the rules-versus-discretion discussion was the seminal contribution by Kydland and Prescott (1977). See also Kopits and Symansky (1998).
4 See Calmfors (2005) or EEAG (2006) for more detailed accounts of the breaches of the stability pact and its subsequent revision.
5 This problem was first discussed by McCallum (1995) and Jensen (1997) in the context of monetary policy and central bank independence. See Debrun (2011), Debrun *et al.* (2013) and Debrun and Kinda (2014) for applications to fiscal policy.
6 See Calmfors (2012).
7 For expositions of the two polar views, see, for example, De Grauwe (2011) and Sinn (2014), respectively.
8 European Commission (2012a, 2013) gives detailed accounts of the reforms. See also Calmfors (2012).
9 The reversed-qualified-majority stipulation does not apply, however, in the case of violations of the debt criterion.
10 It should be noted that international organisations like the IMF and the OECD failed to realise that both Ireland and Spain had unsustainable booms before the outbreak of the international financial crisis in 2008 and therefore judged these countries' cyclically adjusted fiscal balances to be in surplus.
11 Then the automatic reduction in the ratio of government debt to GDP that would otherwise follow from the rise in the denominator (GDP) is small. A falling government debt ratio must then be achieved through further improvements of the fiscal balance, which requires more austerity measures.
12 See Manasse (2015).
13 Hagermann (2010), Calmfors and Wren-Lewis (2011), Debrun *et al.* (2013), Lampreave (2013), and Debrun and Kinda (2014) provide surveys of existing fiscal councils.
14 These, and later, proposals are summarised in Calmfors (2003), Calmfors (2005) and Debrun *et al.* (2009).

15 See Alesina and Tabellini (2007). Some of the proposals sought, however, to address the redistribution issue by letting the independent fiscal agency only decide on the overall fiscal balance, but leaving it to the political system to determine how it would be achieved (Wyplosz 2005) or by confining the power of the agency to vary a specific tax around a base level (Ball 1997).

16 See Calmfors and Wren-Lewis (2011), Debrun *et al.* (2013), and Debrun and Kinda (2014).

17 Lampreave (2013) and Debrun *et al.* (2013) give references to the relevant legal documents.

18 These issues have been discussed by Calmfors and Wren-Lewis (2011), Debrun (2011) and Debrun and Kinda (2014).

19 The logic is similar to the one in the time inconsistency problem of discretionary monetary policy (Barro and Gordon 1983). In that case the monetary policy-maker optimises a loss function with inflation and unemployment (depending negatively on the difference between actual and expected inflation) as arguments, taking inflation expectations as given. This gives an inflation bias but without any reduction in unemployment, as agents in equilibrium rationally expect the government to create inflation. Similarly, an incumbent government that maximises a utility function with the consumption of citizens and its own expected future rents in the case of re-election as arguments, taking the deficit expected (perceived) by voters as given, could be subject to a deficit bias (Persson and Tabellini 2000, Section 4.5). This will be the case if the electorate cannot observe the true deficit and the re-election probability therefore depends on the difference between the actual and the expected (perceived) deficit, for example because this allows the government to 'deliver more' in terms of government consumption, which is taken as a signal of competency by voters. But in equilibrium the actual re-election chances are not increased, because voters rationally anticipate the deficit chosen. If voters, however, have perfect information about the deficit (or the governmnent's competency), the government has no incentive to choose a deficit.

20 See Kopits (2011), Calmfors and Wren-Lewis (2011), Calmfors (2013) and Debrun and Kinda (2014).

21 See, for example, Benassy-Quérè and Vallee (2014).

22 Fuest and Peichl (2012) and Schelkle (2012) provide overviews of different proposals.

23 See, for example, De Grauwe and Moesen (2009).

24 Majocchi and Rey (1993) and Pisani-Ferry (1993) are two early proposals.

25 The argument has been elaborated by Gros (2014).

26 This process is described by Hacker (2013).

References

Alesina, A. and Tabellini, G. (2007), Bureaucrats or Politicians? Part I: A Single Policy Task, *American Economic Review*, 97(1), 169–79.

Barro, R. and Gordon, D.B. (1983), A Positive Theory of Monetary Policy in a Natural Rate Model, *Journal of Political Economy*, 91(4), 589–610.

Ball, L. (1997), A Proposal for the Next Macroeconomic Reform, *Victoria Economic Commentaries,* 14(1) 1–7.

Calmfors, L (2003), Fiscal Policy to Stabilise the Domestic Economy in the EMU: What Can We Learn from Monetary Policy?, *CESifo Economic Studies*, 49(3), 319–53.

Calmfors, L. (2005), *What Remains of the Stability Pact and What Next?* Swedish Institute for European Policy Studies, Stockholm.

Calmfors, L. (2012), Can the Eurozone Develop into a Well-Functioning Fiscal Union, *CESifo Forum*, 13(1), 10–16.

Calmfors, L. (2013), Sweden – Watchdog with a Broad Remit, in Kopits, G. (ed) *Restoring Public Debt Sustainability: the Role of Independent Fiscal Institutions*, Oxford: Oxford University Press.

Calmfors, L. and Wren-Lewis, S. (2011), What Should Fiscal Councils Do? *Economic Policy*, 26(68), 649–95.

Debrun, X. (2011), Democratic Accountability, Deficit Bias and Independent Fiscal Agencies, *IMF Working Paper* 11/173.

Debrun, X., Hauner, D. and Kumar, M.S. (2009), Independent Fiscal Agencies, *Journal of Economic Surveys*, 23(1), 44–81.

Debrun, X., Kinda T., Curristine, T., Eyraud, L., Harris, J., and Seiwald, J. (2013), The Functions and Impact of Fiscal Councils, *IMF Policy Paper*, July.

Debrun, A. and Kinda, T. (2014), Strengthening Post-Crisis Fiscal Credibility: Fiscal Councils on the Rise – A New Dataset, *IMF Working Paper* 14/58.

De Grauwe, P. (2011), The European Central Bank: Lender of Last Resort in the Government Bond Market, *CESifo Working Paper* 3569.

De Grauwe, P. and Moesen, W. (2009), Gains for All: A Proposal for a Common Euro Bond, *Intereconomics*, 44(3), 132–41.

Dullien, S. and Fichtner, F. (2013), A Common Unemployment Insurance System for the Euro Area, *DIW Economic Bulletin*, 1/2013, 9–14.

EEAG (2006), *Report on the European Economy*, Munich: CESifo.

European Commission (2012a), Report on Public Finances in EMU, *European Economy*, 4/2012.

European Commission (2012b), Blueprint for a Deep and Genuine Economic and Monetary Union, Com/2012/0777, Brussels.

European Commission (2013), Report on Public Finances in EMU, *European Economy*, 4/2013.

Fuest, C. and Peichl, A. (2012), European Fiscal Union: What is it? Does It Work? Are There Really No Alternatives? *CESifo Forum*, 13(1), 3–9.

Gros, D. (2014), A Fiscal Shock Absorber for the Eurozone? Lessons from the Economics of Insurance, www.voxeu.org, 19 March.

Hacker, B. (2013), *On the Way to a Fiscal or Stability Union,* Friedrich Ebert Stiftung, December.

Hagermann, R. (2010), Improving Fiscal Performance through Fiscal Councils, OECD ECO/WKP(2010)85.

Jensen, H. (1997), Credibility of Optimal Monetary Delegation, *American Economic Review*, 87(5), 911–20.

Keuschnigg, C. (2012), Should Europe Become a Fiscal Union, *CESifo Forum*, 13(1), 35–43.

Kopits, G. (2011), Independent Fiscal Institutions: Developing Good Practices, *OECD Journal of Budgeting*, 11(3), 1–18.

Kopits, G. and Symansky, S. (1998), Fiscal Policy Rules, *IMF Occasional Paper* 162.

Kydland, F. and Prescott, E. (1977), Rules Rather than Discretion: The Inconsistency of Optimal Plans, *Journal of Political Economy*, 85(3), 473–91.

Lampreave, P. (2013), The New Regulatory Framework in the European Union and the Role of the Independent Fiscal Authority, *Bulletin for International Taxation*, November, 592–600.

Majocchi, A. and Rey, M. (1993), A Special Financial Support Scheme in Economic and Monetary Union. Need and Nature, *European Economy*, 5/1993, 457–80.

Manasse, P. (2015), The EU New Fiscal Flexibility Guidelines: An Assessment, www.voxeu.org, 27 January.

McCallum, B. (1995), Two Fallacies Concerning Central Bank Independence, *American Economic Review*, 85(2), 207–11.

Morris, R., Ongena, H. and Schuknecht, L. (2006), The Reform and Implementation of the Stability and Growth Pact, *ECB Occasional Paper* 47.

OECD (2014), *Recommendations of the Council on Principles for Independent Fiscal Institutions,* Paris.

Persson, T. and Tabellini, G. (2000), *Political Economics*, Cambridge, MA: MIT Press.

Pisani-Ferry, J., Italianer, A., and Lescure, R. (1993), Stabilization Properties of Budgetary Systems: A Simulation Analysis, *European Economy*, 5/1993.

Schelkle, W. (2012), European Fiscal Union: From Monetary Back Door to Parliamentary Main Entrance, *CESifo Forum*, 13(1), 28–34.

Sinn, H.-W. (2014), Responsibilities of States and Central Banks in the Euro Crisis, *CESifo Forum*, 15(1), 3–36.

van Rompuy, H. (2012), Towards a Genuine Monetary and Economic Union, Report by the President of the European Council, 26 June, Brussels.

Wyplosz, C. (2005), Fiscal Policy: Institutions versus Rules, *National Institute Economic Review*, 191(1), 64–78.

PART IV

Trade issues

12

EUROPEAN INTEGRATION AND THE GAINS FROM TRADE

Gianmarco I.P. Ottaviano[1]

1. Introduction

The aim of this chapter is to discuss whether and how an important class of theoretical models, which have been increasingly used to quantify the gains from trade in counterfactual scenarios, can be fruitfully applied to quantify the trade-related welfare effects of further European integration. For lack of a better name, these models will be called 'new quantitative trade models' (henceforth, simply NQTMs), with the understanding that, whereas the models themselves may not be all that new, the novelty resides in the recent formal comprehension of their common policy-relevant implications.

Since the beginning of the century, the field of international trade has become increasingly quantitative due to two major developments. First, thanks to the easier accessibility of individual datasets and to the higher computing power needed to process them, there has been a surge of empirical works studying *ex post* the implications of firms' and workers' heterogeneity for the sources, the patterns and the gains from trade. Second, thanks again to higher computing power, the calibration and the simulation of statistical models have increasingly been used to investigate *ex ante* the implications of trade policies in counterfactual scenarios for which data are necessarily unavailable.

The idea of using mathematical or statistical models to simulate the effects of counterfactual scenarios has a long tradition (Baldwin and Venables, 1995). In particular, 'Computable general equilibrium' (CGE) models remain a cornerstone of trade policy evaluation (Piermartini and Teh, 2005), having also contributed to the design of advanced softwares for their numerical solution such as GAMS or GEMPACK. To this tradition NQTMs contribute a tighter connection between theory and data thanks to more appealing micro-theoretical foundations and careful estimation of the structural parameters necessary for counterfactual analysis (Costinot and Rodriguez-Clare, 2014).

The trailblazer NQTM is arguably the statistical model proposed and structurally estimated by Eaton and Kortum (2002) to quantify the effects of trade liberalization and technological progress in 19 OECD countries. However, by assuming perfect competition, the Eaton-Kortum model does not speak directly to the parallel research line based on individual heterogeneity, of which the main theoretical reference is, instead, Melitz (2003). Introducing heterogeneous firms in the monopolistic competitive model of Krugman (1980), the Melitz model provides a theoretical framework consistent with several stylized facts highlighted by the analysis of firm-level datasets, but its initial applications did not include counterfactual simulations. Early attempts at bridging the two lines of research can be found in Bernard, Eaton, Jensen and Kortum (2003) and Del Gatto, Mion and Ottaviano (2006). On the one side, Bernard et al. (2003) extend the Eaton-Kortum model by introducing heterogeneous firms under oligopostic price competition. The extended Eaton-Kortum model is consistent with fewer stylized facts than the Melitz model but has the merit of pushing the NQTM agenda one step further. On the other hand, Del Gatto et al. (2006), followed up by Corcos, Del Gatto, Mion and Ottaviano (2012), simulate counterfactual scenarios for European integration through a quantitative Melitz model as enriched by Melitz and Ottaviano (2008). Both Bernard et al. (2003) and Corcos et al. (2012) are firmly grounded in the macroeconomic methodology of 'calibration, validation and simulation'. Calibration requires the values of the theoretical parameters to be set such that the model matches some key moments of the data. Validation requires the calibrated model to be able to match other moments of the data different from those used for calibrating. Simulation of counterfactual scenarios can be reasonably performed only if the calibrated model passes the validation checks.

Building on previous theoretical work by Arkolakis, Costinot and Rodriguez-Clare (2012a), Costinot and Rodriguez-Clare (2014) provide the most accomplished attempt at fully bridging NQTMs and firm-level analysis so far. Arkolakis et al. (2012a) are often quoted for showing theoretically that firm heterogeneity is not that important when one is interested in evaluating aggregate gains from trade. Whether they actually do so is debated (Melitz and Redding, 2013). What they do show is, instead, that all models in a specific class share the same predicted 'gains from trade' (defined as welfare with trade relative to welfare with autarky), conditional on the changes in two aggregate statistics: the observed share of domestic expenditure and an estimate of the trade elasticity.[2] These models have four primitive assumptions in common: (a) Dixit-Stiglitz preferences; (b) one factor of production; (c) linear cost functions; (d) perfect or monopolistic competition. They also share three common macro-level restrictions: (a) trade is balanced; (b) aggregate profits are a constant share of aggregate revenues; (c) the import demand system exhibits constant elasticity of substitution (CES). As this set of assumptions is extremely restrictive, one would be forgiven for dismissing the finding by Arkolakis et al. (2012a) as some sort of 'impossibility theorem' with very limited practical relevance. What makes, instead, their finding important is that some of the most popular trade models do satisfy those restrictive assumptions, from the workhorse CGE model by Armington (1969) to the hallmark 'new trade theory' model by Krugman (1980), to the already cited NQTM by Eaton and Kortum (2002) and several variations of the model by Melitz (2003) though not necessarily its original version. In this respect, the main contribution of Arkolakis et al. (2012a) is indeed to theoretically define the class of NQTMs, paving the way to their subsequent empirical implementation by Costinot and Rodriguez-Clare (2014).

The next sections provide a streamlined presentation of some key insights highlighted by Costinot and Rodriguez-Clare (2014), to which the reader is referred for additional details. In particular, Sections 2 and 3 derive the key equations of the Armington model showing how a simple NQTM works as a 'user guide' to possible implementation by the interested reader. Section 4 uses the simple NQTM to evaluate the gains from trade for selected EU countries by comparing the status quo to counterfactual autarky. Apart from being a very peculiar counterfactual, the autarky example also has the limit of not fully exploiting the structure of the model. Subsequent sections therefore present richer counterfactuals. Specifically, Section 5 uses the Armington model to quantify the damages EU countries would suffer from a counterfactual protectionist policy enacted by the US.

Section 6 looks at a counterfactual worldwide protectionist policy to discuss how the predicted welfare changes vary going for the Armington model to richer NQTMs. Section 7 provides a concrete example of how NQTMs can be used to inform the policy debate on the future of European integration, in particular on the possible exit of the UK from the EU (so called 'Brexit').

Section 8 concludes highlighting three main challenges for the use of NQTMs for policy analysis in Europe and beyond. First, the single most delicate choice for policy applications appears to be the one of market structure. As shown by Costinot and Rodriguez-Clare (2014), some cross-country predictions may change dramatically going from perfect to monopolistic competition. Second, current NQTMs do not allow for the 'dynamic' effects of policy intervention on economic growth, through more competition, innovation and adoption of new technologies. Third, the validation of calibrated models before simulating them has increasingly gone missing as recent works tend to favour the implementation of 'exactly identified' NQTMs. These are models in which the number of free parameters to be calibrated equals the number of observed moments of the data, and hence yield a trivially perfect fit. Can simulation based on tautology really help policy design?

2. A simple quantitative trade model

Following Costinot and Rodriguez-Clare (2014), the main components and the working of NQTMs can be usefully illustrated through a simple Armington model.

The economy consists of n countries, indexed $i = 1, \ldots, n$, with each country supplying its own distinct good. There are thus n goods, also indexed $i = 1, \ldots, n$, with country i being the only supplier of good i in fixed quantity Q_i, which corresponds to the country's endowment of the good.

Preferences in country j are captured by a representative consumer with Dixit-Stiglitz utility function:

$$C_j = \left[\sum_{i=1}^{n} \left(\frac{C_{ij}}{\psi_{ij}} \right)^{\frac{\sigma-1}{\sigma}} \right]^{\frac{\sigma}{\sigma-1}} \tag{1}$$

where C_{ij} is country j's consumption of the good supplied by country i, $\psi_{ij} > 0$ is an inverse measure of the appeal of this good for country j, and $\sigma > 1$ is the CES between goods supplied by different countries. According to (1), utility can be interpreted as the level of consumption of an aggregate composite ('quantity index') of the various goods whose 'price index' is

$$P_j = \left[\sum_{i=1}^{n} (\psi_{ij} P_{ij})^{1-\sigma} \right]^{\frac{1}{1-\sigma}} \tag{2}$$

where P_{ij} is the price of good i in country j. Denoting aggregate expenditure by E_j, the price and quantity indices satisfy $P_j C_j = \sum_{i=1}^{n} P_{ij} C_{ij} = E_j$, which is the representative consumer's budget constraint. Utility (1) can then be equivalently rewritten as

$$C_j = \frac{E_j}{P_j} \tag{3}$$

which identifies real expenditure as a measure of country j's welfare.

External trade between countries is subject to trade costs, consisting of frictional and tariff barriers. Frictions are of the *iceberg* type: country i has to ship $\tau_{ij} \geq 1$ units of its good for one unit to reach country j. Tariff barriers are of the *ad-valorem* type with $t_{ij} \geq 0$ denoting the tariff imposed by country j on imports from country i. There are, instead, no trade costs for internal trade: $\tau_{jj} = \tau'_{jj} = 1$ and $t_{jj} = t'_{jj} = 0$.

Markets are perfectly competitive and perfect arbitrage implies that the price of a good at destination equals its price at the origin once trade costs are taken into account: $P_{ij} = (1 + t_{ij})\,\tau_{ij}\,P_{ii}$. This in turn implies that a country's income equals the country's good endowment times its domestic price: $Y_i = P_{ii}Q_i$. Hence, the price at destination satisfies

$$P_{ij} = \frac{\phi_{ij} Y_i}{Q_i} \tag{4}$$

Where $\phi_{ij} \equiv (1 + t_{ij})\tau_{ij}$ denotes the trade costs from country i to country j.

Given (1), utility maximization under the representative consumer's budget constraint determines the value of country j's imports from country i inclusive of the associated tariff revenue

$$X_{ij} = \left(\frac{\psi_{ij} P_{ij}}{P_j}\right)^{1-\sigma} E_j \tag{5}$$

with $E_j = \sum_{i=1}^{n} X_{ij}$. By (2) and (5), the share of expenditure of country j on imports from country i evaluates to

$$\lambda_{ij} = \frac{X_{ij}}{E_j} = \left(\frac{\psi_{ij} P_{ij}}{P_j}\right)^{1-\sigma} = \frac{(\phi_{ij} Y_i)^{-\epsilon}(Q_i/\psi_{ij})^{\epsilon}}{\sum_{i=1}^{n}(\phi_{ij} Y_i)^{-\epsilon}(Q_i/\psi_{ij})^{\epsilon}} \tag{6}$$

where $\epsilon \equiv (X_{ij}/X_{jj})/\tau_{ij} = \sigma - 1$ denotes the 'trade elasticity': the elasticity of imports relative to domestic demand X_{ij}/X_{jj} with respect to bilateral trade costs ϕ_{ij} holding income levels constant. Given (6), equation (5) can be then restated as a standard 'gravity equation'

$$X_{ij} = \lambda_{ij} E_j = \frac{(\phi_{ij} Y_i)^{-\epsilon}(Q_i/\psi_{ij})^{\epsilon}}{\sum_{i=1}^{n}(\phi_{ij} Y_i)^{-\epsilon}(Q_i/\psi_{ij})^{\epsilon}} E_j \tag{7}$$

which expresses the bilateral trade flow from i to j as a function of characteristics of the country of origin (Y_i and Q_i) characteristics of the country of destination (E_j), and bilateral obstacles (ϕ_{ij} and ψ_{ij}).

In equilibrium expenditure equals income plus tariff revenue

$$E_j = Y_j + T_j \tag{8}$$

with

$$T_j = \sum_{i=1}^{n} \frac{t_{ij}}{1+t_{ij}} X_{ij} \tag{9}$$

and

$$Y_j = \sum_{j=1}^{n} \frac{1}{1+t_{ij}} X_{ij} \tag{10}$$

where $X_{ij}/(1 + t_{ij})$ is the tax base. By (6) the share of tariff revenue in country j's expenditure can be expressed as

$$\pi_j = \frac{T_j}{E_j} = \sum_{i=1}^{n} \frac{t_{ij}}{1 + t_{ij}} \lambda_{ij} \tag{11}$$

which allows one to use (8) to state country j's total expenditure as a function of its income

$$E_j = \frac{Y_j}{1 - \pi_j} \tag{12}$$

Plugged together with (7) into (10), (12) implies that good i's market clears as long as

$$Y_i = \sum_{j=1}^{n} \frac{1}{1 + t_{ij}} \frac{\left(\phi_{ij} Y_i\right)^{-\epsilon} \left(Q_i / \psi_{ij}\right)^{\epsilon}}{\sum_{i=1}^{n} \left(\phi_{ij} Y_i\right)^{-\epsilon} \left(Q_i / \psi_{ij}\right)^{\epsilon}} \frac{Y_j}{1 - \pi_j} \tag{13}$$

holds. After using (11) and (6) to substitute π_j with an expression in which income levels are the only endogenous variables, for $i = 1, \ldots, n$, (13) generates a system of n equations in n unknowns that can be solved for the equilibrium income levels $Y = \{Y_i\}$. However, as by Walras' Law, one of those equations is redundant, income levels can be determined only up to a constant pinned down by the choice of the numéraire good. Having determined the equilibrium income levels, the corresponding bilateral prices and price indices $P = \{P_{ij}\}$ can be recovered from (4) and (2) respectively. With the price information at hand, trade flows $X = \{X_{ij}\}$ and expenditures $E = \{E_j\}$ can then be obtained from (5) and $E_j = \sum_{i=1}^{n} X_{ij}$. This also provides information required to compute expenditure shares $\lambda = \{\lambda_{ij}\}$ from (6) and tax revenue shares $\pi = \{\pi_i\}$ from (11). Finally, knowing prices and expenditures, welfare $C = \{C_j\}$ can be measured from (3). This concludes the description of the model and its equilibrium solution.

3. Welfare effects of trade integration

How does trade integration affect national welfare? To answer this question one has to assess what happens to C when trade costs change from actual levels $\phi = \{\phi_{ij}\}$ to counterfactual levels $\phi' = \{\phi'_{ij}\}$. The main insights of Arkolakis et al. (2012a) is that changes in the real expenditure of a country j can be readily computed using only few statistics: the trade elasticity (ϵ) and the changes in the country's shares of expenditure across goods (from $\lambda = \{\lambda_{ij}\}$ to $\lambda' = \{\lambda'_{ij}\}$).

To see this, one needs first to derive three preliminary results on the effects of an infinitesimal change in trade costs. First, given (2), partially differentiating P_j with respect to P_{ij} yields

$$\frac{\partial P_j}{\partial P_{ij}} = \left[\sum_{i=1}^{n} (\psi_{ij} P_{ij})^{1-\sigma}\right]^{\frac{\sigma}{1-\sigma}} (\psi_{ij})^{1-\sigma} (P_{ij})^{-\sigma} = \left(\frac{\psi_{ij} P_{ij}}{P_j}\right)^{1-\sigma} \frac{P_j}{P_{ij}}$$

which, by (5), can be rewritten as

$$\frac{\partial P_j}{\partial P_{ij}} = \frac{X_{ij}}{E_j} \frac{P_j}{P_{ij}}$$

implying the total differential

$$d \ln P_j = \sum_{i=0}^{n} \lambda_{ij} d \ln P_{ij} \tag{14}$$

This change in country j's price index can be further broken down into changes of domestic and import prices as

$$d \ln P_j = \lambda_{jj} d \ln P_{jj} + (1 - \lambda_{jj}) d \ln P_j^M \tag{15}$$

where

$$P_j^M = \left[\sum_{i \neq j} (\psi_{ij} P_{ij})^{1-\sigma} \right]^{\frac{1}{1-\sigma}}$$

is the component of P_j associated with imports, and

$$d \ln P_j^M = \frac{1}{1 - \lambda_{jj}} \sum_{i \neq j} \lambda_{ij} d \ln P_{ij}$$

is its variation. Second, (6) and (5) imply

$$\frac{\lambda_{jj}}{1 - \lambda_{jj}} = \left(\frac{\psi_{jj} P_{jj}}{\psi_{ij} P_j^M} \right)^{1-\sigma} = \left(\frac{\psi_{jj}}{\psi_{ij}} \right)^{1-\sigma} \left(\frac{P_{jj}}{P_j^M} \right)^{1-\sigma}$$

which can be totally differentiated to obtain

$$d \ln P_j^M = d \ln P_{jj} + \frac{1}{1 - \sigma} \left[d \ln(1 - \lambda_{jj}) - d \ln \lambda_{jj} \right] \tag{16}$$

Third, the fact that expenditure shares sum up to one requires

$$\lambda_{jj} + (1 - \lambda_{jj}) = 1$$

the total differentiation of which leads to

$$(1 - \lambda_{jj}) d \ln (1 - \lambda_{jj}) = -\lambda_{jj} d \ln \lambda_{jj} \tag{17}$$

Then, plugging (16) and (17) into (15) gives

$$d \ln P_j = d \ln P_{jj} - \frac{1}{1 - \sigma} d \ln \lambda_{jj} \tag{18}$$

so that the change in country j's real expenditure $C_j = E_j/P_j$ can be written as

$$d \ln C_j = d \ln E_j - d \ln P_j = d \ln E_j - d \ln P_{jj} - \frac{1}{1 - \sigma} d \ln \lambda_{jj} \tag{19}$$

This expression can be further simplified recalling that there are no internal trade costs $(\tau_{jj} = \tau'_{jj} = 1$ and $t_{jj} = t'_{jj} = 0)$ and trade must balance $(Y_j = (1 - \pi_j)E_j)$. Under these conditions, (4) implies $P_{jj}Q_j = Y_j = (1 - \pi_j)E_j$ and thus $d \ln E_j - d \ln P_{jj} = -d \ln (1 - \pi_j)$ since Q_j is a fixed endowment. Given $\epsilon = \sigma - 1$, (19) finally becomes

$$d \ln C_j = -d \ln(1 - \pi_j) - \frac{1}{\epsilon} d \ln \lambda_{jj} \qquad (20)$$

which shows that the welfare change $d \ln C_j$ is driven by the changes in the expenditure share of tariff revenue π_j and in the expenditure share on the domestic good λ_{jj}.

Expression (20) holds only for infinitesimal changes in trade costs, which tend to be of little practical relevance. Nevertheless, it can be readily integrated to characterize the welfare effects of discrete changes. This yields

$$\hat{C}_j = \frac{1 - \pi_j}{1 - \pi'_j} \left(\hat{\lambda}_{jj} \right)^{-\frac{1}{\epsilon}} \qquad (21)$$

where the share of tariff revenues in the actual and counterfactual equilibria are given by

$$\pi_j = \sum_{i=1}^{n} \frac{t_{ij}}{1 + t_{ij}} \lambda_{ij} \text{ and } \pi'_j = \sum_{i=1}^{n} \frac{t'_{ij}}{1 + t'_{ij}} \lambda_{ij} \hat{\lambda}_{ij}$$

Hence, the welfare consequences of any arbitrary change in trade costs can indeed be computed based only on few sufficient statistics: the trade elasticity and the change in the shares of expenditure across goods.

However, knowing that only few sufficient statistics are needed to compute the welfare effects of trade integration would be of little use unless we had a consistent way of identifying the values of those statistics in the counterfactual scenario. This is clearly not much of a problem for the trade elasticity ϵ, which, given utility (1), is constant by assumption. It may look more of a problem for the counterfactual expenditure shares $\lambda' = \{\lambda'_{ij}\}$. Luckily, the structure of the model lends a hand.

Consider (6). As ψ_{ij} is constant, taking log changes gives

$$d \ln \lambda_{ij} = d \ln (P_{ij})^{1-\sigma} - d \ln(P_j)^{1-\sigma}$$

which, by (14), can be rewritten as

$$d \ln \lambda_{ij} = d \ln(P_{ij})^{1-\sigma} - \sum_{i=0}^{n} \lambda_{ij} d \ln (P_{ij})^{1-\sigma} \qquad (22)$$

As Q_i is also constant, (4) implies

$$d \ln(P_{ij})^{1-\sigma} = d \ln \left(\phi_{ij} Y_i \right)^{1-\sigma}$$

which allows one to restate (22) as

$$d \ln \lambda_{ij} = d \ln \left(\phi_{ij} Y_i \right)^{1-\sigma} - \sum_{i=0}^{n} \lambda_{ij} d \ln \left(\phi_{ij} Y_i \right)^{1-\sigma}$$

for infinitesimal changes, or, by integration, as

$$\hat{\lambda}_{ij} = \frac{\left(\hat{\phi}_{ij} \hat{Y}_i \right)^{-\epsilon}}{\sum_{l=0}^{n} \lambda_{lj} \left(\hat{\phi}_{ij} \hat{Y}_l \right)^{-\epsilon}} \qquad (23)$$

for discrete changes given $\epsilon = \sigma - 1$.

In the counterfactual equilibrium, (6), (12) and (10) further imply

$$Y_j' = \sum_{i=1}^{n} \frac{1}{1+t_{ij}'} \lambda_{ij}' \frac{Y_i'}{1-\pi_i'}$$

which can be rewritten as

$$\hat{Y}_j Y_j = \sum_{i=1}^{n} \frac{1}{1+t_{ij}'} \hat{\lambda}_{ij} \lambda_{ij} \hat{Y}_i \frac{Y_i}{1-\pi_i'}$$

so that using (23) to substitute for $\hat{\lambda}_{ij}$ yields

$$\hat{Y}_j Y_j = \sum_{i=1}^{n} \frac{1}{1+t_{ij}'} \frac{\lambda_{ij}\left(\hat{\phi}_{ij}\hat{Y}_i\right)^{-\epsilon}}{\sum_{l=0}^{n} \lambda_{lj}\left(\hat{\phi}_{lj}\hat{Y}_l\right)^{-\epsilon}} \frac{\hat{Y}_i Y_i}{1-\pi_i'} \tag{24}$$

The share of tariff revenues in the counterfactual equilibrium is itself given by

$$\pi_i' = \sum_{i=1}^{n} \frac{t_{ij}'}{1+t_{ij}'} \lambda_{ij}' = \sum_{i=1}^{n} \frac{t_{ij}'}{1+t_{ij}'} \hat{\lambda}_{ij} \lambda_{ij}$$

which, by (23), becomes

$$\pi_i' = \sum_{i=1}^{n} \frac{t_{ij}'}{1+t_{ij}'} \frac{\lambda_{ij}\left(\hat{\phi}_{ij}\hat{Y}_i\right)^{-\epsilon}}{\sum_{l=0}^{n} \lambda_{lj}\left(\hat{\phi}_{ij}\hat{Y}_l\right)^{-\epsilon}} \tag{25}$$

After using (25) to substitute for π_i', (24) generates a system of n equations in n unknown income changes that can be solved for the counterfactual $\hat{Y} = \{\hat{Y}_i\}$ (up to a normalization due the choice of the numeràire good). As the system does not depend directly on the utility parameters $\psi = \{\psi_{ij}\}$ and the endowments $Q = \{Q_i\}$, changes in factor income levels $\hat{Y} = \{\hat{Y}_i\}$ can be determined using only the initial expenditure shares $\lambda = \{\lambda_{ij}\}$, the initial income levels $Y = \{Y_i\}$, and the trade elasticity ϵ. Once the changes in income $\hat{Y}$ have been solved for, the changes in expenditure shares $\hat{\lambda} = \{\hat{\lambda}_{ij}\}$ and the counterfactual tax revenues $\pi' = \{\pi_i'\}$ can be obtained from (23) and (25) respectively. Plugging them into (21) finally determines the welfare change $\hat{C}_j$ in the counterfactual scenario. Hence, the welfare effects of trade cost changes can be evaluated estimating only the trade elasticity and not all the structural parameters of the model.

4. Gains from trade

The counterfactual proposed by Arkolakis et al. (2012a) to assess the contribution of actual trade to welfare is an autarkic scenario in which frictional barriers are prohibitive: $\phi_{ij}' = +\infty$ for all $i \neq j$. In this scenario, domestic goods absorb all expenditures, implying $\lambda_{jj}' = 1$ and thus, $\hat{\lambda}_{jj} = 1/\lambda_{jj}$, and there are no tariff revenues, implying $\pi_j' = 0$. Gains from trade for country j can be measured by the percentage fall in real expenditure due to moving from the actual situation to counterfactual autarky. Using (21) together with $\hat{\lambda}_{jj} = 1/\lambda_{jj}$ and $\pi_j' = 0$ gives

$$G_j = 1 - \hat{C}_j = 1 - \frac{1 - \pi_j}{1 - \pi'_j} (\hat{\lambda}_{jj})^{-\frac{1}{\epsilon}} = 1 - (1 - \pi_j)(\lambda_{jj})^{\frac{1}{\epsilon}} \tag{26}$$

which shows that for this specific counterfactual there is no need to solve the system of equations (24) as λ_{jj} is the observed expenditure share of the domestic good, π_j is the observed expenditure share of tariff revenue, and the trade elasticity ϵ can be estimated from a cross-sectional gravity regression based on (7). In particular, taking (7) in logs and using $P_{ii} = Y_i / Q_i$ gives

$$\ln X_{ij} = \ln(P_{ii})^{-\epsilon} + \ln \frac{E_j}{\sum_{i=1}^{n}(\phi_{ij} Y_i)^{-\epsilon}(Q_i / \psi_{ij})^{\epsilon}} - \epsilon \ln(\phi_{ij}) + \ln(\psi_{ij})^{-\epsilon} \tag{27}$$

which can be empirically implemented treating the first term on the right hand side as an exporter fixed-effect, the second term as an importer fixed-effect, and the fourth term as measurement error in trade flows orthogonal to (ϕ_{ij}) in the third term. Using fixed effects yields a consistent estimate of the trade elasticity ϵ as discussed by Head and Mayer (2014), whose equation (31) embeds (27). Their Table 5 reports the findings of 32 gravity papers that estimate trade cost elasticities. It highlights a large variation in the point estimates with a standard deviation twice as large as the mean. A substantial part of this variation comes from methodological differences across papers. Head and Mayer (2014) choose 5.03 as their preferred estimate, corresponding to the median coefficient obtained using country fixed effects and tariffs for ϕ_{ij}.

Building on Head and Mayer (2014), the rounded value $\epsilon = 5$ is used by Costinot and Rodriguez-Clare (2014) to evaluate G_j for a set of 27 EU countries and 13 other major countries with data on $X = \{X_{ij}\}$ drawn from the World Input-Output Database (WIOD) in 2008 (Timmer, 2012). The results of their computations based on (26) are reported in the first column of their Table 1 $\pi_j = 0$ where is assumed for simplicity. This assumption is motivated by the fact that, despite large trade flows, actual tariff revenues typically account only for a negligible share of aggregate expenditures, at least in the case of most OECD countries. Given (9), $\pi_j = 0$ for positive X_{ij} requires $t_{ij} = 0$.

Figure 12.1 describes the gains from trade for 20 selected EU countries – Costinot and Rodriguez-Clare (2014) place the remaining seven EU members in a residual category comprising both EU and non-EU countries. Percentage gains from trade are measured along the vertical axis and countries are arranged from left to right in decreasing order of gains from trade along the horizontal one. The flat dashed line represents average trade gains at 5.27 per cent. Different fill patterns identify different groups of countries: Southern countries (Greece, Italy, Portugal, Spain) are identified by a checkered fill; Eastern countries (Czech Republic, Hungary, Poland, Romania, Slovakia, Slovenia) by a blank fill; Northern countries (Denmark, Finland, Great Britain, Ireland, Sweden) by a diagonal fill, and Western countries (Austria, Belgium, France, Germany, Netherlands) by a solid fill. All countries are in grey except for the four largest countries that are in black.

The figure shows that: (i) gains from trade are positive for all countries; (ii) all Southern countries and all the largest countries enjoy lower than average gains from trade; (iii) above average gains from trade mostly benefit small non-Southern countries; (iv) within all geographical groups gains from trade fall with country size. Overall, gains from trade tend, therefore, to be smaller for larger or more peripheral countries. The reason is that these countries tend to have larger λ_{jj} since they buy relatively more from themselves. As ϵ is the same for all countries, by (26) larger λ_{jj} translates into smaller computed gains from trade.

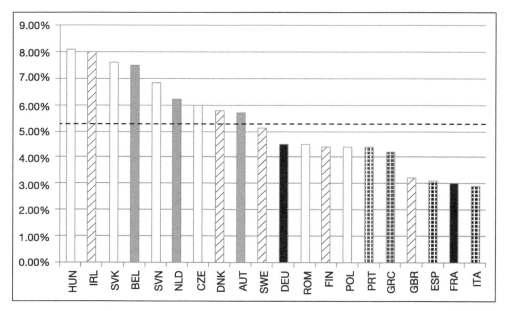

Figure 12.1 Gains from trade for selected EU countries

Source: Author's elaboration based on percentage gains from Table 1 in Costinot and Rodriguez-Clare (2014).

5. Fortress Europe

Using autarky as a counterfactual scenario makes the calculation of the changes in expenditure shares $\hat{\lambda} = \{\hat{\lambda}_{ij}\}$ straightforward. But this is a very specific case. In other scenarios, calculating $\hat{\lambda} = \{\hat{\lambda}_{ij}\}$ requires first solving (24) and (25) for the counterfactual changes in incomes $\hat{Y} = \{\hat{Y}_i\}$. As an example, one can follow again Costinot and Rodriguez-Clare (2014) who consider a counterfactual scenario in which the US unilaterally imposes an import tariff of 40 per cent on all its trading partners: $t'_{IUS} = 0.4$ for any country i other than the US. They point out that this is close to the tariff level observed in the US in the late-nineteenth and early-twentieth centuries.

The welfare changes caused by the 40 per cent tariff in each trading partner of the US are reported in Column 1 of their Table 2. Based on their computations, Figure 12.2 describes the welfare change $\hat{C}_j$ from US protectionism for 19 of the 20 EU countries appearing in Figure 12.1. The excluded country is Ireland. As its welfare loss of 0.91 per cent is more than four times larger than the welfare loss of any other country, its inclusion in Figure 12.2 would have blurred the cross-country variation of welfare changes. Percentage welfare losses are measured (in absolute value) along the vertical axis and countries are ranked from left to right in decreasing order of welfare loss along the horizontal one. The flat dashed line at 0.10 per cent corresponds to the average welfare loss across the selected 19 countries. The different fill patterns have the same interpretation as in Figure 12.1.

The figure shows that: (i) all countries face welfare losses due to US protectionism; (ii) all Southern countries and all Eastern countries except Hungary suffer lower than average welfare losses; (iii) above average welfare losses are mostly concentrated in Northern and Western countries; (iv) all the largest countries besides Germany suffer below average welfare losses. Most of the difference in the group rankings between Figures 12.1 and 12.2 is driven

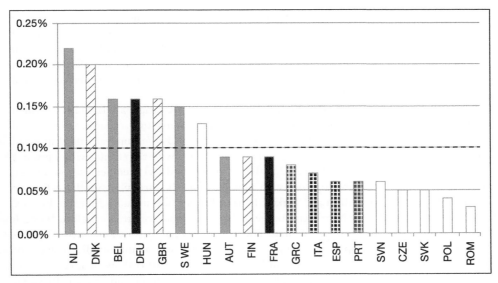

Figure 12.2 Welfare losses from US protectionism for selected EU countries

Source: Author's elaboration based on percentage losses from Table 2 in Costinot and Rodriguez-Clare (2014).

by the shift of Eastern countries from left to right, which reflects the disproportionate orientation of their trade towards EU partners rather than towards the US.

6. Robustness

The Armington model is useful but also too simple. The key insight of Arkolakis et al. (2012a) is that the methodology illustrated in the Armington case can be readily applied to all NQTMs, defined as models that share four primitive assumptions (Dixit-Stiglitz preferences, one factor of production, linear cost functions, perfect competition or monopolistic competition) as well as three macro-level restrictions (balanced trade, aggregate profits as a constant share of aggregate revenues, CES import demand system).

In discussing these issues Costinot and Rodriguez-Clare (2014) show that, when NQTMs feature only one sector, a strong equivalence result holds: conditional on given counterfactual changes in expenditure shares $\hat{\lambda} = \{\hat{\lambda}_{ij}\}$ and the same trade elasticity ϵ, alternative NQTMs must predict the same welfare changes as the Armington model. This does not imply, however, that different models necessarily yield the same predictions on the counterfactual changes in expenditure shares caused by any given policy experiment. It does not imply either that the strong equivalence survives the introduction of additional real world features such as multiple sectors, tradable intermediate goods and multiple factors of production. Hence, the same policy shock may be predicted to have different welfare effects depending on the specific NQTM the analysis relies on.

As a first example one can reconsider the gains from trade. Costinot and Rodriguez-Clare (2014; Table 1) show that introducing multiple sectors and intermediate goods leads to substantial increases in the gains from trade for given trade shares. In the case of perfect competition, introducing multiple sectors increases average gains from trade for our EU countries from the baseline 5.27 per cent reported in Figure 12.1 to 20.10 per cent.

Considering also intermediate goods further increases average gains to 33.78 per cent or 34.83 per cent depending on the chosen measure of intermediate good shares. The effect of intermediate goods (but not of multiple sectors) is amplified under monopolistic competition *à la* Krugman (1980): gains from trade evaluate to 19.11 per cent with multiple sectors and 41.62 per cent with the addition of intermediate goods; they rise to 48.70 per cent when firm heterogeneity is also considered as in Melitz (2003).

Another example can be found in Table 3 of Costinot and Rodriguez-Clare (2014), which compares the predictions of different models for a third counterfactual scenario: a generalized protectionistic surge leading to a 40 per cent increase in worldwide import tariffs. European Countries are sorted into the usual four geographical groups (with zero tariffs within groups) but, differently from Figures 12.1 and 12.2, the list of selected EU members is now longer, and EU countries are bundled together with non-EU ones. In particular: Southern Europe now includes also Cyprus, Malta and Turkey; Eastern Europe also includes Bulgaria, Estonia, Latvia, Lithuania and Russia; Northern Europe includes the same countries as before; Western Europe includes also Luxemburg. Welfare effects are computed for alternative NQTMs featuring perfect or monopolistic competition, with or without intermediates, with or without heterogeneous firms. Costinot and Rodriguez-Clare (2014) show that, consistently across models, the worldwide tariff increase reduces welfare in all countries, with larger average losses predicted by models with monopolistic competition and intermediate goods.

While focusing on averages is interesting, looking at the correlations between countries' losses across models is also important for assessing how sensitive predictions are to model specification. For the 40 per cent increase in worldwide import tariffs, these correlations are reported in Table 12.1. The large correlation between columns 1 and 4 (perfect competition) as well as between columns 2, 3, 5 and 6 (monopolistic competition) show that predictions are fairly robust when alternative models keep the same market structure. They are, instead, not that robust when market structure changes across models: the correlations between columns 1 or 4 on the one side and between columns 2, 3, 5 or 6 on the other are still large

Table 12.1 Correlation of welfare losses from a worldwide tariff increase for 20 European countries

	Without Intermediates	*With Intermediates*				
	Perfect Competition	*Monopolistic Competition*		*Perfect Competition*	*Monopolistic Competition*	
		Krugman (1980)	*Melitz (2003)*		*Krugman (1980)*	*Melitz (2003)*
	(1)	*(2)*	*(3)*	*(4)*	*(5)*	*(6)*
(1)	1	−0.72098	−0.72613	0.998883	−0.63709	−0.72288
(2)		1	0.974937	−0.75233	0.986991	0.933616
(3)			1	−0.75753	0.932363	0.835422
(4)				1	−0.67063	−0.74652
(5)					1	0.955704
(6)						1

Source: Author's elaboration based on percentage losses from Table 3 in Costinot and Rodriguez-Clare (2014).

but negative. Hence, while considering whether or not intermediate goods mostly affects the level of the average welfare effects, the choice of market structure also impacts on the cross-country distribution of those effects.

7. 'Brexit'

The counterfactuals discussed so far illustrate the sort of questions NQTMs can usefully address. In general, these are questions related to effects of possible policy changes that are hard to quantify using econometric techniques either because comparable events never happened or, if they did happen, because data of the right quality are not available. The previous counterfactuals are, however, rather remote from anything currently appearing in the European policy agenda. It is, therefore, interesting to look at a more concrete example.

There is currently major concern over the future relationship between the UK and the EU due to mounting internal political pressure in the former to leave the latter. Predicting the economic effects of an eventual breakup for the UK is, however, quite difficult due the lack of any precedent. This is why, in order to shed some light on the issue, Ottaviano, Pessoa, Sampson and Van Reenen (2014) use a NQTM *à la* Costinot and Rodriguez-Clare (2014). The model quantifies the impact of Brexit on the welfare of UK citizens focusing on effects working through the trade channel. It features perfect competition and considers trade also in intermediates in 35 sectors among the 40 major countries of the world. It investigates two scenarios for how leaving the EU would affect trade costs through changing tariff, non-tariff and regulatory barriers. The first is an 'optimistic scenario' in which the UK maintains a free trade agreement (FTA) with the EU similar to the European Free Trade Association (EFTA) currently involving Norway and Switzerland. The second is a 'pessimistic scenario' in which the UK does not succeed in negotiating comparable terms and trade costs increase much more. In particular, in the optimistic scenario, the UK is assumed to continue enjoying face zero tariffs, to face one-quarter of the reducible non-tariff barriers faced by the US vis-à-vis the EU, and to miss a projected cumulative fall in intra-EU trade costs of 10 per cent thanks to intra-EU regulatory convergence. In the pessimistic scenario, the UK is assumed, instead, to face most favourite nation (MFN) tariffs on goods for UK-EU trade, to face two-thirds of the reducible non-tariff barriers faced by the US when trading with the EU, and to miss a projected cumulative fall in intra-EU trade costs of 5.7 per cent thanks to intra-EU regulatory convergence. The projected falls in intra-EU trade costs are based on the fact that over a period of time trade costs between EU countries have been decreasing roughly 40 per cent faster than trade costs between other OECD countries.

The corresponding findings are reported in Table 12.2. They show an overall welfare loss of 1.13 per cent in the optimistic scenario, mainly determined by current and future changes

Table 12.2 The impact of 'Brexit' on UK welfare

	Pessimistic	Optimistic
Increase in tariffs	−0.14%	0%
Increase in non-tariff barriers	−0.93%	−0.40%
Future falls in non-tariff barriers	−2.55%	−1.26%
Fiscal benefit	0.53%	0.53%
Total welfare change	**−3.09%**	**−1.13%**

Source: Ottaviano, Pessoa, Sampson and Van Reenen (2014).

in non-tariff barriers as these are particularly relevant for services, which are a major UK export category. The overall loss more than doubles to 3.09 per cent in the pessimistic scenario, with a major role again played by non-tariff barriers. The table also shows that the loss coming from shrinking trade more than offsets the fiscal savings from erasing net UK transfers to the EU budget. Moneywise, the loss amounts to a hefty £18 billion in the optimistic scenario and almost triples to £50 billion in the pessimistic one.

8. Conclusion

This chapter has discussed whether and how 'new quantitative trade models' (NQTMs) can be fruitfully applied to quantify the welfare effects of trade liberalization, thus shedding light on the trade-related effects of European integration or disintegration.

On the one hand, the chapter has argued that NQTMs have the potential of being used to supplement traditional CGE analysis thanks to their tighter connection between theory and data, their appealing micro-theoretical foundations, and their enhanced attention to the estimation of structural parameters. On the other hand, further work is still needed in order to exploit their full potential for policy analysis.

First, the predictions of NQTMs seem to be very sensitive to the choice of market structure. This is revealed by comparing perfect competition with monopolistic competition as in Costinot and Rodriguez-Clare (2014). In this respect, more work on the comparison with oligopoly would be useful (see, e.g., Arkolakis, Costinot, Donaldson and Rodriguez-Clare, 2012b) as well as more attention to the actual market structures that characterize different sectors.

Second, NQTMs are mostly silent on the 'dynamic' effects that policy intervention may have on economic growth, through more competition, innovation and technology adoption. While these effects are possibly the most important, including them is a tough challenge. While NQTMs currently embed most 'canonical' static trade models, any specific class of 'canonical' dynamic trade models is yet to be identified.

Finally, from a methodological point of view, the validation checks, which are a crucial passage in macroeconomics from calibration to simulation, have increasingly gone missing in NQTMs. Recent works tend to favour the implementation of models that are 'exactly identified'. These are models in which the number of free parameters to be calibrated equals the number of observed moments of the data, and thus yield a trivially perfect fit. The question is whether simulations based on this sort of tautology are really useful for policy design. In this respect, renewed attention should be devoted to models that are 'overidentified', i.e. models in which the number of free parameters is smaller than the number of moments of the data. For these models the validation checks are not trivially passed, and can thus be used as meaningful evidence that a model is a more or less reasonable representation of reality than its alternatives.

Notes

1 I am grateful to Joao Pessoa and Andres Rodriguez-Clare for useful comments and discussions.
2 See Head and Mayer (2014) as well as Simonovska and Waugh (2014) for recent discussions of methodological issues related to the estimation of the trade elasticity.

References

Arkolakis, C., Costinot, A. and Rodriguez-Clare, A. (2012a), New Trade Models, Same Old Gains? *American Economic Review*, 102, 94–130.

Arkolakis, C., Costinot, A., Donaldson, D. and Rodriguez-Clare, A. (2012b), The Elusive Pro-Competitive Effects of Trade, *Yale University*, mimeo.

Armington, P.S. (1969), A Theory of Demand for Products Distinguished by Place of Production, *IMF Staff Papers*, 16, 159–78.

Baldwin, R.E. and Venables, A.J. (1995), Regional Economic Integration, in: Grossman Gene and Rogoff Kenneth (eds), *Handbook of International Economics*, Vol. 3, Elsevier.

Bernard, A.B., Eaton, J., Jensen, J.B. and Samuel Kortum (2003), Plants and Productivity, in: International Trade, *American Economic Review*, 93, 1268–290.

Corcos, G., Del Gatto, M., Mion, G. and Ottaviano, G.I.P. (2012), Productivity and Firm Selection: Quantifying the 'New' Gains from Trade, *Economic Journal*, 122, 754–98.

Costinot, A. and Rodriguez-Clare, A. (2014), Trade Theory with Numbers: Quantifying the Consequences of Globalization, in: Helpman E., Rogoff K. and Gopinath, G. (eds), *Handbook of International Economics*, Vol. 4, Elsevier.

Del Gatto, M., Mion, G. and Ottaviano, G.I.P. (2006), Trade Integration, Firm Selection and the Costs of Non-Europe, *CORE Discussion Paper*, No. 2006061.

Eaton, J. and Kortum, S. (2002), Technology, Geography, and Trade, *Econometrica*, 70, 1741–79.

Krugman, P. (1980), Scale Economies, Product Differentiation, and the Pattern of Trade, *American Economic Review*, 70, 950–9.

Head, K. and Mayer, M. (2014), Gravity Equations: Workhorse, Toolkit, and Cookbook, in: Helpman E., Rogoff, K. and Gopinath, G. (eds), *Handbook of International Economics*, Vol. 4, Elsevier.

Melitz, M.J. (2003), The Impact of Trade on Intra-Industry Reallocations and Aggregate Industry Productivity, *Econometrica*, 71, 1695–1725.

Melitz, M.J. and Ottaviano, G.I.P. (2008), Market Size, Trade, and Productivity, *Review of Economic Studies*, 75, 295–316.

Melitz, M.J. and Redding, S. (2013), Firm Heterogeneity and Aggregate Welfare, *NBER Working Paper*, No. 18919.

Piermartini, R. and Teh, R. (2005), Demystifying Modelling Methods for Trade Policy, *WTO Discussion Paper*, No. 10.

Ottaviano, G.I.P., Pessoa, J.P., Sampson, T. and Van Reenen, J. (2014), The Costs and Benefits of Leaving the EU, *Centre for Economic Performance*, mimeo.

Simonovska, I. and Waugh, M.E. (2014), The Elasticity of Trade: Estimates and Evidence, *Journal of International Economics*, 92, 34–50.

Timmer, M.P. (ed.) (2012), The World Input-Output Database (WIOD): Contents, Sources and Methods, *WIOD Working Paper*, No. 10.

13

THE EFFECTS OF EUROPEAN INTEGRATION ON THE STABILITY OF INTERNATIONAL TRADE

A duration perspective

Tibor Besedeš

1. Introduction

Since the late 1950s Europe has engaged in an experiment of unparalleled nature in history – the integration of a myriad of cultures, beliefs, and practices in a more cohesive unit. What started as the European Coal and Steel Community has evolved over time into a far broader and encompassing union currently known as the European Union (EU). The creation of the Union was gradual, evolving over time through various incarnations. In the area of international trade, this integration first took root as a customs union of the original member countries before proceeding through two deeper economic integration phases in 1994 and again in 1999 with the adoption of the euro and the creation of the Eurozone.

Every step of the integration process resulted in reduced costs of trading providing for less costly means of exchanging products via the reduction in tariffs, harmonization of standards, practices, and regulation, among other measures. Such reductions in trading costs have had far reaching effects for the growth of aggregate trade. During the time period covered by this study, 1962 to 2005, aggregate trade among the EU-15 countries grew by some 11,000 percent, while their combined GDP grew by less than 900 percent. Reductions in trade costs also have far reaching effects at a disaggregated level as they make it feasible to conduct more trade, by enabling trade which would otherwise be impractical or cost-prohibitive.

The goal of this chapter is to assess the overall effects of European economic integration on international trade at a disaggregated level, focusing on the effects on the stability of trade through the prism of duration of trade. Duration of trade examines how long a country imports a product from its trading partner, where the item of interest is a spell of service – continuous years during which trade is taking place. The pair of countries and the product being exchanged together define a trade relationship, while the number of consecutive years over which the relationship is active constitute a spell of service. Using annual UN COMTRADE data from 1962 combined with the Baier and Bergstrand (2007) Economic Integration Agreements Database as well as key dates pertaining to European integration,

I examine how European integration has affected duration of trade. Duration of trade was first investigated by Besedeš and Prusa (2006a, b) and Besedeš (2008) who focused on duration of US import trade showing it to be surprisingly short. Nitsch (2009) was the first to investigate duration using an EU member country, examining duration of German import trade, finding it to be similarly short. Hess and Persson (2011) examine the duration of EU import trade using the same data as I use, but their focus was not on understanding the impact of the various aspects of EU integration, the sole focus of this chapter.

As Besedeš, Moreno-Cruz, and Nitsch (2014) show, both theoretically and empirically using data for virtually all available countries between 1962 and 2005, economic integration has a dual effect on international trade at a disaggregated level. As economic integration reduces trade costs, one can expect trade to increase and become more stable, or to put it in different words, to last longer. This is precisely the effect Besedeš et al. (2014) find – trade relationships which are active when an economic integration agreement enters into force become longer and are less likely to end or fail. However, lower costs also make it feasible to commence new trade relationships which would otherwise remain dormant. These relationships, by their very nature, are marginal, with small cost advantages realized from trading across borders. Such small cost advantages make for relationships which can easily end as their stability is not backed by large cost differences. As Besedeš et al. (2014) show, on average, trade relationships which begin after two trading partners enter into an economic integration agreement are indeed more fragile displaying a shorter duration and a higher likelihood of failure, a higher hazard of the relationship ceasing. Thus, economic integration agreements have been found to have a dual effect on the stability of trade relationships – they enhance the stability of already active relationships, but reduce the stability of relationships which start after the agreement is in place.

Besedeš et al. (2014) only focused on the effect of a generic economic integration agreement, without differentiating the nature of the agreement. In this chapter I go several steps beyond their basic investigation as the EU presents a unique opportunity to investigate several different aspects of economic integration. First, I explicitly examine whether changes in the nature of European integration have different effects by examining whether the greater extent of integration provided by a common market and an economic union has additional effects beyond those conferred by the free trade agreement engaged into at the onset of European integration. The EU (and its precursors) expanded gradually, adding in several steps, allowing me to examine the effects associated with expansion of the EU between 1962 and 2005. Accession to the EU is a carefully regulated process with each potential member having to apply for membership. This allows me to examine whether there are any anticipation effects stemming from countries announcing their intention to join the integration. In certain cases the EU has a free trade agreement in place with a future member prior to that country joining the EU, allowing me to examine whether such agreements have a differential effect compared to the effect of being in the EU.

2. Data

I use data pertaining to the EU-15, the member countries prior to the eastward expansion which started in the early 2000s: Austria, Belgium, Denmark, Finland, France, Germany, Greece, Ireland, Italy, Luxembourg, the Netherlands, Portugal, Spain, Sweden, and the UK. Such restriction stems from data availability. Trade data are sourced from the UN COMTRADE database. I use bilateral import data reported by the EU-15 member countries at the 4-digit SITC revision 1 level. Trade data are available annually from 1962.

Information on economic integration agreements comes from the Economic Integration Agreements Database compiled by Baier and Bergstrand (2007). The database records the various economic integration agreements that 195 countries have entered into between 1950 and 2005. Economic integration agreements are defined according to Frankel (1997) as being one of six types: non-reciprocal preferential trade agreements, (reciprocal) preferential trade agreements, free trade agreements, customs union, common market, and economic union.

Given the intersection of the two datasets, my investigation spans the time period between 1962 and 2005. Given data on economic integration stop in 2005, I focus on the EU-15 and ignore the eastward expansion due to only being able to observe two years of EU-25 which is not a sufficiently long enough period to be able to obtain results about the effects of that round of expansion on duration of trade. I combine these data with key dates related to the expansion of the EU: dates when the nature of the EU changed, dates when future member countries applied for membership, existence and type of any trade agreement a future member had with the EU prior to joining it, and dates of every round of expansion between 1962 and 2003.

The EU went through four rounds of expansion on the way to becoming EU-15. The original members were Belgium, France, Germany, Italy, Luxembourg, and the Netherlands. The first enlargement occurred in 1973 when Denmark, Ireland, and the UK joined. The next country to join was Greece in 1981 followed by Portugal and Spain in 1986. The last expansion used in the analysis is that of Austria, Finland, and Sweden joining in 1995. For each round of the expansion I identify when the country began negotiating its accession. Denmark, Ireland, and the UK applied for membership twice in 1961 and 1967, as did Spain in 1962 and 1977. As application date I only use the date of the application which resulted in each country joining the union.

Austria, Finland, Portugal, Spain, and Sweden all had a trade agreement in place with the EU prior to joining. Spain had a non-reciprocal preferential trade agreement (PTA) while the other countries had a free trade agreement. I control for these agreements in order to precisely identify the effect of their accession to the EU. While the original formulation of EU in economic terms was that of a customs union, the depth of economic integration was increased in 1994 and again in 1999. According to Frankel's (1997) definition, the creation of the EU by the Maastricht Treaty also signified the creation of a common market, which took effect in 1994. The adoption of the euro and the creation of the Eurozone in 1999 signified increased economic integration, which according to Frankel's (1997) definition is classified as an economic union by Baier and Bergstrand.[1]

Finally, the EU became a common market in 1994 and an economic union in 1999, which I also control for explicitly. I use the standard gravity variables sourced from CEPII to control for country GDP, distance, common language, and common border.

3. Empirical Findings

3.1 Estimation strategy

In order to estimate the likelihood of a spell failing, I convert annual data to spells of service and estimate a random effects probit model, following Hess and Persson (2012) and Besedeš and Prusa (2013). In order to ascertain the magnitude of the effect of any variable I follow Besedeš and Prusa (2013) and Besedeš et al. (2014). I report differences in the fitted hazard at the mean values of all variables with the exception of the variable of interest. To be specific, in order to evaluate the effect of a single variable I will examine the difference in two fitted hazards: one with the value of the variable of interest taking a particular value, such as zero in the case of a dummy variable, and the other with the value of the variable of interest taking a different value, such as one in the case of a dummy variable, while all other variables are held at mean values for the sample or at zero in the case of dummy variables.

3.2 Explanatory variables

The set of explanatory variables follows Besedeš et al. (2014). Along with gravity variables, I include the log of the length of the current year of a spell to allow the hazard to change with duration and the initial volume of trade with which a relationship begins. The next set of variables pertains to economic integration agreements the EU-15 countries or the EU as a whole have with other countries in the world and are defined as in Besedeš et al. (2014). A dummy variable, 'EIA exists,' identifies pairs of countries which have an agreement at some point. Another dummy variable, 'EIA in effect,' identifies the years during which the agreement is active. The 'Start after EIA' dummy variable identifies spells which started after the agreement, while the 'EIA duration' measures how many years have passed since the start of the agreement.

Another set of variables identifies similar effects for intra EU agreements. 'EU pair' identifies instances where countries with a trade relationship are both (eventually) in the EU. Thus, in the instance of trade relationships between Germany, a founding member, and Spain, which joined in 1986, this variable always takes the value of one, irrespective of the year. The 'EU in effect' dummy variable identifies the years when both countries are members of the EU, which in the case of Germany and Spain would be 1986 and beyond. 'Start after EU' identifies spells which started after both countries became members of the EU and 'EU duration' measures the number of years that have passed with both countries as EU members. This set of variables defines the basic specification, the results of which are reported in Table 13.1.

In the remaining columns I sequentially add more variables identifying a particular aspect of the EU integration process. In the second column I add two dummy variables. 'Common market' identifies years during which the EU is a common market, while 'Economic union' identifies years during which the EU is an economic union. These two variables identify how the changing nature of the extent of EU integration affected the duration of intra EU trade relationships. The 'Application' dummy variable identifies years during which future member countries were applicants. The 'Pre-accession agreements' dummy variable identifies instances where future members had a trade agreement with the EU prior to them becoming a member. Finally, there are four dummies, each one identifying years following each round of expansions. 'Accession 1973' identifies all years after 1973 when Denmark, Ireland, and the UK joined the EU, 'Accession 1981' when Greece joined, 'Accession 1986' when Portugal and Spain joined, and finally, 'Accession 1995' when Austria, Finland, and Sweden joined.

3.3 Results

While the EU specific variables are added sequentially, I will focus in my discussion on the specification in the last column of Table 13.1, which includes all variables described above. In Table 13.2 I report the average effect on the hazard corresponding to integration related variables and their effects in the last column of Table 13.1. These were obtained by fitting the hazard and changing the value of the variable of interest as described above. Before focusing on EU specific variables, a short discussion of the effects of other variables is in order.

Table 13.1 Hazard estimates

Regression Estimates

	Basic	Nature of EU	Application period	Pre-accession agreements	Accession
Duration (ln)	−0.527***	−0.527***	−0.527***	−0.530***	−0.532***
Initial volume of imports (ln)	−0.108***	−0.109***	−0.109***	−0.109***	−0.111***
Importer GDP	0.061***	0.060***	0.060***	0.054***	0.062***
Exporter GDP	−0.078***	−0.078***	−0.078***	−0.079***	−0.079***
Distance (ln)	0.113***	0.114***	0.114***	0.114***	0.114***
Common border	−0.252***	−0.253***	−0.253***	−0.242***	−0.191***
Common language	−0.027***	−0.028***	−0.028***	−0.028***	−0.055***
EIA exists	−0.004	−0.001	−0.001	−0.011**	−0.012**
EIA in effect	−0.274***	−0.272***	−0.272***	−0.277***	−0.275***
Start after EIA	0.531***	0.530***	0.530***	0.528***	0.527***
Length of EIA in place (ln)	−0.011***	−0.011***	−0.011***	−0.010***	−0.012***
EU pair	−0.079***	−0.078***	−0.078***	−0.153***	−0.158***
EU in effect	−0.186***	−0.249***	−0.249***	−0.189***	−0.317***
Start after EU	0.077***	0.074***	0.074***	0.076***	0.099***
Length of EU in place (ln)	0.105***	0.147***	0.147***	0.149***	0.160***
Common market		0.026***	0.026***	0.028***	0.048***
Economic union		−0.176***	−0.177***	−0.163***	−0.141***
Application period			0.000	0.057***	0.050***
Pre-accession agreements				0.259***	0.203***
1973 accession					0.179***
1981 accession					0.249***
1986 accession					−0.025***
1995 accession					−0.050***
Constant	0.186***	0.189***	0.189***	0.302***	0.183***
Observations	6,578,177	6,578,177	6,578,177	6,578,177	6,578,177
Number of relationships	611,243	611,243	611,243	611,243	611,243
ρ	0.212***	0.211***	0.211***	0.208***	0.210***

Notes: ***, **, and * indicate significance at the 1%, 5%, and 10% levels.

The length of a spell has a negative effect on the hazard of trade relationships ceasing, indicating that the longer the spell, the less likely it is to cease. Initial volume has a similar effect reducing the hazard. Importer GDP has a positive effect, indicating that the larger the EU member, the shorter lasting are its import relationships. The larger the exporter, the less likely are the relationships to cease. The larger the distance between the two countries in a trading relationship, the higher the hazard. Common language and common border both reduce the hazard and make for longer and more stable relationships. The estimated effects of these variables are stable across all five estimated specifications and are similar to those obtain in the literature.

Table 13.2 Average estimated effects on the hazard

EIA exists	−2.6%
EIA in effect	−48.3%
Start after EIA	203.7%
Length of EIA in place (ln)	−7.9%
EU pair	−32.6%
EU in effect	−52.9%
Start after EU	25.7%
Length of EU in place (ln)	190.7%
Common market	11.6%
Economic union	−28.2%
Application period	13.8%
Pre-accession agreements	58.3%
1973 accession	48.3%
1981 accession	72.6%
1986 accession	−5.1%
1995 accession	−11.6%

Relationships where only one country is an EU member and where the two countries at some point have an economic integration agreement do not have a particularly different hazard than country pairs which never have an integration agreement. In the first three specifications, the estimated coefficient is not significant and is almost equal to zero, while in the last two columns it is statistically significant and small. Estimating the fitted hazard with all variables pertaining to integration agreements and EU specific variables at zero, and changing the 'EIA exists' dummy from zero to one, reveals that that relationships between an EU-15 country and a non-EU trading partner who at some point have an economic integration agreement have a hazard lower by an average of 2.6 percent. The onset of such an agreement significantly reduces the hazard, by an average of 48.3 percent.[2] This indicates that countries which sign a free trade agreement with the EU experience a large positive stability shock to their already active trade relationships which become longer lasting. Despite the large pro-stability shock experienced by already active spells, the spells which begin after such agreements experience more than four times as large a negative shock to stability, having a 203.7 percent higher hazard. The longer the agreement is in place confers a small pro-stability boost of on average 7.9 percent lower hazard per year.

Relationships in which both countries are members of the EU have a significantly lower hazard by an average of 32.6 percent. Spells which are active when both countries join the EU have a significantly lower hazard, experiencing a reduction in the hazard of 52.9 percent. Relationships which begin after both countries are members of EU have a significantly higher hazard by an average of 25.7 percent. Note that the effect of both of these variables is partial in nature as it does not allow for a differential effect that each round of accession might have had, as I discuss below.

The longer both countries have been in the EU, the hazard of their trade relationships increases tremendously, averaging a staggering 190 percent per year. This effect applies to both relationships started before and those started after both countries were in the EU. The size of this effect bears some additional explanation. When calculating the average effect I assume that the effect starts in year one of the spells which is also the first year of both countries being in the EU. Thus, the length of being in the EU increases in parallel with the length of the spell. Over the first ten years, the effect averages to a 57 percent higher hazard, over the next ten years it averages 151 percent, and during the third decade by 221.6 percent. The size of this effect and the rate at which it increases with time indicates that intra-EU trade becomes increasingly less stable and on average of significantly shorter duration.

The conversion of the EU from a free trade agreement to a common market in 1994 resulted in a small and significant increase in the hazard, on average 11.6 percent. Note that the effect of the conversion to a common market is not sufficiently strong to offset the pro-stability effect the EU has on relationships active when both countries join the EU, indicated by the 'EU in effect' variable. The creation of the economic union had the opposite effect, reducing the hazard by a larger magnitude of 28.2 percent, creating significantly longer and more stable relationships. The positive effect of an economic union is sufficiently strong to offset the negative effect the EU has on relationships which start after the EU is stablished or a country joins it, but not the increase in this effect over time. This indicates that an economic union may have a fundamentally different effect on the stability of trade relationships than any other type of economic integration agreement.

During the application period, trade relationships between the applicant country and an EU member have a higher hazard of 13.8 percent, but only after the pre-accession agreement and the accession rounds are taken into account. In terms of the stability of trade relationships, there are no positive anticipation effects, but rather only negative ones increasing the hazard. The existence of a pre-accession agreement significantly increases the hazard of relationships ceasing, on average by 58.3 percent.

Finally, as suggested above, note that each round of expansion of the EU has a different effect on the hazard of trade relationships ceasing. The 1973 and 1981 expansions both significantly increased the hazard for both old and new members, by 48.3 percent and 72.6 percent, the latter of which is the additional effect which starts in 1981. The 1986 and 1995 expansions had very different effects, both reducing the hazard by 5.1 percent after 1986 and by 11.6 percent after 1995. While the last two rounds of expansion reduced the hazard, the magnitude of the reduction was not sufficiently strong to offset the increases caused by the 1973 and 1981 expansions.

The effects of estimated coefficients described in this section are what I will describe as 'pure effects,' occurring in isolation from changes in other variables of interest. For example, the full effect of joining the EU on already active spells is not given just by the 'EU in effect' variable but also by one of the accession dummies. The 'EU in effect' variable identifies the effect of EU common across all observed relationships of that kind. To better ascertain the effect of the various variables in the following section I discuss several specific scenarios of the various effects generated by EU integration.

4. Specific scenarios

In order to examine the various consequences of European integration, I examine the combined effects of the EU integration related variables by examining four specific scenarios. Across all scenarios, I fix all gravity variables at their sample means and all variables specific to economic integration agreements with non-EU countries at zero, thus focusing only on the effect of the variables of interest. I then estimate the fitted hazard for specific values of EU integration variables to ascertain their combined effects and contrast the fitted hazard to the one where the variables of interest are set to zero (i.e., the hazard in the absence of a specific aspect of EU integration). The four scenarios are: (i) the consequence of upgrading the EU from a free trade area first to a common market then to an economic union; (ii) the effect of the 1973 expansion with a 3-year application period; (iii) the effect of the 1986 expansion with a 3-year application period preceded by a 10-year economic integration agreement; and (iv) the effect of all four rounds of expansion, each preceded by a 3-year application period.

In order to examine the differential effect of variables of interest I need to specify the timing of various effects with respect to a given spell. There are two aspects to timing assumptions. One has to do with when during an active spell the integration event takes place, while the other has to do with how long after (joining) the EU the spell starts. As far as the former is concerned, I will assume that the first integration event of interest occurs in the fifteenth year of a spell. As far as the latter is concerned, I will examine two possibilities one having the spell start immediately after the EU is formed or joined, while the other has the spell starting 10 years after the EU is in place. Both of these assumptions are arbitrary in nature, and changing any aspect of the timing would not affect the results qualitatively. In each scenario I set the value of the 'EU pair,' 'EU in effect,' and 'Start after EU' dummy variables to one. For each scenario I plot three fitted hazards, one with the variable(s) of interest set to zero and two with the variable of interest set to one with each plot correspond-ing to a particular set of timing assumptions: one for spells which started in EU's first year and the other for spells which started in EU's tenth year. I then focus on the differences across the three plots. Each fitted hazard is plotted along with the corresponding 99th percentile confidence interval. Should the confidence intervals of any two plotted hazards overlap, then the effect of the variable(s) of interest are not statistically significant.

4.1 Upgrading the EU

The effects of the first scenario are shown in Figure 13.1 and examine the effects of upgrad-ing the EU from a free trade agreement to a common market and then to an economic union, the latter upgrade following the former one after six years, as was actually the case. Aside of the basic EU related variables, all other aspects of EU integration (application period, pre-accession agreements with the EU, and EU expansions) are set to zero.

The effects of upgrading the EU from a free trade agreement to a common market and then an economic union are apparent, but are not particularly large. The conversion to a common market increases the hazard by some 11 percent relative to the EU remaining a free trade agreement. The subsequent conversion to an economic union reduces the hazard more than the increase caused by a conversion to a common market. The hazard under economic union is some 20 percent lower relative to the hazard of the EU as a free trade agreement. While somewhat difficult to read from the picture, both effects are statistically significant.

Note that both effects are significantly smaller in magnitude than the effect on the hazard of having more time pass since the formation of the EU. The only difference over the first fifteen years between the plots in Figure 13.1 is that highest hazard is for spells which start ten years after the EU itself starts. While the difference between the two hazards decreases with duration, starting at 52 percent higher hazard for the later starting spell in year one and decreasing to 20 percent in year fourteen, the difference averages to 33 percent. Spells which start ten years after the EU have by a third higher hazard than spells which started at the same time as the EU itself. Thus, even without any other integration changes within the EU, the establishment of the EU itself increases the hazard by a large amount over time.

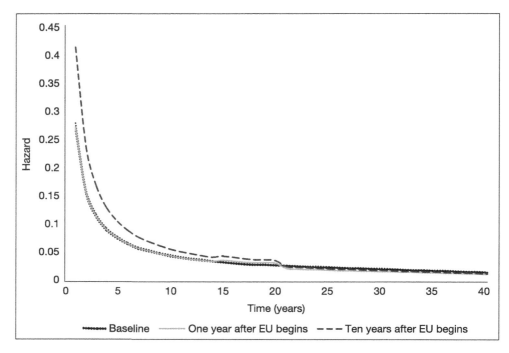

Figure 13.1 EU upgrades

To better examine the increase in the hazard with time after the establishment or accession to the EU in Figure 13.2 I plot three different fitted hazards for EU relationships started after the establishment of the EU, reflecting the effect the age of the EU or joining the EU itself has on the hazard. I compare spells which started immediately after (joining) the EU, spells which started ten years after (joining) the EU, and spells which started twenty years after (joining) the EU. As the figure indicates, the later a spell starts after the establishment of the EU, the higher its hazard. The first year hazard of the spell which starts ten years after the EU is 52 percent higher while the first year hazard of a spell which starts twenty years after the EU is 67 percent higher than that of the spell which starts immediately after the EU. These differences decrease with duration so that the hazard in year ten is 26 percent higher for spells which start in EU's tenth year and 43 percent higher for spells which start in EU's twentieth year. Spells which start in EU's tenth year have on average across the entire length of a spell (43 possible years) a 19 percent higher hazard, while those which start in EU's twentieth year have on average a 32 percent higher hazard. Spells which start in EU's twentieth year have on average 11 percent higher hazard across all years than those which start in EU's tenth year. While the hazard of spells which start after the EU increases the later in the EU a spell starts, the hazard increases at a decreasing rate.

4.2 The 1973 Expansion

The second scenario I examine is the effect of the 1973 expansion of the EU which added Denmark, Ireland, and the UK as members. For this scenario I define the EU as a free trade agreement for the duration of the spell and ignore the upgrade to a common market and an

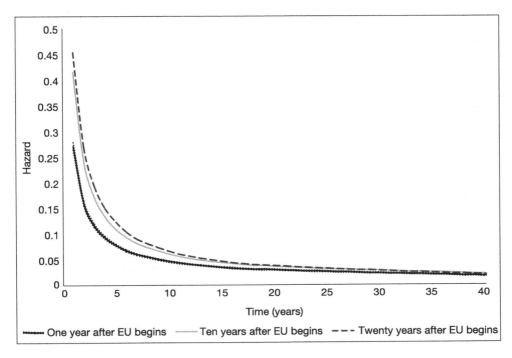

Figure 13.2　The effect of the age of the EU

economic union. I fit the hazard for a spell for which the expansion occurs in the fifteenth year of an active spell assuming there is a three year application period prior to expansion. Figure 13.3 displays the three fitted hazards. The application period increases the hazard slightly, by an average of 13 percent during the application period for spells which started immediately after the EU (one can think of this scenario as examining the effect of the expansion on incumbent members) and by a slightly larger 15 percent for spells which started in the EU's tenth year.

The 1973 expansion increased the hazard by an average of 50 percent for spells which started in the EU's first year, and by 67 percent for spells which start in EU's tenth year relative to the hazard without the expansion.[3] Note that this increase is separate from the application effect as the application effect is present only during the three years immediately preceding the expansion itself.

4.3 Pre-accession agreements with the EU

Spain, Portugal, Austria, Finland, and Sweden all had a trade agreement with the EU in place prior to joining the EU. Spain signed a non-reciprocal PTA with the EU in 1970, sixteen years before joining the EU. Portugal, Austria, Finland, and Sweden signed a free trade agreement with the EU in 1973, thirteen years prior to Portugal joining and twenty two years prior to Austria, Finland, and Sweden joining. I now examine the effect of pre-accession agreements coupled with the 1986 and 1995 expansions when countries that had such agreements joined the EU. The effect on the hazard for the 1986 expansion is shown in Figure 13.4.

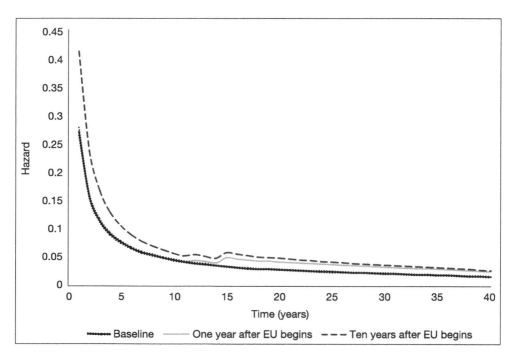

Figure 13.3 The first EU expansion

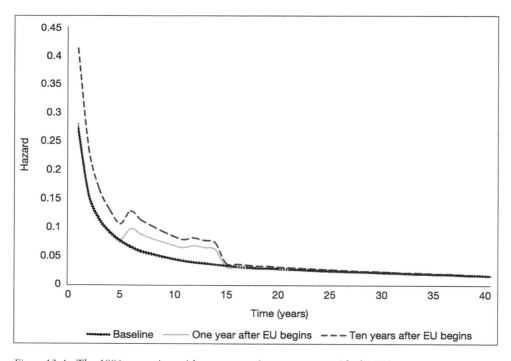

Figure 13.4 The 1986 expansion with a pre-accession agreement with the EU

The pre-accession agreement increases the hazard by an average of 50 percent for spells which started as soon as the EU and by 88 percent for spells which started 10 years after the EU. Roughly a quarter of the increase for the latter spells is due to the higher hazard caused by the EU having been in place for ten years. The three-year long application increases the hazard by an additional 22 percent for the former spells and 16 percent for the latter. The accession eliminates the higher effect of the application period and reduces the hazard to less than what it would be in the absence of the expansion. The reduction is on average about 5 percent for spells which started in the first year of the EU. For spells which started in EU's tenth year there is a reduction in the hazard, but the effect is not strong enough to offset the higher hazard due to a later beginning of the spell with the EU. Such spells have on average a 7 percent higher hazard than would be the case in the absence of expansion. Thus, in the case of the 1986 expansion, the expansion itself had a more stabilizing effect as it reduced the hazard for spells which were affected by the expansion. The corresponding effects for the 1995 expansion are stronger, reducing the hazard after accession by 12 percent for spells starting as soon as the EU is formed and largely having no additional effect on the hazard for spells which start when the EU itself was ten years old.

4.4 All expansions

The last scenario I consider is that of all four rounds of expansion with a three-year application period leading up to every accession. The dummy variable for each accession takes on the value of one in every year after the accession, including years when other accessions occurred. To be more specific, the dummy capturing the 1973 accession takes on a value of one starting in 1973 and stays at one even after the 1981, 1986, and 1995 accessions. Thus, the full effect of the 1981 accession for example combines the effect of the 1973 accession with that of the 1981 accession dummies. The fitted hazards are shown in Figure 13.5.

The effects of the four expansions on the hazard are diverse. The first application period increased the hazard by an average of 13 percent followed by an increase of 47 percent following the expansion. The application period preceding the second round increased the hazard by an additional 20 percent. While the effect of the second application disappears when expansion occurs, the second expansion increased it by an additional 80 percent over the hazard during the second application, and doubles the hazard relative to what it was after the first expansion. At this point, the increase in the hazard relative to what it would be in the absence of both expansions is 147 percent. The application period preceding the third expansion increases the hazard by 32 percent, but the expansion itself reduces it by a slightly larger 37 percent. Thus, the third expansion offsets the entire increase during the third application period and reduces the hazard relative to what it was after the second expansion by roughly 5 percent. The application period before the last expansion increases the hazard by 35 percent, but the actual expansion reduces the hazard by 52 percent relative to the preceding application period and by 17 percent relative to what it was after the third expansion. While the last two rounds of expansion of the EU reduce the hazard, the effects are not sufficiently strong to offset the increased hazard from the first two rounds. After the last expansion the hazard is higher by more than 120 percent relative to what it would have been in the absence of any of the four rounds of expansion.

5. Discussion

The examination of the effects of the various aspects of European economic integration under the EU reveals that additional integration which occurs, and the expansion of the EU,

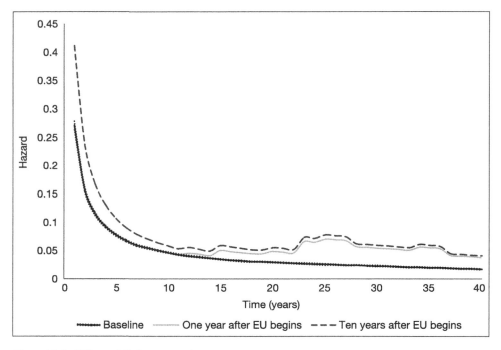

Figure 13.5 Effect of all four expansions

make for a more uncertain and less stable trading environment. The hazard of trade relationships ceasing is higher after every instance of additional integration than it was in earlier times. The magnitude of these effects is in some instances staggering. After the second round of expansion in the early 1980s the hazard of trade relationships increases by almost 150 percent. The subsequent expansion rounds reduce the hazard somewhat, but still leave it more than twice as high as it would be in the absence of any expansion of the EU. The conversion of the EU to an economic union from a common market also reduces the hazard, but by a relatively modest 20 percent. Trade within the EU has become significantly less stable through successive rounds of additional integration.

An obvious question imposes itself considering these results: given the large and potentially counterintuitive effects of European integration on the stability of disaggregate trade patterns, should we consider these effects to be negative and undesirable? To put it differently, what can we say about the economic welfare consequences of European integration when it comes to disaggregated trade? On the one hand we have a staggering growth in aggregate trade of some 11,000 percent between 1962 and 2005, but on the other hand we are confronted with large increases in hazard and have more fragile trade relationships. One could ask the question of where the aggregate growth came from if trade relationships have become significantly shorter on average?

One tantalizing possibility is that European integration has had a large effect on the ability of EU members to start trading with each other by significantly reducing the costs of trading. As discussed above, it is possible trade cost reductions make fringe trade relationships more likely to be attempted as they are no longer cost prohibitive. This is one of the fundamental premises behind any cross-border economic integration – reduce the costs of economic interaction to generate new activity. It is possible that reduced costs have had a significant effect on the extensive margin enabling the creation of many more trade relationships, a large number of which may have been marginal relationships which turned out to be short. But these relationships would not have been possible in the absence of integration. Thus, it is possible that the large increases in hazard post integration are the consequence of integration enabling a large number of what turn out to be short relationships, which would not exist in the absence of integration. If that is the case, then despite the increase in the hazard, integration would have a beneficial effect as it enables trade relationships, however short, which otherwise would never have been realized.

I examine this possibility by calculating the number of new relationships created every year for every country pair in the data and regressing its logged value on the same set of variables used to examine the effect of European integration on the hazard of trade relationships ceasing. The only difference in variables used is that the two 'Started after' dummies can no longer be used since each spell generates a single observation now. In other words, 'EU in effect' and 'Started after EU' are now identical variables. The results are presented in Table 13.3 which contains the same progression of specifications as in Table 13.1.

In my discussion I focus on the last column of Table 13.3. Larger countries form more new relationships as do countries which are closer and surprisingly countries which do not share a border. The border effect may be a function of the data set composed of all EU import relationships, where most EU members share a border, in which case most of the EU related common border effect will be identified by EU related variables. Countries sharing a common language form more relationships. Non-EU member countries who have an economic integration agreement with the EU do not start more relationships, but they do form more relationships after their agreement with the EU begins. The number of newly formed relationships decreases somewhat after an agreement begins.

Table 13.3 Entry estimates

Regression Estimates

	Basic	Nature of EU	Application period	Pre-accession agreements	Accession
Importer GDP	0.160★★★	0.160★★★	0.160★★★	0.160★★★	0.175★★★
Exporter GDP	0.021★★	0.021★★	0.022★★	0.022★★	0.023★★
Distance (ln)	−0.046★★	−0.043★★	−0.043★★	−0.043★★	−0.042★★
Common border	−0.720★★★	−0.741★★★	−0.745★★★	−0.746★★★	−0.731★★★
Common language	0.081★	0.081★	0.081★	0.081★	0.085★
EIA exists	0.070	0.077	0.087	0.087	0.095
EIA in effect	0.492★★★	0.495★★★	0.511★★★	0.507★★★	0.495★★★
Length of EIA in place (ln)	−0.028★★★	−0.029★★★	−0.031★★★	−0.031★★★	−0.031★★★
EU pair	0.066	0.085	0.182★★	0.192★★	0.204★★
EU in effect	4.404★★★	3.010★★★	2.913★★★	2.905★★★	2.723★★★
Length of EU in place (ln)	−0.408★★★	−0.277★★★	−0.275★★★	−0.275★★★	−0.263★★★
Common market		−0.253★★★	−0.260★★★	−0.259★★★	−0.290★★★

(Continued)

Table 13.3 (Continued)

Regression Estimates

	Basic	Nature of EU	Application period	Pre-accession agreements	Accession
Economic union		−0.408★★★	−0.414★★★	−0.414★★★	−0.459★★★
Application period			−0.539★★★	−0.550★★★	−0.561★★★
Pre-accession agreements				−0.045	−0.072
1973 accession					0.068★
1981 accession					0.186★★
1986 accession					−0.019
1995 accession					0.179★★★
Constant	−5.746★★★	−4.567★★★	−4.588★★★	−4.590★★★	−4.684★★★
Observations	77793	77793	77793	77793	77793
No. Subjects	2757	2757	2757	2757	2757
R^2	0.040	0.040	0.040	0.040	0.041

Notes: ★★★, ★★, and ★ indicate significance at the 1%, 5%, and 10% levels.

EU members do create more relationships, both before and after becoming a member. The magnitude of the increase in the number of relationships after both EU members are in the EU is staggering. The semi-elasticity of 2.723 translates to a 1,423 percent increase in the number of relationships under the EU. While the rate of creation of new relationships decreases with the age of the EU, it does so very slowly. Forty years into the EU, the rate of formation of new relationships is still 472 percent higher than it would be in the absence of the EU. Transitions to a common market and an economic union both reduce the rate of formation of new relationships by a modest 25 percent and 37 percent. The number of new relationships is also lower during the application process, by 43 percent, while any integration agreements with the EU prior to joining the EU have had no effect on the number of new relationships. The 1973 expansion had a small, marginally significant, and positive effect on the number of new relationships of 7 percent, while the 1981 expansion had a larger positive effect of 20 percent. The addition of Spain and Portugal in 1986 had no effect on the number of new relationships, while the 1995 addition of Austria, Finland, and Sweden has had a positive and significant effect on the number of new relationships increasing them by 20 percent.

6. Conclusion

European integration has had a largely negative effect on the duration of trade within the EU increasing the instability of disaggregated trade patterns. The evidence presented in this chapter indicates that in the early stages, EU integration had largely negative effects, reducing duration and increasing the hazard. This pattern reversed itself starting with the 1986 expansion which added Portugal and Spain to the ranks of the member countries and continued with the 1995 addition of Austria, Finland, and Sweden. The deeper integration which the EU began in 1993 by creating a common market and then in 1999 by creating an economic union also had a dual effect. The common market initially increased the hazard and reduced duration, but this was more than offset by the creation of the economic union after which the hazard dropped. However, the reduction in the hazard stemming from both the creation of the economic union and the 1986 and 1995 expansions was not large enough to offset the increased hazard from the first two rounds of expansion. The result of all of these changes is that the hazard of trade ceasing experienced by intra-EU relationships after the creation of the economic union in 1999 was higher than the hazard experienced prior to the first expansion.

The evidence presented indicates that European integration while at the same time introducing additional instability into intra EU trade, increasing the hazard and reducing the duration of intra- EU trade relationships, also had a much larger positive effect on the number of new relationships. EU integration has allowed EU member countries to significantly increase the number of trade relationships among themselves by reducing the costs of trade, trade relationships which would likely not exist were it not for the integration processes. The large negative effects on duration of trade are likely largely driven by the large influx of newly created relationships, many of which may be one-off affairs, active for a very short period of time. At first blush such relationships may appear to be inefficient and generating more losses than gains. But in an environment of deep economic integration, where trading costs are very low, even short and small relationships may be efficient and profitable. As such, the reduction in the duration of intra-EU trade observed over the course of sustained EU integration is not a negative development, but rather a consequence of the EU reducing costs of trade and enabling many new relationships which used to be cost-prohibitive.

Data limitations prevented me from exploring the consequences of the eastward expansion of the EU which began in 2004. Given that the majority of new members after 2004 used to be very different economically than the EU-15, once data become available it will be interesting to examine how the effects of continued integration of Europe compare to earlier phases.

Notes

1 The EU has been considered a common market long before 1994. However, in order to be consistent with the extant literature on the determinants and effects of economic integration agreements, I chose to use the categorization of the EU as a common market between 1994 and 1998, and as an economic union beginning in 1999.

2 While the discussion talks about an agreement between an EU member country and a non-member country, I should point out that the EU has a common policy for economic integration agreements which prevents a single member from having standalone agreements with non-members.

3 My choice of spells which start in the EU's first year and the EU's tenth year and then experience the 1973 expansion in its fifteenth year implies that I am looking at spells of countries which joined the EU in 1958 and 1948. Spells which started in 1958 would correspond to the founding members, while spells starting in 1948 do not correspond to any real spell. It is best to think of such spells as thought experiments. I could have chosen to examine spells starting in specific calendar years, but that would make for more difficult comparisons.

References

Baier, S.L. and Bergstrand, J.H. (2007), Do Free Trade Agreements Actually Increase Members' International Trade? *Journal of International Economics*, 71(1), 72–95.

Besedeš, T., Moreno-Cruz, J., and Nitsch, V. (2014), *Trade Integration and the Fragility of Trade Relationships*, Georgia Institute of Technology.

Besedeš, T. and Prusa, T.J. (2006a), Ins, Outs, and the Duration of Trade, *Canadian Journal of Economics*, 39(1), 266–95.

Besedeš, T. and Prusa, T.J. (2006b), Product Differentiation and Duration of U.S. Import Trade, *Journal of International Economics*, 70(2), 339–58.

Besedeš, T. and Prusa, T.J. (2013), Antidumping and the Death of Trade, *NBER Working Paper* 19555.

Frankel, J.A. (1997), *Regional Trading Blocs in the World Economic System*, Washington: Institute for International Economics.

Hess, W. and Persson, M. (2011), Exploring the Duration of EU Imports, *Review of World Economics*, 147(4), 665–92.

Hess, W. and Persson, M. (2012), The Duration of Trade Revisited: Continuous-Time vs. Discrete-Time Hazards, *Empirical Economics*, 43(3), 1083–1107.

Nitsch, V. (2009), Die Another Day: Duration in German Import Trade, *Review of World Economics*, 145(1), 133–54.

14

EU TRADE POLICY

André Sapir

1. Introduction

Global trade has undergone marked changes since the turn of the millennium. In 2013, the European Union (EU) was still the world's largest merchandise trader, but China had reached second place (it was only fifth in 2000), relegating the United States (US) to third position. More significantly, between 2000 and 2013 the share of the old triad economies (EU, US, Japan) fell from 45 to 33 per cent of world merchandise trade with a commensurate gain by the emerging BRICS economies (Brazil, Russia, China, India, South Africa) from 9 to 22 per cent.

The global trade policy regime has also undergone several important developments since 2000. First, the Doha Round of World Trade Organization (WTO) trade negotiations launched in 2001 stalled, becoming the longest ever round of multilateral trade negotiations. Second, the number and scope of regional trade agreements (RTAs) greatly increased. Especially noteworthy are the current negotiations for three mega-regional agreements launched in or after 2010 and involving all the leading players: the Trans-Pacific Partnership (TPP) between the US and a number of Asia-Pacific countries, including Japan; the Transatlantic Trade and Investment Partnership (TTIP) between the EU and the US; and the Regional Comprehensive Economic Partnership (RCEP) between Asia-Pacific countries, including China, India and Japan. The third development is, perhaps surprisingly in light of the previous two developments, the resilience of the WTO liberal trading regime. Despite economic conditions unparalleled since the 1930s, with the global recession of 2008–9 and the ensuing weak global economy, the rise in global protectionism has been relatively modest.

The purpose of this chapter is to analyse the recent evolution of the EU's trade policy. The chapter examines how this core EU policy has adapted to developments within and outside the EU and also how it has impacted the global trade policy regime. The chapter is divided into three parts. The first section provides a description of the change in EU trade flows. The second section examines the evolution of the decision-making process in EU trade policy. The third section analyses the evolution of EU trade policy and in particular how the EU's balancing act between an avowed commitment to multilateralism and a long tradition of preferential trade agreements is changing with the growth of emerging countries.

2. The EU as global trader

The EU has been the world's largest trader of goods and services throughout most of its history.[1,2] From the time of its inception in 1958 until the early 1990s, the EU accounted for more than 20 per cent of total (exports plus imports) global merchandise trade. Since then its share has gradually declined. In 2013, it was only about 15 per cent for merchandise trade, but it was still well above 20 per cent for trade in services. This recent decline is part of a broader trend. From 1958 until the early 1970s, the EU and the US together accounted for well over 40 per cent of total global merchandise trade. Adding Japan, the triad countries accounted for more than 50 per cent of world merchandise trade, a position they retained until the mid-1980s. By 2013, their combined share had fallen to 33 per cent as a result of the growth of emerging countries. In services, however, the share of the triad countries remains well above 40 per cent. See Table 14.1.

Non-agricultural goods account for the lion's share of EU trade (67 per cent of exports and 74 per cent of imports in 2012). Commercial services also represent a significant component (28 per cent of exports and 22 per cent of imports in 2012). By contrast, the share of agricultural goods in EU trade is very small (5 per cent of exports and 4 per cent of imports in 2012). See Table 14.2.

With respect to its trading partners, the EU has undergone important shifts over the years. Until 1994, the group of countries belonging to the European Free Trade Association (EFTA) was the EU's main trading partner, though its importance had gradually declined with the continuous migration of EFTA's members to the EU;[3] in 2012, EFTA had fallen to third position. Since 1995, the largest of the EU's trading partners has been the US, though China already overtook it in 2006 on the import side. In 2012, the EU's main trading partners after the US, China and EFTA were Russia, Turkey and Japan in that order, with the EU's three main European partners (EFTA, Russia, Turkey) accounting for nearly 25 per cent of EU total merchandise trade – far more than the US share of roughly 14 per cent.

Table 14.1 Main trading countries, 1958–2013 (as per cent of world trade)

Year	Exports				Imports			
	EU	US	China	Japan	EU	US	China	Japan
Trade in goods								
1958	23.9	27.8	..	4.3	22.8	21.1	..	4.2
1960	24.5	26.1	..	5.0	23.5	19.7	..	5.1
1970	22.3	21.5	..	9.4	21.6	20.2	..	8.9
1986	22.2	13.8	2.0	13.3	20.5	22.6	2.6	7.6
1990	21.8	15.7	2.6	11.2	22.9	19.1	2.0	8.8
2000	18.5	15.9	5.2	9.4	19.2	24.1	4.0	7.3
2010	16.0	11.2	13.8	6.4	17.3	16.7	11.1	5.8
2013	15.3	10.5	14.7	4.8	14.8	15.4	12.9	5.5
Trade in services								
2013	25.0	18.8	5.9	4.1	19.9	12.7	9.8	4.8

Sources: 1958–2010: Eurostat (2011); 2013: WTO (2014).

Notes: Countries are ordered according to their total (exports + imports) world trade share in 2010. Figures exclude intra-EU trade. EU composition: 1958–1970: EU6; 1990: EU12; 2000: EU15; 2010: EU27; 2013: EU28.

Table 14.2 Product composition of EU trade, 2012 (as per cent of extra-EU27 trade of goods and services)

Product group	Exports	Imports
Agricultural goods	4.9	4.4
Non-agricultural goods	67.3	73.6
Commercial services	27.8	21.9
TOTAL	100.0	100.0

Sources: Own computations based on European Commission, DG Trade (2013).

Table 14.3 Main destinations and origins of EU trade, 1958–2012 (as per cent of total extra-EU trade)

Year	EU exports to						EU imports from					
	US	*China*	*EFTA*	*Russia*	*Turkey*	*Japan*	*US*	*China*	*EFTA*	*Russia*	*Turkey*	*Japan*
					Trade in goods							
1958	10.9	2.0	N/A	1.4	1.0	0.9	17.9	0.7	N/A	1.8	0.6	0.7
1960	11.6	1.2	33.9	2.1	1.2	1.1	19.8	0.8	23.1	2.2	0.7	0.8
1970	13.1	0.8	33.2	3.3	0.9	2.2	19.8	0.6	23.5	2.1	0.6	2.7
1980	12.0	0.8	24.3	3.4	0.8	2.1	16.1	0.7	16.2	4.0	0.4	4.6
1992	16.9	1.6	24.7	2.7	1.9	4.7	17.8	3.4	22.9	3.2	1.4	10.6
2001	24.3	3.1	10.3	2.8	2.1	4.6	19.0	7.4	10.3	4.6	2.0	7.4
2010	18.0	8.4	11.1	6.4	4.5	3.2	11.3	18.7	10.8	10.6	2.8	4.4
2012	17.3	8.5	11.0	7.3	4.5	3.3	11.5	16.2	11.7	11.9	2.7	3.6
					Trade in services							
2012	24.1	4.3	16.9	4.0	1.6	3.6	29.0	3.8	13.9	3.0	3.1	3.3

Sources: 1958–2010: Eurostat (2011); 2012: European Commission, DG Trade (2013).

Notes: Partners are ordered according to their total (exports + imports) EU trade share in 2010. Figures exclude intra-EU trade. EU composition: 1958–1970: EU6; 1980: EU9; 1992: EU12; 2001: EU15; 2010–2012: EU27. EFTA composition: 1960: EFTA7; 1970: EFTA8; 1980: EFTA6; 1992: EFTA7; 2001–2012: EFTA4.

The status of the US as the EU's main trading partner remains far more secure in services. In 2012 the US accounted for more than 25 per cent of EU services trade, compared to about 22 per cent for EFTA, Russia and Turkey combined. Conversely, China's relative position was far weaker in services than in goods, still trailing far behind the US and EFTA. See Table 14.3.

For most of its trading partners, the EU represents one of their top three export destinations and import origins and a significant share of their trade. For instance, in 2012, the EU accounted for more than 50 per cent of EFTA's trade, 45 per cent of Russia's, 40 per cent of Turkey's, 17 per cent of US trade, 14 per cent of China's and 10 per cent of Japan's. The EU's trade policy therefore plays a significant role in the global trading system.

3. The EU as trade policy actor

Trade policy is an exclusive competence of the EU, which means that only the EU, rather than individual Member States, has the authority to legislate on trade issues and conclude international trade agreements. The scope of the EU's Common Commercial Policy (CCP), as set out in the 1957 Treaty of Rome, included changes in tariff rates, trade agreements relating to trade in goods, export policy and measures to protect trade such as those in the event of dumping or subsidies. It was extended to trade agreements relating to trade in services and the commercial aspects of intellectual property by the 2001 Nice Treaty and to foreign direct investment (FDI) by the 2009 Lisbon Treaty.

The main political actors in the process of EU trade policy are the European Commission, the Council of (national) Ministers and, since the Lisbon Treaty, the European Parliament. Their respective involvement depends on the type of trade policy decision. As far as trade agreements are concerned, the Commission negotiates with foreign partners on the basis of a mandate proposed by the Commission and authorized by the Council (by a qualified majority). The Commission must conduct trade negotiations in consultation with the Trade Policy Committee (TPC) (consisting of representatives of the Member States appointed by the Council) tasked with assisting the Commission. Since the Lisbon Treaty, the Commission must also report regularly to the European Parliament on the progress of trade negotiations. After negotiations are completed, the agreement reached by the Commission is subject to the approval of the Council (by a qualified majority)[4] and, since the Lisbon Treaty, of the European Parliament (by a simple majority) rather than national parliaments as was the case previously.[5] Regarding the definition of trade policy on topics such as anti-dumping and anti-subsidy policy the Council and the Parliament are also co-legislators. However, Parliament plays no role in individual trade measures such as those against dumping or subsidies. Here the Commission only submits proposals to the Council. In practice, before submitting proposals the Commission first seeks the opinion of the TPC, which fulfils two roles: it serves as a channel of information to the Commission on the preferences of the Member States, which gives the opportunity to the Commission to alter its proposals before submitting them to the Council; and it monitors the Commission and transmits information to the Council.[6]

The political science literature discusses extensively the EU trade policy setting in terms of a principal-agent framework that focuses on agency autonomy.[7,8] The European Commission is the agent and has preferences that tend to be more liberal than those of the median member among the principals, which have recently expanded in two directions: with the addition of 13 new Member States since 2004 and with the inclusion of the European Parliament in 2009. The literature has examined the impact of these two extensions on the process and outcome of decision-making in EU trade policy. The increase in the number and diversity of EU members does not seem to have resulted in much change to the process or outcome. According to Elsig (2010), the increase in the number and diversity of EU members has not constrained the role of the European Commission as agenda setter, but it has led to an increase in informal processes that have empowered large Member States to the detriment of smaller ones. The effect on outcomes is briefly discussed in the next section.

The more controversial effect concerns the new role of the European Parliament as co-legislator. Formally, the role of Parliament remains less than the Council's. Parliament is not formally involved in the definition of the negotiation mandate for trade agreements and the Commission must only report to Parliament on the progress of negotiations, while the Council's TPC actually assists in the process. In practice, however, Parliament has succeeded in playing an important role both in the definition of the negotiation mandate and during the negotiation itself based on the fact that the Lisbon Treaty gives it equal power to the Council for the approval of trade agreements. The turning point came in 2012, when Parliament used its new power to reject the Anti-Counterfeiting Trade Agreement (ACTA) negotiated by the Commission.[9] The rejection sent a strong signal to the Commission and the Council that Parliament must be actively associated in all stages of the negotiation, starting with the definition of the mandate, a situation which has now become the de facto norm.[10] In the area of trade measures, Parliament plays the same role as the Council in the definition of policy but plays no role at all in individual decisions. The consensus view seems to be that the new and active role of the European Parliament has not lowered the ability of the European Commission to act as agenda setter. But the involvement of Parliament has led to a greater politicisation of EU trade policy.[11] The consequence on outcomes is briefly examined in the next section.

4. The EU trade policy

The EU treaty specifies that the objective of the CCP is to 'contribute, in the common [EU] interest, to the harmonious development of world trade, the progressive abolition of restrictions on international trade *and on foreign direct investment*, and the lowering of customs *and other* barriers'.[12] This objective has been largely met: the EU has contributed to the lowering of trade barriers and the development of world trade.

At every stage the process of European integration – with the EU progressively widening from six to (currently) 28 members and deepening from a customs union with a common external tariff (CET) to a single market with a CCP covering not just trade in goods but also trade in services, intellectual property and FDI – was accompanied by a gradual lowering of the EU's external trade barriers through multilateral trade negotiations. European integration was the main driving force behind the Dillon (1960–2) and Kennedy (1962–7) rounds of multilateral trade negotiations of the General Agreement for Tariffs and Trade (GATT), which produced substantial tariff reductions in non-agricultural products. At the time of the EU's creation, the average tariff of the six members for these products was 13 per cent.[13] Ten years later, when the CET was established, it was 10.4 per cent and the Kennedy Round further reduced it to 6.6 per cent.[14] The simultaneous lowering by the EU of internal and external protection in non-agricultural products did not end with the Kennedy Round. The first EU enlargement in 1973 was followed by multilateral tariff cuts during the Tokyo Round, which was completed in 1978. And the southern EU enlargement in the 1980s was followed by the launching of the Uruguay Round (1986–94), which further reduced the EU average tariff for non-agricultural products to 4.2 per cent, where it stands today. This level is however slightly higher than in the US and Japan. See Table 14.4, panel 1.

It would be a mistake though, to consider that the contribution of the EU to the lowering of non-agricultural tariff during the period from the end of the Kennedy Round in 1968 to today was merely 6.2 percentage points (i.e. 10.4 minus 4.2). In reality its role was far greater since the various EU enlargements tended to bring in countries, which by adopting the CET significantly reduced their external trade protection. This explains a consistent finding in the trade literature, starting with Balassa (1975), that EU integration has led to more trade creation than trade diversion for non-agricultural products, and therefore to net welfare gains for both the EU and third countries.[15] This positive finding, however, is not universal. For instance, Sapir (2001) finds that EFTA's exports to the EU suffered from trade diversion until 1972. Thereafter, with the first EU enlargement and the creation of the EU-EFTA free-trade area, the remaining EFTA countries did much better, their exports to EFTA partners and to EU countries suffering relatively little discrimination compared to intra-EU trade. This situation changed dramatically in the mid-1980s, when the EU further widened (with the southern enlargement) and deepened (with the EU single market project). Starting in 1989, EFTA's exports to EFTA partners or EU countries became significantly less attractive than

Table 14.4 Selected trade policy measures by the main trading countries, latest date available

	EU	US	China	Japan
	MFN tariffs, simple average of applied import duties (%, 2013)			
All goods	5.5	3.4	9.9	4.9
Agricultural goods	13.2	5.3	15.6	19.0
Non-agricultural goods	4.2	3.1	9.0	2.6
	Share of imports, by type of tariff treatment (%, 2008)			
Preferential imports	16.9	23.1	5.8	6.0
Non-preferential imports, MFN zero	56.5	42.8	48.4	80.4
Non-preferential imports, MFN>zero	26.1	33.7	41.7	12.5
Not available	0.4	0.4	4.1	1.1
TOTAL	100.0	100.0	100.0	100.0
	Contingent protection measures in force (2013)			
Anti-dumping (number of measures)	111	241*	118	4
Countervailing (number of measures)	13	52	4	..
Safeguards (number of measures)	0	0	0	0
Imports subject to measures°				
• **Trade weighted share**	1.8	4.0	3.2	<0.1
• **Product line share**	3.1	6.4	1.4	<0.1
	Participation in WTO disputes, number of cases (January 1996–December 2014)			
As complainant	95	107	12	19
As respondent	80	123	32	15
Respondent in EU complaints	–	33	7	6
Complainant against the EU	–	19	3	1

Sources: Panel 1: WTO Trade Profiles; panel 2: Carpenter and Lendle (2010); panel 3: WTO Trade Profiles and Bown et al. (2014); panel 4: WTO Dispute Settlement Database.

Notes: *Measures in force in 2012. °Measures in force in 2011.

intra-EU flows, posing a clear threat to EFTA countries whose exports were mainly destined to the EU market.[16] This finding lends empirical support to the theoretical intuition of Baldwin (1995) that the completion of the EU single market was responsible for a 'domino effect' within Europe, triggering applications to EU membership by nearly all EFTA countries between 1989 and 1992.

But the main exception to the finding that EU integration has led to a parallel decrease of internal and external trade barriers and to positive welfare gains for the EU and the rest of the world is agricultural products. The root of the problem here was the de facto exclusion of agriculture from multilateral trade negotiations prior to the Uruguay Round. As a result, the trade-diverting effect of the Common Agricultural Policy (CAP) progressively increased with successive EC enlargements, starting with the entry of the UK. In the early

1980s, the staggering costs of trade diversion provoked a rising opposition both within and outside the EU, which led to the inclusion of agriculture in the Uruguay Round and resulted in a series of reforms of the CAP and the progressive abolition of restrictions on agricultural trade by the EU and its partners. Despite its successive reforms, the CAP remains the main reason why it is still said today that trade policy in the 'European Union is liberal in some respects, protectionist in others'.[17] In 2013, the average MFN tariff on EU imports of agricultural products was 13.2 per cent, lower than in China and Japan but much higher than in the US. See Table 14.4, panel 1.

In summary, starting with the Dillon Round, the EU was a leading participant in all the last four GATT rounds. It used multilateral trade negotiations to obtain the lowering of foreign trade barriers in exchange for its own external liberalisation in areas where it had already achieved internal liberalisation. On occasion however, like in agriculture, the opposite occurred: the EU used multilateral trade negotiations to reduce trade-distorting domestic support measures. By opening its agricultural market and reducing its agricultural export subsidies, EU negotiators were able to ascertain that foreign partners lower their barriers in sectors like services which now account for a much bigger share of EU exports than agriculture.

During the Doha Round, the first of the WTO era, the EU has continued to be a leading participant in multilateral trade negotiation. It is still, as during GATT rounds, a member of the Quad, the small group of countries that de facto orchestrates the negotiation, though the composition of the group has changed substantially. The old Quad (EU, US, Japan, and Canada) has now been replaced by a new Quad (EU, US, Brazil, and India), with China increasingly playing a key role as well. However the EU's participation in the Doha Round has changed fundamentally compared to the earlier GATT rounds. Previously, the EU was both a leading subject of demands for and a leading demandeur of trade liberalisation measures by major trading partners. This time around the EU still has a defensive agenda – towards agriculture where protection levels remain relatively high – and an offensive one – towards emerging countries where EU market access for non-agricultural products and services remains difficult – but it is neither a prime target of demands nor a prime demandeur. These roles are now played by the large emerging countries (especially Brazil, China and India) and by the US.[18]

There are two ways to judge the EU posture in the Doha Round. One is to see it in a positive light and emphasise that the EU is the largest trading block and as such is in a good position to act as referee in the tussle between the large emerging countries and the US. The other is less positive and ascribes the new EU posture to a lack of leadership in the Doha Round. As one observer noted:

> The EU initially tried to take up the [leadership] role, having been the principal proponent of a new round, but has not played that part very effectively. That was amply demonstrated by the failure of European negotiators to win lasting support for the new issues they had advanced at the start of the round, dropping two of them (labour and the environment) even before the round was launched and jettisoning three others after a few years of fruitless negotiations (investment, competition policy, and government procurement). It is hard for a [WTO] Member to supply leadership when it will not even stick to its own demands.
>
> *(Van Grasstek, 2013)*

There are several possible explanations for this new posture. The first is the loss of economic momentum of all industrial countries to the emerging countries, and of the EU in particular, which has produced a more cautious EU multilateral trade agenda. This was already manifest at the start of the Doha Round but has accelerated since the 2008–9 crisis. This more cautious stance should not be equated however, with protectionist actions like new 'trade defence measures', the EU term for anti-dumping, anti-subsidy and safeguard duties, which have simply not occurred.[19,20] The reason why the 'Great Recession' did not turn into a wave of protectionism in the EU, or in other high-income countries, is twofold: the commitment made by G20 leaders, especially at their London summit at the height of the crisis in April 2009, which has been by-and-large respected by high-income countries;[21] and the changing nature of global production and trade, with the increasing participation of countries to global value chains, which seems to have altered the traditional political economy of trade policy and reduced the demand for import protection.[22] The second explanation is the decreased ability of the EU, which speaks with one voice on trade matters, to use its voice to speak loudly as a result of increased heterogeneity of EU members associated with increased EU membership.[23] The third is the diminished interest of the EU for multilateral trade liberalisation and its increased attraction for bilateral trade deals, which is discussed below.

Although traditionally a prominent participant in multilateral trade liberalisation, the EU has also always been a leading advocate of preferential trade agreements (PTAs). This inclination dates back to two clauses in the founding EU treaty: preferential trade ties between EU members and their colonies or overseas territories; and the EU customs union, itself a preferential trade arrangement.

In 1963, only five years after its creation, the EU signed the Yaoundé Convention giving non-reciprocal preferential treatment (such as zero or low import duties) to products originating in 18 African countries that had just gained independence from Belgium and France. In 1975, after the UK accession, the Lomé Convention extended the non-reciprocal Yaoundé PTA to former UK colonies, giving duty-free access to the EU market to 46 developing countries altogether, formally known as the African, Caribbean and Pacific (ACP) countries. In the meantime, the EU had become in 1971 the first 'donor country' to join the Generalized System of Preferences (GSP) and grant non-reciprocal preferential access to all developing countries. Thus, by 1975 all developing countries received preferential access to the EU market, with ACP countries receiving even better access in the form of lower tariffs or higher duty-free quotas.

Like reciprocal PTAs – customs unions and free-trade areas (FTAs), both often called RTAs – non-reciprocal PTAs are an exception to the most-favoured nation (MFN), non-discrimination GATT principle. However, contrary to RTAs, which are allowed under GATT Article XXIV, the original GATT rules did not allow non-reciprocal PTAs. The Yaoundé/Lomé and GSP PTAs were authorised by separate GATT waivers limited in time to ten years. In 1979, the GATT established a permanent exemption to the MFN obligation by way of the Enabling Clause, which allowed GATT members to grant trade preferences to developing countries that are generalised, non-discriminatory (between beneficiaries) and non-reciprocal.

The ACP–EU PTA, however, did not meet the conditions of the Enabling Clause and required a new waiver when the first one expired. After a series of GATT and WTO waivers, the EU and ACP countries received a last WTO waiver in 2001 giving them until 2007 to implement ACP–EU Economic Partnership Agreements (EPAs) instituting FTAs (hence reciprocal PTAs) between the EU and seven regional groupings of ACP countries. Currently, not all EPAs are operational nor have all ACP countries decided to join an EPA. ACP countries that have not yet joined an EPA still benefit from the EU's GSP programme, which has changed substantially since 1971. The latest reform, introduced in 2014, reduced the number of beneficiaries from 177 developing countries to 88 low- and lower-middle-income countries.[24] The new programme retains the three-tier system introduced in the 2001 reform. The first tier is the standard GSP with duty reductions for roughly 66 per cent of all EU tariff lines; in 2014, 26 countries enjoyed this scheme. The second tier, called GSP+, gives additional preferences to countries that implement core human rights, labour rights and other sustainable development conventions; in 2014 there were 13 GSP+ beneficiaries. The third tier, called Everything But Arms (EBA), gives all least-developed countries (as defined by the UN) full duty-free and quota-free access to the EU for all their exports with the exception of arms and armaments; in 2014 there were 49 EBA beneficiaries.

Over the years, the EU has also built an increasingly vast network of reciprocal PTAs. In 2000, the EU had RTAs with 28 partners: 20 Europeans (of which 12 have since joined the EU), four Mediterraneans, one ACP country (South Africa) and one North American country (Mexico).[25] In 2014, the shift towards countries outside of Europe and its traditional ACP and Mediterranean partners initiated with the EU–Mexico FTA had greatly increased after the launch of the Global Europe strategy in 2006.[26] The EU now had RTAs with 58 partners: 17 Europeans,[27] 8 Mediterraneans, 22 ACP countries, 10 Americans and one Asian (Korea);[28] and it was negotiating RTAs with several other important American (including Argentina, Brazil, Canada and the US) and Asian (including India, Japan, Singapore and Vietnam) partners.[29] This shift was both a deliberate effort to reinforce the EU's presence in emerging economies of Asia and Latin America and a response to policies by other leading trade players, in particular the US, Japan and China. In 2000, the US had only three RTA partners, while Japan had none and China had not yet joined the WTO. By 2014, the US had 20 RTA partners (of which eight were outside of the Americas), Japan 15 (of which four were outside of Asia) and China nine (of which four were outside of Asia).[30] Increasingly, EU and US RTAs cover not only trade in goods but also trade in services, intellectual property and even some areas not covered by WTO agreements, such as investment, competition policy and labour standards.[31]

Figure 14.1 gives the full picture of the EU's so-called 'pyramid of preferences', where partners are ranked from the most (at the top) to the least (at the bottom) preferred. It shows that in 2014 most EU trade partners enjoyed some form of preferential access to the EU market. At the same time, the number of countries trading with the EU on a purely MFN basis substantially increased after the 2014 reform of the EU's GSP scheme: it jumped from seven – Australia, Canada, Hong Kong, Japan, New Zealand, Taiwan and the US, for a long time the only EU's MFN partners – to 32.[32] Today, four out of the six main EU trade partners identified in Table 14.3 are still MFN partners. If EU bilateral negotiations with Japan and the US succeed this number will fall to two, leaving China and Russia as the only major EU partners treated on a MFN basis. It should be noted however that a country treated on a MFN basis is not completely at a disadvantage in terms of EU market access compared to a country with a PTA, at least as far as tariffs are concerned. The reason is that more than half the value of EU imports is at MFN zero, where by definition no preferential treatment can be granted.[33] Also the share of imports with zero MFN duty varies a lot across countries depending on the composition of their exports to the EU. It is 90 per cent for Russia, 45–50 per cent for China, Korea and the US but only 34 per cent for Japan, which implies that Russia suffers little from being treated on a MFN basis compared to PTA partners. By contrast Japan would stand to gain from a PTA with the EU: it would get an edge over countries like China that are treated by the EU on a MFN basis and would make up for its relative competitive disadvantage against countries like Korea which already have a FTA with the EU.[34]

In conclusion, the EU and the global trade regimes now seem on a path dangerously resembling the first option depicted by Sapir (1998) when he suggested that the decision by

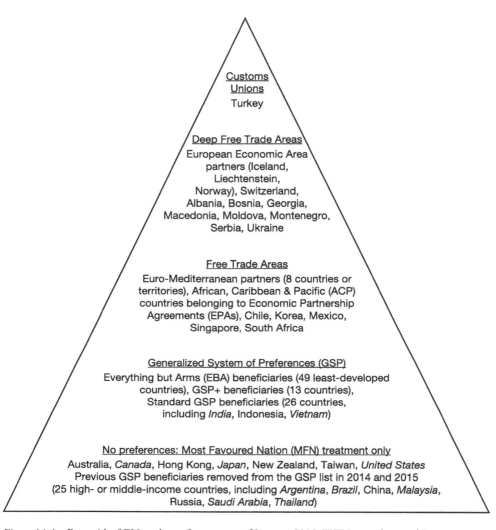

Figure 14.1 Pyramid of EU trade preferences, as of January 2015 (WTO members only)

Notes: Countries with which the EU is currently negotiating FTAs are indicated in italics. The EU and Singapore have initialled the text of their FTA in 2013, but the draft agreement still needs to be agreed upon by the European Commission and the Council of Ministers, and ratified by the European Parliament.

the EU to negotiate RTAs with non-European countries (and therefore for other purposes than potential EU membership) represented a radical step for EU regionalism. He contemplated three possible options. The first

> would see the construction of a EC-centred free-trade area eventually including the EC, the remaining nations of Europe, the Mediterranean countries and some other African countries . . . In total this vast FTA may include 20–25 countries in addition to the 25–30 members of the EC.
>
> *(Sapir, 1998, p. 729)*

The chapter argued that the creation of this EU-centred FTA

> would almost certainly precipitate the formation of the proposed FTAA [the Free Trade Association of the Americas] and transform Asia-Pacific Economic Cooperation (APEC) into a free-trade area. In addition, the inclusion of Russia in [the FTA] is bound to lead to strong political reactions from Washington, which could endanger the North-Atlantic Treaty Organization (NATO).
>
> *(Sapir, 1998, p. 730)*

The way to avoid these problems would be for the EU to

> reinforce its ties with the US by setting TAFTA [the Trans-Atlantic Free Trade Area]. However, because the US has a clear interest in remaining both an Atlantic and a Pacific power, it could not enter into TAFTA without at the same time being part of an Asia-Pacific FTA. The latter would be a clear threat to the economic interests of the EC, unless it succeeded in forming its own free-trade area with Asia. By then, in any event, the WTO-based multilateral trading system would have become devoid of content.
>
> *(Sapir, 1998, p. 730)*

With some caveats (like the fact that there has been no serious discussion to set up a EU–Russia FTA or that the US-led Asia-Pacific negotiations have preceded rather than followed the Trans-Atlantic ones), this scenario closely resembles the present reality: the EU has FTAs (though not yet an overarching one) with many European, Mediterranean and African countries; the US and Asia-Pacific countries are negotiating the TPP; the EU and the US are negotiating the TTIP; the EU has a FTA with Korea and is negotiating FTAs with other Asian countries; and the WTO Doha negotiations are in danger of being scuttled.

The second option considered by Sapir (1998) was viewed as equally extreme but also as the most desirable: having the EU put its weight behind efforts to reach a global free trade pact by 2010. Clearly, this scenario did not materialise nor is it about to happen. The third option, a midway between the first two options, was the continuation of the coexistence of bilateralism/regionalism and multilateralism, viewed as

> a reasonable second-best, provided it involves a substantial strengthening of [GATT] Article XXIV aimed at minimising the discriminatory aspect of RTAs.
>
> *(Sapir, 1998, p. 730)*

This last option is the one which is both favoured and considered as the most realistic by EU trade officials who often claim that the

> bilateral is not the enemy of the multilateral. The opposite may hold truer: liberalisation fuels liberalisation.
>
> *(European Commission, 2010, p. 5)*

History will tell whether they are right or whether, instead, 'discrimination fuels discrimination' and mega-regionals will fuel mega-discrimination and the eventual downfall of the multilateral trading system.[35] But the main threat to the global system may not come from the fact that liberalisation takes place in bilateral rather than multilateral fora. Rather it may result from the shift away from the WTO's dispute settlement mechanism by systemic players like the EU and the US. Since the creation of the mechanism in 1995, the EU has been its second most active participant behind the US.[36] During the period 1995–2014, it was involved in 183 disputes (out of a total of 486 WTO disputes): 93 times as complainant, 90 as respondent. Yet, as noted by Mavroidis and Sapir (2015), only seven of these disputes were with (three) PTA partners. Also bilateral disputes with the US accounted for between one-third and one-quarter of EU WTO litigation. This suggests that the conclusion of TTIP and other bilateral RTAs currently negotiated by the EU with important players could result in a significant shift away from the multilateral resolution of trade disputes and therefore in a weakening of the WTO trading system. A big question mark concerns the role of Brazil, China and India. Will Brazil and India conclude RTAs with the EU? If so will they also conclude RTAs with the US? What about China? Will it also negotiate RTAs with the EU and the US? Or will these three emerging countries remain outside of RTAs with the EU and the US?

5. Conclusion

Trade policy has long been regarded (together with competition policy) as the most successful EU policy largely because it is a field where the EU speaks with one voice. Every Trade Minister around the world knows perfectly well that the number to dial to speak to Europe is the EU Trade Commissioner's. As a result, Europe's weight in trade policy has been fairly commensurate with its share in trade. In particular, its role in multilateral, regional or bilateral trade negotiations has been (almost) on par with the US, until recently the only other global trade giant.

This chapter has shown that EU trade policy has evolved since the turn of the twenty-first century as a result of two related trends that characterize the current phase of globalisation: the growth of emerging countries, and especially China which has now also become a global trade giant; and the growth of global value chains which has significantly increased the interconnectedness of economies.

The first trend had the potential of trade conflicts between old players like the EU and new ones like China, especially in the wake of the global recession. And indeed there have been a number of such conflicts, including the high-profile EU–China solar panel case, but none has degenerated into escalating disputes and trade wars. The reason is primarily the high level of interconnectedness between the EU and emerging countries, especially China, which makes protectionist disputes very costly.

Rather than engage in costly trade wars with China and other emerging countries, the EU has sought to negotiate with them in the context of the Doha Round, but given the lack of progress at the multilateral level the EU (together with the US and other countries) has turned to other avenues to liberalise and regulate trade. One is the plurilateral trade negotiation toward a Trade in Services Agreement (TISA), which unfortunately takes place outside the WTO framework and does not include any of the large emerging countries like Brazil, China or India. The other avenue is a series of bilateral trade negotiations with partners that include not only the US and Japan but also Brazil and India, though the probability of reaching an agreement with these two emerging countries with whom the EU has been negotiating for many years seems fairly low. And so far the EU has refused to negotiate a bilateral trade agreement with China, though it has started to negotiate an investment agreement.

Where does this leave EU trade policy? Despite the growth of China and other emerging countries, the EU is likely to remain an important player on the global trade scene because of the size of its market and its ability to speak with one voice, which has not diminished despite the increased diversity of its Member States and the enlarged power of the European Parliament. It is also likely that the EU will remain a voice and a force in favour of liberal trade. What is less clear is how the EU will combine its two genetic sides, multilateralism and trade preferences, at a time when the multilateral trading system is under stress due to the changing balance of power between advanced and emerging powers. Bilateral preferential negotiations are certainly tempting in the present circumstances if only because they offer the prospect of tangible results. However, they also risk jeopardising the multilateral trading system precisely when it is most needed to ensure that the shift in global power is not accompanied by rising trade tensions.

Notes

1 I use the term European Union throughout to describe the European Economic Community (EEC) founded in 1958 and its successors, the European Community (EC) and the EU, although the three entities cover somewhat different institutional realities.

2 Throughout the chapter the term EU trade refers exclusively to extra-EU trade, i.e. trade with third countries.

3 Denmark and the United Kingdom left EFTA for the EU in 1973, Portugal in 1986 and Austria, Finland and Sweden in 1995. Since then EFTA counts only four members: Iceland, Liechtenstein, Norway and Switzerland.

4 The negotiation and conclusion of trade agreements covering cultural and audio-visual services or social, education and health services require unanimity in the Council.

5 Given the EU's exclusive competence in trade issues since Lisbon, only 'mixed' agreements still need to be ratified by national parliaments. Agreements are mixed if they contain issues for which the EU is not exclusively competent, such as transport policy.

6 See Van Gestel and Crombez (2011).

7 See, in particular, Pollack (1997) and Elsig (2007).

8 There is also an economic history literature on this subject. See especially Coppolaro (2013).

9 ACTA was an agreement negotiated between the EU and most of its Member States, Australia, Canada, Japan, Mexico, Morocco, New Zealand, Singapore, South Korea, Switzerland and the US for the purpose of establishing international standards for intellectual property rights enforcement. Negotiations started in 2006 and were concluded in 2010. The agreement was signed by the European Commission in 2012, but was then rejected by the European Parliament in plenary session by an overwhelming majority.

10 See Van den Putte *et al.* (2014).

11 See, for instance, Podgorny (2013).

12 The text goes back to the 1957 Rome Treaty. The parts in italics were added by the Lisbon Treaty.

13 It was 6.4 per cent in Germany, 9.7 in the Benelux customs union, 17 in France and 18.7 in Italy.

14 See Sapir (1992).

15 See Badinger and Breuss (2011) and Sapir (2011).

16 These findings are confirmed by Baldwin and Rieder (2007).

17 See Young and Peterson (2014).

18 See Martin and Mattoo (2011) for a useful analysis of the Doha Round agenda of negotiations.

19 See Table 14.4, panel 3 and Bown (2014). At the end of 2013, the EU had 111 anti-dumping measures in force, affecting about 20 trading partners. The majority were measures on imports from Asia, in particular China, which alone accounts for half the total measures in force. The biggest trade dispute between the EU and China took place in 2012–13 when the EU threatened to impose AD duties on €21 billion worth of solar panel imports from China. The high-stake dispute was eventually resolved after China threatened to impose AD duties on European wine exports and Germany opposed the Commission's proposed AD measure on grounds that it would have hurt its import and export interests in the solar panel global value chain.

20 At the end of 2013, the EU also had 13 anti-subsidy measures in force against seven trading partners. Again the vast majority affected imports from Asia, in particular China and India. See also WTO (2013).

21 See Vandenbussche and Viegelahn (2010).

22 See, for instance, Gawande *et al.* (2011) and Datt *et al.* (2011). The impact of globalisation on the EU trade discourse and strategy during and after the crisis is well documented by De Ville and Orbie (2014).

23 The number of EU members has increased from 15 to 28 since the launch of the Doha Round. Elsig (2010) writes that: 'Interviews with trade officials suggest that the majority of NMS [New Member States] show only lukewarm support for the multilateral trading system as the backbone of the EU's external trade policy.'

24 According to Van den Putte *et al.* (2014), the removal of high- and upper-middle-income countries from the EU's GSP scheme was the result of a compromise between free traders, protectionists and

developmentalists within the European Commission which also appealed to members of the European Parliament. The exclusion of economically stronger developing countries was welcomed by free traders as an incentive to conclude FTAs, protectionists were happy with lower preferences and developmentalists liked the focus of the new GSP on poorer countries.

25 See Sapir (2000).

26 See European Commission (2006). The EU-Mexico FTA entered into force in 2000 but concluded in 1997 by Leon Brittan, the EU Trade Commissioner during the Santer Commission (1995–9). During the Prodi Commission (1999–2004), a moratorium on new bilateral trade negotiations (except with neighbouring countries) was put in place by the then Trade Commissioner, Pascal Lamy. The 2006 Global Europe strategy was put forward by Peter Mandelson, the Trade Commissioner during the first Barroso Commission (2004–9).

27 Eight partners which already had an RTA with the EU in 2000 but have not joined the EU plus nine new RTA partners.

28 The EU–Korea FTA was the first bilateral free trade agreement that needed approval of the European Parliament following the entry into force of the Lisbon Treaty. Approval of the text negotiated by the European Commission required the addition of a bilateral safeguard clause in the agreement for so-called 'sensitive sectors', including cars, textiles and consumer electronics.

29 The EU maintains or negotiates RTAs not only with individual countries but also with country groupings. In fact the EU, itself a customs union, has tried to promote the creation of other customs unions throughout the world by offering to negotiate free-trade agreements with them. However negotiations between the EU and regional groupings have usually been rather tedious and rarely successful. Examples of still pending negotiations include EU–Gulf Cooperation Council (launched in 1988), EU–Mercosur (launched in 1999) and EU–Central Africa EPA (launched in 2002). The only successful negotiation has been the EU-CARIFORUM EPA concluded in 2009. See Ramdoo and Bilal (2013) for a discussion of the difficulties of negotiating EPAs with African countries.

30 I exclude China's RTAs notified to the WTO under the Enabling Clause which are less demanding than those notified under GATT Article XXIV to which RTAs involving the EU, the US, Japan or other advanced economies must adhere.

31 See Horn *et al.* (2010) for a detailed study of provisions contained in EU and US RTAs, which the authors classify into WTO plus (those already covered by WTO agreements) and WTO extra (those going beyond existing WTO agreements).

32 This number includes four previous GSP beneficiaries which lost their GSP status in January 2015: China, Ecuador, Maldives and Thailand.

33 See Table 14.4, panel 2.

34 All the figures in this paragraph are from Carpenter and Lendle (2010) and were computed using 2008 trade flows and tariffs, which predate the 2014 GSP reform.

35 There is very little empirical evidence on the link between bilateral and multilateral trade liberalisation. One exception is Karacaovali and Limão (2008) who find that the EU's PTAs acted as a stumbling block for multilateral trade liberalisation in the Uruguay Round.

36 See Table 14.4, panel 4.

References

Badinger, H. and Breuss, F. (2011), The Quantitative Effects of European Post-War Economic Integration. In: Jovanovic, M.N. (ed.), *International Handbook on the Economics of Integration, Volume III*. Edward Elgar Publishing Ltd: Cheltenham, UK and Northampton, MA, USA.

Balassa, B. (ed.) (1975), *European Economic Integration*. Contributions to Economic Analysis 89. North-Holland: Amsterdam.

Baldwin, R.E. (1995), A Domino Theory of Regionalism. In: Baldwin, R.E., Haaparanta, P. and Kiander, J. (eds), *Expanding European Regionalism: The EU's New Members*. Cambridge University Press: Cambridge.

Baldwin, R.E. and Rieder, R. (2007), A Test of Endogenous Trade Bloc Formation Theory on EU Data. Centre for Economic Policy Research Discussion Paper 6389. CEPR: London.

Bown, C.P. (2014), Temporary Trade Barriers Database. World Bank: Washington, D.C. Available online at http://econ.worldbank.org/ttbd/

Carpenter, T. and Lendle, A. (2010), How Preferential is World Trade? CTEI Working Paper No. 2010–32, Centre for Trade and Economic Integration, Graduate Institute: Geneva.

Coppolaro, L. (2013), *The Making of a World Trading Power: The European Economic Community (EEC) in the GATT Kennedy Round Negotiations (1963–67)*. Ashgate Publishing Co.: Farnham.

Datt, M., Hoekman, B. and Malouche, M. (2011), Taking Stock of Trade Protectionism since 2008. Economic Premise No. 72, Poverty Reduction and Economic Management (PREM) Network. World Bank: Washington, D.C.

De Ville, F. and Orbie, J. (2014), The European Commission's Neoliberal Trade Discourse since the Crisis: Legitimizing Continuity through Subtle Discursive Change. *British Journal of Politics and International Relations* 16(1), 149–67.

Elsig, M. (2007), The EU's Choice of Regulatory Venues for Trade Negotiations: A Tale of Agency Power? *Journal of Common Market Studies* 45(4), 927–48.

Elsig, M. (2010), European Union Trade Policy after Enlargement: Larger Crowds, Shifting Priorities and Informal Decision-Making. *Journal of European Public Policy* 17(6), 783–800.

European Commission (2006), *Global Europe: Competing in the World.* Communication, COM (2006) 567. European Commission: Brussels.

European Commission (2010), *Trade, Growth, and World Affairs – Trade Policy as a Core Component of the EU 2020 Strategy.* Communication, COM (2010) 612. European Commission: Brussels.

European Commission (2013), *DG Trade Statistical Pocket Guide,* December. European Commission: Brussels.

Eurostat (2011), *External and Intra-EU Trade: A Statistical Yearbook, 1958–2010,* 2011 edition. European Commission: Luxembourg.

Gawande, K., Hoekman, B. and Cui, Y. (2011), Determinants of Trade Policy Responses to the 2008 Financial Crisis. World Bank Policy Research Paper 5862. World Bank: Washington, D.C.

Horn, H., Mavroidis, P.C. and Sapir, A. (2010), Beyond the WTO? An Anatomy of EU and US Preferential Trade Agreements. *The World Economy* 33(11), 1565–88.

Karacaovali, B. and Limão, N. (2008), The Clash of Liberalizations: Preferential vs. Multilateral Trade Liberalization in the European Union. *Journal of International Economics* 74(2), 299–327.

Martin, W. and Mattoo, A. (eds) (2011), *Unfinished Business? The WTO's Doha Agenda.* CEPR: London and the World Bank: Washington, D.C.

Mavroidis, P.C. and Sapir, A. (2015), Dial PTAs for Peace: The Influence of Preferential Trade Agreements on Litigation between Trading Partners. *Journal of World Trade,* forthcoming.

Podgorny, M.-J. (2013), The Negotiation and Adoption of Preferential Trade Agreements in the Lisbon Era: A View from the European Parliament. In: Kleimann, D. (ed.), *EU Preferential Trade Agreements: Commerce, Foreign Policy, and Development Aspects.* European University Institute: Florence.

Pollack, M. (1997), Delegation, Agency and Agenda Setting in the European Community. *International Organization* 51(1), 99–134.

Ramdoo, I. and Bilal, S. (2013), European Trade Policy, Economic Partnership Agreements and Regional Integration in Africa. In: Kleimann, D. (ed.), *EU Preferential Trade Agreements: Commerce, Foreign Policy, and Development Aspects.* European University Institute: Florence.

Sapir, A. (1992), Regional Integration in Europe. *Economic Journal* 102(415), 1491–1506.

Sapir, A. (1998), The Political Economy of EC Regionalism. *European Economic Review* 42(3), 717–32.

Sapir, A. (2000), EC Regionalism at the Turn of the Millennium: Toward a New Paradigm? *The World Economy* 23(9), 1135–48.

Sapir, A. (2001), Domino Effects in Western European Regional Trade, 1960–1992. *European Journal of Political Economy* 17(2), 377–88.

Sapir, A. (2011), European Integration at the Crossroads: A Review Essay on the 50th Anniversary of Bela Balassa's 'Theory of Economic Integration'. *Journal of Economic Literature* 49(4), 1200–1229.

Vandenbussche, H. and Viegelahn, C. (2010), No Protectionist Surprises: EU Antidumping Policy Before and During the Great Recession. In: Bown, Chad P. (ed.), *The Great Recession and Import Protection: The Role of Temporary Trade Barriers.* CEPR: London and the World Bank: Washington, D.C.

VanGrasstek, C. (2013), *Speaking Truth about Power: The Real Problem in the Multilateral Trading System.* In: Evenett, S.J. and Jara, A. (eds), Building on Bali: A Work Programme for the WTO. CEPR: London.

Van den Putte, L., De Ville, F. and Orbie, J. (2014), The European Parliament's New Role in Trade Policy: Turning Power into Impact. CEPS Special Report No. 89, Centre for European Policy Studies: Brussels.

Van Gestel, W. and Crombez, C. (2011), The Role of the Trade Policy Committee in EU Trade Policy: A Political-Economic Analysis. University of Leuven, mimeo.

WTO (2013), *Trade Policy Review: European Union: Report by the Secretariat.* WT/TPR/S/282/Rev.2. World Trade Organization: Geneva.

WTO (2014), Modest Trade Growth Anticipated for 2014 and 2015 Following Two Year Slump. Press Release 721, 14 April. World Trade Organization: Geneva.

Young, A.R. and Peterson, J. (2014), *Parochial Global Europe: 21st Century Trade Politics.* Oxford University Press: Oxford.

15

THE EU AND THE US

TTIP

Gabriel Felbermayr[1]

1. Introduction

Since July 2013, the EU and the US have been in the process of negotiating a Transatlantic Trade and Investment Partnership (TTIP). The objective of the process is to create a common transatlantic market place with low barriers to trade and investment.

After the end of the Soviet Union, the world economy in general and the nature of transatlantic trade in particular underwent a deep transformation towards an increasingly prominent role of value chains and production networks. It has since become clear that the transatlantic relationship needs to be redefined. Therefore, it is no surprise that the TTIP is not the first effort to secure a substantial trade agreement between the world's two biggest trading blocks. The New Transatlantic Agenda in 1995, the Transatlantic Economic Partnership in 1998 and a framework agreed at the Transatlantic Economic Council in 2007 all attempted to make it easier to do business across the Atlantic, however with limited success.

The current attempt is the most credible and the most ambitious so far. At an EU-US Summit meeting in November 2011 both sides agreed to create a high-level working group on jobs and growth led by US Trade Representative Ron Kirk and EU Trade Commissioner Karel De Gucht. In February 2013, a final report from the group recommended:

> [...] to US and EU Leaders that the United States and the EU launch [...] negotiations on a comprehensive, ambitious agreement that addresses a broad range of bilateral trade and investment issues, including regulatory issues, and contributes to the development of global rules.[2]

A little later, in his State of the Union Address in February 2013, US President Obama announced:

> And tonight, I am announcing that we will launch talks on a comprehensive Transatlantic Trade and Investment Partnership with the European Union – because trade that is free and fair across the Atlantic supports millions of good-paying American jobs.[3]

Subsequently, the European Commission adopted the draft mandate for the TTIP talks and a common position between the 27 Member States was negotiated. It was approved unanimously under the Irish presidency of the EU in June 2013. Negotiations started in July 2013. Since then, six rounds have been held, alternating between Brussels and Washington.

While little detail is known about the negotiating process, topics covered, or progress made, officials from both sides of the Atlantic and numerous leaked documents have made fully clear that the envisaged TTIP shall be ambitions, comprehensive, and go beyond existing commitments at the level of the World Trade Organization (WTO). The Commission's mandate states the objective of "realizing the untapped potential of a truly transatlantic market place".

One may wonder why talks on an ambitious TTIP have not started earlier. There are at least three reasons. First, only in 2006 did the EU turn to a more active policy of negotiating bilateral trade agreements based on economic rather than political objectives.[4] This move reflected the incapacity of the WTO to finalize the Doha Round of trade negotiations that was launched in 2001, originally with the aim of achieving an agreement by 2005. Second, while the US and the EU have long commanded substantial influence in the world trading system each on their own, the rise of emerging economies, most notably China, has challenged their pivotal roles. Figure 15.1 shows that, from 1974 to 2003, the joint share of the US and the EU in world GDP (measured in current prices) was very stable, at around 60 percent, and both players had approximately similar weight. From 2003 to 2013, the joint share fell to about 46 percent. Long-run predictions of the OECD see the EU and the US both at about half their 1974–2003 weight by 2060. So, if the traditional "West" wants to retain some influence in the world trade order, transatlantic cooperation is a necessity. Third, the world financial crisis of 2008/09 and the following period of sluggish growth have incentivized policy makers to look for new sources of growth. With little room to loosen fiscal and monetary policies further, it was believed that trade liberalization promises substantial benefits at relatively low political costs.[5]

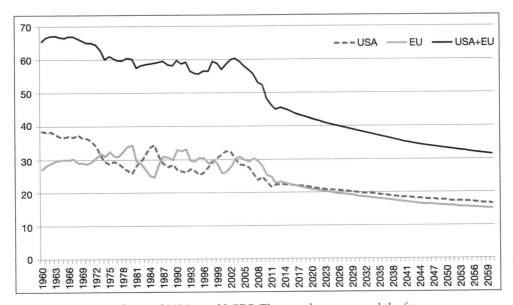

Figure 15.1 Shares of EU and US in world GDP: The past, the present, and the future

2. The nature of EU–US trade

2.1 Trade volume

In 2012, the EU exported goods worth 388 billion dollars to the US, and it imported goods and services worth 264 billion dollars from there. Services exports amounted to about 162 billion and imports to 191 billion dollars. The EU has a bilateral surplus in goods trade, a small deficit in services trade, and an overall bilateral trade surplus of about 95 billion dollars.

Figure 15.2 plots EU goods trade with the US over time. From 1995 to 2013, exports have grown at an annual growth rate of about 6 percent while imports have grown at an annual rate of about 4 percent. These numbers do not compare very favorably to the growth rate of world trade of about 8 percent per annum in the same period.[6]

As shown in Table 15.1, EU exports to the US make up about 8 percent of total EU exports, and they amount to about 3.55 percent of EU GDP. The ratios are slightly smaller for EU imports from the US.

Within the EU, Germany and the UK are the largest trade partners of the US. As shown in Figure 15.3, Germany accounts for 25 percent of exports, the UK for 22 percent. This is higher than the shares of these countries in EU GDP (21 and 15 percent, respectively). The third largest

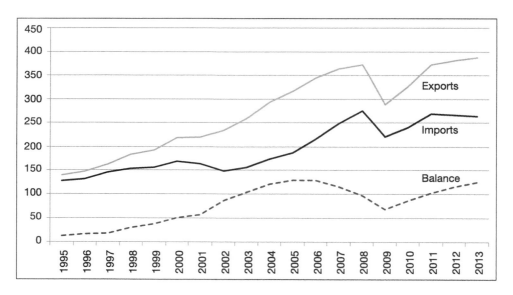

Figure 15.2 EU goods trade with the US over time, volume in bn. current dollars

Table 15.1 Bilateral trade relative to total trade and GDP

	Share in total trade		Share in GDP	
	EU	*US*	*EU*	*US*
Exports	8.06%	22.39%	3.55%	3.05%
Imports	7.07%	21.53%	2.98%	3.64%

Notes: Own calculations based on data from OECD and World Bank.

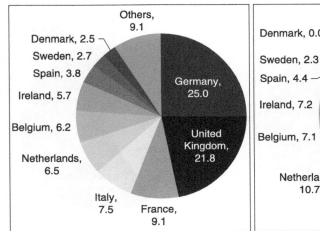 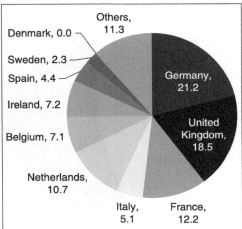

Figure 15.3 Shares of EU Member States in EU exports and imports (goods and services) to and from US, 2012, %

Source: Own calculations based on OECD STAN Bilateral Trade in Goods, and OECD Statistics on International Trade in Services

exporter, France, contributes a share of only 9 percent. On the import side, Germany accounts for 21 percent, the UK for 19 percent, and France 12 percent. Ireland is responsible for 7.2 and 5.7 percent of imports and exports, respectively; this is substantially larger than the country's share in EU GDP, which is a mere 1.2 percent, and almost double the share of Spain. The importance of the US as a trade partner is, therefore, very different for different EU countries.

2.2 Sectoral breakdown

Figure 15.4 shows that, in 2012, services accounted for 36 percent of EU exports to the US and for 40 percent of EU imports. These shares have increased slightly over time; in 2004 they stood at 34 and 39 percent, respectively. On the export side, in 2012, the chemicals, machinery and transport equipment industries accounted for almost 50 percent of total trade (20, 16 and 14 percent, respectively). The same industries also dominate the import side. In 2012, the accounted together for about 44 percent of imports (19, 14, and 11 percent, respectively). These shares have remained remarkably stable over time.

The food and agricultural sectors, despite their prominent role in trade debates, are not important: raw and processed food together amounted to about 15 billion euros of exports and 9 billion euros of imports in 2012; this is about 5 percent of total US trade. In the agri-food sector, the EU has a trade surplus of about 6 billion euros with the US. It is entirely driven by processed food. In raw agricultural goods, the EU has a trade deficit.[7]

The figures shown suggest that transatlantic trade is strongly intra-industry in nature. Indeed, the EU–US link features one of the highest Grubel-Lloyd indices amongst large trading nations. This undisputed fact is very important for the economic analysis.

2.3 The role of multinational firms

Moreover, a large fraction of transatlantic trade occurs within multinational enterprises. According to data from the US Census Bureau, in 2013, 61 percent of European merchandise

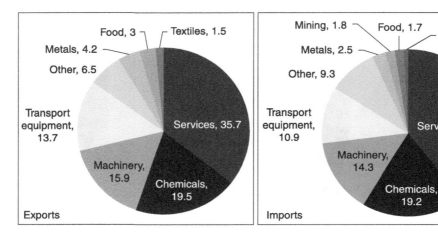

Figure 15.4 Shares of sectors in EU trade with US, 2012, %

Source: Own calculations based on OECD STAN Bilateral Trade in Goods, and OECD Statistics on International Trade in Services

exports to the US have been to related parties (up from 57 percent in 2002).[8] In contrast, only 32 percent of EU imports from the US are from related parties (up from 31 percent). The difference between imports and exports is striking. It has to do with differences in the nature of foreign direct investment (FDI). European FDI in the US is often vertical, so that trade in intermediate inputs between related firms is important. In contrast, US FDI in the EU is more likely horizontal. The share of EU exports to related parties is highest in the chemicals (83 percent), transport (69 percent), plastics (65 percent) and computer (65 percent) industries.

The transatlantic economic relationship is often described as an investment-driven one. Indeed, in 2011, the US outward stock of FDI in the EU amounted to about 50 percent of the US total, and the US inward stock of FDI in the US amounted to about 62 percent of the total. American multinationals earned about 39 percent of their foreign income in Europe and European multinationals accounted for about 63 percent of foreign FDI income in the US. Moreover, about 41 percent of foreign affiliate sales of US multinationals materialized in Europe, while EU multinationals accounted for 52 percent of affiliate sales of foreign firms in the US.[9]

3. How free is transatlantic trade today?

3.1 On the importance of trade costs

The volume of trade between the EU and the US is impressive, at least if one looks at the absolute transaction values. However, to judge the depth of the relationship, one requires a benchmark scenario to compare the status quo with. A rough calculation, inspired by Feenstra (2004, Chapter 5) goes as follows: if trade in the world were entirely free from trade frictions both on the demand and the supply sides, and if trade occurs because of national product differentiation, the level of trade between two countries relative to world GDP is simply the product of the two countries' shares in world GDP. The EU's share in world GDP is a proxy for its supply capacity, and the US' share is a proxy for its demand capacity. So, if both regions account each for a 1/4 of world GDP,[10] their trade should account for about 1/16 of world GDP. Adding flows in both directions, total trade should be 1/8 of world GDP. This number can be compared to observed trade, which amounts to about 1.4 percent of world GDP.[11]

The difference between the benchmark value and the observed value may be due to different preferences, but also due to different trade costs. The fact that the two values differ so much has inspired the literature to talk about a "puzzle of missing trade" (Trefler, 1995). It has spurred a large literature on the importance of trade costs. In their survey article, Anderson and van Wincoop (2004) show evidence that trade costs within the OECD Member States are equivalent to tariffs ranging between 70 and 80 percent. The largest fraction of these costs is not directly induced by trade policies, but is driven by geographical distance, cultural or linguistic differences, or currency related costs. However, the evidence also shows that directly policy-related trade costs are much higher than what data on tariffs suggest. This finding motivates trade policy initiatives in a world where conventional trade barriers (tariffs) are so low.

3.2 Tariffs

Import duties across the Atlantic are already relatively low. According to Felbermayr et al. (2013), in the manufacturing sector, the weighted average customs duties were 2.8 percent for both US imports from the EU and EU imports from the US. In the area of agricultural goods, US imports from the EU were affected by an average tariff of 2.6 percent while EU imports from the US were affected by an average tariff of 3.9 percent (most favored nations tariffs, 2007).

However, this structure hides substantial variation. Figure 15.5 shows data from Berden et al. (2009). EU import tariffs in the processed food and automotive sectors average around 10 percent; US import tariffs are higher than average in processed foods, too, and in other manufactures.

Despite low average tariffs, it would be wrong to conclude that tariffs have no trade-inhibiting role in transatlantic trade. First, trade in intermediate inputs, a significant portion of EU–US trade, can imply double taxation as inputs and final goods are taxed when crossing the border. Second, since tariffs differ substantially across goods, they induce welfare-reducing substitution effects towards low-tariff items. And, third, peak tariffs can be as high as several hundred percentage points, so that they make trade in some (few) goods prohibitively expensive.

Weighted average import tariffs with the US are low, but they are high compared with the weighted average tariff of the EU relative to the world, where it was around 1.41 percent in 2007 (and 1.17 percent in 2012).[12] This is more than half the weighted level for imports from the US, reflecting the facts that EU imports from the US are biased towards products with relatively high tariffs and that the EU already has free trade agreements with important trading partners such as Turkey, Mexico, or non-EU countries in Europe (such as Switzerland, Norway, or Iceland).

3.3 Non-tariff measures

Given these facts, it is not surprising that the focus of trade negotiations has shifted from tariffs to so called non-tariff measures (NTMs). These can be understood as the sum of all policy-related costs that put foreign suppliers of goods and services at a cost disadvantage

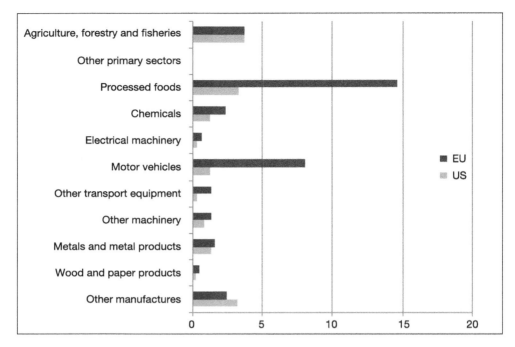

Figure 15.5 Import tariffs, applied MFN, trade weighted, 2007

Source: Data from Francois et al. (2013).

relative to domestic suppliers. Such costs can arise from traditional border measures (costs related to customs procedures, etc.) as well as behind-the-border measures flowing from domestic laws, regulations and practices. Sometimes, the term NTM is used as synonymous to non-tariff *barriers* (NTBs), but it makes sense to view NTBs as including natural barriers (such as distance, language differences . . .) that cannot be changed by trade negotiations besides the policy-related NTMs.

NTMs can reflect the course of history. Legitimate goals can be reached in different ways. This can lead to regulatory divergence. Examples include different regulations across the Atlantic on the design of side mirrors or on the color of blinker lights in cars. Similar divergence exists in the chemicals industry. NTMs may also reflect different policy preferences. For example, in the EU, market access of chemicals has been governed by the so-called precautionary principle, while the US bases regulation on strict liability laws. Third, NTMs may be in place because of simple protectionist motives. In practice, often all three determinants coexist, and NTMs fulfill a multiple purpose. For example, the EU's import ban on chicken washed in a chlorinated solution is in place to protect consumers, but it also effectively protects the EU poultry industry from foreign competition. NTMs are pervasive; they appear in almost every industry, and they take a wide variety of different forms.

There are two main approaches to measure NTMs. The first, a bottom-up approach, is to construct indicators of NTM existence and stringency with the help of firm-level surveys, and to use this information in gravity models to estimate ad valorem tariff equivalents (AVEs) of these barriers. Alternatively, one can use data on NTMs notified to the WTO, e.g., in the areas of technical barriers to trade (TBT) or sanitary and phytosanitary (SPS) measures. In a second step, expert opinion is brought in to decide on the share of those AVEs which is

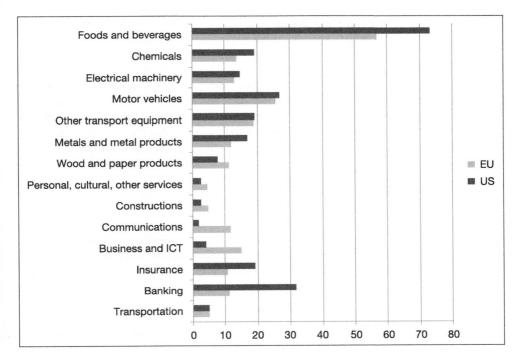

Figure 15.6 Bottom-up estimates of non-tariff measures, tariff equivalents

Source: Berden et al. (2009).

actionable, i.e., which can in principle be reduced by policy reform, and what portion of the actionable share can be realistically lowered within a proposed free trade agreement, such as TTIP. The second approach, a top-down approach, does not aim at measuring the level of NTMs but uses existing free trade agreements to estimate their trade cost reducing effect.

In the context of transatlantic trade, Berden et al. (2009) have used a very careful and comprehensive bottom-up analysis. They have shown that NTMs are very important in EU–US trade, and that their incidence differs strongly from industry to industry. Figure 15.6 provides their data. In the manufacturing industries, AVEs associated with NTMs amount to about 20 percent, with the highest values reached in the areas of food and beverages. While trade weighted tariff rates tend to be higher in the EU than in the US, NTMs are more costly in the US than in the EU.

In the service industry, trade is generally tariff-free, and the main restrictions to trade are of NTM type. In some sectors, such as in construction, they look low; but they can be very substantial, e.g., in the banking industry, where they reach more than 30 percent in the US.

Bottom-up estimates of NTMs are very useful because they can tell negotiators in great detail exactly where the problems lie. They are, however, prone to different problems. For example, it is not clear whether firms actually have incentives to report NTMs when they are asked in a survey. Also, the scope of the underlying NTM concept is often not easily defined. For example, are government procurement or investment restrictions covered?

Top-down estimates of NTM reductions in existing free trade agreements have their own problems, too. First, it is not straightforward to obtain unbiased estimates of average treatment effects. Second, earlier experience need not be informative about a specific agreement in negotiation, such as the TTIP. Third, the ex post, top-down analysis does not inform on the precise channels through which agreements have actually brought down trade costs.

In the empirical trade literature, ex post evaluations of free trade agreements abound. As the theoretical underpinning of the gravity equation has improved, estimation has improved, too. Nonetheless, estimated treatment effects still differ widely. Cipollina and Salvaticci (2010) as well as Head and Mayer (2014) provide meta analyses. Over time, however, estimates have tended to converge as researchers have been able to more successfully deal with the endogeneity of agreements. Overall, it is probably fair to say that the literature agrees on the existence of a positive and substantial treatment effect of agreements on bilateral trade. Depending on sample and period, the effect ranges between 50 and 200 percent.

4. Areas of negotiations

The TTIP negotiations cover three broad areas: (a) market access, (b) regulatory issues and non-tariff barriers (NTMs), and (c) rules. At the time of writing of this chapter (July 2014), some details on the level of ambition and on the state of the negotiations have transpired, but substantial uncertainty still exists. Much of the following is, therefore, to some extent speculative in nature.

4.1 Market access

In the area of trade in goods, the planned agreement strives to eliminate all duties and other requirements (such as taxes, fees, quantitative restrictions, or authorization requirements) on bilateral trade, but it will most likely include phase-in provisions and safeguard "emergency" clauses. It will also contain provisions to harmonize rules of origin, in particular with respect to third countries which already have trade agreements with either the US or the EU. Regarding services, the parties attempt to reduce long-standing market access barriers, while recognizing the sensitive nature of certain sectors. They will also anchor a national treatment clause, by which foreign establishments (subsidiaries of foreign firms) must receive no less favorable treatment than domestic firms. The agreement will contain the mutual recognition of professional qualifications to facilitate services trade. The EU negotiating mandate explicitly excludes audiovisual services.

Concerning investment, uncertainty is large, since the public opinion and even some governments in the EU have expressed doubts about the usefulness of an investment chapter in the TTIP. If the agreement is to be modeled on the publically available texts on the EU–Canada agreement (CETA, comprehensive economic and trade agreement) or on the existing US model text for bilateral investment treaties, it will go beyond the usual bilateral investment treaties in that it not only covers investment protection but also liberalization. It will include provisions that prohibit discriminatory treatment of foreign firms through a national treatment and a most-favored nation clause; it will protect investors against direct and indirect expropriation, including the right for adequate and effective compensation; it will include provisions guaranteeing the free transfer of funds of capital; and it will include an investor-to-state dispute settlement mechanism to enforce the agreement.

The agreement should enhance mutual access to public procurement markets at all levels of government; eliminate domestic production or local content requirements, and achieve transparency in the tendering process.

To date, it is very likely that audiovisual services, and sensitive products in the agri-food sector (chlorinated chicken, beef treated with growth hormones, genetically modified organisms) will be not covered by the treatment.

4.2 Regulatory issues and non-tariff barriers

The agreement will attempt to reach an ambitious level of regulatory compatibility for goods and services through mutual recognition, harmonization, and through enhanced cooperation between regulators. The agreement will cover SPS and measures TBT. The former concerns regulation that sets standards protecting human, animal, and plant health, while the latter deals with technical standards. So far, the negotiators have stressed that the agreement will be without prejudice to the right to regulate in accordance with the level of health, safety, consumer, labor and environmental protection and cultural diversity

It is expected that the agreement will include cross-cutting disciplines on regulatory coherence and transparency for the development and implementation of efficient, cost-effective, and more compatible rules on goods and services. These may include early consultations on regulatory action, impact assessments, or periodic review of existing measures.

The agreement will probably also include sectoral provisions that contain additional commitments or steps aimed at fostering regulatory compatibility in specific areas such as in motor vehicles, chemicals, pharmaceuticals, information and communication technologies, or financial services.

Currently, it appears unrealistic that the agreement will define common standards in any important industry. Mutual recognition of standards is more likely, but will be limited to some industries (for example motor vehicles). At the very minimum, the agreement will contain provisions about the mutual recognition of tests. It will also attempt to improve transparency and predictability of regulatory processes.

4.3 Rules

The agreement will probably cover intellectual property rights. In the EU, geographical indicators are of major importance. Moreover, it will include provisions on customs and trade facilitation. Specifically, these provisions will revise customs rules and procedures or documentation requirements, and improve cooperation between customs authorities. Importantly, the agreement is likely to include provisions on competition policy covering issues such as antitrust, mergers, and state aid. Finally, negotiating parties have announced that they will include a chapter on small and medium-sized enterprises.

Clearly, an agreement between the EU and the US will need an institutional structure to ensure an effective follow-up of commitments. Also, negotiators are talking about a transatlantic regulatory cooperation council whose aim it is to promote the progressive achievement of compatibility of regulatory regimes.

5. Potential economic benefits from a TTIP

At the time of writing this chapter, talks on the proposed TTIP are in full swing. In July 2013, they started with high ambitions, but after six rounds of negotiations it had become increasingly clear that the outcome, if at all positive, was most likely to be more modest than what was initially planned.

Against this backdrop, how can one provide a plausible quantification of the potential economic effects from a TTIP? A number of studies have provided estimates; here, we focus on two exemplary exercises which use different approaches and come, regarding certain aspects, to different conclusions.[13] First, a study ordered by the EU Commission and conducted by Francois et al. (2013) embeds top-down estimates on NTMs described above into a rich multi-sector computable general equilibrium (CGE) model of the world economy.[14] Second, work carried out at the ifo Institute, a think tank in Germany, and summarized in Felbermayr et al. (2015), makes use of a top-down strategy on NTMs in the context of a macro-model with very large country coverage.

All exercises make use of standard general equilibrium models of the world economy. They make use of the so-called Armington assumption by which goods are differentiated by country of origin. Francois et al. (2013) assume monopolistic competition in some industries. These assumptions, while providing different micro structure, do not matter much for quantitative analysis; see Arkolakis et al. (2013). With the exception of Felbermayr et al. (2015), labor markets are assumed competitive. All frameworks compare steady states and abstract from short-run adjustment dynamics. Francois et al. (2013) compare two simulated equilibria, both pertaining to the year of 2027—one with and one without a TTIP—while Felbermayr et al. (2015) compare the observed situation of 2012 with a counterfactual world, also pertaining to 2012, in which a TTIP is in place and fully working. Francois et al. (2013) provide estimates for ten world regions (and a residual aggregate), while Felbermayr et al. (2015) have results for 176 individual countries, including the EU Member States.

The mentioned studies agree that a TTIP could provide a substantial boost to per capita income in both Europe and the US. They also yield very similar estimates on the effects of a tariffs-only liberalization scenario. However, in scenarios going beyond tariffs, they differ strongly from each other with regard to the size of these gains and with regard to the effects on third countries. The main reason for these discrepancies lies in the definition of the deep TTIP scenario.

5.1 Scenario definition

In scenarios of limited integration, all studies assume that tariffs are almost fully eliminated (e.g., in Francois et al. (2013) tariffs are put to zero in 98 percent of all tariff lines), and that some reduction in services NTMs is achieved. The scenarios of comprehensive (or deep) liberalization, however, differ. Francois et al. (2013) assume that, besides elimination of tariffs, costs from NTMs in goods and services trade are reduced by 25 percent, a single market for 50 percent of all public procurement activities is created, and NTMs between TTIP members and third countries as well as NTMs between third countries themselves fall by 30 percent and 20 percent of the reduction achieved within the EU and US.

In contrast, for their comprehensive scenario, Felbermayr et al. (2015) assume that trade costs between the EU and the US fall by exactly the same percentage amount that ex post evaluations have found for existing trade agreements. They follow the econometric analysis of Egger et al. (2011), who have estimated the local average treatment effect for a large number (about 120) of agreements, applying methods that can convincingly deal with the non-random assignment of trade agreements to country pairs. Together with their choice of trade elasticity of seven, the point estimates translates into a reduction of trade costs by 17 percentage points. This approach implies that the TTIP is assumed to be no more and no less ambitious than the average of existing agreements. A bold assumption which is certainly violated in practice, it does have several virtues. First, it is *comprehensive* because it accounts for changed private or public incentives for reductions in bilateral trade costs (e.g., investment into bilateral trading infrastructure, language, or law) and for the administrative costs that tariff exemptions may put on firms (e.g., by requiring exporters to document the origin of their merchandise). Second, it is *feasible*, since the reductions have been possible in other agreements in the past. The approach, however, has drawbacks, too: it strongly relies on the point estimates obtained in econometric analysis and it does not allow disentangling the sources of trade cost reductions. In their main scenario, Felbermayr et al. (2015) do not allow the TTIP to reduce trade costs between country pairs not fully covered by TTIP. That is, they rule out over-effects. Based on a survey contained in the World Trade Report (2012), they argue that there is little existing empirical evidence that would support the existence of such spill-overs. The consequences of this assumption, however, are dramatic: lower NTMs will benefit TTIP insiders in a discriminatory fashion as outsiders see their relative competitiveness in the transatlantic market decline.

5.2 Trade effects of a TTIP

In the tariffs-only agreement, transatlantic free trade would have only very modest effects on trade flows; Francois et al. (2013) predict an increase in bilateral trade of about 6 percent. Effects would be larger in more protected industries, e.g., agri-food and automotive, where Francois et al. (2013) predict an increase of about 18 percent and 14 percent, respectively. However, in a comprehensive agreement, trade effects would be sizeable. According to Francois et al. (2013), EU exports to the US could go up by 28 percent while US exports to the EU could increase by 36 percent. Felbermayr et al. (2015) predict bilateral gains averaging about 80 percent between the EU and the US, and substantial heterogeneity between EU Member States and the US (ranging between 50 and 110 percent). They also report that trade within the EU could reduce by as much as 30 percent on average, and that there would be substantial trade diversion with third countries. Francois et al. (2013), due to existence of spill-over effects, do not find large trade diversion effects.

5.3 Welfare effects of a TTIP

In the tariffs-only scenarios, both studies come to very low welfare gains (defined as equivalent variation measures). Francois et al. (2013) find a gain of 0.10 percent for the EU and of 0.04 percent for the US, while Felbermayr et al. (2015) find 0.32 and 0.41 percent, respectively. Magnitudes differ due to differences in model setup (multi-sector versus macro model), but the overall message is consistent: a tariffs-only agreement would not yield any substantial welfare effects.

Regarding the welfare effects from a comprehensive trade agreement, the studies differ substantially. As shown in Table 15.2 Francois et al. (2013) predict an increase in real per capita income of about 0.5 percent for the EU and 0.4 percent for the US, while Felbermayr et al. (2015) find a plus of about 3.9 percent and 4.9 percent, respectively. Moreover, Francois et al. (2013) report positive welfare effects in third countries, while Felbermayr et al. (2015) find negative effects. For the world in total, the welfare gain is between 0.1 and 1.6 percent, respectively.

Table 15.3 reports more detailed welfare results for 40 selected countries (out of 173) from the Felbermayr et al. (2015) study. It details four different scenarios: the preferred (comprehensive) scenario based on the Egger et al. (2011) estimate; a scenario based on the average effect of trade agreements found in the meta study of Head and Mayer (2014), a tariffs-only scenario, and a scenario where the trade cost savings within TTIP spill over to non-TTIP country pairs in similar fashion than in Francois et al. (2013).

Three lessons stand out: First, the gravity coefficient on trade agreements matters importantly. This becomes clear by comparing columns [1] and [2]. Second, the existence of spill-overs inflates the gains from a TTIP both for insiders and for outsiders, but it does not

Table 15.2 Comparison of welfare effects across studies (comprehensive scenarios)

	Francois et al. (2013)	*Felbermayr et al. (2015)*
EU	+0.48%	+3.94%
US	+0.39%	+4.89%
China	+0.03%	−0.50%
ASEAN	+0.89%	−0.07%
India	+0.04%	−0.31%
Mercosur	+0.01%	−0.83%
World	+0.14%	+1.58%

Notes: equivalent variation measures; for Felbermayr et al. (2015), regional aggregates obtained as GDP weighted averages over countries.

Table 15.3 Welfare effects: selected countries and scenarios

		[1]	*[2]*	*[3]*	*[4]*
		Preferred	*H&M*	*Tariffs only*	*Spillovers*
1	Austria	2.83	0.23	0.22	4.73
2	Belgium	2.25	0.09	0.17	4.12
3	Bulgaria	3.94	0.55	0.33	5.90
4	Croatia	3.53	0.50	0.38	5.49
5	Cyprus	4.36	0.68	0.37	6.33
6	Czech Republic	3.04	0.31	0.24	4.96
7	Denmark	3.45	0.43	0.28	5.38
8	Estonia	4.31	0.73	0.36	6.29
9	Finland	4.60	0.77	0.39	6.58
10	France	3.46	0.33	0.28	5.32
11	Germany	3.48	0.33	0.28	5.28
12	Greece	4.21	0.63	0.35	6.17
13	Hungary	3.50	0.44	0.28	5.44
14	Ireland	4.70	0.64	0.39	6.70
15	Italy	3.86	0.50	0.32	5.74
16	Latvia	4.10	0.65	0.34	6.09
17	Lithuania	3.97	0.61	0.33	5.94
18	Luxembourg	2.57	0.19	0.20	4.48
19	Malta	4.84	0.96	0.41	6.86
20	Netherlands	2.85	0.22	0.22	4.73
21	Poland	3.51	0.45	0.28	5.44
22	Portugal	4.80	0.79	0.40	6.80
23	Romania	3.87	0.65	n.a.	5.82
24	Slovak Rep.	3.40	0.41	0.27	5.34
25	Slovenia	3.14	0.32	0.25	5.06
26	Spain	5.56	1.13	0.48	7.55
27	Sweden	4.25	0.71	0.35	6.20
28	United Kingdom	5.14	0.80	0.44	7.05
EU average		**3.94**	**0.51**	**0.32**	**5.83**

		[1]	[2]	[3]	[4]
		Preferred	*H&M*	*Tariffs only*	*Spillovers*
29	**United States**	**4.89**	**0.59**	**0.41**	**5.95**
30	Australia	−2.01	−0.09	−0.17	−0.93
31	Brazil	−0.77	−0.08	−0.05	0.06
32	Canada	−3.09	−0.44	−0.27	−1.82
33	China	−0.50	−0.03	−0.04	0.13
34	India	−0.31	−0.05	−0.03	0.65
35	Japan	−0.51	−0.05	−0.05	−0.04
36	Mexico	−2.56	−0.41	−0.22	−1.37
37	Norway	−1.91	−0.27	−0.17	−1.05
38	Russian Fed.	−1.01	−0.12	−0.08	−0.16
39	South Africa	−1.69	−0.12	−0.14	−0.82
40	Turkey	−1.56	−0.17	−0.14	−0.72
	Non–TTIP average	**−0.92**	**−0.10**	**−0.08**	**−0.07**
	World average	**1.58**	**0.21**	**0.13**	**2.73**

Source: Felbermayr et al. (2015). No tariff data available for Romania in 2012. H&M refers to a simulation where the trade cost reducing effect of TTIP is taken to equal the meta-study average for free trade agreements reported by Head and Mayer (2014).

fully undo negative third country effects. Third, as mentioned above, a tariffs-only agreement yields very limited benefits for insiders and very limited losses for outsiders.

5.4 Labor market effects

The quantitative literature on trade policy reform in models with non-competitive labor markets is still at its beginning. However, when a recent model with search frictions and wage bargaining is brought to the data (Heid and Larch, 2013), a TTIP looks as if – in the long-run – it could create jobs in the transatlantic economy, and destroy jobs elsewhere. The logic for this result is that, with bargaining, gains from trade are divided between workers and firms, and, assuming free entry, the latter use the windfalls to create more jobs. Empirical literature supports this long-run result; see Felbermayr et al. (2011). Nonetheless, there is a wide-spread consensus that the short-run effect of a big trade agreement such as a TTIP is likely to lead to substantial reallocation and displacement effects. Since transatlantic trade is so strongly intra-industry, there is reason to hope that the costs of these reallocation effects will be comparably small since most of the effects will happen within rather than between industries.

6. Potential risks caused by a TTIP

The public debate has come up with at least three important points of critique. First, the TTIP will lead to a lowering of standards, second, the TTIP will limit the sovereignty of countries, and third, the TTIP harms third countries and the multilateral system. There are more areas of concern, for example on how the negotiations are conducted (secret, and non-democratically); but these issues are procedural and political and the economic analysis in this chapter will not touch on them.

6.1 Standards

If a TTIP leads to the mutual recognition of standards, and one country has less stringent regulation than the other, the agreement will put firms from the more stringent countries at a competitive disadvantage. In turn, one can expect political pressure to bring standards in line with the lowest existing ones. However, in many areas, it is not straightforward to say whether the EU or the US have the more demanding standards, but it is clear that standards differ. It is in these areas that a TTIP could make progress. In other areas, where differences in stringency are strong, such as in the agri-food industry, mutual recognition will be very hard to achieve. Remarks by the lead negotiator of the EU, Ignacio Garcia Bercero, point in this direction. In December 2013, he said that "TTIP is not and will not be a deregulation agenda. Neither side intended to lower its high standards of consumer, environment, health, labour or data protection." US officials have made similar remarks. In difficult industries, rather than agreeing on mutual recognition of standards, the negotiators could at least agree on mutual recognition of test results on which different standards could be applied. Also, by agreeing on a set of commitments on transparency and regulatory stability, transatlantic trade could be facilitated.

6.2 Sovereignty

International agreements necessarily limit the policy space of democratically elected governments. Politicians may want to voluntarily give away some discretion, for example, on exchange rates (in currency unions), or tariffs (in trade agreements), to reduce uncertainty and to avoid opportunistic behavior that could be harmful in the long-run (e.g., devaluation or tariff wars). However, many observers are increasingly skeptical as to the advantages of such commitment devices, in particular in the context of globalization. They criticize the use of so called "negative lists", which specify exemptions from general rules rather than "positive lists" which provide an exhaustive enumeration of configurations to which a rule applies. Indeed, the problem with negative lists is that future regulatory needs are very hard to predict as they may depend on products or techniques that do not yet exist.

Many observers are also very skeptical regarding the usefulness of so-called investor-state dispute settlement (ISDS) provisions in a TTIP. ISDS enables foreign investors to sue governments when the latter expropriate them in a discriminatory fashion and without providing compensation. ISDS clauses may include indirect expropriation, which refers to changes in regulation that reduce the economic value of an investment by a foreign firm.

Between 1990 and 1998, nine EU Member States, all of them formerly communist countries, have signed bilateral investment treaties (BITs) with the US.[15] The remaining EU Member States do not have bilateral investment agreements with the US. However, all together, the EU countries maintain about 1,400 agreements, most of them with developing countries.[16] Since the entry in force of the treaty of Lisbon in 2009, the EU has acquired competence on foreign direct investment affairs, so that Member States no longer negotiate their own BITs.

Critiques fear that ISDS provisions lead to regulatory chill, i.e., to a reluctance of governments to enact laws protecting consumers, workers, or the environment due to fear that foreign investors could demand large sums of compensation. Through this mechanism, ISDS limits the sovereignty of countries regarding future regulation. This is more problematic the broader the scope of an investment chapter in a TTIP is. Conventional investment treaties concern only FDI, but if portfolio investment and public debt is also covered, sovereignty concerns become even more important.[17] Also, one may criticize the way that ISDS is organized: in private tribunals rather than in public courts, behind closed doors, and without providing for the possibility of appeal. Finally, while investment liberalization and protection is important to facilitate trade in services, it is unclear whether bundling investment issues and more conventional trade policy issues into a single agreement is sensible when investors from both sides can actually trust the official legal systems in both countries to protect their rights.

For these reasons, the German government, some economists, and the former US chief negotiator Robert Zoellick, have demanded to exclude ISDS from a potential TTIP. The European Commission has launched a three month moratorium on negotiations regarding the investment chapter and has engaged in public consultations during this period.

The calculations in the economic assessment studies covered in this chapter do not assume that an ISDS is in place. Neither do they assume that common standards or mutual recognition of standards will be achieved in all areas of economic activity. So, even an agreement that is much closer to existing agreements of both the EU and the US than to the negotiators' initial ambitions can generate substantial welfare gains.

6.3 Third country effects and multilateralism

A comprehensive TTIP could harm outsiders. This is an important message from economic modeling that goes back to Viner (1950). Indeed, multilateral agreements, that lead to lower trade costs relative to all trade partners, are strictly preferable to bilateral ones. While this remains true, there has been virtually no progress at the multilateral level since the creation of the WTO in 1995. This paralysis is one of the reasons why a TTIP is being negotiated. However, if a TTIP – by its sheer size – causes negative effects for many poor countries, it counteracts other policies by the EU or the US that aim to promote development.

Indeed, the negative effects calculated by Felbermayr et al. (2015) are impressive. However, three comments are in order. First, the TTIP scenario is a ceteris paribus scenario. It does not factor in that third countries will react, either by signing free trade agreements amongst themselves or with TTIP partners, or by making stronger efforts to bring down trade costs multilaterally. Such actions could reduce the negative effects of a TTIP. If, however, a TTIP leads to even more free trade within the OECD, for example, by bringing Mexico, Canada, or Japan into the agreement at some future date, negative effects for outsiders would grow.

Second, the calculations assume that NTM reform within a TTIP will be fully discriminatory. This need not be the case. For example, under mutual recognition, the EU and US could admit products from third countries to their markets when they conform either to EU or US standards. Also, the degree of discrimination depends on the design of rule of origin: the more generous they are, the lower adverse third country effects will be. And, finally, as discussed above (section 5.1), the picture looks more benign if there are regulatory spill-overs. Negotiators can make a TTIP more or less conducive to such spill-overs.

Regarding the multilateral system, it is true that neither the EU nor the US have much negotiating capacity available for multilateral initiatives while a TTIP (and other so-called mega regionals) are being negotiated. Also, their interest in the WTO may fall as a smaller share of trade falls under WTO provisions. While these arguments imply that the WTO may lose some of its appeal as a trade legislating forum, it remains important as the world's trade police. Moreover, many trade economists (most vocally, maybe, Richard Baldwin) see bilateral agreements as stepping stones rather than stumbling blocs for multilateralism, because they increase the incentives of third countries to make concessions.

As a final remark, a comprehensive TTIP will quite obviously reshape the political power game in the world trade system. It will give the EU and the US more power in the necessary review of existing trade rules and in the design of new ones. This may not necessarily harm third countries economically, but it does hurt them politically.

7. Conclusions

A TTIP would create the world's largest free trade area. If comprehensive, it could have strong effects on real per capita GDP around the world. The sheer size of TTIP makes it a very special undertaking. This leads to a lot of uncertainties in the economic ex ante analysis and to large discrepancies in the trade and welfare effects of a TTIP in different studies. However, studies agree that economic effects for TTIP insiders from a deep agreement would be unambiguously positive in the long-run, that a tariffs-only agreement is not worth much, and that discriminatory elements in a TTIP should be minimized. Studies suggest that insiders could harvest substantial gains, ranging between 0.5 and 5 percent, world GDP could go up by between 0.1 and 1.6 percent, but non-TTIP countries could potentially register large losses.

Although still in negotiation, the prospect of a TTIP has triggered a lot of criticism. Much of it is to be taken very seriously. A TTIP could lead to a lowering of standards in both the EU and the US, it will most likely lead to some loss of policy space, and it will probably not be helpful for third parties. However, there are remedies to these concerns. Even if a TTIP does not come up with investor-state dispute settlement provisions, and even if it limits mutual recognition of standards to areas where standards are deemed of equal stringency, will economic benefits be sizeable.

TTIP would shape the world trading system for the next few decades. It would give the EU and the US a more pivotal role in revising old rules and institutions and in designing new legislation. It could turn out to be the corner stone for a WTO 2.0 (Baldwin, 2012), but it could also lead to a fragmentation of the world economy into large and opposed blocs.

Notes

1 I wish to thank Sebastian Benz, Fritz Breuss, Kerem Cosar, Anne-Célia Disdier, Heribert Dieter, Lionel Fontagné, Joe Francois, Benedikt Heid, Len-Kuo Hu, Sébastien Jean, Mario Larch, Sybille Lehwald, Jacques Pelkmans, Laura Márquez Ramos, Uli Schoof, Erdal Yalcin, and seminar participants at various places for many informative and inspiring discussions on transatlantic trade and investment. All remaining errors are mine.

2 The document is available at trade.ec.europa.eu/doclib/html/150519.htm.

3 The speech is available under www.whitehouse.gov/state-of-the-union-2013.

4 The "Global Europe" strategy report from 2006 by the EU Commission describes the role of bilateral free trade agreements and ends a de facto moratorium on bilateral deals; see http://trade.ec.europa.eu/doclib/docs/2006/october/tradoc_130376.pdf.

5 Indeed, EU President Manuel Barroso has called the "TTIP the cheapest stimulus program one can imagine" (EC-MEMO/13/569 from June 15, 2013).

6 WTO, World Trade Report, 2013.

7 See Bureau et al. (2014) for a detailed account of EU-US agri-food trade and the potential effects of TTIP in this sector.

8 Data is available freely on http://sasweb.ssd.census.gov/relatedparty/.

9 Hamilton and Quinlan (2013).

10 See Figure 15.1 for exact data.

11 In 2012, total EU–US trade is about 1,000 billion dollars; world GDP is about 72,000 billion dollars.

12 According to Eurostat, total tariff income in the EU was 20.3 billion euro in 2007. Total (extra-EU) imports amounted to 1,446.8 billion euro.

13 Breuss (2014) provides a balanced discussion of different studies.

14 A study by Fontagné et al. (2013) also applies a bottom-up approach and uses a CGE model developed at the CEPII in Paris called Mirage.

15 These countries are (in order of the date of signing): Poland, Czech Republic, Slovakia, Romania, Bulgaria, Estonia, Latvia, Croatia, and Lithuania.

16 Germany has 137 active BITs, France has 102, Italy and the UK have 94 each.

17 Such broad scope, however, would turn a TTIP into a mixed agreement which the EU Parliament and national parliaments would have to vote on separately.

References

Anderson, J.E. and van Wincoop, E. (2004), Trade Costs, *Journal of Economic Literature*, 42(3), 691–751.

Arkolakis, C., Costinot, A., and Rodríguez-Clare, A. (2012), New Trade Models, Same Old Gains?, *American Economic Review*, 102(1), 94–130.

Baldwin, R. (2012), WTO 2.0: Global governance of supply-chain trade, *CEPR Policy Insight* 64.

Berden, K., Francois, J., Thelle, M., Wymenga, P., and Tamminen, S. (2009), Non-Tariff Measures in EU-US Trade and Investment – An Economic Analysis, Report OJ 2007/S 180-219493 for the European Commission: Directorate-General for Trade.

Bureau, J.-C., Disdier, A.-C., Emlinger C., Felbermayr, G., Fontagné, L., Fouré, J., and Jean, S. (2014), Risks and Opportunities for the EU Agri-food Sector in a Possible EU-US Trade Agreement, Study IP/B/AGRI/IC/2013_129 for the European Parliament.

Breuss, F. (2014), TTIP und ihre Auswirkungen auf Österreich: Ein kritischer Literaturüberblick, *WIFO Working Papers* 468/2014.

Cipollina, M. and Salvatici, L. (2010), Reciprocal Trade Agreements in Gravity Models: A Meta Analysis, *Review of International Economics*, 18(1), 63–80.

Egger, P.H., Larch, M., Staub, K., and Winkelmann, R. (2011), The Trade Effects of Endogenous Preferential Trade Agreements, *American Economic Journal: Economic Policy*, 3(3), 113–43.

Feenstra, R. (2004), *Advanced International Trade: Theory and Evidence*, Princeton: Princeton University Press.

Felbermayr, G., Heid, B., Larch, M., and Yalcin, E. (2015), Macroeconomic Potentials of Transatlantic Free Trade: A High Resolution Perspective for Europe and the World, *Economic Policy*, doi.org/10.1093/epolic/eiv009.

Felbermayr, G., Larch, M., Flach, L., Yalcin, E., and Benz, S. (2013), Dimensionen und Auswirkungen eines Freihandelsabkommens zwischen der EU und den USA, *ifo Forschungsbericht* 62.

Felbermayr, G. and Larch, M. (2013), The Transatlantic Trade and Investment Partnership (TTIP): Potentials, Problems and Perspectives, *CESifo Forum*, 14(2), 49–60.

Felbermayr, G., Schmerer, H.-J., and Prat, J. (2011), Trade and Unemployment: What Do the Data Say, *European Economic Review*, 55, 741–58.

Fontagné, L., Gourdon, J. and Jean, S. (2013), Transatlantic Trade: Whither Partnership, Which Economic Consequences? *CEPII Policy Brief* 2013-01.

Francois, J., Manchin, M., Norberg, H., Pindyuk, O., and Tomberger, P. (2013), Reducing Transatlantic Barriers to Trade and Investment: An Economic Assessment, Report TRADE10/A2/A16 for the European Commission.

Hamilton, D. and Quinlan, J. (2013), The Transatlantic Economy 2013: Annual Survey of Jobs, Trade and Investment between the United States and Europe, Center for Transatlantic Relations.

Head, K. and Mayer, T. (2014), Gravity Equations: Workhorse, Toolkit, and Cookbook, in Gopinath, G., Helpman, E. and Rogoff, K. (eds) *Handbook of International Economics 4*, Amsterdam: Elsevier.

Heid, B. and Larch, M. (2013), International Trade and Unemployment: A Quantitative Framework, *CESifo Working Paper* 4013.

Trefler, D. (1995), The Case of the Missing Trade and Other Mysteries, *The American Economic Review*, 85(5), 1029–46.

Trefler, D. (2004), The Long and Short of the Canada-U.S. Free Trade Agreement, *American Economic Review*, 94(4), 870–95.

Viner, J. (1950), *The Customs Union Issue*, New York: Carnegie Endowment for International Peace.

World Trade Organization (2012), World Trade Report 2012 – Trade and Public Policies: A Closer Look at Non-Tariff Measures in the 21st Century, available at www.wto.org/ENGLISH/res_e/reser_e/wtr_e.htm.

16

THE EU AND THE ACP COUNTRIES

Ludger Kühnhardt

1. Post-Cotonou: A time of intensive stock taking

The future has already begun: Intensive stock taking of possible options beyond 2020 has started for the European Union (EU) and the African, Caribbean and Pacific group of states (ACP). "In 2012, the ACP figured as the EU's fifth most important trading partner, loosely followed by ASEAN and far behind the USA, China, European Free Trade Association and Russia."[1] Elisabeth Pape's (2013, p. 736) analysis continues: "For the ACP countries, the EU as a group remained the most important single trading partner, despite a dramatic increase of their trade with China." EU-ACP relations constitute a unique feature in the global economy, but also in world politics. The only regional arrangement stretching over three continents it is primarily perceived as a component of development policies, but it is far more than that. The EU with 28 member states and the ACP group with 79 member states represent almost half of all states in the world. The current frame of this relationship – the Cotonou Agreement – will expire on February 29, 2020.

Since the ACP Summit in Malabo in 2012, an Eminent Persons group of politicians and academics reflected on possible post-Cotonou options.[2] In 2015, the ACP leadership – that is the heads of state and government of all ACP member states – will draw their final conclusions. A planned ACP summit in Suriname had to be postponed in the autumn of 2014 because of the Ebola outbreak in West Africa. The 2015 ACP Summit will endorse the group's strategy for the upcoming negotiations with the EU. Thus, the ACP is ahead of the EU in preparing for possible post-Cotonou negotiations. This is not surprising: After all, the EU finances most of the ACP's infrastructure and activities across the ACP regions with a budget of roughly 31.5 billion euro, through the 11th European Development Fund (2014–2020). As for the EU, in autumn 2014 Commission President Jean-Claude Juncker mandated to his Commissioner for International Cooperation and Development, Neven Mimica, for "preparing and launching negotiations for a revised Cotonou agreement," replacing the current Cotonou Agreement which was signed in 2000.[3] For the time being, the EU collects data, opinions and ideas for possible scenarios before defining a clear mandate for formal negotiations with the ACP group.[4]

In spring 2015, the post-Cotonou issue was discussed for the first time by all EU Commissioners dealing with external actions of the EU (including trade, development and foreign and security affairs). A "Green Paper" will be presented by the EU Commission, coordinated by the DG Development and Cooperation (DEVCO) together with the European External Action Service and other Commission units, in late 2015. This will be followed by a "Communication" in 2016 (indicating the way forward and probably the negotiation framework), then by "EU Council conclusions" and eventually by a proposal for a "Council decision" which will define the precise mandate for the formal opening of negotiations. As a first step to start the preparatory process and connect with interested EU citizens, the Commission is planning a "Consultation" for 2015, engaging stakeholders, scholars, NGO activists and others, primarily via the Internet. This process will be more public, transparent and serious than anything in the past, yet it can be predicted that eventually political actors, especially those with the potential to polemically undermine EU policy timelines, along with NGO's, especially those representing the development lobby and, partly, the anti-globalization lobby in the EU, will complain about back-door policies, disrespect for the "real citizens" and the negative impacts of development policies in the context of globalization. In the EU bureaucracy will dominate: about 20 DGs and services will have to be heard, along with all member states who are party to a possible "mixed" agreement (meaning that a post-Cotonou Agreement will fall both under EU competencies in the area of trade and development aid as well as under national prerogative rights, thus requiring approval of the EU organs and ratification in all 28 EU member states), along with the European Parliament, whose delegates represent the EU in the EU-ACP Joint Parliamentary Assembly. It should be assumed that EU partner countries who are outside the Cotonou Agreement, but affected by it – such as the countries of Latin America and the remaining eight least developed countries who are not members of the ACP – will also want to be consulted. The process will be as rigorous as it is daunting and complex.

Formal negotiations between the EU and the ACP group of states may not commence before 2017 or even in 2018. This leaves only a short period of time for their successful conclusion (including approval in the European Parliament and the EU Council, followed by the ratification process in all EU member states) before the beginning of the next election campaign to the European Parliament in early 2019 and the establishment of the next EU Commission in late 2019. Furthermore, the current financial base for EU–ACP relations will expire in late 2020, while a possible merger between the European Development Fund (EDF) – the main financial instrument for EU–ACP activities – and the general EU budget – which has been long demanded by the European Parliament ("budgetization of the EDF") – needs to take place before the next fiscal frame for the period 2021–2027 will be formalized.

Reflections in the ACP group focus around the following possible scenario: renewing the EU–ACP relationship but deepening its political content and broadening its outreach to new ACP partners among other emerging countries, including the BRICS group of states. As for the EU, the debate focuses more on principles and touches on the very rationale for a continuation of EU–ACP relations: Critics question the economic benefit of the EU–ACP relationship, demanding more concrete actions and results on the side of the ACP and prefer regional approaches which reflect the diverse realities in Africa, the Caribbean, and the Pacific. As it is still too early to say which path will eventually be taken in the context of proper negotiations, it is worth recalling the reasoning for EU–ACP relations and the context in which this genuine multi-continental relationship has developed.

2. Colonial and post-colonial legacies from Rome to Lomé

EU–ACP relations are still organized in the shadow of their colonial and post-colonial beginnings.[5] With the establishment of the European Economic Community (EEC) in 1957, a formalized association was established between the emerging European common market and the overseas territories and colonies of its member states. France with its two colonial empires in Africa and the ongoing inclusion of Algeria as an integral part of the French republic, but also Belgium with its colonial rule over Congo and Italy with its trust-territory Somaliland demanded the association of their African possessions.[6] Reluctantly, Germany accepted the association status while insisting on its preference for decolonization and self-determination. The Treaty of Rome (Article 131, 1) laid the ground for the association of the EEC with the overseas territories of its member states, establishing the first EDF (guaranteeing $581 million for the period 1959–64 in support of investment in the overseas territories), aimed at supporting the process of market development in the overseas territories, and facilitating access of African products into the emerging EEC. Following the wave of independence across Africa during the late 1950s/early 1960s, the association approach came to an end. The Yaoundé Agreement of 1963[7] (and its successor arrangement, the Yaoundé II Agreement of 1971[8]) echoed the experiences of the first few years with the double objective of aid and trade, while giving more institutional structure to the EEC/EC[9]-(independent)Africa link: an Association Council, a Parliamentary Conference and an Arbitration Court could not however overcome the asymmetric trade and power relationship between the EEC and its independent partners tied together by customs free access to the European market.

Colonial rule over much of Africa had come to an end and the association shifted toward post-colonial parameters, that is to say: formal independence for the African countries coupled with continued economic dependency and burning "underdevelopment" issues (extreme poverty and a lack of economic production beyond the level of subsistence). The transformation of France's role in Africa is symbolized by the change in the meaning of the term "CFA" used for the African currency CFA franc to this day: From *Communauté Franco-Africaine franc* (established in 1945) to *Communauté financière Africaine franc* (existing since 1994 as a West African CFA franc under the auspices of the Economic and Monetary Community of West African States UEMOA and as a Central African CFA franc under the auspices of the Economic and Monetary Community of Central African States CEMAC).[10] The transformation of the British role in Europe as well as in Africa was symbolized by British EC membership in 1973 (along with Ireland and Denmark) and the expansion of the Yaoundé Agreement through a new arrangement with initially 46 African, Caribbean, and Pacific states in 1975. Signed in the capital of Togo, Lomé, the preferential trade agreement of 1975 reflected not only changes in EC relations with former colonies, but also global North-South debates in the shadow of the growing awareness of the limits of growth (Club of Rome Report 1972) and the oil crisis of 1973. One special feature of the effect of Franco-British reconciliation inside Europe was the establishment of the Economic Community of West African States (ECOWAS) in 1975, bringing together for the first time Francophone and Anglophone countries of Africa under the umbrella of one regional economic community. Another feature was the Georgetown Agreement, also signed in 1975 by the 46 African, Caribbean and Pacific signatory states to the Lomé Agreement, thus founding the ACP group of states.[11] Commonwealth links ensured that six Caribbean and three Pacific states (the majority of them Anglophone and reasonably stable, Westminster-type democracies) extended the geographical scope of the EC-Africa policy by creating the ACP group; the ACP group, in turn, helped the EC to rationalize its partnership with the geographically widely spread group of former colonies and overseas territories. While British EC membership was giving hope of a stronger free trade orientation in EC relations with the developing world, in reality, the protectionist French approach to the post-colonial relationship since the association under the Rome Treaties did not wither away. In fact, it continued to dominate EC–ACP ties: The Lomé Treaty of 1975 (and subsequent Lomé Treaties of 1980, 1985 and 1990) facilitated free trade between the EC and the ACP group thus protecting European investment in the ACP region as much as guaranteeing free access for ACP goods into the European common market. The ACP grouping established its secretariat in Brussels and a trade office in Geneva at the seat of GATT. Most ACP operations and programs were (and are) financed by the European Community through subsequent EDFs.

The artificial "coalition of the poor," as the ACP group likes to be seen, engaged with the European Community in a series of treaties, providing privileged aid and trade relations – which was as much in the interest of post-colonial elites across the developing world as in the interest of European investors and importing companies, enhancing the reliability of trade ties with former European colonies. The notion "not aid but trade" was translated into a preferential system of import conditions from the ACP region into the European common market; stabilizing the market price of agricultural goods through STABEX (Stabilization of Export Earnings) and of mineral commodities through SYSMIN (System for Stabilization of Export Revenues in Minerals) guaranteed stability of trading ties between European companies and their subsidiaries or partners across the ACP region. Over time, the counter-productive effects of these subsidy systems have become evident: Preferential EU–ACP trade relations prolonged post-colonial ties between raw or semi-raw material producers on the one hand and the benefits for value-chains located primarily in Europe.[12] The Lomé Treaties did not contribute to the diversification, de-monopolization and industrial production across the ACP region. Between 1980 and 2000, the ACP share of exports from the EC/EU went down from 8.5 percent to merely 2.8 percent. At the same time, and in spite of unilateral trade preferences, the share of imports from the ACP group of countries to the EC/EU went down from 8.1 percent to 3.4 percent.[13] Moreover, preferential trade conditions established under the Lomé Treaties antagonized other developing countries outside the ACP group. They demanded an end to these exclusive privileges which the EC, after all, was granting to only a selected number of developing countries. To this day, honest stock-taking about the economic effects of EU–ACP trade relations includes the assessment of the dilemma of asymmetric trade relations, post-colonial dependencies and the structural preservation of production-chains to the benefit of the EU. Overcoming the post-colonial donor-recipient-equation remains an ongoing challenge for any possible perspective post-2020.

3. Cold War leftovers: governance-issues and growing skepticism toward the West

A second set of issues has penetrated EC–ACP relations since the beginning and intensified during the 1980s: the European demand to link economic development to good governance and human rights. After a decade of often ideological debates about a New World Economic Order, the Western world responded with a counter-strategy: "Political dialog" became a mantra for the growing demand in Europe (in parallel with similar policies of the World Bank and the IMF) not only for structural economic reforms, but also for political reforms in the developing world. This policy priority came as an indirect result of the Cold War and its Third World proxy wars. Progress in development was considered a function of good governance and human rights. While incentives were difficult to impose on Third World partners – as was often tried throughout the Cold War – sanctions were no less popular overseas as they were limited in easing Western frustration about the slow speed of their impact on governance reforms in developing countries. "Conditionality" became the key word of Lomé III (1985) and Lomé IV (1990).[14] With the end of the Cold War, the quest for political democratization and economic liberalization received an additional boost in the development agenda, with intensified neo-liberal structural adjustment policies executed by World Bank and IMF, echoed in the EU's policy of conditionality.

But conditionality and the search for effective incentives to promote good governance were not the only Cold War legacies. The end of the Cold War coincided with an increasing debate about globalization.[15] One of its features was the growing demand from non-ACP developing countries as well as other industrialized countries, including the US, for the EU to abandon its preferential trade relations with the ACP group of states in favor of a general and globalized free trade approach. This resulted in several GATT Panels where the EU was charged and whose rulings forced the EU to eventually re-consider its privileged subsidies and protective trade relations with ACP countries.[16] Gradually, agricultural products (i.e. sugar, coffee, tea, banana, and cocoa) but also raw materials were considered to be protected in unacceptable ways against the interests of other players in the global economy. The issue of "blood diamonds," especially in war-torn areas of Western and Central Africa, added to the moral delegitimization of the privileged post-colonial relations of the EU-ACP arrangement.

Surprisingly enough, with the demise of the Soviet bloc – including its ramifications for Third World developments – a new wave of anti-Western sentiment emerged in the developing world. The EU was no longer the good guy, providing the largest amount of development aid (which it does), but was considered a paternalistic bullying bloc with a tendency to become a trade fortress not ready to open its markets sufficiently for goods and products from developing countries. EU migration policies added to the list of frustrations, while the role of China was often exaggerated as a systemic alternative in terms of development model and geopolitical partnership.[17] Indeed, some of the moral high ground of the EU during the immediate post-Cold War days was lost, with the growing presence of China across much of the developing world, offering a distinctly different set of trade relations without political conditions and lecturing on human rights and good governance. Yet, Chinese development aid came and comes with the danger of a new wave of indebtedness across ACP regions. But without a doubt, the new debate on development models and possible alternatives forced the traditional EU–ACP relationship onto the defensive.

4. Post-Cold War stalemate: Cotonou and economic partnership agreements

In 2000, the series of Lomé Treaties came to an end and were replaced by the Cotonou Treaty which was designed to cover a period of altogether twenty years until 2020.[18] Quite uncommon for such an international cooperative agreement, the Cotonou Agreement was intended to structure EU–ACP long-term relations across three baskets: aid, trade, and political dialog. The aid approach coincided with and reinforced the UN Millennium Development Goals, while the trade agenda introduced a certain deconstruction of the ACP grouping with the focus on regional economic developments and political trends, thus taking into consideration the growing role of regional economic communities within the different sub-regions of the ACP grouping. Article 96 of the Cotonou Treaty became the notorious instrument for imposing sanctions against those ACP countries who do not comply with EU political norms; inter alia, in the case of Fiji after a military coup in 2006. Less known is Article 8, which also enables the ACP countries to invoke a political dialog if they wish to discuss any pending EU policy matter.

The Cotonou Agreement was revised in 2005 and, again, in 2010. The first revision – concluded in Luxembourg on June 25, 2005 entered into force on July 1, 2008 – introduced new issues such as climate change and security (post 9/11) to the EU–ACP agenda. The second revision of the Cotonou Agreement – signed on June 22, 2010 and entering provisionally into force on November 1, 2010 (still being subject to ratification in some countries) – intended to further improve the effectiveness of EU aid and trade policies. In the meantime, the ACP group of states has grown to a membership of 79 states across Africa, the Caribbean and the Pacific.[19]

More debated than anything else in the context of the EU–ACP Cooperation Agreement of 2000 was (and still is) the concept of Economic Partnership Agreements (EPAs). The Cotonou Agreement stipulated the negotiation of regional free trade arrangements between the EU and several ACP regional subgroups to be concluded by 2007. The debate surrounding Economic Partnership Agreements consumed most of the first decade of the Cotonou Agreement.[20] While the EU insisted that bi-regional economic free trade arrangements were inevitable to bring the EU–ACP relationship in line with the requirements of the WTO (reciprocity, non-discrimination of third parties, rules of origin),[21] the officials of the ACP group felt almost betrayed by the pressure exercised on them by the EU. Solidarity among the "coalition of the poor" came under pressure too, as individual countries ended up in negotiating free trade arrangements unilaterally with the EU instead of with their respective regional community. Further, the EU practiced cherry-picking by organizing regional groups to its own liking, not fully accepting the realities of regional integration as they have evolved across Africa, the Caribbean and the Pacific islands region. By the 2007 deadline, only one EPA had been signed, between the EU and CARIFORUM, an artificial arrangement of most CARICOM countries plus the Dominican Republic and Cuba.[22] To the surprise of many, 2013 ended with the conclusion of negotiations on a second comprehensive EPA between the EU and ECOWAS.[23] In the meantime, the EU extended the deadline for EPA negotiations to 2016, when the privilege of duty-free export to the EU for "everything but arms" will expire. But as of late 2014, the overall "state of play" in EPA negotiations was not at all impressive:

West Africa: West Africa–European Union negotiations of an Economic Partnership Agreement were closed by the Chief Negotiators on February 6 in Brussels. The text was initialled on June 30 and on July 10, 2014 the ECOWAS Heads of State endorsed the EPA for signature.

Central Africa: Cameroon signed the interim EPA for Central Africa as the only country in the region on January 15, 2009. The European Parliament gave its consent in June 2013. In July 2014 the Parliament of Cameroon approved the ratification of the Agreement and on August 4, 2014 the agreement entered into provisional application.

Eastern and Southern Africa: In 2009 Mauritius, Seychelles, Zimbabwe, and Madagascar signed the interim EPA. The Agreement has been provisionally applied since May 14, 2012. The European Parliament gave its consent on January 17, 2013.

East African Community (EAC): In June 2010, a Ministerial meeting held in Dar Es Salaam noted that EAC was not ready to sign the Framework EPA initialled in November 2007 and both sides agreed to seek a successor agreement to their framework (interim) agreement. The ministerial EPA meeting held in January 2014 was a key step towards conclusion of the negotiations and three rounds with Senior Officials resolved the few outstanding issues to bring the deal to conclusion on October 16, 2014.

Southern African Development Community (SADC): On July 15, 2014 the EPA negotiations were successfully concluded in South Africa. This ended ten years of negotiations and produced an agreement that will replace the interim EPA signed by the EU and by Botswana, Lesotho, Mozambique, and Swaziland in June 2009. That agreement was never ratified.

Caribbean: The CARIFORUM – EU EPA was signed in October 2008 and approved by the EP in March 2009. The agreement: opens up trade in services as well as in goods; seeks to spur more investment in the Caribbean; commits governments to other trade-promoting measures, like ensuring free and fair competition; promotes development that respects the environment and people's rights at work. The EPA also sets up several joint institutions. These have met regularly since 2010. In September and October 2012, two of these met for the second time: first the Trade and Development Committee (senior officials), and then the Joint CARIFORUM-EU Council (ministers).

Pacific: Signed by the EU and Papua New Guinea (PNG) on July 30 and by Fiji on December 11, 2009. EP ratified on January 19, 2011. EU ratification completed by Council on February 15, 2011. The third meeting of the Trade Committee established under the interim EPA took place in Brussels in July 2013. The Parliament of Papua New Guinea ratified the interim EPA on May 25, 2011. On July 17, 2014 Fiji decided to start provisionally applying the agreement. In negotiations on a comprehensive regional Economic Partnership Agreement, four technical rounds have taken place since October 2012, the latest one in Brussels from June 24 to July 5, 2013 on fisheries, trade in goods, development cooperation, sustainable development, and rules of origin.[24]

In conclusion: EPAs as a new core concept of EU-ACP relations and the EU's way of negotiating EPAs has been a failure.[25] Patrick I. Gomes (2013, p. 721), the new ACP Secretary General and former Ambassador of Guyana to the European Union, summarized the ACP's stand in a nutshell:

> Throughout the negotiations, the EU side failed to articulate an understanding of trade as an instrument of development. This was of course the overriding concern of ACP states and is alleged to be a reason why some turn to countries such as China for the requisite action where large infrastructure projects are needed.

The EPA legacy has left traumatization on both sides. While the EU felt disappointed that many of its traditional ACP partners did not accept the approach the EU had asked them to take without too much arguing, most ACP countries became aware that EU interests and their own interests might clash more often than in the past. The idea of establishing unprotected free trade relations between the powerful single market of 505 million consumers in 28 industrialized countries and several sub-regions of 79 of the poorer or even poorest countries on earth without any solid base of production and inclusion into the world economy remains a matter of intensive controversy; from the side of NGOs both in the EU and in ACP countries. For those least developed countries among ACP states who did not sign an EPA in time, the preferential duty-free trade access to the EU market under the "everything but arms" initiative remained a safe haven which did not force them to compromise beyond their preferences in negotiations with the EU – at least for the time being.

The 2010 mid-term evaluation of the EU–ACP relationship did not result in convincing conclusions.[26] In spite of much partnership rhetoric, the donor–recipient relationship has not substantially changed. Most of the ACP is still dependent upon financial support from the EU, the ACP infrastructure as much as ACP member state budgets. While growing regionalization in the ACP regions has contributed to the growing rise of region-building across the world, the EU obviously does not take the existing regional groupings as seriously as it appears to. In turn, the ACP group of states has a hard time to convincingly demonstrate its readiness and capability of being a political partner for the EU in international fora. Moreover, the economic effect of the ACP group on EU import and export figures remains suboptimal, some critics may say: marginal.

5. New realities: The EU at 28 and the emergence of the BRICS

Since the Cotonou Agreement was signed in 2000, the EU and the ACP countries have undergone manifold transformations. The EU has been enlarged to include 11 post-communist countries plus two former British colonies (Malta and Cyprus). None of whom entertains relations with the ACP states comparable with those of former West European colonial powers and Northern European development aid empires. For post-communist countries, the priority of catching up with the value chain of Western Europe and enhancing the competitiveness of their industrial potential in the global economy has been more of a priority than any reflection on the future of the South. The Lisbon Treaty (signed in 2007, in force since December 2009) does not mention the ACP group as a special concern of the EU. It outlines foreign policy principles – and development policy objectives, too – but does not make any specific reference to the ACP group of states.

The EU external trade agenda is dominated by ties to the US, to emerging markets, China in particular, and to other larger populations in the world with a relevant effect on EU trade patterns. The ACP group of states clearly falls behind in terms of economic significance and hence is often neglected. The emotional ties of decades gone by do not play a significant role any more in the corridors of decision-making and policy-implementation in Brussels and in most EU member states – with the possible exception of special interests still represented and emotionally linked to policy circles in Paris and London.

The ACP group of states has observed the past twenty years of EU internal development with mixed feelings. On the one hand, the EU has been immersed in the post-communist transformation rhetoric of market-driven democratic change which also resonated in its development policy. On the other hand, the EU has redirected funds in support of its Eastern neighbors and its new member states – to the detriment of its commitments to the ACP regions, so they believe. Almost nostalgic efforts to preserve ties with France and the UK, as well as with Belgium, and in part with the Netherlands, and Italy can be found across the ACP group of states, especially among political and diplomatic actors reflecting their uneasiness about a growing Europeanization of EU policies which, so it seems, no longer considers the post-colonial ties to be essential part of its own identity.

The ACP group of countries neighbors the biggest emerging markets, especially the BRICS group of countries. But ACP relations with the BRICS are a mixed bag.[27] On the one hand, investment from China, India, Brazil, South Africa and Russia is welcome across ACP regions, especially in the absence of EU investment in future oriented infrastructure. On the other hand, the ACP group internal solidarity is not reinforced by the emergence of BRICS, but rather torn apart: South Africa is both an ACP and a BRICS state, without any visible effect on the stature of the ACP in the world; its trade volume – accounting for a third of all EU trade with the 79 ACP countries[28] – adds to the distortive asymmetries across the ACP regions. Some ACP countries rush to be faster in forming new relationships with China especially. Others in turn are worried that too much Chinese influence and too much bilateralism with any emerging market may lead to a loss of autonomous decision-making if the ACP group is not going to stay together. Finally, new centers of gravity have emerged in each of the ACP regions – from the African Regional Economic Communities (RECs) and CARICOM with its common market, to the Pacific Islands Forum (PIF) and, most recently, to the Small Island Development States (SIDS) group of 36 ACP states which organized their first ever summit meeting in the autumn of 2014 in Samoa.[29]

6. Key Actors: A new ACP leadership meets the Juncker commission

While the ACP and the EU are engaged in stock taking as a first step to beginning solid negotiations for a new agreement, they are both confronted with changing leadership environments. The EU leadership as it has emerged in 2014 will define the post-Cotonou process a great deal. A European Commission, committed to concluding a new agreement but so far without a clear profile about what it could contain; a European Parliament, more self-confident than ever, but under the pressure of Eurosceptics – who tend to be protectionist, and who also look critically at migration from the ACP region and often at development aid in general – and led by a grand coalition of mainstream parties who pursue traditional EU normative discourses – such as promotion of human rights, conditionality in development, or reciprocal trade advantages; a European Council representing all 28 EU member states who have overcome a daunting period of soul-searching, yet are still heavily under pressure to mobilize jobs and growth for themselves instead of engaging too much with the concerns and interests of distant places. This constellation may have two consequences for further EU deliberations with the ACP group of states and its related issues: Either the EU will remain restrained and thus tight to the well-known and established stakeholder community in development matters or it will have the courage to enlarge its circle of stakeholders substantially by also engaging with traditional foreign policy discourses, investment and innovation policies, the private sector and those in civil society who tend to represent scepticism towards the fear of a declining West. Neither of the two projections provide reassuring insights into the possible outcome of the European reflection on the dialog with the ACP group of states.

The ACP in turn needs to broaden its visibility across three continents, all of them engaged in their own complex agendas. This could easily water down any substantial offer for partnership with the EU or increase the EU perception that the rhetoric of solidarity among ACP countries does not stand the test of time when individual national interests somewhere across the vast ACP region are touched upon.

Harmonizing ACP interests and communicating them properly with the EU representatives is essential for any ACP leverage in the forthcoming years. In December 2014, the ACP Ministerial meeting held in Brussels elected Dr. Patrick Gomes as new ACP Secretary General, serving from March 2015 until February 2020. Gomes has been a long-standing Ambassador of Guyana to the European Union and a member of the ACP Eminent Persons Group. He also authored a report of the group of ACP Ambassadors to the EU on the prospects for restructuring the ACP Secretariat in Brussels. So far, almost only Caribbean news media noted the election of Ambassador Gomes by the ACP Ministerial meeting (against two other Caribbean candidates). The rotating system of the ACP has brought the Caribbean into the driver's seat ahead of the formalized EU–ACP negotiations toward a post-Cotonou agreement. Given the insider knowledge of Patrick Gomes, the other ACP regions seem well represented by him. Yet, given his personal background, a stronger Caribbean perspective as otherwise expected could occur in the course of his work of coordinating negotiations on a post-2020 agreement with the EU.

For the EU, Africa obviously is of greatest importance. The EU will have to connect its well-developed strategic partnership with the African Union, in existence since 2007, with the overall ACP perspective. It will also have to accommodate special features of the Northern African dimension, usually covered by the EU's Neighborhood Policy, yet an integral aspect of the EU–Africa partnership. The ocean economies in the Pacific resonate in the EU only when issues related to climate change are addressed. But distance and size minimize the moral high ground which is touched upon when the survival of Pacific islands is mentioned. The EU may enhance its engagement with the Pacific islands states also in reaction to the increasing geopolitical and geo-economic interest of other players in the region, including Australia and New Zealand, China, India, and the US. The Caribbean is no longer a geopolitical issue as it was during the Cold War, when Cuba was pointing at the East-West divide; with the normalization of relations between the US and Cuba, the EU will be confronted with new competition over Caribbean markets, thus linking the post-2020 negotiations with the ongoing negotiations for a "Transatlantic Trade and Investment Partnership," currently negotiated between the EU and the US. The Caribbean market or the resources in the Gulf of Mexico are not in any way comparable to the trade relevance of EU-US relations and of EU-Mercosur relations. The possible global diplomatic capital for the EU that could be seen in the continuous existence of the ACP group is minimized by rather sober experiences in past decades regarding the global support of EU positions – including the notorious reservation of CARICOM member states in 2010 to accept an enhanced observer status of the EU in the UN General Assembly (which was eventually accepted in May 2011 only after some arm twisting and compromises reducing the EU claim for exceptionalism in its UN representation). Against this backdrop, the Caribbean leadership in the ACP Secretariat during the period of negotiations for a post-Cotonou agreement may turn out to be significant.

The possible merger of the EDF with the general EU budget – due not before 2021 – is a matter of concern among ACP representatives: They fear that although oversight rights of the European Parliament will enhance the African priority, the European Parliament will also demand more deliverables from the ACP group in return for fresh EU money. Moreover, the problem of duplicating tasks which other national, regional or even global institutions can cope with in a more effective way looms large over the ACP grouping. Becoming recognized as a pole of global stability would require the ACP to practically reinvent itself – and this time neither as an appendix to the EU nor as the EU's nemesis. Common institutional ties such as the EU–ACP Joint Parliamentary Assembly will play a critical role in advancing the upcoming negotiation process toward a reasonably consensual outcome.

7. What to expect in the years ahead

The reflection on a possible future of EU–ACP relations beyond 2020 will remain linked to the three priorities currently defined by the Cotonou Agreement, such as:

Aid: The Cotonou agenda still exists. Aid to remedy poverty remains an issue beyond the global reflection on the achievements of the UN Millennium Development Goals. The challenge will be to redefine the very notion of development, beyond the simplistic focus on GDP and even criteria such as those of the Human Development Index. Also the industrialized countries of the Northern hemisphere are developing countries in their own way. Only a universal and inclusive definition of development can be appropriate in the age of globality.[30] EU and ACP partners could promote the reflection on a new notion of development, realizing that eventually it will be the small and the big, the peripheral and the core countries of the global community to advance such a debate.

Trade: Bi-regional arrangements toward free trade can facilitate success in the global promotion of free trade and a return to structured multi-lateralism beyond the Doha Round and the Bali process. Whether the ACP-EU format as such may contribute in any way to a consolidated and pragmatic multilateralism is debatable.[31] Certainly, regional groupings across the three ACP regions can play a growing role in the years ahead.[32] This implies that the EU must take them more seriously just the way they are (instead of restructuring them to its own liking, as happened during the unsuccessful EPA negotiations).

Political dialog: The term is as broad as it is inconclusive. It could touch upon the classical notion and idea of development – including issues of good governance and their preconditions – but it could also go beyond and promote reflections on the management of a global order which includes freedom and authority, rule of law and basic rights, a human centred understanding of development, human security and sustainable peace. Whether the EU–ACP format can contribute to this reflection, again, depends on the readiness of both sides to engage in a joint political effort which could impact the agenda of the United Nations and its institutions.

In any case, the EU and the ACP group of states need to broaden their stakeholder communities for a fresh beginning – even more so should they opt to dissolve the traditional format and advance regional groupings and bi-regional cooperation (both North-South and South-South).

The twofold dilemma which the EU and the ACP group of states are facing is easier to describe than to overcome: The EU needs to broaden its stakeholder community internally to update its contribution to the global debate for it to have any relevance for progress in the ACP group of countries. The ACP group of countries needs to engage more players, both officials as well as civil society activists, within and among countries across a huge territory and a vast set of agendas, in order to regain respect and be taken seriously by anybody beyond the donor community. Streamlining priorities internally and subsequently coming to terms with each other – nobody has ever suggested that the challenges ahead in advancing relations between the EU and the ACP group of countries would be easy. Whether both the EU and the ACP can draw diplomatic capital and economic benefits from the potential opportunities attributed to the challenges ahead remains dependent on the top-down will of political actors, but likewise on the bottom-up engagements of the private sector and civil society groups.

As for the EU, if it wants to be coherent and credible globally, recognizing regional communities the way they are ought to be the first priority. This recognition of non-European regional communities as actors in their own right requires a substantial renewal of the EU perspective and agenda; in most regions, traditional economic ties and development concerns overlap with geopolitical issues and new thematic challenges which go beyond the usual rhetoric and agenda of the EU. The end of the post-colonial era compels the EU to globalize its strategic orientation, linking traditional development concerns and trade interests with geopolitical and security considerations. The role which a renewed ACP partnership could play has to be addressed in multidimensional ways, and not only through the lens of political economy. Trying to advance the EU–ACP relationship from a post-colonial forum into a sincere element of global economic governance – compatible with the WTO, yet with a special focus on human development needs – is worth the effort. For the time being, only one thing is clear: The Cotonou Agreement, the foundation for a structured multidimensional relationship between the European Union and the African, Caribbean and Pacific group of states, will expire on February 28, 2020.

Notes

1 See Pape (2013, p. 736).
2 See Van Reisen (2011, 2012), Laporte (2012), Keijzer et al. (2013), and Van Reisen (2014). See also Piebalgs (2012).
3 Mission Letter of EU Commission President Jean-Claude Juncker to Commissioner for International Cooperation and Development, Neven Mimica, Brussels, November 1, 2014, available at www.ec.europa.eu/commission/2014–2019/mimica_en.
4 See Nickel (2012), Deutsches Institut für Entwicklungspolitik (2013), and Manrique Gil (2013).
5 See Abernethy (2000), Broberg (2011), and Vogt (2011).
6 On the French discourse, see Bitsch and Bossuat (2005).
7 In force from 1964 to 1969 and signed with 18 independent African countries: Burundi, Dahomey, Democratic Republic Congo, Gabon, Cameroon, Congo-Brazzaville, Ivory Coast, Madagascar, Mali, Mauretania, Niger, Upper Volta, Rwanda, Senegal, Somalia, Togo, Chad, and Central African Republic.
8 In force from 1972 to 1975 and additionally signed by Mauritius, while the planned membership of Kenya, Tanzania, Uganda (initiated with the Arusha Agreement of July 26, 1968 which was never ratified by the three member states of the East African Community) and of Nigeria (planned by the Lagos Agreement of Cooperation of July 16, 1966 but torpedoed by the effects of the Biafra War 1967–1970) did not work out as expected, in spite of the strong interest of Great Britain, who joined the EEC in 1973, to extend special relations to Anglophone countries in Africa.
9 The fusion treaties between the European Economic Community, Euratom and the European Community of Coal and Steel (ECCS) of 1967 turned the EEC into the EC (European Communities).
10 The literature on the CFA franc and the effect of being pegged to the euro is surprisingly limited; see Stasavage (2003), Van den Boogaerde and Charalambros (2005) and Zafar (2005).
11 See Georgetown Agreement (1975).
12 See Wolf (1996).
13 See Gieg (2010, p. 85).
14 See McQueen (1999), Holland (2002), and Slocum-Bradley and Andrew Bradley (2010).
15 In the African context, see Cheru (2002).
16 For a significant aspect, see Clegg (2002).
17 For the larger context of African relations with its global partners, see Kühnhardt (2014).
18 See Partnership Agreement (2000).
19 Africa: Angola, Benin, Botswana, Burkina Faso, Burundi, Cameroon, Cape Verde, Central African Republic, Chad, Comoros, Democratic Republic of the Congo, Djibouti, Equatorial Guinea, Eritrea, Ethiopia, Gabon, Gambia, Ghana, Guinea, Guinea-Bissau, Ivory Coast, Kenya, Lesotho, Liberia, Madagascar, Malawi, Mali, Mauritania, Mauritius, Mozambique, Namibia, Niger, Nigeria, Republic of the Congo, Rwanda, São Tomé and Príncipe, Senegal, Sierra Leone, South Africa, Tanzania, Togo, Uganda, Seychelles, Somalia, Sudan, Swaziland, Zambia, Zimbabwe; Caribbean: Antigua and Barbuda, Bahamas, Barbados, Belize, Cuba, Dominica, Dominican Republic, Grenada, Guyana, Haiti, Jamaica, Saint Kitts and Nevis, Saint Lucia, Saint Vincent and the Grenadines, Suriname, Trinidad and Tobago; Pacific: Cook Islands, Timor-Leste, Fiji, Kiribati, Marshall Islands, Federated States of Micronesia, Nauru, Niue, Palau, Papua New Guinea, Samoa, Solomon Islands, Tonga, Tuvalu, Vanuatu.
20 See Bilal and Rampa (2006), Grant (2006), Stevens (2006), Borrmann and Busse (2006), Jones and Martí (2009), and Engel (2012).
21 See Borrmann, Großmann, and Koopmann (2005), Naumann (2006), and Genin (2010).
22 For an assessment, see Günther (2011).
23 See *Euractiv* (2014).
24 See European Commission (2014).

25 See Reich (2011), De Benedictis and Salvatici (2011), and Morrissey (2011).
26 See Grimm and Makhan (2010).
27 See also Mackie, Byiers, Niznik, and Laporte (2011).
28 See Pape (2013, p. 734).
29 On the Pacific context, see Hassall (2011).
30 See Rist (2008) and Olopade (2014).
31 See Ngangjoh-Hodu and Matambalya (2010) and Nyomakawa-Obimpeh (2012).
32 See Kühnhardt (2010) and Telò (2014).

References

Abernethy, D.B. (2000), *The Dynamics of Global Dominance: European Overseas Empire 1915–1980*, Yale: Yale University Press.

Bilal, S. and Rampa, F. (2006), Alternative to EPAs. Possible Scenarios for the Future. ACP Trade Relations with the EU, *ECDPM Policy Management Report* 11.

Bitsch, M.-T. and Bossuat, G. (eds) (2005), *L'Europe unie et l'Afrique. De l'idée d'Eurafrique à la Convention de Lomé I*, Bruxelles: Bruylant.

Borrmann, A. and Busse, M. (2006), The Institutional Challenge of the ACP/EU Economic Partnership Agreements, *HWWA Research Paper* 2–3.

Borrmann, A., Großmann, H., and Koopmann, G. (2005), *The WTO Compatibility of the Economic Partnership Agreement between the EU and the ACP States*, Eschborn: Deutsche Gesellschaft für Technische Zusammenarbeit.

Broberg, M. (2011), The EU's Legal Ties with its Former Colonies. When Old Love Never Dies, *DIIS Working Paper* 2011:01.

Cheru, F. (2002), *African Renaissance: Roadmaps to the Challenge of Globalization*, London, New York: Zed Books.

Clegg, P. (2002), From Insiders to Outsiders: Caribbean Banana Interests in the New International Trading Framework, in Dearden, S.J.H. (ed.) *The European Union and the Caribbean*, Aldershot: Ashgate.

De Benedictis, L. and Salvatici, L. (eds) (2011), *The Trade Impact of European Preferential Policies*, Berlin: Springer.

Deutsches Institut für Entwicklungspolitik (ed.) (2013), AKP-EU-Beziehungen nach 2020: Auf der Suche nach einer europäischen Haltung, *Analysen und Stellungnahmen*, 5/2013, available at www.die-gdi.de/uploads/media/AuS_5.2013.pdf.

Engel, L. (2012), *EPAs als Entwicklungsinstrumente? Ideen und Diskurse in den Verhandlungen der Wirtschaftspartnerschaftsabkommen zwischen der EU und den AKP-Staaten*, Marburg: Tectum Verlag.

Euractiv (2014), EU Seals Free Trade Deal with West Africa, 7 February, available at www.euractiv.com/development-policy/eu-seals-free-trade-deal-west-af-news-533293.

European Commission (2014), Overview of EPAs – State of Play, available at www.ec.europa.eu/trade/policy/countries-and-regions/development/economic-partnerships.

Genin, A. (2010), *Von Lomé zu den Wirtschaftspartnerschaftsabkommen. Die Zukunft der gemeinschaftsrechtlichen Präferenzsysteme zugunsten der Entwicklungsländer im Rahmen der WTO am Beispiel der AKP-EG-Handelszusammenarbeit*, Stuttgart: Boorberg.

The Georgetown Agreement on the Organization of the African, Caribbean and Pacific Group of States (1975), available at www.wipo.int/wipolex/en/other_treaties/details.jsp?treaty_id=220.

Gieg, P. (2010), *Great Game um Africa? Europa, China und die USA auf dem Schwarzen Kontinent*, Baden-Baden: Nomos.

Gomes, P.I. (2013), Reshaping an Asymmetrical Partnership: ACP-EU Relations from an ACP Perspective, *Journal of International Development*, 25(5), 714–26.

Grant, C. (2006), Ongoing Trade Negotiations – EPA, Stellenbosch: Tralac.

Grimm, S. and Makhan, D. (2010), Überarbeitung des Cotonou-Abkommens: nichts Neues unter der Sonne?, *DIE Die aktuelle Kolumne*, 5 July, available at www.die-gdi.de/die-aktuelle-kolumne/article/ueberarbeitung-des-cotonou-abkommens-nichts-neues-unter-der-sonne/.

Günther, E. (2011), Regionale Integration und die Economic Partnership Agreements der EU: Das EPA mit der Karibik am Fallbeispiel CARICOM, Saarbrücken: VDM.

Hassall, G. (2011), 'Including the Excluded in Global Politics': The Pacific Island Micro-States and Global Politics, Victoria University of Wellington.

Holland, M. (2002), *The European Union and the Third World*, Houndmills: Palgrave.

Jones, E. and Martí, D.F. (eds) (2009), Updating Economic Partnerships Agreements to Today's Global Challenges, German Marshall Fund of the United States *Economic Policy Paper Series* 09.

Keijzer, N., Lein, B., Negre, M., and Tissi, N. (2013), ACP-EU Relations Beyond 2020: Exploring European Perceptions, *DIE Briefing Paper* 11/2013.

Kühnhardt, L. (2010), *Region-Building*, Oxford, New York: Berghahn Books.

Kühnhardt, L. (2014), *Africa Consensus. New Interests, Initiatives, and Partners*, Washington, Baltimore: Woodrow Wilson Center Press with Johns Hopkins University Press.

Laporte, G. (2012), What Future for the ACP and the Cotonou Agreement? Preparing for the Next Steps in the Debate, *ECDPM Briefing Note* 34.

Mackie, J., Byiers, B., Niznik, S., and Laporte, G. (ed.) (2011), Global Changes, Emerging Players and Evolving EU-ACP Relations: Towards a Common Agenda for Action? *ECDPM Policy and Management Report* 19.

McQueen, M. (1999), After Lomé IV: ACP-EU Trade Preferences in the 21st Century, *Intereconomics*, 34(5), 223–32.

Manrique Gil, M. (2013), ACP-EU Relations After 2020: Review of Options, Policy briefing, European Commission, Directorate General for External Policies, available at www.europarl.europa.eu/RegData/etudes/briefing_note/join/2013/491488/EXPO-DEVE_SP(2013)491488_EN.pdf.

Morrissey, O. (ed.) (2011), *Assessing Prospective Trade Policy: Methods Applied to EU-ACP Economic Partnership Agreements*, London: Routledge.

Naumann, E. (2006), Comparing EU Free Trade Agreements: Rules of Origin, *ECDPM InBrief* 61.

Ngangjoh-Hodu, Y. and Matambalya, F.A.S.T. (eds) (2010), *Trade Relations Between the EU and Africa: Development, Challenges and Options Beyond the Cotonou Agreement*, London, New York: Routledge.

Nickel, D. (2012), Was kommt nach Cotonou? Die Zukunft der Zusammenarbeit zwischen der EU und den Afrika-, Karibik- und Pazifikstaaten, *SWP-Studie* S13.

Olopade, D. (2014), Forget 'Developing': Fat Nations Must Go Lean, *New York Times*, 1–2 March.

Pape, E. (2013), An Old Partnership in a New Setting: ACP-EU Relations from a European Perspective, *Journal of International Development*, 25(5), 727–41.

Partnership Agreement between the members of the African, Caribbean and Pacific Group of States of the one part, and the European Community and its Member States, of the other part (2000), signed in Cotonou on 23 June 2000, *Official Journal of the European Communities*, L317/3, available at www.acp.int/content/acp-ec-partnership-agreement-cotonou-agreement-accord-de-partenariat-acp-ce-accord-de-cotonou.

Piebalgs, A. (2012), Challenges and Opportunities Ahead for the African, Caribbean and Pacific Group of States, speech delivered at the ACP Summit in Malabo, 13 December, available at www.eu-un.europa.eu/articles/en/article_12958_en.htm.

Reich, P. (2011), *EU-AKP Partnerschaftsabkommen – eine Bilanz. Das Abkommen von Cotonou zwischen Anspruch und Wirklichkeit*, Hamburg: Führungsakademie der Bundeswehr.

Rist, G. (2008), *The History of Development: From Western Origins to Global Faith*, London: Zed Books.

Secretariat of the African, Caribbean and Pacific Group of States (ed) (2011), Strategy for Renewal and Transformation 2011–2014, Brussels: Secretariat of the ACP Group of States.

Slocum-Bradley, N. and Bradley, A. (2010), Is the EU's Governance 'Good'? An Assessment of EU Governance in Its Partnership with ACP States, *Third World Quarterly*, 31(1), 31–49.

Stasavage, D. (2003), *The Political Economy of a Common Currency: The CFA Franc Zone Since 1945*, Aldershot: Ashgate.

Stevens, C. (2006), The EU, Africa and Economic Partnership Agreements: Unintended Consequences of Policy Leverage, *Journal of Modern African Studies*, 44(3), 441–58.

Telò, M. (2014), *European Union and New Regionalism: Competing Regionalism and Global Governance in a Post-Hegemonic Era*, Farnham: Ashgate.

Van den Boogaerde, P. and Charalambros, T. (2005), Ten Years After the CFA Franc Devaluation: Progress Toward Regional Integration in the WAEMU, *IMF Working Paper* 05/145.

Van Reisen, M. (2011), The Old Man and the Seas: The Future of the EU-ACP Relationship, *The Broker*, available at www.thebrokeronline.eu/Special-Reports/Special-Report-The-ACP-EU-Relationship/The-old-man-and-the-seas.

Van Reisen, M. (2012), The Future of the ACP-EU Relationship, *European Ideas*, 29 May, available at www.europeanideas.eu/pages/economics/international-trade/the-future-of-the-acp-eu-relationship.php.

Van Reisen, M. (2014), Study on the Future Perspectives of the ACP Group, *ACP Secretariat Report* 05/2014.

Vogt, D. (2011), *Die Integration der ultra-peripheren Regionen in die Europäische Union: Wandel der europäischen Politik gegenüber den überseeischen Besitzungen von Rom (1957) bis Lissabon (2009)*, Baden–Baden: Nomos.

Wolf, S. (1996), *Begrenzter Erfolg der Lomé-Abkommen: Eine empirische Untersuchung der Wirkungen der EU-Zollpräferenzen auf den Haushalt der AKP-Staaten*, Frankfurt am Main: Peter Lang.

Zafar, A. (2005), The Impact of the Strong Euro on the Real Effective Exchange Rates of the Two Francophone African CFA Zones, *World Bank Policy Research Working Paper* 3751.

PART V

Selected policy areas

17

REGIONAL POLICY

Sascha O. Becker, Peter H. Egger and Maximilian von Ehrlich

1. Introduction

The European Union's regional policy has the goal to foster convergence in per-capita earnings at purchasing power parity, to limit poverty and unemployment in peripheral regions, and to foster economic as well as social cohesion at large, while upholding environmental protection and respecting fiscal autonomy (see European Union, 1987). The removal of barriers to international transactions among the EU member countries and, in particular, the inception of the four fundamental freedoms of movement – of people, goods, services, and capital – between all member countries through the Single Market Program paved the way for some convergence in factor prices and incomes with the expected benefits (to consumers, firms, etc.) and costs (increased tax competition, the export and import of consequences of market imperfections such as credit constraints and unemployment). It is unquestioned that the fundamental heterogeneity among the member countries and regions (in institutions, climate, geography, the endowment with immobile factors, the age profile of the populations, in currencies, etc.) creates an obstacle to such convergence that market forces established by the four freedoms may not be able to surmount. Hence, it is held at the European Commission – as in all national federations – that a system of transfers should be established in order to extend equalization (in purchasing power parity and fiscal capacity) to where the market itself cannot provide it, at least not in the short run.

Beyond its Common Agricultural Policy (CAP) the European Commission administers such equalization mainly through the Structural and Cohesion Funds (SCF; collectively the second biggest item in the EU's budget after the CAP), accounting for 29–36 percent of the EU's total expenditure between 2000 and 2013.[1] The SCF consist of three main funds: the European Regional Development Fund (ERDF), the European Social Fund (ESF), and the Cohesion Fund (CF). Putting the expenditures in a long-term perspective the Union's expenditure share on regional policy steadily increased. The average annual share of structural funds expenditure amounted to 4.9 percent of the total budget in the period 1961–72 (EU6), 8.2 percent during 1973–80 (EU9), 16.2 percent during 1981–5 (EU10), 22.1 percent during 1987–94 (EU12), and 32.4 percent during 1995–9 (EU15) where these figures include cohesion fund expenditures from 1993 onwards. For the ongoing period 2014–20, regional policy expenditure is budgeted at €351.8 billion or 32.5 percent of total budget (see European Commission, 2014a).

2. The history and administration of EU regional policy

While the principal foundations for the EU's regional policy were laid already in one of its (or better the European Economic Community's) founding documents, namely the Treaty of Rome, regional policy lacked funding and bite in the EU's wake, even though the Directorate-General of the European Commission was founded as early as 1968. Specific regional instruments were absent at this stage, but the Community focused on social cohesion (by the foundation of the European Social Fund) and general (e.g., transport-related) or specific sectoral aid (by the foundation of the European Investment Bank and the associated financed projects).

The first specific instrument towards regional policy was created with the establishment of the ERDF in 1975 – a consequence of the EU's first enlargement in 1973 by Denmark, Ireland, and the UK. The ERDF explicitly focuses on economic and social cohesion in the EU by aiming to correct imbalances between the EU's (sub-national) regions. It does so by providing direct aid to investments in (particularly small and medium-sized) companies for the sake of creating sustainable jobs; by financing infrastructure, in particular when related to research and innovation, telecommunications, energy, transport, and the environment; by providing financial instruments to regions (such as capital risk funds, local development funds, etc.) to support development and to foster cooperation between sub-national units; and by providing technical assistance. Three main objectives of the ERDF are convergence, regional competitiveness and employment (with special emphasis on education-, skill- and innovation-intensive activities, information and communication, culture, environment, tourism, health, and risk-prevention in general), and territorial cooperation within Europe (economically and socially).

However, only with the enlargements in 1981 (by Greece) and in 1986 (by Portugal and Spain) did the need for a significant increase in the funding of regional policy and the desire for an overarching cohesion policy with the ESF and the ERDF as its two key pillars take form. It materialized in a commitment to foster convergence and cohesion by way of targeted project funding during 5–7-year programming periods, ensuring a strong involvement of local (national and sub-national) partners. In the aftermath of the so-called southern enlargements in 1981 and 1986, it became clear that the integration of poorer regions in the EU called for means that went beyond the capacities of the ESF and the SF at the time. Therefore, the CF was established in 1993, administering funds of about one-tenth of the ones in the SF at the time, and providing special aid for convergence and development in regions of Greece, Ireland, Portugal, and Spain. Overall, the budgetary periods distinguished between numerous objectives and strategies outside of those in the periods 1989–93 and 1994–9 which were condensed in 2000–6 and recast in 2007–13. See Tables 17.1 and 17.2 for a summary of the activities, budgets, and main objectives of the SF in the last four budgetary periods. The administration of the SCF rests on five main pillars: the ERDF, the ESF, the EAGG-F (European Agricultural Guidance and Guarantee Fund), the FIF (Financial Instrument for Fisheries), and the CF (see Table 17.3 for the relative importance of those across the previous budgetary periods).

While in a broad sense, regional policy had the fundamental goal to reduce unemployment and raise wealth and well-being, in particular, in the least-developed regions, the particular channels (objectives) changed from programming period to programming period. While structural issues (specialization, industrial change) were important early on, the Commission gradually put greater emphasis on social, technological, and environmental issues in the course of years.

Table 17.1 Program periods

Program period	Activity	Regional policy budget
1989–93	Formulation of overarching cohesion policy goal with 4 key principles: (i) focusing on the poorest and least-advanced regions; (ii) multi-year programming periods; (iii) strategic investments; (iv) participation of regional and local partners. Maastricht Treaty (1993): Foundation of the Cohesion Fund; Foundation of the Committee of the Regions; Introduction of the principle of subsidiarity.	ECU 70.3bn.
1994–99	Resources for SCF were significantly increased. Introduction of a special objective in 1995 to support sparsely-populated regions of Finland and Sweden.	ECU 145bn. [of which ECU 11.8bn. CF]
2000–06	Stronger emphasis on growth, jobs, and innovation.	€201bn. [of which €16.5 bn. CF]
2007–13	Stronger emphasis on innovation and environmental infrastructure as well as climate change.	€347.4bn. [of which €69bn. CF expenditures]

Sources: European Commission (2007a: 41–42), and European Commission (2007b: 25) for 2007–13.

Table 17.2 Objectives by period

Budgetary period	Main objectives	Percentage of SCF funding
1989–93	Objective 1 – Convergence & structural adjustment (ERDF, ESF)	61.40
	Objective 2 – Industrial decline (ESF)	8.59
	Objective 3 – Long-term unemployment and labor market re-integration (ESF)	9.35 (Obj. 3&4)
	Objective 4 – Adapting workforce to industrial change; youth unemployment (ESF)	
	Objective 5a – Agricultural and fishery structure adjustment	4.94
	Objective 5b – Rural adjustment (ESF)	3.13
	CF	2.20
	IMP outside Objective 1	2.19
	Community initiatives	7.41
1994–99	Objective 1 – Convergence & structural adjustment (ERDF, ESF)	56.38
	Objective 2 – Industrial decline (ESF)	9.21
	Objective 3 – Long-term unemployment and labor market re-integration (ESF)	3.11 (Obj. 3&4)
	Objective 4 – Adapting workforce to industrial change (ESF)	
	Objective 5a – Agricultural and fishery structure adjustment	3.68
	Objective 5b – Rural adjustment (ESF)	4.12

(Continued)

Table 17.2 (Continued)

Budgetary period	Main objectives	Percentage of SCF funding
	Objective 6 – Developing regions with extremely low population density	0.42
	CF	8.67
	Community initiatives	8.41
2000–06	Objective 1 – Convergence (ERDF, ESF, EAGGF Guidance Section)	67.04
	Objective 2 – Socio-economic restructuring (ERDF, ESF)	10.06
	Objective 3 – (ESF)	10.71
	Objective F (FIF)	0.46
	CF	6.86
	Community initiatives	4.88
2007–13	Convergence (ERDF, ESF, CF)	81.46
	Regional competitiveness & employment (ERDF, ESF)	15.83
	European territorial cooperation (ERDF)	2.59

Sources: European Commission (1997: 154–155) for 1989–93 and 1994–99, European Commission (2007a: 41–42), European Commission (2007c: 202–229) for 2000–06, and http://ec.europa.eu/regional_policy/thefunds/funding/index_en.cfm for 2007–13.

Table 17.3 Funds by period

Funds	Established	Percentage of budget in all SCF			
		1989–93	*1994–99*	*2000–06*	*2007–13*
ERDF	1975	46.74	43.19	40.25	58
ESF	1957	27.89	24.75	21.97	22
CF	1993	1.13	8.15	8.25	20
EAGG-G	1957	15.68	13.27	7.47	–
FIF-G	1993	–	1.75	1.40	–
SCF in percent of total EU Budget		26.01	31.64	30.37	37.54

Sources: EU Commission (2007a: 41–42), and http://ec.europa.eu/regional_policy/thefunds/funding/index_en.cfm for 2007–13. Note that these shares do not sum up to 100 percent as parts of the expenditures capture completions of earlier programs.

3. Counterfactual evaluation of the EU's regional policy

It is no trivial task to evaluate the success of EU Regional Policy. Poor regions going through a catch-up phase might grow faster than rich regions, independently from the receipt of EU transfers. A simple comparison of the growth rates of regions that receive EU transfers and those that do not is insufficient to draw any accurate conclusions about the causal effect of EU transfers on regional growth.

In the past, the European Commission tried to dissuade any concerns that EU money is being spent in an inappropriate manner by reducing the issue to one of proper accounting for projects that have been approved to receive funding (see European Commission, 2011). Only in 2008 the Commission started its own counterfactual impact evaluations, which so far have concentrated on the evaluation of specific funding initiatives in selected regions or countries (see http://ec.europa.eu/regional_policy/information/evaluations/impact_evaluation_en.cfm for an overview).

Academic research has looked into the growth effects of EU Regional Policy in various ways. Sala-i-Martin (1996) compared the regional growth and convergence pattern in the EU to that of other federations which lack a similarly extensive cohesion program and concluded that the EU's structural policy was a failure. Such a conclusion requires comparability of federations and their regions in all other respects, which is empirically challenging. Boldrin and Canova (2001) came to similar conclusions when comparing regional growth within the EU in recipient and non-recipient regions.

Midelfart-Knarvik and Overman (2002) took a more positive stance based on their finding of a positive impact of the Structural Funds Program on industry location and agglomeration at the national level. Beugelsdijk and Eijffinger (2005) and Ederveen, de Groot and Nahuis (2006) used national data and found a positive relationship between Structural Funds Program spending and GDP-per-capita growth (at least, in countries with favorable institutions). Based on regional data at the NUTS1 or NUTS2 level, Cappelen, Castellacci, Fagerberg and Verspagen (2003) as well as Ederveen, Gorter, de Mooij and Nahuis (2003) detected a significant positive impact of structural funds on regional growth.

In a Commission Staff Working Document entitled "Common methodology for state aid evaluation", SWD(2014) 179 final (published on May 28 in 2014, Brussels), The European Commission provides a generic review of some methods for program evaluation that could and would ideally be used to evaluate state aid programs at large and specifically the EU's transfer programs. The literature review in this document reveals that relevant parties in the Commission are unaware of a recent body of work, started off by the contributions of Becker, Egger, and von Ehrlich (2010, 2012, 2013), which applies exactly the methods surveyed and discussed in that document to evaluate regional EU funding schemes.

Becker, Egger and von Ehrlich (2010) concentrate on the growth effects of EU Objective 1 funds. Those are the most important category in the EU's Regional Policy in the programming periods 1989–93, 1994–9 and 2000–6 and make up more than two-thirds of the whole EU Regional Policy budget. They are targeted at the poorest EU regions and are assigned by a clearly defined rule: NUTS2 regions, whose GDP per capita is less than 75 percent if EU average, are eligible. This rule gives rise to a so-called regression discontinuity design to evaluate the growth effects of Objective 1 funds. In fact, on paper, a region whose GDP per capita relative to the EU average is 74.99 percent qualifies for potentially billions of Euros in EU Objective 1 funding, whereas a region whose GDP per capita relative to the EU average is 75.01 percent does not qualify for Objective 1 funding. To the extent that regions to the left and right of the 75 percent threshold only differ minimally in their GDP per capita, Objective 1 funds are essentially randomly assigned, yielding a quasi-experimental setting which can be exploited in statistical analysis. If the 75 percent rule was strictly applied, we would have a sharp regression-discontinuity design. In reality, however, the number of observations which comply with the 75 percent-rule is (only) 628 out of 674 observations at the NUTS2 level. About 7 percent of all observations are exceptions from the rule. There are two types of exceptions. First, some eligible regions fail to obtain Objective 1 status. For instance, the UK did not deliver GDP data at the NUTS2-level at the time Objective 1 status was determined in the programming period 1989–93, so some British NUTS2 regions failed to obtain Objective 1 funds. Second, some governments negotiated exceptions from the 75 percent rule for regions which were too rich to be formally eligible (see Becker, Egger and von Ehrlich, 2010, footnote 3 for further details).

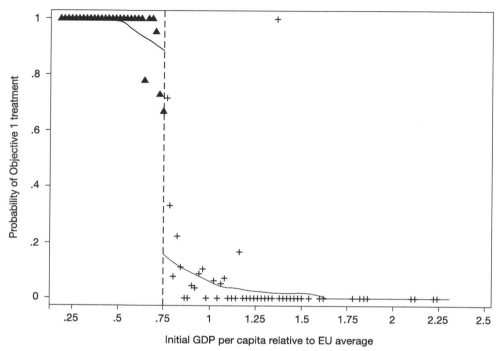

Figure 17.1   Objective 1 treatment and the 75% threshold

Note: This figure corresponds to NUTS2 region data pooled for the program periods 1989–93, 1994–99, and 2000–06. The dots refer to local averages in the probability to receive Objective 1 status for observations within equally sized bins of 2% which are plotted against the per capita GDP that applied in the years relevant for the decision about Objective 1 status. The figure is taken from Becker, Egger, von Ehrlich (2010).

Figure 17.1 shows the average treatment rates in equally sized bins of 2 percent which are plotted against the per capita GDP that applied in the years relevant for the decision about Objective 1 status.

The partial non-compliance with the 75 percent-rule gives rise to a so-called fuzzy regression discontinuity design. From an econometric perspective, the effect of Objective 1 funding on regional growth is estimated via an instrumental-variables estimator, where regional growth is regressed on a dummy for Objective 1 status, which in turn is instrumented by a dummy variable equal to 1 for regions that are formally eligible and 0 otherwise. A polynomial function in initial GDP per capita relative to the EU average serves to control for the relationship between regional GDP per capita and growth away from the 75 percent threshold and thus helps to isolate the jump at the 75 percent threshold in both the first stage (with Objective 1 treatment as the outcome) and in the second stage (with growth as the outcome variable).

The results in Becker, Egger and von Ehrlich (2010) show that Objective 1 funds are, on average, helping recipient regions to grow faster: Objective 1 funds are effective, on average, in generating additional growth. A crucial question is, however, whether Objective 1 gives value for money from a cost-benefit perspective. Our reference estimate for the additional growth generated by Objective 1 funding is 0.016. Accordingly, Objective 1 treatment raised average growth of real GDP per capita by about 1.6 percentage points in recipient regions. This compares with an average transfer of 1.4 percentage points of beginning-of-period GDP per capita, yielding a multiplier of about 1.2. In other words, every Euro spent on Objective 1 transfers leads to 1.20 EUR of additional GDP. The analysis thus shows that, on average, Objective 1 transfers during the years 1989 and 2006, under the EU's Structural Funds Program are effective in generating additional growth and – in net terms – not wasteful.

Interestingly, while Objective 1 funds generate additional GDP growth, there is no additional employment growth. One reason for this could be that Objective 1 transfers mainly stimulate the volume and change the structure of investment. But another potential reason could be that job creation takes longer than the duration of a programming period of five to seven years.

Pellegrini et al. (2013) repeat the analysis in Becker, Egger, and von Ehrlich (2010) and, not surprisingly, come to the same conclusions.

The finding in Becker, Egger and von Ehrlich (2010) of positive growth effects on average does, however, leave open the question whether some regions are more successful in turning Objective 1 funds into additional growth than others and what are factors driving such hetero-geneity. This is the focus of further work in Becker, Egger and von Ehrlich (2013), which looks at the role of absorptive capacity in generating additional growth from Objective 1 transfers.

Absorptive capacity has been highlighted as important to understand the effectiveness of aid programs to developing countries. Starting with the work of Burnside and Dollar (2000, 2004), it has been hotly debated whether (and under what conditions) foreign aid actually leads to more growth. Easterly (2003) questions the effectiveness of aid with respect to economic growth, while Dalgaard et al. (2004) argue in favor of an aid-growth link.

The aid literature in general seems to suggest that low levels of education and poor performing institutions (such as corrupt politicians, bad administrations, etc.) are measures of (the absence of) absorptive capacity that bode ill for a growth effect of foreign aid. In the EU context, such institutions are also mentioned as one reason why regional transfers are not as effective as they could be. Pisani-Ferry et al. (2011) argue that poor performing institutions in Greece are responsible for the country's repeated failure to use up the EU funding that had already been assigned. Capital-skill complementarities are the reason why human capital is important as a factor facilitating growth effects of EU transfers: a lack of skilled workers in some recipient regions should be considered an important source of lower returns on investment (Duffy et al., 2004).

Based on these arguments, Becker, Egger and von Ehrlich (2013) look at human capital and the quality of government as two dimensions of absorptive capacity which affect the effectiveness of EU transfers more. The logic of this analysis is illustrated in Figure 17.2.

Figure 17.2 features two "planes," one to the left of the 75 percent threshold and one to the right. The wedge between these two planes follows the direction of the axis displaying the human capital endowment of the work force in a region, relative to the EU average. The size of the wedge at any given value of a region's human capital endowment shows the additional growth generated in a recipient region with such human capital endowment. As before, not all regions to the right of the wedge receive Objective 1 funds despite their eligibility and some regions to the left of the wedge do receive Objective 1 funds. The instrumental variables estimation procedure adjusts for this by the first-stage estimation of the treatment probability. The result of this procedure is the curve displayed in Figure 17.3 which shows how additional growth generated by Objective 1 transfers varies across regions with different level of human capital endowment. Human capital endowment is measured as the share of the region's work force with at least upper-secondary education, as measured in the European Labour Force survey.

Figure 17.3 shows that only regions with above-average human capital endowment are successful in generating additional GDP growth from Objective 1 transfers. Regions with

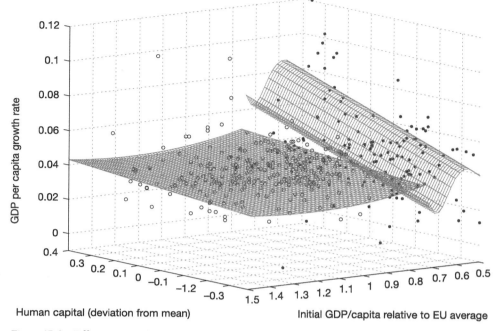

Figure 17.2   Effectiveness of Objective 1 transfers and human capital

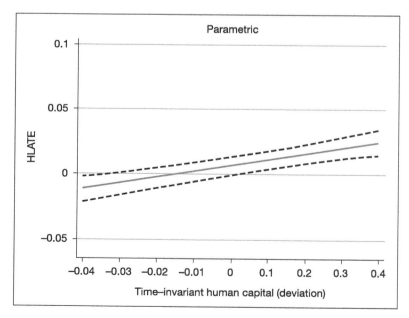

Figure 17.3   Effectiveness of Objective 1 and human capital

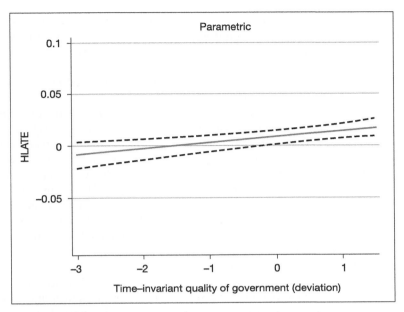

Figure 17.4 Effectiveness of Objective 1 and quality of government

below-average human capital endowment, in contrast, do not turn Objective 1 transfers into growth.

An alternative measure of a region's absorptive capacity is quality of government. It is based on an EU-wide survey on perceptions (Charron, Dijkstra and Lapuente, 2014) of 34,000 EU citizens, to date the largest survey ever undertaken to measure quality of government at the sub-national level. The index is based on 16 separate survey questions concerning three key public services: education, health care, and law enforcement. The respondents were asked to rate the quality, impartiality, and level of corruption of those services. The idea being that governments that score high on the quality of government along these lines are also likely to be better at attracting and administering EU funds.

Using quality of government as a measure of absorptive capacity, a similar result emerges: regions with high quality of government are able to turn transfers under the Union's Objective 1 Structural Funds Program into faster growth whereas those with low quality of government do not. This is shown in Figure 17.4.

Considering these results in connection with our earlier work, it turns out that Objective 1 recipient regions with above-average human capital and/or above-average quality of government are the ones driving the overall positive average effect of the Objective 1 Program.

Notice that these conclusions, while plausible, stand in stark contrast to those in other work which did not employ techniques to avoid the endogeneity of Structural Funds transfers. For instance, Le Gallo, dall'Erba, and Guillain (2011, p. 483) found that some regions "in the UK, in the Southern part of Italy, and in Greece did benefit positively from structural funds while some core regions in Germany, the Netherlands, Belgium, France, and Denmark did not." However, they admit, on the same page, that "structural funds are not allocated randomly but depend, among others, on the regional GDP level, structural funds are possibly not exogenous" but that "this endogeneity problem cannot be solved" within their approach. Addressing this endogeneity problem, Becker, Egger, and von Ehrlich (2013) arrived at more or less exactly the opposite conclusion: the regions in the "South" fared worst while those in Germany and other "Northern" countries fared best in responding positively to EU transfers as an outcome of better governance and absorptive capacity in the North than in the South, on average.

A further question of importance in connection with EU Structural Funds as a whole is whether more funds mean more additional growth?

Becker et al. (2012) provide an answer to this question by looking at the total amount of transfers received under Objectives 1, 2 and 3 combined, relative to regional GDP, i.e. the transfer intensity, and its effect on regional growth. Data on the amount of transfers received is available for the two last completed programming periods only, 1994–9 and 2000–6, but at the more disaggregated NUTS3 level. Interestingly, about 90 percent of all EU regions received transfers under the auspices of the EU's Regional Policy. In some cases, the amounts received were tiny: in the programming period 2000–6, the Swedish region of Hallands län received EU transfers of 5,345 Euros, equivalent to only 0.00009 percent of its GDP. At the other extreme, the Greek region of Grevena displayed a transfer intensity of 29.057 percent in the 1994–9 programming period. Table 17.4 gives an overview of the amounts of EU funding received across EU regions.

In theory, more EU transfers might be expected to generate greater additional growth, but in reality it appears there may well be decreasing returns from investment and investment-stimulating transfers. One argument backing up this view – and, ultimately, the conclusion that there exists a *maximum desirable level* of regional transfers – comes naturally from neoclassical production theory and the assumption of diminishing returns (Hirshleifer, 1958). Supposing that investment projects are financed and undertaken in the order of their expected returns on investment, then a larger number of investment projects would be associated with a lower return on investments or transfers. If diminishing returns from transfers were relevant, a maximum desirable level of the treatment intensity of EU transfers could be identified. Above that level, no additional (or even lower) per capita income growth effects would be generated than at or below that threshold.

There is a similar argument for a minimum necessary level of regional transfers. It is based on the big-push or poverty-trap theory of development which states that transfers (or aid)

Table 17.4 EU funding received across EU regions

	Mean	Std.dev.	Min	Max	Treated obs.
Annual transfers per treated region					
Sample: all regions receiving EU transfers from either Structural Funds or Cohesion Funds budget					
Total EU transfers (mn. Euros)	23.141	49.744	0.005	778.531	2078
Total EU transfers/GDP (%)	0.759	1.512	0.00009	29.057	2078
Sample: regions receiving EU transfers from the Structural Funds budget under the Objective 1 heading					
Objective 1 transfers (mn. Euros)	52.131	68.869	0.603	778.531	702
Objective 1 transfers/GDP (%)	1.991	2.103	0.076	29.057	702
Sample: regions receiving EU transfers from the Cohesion Funds budget					
Cohesion Fund transfers (mn. Euros)	21.479	36.090	0.018	334.935	363
Cohesion Fund transfers/GDP (%)	0.659	0.950	0.002	6.338	363
Annual GDP per-capita growth	0.042	0.017	−0.039	0.138	2078

Source: Becker, Egger, and von Ehrlich (2012), Table 1.

have to exceed a certain threshold in order to become effective. There are two primary reasons for such minimum thresholds. First, the marginal product of capital might be extremely low and at levels of infrastructure or human capital that are too small (Sachs et al., 2004). Second, regions lagging behind might be isolated from other developed regions (Murphy et al., 1989).

In the context of EU Structural Funds, it would be greatly beneficial to pinpoint both a maximum desirable level of the treatment intensity and a minimum necessary level of regional transfer intensity. This would lead to significant efficiency gains by cutting transfers above the maximum desirable level and redistributing funds to regions whose transfer intensity is below the optimum level.

The relationship between the transfer intensity (the "dose") and the growth effect can be analyzed by way of estimating dose-response functions. Figure 17.5 shows that, on average, a

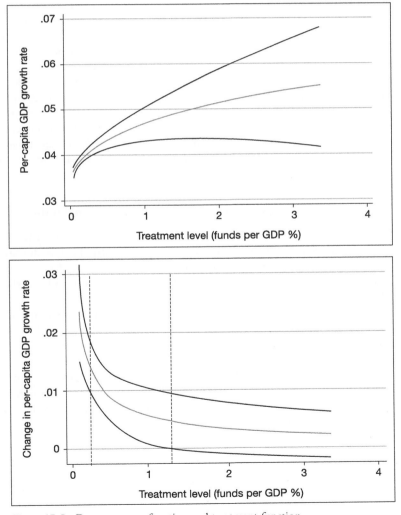

Figure 17.5 Dose-response function and treatment function

higher treatment intensity is associated with a faster growth rate. However, the confidence bands plotted around the average response indicate that, beyond a treatment intensity of 1.3 percent, per capita income growth no longer necessarily leads to additional economic expansion. In other words, beyond this maximum desirable treatment intensity, the null hypothesis of zero (or even negative) growth effects induced by additional transfers can no longer be rejected. This is plotted in the bottom graph in Figure 17.5, where the additional growth effect is plotted against the treatment intensity.

About 18 percent of NUTS3 recipient regions received transfers above the maximum desirable treatment intensity in the programming periods 1994–9 and 2000–6. A reallocation of transfers from those regions, most of them in the periphery of the EU, would therefore not be detrimental, and could well be of benefit to other regions. By contrast, at the lower end of treatment intensity levels, there is no evidence for a big push theory. Even for low levels of treatment intensity, additional transfers generate a significant amount of additional growth.

The research by Becker, Egger, and von Ehrlich (2012) is related to the one of Mohl and Hagen (2010), who analyze the effects of Objectives 1–3 on regional economic growth. They exploit the availability of the data in panel form (across regions and years), taking into account contagion in the sense of spatially correlated growth rates of regions as well as serial correlation, and find that Objective 1 transfers raise growth while Objective 2 and 3 transfers do not. One caveat with respect to their results is that they do not take the endogeneity of structural funds into account and this is an issue since these funds are determined at the beginning of a programming period with full knowledge of the recipient regions. Another caveat relates to the timing of funding expenditures versus the one of their effects on GDP and its growth. The latter is hard to identify in the framework of Mohl and Hagen (2010), since only those effects can be identified which materialize within a year from the Objective 1–3 expenditures.

4. Towards greater transparency of the EU's regional policy

One fundamental problem with the evaluation of the effectiveness of the EU's Structural Funds was a certain lack of transparency regarding (i) the rationale behind allocating funds to regions which apparently did not comply with the ruling, (ii) the data not only made available to researchers but even actually available to the Commission, and (iii) the support of independent research on the matter.

However, recent action has been taken and the European Commission has put out guidelines for the monitoring and evaluation of European Cohesion Policy (European Commission, 2014b).

As to the future of the institutions of regional transfers, there is some hope that greater transparency will lead to a recognition of earlier findings (regarding factors such as governance and skill abundance which co-determine the effectiveness and efficiency of transfers, the nonlinear relationship between the amount of transfers and their effectiveness, and the greater effectiveness of public rather than firm-specific transfers).

Note

1 The overall EU budget amounted to € 733.5bn and € 925.3bn for the periods 2000–6 and 2007–13, respectively (see European Commission, 2007a).

References

Becker, S.O., Egger, P.H. and von Ehrlich, M. (2010), Going NUTS: The Effect of EU Structural Funds on Regional Performance, *Journal of Public Economics*, 94(9–10), 578–90.

Becker, S.O., Egger, P.H. and von Ehrlich, M. (2013), Too Much of a Good Thing? On the Growth Effects of the EU's Regional Policy, *European Economic Review*, 56(4), 648–68.

Becker, S.O., Egger, P.H. and von Ehrlich, M. (2013), Absorptive Capacity and the Growth Effects of Regional Transfers: A Regression Discontinuity Design with Heterogeneous Treatment Effects, *American Economic Journal: Economic Policy*, 5(4), 29–77.

Beugelsdijk, M. and Eijffinger, S.C.W. (2005), The Effectiveness of Structural Policy in the European Union: an Empirical Analysis for the EU-15 in 1995–2001, *Journal of Common Market Studies*, 43(1), 37–51.

Boldrin, M. and Canova, F. (2001), Inequality and Convergence in Europe's Regions: Reconsidering European Regional Policies, *Economic Policy*, 16(32), 207–53.

Burnside, C. and Dollar, D. (2000), Aid, Policies, and Growth, *American Economic Review*, 90(4), 847–68.

Burnside, C. and Dollar, D. (2004), Aid, Policies, and Growth: Revisiting the Evidence, World Bank Policy Research Working Paper No. 3251.

Cappelen, A., Castellacci, F., Fagerberg, J. and Verspagen, B. (2003), The Impact of EU Regional Support on Growth and Convergence in the European Union, *Journal of Common Market Studies*, 41(4), 621–44.

Charron, N., Dijkstra, L. and Lapuente, V. (2014), Regional Governance Matters: Quality of Government within European Union Member States, *Regional Studies*, 48(1), 68–90.

Dalgaard, C.-J., Hansen, H. and Tarp, F. (2004), On the Empirics of Foreign Aid and Growth, *Economic Journal*, 114(496), 191–216.

Duffy, J., Papageorgiou, C. and Perez-Sebastian, F. (2004), Capital-Skill Complementarity? Evidence from a Panel of Countries, *Review of Economics and Statistics*, 86(1), 327–44.

Easterly, W. (2003), Can Foreign Aid Buy Growth? *Journal of Economic Perspectives*, 17(3), 23–48.

Ederveen, S., Gorter, J., de Mooij, R. and Nahuis, R. (2003), Funds and Games: The Economics of European Cohesion Policy, *European Network of Economic Policy Research Institutes Occasional Paper* No. 3.

Ederveen, S., de Groot, H.L.F. and Nahuis, R. (2006), Fertile Soil for Structural Funds? A Panel Data Analysis of the Conditional Effectiveness of European Cohesion Policy, *Kyklos*, 59(1), 17–42.

European Union (1987), The Single European Act. Official Journal of the European Union 169 of 29.6.1987.

European Commission (1997), Regional Development Studies – The Impact of Structural Policies on Economic and Social Cohesion in the Union 1989–99. Office for Official Publications of the European Commission, Luxembourg.

European Commission (2007a), EU Budget 2006 Financial Report. Available for download at www.europarl.europa.eu/meetdocs/2004_2009/documents/dv/tran20071120accountscom2006_/tran20071120accountscom2006_en.pdf

European Commission (2007b), Cohesion Policy 2007–13: Commentaries and Official Texts. Available for download at http://ec.europa.eu/regional_policy/sources/docoffic/official/regulation/pdf/2007/publications/guide2007_en.pdf

European Commission (2007c), 18th Annual Report on Implementation of the Structural Funds (2006), Annex. Available for download at: http://ec.europa.eu/regional_policy/sources/docoffic/official/reports/pdf/annex/2006_sf_annex_en.pdf

European Commission (2011), EU SPENDING. A Myth-buster. Available for download at http://ec.europa.eu/budget/explained/myths/myths_en.cfm

European Commission (2014a), A Reformed Cohesion Policy for Europe. Available for download at http://ec.europa.eu/regional_policy/thefunds/funding/data/graphics/cohesionpolicy20142020_full_highres.png

European Commission (2014b), The Programming Period 2014–2020: Monitoring and Evaluation of European Cohesion Policy Available for download at http://ec.europa.eu/regional_policy/sources/docoffic/2014/working/evaluation_plan_guidance_en.pdf

Hirshleifer, J. (1958), On the Theory of Optimal Investment Decision, *Journal of Political Economy*, 66(4), 329–52.

Le Gallo, J., Dall'Erba, S. and Guillain, R. (2011), The Local versus Global Dilemma of the Effects of Structural Funds, *Growth and Change*, 42(4), 466–90.

Midelfart-Knarvik, K.H. and Overman, H.G. (2002), Delocation and European Integration—is Structural Spending Justified?, *Economic Policy*, 17(35), 323–59.

Mohl, P. and Hagen, T. (2010), Do EU Structural Funds Promote Regional Growth? New Evidence from Various Panel Data Approaches, *Regional Science and Urban Economics*, 40(5), 353–65.

Murphy, K.M., Shleifer, A. and Vishny, R.M. (1989), Industrialization and the Big Push, *Journal of Political Economy*, 97(5), 1003–26.

Pellegrini, G., Terribile, F., Tarola, O., Muccigrosso, T. and Busillo, F. (2013), Measuring the Effects of European Regional Policy on Economic Growth: A Regression Discontinuity Approach, *Papers in Regional Science*, 92(1), 217–33.

Pisani-Ferry, J., Marzinotto, B. and Wolff, G.B., (2011), How European Funds can Help Greece Grow, *Financial Times*, 28 July 2011.

Sachs, .D., McArthur, J.W., Schmidt-Traub, G., Kruk, M., Bahadur, C., Faye, M. and McCord, G. (2004), Ending Africa's Poverty Trap, *Brookings Papers on Economic Activity*, 35(1), 117–240.

Sala-i-Martin, X. (1996), Regional Cohesion: Evidence and Theories of Regional Growth and Convergence, *European Economic Review*, 40(6), 1325–52.

18

THE COMMON AGRICULTURAL POLICY

Johan Swinnen

1. Introduction

Policies designed to protect and subsidize agriculture have been a key part of the EU throughout its history, primarily through its Common Agricultural Policy (CAP). And for much of the past 50 years, critics have argued that the CAP distorted world markets and contributed to global poverty and food insecurity by exerting downward pressure on agricultural commodity prices in world markets. As the EU subsidized its own production and exports of agricultural commodities, it caused a decline in world prices. However the CAP of today is a very different policy than the CAP of the 1970s and 1980s – with much less distortive effects.

Pressure to reform EU agriculture policies increased as the EU grew in size and the CAP transformed EU agriculture in the late twentieth century. With high subsidies for agricultural production and exports and taxes on imports, production increased and imports declined. As a result the EU shifted from being a major importer to a major (subsidized) exporter of agricultural products. This upset traditional agricultural exporters in world markets. It also caused budget concerns within the EU with declining revenue from import taxes and growing expenditures on subsidies, and the CAP taking up a major share of the EU budget.

The EU not only grew in size but also grew institutionally. In the early years of the CAP, ministers of agriculture met once a year to fix the EU agricultural prices and to decide on the level of the subsidies. All decisions were made unanimously – a difficult task with countries having quite diverse agriculture and food interests. However, since then much has changed. CAP decisions are no longer made by unanimity but by qualified majority voting, while major policy issues are set through multiyear policy agreements rather than at annual talks. In addition, an elected EU Parliament now has co-decision-making power. Moreover, European society also became more concerned about the safety and quality of its food, and about environmental issues. A series of food-safety scares in the 1990s shocked EU consumers and society. All these changes have affected EU agriculture and food policies.

Various pressures for policy change from inside and outside the EU led to a series of reforms over the past three decades. These reforms caused a shift in the nature of the subsidies, from taxing imports and subsidizing production and exports to subsidizing first land and animals, and later to subsidizing farms directly. These subsidies have a much smaller impact on production and trade, while maintaining support for farmers. At the same time, more stringent food safety and quality standards have been introduced and farm subsidies have been increasingly linked to achieving environmental objectives.

After these reforms of the CAP, the EU now faces a somewhat paradoxical situation: while its agricultural policies no longer push global agricultural and food prices down, global food security problems are now attributed to high food prices (Swinnen and Squicciarini, 2012). Surpluses have declined to the extent that there is hardly any food aid being given by the EU to poor countries during the global "food crisis" of recent years.

The most recent reform was decided in 2013, setting the CAP framework until 2020. There was pressure to re-introduce more market regulation, in response to recent price volatility in global markets. But the 2013 agreement kept the EU largely on its long-term trajectory towards market-based agriculture, while retaining large subsidies to enhance farm incomes directly and to incentivize environmental objectives.

In this chapter I first review the history of the EU's agricultural policy starting with the creation of the CAP and its initial effects[1] (section 2), the reforms over the 1980–2010 period and their effects (section 3) and the last decisions on the future CAP (section 4).

2. The creation of the Common Agricultural Policy and the growth of agricultural protection in Europe

In 1957 the Treaty of Rome was signed by the six founding EU member states: Belgium, France, Germany, Italy, Luxembourg, and the Netherlands. This treaty provided the foundations of the "European Economic Community." Agriculture was an important sector and element in the initial discussions and was the first sector to have a true "common policy."

In 1958, at a conference in Stresa, Italy, the ministers agreed on a set of policy principles, which in the course of the next ten years were developed into specific policy measures that would form the "Common Agricultural Policy" (CAP). The policy decisions taken clearly reflected the decision-makers' experience of living with food shortages and upheaval during the still-recent war years. They also reflected concern about the fast-growing rural-urban income disparities of the 1950s, when economic growth took off and relative incomes in agriculture fell rapidly (Swinnen, 2009; Tracy, 1989).

The official objectives as stated in Article 33 (39) of the Rome Treaty were: (1) to increase agricultural productivity by promoting technical progress and ensuring the optimum use of the factors of production, in particular labor; (2) to ensure a fair standard of living for farmers; (3) to stabilize markets; (4) to assure the availability of food supplies; (5) and to ensure reasonable prices for consumers.

Objective 5 reflects the wartime experience of high food prices and the fact that despite robust growth in the European countries in the 1950s, there remained many poor people for whom food was a dominant budget item. However, this objective arguably soon became the least important in policy-makers' minds. Only the brief upheaval on global food markets in the early 1970s, when prices spiked following the first oil crisis, brought it back to the forefront.

For most of the next 50 years, the European agricultural discussion focused on the protection of farmers and its implications for global markets. The CAP resulted from the integration of various pre-EU member state policies that had been introduced to protect EU farmers' income from foreign competition and market forces. One of the main debates was between the two countries that were the driving forces behind the European integration, France and (then) West Germany. France was a major agricultural producer and exporter while West Germany had no comparative advantage in agriculture since after the war, what had been Germany's most important farmland was now in East Germany and Poland. West Germany's economic growth came from its industry and it was supporting its smaller farms.

However, other actors played a key role as well. Knudsen (2009) and Ludlow (2005) provide an in-depth analysis of "the making of Europe's Common Agricultural Policy," explaining how a coalition of France, the Netherlands and the European Commission – with different objectives, but aligned in their support of the CAP – was crucial in the establishment of the CAP. The resulting compromise was one where the agricultural prices throughout the CAP were raised close to (higher) German prices. Germany, as the main contributor to the EU budget, paid much of the costs, while France and the Netherlands, as the main agricultural producers and exporters, benefitted most from the policy. The Commission saw the first truly common policy as an important step in its strategic goal for a European political federation.[2]

The mechanism of government support for agriculture was through export subsidies, high import tariffs, and guaranteed prices for agricultural commodities, which were well above world market prices. This system was particularly important for key commodities such as cereals, oilseeds, beef, sugar and dairy products.[3] While this largely achieved the third CAP objective of a stable market within the EU market, it also created much instability on world markets.[4] The high import tariffs and growing surplus stocks, which were exported with subsidies, caused global agricultural prices to decline. In addition the budgetary cost of the CAP grew as imports declined (bringing in less tax revenue) and surpluses and exports increased (requiring more subsidies). In those years, the EU was described as the land of "butter and sugar mountains," "wine lakes," and so on, referring to the large surpluses and stocks generated by subsidies.

The increase in agricultural protection in Europe in the post-Second World War decades is clearly illustrated in Figure 18.1. The nominal rate of assistance (NRA), an indicator that measures how large government support is compared to market revenues for farmers, increased from close to zero in the 1940s to around 80 percent in the mid-1960s when the CAP was implemented. This means that farms were receiving almost as much gross revenue through government support as from the market at that time.

This growth in protection was caused by a combination of several factors (Swinnen, 1994, 2009). First, while farm incomes grew after the Second World War, incomes in the rest of society grew much faster with the rapid economic growth of the 1950s and 1960s. This created a growing urban-rural income gap. Political economists have shown that interest groups turn to governments to assist them when market conditions turn against them and that there are political incentives for decision-makers to introduce or adjust policies to assist these groups (for example, Swinnen and de Gorter, 1993).[5] Hence, European farmers increasingly pressed their governments to introduce support policies to reduce the urban-rural income gap.

Second, the most important opposition to governments raising prices for farmers came from consumers (workers) and from industry (which was concerned about the inflationary impact of food costs on wages). With economic growth, the share of food in consumer budgets became less important, and thereby the inflationary effect of food on wages was also diminished. These factors reduced the opposition of workers and industry (Swinnen et al., 2001).

A third factor was the enhanced political organization of farms and agribusiness interests. One element was the growth of farmer cooperatives as major forces in rural credit, input purchasing, processing and marketing. Such organizations not only played an important role in improving the economic situation of farmers but also in their political influence. At the same time improvements in rural infrastructure, including in communication, allowed farmers to better organize. Together, these factors led to a strong increase in government support to

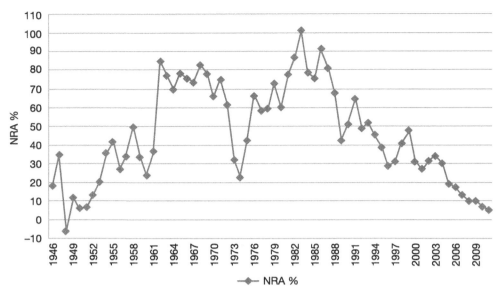

Figure 18.1 Government support to agriculture (NRA) in the EU*

Source: Anderson and Nelgen (2013) and Swinnen (2009).

Note: * NRA = nominal rate of assistance, which is an indicator of (market distorting) government support to agriculture and is measured as the price of a product in the domestic market (plus any subsidy) less its price at the border, expressed as a percentage of the border price (adjusting for transport costs, quality differences etc) – see Anderson (2009).

agriculture, as government tried to protect employment and incomes in a sector in (relative) economic decline from market forces.

3. Three decades of CAP reforms

The EU's impact on the world market increased as it expanded, and as subsidies and tariffs turned the region into a net exporter of food. The EU had previously been a major net importer of agricultural and food products, but the CAP caused a strong reduction in net imports as exports of the agricultural products receiving government support increased. As Figure 18.2 illustrates, the net trade (ratio of exports over imports) increased from less than 40 percent in the early 1960s to more than 80 percent by the end of the 1970s. While the EU is still the largest agricultural importer in the world, its increasing net trade has been due to a combination of both increased exports and falling imports.

In the 1970s and 1980s, pressure increased on EU policy-makers to reform the CAP. The pressure came both from inside the EU, primarily from ministers of finance concerned about the cost of subsidies, and from outside actors concerned about depressed global prices. The most important outside pressure came from exporting nations such as the US and Australia, and from developing countries and international organizations that accused the EU of causing poverty and hunger in poor rural households.[6] In response to these internal and external pressures, the EU introduced a series of reforms, spanning three decades, to reduce the impact of its CAP on international markets (Josling, 2008; Moehler, 2008).

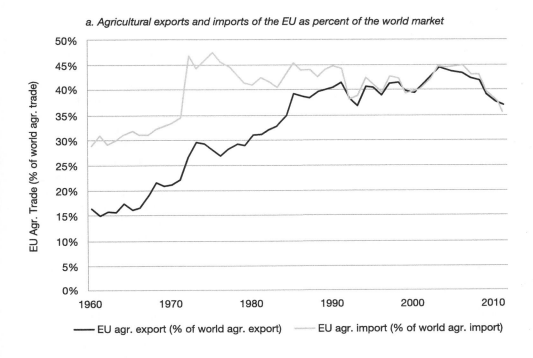

Figure 18.2 Agricultural exports and imports of the EU as percent of the world market

The first reforms came in the 1980s with the introduction of production quotas (i.e. maximum quantities that could be produced with subsidies) in the sugar and dairy sectors. These quotas limited the size of subsidies and surpluses, but did not eliminate them. Most production was still subsidized and a substantial amount was still exported with subsidies.

More fundamental problems remained in sectors such as oilseeds and grains where it was more difficult to implement quotas because these products were easier to store and were used in animal feed complicating the enforcement of supply controls. It took until the early 1990s before policy changes were introduced here: it was decided to replace price support and export subsidies by payments based on the area of land under cultivation, the so-called "direct payments." These reforms were strongly influenced by the GATT[7] negotiations at the time. The Uruguay Round of GATT/WTO negotiations for the first time included agriculture in the discussions – largely because of pressure from other countries that wanted to reduce the impact of the CAP on world markets. The negotiations were long and difficult and ultimately lead to the so-called "Uruguay Round Agreement on Agriculture" (URAA) in 1992. This agreement imposed limits, among others, on the value of agricultural subsidies that were "trade distorting" (such as import tariffs and production subsidies) and on the volume of subsidized exports. In order to reach an agreement the EU had to change the nature of the CAP subsidies. Under the so-called "MacSharry Reforms" a significant share of the price support and trade interventions were replaced by farm payments on the basis of land use and the number of animals. Subsidies linked to land (and animals) still stimulated production and exports but less so than subsidies directly linked to production, such as price supports. The compromise in the URAA allowed the EU (and also the US) to continue large subsidy payments linked to land used by farmers, while freeing global markets at least partially from the downward price pressure.

Figure 18.3 clearly illustrates the resulting changes in EU budget expenditures on the CAP: the value of subsidies going to exports and other market support declined significantly in the early 1990s, while the share of "coupled direct payments," i.e. the subsidies coupled to land use for specific agricultural production, increased strongly. In Figure 18.3 these are defined as "coupled direct payments." (Later, these coupled subsidies would be largely replaced by "decoupled" direct payments, as explained further.)

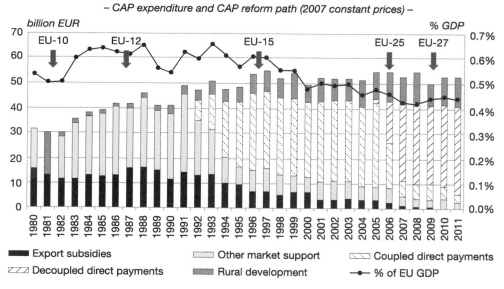

Figure 18.3 CAP budget expenditures (1980–2012)★

Source: European Commission.

Note: ★in 2007 constant prices.

Eastern enlargement and the CAP

In the late 1990s the EU was facing the most challenging extension in its history. Agriculture was a big concern (Burrell and Oskam, 2000; Swinnen, 2001). This "Eastern enlargement" added around 50 percent to the EU's farmland and more than doubled the number of farmers. This created all kinds of challenges for the EU. One challenge was finding money for all the farmers who would become eligible for EU subsidies (Ackrill, 2003). Another challenge was that the increase in the total value of subsidies given to the enlarged agricultural sector would put the EU into conflict with the constraints imposed by the URAA. Internally, the old (Western) farms feared that the new (Eastern) farms would flood the newly integrated market with cheap products, while Eastern farmers feared that rich Western farmers and investors would buy up all their land.

Negotiations on the conditions of accession for the Eastern countries and on CAP reforms were conducted simultaneously. The outcomes included: (a) further reductions in price support and export subsidies for all EU farmers (to satisfy GATT/WTO conditions) under the so-called Agenda 2000 reforms; (b) an extension of the direct payments to Eastern farmers but at considerably lower levels than Western farmers received; and (c) a temporary prohibition for Western farmers and investors to buy agricultural land in Eastern countries.[8]

Figure 18.4 clearly shows that even though payments to East European farmers in 2011 have significantly increased compared to the levels when the Eastern countries joined in 2004, Eastern payment levels are still considerably below those in the Western member states. Not surprisingly, one of the demands of the Eastern countries for changes during the recent CAP reform discussions was to make these payments more equitable.

Eastern enlargement also significantly increased the heterogeneity of the EU's agriculture. Despite a "common" agricultural policy, there were always substantial differences in EU agriculture. This applies to everything from the commodities produced and consumed, to farm structures, land use, the importance of agriculture in the regional/national economy, income levels, and more (Swinnen and Knops, 2013). The "European farm model" concept, of small-scale local family farmers needing government protection from (presumably) "large-scale capitalist farms" was increasingly difficult to maintain. While large-scale farms in France

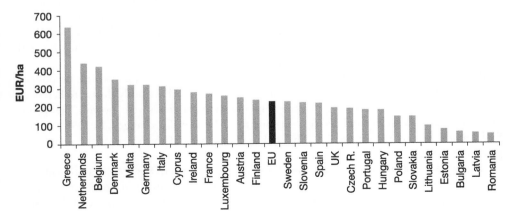

Figure 18.4   Direct Payments in the EU Member States in 2011 (€/ha)

Source: Eurostat and European Commission.

and the UK had always been happy to hide behind this political construct, the integration of the large-scale corporate farms that dominate many regions in the Czech Republic, Slovakia, and the former East Germany made doing so less feasible. EU's agriculture became much more diverse.

The 2003 "Fischler reforms": A perfect storm

Many experts identified the 2003 CAP reform,[9] presided over (and guided) by then-Commissioner for Agriculture and Rural Development Franz Fischler, as the most radical reform in CAP history. This was caused by what I have termed a "perfect storm" (Swinnen 2008). Several factors came together in the period around 2002, creating a strong pressure for radical changes in the CAP and the conditions to overcome opposition.

Commissioner Fischler argued that the CAP needed significant reform because "the CAP had lost its legitimacy among the EU public." The CAP was seen as hurting EU trade interests, as it had been a major stumbling block in trade negotiations (the EU expected that further cuts in agricultural subsidies would be needed to reach a new trade agreement in the Doha WTO Round). In addition, there were increasing concerns about the negative effects of agriculture on the environment. Moreover, when several food safety and animal welfare crises hit the EU in the late 1990s, the CAP not only appeared to be ineffective in addressing the problems and the food safety concerns of EU consumers, but instead appeared to worsen the situation. Hence, when Ministers of Finance were searching for budget cuts the CAP immediate came into focus as it was seen as using a disproportionate amount of the EU funds given the problems with the policy. In response, Commissioner Fischler and his team designed a strategy to maintain support for European agriculture by creating a new legitimacy for the CAP by addressing trade, environmental and food safety concerns.

The main element of the reform was a shift towards a policy system that continued to support farmers but which created fewer distortions in international markets. The proposal was to fully "decouple" farm payments through a "single farm payments" (SFP) system. Subsidies would no longer be related ("coupled") to what was produced or the land that was used, but farmers were given a fixed payment. Moreover, farm payments would be conditional certain environmental conditions, such as preventing soil erosion, managing water and taking measures to avoid the deterioration of habitats – the so-called "cross-compliance" requirements. Food safety concerns were addressed in a separate policy and there was a significant increase in funding for rural development policies – the so-called Pillar II of the CAP (Thomson et al., 2011).[10]

A key factor in the 2003 CAP reform was the 2001 Treaty of Nice, which introduced (qualified) majority voting in the decision-making on the CAP. Previously, decisions had been made by unanimous agreement, effectively giving member states veto power. The agents involved in agenda setting and decision-making for CAP had also changed. In 1995 Sweden, Finland and Austria joined the EU. This reduced the share of the votes of the established players in the EU.

The 2003 negotiations also transformed the politics-as-usual of the CAP. Traditionally, the main pressure group had been the farm unions. Fischler and his team purposely tried to include consumer and environmental groups to enhance the broader legitimacy of the future CAP among an increasingly urban EU society.

Fischler and his team saw their reforms not as an instrument to reduce the importance of the CAP, but as a way of saving it, and its role in supporting sustainable rural development.

They sought bold reforms to reduce its negative effects on the environment, on market distortions and on the WTO negotiations in order to create new support for CAP and reduce the pressure for large budget cuts. Major budget cuts for the next financial period were in fact avoided. From this perspective, the Fischler reforms contributed to the survival of the CAP, rather than to its demise.

Impact of the CAP reforms

The combined reforms resulted in an overall decline in agricultural subsidies affecting production and trade. Figure 18.1 illustrates how the nominal rates of assistance to agriculture (NRA, explained above p. 272) fell strongly over the past two decades: from on average of more than 50 percent in 1991–5 to just 11 percent in 2005–10. In particular the reduction in coupled farm support has been strong. The same conclusion comes from OECD (2012) estimates on agricultural support in the EU. Their measure, the producer support estimate (PSE), declined from on average 36 percent in the period 1991–3 to 20 percent in 2009–11; the PSE for agricultural support that affects production and trade (the so-called "coupled support") fell below 10 percent.

The dramatic change in the nature of the agricultural subsidies can also be seen from Figure 18.2 which illustrates the change in the nature of the subsidies on the EU budget. From the mid-2000s onwards the vast majority of EU farm support (35 billion euros out of a total of slightly more than 50 billion euros per year) occurs as decoupled direct payments.

After the reforms, prices in the EU are close to those on world markets and the impact of the current CAP on global prices is much smaller than in the past. Recent studies show that EU policies no longer have a significant impact on the price volatility of major food commodities (Anderson and Nelgen, 2012; Anderson et al., 2012).[11] Unlike other countries, such as Russia and China, the EU has also not introduced export constraints for food during the recent price spikes.

Hence, somewhat paradoxically, after the EU had gone through decades of reforms to reduce the negative impacts of the CAP pushing global food prices downward, the world became concerned with food prices heading in the other direction. After the price spikes of 2007–8, international organizations, NGOs and many experts pointed at the hunger and poverty effects of high food prices.[12]

The CAP of the 1970s and 1980s would have had a much stronger effect in countering high food prices than the current CAP. The former surplus production and the large food stocks in the EU could have been used to export food, including cereals, and thus to reduce prices when they were rising, both as commercial exports and as food aid. The policy reforms over the past two decades, which have reduced the distortionary effects of EU policies on world food markets, have also reduced the EU's capacity to quickly increase food exports during price spikes. In fact, EU food aid to developing countries was at its lowest during the past five years, when food prices spiked. Despite high food prices EU food aid declined from peaks of more than 3.5 million tons per year in the early 1990s to close to zero tons in recent years. Agricultural surpluses and food stocks have largely disappeared and the EU moved to providing aid through budget support.

4. The CAP for 2014–20[13]

The food price spikes of the late 2000s coincided with negotiations on the future of the CAP. The first global price increase coincided with the conclusion of the so-called health check reforms in 2008. The "health check" reform of the CAP further decoupled support and reduced government intervention in several commodity markets. This included the important decision to continue the gradual abolition of dairy and sugar quotas, and to keep moving toward a more market-based CAP. The aim, according to the European Commission, was to "modernize, simplify and streamline the CAP and remove restrictions on farmers, thus helping them to respond better to signals from the market and to face new challenges" (European Commission, 2008).

The CAP's continuing large share of total EU expenditures was one of the main issues in negotiations over the EU budget for the 2013–20 period. In 2011, the CAP budget amounted to €58.7 billion out of a total of €141.9 billion, or around 40 percent.[14] The budgetary discussions were given extra impetus by the global financial and economic crisis.

The 2007 Lisbon Treaty gave the EU Parliament "co-decision powers" on CAP and budgetary issues. These co-decision powers were expected to transfer power from the European Commission (which proposes policy reforms to be voted on by the Council of Ministers) to the EU Parliament (which to that point had only a consulting role, with very little effective influence on final decisions) (Crombez et al., 2012).

There was considerable uncertainty about the way the European Parliament would handle this first CAP co-decision experience, and its influence. Some, such as Roederer-Rynning (2010) argued that the European Parliament would push for a more interventionist policy because farmers associations were influential in the European Parliament's Agricultural Committee.

In October 2011, the European Commission published its proposal on the CAP for the 2013–20 period. The Commission essentially proposed to maintain the key elements of the CAP, with some changes in the nature, structure and distribution of the payments but without a return to market interventions. The changes in the payments can be summarized in three key words: *convergence*, *greening* and *capping*. Support is to be more equally distributed (convergence), better linked to environmental objectives (greening) and with a maximum ceiling to any individual producer (capping). The proposals used the increased price volatility in agricultural markets as a justification to maintain the CAP direct payments (as a "safety net") to protect farmers against price volatility: they give "basic financial security to farmers, without distorting international markets" (European Commission, 2011).

The proposals were amended by the European Parliament and the Council of Ministers (where qualified majority applies). Both came to a final agreement on a joint version of the proposals in the summer of 2013. The 2013 agreement implied still considerable uncertainty on the precise outcome of the CAP decision, since the implementation of several general principles had to be decided at the Member State level (Anania and Pupo, 2015).

That said, experts argue that the amendments weakened the Commission proposals in some areas but had relatively little impact on the market strategy proposed by the Commission (Bureau and Mahé, 2015). While the future CAP includes more subsidies that can be linked to production than under the 2003 reforms, the main policy decisions are largely in line with the fundamental long-term strategy towards market-based agriculture. In this latest round of CAP reform, the EU has reaffirmed its commitment towards an open trade policy, while also underlining the harm done by the restrictive export policies implemented by some countries in response to price volatility. It has also stayed on course with its reform proposals in specific sectors such as phasing out the quota regime in dairy and sugar. The reforms also reduced the gap in payments between regions and farmers within member states and across member states. The payments were particularly increased for member states with the lowest payments, such as the Baltic countries.

Despite the consolidation of these general principles many were disappointed that the reforms were not more ambitious in particular in terms of (a) the failure to shift more of the funding towards (genuine) rural development policies, (b) the limited environmental ("real greening") achievements; and (c) the possibility that implementation details will give member states too much freedom in (re-)implementing market distorting measures (Matthews, 2013, 2015). In particular the watering down of proposals to link the subsidies more closely to environmental objectives, after the CAP budget was secured, caused much disappointment (Brunner 2014; Erjavec et al., 2015; Pe'er et al., 2014).

5. Conclusions

The original CAP resulted from the integration of various pre-member state policies, which in turn were introduced to protect farm income from foreign competition and market forces. The mechanism of government support was through high import tariffs, export subsidies and guaranteed prices for products, which were well above world market prices. While this regime created a stable EU market, it also created much instability on world markets. The high import tariffs and growing surplus stocks, which were exported with subsidies, caused global agricultural prices to decline.

With its expansion, the EU increased its impact on world food markets. In response to internal and external pressures, the EU introduced a series of reforms, spanning three decades, to reduce the impact of its CAP on international markets. The main element of the reform was a shift towards a policy system that continued to support farmers but which created less distortion in international markets. To address environmental concerns, payments were made conditional on farmers addressing certain environmental conditions. Food safety concerns were addressed in a separate policy. Reforms to reduce the CAPs negative effects on the environment, on market distortions and on the WTO negotiations, and to make it consistent with sustainable rural development, reduced the pressure for large budget cuts and created a new support base for the CAP. From this perspective, the reforms contributed to the survival of the CAP.

The combined reforms resulted in a decline in agricultural support in the EU, and in particular in a strong decline in the use of subsidies that affect production and trade. After the reforms, prices in the EU are close to those on world markets and the impact of the current CAP on global prices is much smaller than in the past. EU policies had no significant impact on the recent price volatility of major food commodities. Hence, somewhat paradoxically, after the EU had gone through decades of reforms to reduce the CAP's (negative) impact on global food prices, the world became concerned with the implications of high food prices. The policy reforms over the past two decades, which have reduced the distortionary effects of EU policies on world food markets, have also reduced its capacity to quickly increase food exports during price spikes.

The food safety crises in the 1990s were crucial in a new food safety initiative which led to major legislative changes such as the *Basic Food Law Regulation*, including a recast of EU veterinary rules, and the creation of the European Food Safety Authority (EFSA). The new food safety policies introduced a from-farm-to-fork approach, imposing strict traceability requirements throughout the EU food chains.

For the future, the EU has (i) reaffirmed the engagement of the EU towards an open trade policy – also by underlining the harm done by the restrictive export policies implemented by some countries in response to price volatility; and (ii) stayed on course with its reform proposals in specific sectors, despite a slight change in argumentation, i.e. by also linking the motivation to price volatility. Until 2020 the new CAP will reduce differences in payments between member states. However, although there is still some uncertainty on the implementation specifics, it will probably not contribute to significantly better environmental outcomes or more investment in rural development, and is almost certainly becoming a more complex set of regulations and policies with more opportunities for member state initiatives.

Notes

1   For more detailed analyses of the CAP see Josling and Swinbank (2013), Oskam et al. (2011) and Swinnen (2008, 2015) and for earlier periods see Grant (1997) and Ritson and Harvey (1997); for an analysis of pre-CAP agricultural and food policies in Europe see Tracy (1989) and Swinnen (2009).
2   These differences in costs and benefits associated with common policies have remained important in the political discussions on the CAP to this day. The "net contribution" status of a country is a highly politically sensitive issue with some countries benefiting more from the CAP support as large agricultural producers and others contributing more to the budget. The issue became especially sensitive after Margaret Thatcher insisted, "I want my money back." This resulted in a reduction of UK budgetary contributions to the EU from 1984 – the so-called "UK rebate."
3   Another highly regulated market is the vineyard and wine market (see Meloni and Swinnen (2013) for a review).
4   EU import tariffs and export subsidies varied to capture the difference between (fixed) domestic prices and (fluctuating) world market prices. This system of variable tariffs and subsidies ensured stable prices inside the EU, but intensified fluctuations outside the EU since export subsidies would be even higher when world market prices were lower.
5   This so-called "anticyclical policy pattern" is well documented in agri-food markets, both in Europe (e.g. Olper, 1998; Swinnen et al., 2001; Swinnen, 2009) and elsewhere (Anderson and Hayami, 1986; Gardner, 1987; Anderson et al., 2013).
6   For example, organizations such as the OECD and the World Bank emphasized how the EU (and other countries including the US) were hurting the poor by contributing to low agricultural and food prices through their agricultural subsidies:

> Many (developed countries) . . . use various forms of export subsidies that drive down world prices and take markets away from farmers in poorer countries . . . Much of this support depresses rural incomes in developing countries while benefiting primarily the wealthiest farmers in rich countries.
>
> *(OECD, 2003)*

Non-governmental organizations (NGOs) took the same position. For example, Oxfam International (2005) argued that: "Europe's surplus production is sold on world markets at artificially low prices, making it impossible for farmers in developing countries to compete. As a consequence . . . farmers are losing their livelihoods." See Swinnen (2011) for more details.
7   General Agreement on Tariffs and Trade.
8   The transition period was initially for 7 years with an exceptional 13 years for Poland (Swinnen and Vranken 2009).
9   The 2003 reform was initially referred to as the "Mid Term Review" because it had the original objective to monitor, at the halfway period, the effectiveness of the Agenda 2000 reforms, which had been insufficient in addressing the problems facing the CAP (e.g. Buckwell and Tangermann, 1999; Burrell, 2000, Núñez Ferrer and Emerson, 2000).
10 EU consumers in the twenty-first century are particularly concerned about the safety and quality of food (Swinnen et al., 2011). These concerns were triggered by the food scares that plagued the EU in the second half of the 1990s, such as bovine spongiform encephalopathy (BSE, or "mad cow disease"), food and mouth disease (FMD) and episodes of toxic contamination, including the dioxin crises. Previously, food safety and quality policies were mainly the responsibility of member states, except for some veterinary directives from the EC. The food safety crises in the 1990s, particularly

the emergence of BSE in 1996 and the dioxin contamination crisis in 1998, were crucial in changing this. In 1997, a year after the BSE crisis, the Commission launched a new food safety initiative. This resulted in major legislative changes such as the Basic Food Law Regulation, including the creation of the European Food Safety Authority (EFSA) (van der Meulen and van der Velde, 2011). The main goal of the new food safety policies is to protect consumer health by the introduction of a farm-to-fork safety approach, imposing strict traceability requirements throughout EU food chains. At the same time, the policies aim to ensure the smooth operation of the "single market" and to take into account existing or planned international agreements. These include the sanitary and phytosanitary (WTO-SPS) and technical barriers to trade (TBT) agreements under the WTO.

Not only has the public sector responded to the crises, but there has also been a rapid growth in private sector initiatives in the field of food safety and quality standards. These include the Global GAP standard which is now used by a large number of the major retailers in the EU (and the world). Furthermore, there is a rise in public-private partnerships in establishing quality assurance schemes (Maertens and Swinnen, 2011; Velthuis et al., 2011).

11 Interestingly, they find some impact in the maize market. This is because global maize price increases triggered some policy adjustments, including a reduction in EU import constraints, which contributed to higher world market prices. Hence, even here it is the reduction in import constraints which contributed to higher prices – which in the pre-2008 world would have been considered a positive development.

12 See Swinnen, Squicciarini and Vandemoortele (2011) for a political economy explanation.

13 For excellent discussions on the latest CAP reform, see the comments by leading economists, such as Alan Matthews, JC Bureau, Emil Erjavec and their colleagues, at the weblog CapReform.eu, and various chapters in Swinnen (2015).

14 European Commission, Financial Programming and Budget, *The 2011 Budget in Figures*, http://ec.europa.eu/budget/figures/2011/2011_en.cfm

References

Ackrill, R. (2003), EU Enlargement, the CAP and the Cost of Direct Payments: A Note, *Journal of Agricultural Economics*, 54(1), 73–8.

Anania, G., and Pupo, M.R (2015), The 2013 Reform of the Common Agricultural Policy, in: Swinnen J. (ed.), *The Political Economy of the 2014–2020 Common Agricultural Policy: An Imperfect Storm*, Brussels: Centre for European Policy Studies.

Anderson, K., and Hayami, Y. (1986), *The Political Economy of Agricultural Protection: East Asia in International Perspective*, London: Allen and Unwin.

Anderson, K., M. Ivanic, and Martin, W. (2012), Food Price Spikes, Price Insulation and Poverty. Paper presented at the NBER conference on The Economics of Food Price Volatility, 15–16 August. Seattle.

Anderson, K., and Nelgen, S. (2012), Agricultural Trade Distortions during the Global Financial Crisis'. *Oxford Review of Economic Policy*, 28(1), 235–60.

Anderson, K., and Nelgen, S. (2013), Updated National and Global Estimates of Distortions to Agricultural Incentives, 1955 to 2011, Washington, D.C., June 2013. (Available at www.worldbank.org/agdistortions website)

Brunner, A. (2014), Birdlife: CAP reform is dead. *CAP Reform*. EU [web log]. http://capreform.eu/birdlife-cap-reform-is-dead/

Buckwell, A., and Tangermann, S. (1999), The Future of Direct Payments in the Context of Eastern Enlargement, *MOCT-MOST: Economic Policy in Transition Economies*, 9(3), 229–52.

Bureau, J.C., and Mahé, L.P. (2015), Success and/or Failure of the Reform? in: Swinnen J. (ed.), *The Political Economy of the 2014–2020 Common Agricultural Policy: An Imperfect Storm*, Brussels: Centre for European Policy Studies.

Burrell, A. (2000), The World Trade Organization and EU Agricultural Policy, in: Burrell A. and A. Oskam (eds.), *Agricultural Policy and Enlargement of the European Union*, Wageningen: Wageningen University Press, 91–110.

Burrell A., and Oskam, A. (2000), *Agricultural Policy and Enlargement of the European Union*, Wageningen: Wageningen University Press, 91–110.

Crombez, C., L. Knops, and Swinnen, J. (2012), Reform of the Common Agricultural Policy Under the Co-decision Procedure, *Intereconomics*, 47(6), 336–42.

Erjavec, E., M. Lovec, and Erjavec, K. (2015), From "Greening" to "Greenwash": The Drivers and Discourses of CAP 2020 Reform?, in: Swinnen J. (ed.), *The Political Economy of the 2014–2020 Common Agricultural Policy: An Imperfect Storm*, Brussels: Centre for European Policy Studies.

Eurobarometer (2010), Europeans, Agriculture and the Common Agricultural Policy. (Special Eurobarometer 336, Wave EB72.5), Brussels: European Commission, Directorate General for Agriculture and Rural Development.

European Commission (2008), The Health Check of the Common Agricultural Policy. Proposal for a council regulation establishing common rules for direct support schemes for farmers under the common agricultural policy and establishing certain support schemes for farmers, on modifications to the common agricultural policy by amending Regulations (EC) No 320/2006, (EC) No 1234/2007, (EC) No 3/2008 and (EC) No [...]/2008, amending Regulation (EC) No 1698/2005 on support for rural development by the European Agricultural Fund for Rural Development (EAFRD), amending Decision 2006/144/EC on the Community strategic guidelines for rural development (programming period 2007 to 2013), Brussels.

European Commission (2011), Press Release, Commissioner Dacian Ciolos, Member of the European Commission Responsible for Agriculture and Rural Development, Delivering sustainability and resource efficiency in Europe's farms, fields and forests. Koli Forum Joensuu, 15/09/2011, Brussels.

European Commission, (2013), *The 2011 Budget in Figures.* http://ec.europa.eu/budget/ figures/2011/2011_en.cfm

Gardner, B.L. (1987), *The Economics of Agricultural Policies*, New York: Macmillan.

Grant, W. (1997), *The Common Agricultural Policy*, New York: MacMillan Press.

Josling, T. (2008), External Influences on CAP Reforms: An Historical Perspective, in: J. Swinnen (ed.), *The Perfect Storm: The Political Economy of the Fischler Reforms of the Common Agricultural Policy*, Brussels: Centre for European Policy Studies, 76–82.

Josling, T., and Swinbank, A. (2013), EU Agricultural Policies and European Integration: A Thematic Review of the Literature, in: Verdun, A. and Tovias, A. (eds) *Mapping European Economic Integration*, Houndmills, Basingstoke: Palgrave Macmillan, 18–37.

Knudsen, A.C., (2009), *Farmers on Welfare,* Cornell University Press.

Ludlow, P. (2005), The Making of the CAP, *Contemporary European History*, 14(3), 348–71.

Maertens, M., and Swinnen, J. (2011), European Standards in Trade and Development, in: Oskam, A., Meester, G., and Silvis, H. (eds), EU Policy for Agriculture, Food and Rural Areas, Wageningen: Wageningen Academic Publishers, 107–14.

Matthews, A. (2013), The Ciolos CAP Reform, December 17, 2013, CapReform.eu

Matthews, A. (2015), The Multi-Annual Financial Framework and the 2013 CAP reform, in: Swinnen J. (ed.), *The Political Economy of the 2014–2020 Common Agricultural Policy: An Imperfect Storm*, Brussels: Centre for European Policy Studies. Forthcoming.

Meloni, G., and Swinnen, J. (2013), The Political Economy of Wine Regulations, *Journal of Wine Economics*, 8(3), 244–84.

Moehler, R. (2008), The Internal and External Forces Driving CAP Reforms, in: J. Swinnen (ed.), *The Perfect Storm: The Political Economy of the Fischler Reforms of the Common Agricultural Policy*, Brussels: Centre for European Policy Studies, 76–82.

Núnez Ferrer, J., and Emerson, M. (2000), Goodbye Agenda 2000, Hello Agenda 2003. CEPS Working Document No. 140, CEPS, Brussels.

OECD (2003), Cancún and the Doha agenda: The key challenges. 10–14 September 2003 [also repeated in the Declaration by the Heads of the IMF, OECD and World Bank, 4 September 2003] www.bfsbbahamas.com/photos/old_images/Declaration.pdf

OECD (2012), Producer and Consumer Support Estimates Database. Paris: Organisation for Economic Co-operation and Development.

Olper, A. (1998), Political Economy Determinants of Agricultural Protection Levels in the EU Member States: An Empirical Investigation, *European Review of Agricultural Economics*, 25(4), 463–87.

Oskam, A., Meester, G., and Silvis, H. (2011), *EU Policy for Agriculture, Food and Rural Areas*, Wageningen: Wageninge Academic Publishers.

OXFAM International (2005), International celebrities get dumped on at the WSF. 1 November 2005. www.oxfam.org/en/node/283.

Pe'er, G., Dicks, L.V., Visconti, P., et al. (2014), EU Agricultural Reform Fails on Biodiversity, *Science*, 344(6188), 1090–92.

Ritson, C., and Harvey, D.R. (1997), *The Common Agricultural Policy*, Wallingford: CAB International.

Roederer-Rynning, C. (2010), The Common Agricultural Policy: The Fortress Challenged, in: H. Wallace, M.A. Pollack and A.R. Young (eds), *Policy-Making in the European Union*, 6th edition, Oxford: Oxford University Press.

Swinbank, A., and Daugbjerg, C. (2006), The 2003 CAP Reform: Accommodating WTO Pressures, *Comparative European Politics*, 4(1), 47–64.

Swinnen, J. (1994), A Positive Theory of Agricultural Protection, *American Journal of Agricultural Economics*, 76(1), 1–14.

Swinnen, J. (2001), Will Enlargement Cause a Flood of Eastern Food Imports, Bankrupt the EU Budget, and Create WTO Conflicts? *EuroChoices*, Spring 2001.

Swinnen J. (ed.) (2008), *The Perfect Storm: The Political Economy of the Fischler Reforms of the Common Agricultural Policy*, Brussels: Centre for European Policy Studies.

Swinnen, J. (2009), The Growth of Agricultural Protection in Europe in the 19th and 20th Centuries, *The World Economy*, 32(11), 1499–1537.

Swinnen, J. (2011), The Right Price of Food, *Development Policy Review*, 29(6), 667–88.

Swinnen J. (ed.) (2015), *The Political Economy of the 2014–2020 Common Agricultural Policy: An Imperfect Storm*, Brussels: Centre for European Policy Studies.

Swinnen, J., and de Gorter, H. (1993), Why Small Groups and Low Income Sectors Obtain Subsidies: The "Altruistic" Side of a "Self-Interested" Government. *Economics and Politics*, 5(3), 285–96.

Swinnen, J., Banerjee, A. and de Gorter, H. (2001), Economic Development, Institutional Change and the Political Economy of Agricultural Protection: An Empirical Study of Belgium since the 19th Century, *Agricultural Economics*, 26(1), 25–43.

Swinnen, J., and Vranken, L. (2009), *Land & EU Accession: Review of the Transitional Restrictions by New Member States on the Acquisition of Agricultural Real Estate*, Brussels: Centre for European Policy Studies.

Swinnen, J., P. Squicciarini, and Vandemoortele, T. (2011), The Food Crisis, Mass Media and the Political Economy of Policy Analysis and Communication, *European Review of Agricultural Economics*, 38(3), 409–26.

Swinnen, J., and Squicciarini, P. (2012), Mixed Messages on Prices and Food Security, *Science*, 335(6067), 405–6.

Swinnen, J., and Knops, L. (eds.) (2013), *Diversity Under A Common Policy: Land, Labour and Capital Markets in European Agriculture*, Brussels: Centre for European Policy Studies.

Tracy, M. (1989), *Government and Agriculture in Western Europe 1880–1988*, New York: Harvester Wheatsheaf.

Thomson, K., Berkout, P., and Constantinou, A. (2011), Balancing between Structural and Rural Policy, in: Oskam, A., Meester, G. and Silvis, H. (eds), *EU Policy for Agriculture, Food and Rural Areas*, Wageningen: Wageningen Academic Publishers, 121–38.

van der Meulen, B.M.J., and van der Velde, M. (2011), The General Food Law and EU Food Legislation, in: A. Oskam, G., Meester, H. Silvis, (eds), *EU Policy for Agriculture, Food and Rural Areas*, Wageningen Academic Publishers.

Velthuis, A., W. Verbeke, and Marette, S. (2011), Food Quality, Food Safety and Certification, in: A. Oskam, G. Meester, H. Silvis (eds.), *EU Policy for Agriculture, Food and Rural Areas*, Wageningen: Wageningen Academic Publishers, 285–95.

19

LABOR AND SOCIAL POLICY

Giuseppe Bertola

By removing international market barriers the European Union intends to foster not only economic, but also social and political interactions among its member countries' citizens. Labor and social policies are essential elements of those countries' histories and political identities, and economic integration interacts uneasily with national Welfare States. This chapter reviews sources and consequences of the tension between Europe's social policy reform and economic integration processes.

Section 1 briefly characterizes the motivation and effects of national labor and social policies, and their interaction with international economic integration. Section 2 outlines the configuration of labor and social policies in the EU, highlighting their heterogeneity across member countries and the lack of supranational action. Section 3 reviews evidence from the early Economic and Monetary Union experience, Section 4 discusses lessons from the crisis, and Section 5 outlines the difficult problems that remain to be addressed.

1. Welfare policy and economic integration

One might view labor and social policies as market distortions, and advocate their deregulation. To assess these policies' implications and interpret their evolution in Europe, however, it has to be recognized that their objectives were important when they were introduced. Social and labor policies can be motivated by solidarity towards one's neighbors or by the unpleasant implications of extreme poverty within reach of one's property. But they also provide security over each individual's lifetime (Agell, 2002): labor income is most households' most important resource, and labor market risk cannot be easily diversified in financial markets. Hence, policies and institutions often aim at increasing and stabilizing wages (Bertola, 1999).

Imperfect markets can be improved if collective action exploits better information than is available to individuals, and coordinate their behavior. Providing public goods and stabilizing macroeconomic fluctuations, governments can correct externalities and prevent coordination failures; their superior powers of observation and enforcement can similarly make it possible to smooth incomes across individuals and within individual lifetimes. Policymakers, however, face some of the same asymmetric information problems as labor and financial market participants, and policies aimed at reducing risk and inequality also decrease effort, employment, and aggregate production.

Labor and social policies interact with economic integration. On the one hand, international trade and factor mobility influence the inequality and instability of incomes within each country. If wealth is more unequally distributed than other income sources, inequality increases in capital-rich countries, where wealthier individuals can enjoy the higher rate of return offered by investment in capital-poor countries, and declines in countries where capital inflows bid down returns on wealth and increase the marginal productivity of complementary labor. Removal of international market barriers opens the way to new shocks as well as to new adjustment channels, and can amplify income fluctuations. For these reasons, labor and social policies may be equally or more appealing within internationally integrated countries.

On the other hand, market competition across the borders of areas where policies are chosen and enforced reduces the effectiveness of policy instruments meant to reduce risk and inequality (Bean et al., 1998, and Bertola et al., 2001). International competitiveness is damaged by the production efficiency losses that labor and social policies typically entail, and the freedom of choice afforded by goods and factor mobility makes it easier for private agents to escape supposedly mandatory policy prescriptions. When transfers benefit foreigners (directly through immigration, or indirectly through product and labor market interactions), and high-earning individuals can relocate abroad to escape regulation and taxes, social policy is unappealing and ineffective: its objectives may still be valuable, but entail larger economic efficiency costs.

The intensity and character of these effects varies across policies. Any regulation that enhances productivity should in fact be even more attractive for competing systems, and this may be applicable to some labor and social policies: a welfare safety net may encourage entrepreneurial innovation, and job security may similarly give appropriate risk-taking incentives to employees. If these were the prevalent effects of social and labor policies, international competition would trigger a race to the top. In the absence of coordinated collective action throughout the integrated market areas, however, welfare policies that trade equal and stable income off production efficiency are subject to race-to-bottom pressure.

International competitive pressure may be welcome when it prevents policy from favoring small groups at a large cost in terms of aggregate production efficiency. It may also ease reforms of policies that have become obsolete because demographic and technological trends, or development of private financial and insurance markets, have made generous and pervasive redistribution and regulation schemes more costly and less useful than they were when introduced.

Deregulation pressure, however, is both politically and economically damaging when it is applied to policies that benefit large segments of society, and aim at goals that markets remain poorly equipped to pursue. Competition among individuals in well-regulated markets fosters efficiency, but competition among policymakers replicates across policy systems the market failures that collective action is meant to correct (Sinn, 2003).

2. Social Europe?

Like old-age pensions, labor and social policies shelter households from problems that imperfect financial markets cannot solve, and are part of the Welfare States that in industrialized and urbanized nations replaced the traditional risk-sharing channels of extended families. Legislation meant to endow workers with some bargaining power and to insure them against health, unemployment, and old-age hazards was introduced at times of actual or feared social unrest, such as Bismarck's industrializing Germany or Lord Beveridge's wartime UK. In

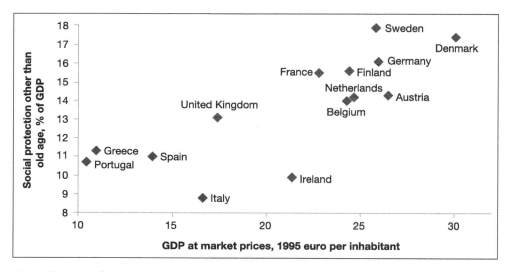

Figure 19.1 Social expenditure and income levels in the EU15, 2000

Europe, a history of revolutions, dictatorships, and wars puts "cohesion" and "stability" at the same level as "growth" among the objectives of collective action.

Like histories, so Welfare State configurations differ across European nations. The most obvious and perhaps most important dimension of heterogeneity is the dispersion of per-capita income levels. As Figure 19.1 shows, social expenditure as a fraction of GDP increases with per capita income levels across EU member countries. This is not surprising, because generous social spending is a luxury: subsidies have to be financed by taxes that reduce incentives to work, an efficiency cost that a richer economy finds easier to bear.

Other socio-political characteristics of countries also matter. In the US, per capita income is higher than in the richest of the European countries in Figure 19.1, but the social expenditure share of GDP is lower than in the poorest of those countries. This indicates that social policy is more important for Europeans than for Americans, but also that its generosity depends on economic development in ways that make its harmonization very problematic: across American States, and across regions of EU member countries, the share of social expenditure in income is negatively rather than positively related to per capita income levels, because the resulting geographically unbalanced funding needs are offset within an integrated rather than local budget.

An additional problem is that EU member countries not only devote different resources to social objectives, but also use different instruments. Figure 19.2 shows that the generosity of unemployment insurance and the stringency of employment protection legislation differ widely across Europe. Some countries offer little of both. Among the others, historical tradition and administrative capacity make it preferable to use explicit subsidies and contributions and preserve flexibility of employment relationship, or to enforce employment protection regulation that shifts labor market income risk away from workers and towards firms with better access to financial markets.

Four different Welfare State "models" can be identified more generally in Europe (Esping-Andersen, 1990, and Bertola et al., 2001). In the EU15, Sweden, Finland, Denmark, and also the Netherlands implement a Scandinavian model of full employment and universal welfare provision, with generous unemployment insurance benefits and a very important role for

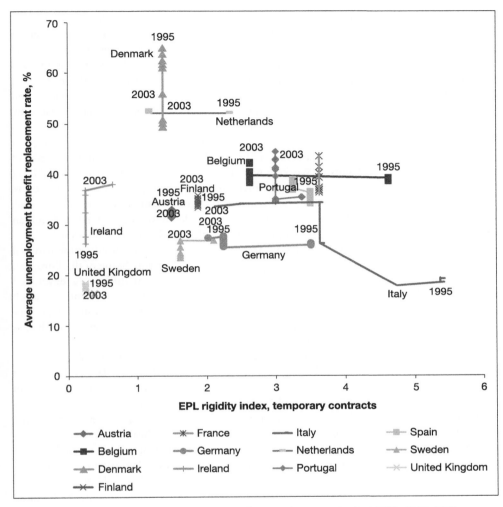

Figure 19.2 Employment protection and unemployment insurance in the EU15, 1995–2003

active labor market policies (including job creation in the public sector). Continental countries (such as Austria, Belgium, France, and Germany) adopt a Bismarckian system of centralized wage determination, stringent employment protection legislation, and contribution-financed occupational pensions, health services, and unemployment benefits. In Scandinavian and Continental Welfare States benefits are universal and there is only a residual role for social assistance safety nets, targeted to low-income individuals, which instead play a key poverty-prevention role in the UK and Ireland: in these Anglo-Saxon, Beveridgean countries private insurance schemes play a more important role, and unregulated labor markets feature relatively low unemployment insurance benefits, little employment protection, and decentralized wage-setting. Southern European countries (such as Greece, Italy, Portugal, and Spain) feature more recent and less precisely defined Welfare States, where public social expenditure plays a small redistributive role and safety is still largely provided by transfers within extended families.

The issues addressed by labor and social policy concern not only country-level policymakers but also the European Union. Production efficiency (or "growth") is only one of the objectives of a process that, in the tragic aftermath of the Second World War, deployed economic integration to pursue cultural and political objectives. Removal of market barriers is a means to an end of fostering "cohesion" and "stability" through convergence not only of incomes but also of institutions, cultures, and policies that, with or without explicit coordination and political agreement, could be expected to become increasingly similar across nations faced by similar problems and interacting in common markets.

Social and labor policy objectives are very prominent in EU documents. The European Social Charter was signed at Turin as early as 1961, and in 1989 the Community Charter of the Fundamental Social Rights of Workers was annexed to the Treaties: Article 149 TFEU states as objectives "the promotion of employment, improved living and working conditions, so as to make possible their harmonization while the improvement is being maintained, proper social protection, dialog between management and labor, the development of human resources with a view to lasting high employment and the combating of exclusion."

Labor and social policy instruments, however, are practically absent from the supranational layer of the European policy framework reviewed by Sapir et al. (2004). Some of the European budget finances structural programs meant to ease integration of differently developed economies, and a Social Fund component is explicitly devoted to education, training, and job search. But at less than 10 percent of the European Union's budget, itself around 1 percent of the region's GDP, structural funds are negligible next to national social spending that, as seen in Figure 19.1, is about a hundred times larger.

And while relaxation of work and safety rules is prevented by binding legislation, policy competition is essentially accepted in social and employment policy. Article 151 TFEU and Article 153 TFEU identify social and employment policy areas where EU legislation competence might or might not ". . . implement measures which take account of the diverse forms of national practices," and classify them in different categories according to the scope and method of supranational legislation. In the fields of workers' health and safety, working conditions, information and consultation of workers, integration of persons excluded from the labor market, and equality between women and men, directives and minimum requirements can be introduced with the standard co-decision legislative procedure, where the member countries decide by qualified majority in the European Council. Unanimity of the Council is required instead for any action on social security and social protection of workers, as well as (unless the Council unanimously decides to adopt render the ordinary legislative procedure applicable, without a Treaty revision) employment contract termination, collective representation and defense of workers and employers, and employment of third-country nationals. And "any harmonization of the laws and regulations of the Member States" is explicitly ruled out for social exclusion and social protection schemes. In these fields, only measures aimed at cooperation, knowledge sharing, and exchanges of information and best practices are allowed. This "open method of coordination" is implemented by the European Employment Strategy's requirement that Member States report jointly on set, verifiable, regularly updated targets (Van Rie and Marx, 2012), and access to the European Social Fund and other small financial sources can be conditioned on preparing and filing those reports: but not even this "soft" supranational action may be taken for "pay, the right of association, the right to strike or the right to impose lockouts."

It is not immediately obvious that supranational harmonization of various labor and social policies should be regulated differently: all aim to strike a balance between objectives of production efficiency (or "growth") and equity (or "cohesion"), and all are similarly influenced by economic integration. But the Article's classification of policies is tightly related to the key problem facing the European project. The areas viewed as subsidiary, and subject only to non-binding monitoring and comparison procedures, are those where national histories and traditions resulted in very heterogeneous institutional configurations across the member countries: employment protection, collective wage bargaining, minimum wages. EU-level policy is instead envisioned for fields that are more directly relevant to product market competitiveness. Already in 1957 the Treaty of Rome stipulated harmonization of pay non-discrimination across genders and of paid holiday schemes, both of which were already protected by law in France: free trade would not have been acceptable to the French if foreign competition had been allowed to endanger such worker rights. Like many other working conditions and safety provisions, measures that ensure a "level playing field" in product markets have ever since been enshrined in the *acquis communautaire* body of legislation that all current and any prospective member country must adopt and enforce.

Elimination of market barriers increases productivity through trade and factor mobility, and allows external competition to counter any rent-seeking tendencies in national policy-making processes. Hence, adoption of the *acquis* makes it possible to achieve the EU's "growth" objective. But the EU policy framework is not as conducive to the "cohesion" and "stability" objectives targeted by country-level policies in all member countries. Because political support for and technical implementation of labor and social policies are firmly rooted in the history of European nations, "positive" supranational harmonization of social and labor market policies is very difficult, while elimination of market boundaries allows "negative" international market integration to undermine national policies.

It is well understood that uncoordinated macroeconomic policies, a fixed exchange rate, and free capital mobility were mutually inconsistent before Economic and Monetary Union (EMU) (Padoa-Schioppa et al., 1987). It is equally clear that free mobility of goods and/or factors, local decision-making powers in the social protection area, and social inclusion cannot coexist consistently, because pursuing two of the three necessarily implies forsaking the third: removal of market boundaries makes it easier for individuals to opt out of supposedly mandatory redistributive schemes, and race-to-the-bottom tensions are unavoidable if uncoordinated policy choices are made locally within the integrated market. Social objectives beyond the reach of imperfect markets cannot be achieved together with full economic integration in the absence of centrally agreed and enforced labor and social policies.

3. Policy trajectories

European labor markets, especially those of Continental countries, are characterized by more unionized wage setting and more stringent regulation of employment relationships than those of other developed countries. In the 1960s, however, unemployment in European countries was much lower than in the US. Around 1970, the unemployment rate was about 3 percent on average in the OECD, and 5 percent in the US, but only 2.2 percent on average in the 11 core European Union countries that were the first to join EMU. In the 1970s it rose steadily, reaching the US level in the early 1980s and hovering around 12 percent until the 1990s: while both the US and the OECD aggregate unemployment rates fluctuated in the 4–9 percent range, European countries experienced "eurosclerosis." Labor market rigidities can be blamed for the relatively poor performance of European labor markets in the last twenty years of the twentieth century, but this experience was to some extent a predictable consequence of Europe's fast and stable post-War growth. Social protection and labor market regulation do reduce employment and production, and these

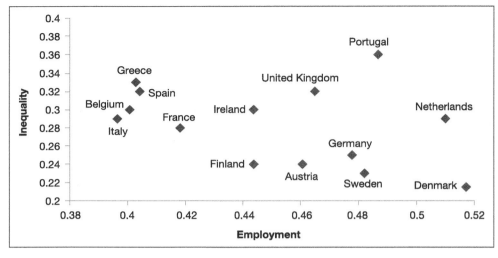

Figure 19.3   Inequality and employment in the EU15, 2000

costs are more easily affordable for richer societies. By the 1970s, stringent labor market regulation and generous social benefits were political winners in the typical European country (Bertola, 2014).

Around this common trend institutions and outcomes varied across European countries, in ways that can be explained on country-specific socio-economic characteristics. Even when eurosclerosis ravaged their neighbors' labor markets, smaller countries (Austria, Ireland, Portugal, and the Netherlands) displayed enviably low unemployment, while in large and heterogeneous countries nationally uniform social benefits tended to disproportionately reduce work incentives in poorer regions, where centrally negotiated wages and job security provisions implied high unemployment. The historical heterogeneity of Welfare States also contributes to explaining their different labor market performance and inequality levels, which as shown in Figure 19.3 do not conform to what one would expect if the data were generated by country-specific choices along a common tradeoff between "growth" and "cohesion" (Sapir, 2006): Denmark has both the lowest inequality and the highest employment rate, while Italy, Belgium, Spain, and Greece do worst in both respects; Anglo-Saxon and Mediterranean countries feature very similar income inequality, but the latter also display low employment rates (especially for youth and females); and Scandinavian countries are better than Continental European ones in both respects.

It would be naïve, of course, to suppose that if Greece adopted a Scandinavian Welfare State it would become similar to Denmark in all respects. Policies are implemented in country-specific conditions, and have country-specific motives and effects. Countries face their own tradeoffs between "growth" and "cohesion" objectives. As discussed above and shown in Figure 19.2, European Welfare States are deeply rooted in each country's level economic and political system, and very different in terms of generosity as well as of institutional structure and technical implementation. Over time, however, the relevant tradeoffs and countries' policy choices change in ways that are broadly similar across countries. Figure 19.2 also shows that each country's Welfare State configuration is not immobile. Over a period of increasingly tight integration, there is a tendency to steer policies towards unemployment insurance: when competitiveness becomes more important, it is more difficult for firms to bear the production efficiency losses implied by job security provisions, and more important for countries with relatively poor administrative capacity to modernize their welfare systems.

Deregulation is a theoretically plausible implication of the pressure exerted by globalization and enlargement, as well as by EMU, on country-specific policymaking choices. Around the turn of the millennium, and until the crisis, unemployment in Europe started to converge towards the US level, and declined below it. This was partly due to the flexibility-oriented reforms of national labor and social policies that ever tighter economic integration implies. In a comparison of countries that did and did not join the euro area, and of the 1995–9 and 2000–4 periods, the tighter economic integration implied by a common currency was indeed associated with substantially faster deregulation of their product markets, some deregulation of their labor markets, and lower social policy expenditure (Bertola, 2010b). Reforms of national policies were plausibly shaped by policy competition, and largely explain why disposable income inequality grew faster in countries adopting the single currency (Bertola, 2010a).

Deregulation trajectories were heterogeneous across countries. In theory, small countries are more likely to undertake flexibility-oriented reforms. The Netherlands was the first Continental European country to implement them in the early 1980s, when not only trade and capital mobility were completely liberalized but in the D-Mark block the exchange rates was also, in effect, irrevocably fixed. A little wage moderation could attract much cross-border business, and yield large employment gains. The resulting more attractive tradeoff between labor market flexibility and worker protection explains why already in 1982 the Wassenaar agreement substantially deregulated the Dutch labor market. The German "Agenda 2010" reform framework only took a similar path in the first half of the 2000s (Rinne and Zimmermann, 2012): deregulation was the politico-economic outcome only after the country's reunification, euro adoption, and Eastern enlargement had changed the trade-off between high wages and idle labor on the one hand, and better competitiveness on the other.

Up to the mid-2000s, the EU policy framework envisioned social-policy convergence and coordination as the automatic result of economic integration and of National reforms by countries sharing a common social model, facing common challenges, and sharing information through "soft" coordination processes. Of course, it is not easy to reform and harmonize the welfare systems developed in each EU Member State when industrial plants and cities replaced farms, workshops, and villages. Suitable harmonization of heterogeneous welfare schemes is unlikely to result spontaneously from policy competition, especially in the absence of positive integration "carrots" countering the negative integration constraints imposed by market integration on national policies. Striving towards complete economic integration while maintaining subsidiarity of labor and social policies, the EU accepted lower levels of social protection. This choice, while certainly not explicit, was appropriate if European Welfare States were still addressing Industrial Revolution problems in a "new economy" situation where flexibility and adaptability were particularly useful, financial market development made it less urgent to protect workers from labor market risk, and labor markets had to respond to shocks that were more likely to be region- or industry-specific than country-specific.

4. The crisis

The financial and economic crisis that started in 2008 and evolved in to the euro debt crisis highlights both the still very important role of collective stabilization and regulation policies in the presence of market imperfections, and the shortcomings of the EU's approach to those policies. Within each country, households and firms are tied together by geographical location as well as by institutional and cultural features. Not only financial and insurance contracts, but also taxes, transfers, and other public policies transfer resources so as to smooth out shocks that imperfect financial markets cannot absorb, and often can magnify. But in the EU heterogeneous social insurance schemes are implemented independently and are subject to international competition, and almost only financial markets transfer resources across national borders.

The crisis has shown the fragility of international financial markets in the face of country-specific shocks, and made it clear that international policy coordination has a crucial role to play when markets span the borders of nations. The idea that welfare policies and bank supervision could be left to national subsidiarity was always theoretically dubious, and was shattered by a crisis that forced some countries to relinquish much of their sovereignty in the labor and social policy area. It is also interesting to note that in 2013 bankers' bonuses were regulated at the EU level, in apparent violation of the Article 151 TFEU prohibition of community regulation of pay: the measure survived legal challenges because it does not regulate total pay, and is motivated by prudential concerns in financial markets rather than by social policy. Public finance problems arising in the euro debt crisis have also begun to erode the notion that direct taxation should be a subsidiary prerogative of national governments (Article 26 TFEU): the European Commission's October 2014 decision against Luxembourg's selective favorable taxation of a specific multinational corporation was based on the prohibition of measures that "distort or threaten to distort competition and have the potential to affect trade between Member States" (Article 107–1 TFEU), which would in principle be applicable to essentially all policies and ultimately call for their supranational coordination.

The crisis also shone some new light on the advantages and disadvantages of the EU member countries' diverse approaches to labor and social policies. The Danish framework of conditional unemployment benefits, low employment protection, active labor market policies, and decentralized wage setting was fashionable in the early 2000s when it proved capable of reducing unemployment, albeit at substantial fiscal cost. That model however did not perform well in a crisis that saw Danish unemployment increase by some five percentage points in just three years. In Germany, the Hartz reforms that before the crisis reduced the generosity of social benefits and introduced some labor market flexibility were spurred by international competitive pressures, as discussed above. But they were also meant to modernize policies better suited to old-fashioned lifelong manufacturing employment than to modern lifelong-learning in innovation-driven economies. Ironically, the crisis hit "new economy" sectors more permanently than manufacturing: exports fell sharply, but recovered as emerging country growth resumed; unreformed policies that appeared obsolete before the crisis – such as temporary layoff programs – did play a useful role in this type of crisis (Rinne and Zimmermann, 2012). Country-specific experiences during a crisis when outcomes were determined by shocks as much as by institutions offer useful information for employment and social policy reforms, but of course need not inspire them unconditionally: future shocks will likely be different, and countries facing the worst crises should not rush to imitate the labor market configuration of more fortunate countries.

5. The future

Redistribution can be excessive or perverse, and is certainly not liked by all, but labor and social policies are not generally harmful. Regulations and tax-and-subsidy programs that reduce production efficiency do so for the sensible purposes of smoothing consumption over individual lifetimes, or redistributing resources across individuals. The regions and individuals of European nation-states were put together by wars, and amalgamated by Welfare States as well as by cultural assimilation, internal markets, and migration. National labor market and social policies still have vastly different implications across regions of internally diverse countries, and any redistribution-oriented scheme has even larger implications across households and individuals. Within each country, economically strong areas and individuals coexist with weaker ones, shocks have asymmetric effects, and not only private but also public financial instruments fill gaps between consumption and income levels. Uneasy compromises between homogeneity and diversity are the price of economic and social cooperation beyond (and even within) the boundaries of one's immediate family.

In Europe, the income stabilization role of taxes, transfers, and regulation is too important to be exposed to the system competition pressure exercised by integrated markets, especially when imperfect financial markets cannot be relied upon to address distributional issues. It would in principle be possible for a coherent EU policy framework to deploy the same instruments that address such policy issues within the member countries, where labor and social policies smooth out the migration and product-market competition implications of regional heterogeneity. But while average income differences across countries are not always larger than those across regions within a country, they are certainly large enough to make it unthinkable to implement welfare schemes as homogenous as those of each member states across the whole EU.

The EU's attempt to remove national economic boundaries peacefully faces issues that make devising a harmonized and integrated supranational social and employment policy framework even more difficult than, but arguably as necessary as, adopting a single monetary policy. Market integration is fragile when it implies policy competition and race-to-the-bottom tensions. It should be complemented by coordinated minimum welfare benefits, co-financed centrally to prevent systems competition from resulting in unacceptably low levels of welfare provision, and set at levels compatible with suitable work and mobility incentives within and across differently developed areas. It would also be desirable to implement unemployment benefits and pension schemes that, while designed so as not to redistribute resources ex ante and not to require central funding, are mandatory and comprehensive enough to provide the insurance against life events that private financial markets cannot supply (Bertola et al., 2001).

In the US, the federal government not only ensures freedom of interstate commerce but also regulates and co-finances welfare provision schemes that are administered at the State level, and complemented by a fully federal Social Security scheme. This framework suitably complements labor mobility: in response to local shocks, migration stabilizes labor supply and wages, and reduces the need for location-specific fiscal and monetary policy; but it destabilizes public finances inasmuch as it reduces the contribution basis of depressed areas. As in the US, unemployment benefits funded by payroll taxes across all EU countries could smooth the implications not only of local but also of aggregate shocks (European Commission, 2013): only public balance sheets backed by area-wide production, rather than by local tax bases vulnerable to systems competition and asymmetric shocks, can provide a safe asset to the area's financial system and allow tax smoothing in the face of area-wide shocks.

The design and implementation of suitably integrated social policies entails formidable political and technical problems. A politically difficult treaty revision would be necessary for even the smallest harmonization or joint administration efforts: payroll contributions could arguably be viewed as a technical policy instruments, certainly more similar to value added than to income or wealth taxes, but the current Treaties explicitly exclude Union competence for them. It would be technically difficult to design a supranational scheme that could replace or be added to the heterogeneous payroll tax and benefit schemes of the member countries. And it would be both technically and politically difficult to control subsidy disbursement in countries with very different administrative capacities.

But just like a single money was the logical consequence of product market integration (that needs stable exchange rates) and capital market integration (that equalizes rates of return), so a common employment and social policy framework should logically be enforced in an integrated area throughout which not only goods but also persons, services, and capital are free to move.

Steps in that direction are needed for an European integration process that is first and foremost a political project, meant to prevent further wars, to ensure commitment to democracy in countries that (like Spain, Portugal, and Greece) had experienced dictatorship, and to ease the post-Communist transition of Central and Easter European countries. The project has so far used market unification as a tool to achieve the ultimate "growth, stability, and cohesion" objectives of European societies, but the crisis has shown the limits of that approach.

References

Agell, J. (2002), On the Determinants of Labor Market Institutions: Rent Seeking vs Social Insurance, *German Economic Review*, 3(2), 107–35.

Bean, C., Bentolila, S., Bertola, G., and Dolado, J.J. (1998), Social Europe: One for All? CEPR, *Monitoring European Integration* 8. London: Centre for Economic Policy Research.

Bertola, G. (1999), Microeconomic Perspectives on Aggregate Labor Markets, in Ashenfelter, O. and Card, D. (eds) *Handbook of Labor Economics 3*, Amsterdam: North-Holland.

Bertola, G. (2010a), Inequality, Integration, and Policy: Issues and Evidence from EMU, *Journal of Income Inequality*, 8(3), 345–65.

Bertola, G. (2010b), Labor Markets in EMU: What has Changed and What Needs to Change, in Buti, M., Deroose, S., Gaspar, V., and Nogueira Martins, J. (eds) *The Euro: The First Decade*, Cambridge: Cambridge University Press.

Bertola, G. (2014), Labor Market Policies and European Crises, *IZA Journal of Labor Policy*, 3(5), 1–11.

Bertola, G., Jimeno, J.F., Marimon, R., and Pissarides, C. (2001), EU Welfare Systems and Labour Markets: Diverse in the Past, Integrated in the Future? in Bertola, G., Boeri, T., and Nicoletti, G. (eds) *Welfare and Employment in a United Europe*, (pp.23–122) Cambridge, MA: MIT Press.

Esping-Andersen, G. (1990), *The Three Worlds of Welfare Capitalism*, Cambridge: Polity Press.

European Commission (2013) *Strengthening the Social Dimension of the Economic and Monetary Union*, COM(2013) 690.

Padoa-Schioppa, T., Emerson, M., King, M., Milleron, J.C., Paelinck, J.H.P., Papademos, L.D., Pastor, A., and Scharpf, F.W. (1987), *Efficiency, Stability and Equity: A Strategy for the Evolution of the Economic System of the European Community*, Oxford: Oxford University Press.

Rinne, U. and Zimmermann, K.F. (2012), Another Economic Miracle? The German Labor Market and the Great Recession, *IZA Journal of Labor Policy*, 1(3), 1–21.

Sapir, A., Aghion, P., Bertola, G., Hellwig, M., Pisani-Ferry, J., Rosati, D., Vials, J., and Wallace, H. (2004), *An Agenda for a Growing Europe – The Sapir Report*, Oxford: Oxford University Press.

Sapir, A. (2006) Globalization and the Reform of European Social Models, *Journal of Common Market Studies*, 44(2), 369–90.

Sinn, H.-W. (2003), *The New Systems Competition*, Oxford: Basil Blackwell.

Van Rie, T. and Marx, I. (2012), The European Union at Work? The European Employment Strategy from Crisis to Crisis, *Journal of Common Market Studies*, 50(2), 335–56.

20

TAX COMPETITION AND
TAX COORDINATION[1]

Christian Keuschnigg, Simon Loretz and Hannes Winner

1. Introduction

Although the European Union was ultimately grounded on political motives, it was mainly promoted by economic means and measures. This is also reflected in the institutional design of the European Union (EU), which initially was approached as economic community, but slowly proceeded into broader political and societal areas.[2] According to Article 3 of the Treaty on the European Union (TEU), the EU intends to, "... offer its citizens an area of freedom, security and justice without internal frontiers ...," and to "... establish a common market." To achieve these goals, the Union relies heavily on market competition, largely eliminating trade impediments and distortions of consumer and producer choices. This, in turn, requires a substantial degree of policy coordination and, among others, a strong mandate to harmonize taxes, even if the TEU does not stipulate explicit taxing rights at the European level.

Before proceeding further, we would like to define three important concepts regarding the European tax policy. The first is *tax competition*, which is originally based on the analysis of optimal tax assignment in federal states as developed by Oates (1972) and the subsequent research on fiscal federalism, showing that tax rates on mobile factors might end up at inefficiently low levels. Subsequent theoretical developments extend this approach to competition between independent jurisdictions, with widely varying policy implications depending on the particular assumptions made. For the purposes of this chapter, we rely on this notion of inter-country competition defining tax competition in a broad sense and along the lines of Devereux and Loretz (2013, p. 746) as "... the uncooperative setting of taxes where a country is constrained by the tax setting behaviour of other countries." *Tax coordination* refers to a cooperative tax setting, where countries or a group of them build on domestic tax systems to render them compatible with the aims of the Union as formulated in the TEU. Consequently, countries deliberately give up parts of their autonomy in tax matters. *Harmonization* is viewed as tighter coordination, leading to almost identical or at least similar tax systems, tax bases and tax rates within a Union.

The reason why tax competition may lead to undesirable outcomes lies mostly in two externalities inherent to international taxation. First, an increase in a country's tax burden might induce to a relocation of mobile tax bases to adjacent economies, representing a *positive externality*. If tax policies are adjusted uncooperatively, policymakers ignore this externality in neighboring countries and, therefore, set tax rates at inefficiently low levels. The second effect comprises a *negative externality* when taxes imposed by one country are borne partly by the residents of another country. It is known as tax exporting and appears if a country imposes source based taxes on natural resources (e.g., land), income or consumer activities of non-residents. In this case, the tax burden tends to be higher than optimal from a social point of view.[3] Tax competition may lead to over- or under-taxation, depending on which of these countervailing effects is the dominating one.

The European integration affects the intensity of both externalities. First, the establishment of a common market and the abolition of borders fosters the mobility of tax bases and, consequently, reinforces positive tax externalities in each Member State. At the same time, impediments on the free movement of goods, services, persons and capital are amongst others eliminated by ruling out discrimination because of nationality. This reduces the possibilities to raise taxes particularly on foreigners and, in turn, lowers the negative effects of tax exporting. Taken together, it seems that the existence and development of the EU increases tax competition and exerts downward pressures on tax rates.

A race to the bottom due to increased tax competition was feared since the very beginning of European integration. It was one of the driving forces behind any attempts to harmonize taxes at the European level. However, tax harmonization succeeded only moderately so far. The main reason was that Member States did not agree on the necessity and also the scope of harmonization, apart from the fact that tax matters remain one of the few areas where a proposal needs unanimity to pass the Council of the EU.

The next section briefly reviews the historical development of EU tax policy highlighting the implemented directives to harmonize taxes. Section 3 summarizes the state of theoretical and empirical research on tax competition, focusing on whether the observed differentials in cross-country tax rates give rise to a stronger coordination of EU tax policy. Section 4 summarizes and draws some policy conclusions.

2. A brief history of tax harmonization

The original intention of the EU to establish a customs union translates into very different legal mandates for direct and indirect taxation.[4] In particular, cross border flows of goods and services are not only influenced by tariffs and technical trade barriers, but also by commodity taxation. Therefore, a legal mandate for the EU to harmonize indirect taxes was necessary to guarantee the functioning of a customs union. Personal and corporate income taxes, in contrast, mainly affect the mobility of capital and labor and are, therefore, important to establish the common market. As a result, harmonization is widely advanced for commodity taxation and relatively less developed for direct taxes, where the EU mainly tried to commit the Member States to a levelling of the playing field via the abolition of unfair tax practices.[5]

2.1 Indirect taxation

The fact that non-uniform indirect taxes may lead to substantial intra-Community trade impediments was recognized from the very beginning of European integration. The Tinbergen Committee was already the first expert group requested to tackle unresolved issues of commodity taxation in the European Coal and Steal Community (Tinbergen 1953). One of its particular mandates was to assess the economic effects of two taxing principles governing general sales taxation on intra-Community trade. Under the *destination principle*, commodities are taxed by the country where they are finally consumed; also, the revenues are attributed to this jurisdiction. Exports are free of taxes and imported goods are subject to sales taxation once they cross the border. Consequently, the application of the destination principle leads to equal relative prices between in-state and out-of-state produced goods and services. The *origin principle*, in contrast, taxes goods and services in the country of production, and the revenues are distributed according to the value added in each country. Commodities produced in one Member State would bear the same tax burden within the EU, irrespective of where they are consumed. Under this principle, no border adjustments are needed, making it more consistent with the operation of a common market. Under arbitrage conditions and different commodity tax rates across countries, the destination principle balances producer prices (before taxes), therefore maintaining *production efficiency*, while the origin principle promotes *exchange efficiency* via the equalization of after tax (consumer) prices (see, e.g., Razin and Sadka 1991).[6] Further, the revenue consequences for each Member State are very different under both systems, depending on whether a country is a (net) importer or exporter and/or levying high or low tax rates.

The Tinbergen Committee arrived at the conclusion that both principles are equivalent under certain conditions (e.g., uniform tax rates and tax bases) and, since the destination principle was commonly used in international trade at that time, there was no need to substitute the destination by the origin principle (Tinbergen 1953, p. 132). Ten years later, the Neumark Report (1963) recognized that the destination principle is not sustainable once the single market is completed. Therefore, it explicitly advocated a change to the origin principle. For similar reasons, the Neumark Committee recommended replacing the gross turnover tax by a net turnover or *value added tax* (VAT).[7] The European Economic Community (EEC) followed this advice and released the First and Second VAT Directives in 1967 (Council Directives 67/227/EEC and 67/228/EEC), which laid down the general structures of the VAT system but left it to the Member States to determine the coverage of the VAT and its rate structure. It took many years to implement the VAT uniformly, with some countries being able to introduce this system only a decade after the enactment of the directives (see Table 20.1).[8] In 1977, the EEC adopted the Sixth VAT Directive establishing a widely uniform coverage of the VAT (Council Directive 77/388/EEC). However, the directive refrained from narrowing national exemptions and product-specific VAT rates, leaving the core of systematic imbalances untouched.

The completion of the Single European Market (SEM) in 1993 induced a substantial change in EU tax policy, especially with regard to commodity taxes. The removal of borders implied that it was impossible to maintain the destination principle any longer and let the European Commission fear that cross border shopping of individuals and illegal arbitrage activities for commercial purposes would increase massively. The Commission launched two draft directives, the first in 1987 and a modified version in 1989, proposing to replace the destination by the origin principle and to introduce a two-rate VAT system.[9] Switching to the origin principle would have changed the distribution of tax revenues within EU Member States dramatically. To circumvent this problem, the Commission proposed a "clearing mechanism" based on single purchases (1987; *micro* clearing) or trade statistics (1989; *macro* clearing). The purpose of the clearing mechanism was to restore the Member States' revenue distribution according to the destination principle. The clearing system never was implemented as the Member States were concerned to lose sovereignty in taxing rights but also feared additional administrative burdens to govern the mechanism.

In 1993, the Member States reached a compromise and agreed upon a "transitional" scheme, which attempts to mirror border adjustments on cross-border trade between registered businesses via a deferred payment or postponed accounting basis (Council Directive 91/680/ EEC). Accordingly, exports are free of VAT; importers of goods and services declare their purchases, apply the corresponding VAT and take credit for the same amount. A VAT Information Exchange System (VIES) requires registered businesses to file quarterly reports on exports and imports. While this system in effect leads to the application of the destination principle for businesses, over-the-counter sales to nonregistered traders and consumers (accounting for the minor share of total intra-EU trade) are taxed on an origin basis.[10] Finally, minimum rates of 15 percent (standard rate) and 5 percent (reduced rate) were agreed upon (Council Directive 92/77/EEC). Apart from this, the existing zero rates applied in certain countries and for specific necessities were allowed to continue (e.g., for food products, medicines or newspapers). Many observers have argued that the deferred payment system not only creates additional bureaucracy and expenses for firms, but also increases the danger of cross-border shopping and tax fraud (see, e.g., European Parliament 2001).

The transitional system was planned to be in effect until 1996 and thereafter to be replaced by a "definitive" solution. This never happened and so the transitional system continues to work even today.[11] The co-existence of the destination principle for VAT-registered traders and the origin principle for final consumers increases a country's incentives to attract foreign consumers by lowering its commodity tax rates, which in turn might intensify cross-border shopping and tax competition (see Haufler 2001, p. 151).

Table 20.1 reports the VAT rates currently in use. First, it shows a great deal of disparities with regard to the number and the levels of specific VAT rates applied in the Member States. There is also large variation in standard VAT rates, ranging from 15 (Luxembourg) to 27 percent (Hungary). Generally, the standard VAT rate has been increased over the course

Table 20.1 VAT rates in EU Member States

Member State	VAT introduction	Specific rates				Standard rate		
		Zero rate	Super reduced	Reduced	Parking	2009	2014	Change
Austria	1973		–	10	12	20	20	0.0
Belgium	1971	yes	–	6/12	12	21	21	0.0
Bulgaria	1994		–	9	–	20	20	0.0
Croatia	1998		–	5/13	–	–	25	–
Cyprus	1992		–	5/9	–	15	19	4.0
Czech Republic	1993		–	15	–	19	21	2.0
Denmark	1967	yes	–	–	–	25	25	0.0
Estonia	1991		–	9	–	18	20	2.0
Finland	1994	yes	–	10/14	–	22	24	2.0
France	1954		2.1	5.5/10	–	19.6	20	0.4
Germany	1968		–	7	–	19	19	0.0
Greece	1987		–	6.5/13	–	19	23	4.0
Hungary	1988		–	5/18	–	20	27	7.0
Ireland	1972	yes	4.8	9/13.5	13.5	21.5	23	1.5
Italy	1973	yes	4	10	–	20	22	2.0
Latvia	1995		–	12	–	21	21	0.0
Lithuania	1994		–	5/9	–	19	21	2.0
Luxembourg	1970		3	6/12	12	15	15	0.0

Member State	VAT introduction	Specific rates				Standard rate		
		Zero rate	Super reduced	Reduced	Parking	2009	2014	Change
Malta	1995	yes	–	5/7	–	18	18	0.0
Netherlands	1969		–	6	–	19	21	2.0
Poland	1993			5/8	–	22	23	1.0
Portugal	1986		–	6/13	13	20	23	3.0
Romania	1993			5/9	–	19	24	5.0
Slovak Republic	1993		–	10	–	19	20	1.0
Slovenia	1999		–	9.5	–	20	22	2.0
Spain	1986		4	10	–	16	21	5.0
Sweden	1969		–	6/12	–	25	25	0.0
United Kingdom	1973	yes	–	5	–	15	20	5.0
Average						19.5	21.5	1.9

Source: European Commission (2009, 2014).

Notes: All entries represent percentage rates.

of the years, especially since the recent financial and debt crisis, which might be viewed as suggestive evidence against the notion of increased competition in commodity taxation. Overall, we do not observe any remarkable convergence in VAT rates, which, together with inefficiencies from the deferred payment system, still may represent one major impediment for intra-EU trade.

The harmonization of special consumer taxes (excise duties) dates back to the early 1970s. However, and similar to the VAT, the most important steps to a uniform system of excise duties were taken under the SEM-program. Since then, several directives have been issued covering the products subject to taxation (i.e., mineral oils, alcohol and alcoholic beverages, tobacco products and energy), the general arrangements of taxation (among others, the uniform application of the destination principle as the general scheme for cross-border consumption), and the corresponding minimum tax rates (including zero rates for specific products, for example wine). Apart from wide dispersions in tax rates, one may assert a stronger harmonization for these taxes than for the VAT, implying less administration and lower compliance costs associated with the functioning of the actual system.[12]

2.2 Direct taxation

As early as in the Neumark Report (1963) and in the Van den Tempel Report (1970) the long run goal of full harmonization of corporate taxation and a minimum tax burden of 50 percent on retained earnings were debated. However, due to the lack of a direct mandate to harmonize direct taxes, these proposals were never implemented. It is only in 1992, when the Ruding Report systematically reviews the distortions to the common market imposed by differences in corporate taxation. The conclusion that "[. . .] the threat of overall tax atrophy does not seem to provide a sufficiently strong justification for the total harmonization of corporate taxes within the Community" (Ruding Report 1992, p. 26) points to an important change in the approach towards EU tax policies in the area of direct taxation. While the

Ruding Report still proposes a bandwidth for corporate income tax rates between 30 and 40 percent, the focus starts to shift on abolishing preferential tax regimes for foreign corporations and tax obstacles to cross border activities. This tendency is reiterated by the European Commission (1997), suggesting a package to tackle harmful tax competition. The subsequent Bolkestein Report (2001) switched the general harmonization strategy pursuing a policy of aligning the corporate tax base rather than tax rates. At the same time, the difficulties of finding unanimous decisions in tax matters are acknowledged and the idea of enhanced cooperation between a subgroup of Member States gained momentum.

Out of the Bolkestein Report, a common consolidated corporate tax base (CCCTB) emerged as the preferred measure of the European Commission. After assessing the possibilities of a CCCTB in depth, the Commission formally proposed the CCCTB in March 2011.[13] However, the deep economic impact of the financial crises overshadowed the attempts of corporate tax harmonization, so that the future of the CCCTB proposal is still uncertain.

Apart from tax rate and tax base harmonization, the EU passed three directives intending to remove obstacles on cross-border activities of multinational firms (MNEs). First, the Mergers Directive (90/434/EEC last amended in Council Directive 2005/19/EC) rules out additional taxes on cross border transfers of assets in the case of mergers between two companies in different Member States. Second, the Parent Subsidiary (Council Directive 2003/123/EC) abolishes withholding taxes on payments and legal double taxation of dividends between associated companies of different Member States. Finally, the Interest and Royalty Directive (Council Directive 2003/49/EC) rules out withholding taxes on interest and royalty payments between associated companies of different Member States.

The incomplete tax harmonization process in the European Union has changed the surroundings for tax competition in a number of ways. The Parent and Subsidiary Directive and the Interest and Royalty Directive largely eliminate negative externalities from tax exporting (for example, arising from double taxation on dividend payments of foreign firms). Further, the abolition of withholding taxes increases the attractiveness of low tax countries and thereby influences the positive externality because of tax base flight. Therefore, one would expect a stronger downward pressure on corporate taxes within the European Union.

At the same time, the European Monetary Union and in particular the Stability and Growth Pact stipulates that the Members of the Eurozone ultimately have to balance their budgets and to maintain their debt to GDP ratios below 60 percent. This induces a strong restriction on tax policies of EU Member States, especially in times of the recent financial and debt crisis. Tax revenues are strongly needed in many countries, which may well contribute to the mixed picture in Table 20.2, presenting the status quo and recent trends in both corporate and personal income taxation. Out of the 28 EU Member States, there are four countries having increased their top statutory corporate tax rate, while seven countries have lowered it during the course of the last five years. Some of the tax increases can be attributed to increased revenue needs (e.g., Cyprus and Greece) while some of the countries lowering their tax rate can be seen as traditionally high tax Nordic countries converging to a European average (Denmark, Sweden and Finland). Linking changes in corporate tax rates to ones in the corresponding tax bases reveals that only the United Kingdom and Denmark experienced rate-cut-cum-base-broadening reforms. This is somewhat surprising, as this type of reform has been prominently placed in many tax policy discussions over the last two decades.[14] At the same time, the way the corporate tax base is measured may also underestimate the extent of base broadening, since a number of countries have broadened their tax base by restricting the deduction of financing costs, limiting the loss offset or abolishing lower tax rates for smaller businesses. In a similar vein, the relative small number of countries reducing tax rates

Table 20.2 Status quo and recent development of direct taxation in EU Member States

Country	Corporate income tax rate			Personal income tax rate		
	statutory	*effective*	*development*	*statutory*	*effective*	*development*
Austria	25.00	18.56	B: → R: →	50.00[b]	49.12	B: → R: →
Belgium	33.99	22.62	B: → R: →	53.70	55.80	B: → R: →
Bulgaria	10.00	6.36	B: ↘ R: →	10.00	n.a.	R: →
Cyprus	12.50	8.62	B: ↘ R: ↗	35.00	n.a.	R: ↗
Croatia	20.00	12.91	B: → R: →	47.20	n.a.	R: ↘
Czech Republic	19.00	15.23	B: → R: →	22.00	42.38	B: → R: ↗
Denmark	24.50	18.72	B: ↗ R: ↘	55.60	38.24	B: ↗ R: ↗
Estonia	21.00	24.66	B: → R: →	21.00	39.90	B: → R: →
Finland	20.00	13.31	B: → R: ↘	51.50	43.12	B: → R: ↗
France	34.43[a]	24.00	B: → R: →	50.30	48.92	B: ↘ R: ↗
Germany	29.58	23.65	B: ↗ R: →	47.50	49.33	B: → R: →
Greece	26.00	20.42	B: ↗ R: ↗	46.00	41.56	B: ↘ R: ↘
Hungary	19.00	12.00	B: → R: →	16.00	49.03	B: ↗ R: ↘
Ireland	12.50	9.59	B: → R: →	48.00	26.60	B: ↗ R: ↗
Italy	27.50	24.28	B: → R: →	47.90	47.78	B: → R: ↗
Latvia	15.00	9.63	B: → R: →	24.00	n.a.	R: ↘
Lithuania	15.00	9.24	B: → R: →	15.00	n.a.	R: →
Luxembourg	29.22	20.00	B: → R: ↗	43.60	37.01	B: ↗ R: ↗
Malta	35.00	24.56	B: → R: →	35.00	n.a.	R: →
Netherlands	25.00	17.44	B: → R: ↘	52.00	36.94	B: ↘ R: →
Poland	19.00	15.30	B: → R: →	32.00	35.56	B: → R: →
Portugal	23.00	15.46	B: → R: ↘	56.50	41.15	B: ↘ R: ↗
Romania	16.00	11.31	B: → R: →	16.00	n.a.	R: →
Slovak Republic	22.00	16.12	B: → R: ↗	25.00	41.13	B: ↗ R: ↗
Slovenia	17.00	11.13	B: → R: ↘	50.00	42.34	B: → R: ↗
Spain	30.00	23.60	B: → R: →	52.00	40.66	B: → R: ↗
Sweden	22.00	15.66	B: → R: ↘	56.90	42.93	B: → R: ↗
United Kingdom	21.00	18.19	B: ↗ R: ↘	45.00	31.48	B: ↘ R: ↘

Notes: [a]Including the temporarily levied 10.7 % surtax for entities with a sales turnover greater than 250 million Euros raises this rate to approx. 38%. [b]Taking into account the special tax treatment of the 13th and 14th salary the top statutory tax rate is at 43.71%.

All rates are in percentages. "B" represents the tax base, "R" tax rates, "n.a." ... not available.

Effective corporate tax rates refer to a weighted EATR measure as proposed by Devereux and Griffith (1999) and are based on the same assumptions as in Loretz (2009). Effective personal income tax rates are from the OECD taxing wages publication and refer to the tax burden including social security contributions of a single tax payer at the average earnings. Development refers to the change over the last five years. ↘ (↗) refers to a narrowing (broadening) of the tax base, which is defined as depreciation allowances for the corporate income tax and the progressivity for personal income tax.

might understate any general downward tendencies in corporate taxation as mirrored in a growing number of special provisions for tax treatment of R&D expenditures and related revenues.[15]

The swelling need for tax revenues with a potentially intensified corporate tax competition may result in an increased tax burden on less mobile labor. The last three columns of Table 20.2 report the top statutory personal income tax rate, the effective tax burden (including social security contributions) on a single taxpayer earning the country-specific average income, and the corresponding development of tax rates and tax bases over the last five years. Out of the 28 EU Member States, 13 countries increased their top personal income tax rate, while five of them reduced these rates. Countries with unchanged top income tax rates are mainly Eastern European ones with partly flat taxes on personal income. Although there is no clear development of tax rates and tax bases reported in the last column of Table 20.2,[16] we might assert a general increase in personal income tax burden over time, which, together with the observed pattern in corporate taxation, is broadly consistent with a shift in tax burden from (mobile) capital to (immobile) labor.

3. Tax competition: Lessons from economic research

Since the mid-1980s, there has been a remarkable theoretical and empirical literature on tax competition, not only providing important insights into strategic interactions among jurisdictions, but also pointing to the policy implications of increased factor mobility and, more generally, globalization of markets. Many results from this research have been proved as theoretically robust and in line with empirical observations (Wilson 1999, Zodrow 2003 or Keen and Konrad 2013 provide comprehensive surveys over this research). For instance, there is a bulk of papers finding that tax competition leads to inefficiently low tax rates on mobile tax bases, with the tax burden shifted to less mobile factors. Further, it is shown that a country's ability to engage in the international tax game crucially depends on its country size. However, it is less clear whether tax competition leads to positive or negative welfare effects, and whether the tax reaction functions of countries are positively or negatively sloped, i.e., whether tax rates of competing countries are strategic complements or substitutes. Both aspects are relevant for European tax harmonization and discussed in the subsequent sections.

3.1 Theory

The concept of tax competition originally dates back to Tiebout (1956), who developed a model with autonomous regions and citizens who *vote with their feet* to choose the jurisdiction with the optimal combination of tax burdens and provision of public goods. Under a set of strict assumptions, this leads to an efficient sorting and, therefore, to welfare enhancing tax competition relative to unified tax rates across all jurisdictions.[17] Intuitively, if a monopolist can segment its market and the customers sort themselves without frictions into the best fitting segment, the outcome will dominate the non-discriminating case. Bradford and Oates (1971) and Oates (1972) took a less optimistic view on tax competition, predicting that governments underprovide local public goods in an attempt to attract mobile factors. This line of reasoning is formalized in the seminal contributions of Zodrow and Mieszkowski (1986) and Wilson (1986), who assume a large number of jurisdictions competing for perfectly mobile capital. A tax cut in one region creates an inflow of mobile factors, increasing its tax base and, consequently, tax revenues. This revenue gain comes at the expense of all other jurisdictions, which are faced with shrinking tax bases representing a negative fiscal externality. In the Nash-equilibrium, capital tax rates are competed down to zero, a result that is known as "race to the bottom." Much like a perfect competition case, these models have become the benchmark and starting point for extensions into various directions.[18]

Starting from the assumption of a benevolent government, the lack of monopoly power to impose taxes necessarily implies a loss in welfare. Brennan and Buchanan (1980) were more skeptical arguing that the governments act as *Leviathan* primarily interested in raising tax revenues. Under such a perspective, tax competition is beneficial as it helps to limit an over-expansion of the state. Edwards and Keen (1996) formalize this argument assuming that government officials not only maximize the welfare of their residents but also act in their self-interest. They show that tax harmonization fosters collusive behavior of governments, leading to excessive spending. However, from a voter's perspective, it is not clear whether this is welfare-reducing or -enhancing, depending on whether the distortions from harmonized taxes outweigh the revenues from previously uncoordinated taxes. Hence, if competition between jurisdictions does not imply very large excess burdens, there is room for beneficial tax competition in addition to the welfare enhancing differentiation of tax policy amongst European Member States.

The second key aspect where the tax competition literature seemingly fails to come to an agreement is the question whether tax rates are strategic complements or substitutes. In the former case, the tax reaction functions have a positive slope, i.e., a jurisdiction will lower (increase) its tax rate when tax rates of neighboring jurisdictions are falling (increasing). In contrast, if tax rates are strategic substitutes, a country that is faced with decreasing tax rates in neighboring countries and, hence, with a decline of the tax base due to relocations of mobile factors, would increase its tax rate to maintain a certain level of public expenditures (see Wildasin 1988). Hence, the tax reaction function is negatively sloped. The ambiguity regarding the slope of the tax reaction functions can be explained through one key modeling assumption, namely whether the level of expenditure is exogenously given or determined by the ability to raise revenues. Early tax competition models treat expenditure as endogenous and find that tax rates are strategic complements, implying the race to the bottom result. In contrast, Wildasin (1988) shows that tax rates would be strategic substitutes if public expenditure were used as strategic variable. Rather than a race to the bottom, this would imply specialization into high tax and low tax countries. The reality is most likely a mixture of governments deciding on expenditure levels independently of the individual tax rate decisions, as well as countries adjusting expenditures because of difficulties to raise tax revenues. Hence, whether there is a race to the bottom or increasing differences in the tax rates depends amongst others on the rigidity of the expenditure level and availability of other tax instruments.

While the classical tax competition models only consider one tax instrument, Bucovetsky and Wilson (1991) focus on two tax instruments, i.e., immobile labor and perfectly mobile capital. They find that tax competition forces the optimal capital tax rate down to zero, while the remaining tax burden entirely falls on the immobile factor. The presence of a less mobile tax base will also weaken the link between the tax rate on a particular tax base and expenditure levels. Hence, with the availability of other tax instruments, tax rates on more mobile factors more likely become strategic complements. However, it should be noticed that this result is no longer valid if labor is mobile as well. For instance, Kleven, Landais and Saez (2013) show that the mobility of high skilled labor limits a country's ability to raise taxes on top incomes. Further, one cannot sharply distinguish between labor and capital mobility. In particular, generous replacement rates in social insurances push up reservation wages and inflate wage costs, which might have an equivalent effect on foreign direct investment (FDI) than a given increase in corporate tax rates (see Keuschnigg 2009). In the same vein, Keuschnigg and Ribi (2009) have demonstrated that labor taxation and social insurance magnifies outsourcing and offshoring of domestic employment. The upshot is that international fiscal competition might be as much driven by high labor taxes as by high corporate taxes.

The relative mobility of tax bases also depends on country size, as shown by Bucovetsky (1991) and Wilson (1991), modeling tax competition between jurisdictions of different size. They find that smaller regions will set lower tax rates on mobile factors and, consequently, win through tax competition. Further developments in the theoretical tax competition literature stress that even perfectly mobile tax bases can be de facto immobile because of agglomerations rents.[19] These, in turn, reinforce the taxing power of jurisdictions and dampen the negative consequences of tax competition. Further, the downward pressure on corporate tax rates might be limited if the corresponding revenues are used to finance infrastructure and other public services (e.g., Sinn 1997, Keen and Marchand 1997). In a similar vein, Egger et al. (2014) argue that a country with high institutional quality and well developed capital markets leads firms to invest more in that country. In other words, if there are sound business reasons to be located in a particular country, it is possible to tax the accruing rents. Countries may thus be able to sustain higher tax rates as they offer other compensating advantages via a favorable institutional environment fostering international investment. However, the possibility to relocate the tax base abroad through profit shifting may undermine even the taxation of de facto immobile production factors. This most harmful aspect of tax competition has also moved increasingly into the focus of initiatives of international organizations like the EU or the OECD.[20]

In addition to a broad literature on direct taxes, there is also theoretical research on commodity tax competition. One of the first contributions in this regard is by Mintz and Tulkens (1986), who model competition between two regions that are interlinked through cross-border shopping. Public goods are financed by a consumption tax based on the origin principle, which in turn gives rise to cross-border shopping of consumers. Tax competition arises if tax rate differentials are sufficiently large to compensate transportation costs. If a high tax country increases its commodity tax rate in this setting, it loses cross-border shoppers to neighboring countries with lower tax rates. This represents a positive externality, leading to inefficiently low tax rates in the high tax country. From this, one might conclude that tax harmonization is efficiency-enhancing. However, a tax increase in the low tax country also induces a negative externality as cross-border shoppers are now faced with higher prices. Hence, a coordinated tax policy is not necessarily associated with a welfare improvement in the Mintz-Tulkens setting (see also Haufler 1998).

Kanbur and Keen (1993) extended the Mintz and Tulkens framework focusing on spatial competition between revenue maximizing governments. Countries are treated as asymmetric, distinguished by their population size (see Ohsawa 1999 and Nielsen 2001 for similar analysis). One finding of the model is that commodity tax rates are positively related to tax rates in neighboring countries (i.e., tax reaction functions are upward sloping). Further, it is shown that smaller countries strictly set lower tax rates than their larger counterparts, which is consistent with models on capital tax competition. Intuitively, a small country that lowers its tax rate produces revenue gains from a large mass of foreign consumers, which outweighs the revenue loss from (relatively less) domestic individuals. The opposite is true for the large economy, so that it has no incentives to undercut the tax rates of a small country. After all, this result indicates that welfare implications of tax coordination are not symmetric, being particularly important if countries of an economic union are heterogeneous.

What is common to all theoretical models on commodity tax competition is that cross-border shopping is mainly driven by transportation costs, influencing the incentives for purchasing abroad. Economic integration is associated with a reduction of transportation costs thereby intensifying tax competition and generally reducing tax rates. One way to avoid the negative consequences of such a race to the bottom is to ascertain minimum tax rates within the customs union, a policy the EU has been incorporated in commodity taxation. Kanbur and Keen demonstrated that such a policy is clearly welfare improving as the high tax country is now able to maintain higher tax rates, leading to revenue gains sufficiently large to compensate the low tax country for its revenue losses from cross-border shoppers.

3.2 Empirical evidence

The empirical literature on tax competition has been grown extensively in recent years, covering many different aspects of personal and corporate income taxes as well as commodity taxation. It goes beyond the scope of this chapter to address all of the related issues. We rather highlight some of the key findings associated with European tax harmonization.

Despite contributing only a moderate share of tax revenues, the bulk of the empirical research is concerned with two main aspects of business and corporate taxation. First, there is an extensive literature addressing the *elasticity of the corporate tax base*. Early contributions in this field were restricted by data availability and only investigate cross-country variations in statutory corporate tax rates and their impact on US inbound and outbound investment of multinational firms (see, e.g., Grubert and Mutti 1991, Hines and Rice 1994 and Hines 1996). Subsequent papers referred to a larger cross section of countries and exploited information on various elements of tax codes and tax treaties as reflected in (bilateral) effective tax rates (see, e.g., Devereux and Griffith 1998 or Egger et al. 2009). Generally, these papers find a systematic and robust impact of corporate taxation on foreign direct investment (De Mooj and Ederveen 2003 and Feld and Heckemeyer 2011 provide comprehensive meta-studies over this research).

As firm-level data became increasingly accessible, researchers started to analyze more directly cross border profit shifting activities of MNEs. In this regard, Egger, Eggert and Winner (2010), relying on a large cross section of European firms, find that foreign-owned subsidiaries of MNEs pay significant lower taxes than their domestic counterparts. Many explanations have been provided to explain this observation, where transfer pricing and debt shifting probably have attracted most attention so far (see Gresik 2001 and Devereux 2007 for comprehensive surveys). Transfer pricing allows MNEs to exploit international tax rate differentials by determining prices for intermediate goods or by charging license fees and royalties for headquarter services (see Dischinger and Riedel 2011 or Karkinsky and Riedel 2012 for recent evidence using European data). Under debt shifting, MNEs reduce their overall tax liability by shifting debt from low- to high-tax countries taking advantage of the high-interest deduction in high-tax jurisdictions (see, e.g., Huizinga, Laeven and Nicodème 2008, Egger et al. 2010 or Mintz and Weichenrieder 2010 for recent research). However, part of this profit shifting may occur for good economic reasons. In spite of obvious tax disadvantages, multinationals may shift profit to high tax countries because they need funds there to self-finance investment and to circumvent the difficulties of local financing due to bad institutional environment (see Egger et al. 2014), or underdeveloped capital markets (Keuschnigg and Devereux, 2013). After all, countries may compensate tax disadvantages and facilitate investment by offering high quality in institutional matters.

Apart from the literature on the impact of corporate taxation on location and production decisions of MNEs, there is an eminent line of research investigating *determinants of corporate tax policies* and the role of *strategic interaction* therein. Two strands of literature might be distinguished here. One group of authors investigates whether economic integration as measured by the increased mobility of factors is associated with in a decrease of tax burdens, as suggested by early tax competition models. Most of these studies find a negative relationship between those variables, suggesting that tax competition leads to a downward pressure on tax rates (see Leibrecht and Hochgatterer 2012 for a survey). However, one should interpret such results very cautiously as it is difficult to capture economic integration, factor mobility and the corresponding tax burdens without measurement error. Further, a (reduced-form) regression of a tax burden measure on factor mobility may hide any endogeneity issues,[21] probably leading to wrongful conclusions on the consequences of international tax competition.

Perhaps a more promising way to identify international tax competition is to directly test for strategic interaction in tax rate setting. Following the discussion about strategic complementarity above, it is not entirely clear whether we would expect a positive or a negative sign on the reaction functions, although the majority of the literature leans towards the idea of positively sloped reaction functions. The use of spatial econometric methods to test for reaction functions was established first in the local tax competition literature as surveyed by Brueckner (2003). More recently, Devereux, Lockwood and Redoano (2008) extend the empirical test to a panel of 21 OECD countries and find evidence for a positively sloped reaction functions in corporate tax rates. Subsequent research mainly refined this analysis and found that Eastern European countries are a driving force of the tax competition process (see, e.g., Cassette and Paty 2008). Further, Davies and Voget (2010) fund that EU Membership in general increases any pressures from fiscal competition. More recently, the empirical identification strategy of spatial models has been criticized by some authors. Gibbons and Overman (2012) emphasize that confounding factors may induce spatial correlation and propose natural experiments for credible identification. So far, there is only one study by Parchet (2013) using tax rate variation from neighboring jurisdictions in Switzerland to identify strategic interactions among jurisdictions. He finds negatively sloped reaction functions, implying that Swiss municipalities are competing over expenditures rather than tax rates. This result is somewhat corroborated by Egger, Pfaffermayr and Winner (2009), who present evidence for more subtle strategic interactions in personal and corporate income tax rates among OECD countries. In particular, although they estimate positive reaction functions for both types of taxes, it seems that a reduction in corporate tax rates might be compensated by an increase in personal income tax rates, and vice versa. This finding is in line with theory predicting a shift in tax burden from mobile to less mobile factors.

With regard to commodity taxation, there is firstly literature estimating tax reaction functions at the international level. For instance, Egger, Pfaffermayr and Winner (2005) use spatial panel data techniques to test empirically the implications of the above-mentioned Ohsawa model. They find that VAT rates are strategic complements and that smaller countries tend to set lower VAT rates than their larger counterparts,[22] which, again, indicates that all countries will benefit equally from tax coordination.[23] Apart from this, there is also empirical research on cross-border shopping within EU Member States, mainly considering the situation before the completion of the SEM. Relying on consumer surveys at sensitive borders with serious VAT differences (e.g., Ireland–UK or Denmark–Germany), they show that cross-border shopping does not much account on volumes of intra-EU consumption (see, e.g., FitzGerald, Johnston and Williams 1995, Copenhagen Economics 2007).

5. Conclusions

At the time the TEU was negotiated, Sinn (1990, p. 501) discussed the problems lying ahead with the next step of economic integration and came to the rather gloomy conclusion, that the "... effect will be the death of Europe's welfare states if the unmitigated competition of tax systems is allowed." Two and a half decades later, one might revisit the situation of tax competition in the European Union evaluating to which extent these fears were met. Indeed, we find that the integration process within Europe provides a fertile ground for tax competition, with increased mobility and reduced possibilities to tax foreign citizens. The call for tax coordination has certainly been around, but we observe a significant harmonization progress mainly for indirect taxes. For direct taxation, we have to conclude that Member States were reluctant to give up their tax autonomy and, therefore, it is not surprising that the harmonization process seems to be more or less suspended with regard to theses taxes.

Absent significant harmonization in the area of direct taxation and with the increased factor mobility one would expect a strong downward trend in tax rates. This, however, is not really observed in the last two decades. While there was a period of strong corporate tax rate reductions, in particular around the time of the Eastern enlargement of the EU, this process has been slowed down significantly in recent years. This development is still consistent with the idea of tax competition taking place. If one looks at the world as a whole, this observation simply mirrors the fact that Europe became more competitive from a tax perspective. Taken into account that the completion of the SEM generally increased the attractiveness of Europe for international investment, it seems plausible that EU Member States can maintain their now moderate level of corporate taxation in the future.

In some aspects, the predictions of Sinn (1990) are also borne out in reality. Tax competition has resulted in an observed shift away from capital and corporate taxation towards consumption taxes, which certainly creates winners and losers. However, in contrast to the prediction that landowners will be the losers because of higher taxes on immovable property, it appears that the burden currently falls on the next generation via excessive debt making.

Notes

1 Keuschnigg thanks the Swiss National Fund for financial support as part of the SNF Sinergia grant no. 147668.
2 The aim to: "... make war not only unthinkable but materially impossible ..." (Robert Schuman) was achieved by regional integration creating a common market for coal and steel, especially in the Ruhr area. This idea was extended further to a general customs union (Treaty of Rome, 1957) and, more recently, to the creation of the Economic and Monetary Union (Treaty of Maastricht, 1992), which is often viewed as the final step of economic integration, but at the very same time, explicitly was thought as a first step to establish a political union.
3 See Haufler (2001), for a comprehensive discussion of the externalities with regard to capital taxation.
4 In the following, we subsume commodity taxes (i.e., the value added tax and excise duties) under *indirect taxation*, while assigning personal and corporate income taxes to *direct taxation*. This is also in line with the usual classification of taxes as used, for example, in the OECD's Revenue Statistics (e.g., OECD 2014).
5 This difference also translates into a stronger legal mandate in the TEU to harmonize commodity taxes. In particular, Article 110 TEU states that "[N]o Member State shall impose, directly or indirectly, on the products of other Member States any internal taxation of any kind in excess of that imposed directly or indirectly on similar domestic products." Further, Article 113 TEU calls for the European Council do adopt unanimously measures regarding "... [the] harmonisation of legislation concerning turnover taxes, excise duties and other forms of indirect taxation to the extent that such

harmonisation is necessary to ensure the establishment and the functioning of the internal market and to avoid distortion of competition."

6 Diamond and Mirrlees (1971) have demonstrated that the goal of production efficiency has to be preferred over the one of exchange efficiency. Therefore, the destination principle is more desirable from a welfare perspective.

7 The former was applied in five out of the six original Member States, the latter only in France. See Ebrill, Keen and Summers (2001) for more technical and historical details on the VAT.

8 Subsequently, the adoption of the VAT became a non-negotiable pre-requisite to join the EU.

9 While the 1987 draft directive planned to restrict the Member States to bandwidths of 14 to 20 percent for the standard rate and of 4 to 9 percent for a reduced rate on basic goods, the Commission proposed a system of minimum rates of 14 (standard rate) and 9 (reduced rate) percent in the 1989 proposal.

10 Exceptions are household purchases of motor vehicles, mail-order sales and intra-EU acquisitions of intermediate inputs by VAT-exempted firms. In all these cases, the destination principle still applies to cross-border consumption.

11 Subsequent research also discusses additional alternatives, either based on some forms of clearing mechanisms (e.g., European Commission 1996) or on more centralized VAT systems, including the compensating VAT (CVAT, McLure 2000) and the viable integrated VAT (VIVAT, Keen and Smith 1996). See Bird and Gendron (2000) for a detailed discussion.

12 In the following, we do not discuss harmonization issues of excise duties any further. The interested reader is referred to Cnossen (2001, 2006, 2007).

13 With the CCCTB, multinational companies would calculate the corporate tax base for their overall European activities and thereby overcome problems allocating activities to specific Member States. In a second step, the overall tax base would be allocated to the Member States according to formulas, which reflect the economic activities (e.g., employment, tangible assets or sales). See Bettendorf et al. (2010) for an in-depth discussion of the CCCTB.

14 See, for example, Devereux, Griffith and Klemm (2002) and Loretz (2008).

15 See, for example Evers, Miller and Spengel (2015) for a discussion of the recent rise of patent boxes in Europe.

16 We measure the personal tax base as the progressivity of the tax system, defined as the ratio of the total tax wedges for single persons with above (167 percent) and below (67 percent) average incomes. This implies that our measure only captures some aspects of the breadth of the personal tax base.

17 It is worth noting that the original Tiebout model is not concerned about redistributive policy, which may reverse the overall desirability of the outcome.

18 See also Devereux and Loretz (2013) for analogies between tax competition models and competition models in the goods market.

19 See, for example, Baldwin and Krugman (2004) for linking the new economic geography models with the tax competition literature.

20 In May 2013, the OECD adopted a declaration to combat base erosion and profit shifting (BEPS) and developed an action plan, which is supported by the finance ministers of the G20 countries.

21 For instance, it might be the case that causality runs not only from capital mobility to corporate tax rates but also in the opposite direction, leading to potentially biased estimation results in such a regression.

22 Lockwood and Migali (2009) provide similar evidence for excise taxes.

23 This finding seems to be confirmed by Heinemann and Osterloh (2013), who did a survey on members of the European Parliament, asking on whether they would support a minimum corporate tax rate. As expected, they find that such a proposal would be refused mainly by politicians from high-tax countries.

References

Baldwin, R.E. and Krugman, P. (2004), Agglomeration, Integration and Tax Harmonization, *European Economic Review* 48(1), 1–23.

Bettendorf, L., Devereux, M.P., van der Horst, A., Loretz, S. and de Mooij, R. A. (2010), Corporate Tax Harmonization in the EU, *Economic Policy* 25(63), 537–90.

Bird, R. and Gendron, P.-P. (2000), CVAT, VIVAT and Dual VAT: Vertical Sharing and International Trade, *International Tax and Public Finance* 7(6), 753–61.

Bradford, D.F. and Oates, W.E. (1971), The Analysis of Revenue Sharing in a New Approach to Collective Fiscal Decisions, *The Quarterly Journal of Economics* 85(3), 416–39.

Brennan G. and Buchanan, J. (1980), *The Power to Tax: Analytical Foundations of a Fiscal Constitution*, New York: Cambridge University Press.

Brueckner, J.K. (2003), Strategic Interaction among Local Governments: An Overview of Empirical Studies, *International Regional Science Review* 26(2), 175–88.

Bucovetsky, S. (1991), Asymmetric Tax Competition, *Journal of Urban Economics* 30(2), 167–81.

Bucovetsky, S. and Wilson, J.D. (1991), Tax Competition with Two Tax Instruments, *Regional Science and Urban Economics* 21(3), 333–50.

Cassette, A. and Paty, S. (2008), Tax Competition Among Eastern and Western European Countries: With whom do Countries compete? *Economic Systems* 32(4), 307–25.

Cnossen, S. (2001), Tax Policy in the European Union: A Review of Issues and Options, *FinanzArchiv/Public Finance Analysis* 58(4), 466–558.

Cnossen, S. (2006), Tobacco Taxation in the European Union, *CESifo Working Paper* No. 1718.

Cnossen, S. (2007), Alcohol Taxation and Regulation in the European Union, *International Tax and Public Finance* 14(6), 699–732.

Commission European Economic Community (1963), *Report of the Fiscal and Financial Committee*, Brussels (Neumark Report).

Commission of the European Community (1970), *Corporation tax and individual income tax in the European Communities*, Competition – Approximation of legislation series 15, Luxembourg (van den Tempel Report).

Commission of the European Communities (1985), *Completing the Internal Market: White Paper from the EC Commission to the Council*, COM (85) 310 Final (June (1985)).

Copenhagen Economics (2007), *Study on Reduced Vat Applied to Goods and Services in the Member States of the European Union*, Brussels, European Commission.

Davies, R.B and Voget, J. (2010), Tax Competition in an Expanding European Union, *GEE Papers 0033*, Gabinete de Estratégia e Estudos, Ministério da Economia e da Inovação, Lisbon, Portugal.

de Mooij, R.A. and Ederveen, S. (2003), Taxation and Foreign Direct Investment: A synthesis of Empirical Research, *International Tax and Public Finance* 10(6), 673–93.

Devereux, M.P. (2007), The Impact of Taxation on the Location of Capital, Firms and Profit: A Survey of Empirical Evidence, *Working Paper* No. 07/02, Oxford University Centre for Business Taxation.

Devereux, M.P. and Griffith, R. (1998), Taxes and the Location of Production: Evidence from a Panel of US Multinationals, *Journal of Public Economics* 68(3), 335–67.

Devereux, M.P. and Griffith, R. (1999), The Taxation of Discrete Investment Choices, *The Institute for Fiscal Studies Working Paper Series* W98/16.

Devereux, M.P., R. Griffith and Klemm, A. (2002), Corporate Income Tax Reforms and International Tax Competition, *Economic Policy* 17(35), 449–95.

Devereux, M.P., B. Lockwood and Redoano, M. (2008), Do Countries Compete over Corporate Tax Rates? *Journal of Public Economics* 92(5–6), 1210–35.

Devereux, M.P. and Loretz, S. (2013), What Do We Know about Corporate Tax Competition? *National Tax Journal* 66(3), 745–74.

Diamond, P. and Mirrlees, J. (1971), Optimal Taxation and Public Production I: Production Efficiency, *American Economic Review* 61(1), 8–27.

Dischinger, M. and Riedel, N. (2011), Corporate Taxes and the Location of Intangible Assets within Multinational Firms, *Journal of Public Economics* 95(7–8), 691–707.

Ebrill, L.P., M. Keen and Summers, V.P. (2001), *The Modern VAT*, Washington D.C.: International Monetary Fund.

Edwards, J. and Keen, M. (1996), Tax Competition and Leviathan, *European Economic Review* 40(1), 113–34.

Egger P.H., W. Eggert, C. Keuschnigg and Winner, H. (2010), Corporate Taxation, Debt Financing and Foreign Plant Ownership, *European Economic Review* 54(1), 96–107.

Egger P.H., W. Eggert and Winner, H. (2010), Saving Taxes Through Foreign Plant Ownership, *Journal of International Economics* 81(1), 99–108.

Egger, P.H., C. Keuschnigg, V. Merlo and Wamser, G. (2014), Corporate Taxes and Internal Borrowing Within Multinational Firms, *American Economic Journal: Economic Policy* 6(2), 54–93.

Egger, P.H., S. Loretz, M. Pfaffermayr and Winner, H. (2009), Bilateral Effective Tax Rates and Foreign Direct Investment, *International Tax and Public Finance* 16(6), 822–49.

Egger, P.H., M. Paffermayr and Winner, H. (2005), Commodity Taxation in a Linear World: A Spatial Panel Data Approach, *Regional Science and Urban Economics* 35(5), 527–41.

Egger, P.H., M. Pfaffermayr, and Winner, H. (2009), Competition in Corporate and Personal Income Taxation, *Unpublished Working Paper*, University of Innsbruck.

European Commission (1992), Report of the Committee of Independent Experts on Company Taxation, Luxembourg (Ruding Report).

European Commission (1996), *A Common System of VAT: A Programme for the Single Market*, COM 328(96) final, Brussels.

European Commission (1997), *A Package to Tackle Harmful Tax Competition in the EU*, COM(97) 564 final, Brussels.

European Commission (2001), *Company Taxation in the Internal Market*, COM (2001) 582 final, Brussels (Bolkestein Report).

European Commission (2009), *VAT Rates Applied in the Member States of the European Community*, Situation at 1st January 2014, Brussels.

European Commission (2014), *VAT Rates Applied in the Member States of the European Union*, Situation at 13th January 2014, Brussels.

European Parliament (2001), *Tax Coordination in the EU – The Latest Position*, Working Paper, ECON 128, DG Research.

Evers, L., H. Miller and Spengel, C. (2015), Intellectual Property Box Regimes: Effective Tax Rates and Tax Policy Considerations, *International Tax and Public Finance*, 22(3), 502–30.

Feld, L.P. and Heckemeyer, J. (2011), FDI and Taxation: A Meta Study, *Journal of Economic Surveys* 25(2), 233–72.

FitzGerald, J., J. Johnston and Williams, J. (1995), Indirect Tax Distortions in a Europe of Shopkeepers, *Working Paper* No. 56, Dublin, The Economic and Social Research Institute.

Gibbons, S. and Overman, H.G. (2012), Mostly Pointless Spatial Econometrics, *Journal of Regional Science* 52(2), 172–91.

Gresik, T.A. (2001), The Taxing Task of Taxing Transnationals, *Journal of Economic Literature* 39(3), 800–38.

Grubert, H. and Mutti, J. (1991), Taxes, Tariffs and Transfer Pricing in Multinational Corporate Decision Making, *Review of Economics and Statistics* 73(2), 285–93.

Haufler, A. (1996), Tax Coordination with Different Preferences for Public Goods: Conflict or Harmony of Interest? *International Tax and Public Finance* 3(1), 5–28.

Haufler, A. (2001), *Taxation in a Global Economy*, Cambridge, NY: Cambridge University Press.

Heinemann, F. and Osterloh, S. (2013), The Political Economy of Corporate Tax Harmonization – Why Do European Politicians (Dis)Like Minimum Tax Rates?, *European Journal of Political Economy* 29, 18–37.

Hines, J.R. (1996), Altered States: Taxes and the Location of Foreign Direct Investment in America, *American Economic Review* 86(5), 1076–94.

Hines, J.R. and Rice, E.M. (1994), Fiscal Paradise: Foreign Tax Havens and American Business, *Quarterly Journal of Economics* 109(1), 149–82.

Huizinga, H., L. Laeven and Nicodème, G. (2008), Capital Structure and International Debt Shifting, *Journal of Financial Economics* 88(1), 80–118.

Kanbur, R. and Keen, M. (1993), Jeux sans frontières: Tax Competition and Tax Coordination when Countries Differ in Size, *American Economic Review* 83(4), 877–92.

Karkinsky, T. and Riedel, N. (2012), Corporate Taxation and the Location of Patents within Multinational Firms, *Journal of International Economics* 88(1), 176–85.

Keen, M. and Konrad, K. (2013), The Theory of International Tax Competition and Coordination, in: Auerbach, A.J., Chetty, R., Feldstein, M. and Saez, E. (eds.) *Handbook of Public Economics*, Volume 5, Amsterdam & Oxford: Elsevier, 257–328.

Keen, M. and Marchand, M. (1997), Fiscal Competition and the Pattern of Public Spending, *Journal of Public Economics* 66(1), 33–53.

Keen, M. and Smith, S. (1996), The Future of Value-added Tax in the European Union, *Economic Policy* 11(23), 373–420.

Keuschnigg, C. (2009), Corporate Taxation and the Welfare State, *CESifo Working Paper* No. 2557.

Keuschnigg, C. and Devereux, M.P. (2013), The Arm's Length Principle and Distortions to Multinational Firm Organization, *Journal of International Economics* 89(2), 432–40.

Keuschnigg, C. and Ribi, E. (2009), Outsourcing, Unemployment and Welfare Policy, *Journal of International Economics* 78(1), 168–76.

Kleven, H., C. Landais and Saez, E. (2013), Taxation and International Mobility of Superstars: Evidence from the European Football Market, *American Economic Review* 103(5), 1892–1924.

Leibrecht, M. and Hochgatterer, C. (2012), Tax Competition as a Cause of Falling Corporate Tax Rates: A Survey of Empirical Literature, *Journal of Economic Surveys* 26(4), 616–48.

Lockwood, B. and Migali, G. (2009), Did The Single Market Cause Competition in Excise Taxes? Evidence From EU Countries, *Economic Journal* 119(536), 406–29.

Loretz, S. (2008), Corporate Taxation in the OECD in a Wider Context, *Oxford Review of Economic Policy* 24(4), 639–60.

McLure, C.E. (2000), Implementing Subnational Value Added Taxes on Internal Trade: The Compensating VAT (CVAT), *International Tax and Public Finance* 7(6), 723–40.

Mintz, J. and Tulkens, H. (1986), Commodity Tax Competition between Member States of a Federation: Equilibrium and Efficiency, *Journal of Public Economics* 29(2), 133–72.

Mintz, J. and Weichenrieder, A. (2010), *The Indirect Side of Direct Investment*, Cambridge, MA: The MIT Press.

Nielsen, S.B. (2001), A Simple Model of Commodity Taxation and Cross-border Shopping, *Scandinavian Journal of Economics* 103(4), 599–623.

Oates, W. E. (1972), *Fiscal Federalism*, New York: Harcourt Brace Jovanovich.

OECD (2014), *Revenue Statistics 2013*, Organization of Economic Co-operation and Development, Paris: OECD Publishing.

Ohsawa, Y. (1999), Cross-border Shopping and Commodity Tax Competition Among Governments, *Regional Science and Urban Economics* 29(1), 33–51.

Parchet, R. (2013), Are Local Tax Rates Strategic Complements or Substitutes? *Unpublished Working Paper*, University of Lausanne.

Razin, A. and Sadka, E. (1991), International Tax Competition and Gains from Tax Harmonization, *Economics Letters* 37(1), 69–76

Sinn, H.-W. (1990), Tax Harmonization and Tax Competition in Europe, *European Economic Review* 34(2–3), 489–504.

Sinn, H.-W. (1997), The Selection Principle and Market Failure in Systems Competition, *Journal of Public Economics* 66(2), 247–74.

Tiebout, C. (1956), A Pure Theory of Local Expenditures, *Journal of Political Economy* 64(5), 416–24.

Tinbergen, J. (1953), *Report on Problems Raised by Different Turnover Tax Systems Applied within the Common Market*, High Authority of European Coal and Steel Community, Brussels (Tinbergen Report).

Wildasin, D.E. (1988), Nash Equilibria in Models of Fiscal Competition, *Journal of Public Economics* 35(2), 229–40.

Wilson, J.D. (1986), A Theory of Interregional Tax Competition, *Journal of Urban Economics* 19(3), 296–315.

Wilson, J.D. (1991), Tax Competition with Interregional Differences in Factor Endowments, *Regional Science and Urban Economics* 21(3), 423–52.

Wilson, J.D. (1999), Theories of Tax Competition, *National Tax Journal* 52(2), 269–304.

Zodrow, G.R. (2003), Tax Competition and Tax Coordination in the European Union, *International Tax and Public Finance* 10(6), 651–71.

Zodrow, G.R. and Mieszkowski, P. (1986), Pigou, Tiebout, Property Taxation and the Underprovision of Local Public Goods, *Journal of Urban Economics* 19(3), 356–70.

21

FINANCIAL MARKET INTEGRATION, REGULATION AND STABILITY

Angel Ubide[1]

1. Introduction

The creation of a single market in financial services has been, since the early years of the European Economic Community, one of the key objectives of the process of European integration. The so-called Segre Report[2] is an example of the early efforts – the report is dated November 1966 – to foster the lowering of restrictions to capital mobility and the integration of financial markets. After the launching of the euro, the decade prior to the 2007 crisis saw a rapid integration in the areas of money markets and government bonds. However, the crisis generated a rapid process of fragmentation in euro area financial markets, which remains unsolved. This chapter outlines the main drivers of the process of integration and the subsequent fragmentation, describes the policy measures adopted during the crisis in the areas of supervision and regulation, and assesses their effectiveness and their impact on current and future euro area financial market integration, regulation and stability.

2. The creation of the single market for financial services

A key objective of the European Union was the creation of an internal market via the dismantling of internal trade restrictions to promote the freedom of movement of people, capital, goods and services.[3] This was further promoted by the creation of a common currency, the euro, and the focus on the integration of the market for financial services. In December 1998, at the European Council meeting in Vienna, the leaders of the EU called for the prompt integration of the financial services sector among member nations, which led to a Financial Services Action Plan ("FSAP") that outlined specific steps to be taken to create an internal market for financial services. The heads of state of the EU approved the FSAP with a goal to integrate all EU financial markets by 2005. With this objective in mind, EU bank supervision was designed to be based on the legal principles of home country control, mutual recognition and minimum harmonization of laws. To accelerate this process, the Council of Ministers created a Committee of Wise Men led by Alexandre Lamfalussy, which issued a report recommending changes in the process of enacting legislation governing the securities markets in Europe. This process was extended to the other parts of the financial services sector – namely, banking and insurance. A similar group – the Giovannini Group – presented, in two reports published in 2001 and 2003, recommendations to lower barriers in cross-border clearing and settlement of securities in the EU.

3. The euro area financial markets prior to the crisis

Euro area financial markets expanded rapidly in the run up to the euro (see Table 21.1) and accelerated their integration after the introduction of notes and coins in 2002. By 2013, total stock market capitalization amounted to 65 percent of GDP, three times bigger than in 1992, while the amount of debt securities as share of GDP doubled over the same period. Despite this increase, euro area capital markets remain underdeveloped with respect to other countries, especially the US, Japan or Switzerland (see Figure 21.1).

Table 21.1 A comparison of financial market indicators

Size of capital markets

Percentage of GDP

Date	Euro Area	Switzerland	Sweden	United Kingdom	Japan	United States
1990–1994	1.50	3.01	1.62	2.36	3.02	1.85
1995–1999	1.76	4.07	2.06	3.10	3.07	2.70
2000–2004	2.27	4.52	2.57	3.57	2.31	3.07
2005–2009	2.63	4.56	3.38	4.37	2.32	3.28
2010–2013	2.80	4.23	3.88	5.00	2.13	3.16

Debt securities issued by non–financial corporations

Percentage of GDP

Date	Euro Area	Switzerland	Sweden	United Kingdom	Japan	United States
1990–1994	5.45	9.11	7.66	6.28	14.09	21.99
1995–1999	4.98	13.41	6.84	7.41	14.96	23.12
2000–2004	7.15	12.28	12.83	11.31	17.27	25.21
2005–2009	7.60	6.57	13.74	11.13	16.73	25.24
2010–2013	10.06	10.75	16.70	14.79	7.08	16.03

Venture capital financing (early stage)

Percentage of GDP

Date	Euro Area	Switzerland	Sweden	United Kingdom	United States
1996–1999	2.03	2.78	2.90	1.10	8.80
2000–2003	3.60	3.05	8.40	5.75	11.18
2004–2007	1.58	3.10	6.85	8.50	4.18
2008–2012	1.56	3.76	3.70	2.50	5.40

Source: ECB Financial Integration Indicators.

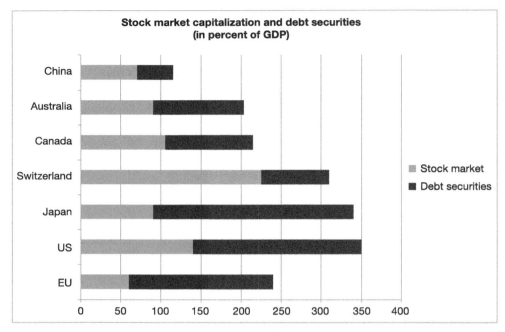

Figure 21.1 Stock market capitalization and debt securities (in percent of GDP)

The initial linking of national markets and structures was succeeded by veritable integration. For example, the 15 national large-value payment systems that were originally linked in 1999 to form TARGET were superseded in 2008 by a technically centralized, much more efficient system called TARGET2, which now links over 1000 banks in more than 20 countries.

Overall, the degree of integration varied greatly depending on the market segment. The unsecured money market has been fully integrated since shortly after the introduction of the euro. Trading, quoting and settlement operations became denominated in euros. EURIBOR (euro interbank offered rate, the rate at which euro interbank term deposits are offered by one prime bank to another), EONIA (euro overnight index average) and EUREPO (the rate at which one prime bank offers funds to another in exchange for collateral) became the reference interest rates in the euro area and the cross country standard deviation of these reference rates across euro area countries collapsed towards zero.

Government bond markets were significantly integrated, but some yield differentials remained. At the time, this convergence in long term yields towards the German yield curve was hailed by the ECB as a sign of success of the euro. However, during the crisis, some would criticize this narrowness of yield differentials as a market failure. Measures of beta convergence (the correlation of changes in the 10 year rate of a given country with respect to the German 10 year rate) moved towards 1, signaling "perfect integration".[4] Corporate bond markets, which grew considerably since the advent of the single currency (see Table 21.1), also displayed a high degree of integration (measured as the declining share of variation explained by individual country effects). Similarly, equity returns became increasingly determined by common factors – although the ownership of listed companies remained predominantly national.

However, retail banking markets remained generally much less integrated, with high segmentation along national lines, mostly the result of domestic consolidation, with very few cross border groups (Dexia and Fortis being the most prominent). A national champions doctrine prevailed,[5] fending off proposals for the formation of cross border groups (for example the strong opposition by the Bank of Italy to BBVA's bid for Banco di Napoli, which derailed the operation). Concentration remained high, especially in small countries, with the top five banks holding more than 50 percent of market share, while the penetration of foreign banks remained very low, with average shares around 10–15 percent (though larger in smaller countries).[6]

In hindsight, the pattern of integration of euro area financial markets presented two problematic aspects. First, despite the development of the European corporate bond market, the funding of the euro area economy, especially of small and medium-sized enterprises (SMEs), remained dominated by large domestic banks. In addition, the domestic consolidation of banks, combined with the rapid expansion of credit in some countries, created banking groups that, in some cases, became very large as shares of national GDP (with several euro area countries, at the peak of the crisis, having banking sectors with assets well above 300 percent of GDP). This nationalization of banking was at the heart of the vicious link between sovereigns and banks that drove the crisis.[7] Second, the combination of national banking and euro area monetary policy implied that the geographical domain of monetary policy and that of prudential supervision no longer coincided. Supervision was based on the principles of mutual recognition and home country control, with domestic banks, subsidiaries of foreign banks and branches of non EU banks supervised by the domestic authorities, while branches of EU banks were supervised by their home supervisors. Different countries had different supervisory structures, some at the central bank, some separated by sectors, others integrated in a supervisory authority. In addition to national supervisors there was a EU-level superstructure (albeit with rather limited scope), with the Banking Advisory Committee advising the Commission on broad supervisory issues, and the Banking Supervisory Committee at the ECB advising on broad issues of financial stability. Deposit insurance remained strictly domestic, with a minimum €20,000 coverage amount harmonized across EU countries. Several reports, most notably the so called "Brouwer report",[8] suggested room for improvement, including deeper exchange of confidential supervisory information, enhanced convergence of supervisory practices and stronger involvement of central banks in supervisory coordination, especially in times of stress. Belaisch et al. (2001) highlighted the need to improve the structure to deal with cross country exchanges of information, the management of potential liquidity crises, and the potential moral hazard issues that could arise from the combination of too big to fail local banks and domestic provision of liquidity by the national central banks. The crisis showed that some of these warnings were well founded.

4. The crisis and the fragmentation of the euro area financial system

This pre-crisis framework proved to be unable to withstand the financial crisis, in particular its systemic nature. By the time the financial crisis spread to Europe in 2008, there were 27 different regulatory systems for banks in place, largely based on national rules and national rescue measures with some limited European minimum rules and coordination mechanisms. There were no clear tools in place to efficiently deal with the collapse of large cross-border banks. This lack of a common and shared approach to banking crisis management, exacerbated by the lack of political solidarity that led to the decision, in 2010, not to mutualize the management and resolution of the banking crisis,[9] amplified the impact of the crisis by creating a vicious loop between sovereigns and banks and delayed the recovery by creating the "legacy assets" doctrine. This legacy assets doctrine – namely that countries would have to deal with the losses induced by the crisis at the national level before any mutualization could take place – has been at the core of the decision not to allow the ESM to directly recapitalize banks, something that would have softened the impact of the crisis in the hardest hit countries. The lack of homogeneous and integrated supervision became an impediment for the implementation of early and credible stress testing, recapitalization and resolution of banks across euro area. The insufficient risk sharing properties of the euro area economy, mostly the lack of cross border ownership of banks, which concentrated the losses at the national level, and the lack of a eurobond that would break links between governments and banks, and would have allowed policy to remain countercyclical, exacerbated the impact of the crisis.

The combination of these institutional and economic shortcomings, combined with the ECB's decision not to undertake quantitative easing (interpreted by markets as unwillingness to be a buyer of last resort and, thus, to defend the euro) and the German decision to push for PSI (Private Sector Involvement, namely requiring debt restructuring as a condition for a rescue package) in Greece and openly contemplate Greece's exit from the euro (which led markets to price redenomination risk) created the conditions for contagion to other countries susceptible to be bailed out – such as Spain or Italy – resulting in their bonds being priced as credit (thus based on default probabilities and loss given default) rather than bonds (based on expected nominal GDP growth), leading to a procyclical behavior of interest rates (increasing as growth prospects deteriorated) in some countries and a sharp fragmentation of euro area financial markets.[10]

In addition to these macro factors, financial fragmentation was boosted by the presence of elevated bank counterparty risks, regulatory hurdles (for example higher liquidity ratios and "bail-in" procedures), and the increased subsidiarization of banks' business models (exacerbated by the regulatory "ring-fencing" in some countries that fostered home bias). This undermined cross-border bank flows, particularly to the periphery, and contributed to diverging term funding costs with the core.

As a result there was a sharp increase in sovereign bond spreads. Fragmentation could also be observed in several areas at the micro level: First, a sharp decline in cross border banking flows (see Table 21.2). Both core and periphery banks retrenched throughout the crisis, withdrawing capital to domestic markets and reducing their foreign lending, especially in core countries. Most periphery banks also scaled back their lending to each other, while the volume of euro area unsecured overnight interbank activity more than halved since the

Table 21.2 Change in cross-border bank holdings during the crisis

To \ From	Germany	France	Italy	Spain	Portugal	Ireland	Greece
Germany		−1.8	−5.2	−10.3	−8.2	−43.2	−10.6
France	−2.1		−5.2	−4.1	−4.2	−17.6	−5
Italy	−4.1	−0.5		−0.4	−3	−5.5	−2.4
Spain	0.1	−0.8	−0.4		2.3	−4.6	0
Portugal	−0.3	0	0	−0.2		0.7	0.7
Ireland	−1.5	−0.9	−2.2	−2.1	−2.1		−2.9
Greece	0	0.2	0	0	0	0	

Source: BIS and own calculations.

Notes: Holdings in percent of counterparty country GDP, 2008Q1–2012Q2.

start of the crisis. Second, a material increase in banks' funding costs, with growing divergence between core and periphery driven mainly by rising sovereign periphery spreads (see Figures 21.2 and 21.3). The average spread (to benchmark rates) for periphery banks at issuance was about 380 basis points in early 2013, about 250 basis points above their counterparts in the core. Prior to the crisis, the spread between core and periphery banks was negligible. Third, a large increase in the reliance of periphery banks on deposits. In particular, the spreads over Germany have increased substantially for term deposits (over two years), reflecting the squeeze in term funding and adding further pressure to bank profitability. Fourth, a sharp divergence in lending conditions across euro area countries, with strong differences in lending rates and in the likelihood of receiving a credit across different countries (see Figure 21.4).[11]

Fragmentation was also affected by the pricing by markets of "redenomination risk". This could be observed in the increase in the number of speculative short future contracts in euros and a widening of the spread in bonds issued by periphery banks in different jurisdictions, suggesting some currency related risk premium. This currency risk premium declined markedly after Draghi's famous "whatever it takes" London speech convinced market participants that the probability of euro break up was small.

The combination of these and other factors were reflected in periphery bank CDS spreads, with a sharp increase in the divergence between core and periphery. After showing some improvement in the immediate wake of the OMTs announcement, spreads reached 430 basis points at the end of March 2013 (about 375 basis points above early 2008 levels), declining thereafter as financial conditions, especially sovereign spreads, improved. This rise in spreads coincided with lower bond issuances, for both core and periphery banks. At the same time, the relative volume of euro area corporate bond issuance increased, pointing to a degree of disintermediation and unmet demand by banks for corporate borrowing.

5. The crisis response

In response to the financial crisis the euro area and the EU pursued a number of initiatives to create a safer and sounder financial sector, in two stages.[12] Initially, the response was directed towards strengthening EU supervisory institutions and the creation of a single rulebook for all financial institutions, including stronger prudential requirements for banks, improved depositor protection, and rules for managing failing banks. As the crisis deepened and the future of the euro area was at risk, new euro area institutions were created in the context of the banking union project, and the Single Supervisory Mechanism (SSM), the Single Resolution Mechanism (SRM) and the Single Resolution Fund (SRF) were established.

5.1 Reinforcing the European Union supervisory and regulatory framework

The report of a high level group chaired by Jacques de Larosière in February 2009 led to the creation of three EU supervisory authorities (ESAs), which were established on January 1 2011 to create an EU supervisory architecture: (1) the European Banking Authority (EBA), to deal with bank supervision, including the supervision of the recapitalization of banks; (2) the European Securities and Markets Authority (ESMA), to deal with the supervision of capital markets and credit rating agencies and trade repositories; and (3) the European Insurance and Occupational Pensions Authority (EIOPA), to deal with insurance supervision.

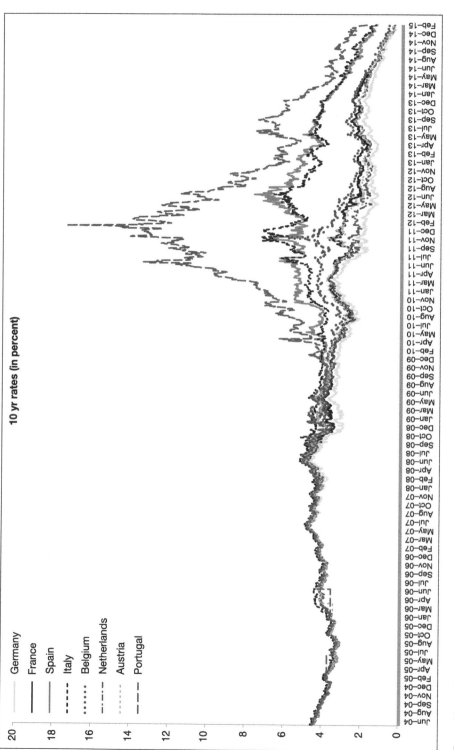

Figure 21.2 Ten year rates (in percent)

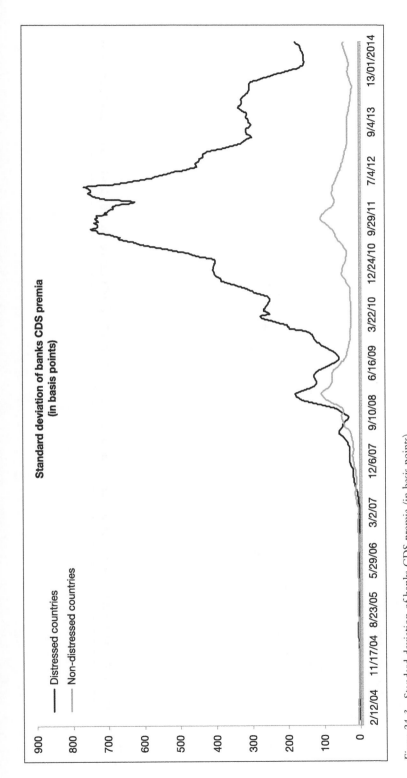

Figure 21.3 Standard deviation of banks CDS premia (in basis points)

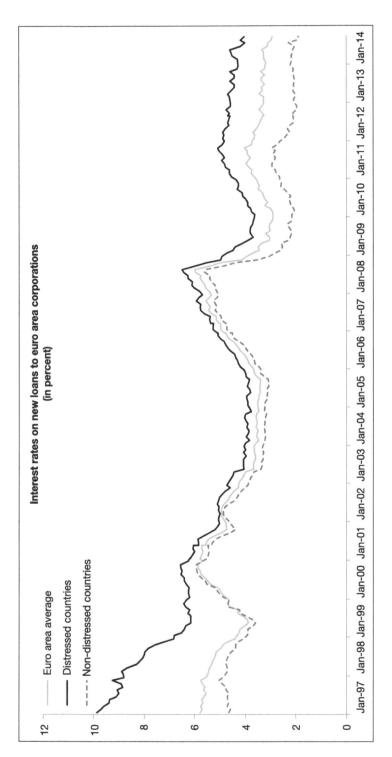

Figure 21.4 Interest rates on new loans to euro area corporations (in percent)

In addition, a European Systemic Risk Board (ESRB) was established to monitor and assess potential threats to financial stability that arise from macro-economic developments and from developments within the financial system as a whole ("macro-prudential supervision").

The European Council of June 2009 decided to create a single rulebook applicable to all financial institutions in the Single Market, with the aim to close regulatory loopholes and guarantee a level playing field for banks. The backbone of the single rulebook was stronger prudential requirements, via a new Capital Requirements Directive (CRD IV), which would transpose the new global standards on bank capital (the Basel III agreement) into the EU legal framework and tackle some of the vulnerabilities shown by the banking institutions during the crisis, namely the insufficient level of capital, both in quantity and in quality. These new rules were scheduled to apply from January 1 2014.

In addition, and in an attempt to minimize the use of budgetary resources in the resolution of banks and thus break the link between banks and sovereigns, the European authorities adopted the Directive on Bank Recovery and Resolution (BRRD). This directive determines the rules for how EU banks in difficulties are restructured, and how losses and costs are allocated to the banks' shareholders and creditors. In a nutshell, if a bank needs to be rescued, the authorities will follow a pre-determined bail-in order. Shareholders and other creditors who invest in bank capital (such as holders of convertible bonds and junior bonds) will bear losses first, for an amount of up to 8 percent of the bank's assets. Deposits under €100,000 would be protected[13] and the deposit guarantee scheme would make a contribution equivalent to the amount it would have born if the institution had been liquidated. If after this bail-in further public resources are needed, the Directive relies on a network of national authorities and resolution funds to resolve banks, in the context of the SRM and SRF (see discussion below).[14]

5.2 The banking union

As the crisis worsened in 2011 and markets started to doubt the future viability of the euro area, it became clear that a deeper integration of the euro area banking system supervision and regulation was needed in order to break the links between banking sector fragilities and sovereign risk. In June 2012, the European leaders agreed to start the process to form a banking union (for countries of the euro area, but non-euro area countries could also join), starting by establishing an SSM and an SRM for banks, including a SRF.

The SSM creates a new system of financial supervision comprising the ECB and the national competent authorities of participating EU countries, which include all euro area countries but also some non-euro area countries who have decided to participate. Specific tasks relating to the prudential supervision of credit institutions are conferred on the ECB according to Article 127(6) of the Treaty on the Functioning of the European Union. The ECB became responsible for the effective and consistent functioning of the SSM, cooperating with the national competent authorities of participating EU countries, and assumed its new banking supervision responsibilities in November 2014, 12 months after the SSM Regulation creating the supervisor entered into force.

The decision on which credit institutions were to be supervised by the SSM was based on four main criteria: (1) the total value of their assets; (2) the importance for the economy of the country in which they are located or the EU as a whole; (3) the significance of their cross-border activities; and (4) whether they have requested or received public financial assistance from the European Stability Mechanism (ESM) or the European Financial Stability Facility (EFSF). The result is that the ECB will directly supervise around 130 credit institutions, representing almost 85 percent of total banking assets in the euro area and holding assets worth about 250 percent of euro area's GDP. In each participating country, at least the three most significant credit institutions are subject to direct supervision by the ECB, irrespective of their absolute size. All other credit institutions in the participating countries will continue to be supervised by the national competent authorities.[15] The ECB can decide at any time to exercise direct supervision of any one of these credit institutions in order to ensure consistent application of a high supervisory standard.[16]

During the transitional phase to the creation of the SSM and to allow the ECB to start its supervisory mandate with a clean sheet, the ECB decided to embark in a "comprehensive assessment" of the euro area banking sector, built on two pillars. The first was an asset quality review (AQR) of banks' assets as per December 31 2013. The assessment was based on a capital benchmark of 8 percent common equity Tier 1. The second pillar was a stress test, to provide a forward-looking view of banks' shock-absorption capacity under stress.[17] The capital thresholds for the baseline and adverse scenarios were decided to be 8 percent and 5 percent common equity Tier 1 respectively. The methodology and underlying assumptions covered a wide range of risks including credit and market risks, exposures towards securitization, sovereign and funding risks. The adverse scenario included four systemic risks assessed as the most pertinent threats to the stability of the EU banking sector. First, an increase in global bond yields amplified by an abrupt reversal in risk assessment, especially towards emerging market economies; second, a deterioration of credit quality in countries with feeble demand; third, a stalling of policy reforms jeopardizing confidence in the sustainability of public finances; and fourth, the lack of necessary bank balance sheet repair to maintain affordable market funding. Banks were expected to raise capital (CET1) to cover a capital shortfall arising from the AQR or baseline scenario within six months. For capital shortfalls arising from the adverse scenario, banks would have nine months to raise capital, on the basis of an agreed capital plan, so long as regulatory minima are respected. The periods of six or nine months would start from the release of the comprehensive assessment results.[18] The banks' capital plans should reflect the BBRD directive provisions and show that they will first draw on private sources of funding to strengthen their capital positions so as to meet the required targets, including retained earnings, reduced bonus payments, new issuances of common equity, suitably strong contingent capital, and sales of selected assets at market prices or reductions of RWAs associated with restructuring plans agreed with the European Commission.

Following the creation of the SSM, and in line with the recommendations of several analysts[19] that suggested the need for matching the perimeter of supervision and resolution, the European authorities created the SRM,[20] foreseeing that resolution decisions will be prepared and monitored centrally by a Single Resolution Board (SRB), which will be charged with applying the Single Rulebook on bank resolution provided for in the BRRD Directive to the banks in the participating Member States.

The SRM will be directly responsible for the resolution of all banks (about 6,000) in Member States participating in the banking union, with a structure mirroring that of the SSM. The SRB is directly responsible for the resolution of entities directly supervised by the ECB and cross-border groups, while the national resolution authorities are responsible for all other entities, except where a resolution scheme foresees the use of the SRF. In such cases, the SRB becomes competent for the resolution of the entity concerned regardless of its size.

Decision-making at SRM is built around a Board consisting of a Chairman, a Vice Chair, four permanent members, and the relevant national authorities, with the ECB and the

European Commission as permanent observers. Upon notification from the ECB that a bank is failing or likely to fail the Board will adopt a resolution scheme including relevant resolution tools and any use of the SRF. Three conditions need to be determined for resolution: (1) that a bank is failing or likely to fail, (2) that there are no alternative private solutions, and (3) that a resolution action is necessary in the public interest (the Board remains ultimately responsible to determine whether the resolution action is necessary in the public interest). All this is foreseen to happen within very tight deadlines, in total 32 hours, in order to allow resolving an ailing bank over the weekend. National authorities are in charge of implementing the resolution decisions in line with national company and insolvency law, under the monitoring of the Board who, should a national resolution authority not comply with its decision, can directly address executive orders to the troubled banks.

The bank SRF is set up under the control of the SRB to ensure the availability of medium-term funding support to enable the bank (either in its original form, through a bridge bank or as an asset management vehicle – bad bank) to continue operating while it is being restructured. The SRF is composed of national compartments for a transitional phase of eight years, and is expected to be built up over time by contributions from the banking sector raised at the national level by the national resolution authorities. All the banks in the participating Member States are expected to contribute to the SRF. The SRF has a target level of €55 billion, or 1 percent of deposits of the banking system (vs. current assets of the financial system of about €25 trillion and capital of about €1 trillion) and can borrow from the markets if decided by the Board. The resources accumulated in the national compartments would be progressively mutualized over the eight year period, starting with 40 percent of these resources in the first year and 60 percent the second year (an improvement with respect to the initial plan of a 10 year transition period with a linear mutualization schedule).

In order to avoid any risk of legal challenges, certain elements related to the functioning of the SRF are regulated in an intergovernmental agreement between the participating Member States. These include the transfer of the contributions raised by the national resolution authorities to the national compartments; the mutualization schedule of the funds available in the national compartments; the replenishment of the compartments; the order in which financial resources are mobilized to cover resolution costs ("waterfall"); the temporary lending among national compartments; the possible participation of the non-euro area Member States into the SRM; the bail-in conditionality; and the compensation provisions to the benefit of those Member States which do not participate in the SRM. The SRM is expected to become fully operative in January 2016 once the intergovernmental agreement has been ratified by Member States participating in the SSM/SRM that represent 90 percent of the aggregate of the weighted votes of all participating Member States.

6. An assessment of the banking union and its economic impact

The banking union has been hailed as one the key European achievements of the last few years.[21] No doubt, it has been a major change in the economic infrastructure of the euro area. But process should not be confused with outcomes. In order to assess the banking union project and its potential impact, there are three benchmarks. First, assess it versus its original purpose as stated at its launch. Second, assess it as regards the potential medium-term implications of the current state of the banking union project, regardless of its original purpose. Third, assess it as far as pending issues in order to make it a more perfect banking union. This section discusses these three issues in turn.

First we start by clarifying the original purpose of the banking union. The banking union project was launched at the June 29 2012 Euro Area Summit with the objective to "break the vicious circle between sovereigns and banks", and with a commitment to launch the SSM and establish a mechanism at the European Stability Mechanism (ESM) for the direct recapitalization of banks. This provides a benchmark to evaluate whether the banking union has delivered in the near term. The answer is both no, and yes.

No, because the vicious circle between sovereigns and banks was broken by the decision to end the discussion on Greek exit from the euro area and by the actions of the ECB (especially the launching of OMT), not by the launching of the banking union. In fact, one of the key measures intended to break the vicious circle, namely the direct bank recapitalization by the ESM, was quickly eliminated from the decision set, and the SSM only became effective in late 2014. Yes, because the decision to launch the banking union might have been a necessary condition for the ECB's decision to launch the OMT,[22] and because the SSM has led to a more rigorous AQR and stress test that will likely end doubts about the solvency of the euro area banking system. Therefore, the banking union has likely been a positive development, but not for the reasons that were envisaged initially.

Second, beyond the crisis management impact in the near term, the banking union is a permanent change to the economic infrastructure of the euro area, with an important potential impact over the medium term. As discussed above, banking in the euro area was organized along national lines, in many respects. For example, the proliferation of national champions, which reduced the cross border risk sharing via equity holdings. The national supervisory frameworks, which lead to different approaches to supervision and to practices that amplified the fragmentation during the crisis. The national approach to crisis management, with a conscious decision to harmonize but not mutualize the resolution of the banking crisis. And the national approach to crisis resolution, with the creation of the so called "legacy assets" doctrine.

The banking union has made some changes to this national approach to banking, with the creation of the SSM, the SRF, and the BRRD legislation. Therefore there have been plenty of institutional changes. But, again, process should not be confused with outcomes. It is important to take a step back and discuss the political context in which these decisions have taken place. The banking union was launched during the acute phase of the euro area crisis because it was politically easier than what would have been the optimal strategy, starting a program of eurobonds – establishing the SSM didn't require a Treaty change, as the Maastricht Treaty already allowed for the ECB to have supervisory functions. The design of the banking union contained three key political imperatives: (1) minimizing the near term use of tax payer money; (2) minimizing the moral hazard at the national government level by designing a minimalistic European backstop; and (3) minimizing moral hazard at financial market level by introducing mandatory bail-ins via the BRRD legislation. These political premises could be summarized in one sentence: maximizing national bail-ins (as most investors in banks are domestic) to minimize European bail outs.

Therefore, this banking union was born out of these political restrictions at a time of maximum stress, rather than designed with optimality in mind, and thus it was bound to be suboptimal. In fact, it should be clear that the key objective of the banking union should have been to minimize the GDP cost of a systemic crisis, not to minimize the near term use of tax payer money. This is an example of what happens when new systems are designed in a backward looking manner, to avoid a repetition of past crises, and not to maximize efficiency in future crises. This suboptimal design implies that there are positive and negative outcomes of this banking union project.

The potential positive outcomes from the banking union project include better and more efficient supervisory information sharing – recall that until the establishment of the SSM there was very little cross country exchange of supervisory information, at times due to legal restrictions but often reflecting reputational fears. There should also be an end to supervisory fragmentation, both in methods (thus leveling the playing field) and in practices (during the crunch of the crisis, some national supervisors exacerbated the fragmentation by forcing banks to curtail cross border exposures to other euro area countries), and a reduction in national supervisory capture. In the end, the supervisory and regulatory framework of the European banking system will be more homogeneous and, likely, stronger and more robust.

However, there are also potentially negative aspects of the current banking union framework. As the resolution leg of the banking union remains mostly domestic, the national fragmentation in banking ownership is likely to continue. National authorities will likely ensure that banks don't grow too big for the national GDP, creating a banking sector that may be efficient for each individual country but that is likely to be inefficient for the euro area as a whole. There is no reason why banking should represent similar shares of GDP in all euro area countries. In addition, it is likely that national governments will press banks not to invest cross borders as the potential repercussions of a failure will be borne by national budgets. After all, the resolution framework with mostly centralized decision-making but national budgetary repercussions is akin to taxation without representation. We may have already seen this process at work: in none of the euro area countries that have suffered a banking crisis in the last few years has there been major foreign acquisitions of banks as a result of the process. The banking sectors of these countries (Spain, Ireland, Portugal, Greece) are smaller and more concentrated, but remain nationally owned. Thus, the clearest risk is that there will be European supervision but the business of banking will remain national. European supervisions for national banking. That would not be a banking union.

There are important pending issues to address in the current banking union project. First, this is a banking union to deal with small problems, not to deal with systemic events, as there is no access to a budget or central bank. An ESM line of credit for the SRF would have been an important step in this direction (as recommended in Ubide (2013a)). In some sense, this project is born under the assumption of no further systemic crises and, if and when they happen, something will have to be improvised. Second, for as long as insolvency frameworks remain national, the SRM will have to rely on national resolution authorities and thus will be European only in name.[23] Third, the legislation imposing forced bail-ins (BRRD) includes many provisions that haven't been tested in practice and could be very risky in a systemic crisis, as it is impossible to foresee ex ante what will be systemic.[24] Fourth, national champions will continue to be prevalent – in fact bigger, as we have seen in the consolidation process in the crisis countries, with very little foreign participation, as discussed above. It is logical: after all, resolution is a very politically sensitive issue that deals with the allocation of losses and property rights, and may make sense to keep it domestic. But the outcome is no increase in risk sharing via cross equity holdings. Similarly, the national home bias with government bonds will remain intact. It is logical: unless there are eurobonds, it will be optimal from a business perspective for banks to hold national bonds.

Fifth, it will be challenging for the SSM to perform supervision from a truly European perspective. Supervisors at the ECB will come from diverse backgrounds and nationalities, but the supervisory culture should be European. The SSM regulation contains provisions regarding independence and the ECB has created Joint Supervisory Teams consisting of supervisors from different countries, to be able to blend local expertise and a European view. The first crisis that the SSM has to deal with will show the strength of this new culture. Finally, there are legitimate question marks about institutional design. The ECB could be confronted with potential conflicts between monetary policy and supervision – and not just when facing an inflationary threat, as the old literature on separation of monetary policy and supervision argued, but also in a deflationary situation, as the low inflation environment of 2013–15 showed. One could argue that the supervisory mandate and the desire to implement as tough an AQR as possible have interfered with the ECB's monetary policy mandate and been one of the reasons why the ECB was failing to meet its price stability mandate. In addition, failure to properly manage a banking crisis could generate negative credibility spillovers on the ECB's monetary policy mission. Given the magnitude of the enterprise, especially in terms of managing teams of supervisors of different nationalities and, at times, likely conflicting loyalties, the probability of failure should not be overlooked. This institutional complexity may be compounded by the fact that the perimeter of monetary policy may not coincide with the perimeter of the banking union (for example, Bulgaria recently requested to join the SSM). Once the SSM is up and running, it will be necessary to have another look about the appropriateness of the institutional design and, possibly, relocate supervision outside of the ECB and into an independent agency.

Finally, the economic impact of the new bail-in culture that stems from the BRRD remains very unclear. It is possible that this segments the banking sector into bail-in-able small banks with higher financing costs and systematically important financial institutions (SIFIs) that avoid the bail-ins by paying in advance, via higher capital requirements, for their too big to fail nature. If so, unless capital market financing develops efficiently for SMEs, this could constrain the size of euro area SMEs, jeopardizing productivity growth (it has become more evident that size and scalability of SMEs is the key to productivity growth). This could offset any benefit that could derive from a reduction of moral hazard risk.

7. Conclusion

The euro area crisis has left many scars and a fragile financial sector with a high degree of fragmentation. Five years after the start of the financial crisis the euro area financial sector was barely starting to heal after a very intense credit crunch. At the same time, the lack of contagion to the rest of the euro area from the volatility generated by the 2014 Greek elections and the uncertainty arising from the new Syriza government in early 2015 suggests that the cumulative effect of the many policy actions since the crisis, supported by the ECB's quantitative easing program, were having the desired positive effect.

The AQR and the stress tests undertaken prior to the launching of the SSM served to end the debate on the capitalization of the European banking sector which, combined with the new supervisory and regulatory structure, should create the foundation for a sustainable economic recovery. But the euro area financial market remains too bank centric and that has detrimental consequences for growth.[25] The ECB decision to start purchasing Asset Backed Securities (ABS) and Covered Bonds to foster the creation of a liquid market in these instruments should contribute to diversifying the sources of funding for the euro area economy, and the initiatives to foster the creation of a capital markets union should ensure that funding for small firms becomes more balanced and resilient to shocks to specific institutions.[26] There are many areas where euro area capital markets can become more efficient and harmonized, such as data provision, regulatory and supervisory design and enforcement, corporate governance and legislation, insolvency provisions, and tax treatment of assets. This will generate a better allocation of capital within the euro area and within sectors and a more effective management of risks.

Nevertheless, this has to be complemented with a more balanced policy mix that combines demand stimulus and productivity increasing reforms to regenerate growth.[27] Insufficient growth will continue to be a major financial stability risk in the euro area. The ECB's quantitative easing program is a very welcome step in that regard, as it has broken a very detrimental taboo – that the ECB couldn't possibly buy government bonds – and has a high probability of success in contributing to lifting euro area growth

The banking union and the capital markets union project are good steps in the right direction towards completing the economic infrastructure of the euro area, but a lot remains to be done in order to restore euro area financial intermediation to pre-crisis levels of efficiency. For example, as the SSM starts to operate, it will be important to assess if the expected lowering of barriers to intra euro-area liquidity materializes and if cross border barriers to ownership of financial groups are softened. In addition, the euro area needs to continue to work towards completing its economic infrastructure, and that must include the establishment of eurobonds. The banking union is a complement, not an alternative, to eurobonds. Without eurobonds, the euro area will just be a fixed exchange rate regime, not a monetary union.

Notes

1 I would like to thank Jacob Kirkegaard, Nicolas Veron and participants at the PIIE European Breakfast for many discussions on this issue. All views and errors are my own.
2 See European Commission (1996).
3 See the extensive discussion in European Commission (1996).
4 See ECB (2005).
5 See the discussion in Belaisch et al. (2000).
6 See the discussion in Sapir and Wolff (2013).
7 Belaisch et al. (2000) were already alerting against the financial stability implications of the trend towards domestic consolidation.
8 See Economic and Financial Committee (2001).
9 This issue is elaborated in detail in Bastasin (2012) and Ubide (2013a).
10 For further discussion on fragmentation see, for example, Ali Al-Eyd and Berkmen (2013).
11 See OECD (2013).
12 The creation of firewalls, first the EFSF and then ESM, and the Troika programs in Greece, Ireland, Portugal and Cyprus, was certainly part of this process, but its discussion remains outside the scope of this chapter. For an extensive discussion see, for example, Cline (2014).
13 This protection of deposits under 100,000 EUR was made explicit after the chaotic management of the rescue program in Cyprus.
14 The Spanish bank rescue program, based on the triangle of bail-ins, a dedicated rescue fund (the FROB) and a bad bank (the SAREB) funded by a public-private consortium with a private majority stake (so that it doesn't have to be accounted as public debt), has become the benchmark for rescues in the euro area.
15 The decision on where to set the lower boundary in order to exclude smaller banks was explicitly targeted at excluding the German Sparkassen from the SSM supervision, in an example of the German dominance of the process.
16 The list of supervised institutions can be found at ECB (2014).
17 The stress test methodology and the scenarios were published by the EBA in mid-2014, see www.eba.europa.eu/-/eba-publishes-common-methodology-and-scenario-for-2014-eu-banks-stress-test.
18 To illustrate the scope and the comprehensiveness of the AQR, a total of around 760 banking book portfolios were selected from the 128 banks for a detailed examination. The AQR covered €3.72 trillion of risk-weighted assets (RWA), representing 58 percent of the total credit RWA of all banks

in the exercise. The examination involved the review of approximately 135,000 credit files, involving over 6.000 supervisors, external auditing staff, consultants and independent specialist appraisers.

19 See, for example, Ubide (2014).
20 The legal basis for the SRM Regulation is Article 114 of the Treaty on the Functioning of the European Union (TFEU), which allows the adoption of measures for the approximation of national provisions aiming at the establishment and functioning of the Single Market.
21 For an assessment of the banking union, see Veron (2013) and Ubide (2013a,b).
22 Veron (2014) makes this argument forcefully. Others are more skeptical.
23 See Veron (2014).
24 This is a similar mistake to the IMF's recent policy proposals to deal with programs in situations of uncertainty about debt sustainability, see Goyal et al. (2013) and Rediker and Ubide (2014).
25 See, for example, Langfield and Pagano (2014).
26 See European Commission (2015).
27 See Posen and Ubide (2014).

References

Al-Eyd, A. and Berkmen, S.P. (2013), Fragmentation and Monetary Policy in the Euro Area, *IMF Working Paper* 13/208.

Bastasin, C. (2012), *Saving Europe: How National Politics Nearly Destroyed the Euro*, Washington: Brookings Institution Press.

Belaisch, A., Kodres, L., Levy, J., and Ubide, A. (2001), Euro Area Banking at the Cross Roads, *IMF Working Paper* 01/28.

Cline, W.R. (2014), *Managing the Euro Area Debt Crisis*, Washington: Peterson Institute for International Economics.

ECB (2005), *Indicators of Financial Integration in the Euro Area*, Frankfurt: European Central Bank.

ECB (2014), List of Supervised Entities Notified of the ECB's Intention to Consider them Significant, available at www.bankingsupervision.europa.eu/banking/list/who/html/index.en.html.

Economic and Financial Committee (2001), Report on Financial Crisis Management/Brouwer Report, Brussels: Economic and Financial Committee.

European Commission (1996), The Development of a European Capital Market, Brussels: European Commission.

European Commission (2015), Initial Reflections on the Obstacles to the Development of Deep and Integrated EU Capital Markets, Commission Staff Working Document.

Goyal, R., Brooks, P.K., Pradhan, M., Tressel, T., dell'Arriccia, G., Leckow, R., and Pazarbasioglu, C. (2013), A Banking Union for the Euro Area, *IMF Staff Discussion Note* 13/01.

Langfield, S. and Pagano, M. (2014), Bank Bias in Europe: Effects on Systemic Risk and Growth, European Central Bank and Università die Napoli Federico II.

OECD (2013), *Financing SMEs and Entrepreneurs: An OECD Scoreboard*, Paris: OECD Publishing.

Posen, A. and Ubide, A. (2014), Rebuilding Europe's Common Future: Combining Growth and Reform in the Euro Area, *PIIE Briefing* 14–5.

Rediker, D. and Ubide, A. (2014), The IMF is Courting New Risks with a Change in Policy on Debt Restructuring, *RealTime Economic Issues*, available at http://blogs.piie.com/realtime/?p=4220.

Sapir, A. and Wolff, G.B. (2013), The Neglected Side of Banking Union: Reshaping Europe's Financial System, presented at the informal ECOFIN meeting in Vilnius on 14 September 2013.

Ubide, A. (2013a), How to Form a More Perfect Banking Union, *PIIE Policy Brief* 13–23.

Ubide, A. (2013b), Reengineering EMU for an Uncertain World, *PIIE Policy Brief* 13–4.

Ubide, A. (2014), Is the ECB failing its Price Stability Mandate?, *PIIE Policy Brief* 14–5.

Veron, N. (2013), A Realistic Bridge Towards European Banking Union, *PIIE Policy Brief* 13–17.

Veron, N. (2014), European Banking Union: Current Outlook and Short-Term Choices, presented before the Portuguese Parliament on 26 February 2014.

PART VI

The crisis

22

THE CRISIS IN RETROSPECT

Causes, effects and policy responses

Fritz Breuss

"Why No One Predicted the Crisis?" Her Majesty The Queen at a visit to the LSE, London,
5 November 2008

1. Introduction

In recent years we witnessed not only "the crisis" but a sequence of crises: the US subprime
and banking crises triggered the global financial crisis (GFC) in 2008/09 which in turn
caused the "Great Recession"[1] in 2009 with the biggest drop in GDP since the Second World
War in the industrialized world. The Euro area has been hit by two crises. The first, the GFC
had external (US) origin and caused a deep recession. The second, the "Euro crisis" was
homemade. It was the result of systemic failures of the European Monetary Union's (EMU's)
policy design and due to the lack of necessary structural adjustments.

2. The Global Financial Crisis

It seems to be the peculiarity of great events that – although the facts are clear – the narrative
of the reasons are manifold.[2] This was true in explaining the reasons for the "Great Depression"
in the 1930s and it happens again in the case of the GFC, starting in 2008, followed by the
"Great Recession" in 2009 (see Lo, 2012).

2.1 The causes

The best and most compact summary of the description of the causes and the emergence of
the GFC is provided by the "Financial Crisis Inquiry Commission" (2011: XVI):

> It was the collapse of the housing bubble – fuelled by low interest rates,[3] easy and
> available credit, scant regulation, and toxic mortgages – that was the spark that ignited
> a string of events, which led to a full-blown crisis in the fall of 2008. Trillions of dollars
> in risky mortgages had become embedded throughout the financial system, as
> mortgage-related securities (CDOs) were packaged, repackaged, and sold to investors
> around the world. When the bubble burst,[4] hundreds of billions of dollars in losses in

mortgages and mortgage-related securities shook markets as well as financial institutions that had significant exposures to those mortgages and had borrowed heavily against them. This happened not just in the United States but around the world. The losses were magnified by derivatives such as synthetic securities.

The crisis reached seismic proportions in September 2008 with the failure of Lehman Brothers and the impending collapse of the insurance giant American International Group (AIG). Panic fanned by a lack of transparency of the balance sheets of major financial institutions, coupled with a tangle of interconnections among institutions perceived to be "too big to fail," caused the credit markets to seize up. Trading ground to a halt. The stock market plummeted. The economy plunged into a deep recession.

Figure 22.1 summarizes this story of the evolution of the multiple crises.

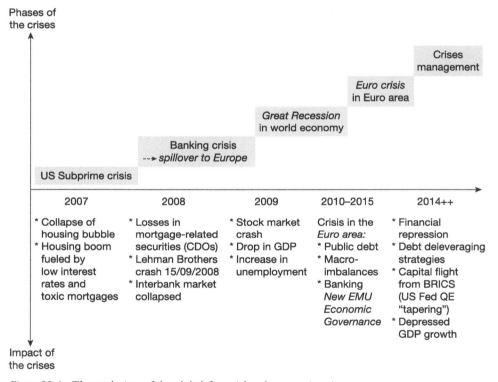

Figure 22.1 The evolution of the global financial and economic crises

2.2 The Great Recession

Financial crises have large economic costs. The "Great Recession" in 2009 caused the biggest drop in real GDP[5] in the US and in Europe (see Figure 22.2). Although the Great Recession was associated with the greatest slump of GDP since the Second World War, in comparison with the Great Depression, however, the downturn of world trade and real GDP was much shorter and the recovery started soon in 2009/2010, faster in the US than in Europe (see Eichengreen and O'Rourke, 2012; Aiginger, 2010[6]).

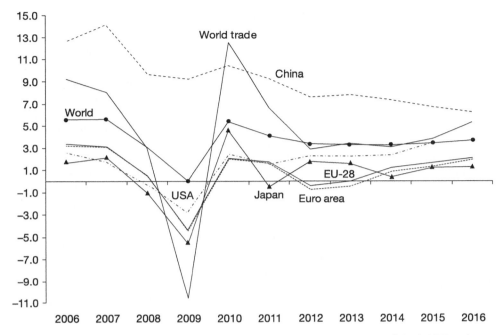

Figure 22.2 GDP and world trade during and after the "Great Recession 2009" (real GDP and world trade volume of goods and services; % changes)

Sources: European Commission (2015) and IMF (2014B and 2015) for China, world GDP and world trade.

2.3 Lessons learnt

2.3.1 Keynes reloaded and unconventional monetary policy

The main reason why the GFC did not trigger a crash as serious as the Great Depression is that this time the governments and central banks of the industrial countries did not allow the financial system to collapse. The Great Depression, hence, was the grand master concerning crisis policy in many areas: fiscal policy acted anti-cyclically à la Keynes,[7] monetary policy reacted very quickly and was supportive with conventional (sharp drop of the key policy rates) and unconventional measures (e.g. quantitative easing (QE) by the Fed[8] and non-standard measures by the ECB[9]) and protectionism – due to WTO commitments – were largely avoided.[10] All together this helped to mitigate the recession in 2009 and enabled a relatively quick recovery.

2.3.2 The need for a new macroeconomics

Most of the economic profession were unable to foresee the consequences of the financial crash after the failure of Lehman Brothers and also could not forecast the full depth of the Great Recession in 2009.[11] The Great Recession in 2009 is largely considered to have been caused by financial shocks (or restrictions) and not by a technology shock as postulated by the pure real business cycle (NK) models. A "new macroeconomics" is necessary with a more adequate modeling of the financial-real sector nexus. Beside private initiatives (e.g. George Soros sponsors the project "Institute of New Economic Thinking" (NET[12])) also much academic endeavor is put into this project (see e.g. Blanchard et al., 2010; Brunnermeier and Sannikov, 2014; Kollmann et al., 2013; Breuss et al., 2015).

3. The Euro crisis

The GFC, triggered by the US subprime and banking crisis (the failure of Lehman Brothers) acted like an asymmetric external shock to the Euro area (now with 19, at the outbreak of the crisis only with 12 Member States) which consists of highly heterogeneous economies lacking a "European business cycle." The economically weakest countries in the periphery (the PIIGS[13] countries) suffered the most from the asymmetric external shocks:[14] Ireland and Spain were hit by a housing crisis, combined with a banking crisis. In Greece and Italy, less so in Portugal and Spain, primarily the increasing public debt became unsustainable. The yield rates of their sovereign bonds increased dramatically (see Figure 22.3).

Whereas the US economy recovered from the Great Recession relative quickly (see Figure 22.2), Europe and in particular the euro area has been stuck in a crisis of its own since 2010, which was named the "Euro crisis". The Euro crisis, however, is not a crisis of the euro as a currency but an economic crisis in some parts (in the peripheral countries) of the Euro area.

3.1 Systemic weakness of EMU's governance

One reason why the Euro area suffered most from the Great Recession and ran into the Euro crisis after the external shock of the GFC is due to the imperfect political architecture of the EMU.[15] The asymmetric policy design of EMU with a centralized monetary policy by the ECB paired with a decentralized (and only co-ordinated) fiscal policy by the Member States worked well in the nice weather period 1999 to 2008 but lacks a crisis-proven framework.

3.1.1 Misperception of sovereign default risks

One precondition of a monetary union with a centralized monetary policy is the harmonization of short-term interest rates. Before entering EMU the high rates of the PIIGS countries had to be adjusted downwards to the lower-level rates of the Euro area which were greatly determined by the German rates. This discretionary monetary policy created an "interest rate" bonus for their economies. The downward trend in short-term interest rates also translated into the long-term lending rates and created an artificial "harmonization" of government bond yields (see Figure 22.3).

The interest rate bonus in the PIIGS led to a misallocation of resources by private households and governments. This triggered the accumulation of debt.[16] The artificially harmonized government bonds yields induced a misperception of sovereign default risks in the Euro area. Rating agencies believed that government bonds of periphery countries would be equally non-risky as German bonds. They believed into the "no-bail-out" lie.[17] Only after the outbreak of the Euro crisis early in 2010 did rating agencies estimate the risks of the PIIGS countries more realistically than before.

3.1.2 Diverging competitiveness

Since the inception of EMU, the Euro area witnessed a divergence in competitiveness (measured by relative unit labor costs) between the Euro area core countries like Germany and Austria and the periphery PIIGS countries (see Table 22.1 on p. 338). This secular trend in competitive heterogeneity (with rising macroeconomic and current account imbalances) was another reason why the PIIGS countries were hit the most by the GFC and the Great Recession.

3.1.3 No crisis-proven instruments in EMU

The succession of the crises since 2008/09 has brutally revealed the weaknesses of the policy design of EMU. The EU Treaty had no crisis instruments at hand when the Euro crisis broke

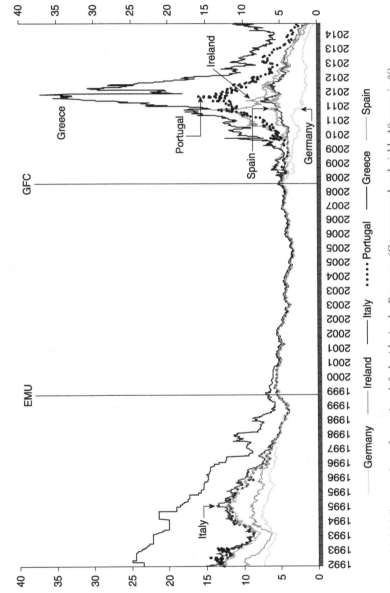

Figure 22.3 Misperception of sovereign default risks in the Euro area (Government bond yields, 10 years, in %)

Source: MACROBOND.

out. Only step-by-step – firstly intergovernmental, then by the Community method – rescue instruments (ESM) and new governance structures were implemented.

REVENGE OF THE OPTIMUM CURRENCY AREA

The crises since 2008 exhibited clearly that the Euro area is not (yet) an Optimum Currency Area (OCA) in the sense of Mundell (1961) and Kenen (1969). The Euro area is inadequately designed for external asymmetric shocks. There are many suggestions of how to make the Euro area more consistent with a functioning OCA (see e.g. Breuss, 2011b, 2013c; De Grauwe, 2011; Krugman, 2012; Sinn, 2014).

3.2 A trinity of causes

In his State of the Union 2012 Address to the European Parliament on 12 September 2012, José Manuel Durão Barroso (2012), the then-President of the European Commission identified three main causes for the GFC and the following Euro crisis:

- unsustainable public debt (*public debt crisis*),
- a lack of competitiveness in some Member States (*macro-imbalances crisis*), and also
- irresponsible practices in the financial sector (*banking crisis*).

The different ingredients of the Euro crisis are summarized in Figure 22.4.

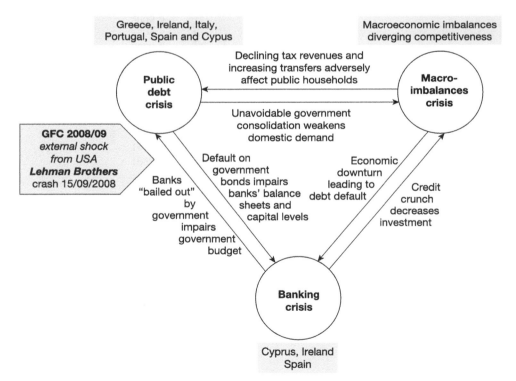

Figure 22.4 The "Euro crisis" consisting of multiple crises in the Euro area (vicious circle of debt, macroeconomic imbalances, and banking crises)

Source: German Council of Economic Experts (2012), p. 1 plus own amendments.

3.2.1 Public debt crisis

Most Euro area countries were able to stabilize their public debt dynamics before the outbreak of the Euro crisis. However, the peripheral PIIGS countries (with the exception of Ireland, Portugal and Spain) started into the crisis with levels much above the Maastricht target of 60 percent of GDP (see Figure 22.5).

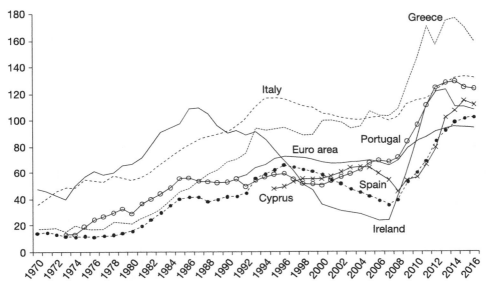

Figure 22.5   Public debts in the Euro area periphery (gross public debt in % of GDP)

Source: European Commission (2015), AMECO database.

When the newly elected government in Greece in late 2009 "discovered" that the fiscal position of its country was much worse than previously reported to Eurostat the "Greek crisis" broke out and triggered the Euro crisis.[18] The Greek public debt was unsustainably high and the interest rates for government bonds rose much above the "death zone" of 7 percent (see Figure 22.3) so that the country could no longer finance its debt on the capital market. The Euro area partner countries had to intervene despite the "no-bail-out" provisions in the Article 125 of the TFEU.

3.2.2 Macro-imbalances crisis

In the run-up to the crisis most of the PIIGS countries did not completely realize that the loss of the exchange rate instrument requires adjustments in the wage policy towards a more productivity oriented path. As a consequence since the inception of the EMU in 1999 competitiveness within the Euro area diverged continuously: the core countries – in particular Germany and Austria – steadily improved their unit labor costs relative to their competitors (e.g. they devalued their real exchange rate – REER), whereas the countries in the periphery (the PIIGS) and also those in the rest of the Euro area (in particular the Baltic States and Slovakia) lost ground continuously.

Table 22.1 Macroeconomic imbalances in the Euro area

	REER			Current account balance		
	1999–2008	*2009– 2016*	*1999/08– 2009/16 Change*	*1999–2008*	*2009–2016*	*1999/08– 2009/16 Change*
	% p.a.			% of GDP		
Belgium	0.59	−0.37	−0.96	3.97	0.30	−3.67
Germany	−1.35	0.47	1.82	2.80	6.94	4.14
Estonia	5.01	0.18	−4.83	−10.22	−0.15	10.07
Ireland	3.26	−3.57	−6.83	−2.52	1.78	4.30
Greece	1.44	−1.95	−3.39	−10.98	−5.79	5.19
Spain	1.95	−2.05	−4.01	−6.01	−1.17	4.84
France	0.51	−0.57	−1.09	0.47	−1.87	−2.34
Italy	1.36	−0.27	−1.63	−0.80	−0.14	0.66
Cyprus	0.75	−1.67	−2.43	−5.47	−3.86	1.61
Latvia	5.36	−1.92	−7.29	−12.02	−0.85	11.16
Luxembourg	1.68	1.02	−0.66	9.77	5.56	−4.21
Malta	1.42	0.52	−0.89	−5.13	−0.55	4.58
Netherlands	0.90	−0.13	−1.03	5.99	7.75	1.77
Austria	−0.47	0.52	0.99	1.43	2.49	1.06
Portugal	0.89	−1.44	−2.33	−9.85	−3.52	6.33
Slovenia	0.26	−0.19	−0.46	−2.64	3.20	5.84
Slovakia	4.24	0.43	−3.81	−6.25	−1.03	5.22
Finland	0.26	0.58	0.32	5.49	−0.57	−6.05
Euro area (18)	**0.67**	**−0.60**	**−1.27**	**0.19**	**1.83**	**1.64**
PIIGS (5)	1.78	−1.86	−3.64	−6.03	−1.77	4.26
CORE (6)	0.07	0.08	0.01	3.36	2.51	−0.85
Rest-EA (7)	2.67	−0.23	−2.91	−4.56	0.33	4.90

Source: European Commission (2015); AMECO data base.

Notes: REER = Real effective exchange rate, based on ULC relative to the rest of 37 industrial countries.
ULC = unit labour costs of the total economy; PIIGS = Portugal, Ireland, Italy, Greece and Spain.
CORE = Belgium, Germany, France, Netherlands, Austria and Finland.
Rest-EA = Estonia, Cyprus, Latvia, Luxembourg, Malta, Slovenia and Slovakia.

In the pre-crisis period 1999 to 2008, Germany and Austria were the only Euro area members with declining real exchange rates. In the PIIGS on average competitiveness deteriorated in this period by 1.8 percentage points per annum, whereas it stagnated in the core more or less (in the remaining Euro area countries +2.7 percent). During the Euro crisis and also due to the austerity commitments ordered by the Troika a considerable adjustment of unit labor costs (the necessary "internal devaluations") took place in the PIIGS (−1.8 percent in the period 2009–16). This helped to diminish the macro-imbalances, measured by the balances of current account. The strong negative relationship ($R^2 = 0.57$) between the change of the current account balances (last column in Table 22.1) and the change of the REER (4th column in Table 22.1) from the pre- to the post-crisis period demonstrates this improvement.

3.2.3 Banking crisis

The US banking crisis was contagious for the European banking sector (e.g. in Cyprus, Ireland and Spain). The IMF (2013: 17), when analyzing the European banking sector, came to the conclusion that the banking sector of the Euro area periphery needs urgent adaptation (the banking sector is too big; banks have too many non-performing loans (NPLs) and many other failures). On both sides of the Atlantic the "too-big-to-fail" (TBTF) problem is still far from being solved.

During the European banking crisis, European States played the role of the "lender of last resort" causing high public debt through bank bailouts. The government interventions to repair the banking sector since the onset of the GFC in 2008/09 has reached dramatic proportions. According to Eurostat (Baciulis, 2013) the net cost of the bank bail-out programs are reflected in a cumulative increase in the national debt by 2012 to 690 billion euros in EU-27 (or 5.2 percent of GDP) and around 520 billion euro in the Euro zone (or 5.5 percent of GDP). They increased the budget deficit of the EU-27 by 0.5 percent of GDP in 2010 (peak) and in 2012 it still amounted to 0.4 percent (0.7 percent and 0.6 percent respectively in the Euro area). Due to the nationalization of the banks, the overall deficit of Ireland jumped to 30 percent in 2010, including 20 percent of GDP by the bank nationalization. In Portugal, the budget deficit in 2010 rose to 10 percent of GDP, the share of bank rescue was relatively low at 1 percent. In 2012, the contribution of the bank bail-out in Greece was particularly large, leading to an increase of the budget deficit by 4 percentage points of GDP; this was followed by Spain with 3.6 percentage points. In other EU countries (Belgium, Latvia, Austria, Portugal and Cyprus – not counting the bail-out of March 2013), the cost of the bank bail-out increased the budget deficit by 0.2 percentage points.

3.3 Economic and political effects

The Euro crisis since early 2010 caused not only a severe economic setback for some of its Member States but the whole euro project has been questioned politically. The exit of Greece ("Grexit") could have caused the break-up of the whole Euro zone.

3.3.1 Deep economic impact

In the 'Great Recession' all Euro area members experienced a drop in real GDP (see Table 22.2), the deepest recession was exhibited in the Baltic States of Estonia and Latvia, followed by Finland, Slovenia and Ireland. On average, in 2009 the Euro area's real GDP dropped by 4.5 percent and hence with the same rate as in EU-28. Poland was the only EU country which suffered no drop in GDP. In the US, where the GFC had its origin, the drop in real GDP was only 2.8 percent in 2009.

Not all industrial countries – inside and outside the EU – managed the crises so that their real GDP levels for 2016 come to lie above those of the pre-crisis year 2008. In the Euro area (EUR-18) only half of the Member States succeed in this respect. Greece – with –21 percent – is lagging the most behind this target, followed by Cyprus, Italy, Portugal, Slovenia, Finland, Spain, Ireland and Latvia.

Table 22.2 The Great Recession 2009 and its overcoming in Europe and selected countries (real GDP, % change)

	1999–2008 Pre crisis % p.a.	*2009 Great Recession % p.a.*	*2010–2016 Post crisis % p.a.*	*2016 GDP above pre crisis 2008 level in %*
EU-28	2.33	−4.39	1.20	3.93
EU-15	2.20	−4.46	1.12	3.28
EUR-18	2.10	−4.51	0.92	1.84
PIIGS	3.01	−4.56	−0.09	−4.76
Euro area countries				
Belgium	2.25	−2.62	1.15	5.50
Germany	1.58	−5.64	1.87	7.42
Estonia	5.70	−14.74	3.43	7.94
Ireland	5.13	−6.37	2.01	7.61
Greece	3.51	−4.39	−2.63	−20.69
Spain	3.57	−3.57	0.31	−1.43
France	2.04	−2.94	1.12	4.91
Italy	1.23	−5.48	−0.08	−6.02
Cyprus	4.12	−2.04	−1.01	−8.73
Latvia	6.70	−14.19	2.86	4.52
Luxembourg	4.39	−5.33	2.56	13.01
Malta	2.99	−2.46	2.88	18.97
Netherlands	2.49	−3.30	0.60	0.80
Austria	2.40	−3.80	1.21	4.68
Portugal	1.62	−2.98	−0.05	−3.29
Slovenia	4.32	−7.80	0.69	−3.24
Slovakia	5.02	−5.29	2.66	13.79
Finland	3.29	−8.27	0.72	−3.56
Non–Euro area countries				
Bulgaria	4.50	−5.01	1.04	2.15
Czech Republic	4.04	−4.84	1.43	5.10
Denmark	1.72	−5.09	0.89	0.95
Croatia	3.71	−7.38	−0.63	−11.38
Lithuania★)	6.21	−14.81	3.46	8.10
Hungary	3.38	−6.55	1.46	3.41
Poland	4.08	2.63	3.11	27.21
Romania	5.39	−7.07	1.83	5.51
Sweden	2.98	−5.18	2.32	11.34
United Kingdom	2.68	−4.31	1.94	9.43
Third countries				
Turkey	3.80	−4.83	4.92	33.19
Norway	2.19	−1.62	1.48	9.03
Switzerland	2.34	−2.13	1.80	10.90
United States	2.55	−2.78	2.54	15.90
Japan	1.08	−5.53	1.49	4.80

Source: European Commission (2015); AMECO data base.

Note: PIIGS = Portugal, Ireland, Italy, Greece and Spain (unweighted averages).
★) As of 1 January 2015 Lithuania became the 19th member of the Euro area.

Whereas the US economy recovered without interruption since 2009/2010, the Euro area's recovery was interrupted by the double-dip recession (2012 to 2014). The burden of the Euro crisis is manifested in rising unemployment and high public debt. The highest unemployment rates for 2016 will still be recorded in Greece (22 percent), Spain (21 percent), Portugal and Italy (13 percent) and Ireland (9 percent).

According to forecasts by the European Commission (2015), in 2016, the unemployment rate in EU-28 will be 9.3 percent (in the US only 5 percent) and in the Euro area 10.6 percent. That corresponds to 24.8 million in EU-28 and 18.5 million in the Euro area. Much more explosive is the high rate of youth unemployment. In 2014 the youth unemployment rate was 53.2 percent in Spain, 52.4 percent in Greece, 23.9 percent in Ireland, 42.7 percent in Italy and 34.7 percent in Portugal (Euro area 23.8 percent).

The biggest handicap for growth in the Euro area is the high public debt. The deleverage processes (austerity policy, "financial repression"[19]) impede a quick upswing in the Euro area. According to Reinhart and Rogoff (2010) – although contested by other authors[20] – public debt above the benchmark of 90 percent of GDP can reduce growth perspectives. According to forecasts by the European Commission (2015), the Euro area on average will consolidate its debt-to-GDP ratio at around 93 percent in 2016 with some Member States much above this level (Greece 159 percent, Italy 132 percent, Portugal 124 percent, Cyprus 112 percent, Ireland 108 percent and Spain 103 percent). This might explain why one must assume that the growth rates in the Euro area in the medium-term will be around one percentage point below that of the US (see IMF, 2014a).

3.3.2 Unequal burden of the Euro crisis and danger of deflation

The economic and social burden of the Euro crisis is unequally distributed in the Euro area. The periphery countries (the PIIGS) suffered the most in terms of GDP loss, unemployment, current account deficit and public debt. This unequal impact of the Euro crisis led to a split in the Eurozone with a less successful South and a more successful North. Additionally, according to estimates by the European Commission (2015), the peripheral countries are close to or already in a phase of *deflation* (e.g. Greece −1.4 percent HICP in 2015) and also in the core countries the inflation rate hovers between zero and 1 percent (Euro area −0.1 percent). This is already below the ECB's own target of 2 percent or near below it.

3.3.3 Eurozone breakup?

Shortly after the outbreak of the Euro crisis in 2010 a deep political split occured in the Euro zone. Starting with Greece, step by step the periphery countries of the Euro area needed support either to finance their public debt (Ireland and Portugal) or to bail-out their banks (Cyprus and Spain).

At the beginning of the Euro crisis (in 2010 to 2012) many experts believed that an exit of Greece from the Euro zone would be unavoidable. Many economists began to calculate the costs of such a "Grexit" for Greece and the partners of the Euro area.[21] But also the economic and political costs of averting the Euro zone breakup were tremendous. Several governments had to resign and were substituted by a government of experts (Greece and Italy). The very strong conditions to stabilize the economy (austerity policy with the need of structural change in labor markets and tax collection) provoked political protest. The strongest movements in this direction were seen in Greece, Portugal and Spain. The election of the

European Parliament on 23–25 May 2014 awakened many extremist political movements towards the right (in France) or to the left (in Greece) and saw a strengthening of anti-EU, anti-Euro parties (e.g. in Germany the AfD; in the UK – UKIP). These new anti-Europe movements may also be a reaction to the Euro crisis management at EU level. At the beginning of the Euro crisis nearly all the rescue operations were conducted intergovernmentally by the EU/Euro area Member States. The European Parliament was rarely involved. In the Euro crisis intergovernmentalism (where the EU Member States decide alone) dominated the Community method (based on EU law mechanism involving all EU institutions: the European Commission, Parliament and Council).

Some authors, like Sinn (2014), advocate more flexibility in leaving and entering the Euro area. Breuss (2013c) suggested an amendment to the TFEU, namely in addition to Article 50, ruling the exit of an EU Member State, and also an Article 50a, ruling the exit of only the Euro area. This would allow Euro area members to leave the Euro zone temporarily to gain competitiveness via devaluating their currency and to re-enter afterwards.

3.4 New EMU economic governance

The Great Recession of 2009 and more so the Euro crisis made it clear that the policy design of EMU and hence its Economic governance had to be overhauled (see Breuss, 2013a; Juncker et al., 2015). The European Commission (2008) in its report on "EMU@10 – Successes and challenges after 10 years of Economic and Monetary Union" identified already before the outbreak of the GFC 2008/09 the necessary areas of reforms. Since 2010 the EU by EU law (community method) and partly only the Euro area Member States (intergovernmental) have developed new instruments for a "New Economic Governance" of EMU which can be grouped into measures in the context of the (A) *"European Semester"* and (B) *"Rescue measures"* for states and banks (see the overview in Figure 22.6). The New Economic Governance of EMU aims at targeting and solving the problems of the three forms of the Euro crisis (see Figure 22.4).

(A) European Semester

The European Semester[22] is now the major instrument of economic policy coordination for short-term (fiscal policy of EU Member States) and medium-term issues (the "growth and job programme" of *"Europe 2020"*;[23] see European Commission, 2010). It is a six-month cycle of economic policy coordination in the first half of each year (it started in spring 2011) which covers all 28 EU Member States. It relates to a procedure for the *ex ante* assessment of Member States' structural reforms, budget plans, and macroeconomic imbalances. The main innovation introduced by the European Semester is that the enforcement of economic policy coordination is now being extended right through to the budgetary process of all the Member States. The tools of the European Semester are firmly rooted in the jointly agreed Europe 2020 Strategy and in the reformed Stability and Growth Pact.

- The *public debt crisis* is being fought by a reform of the fiscal policy coordination mechanism: the Stability and Growth Pact (SGP-III) within the legal framework of the "Six-Pack"[24] and additionally an early monitoring of Euro area countries in the "Two-Pack" arrangements. An intergovernmental treaty, the "Fiscal Compact," complements the reform of the SGP in targeting a reduction of the structural budget deficits and in slowing down the public debt dynamic by installing a "debt break."

- The *macro-imbalances crisis* (the diverging development of competitiveness and performance in the current account) is for the first time monitored by a Macroeconomic Imbalance Procedure.[25]

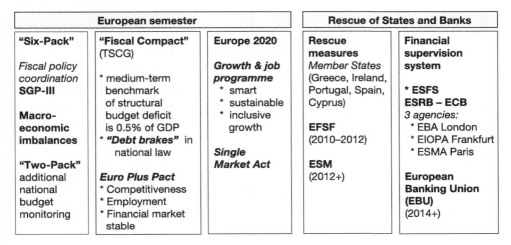

European semester			Rescue of States and Banks	
"Six-Pack" *Fiscal policy coordination* **SGP-III** **Macro-economic imbalances** **"Two-Pack"** additional national budget monitoring	**"Fiscal Compact" (TSCG)** * medium-term benchmark of structural budget deficit is 0.5% of GDP * ***"Debt brakes"*** in national law ***Euro Plus Pact*** * Competitiveness * Employment * Financial market stable	**Europe 2020** ***Growth & job programme*** * smart * sustainable * inclusive growth ***Single Market Act***	**Rescue measures** *Member States* (Greece, Ireland, Portugal, Spain, Cyprus) **EFSF** (2010–2012) **ESM** (2012+)	**Financial supervision system** * **ESFS** **ESRB – ECB** *3 agencies:* * EBA London * EIOPA Frankfurt * ESMA Paris **European Banking Union (EBU)** **(2014+)**

Figure 22.6 New economic governance of EMU since 2010 ("EU economic government")

Notes: SGP = Stability and Growth Pact; EFSF = European Financial Stability Facility; ESFS = European System of Financial Supervision; ESM = European Stability Mechanism; ESRB = European Systemic Risk Board; EBA = European Banking Authority; EIOP = European Insurance and Occupational Pension Authority; ESMA = European Securities and Markets Authority; TSCG = Treaty on Stability, Coordination and Governance in the EMU ("Fiscal Compact").

(B) Rescue of States and Banks

The EMU policy design did not foresee any rescue measures for Member States in danger of insolvency because of over-indebtedness. In contrast, Article 125 of the TFEU prohibits Member States of the EU/Euro area to bail-out other Member States. This "no-bail out" clause had to be overruled during the Euro crisis, starting with the Greek crisis in 2010. New rescue instruments had to be created (EFSF and the permanent ESM[26]) to help failed Euro area members (see Breuss, 2013a). Furthermore, the financial sector, one of the originators of the crisis had to be stabilized.

The *banking crisis* is addressed by the installation of a financial supervision system (ESFS with three agencies since 2011; see Figure 22.6). Finally, the banking sector should be better supervised and in case of failure more efficiently liquidated within the framework of the "European Banking Union" (EBU; see Breuss, 2012b; Breuss, forthcoming; Breuss et al., 2015). By switching from the principle of "bail-out" to "bail-in" one hopes to break the vicious circle of bank failures and public intervention at the expense of the taxpayer.

"More Europes" or "More Europe"?

The Euro crisis has led to a diversification of the EU in several respects: (i) the burden of the Euro crisis was shouldered solely by the Euro Member States (primarily by the core countries); (ii) most of the new crisis instruments (EMS) and the main elements of the new EMU governance (Fiscal Compact; EBU) refer only to members of the Euro zone. In this sense the Euro crisis has further enhanced the already existing EU as a "Europe à la carte" (ins and outs of the euro and Schengen). This raises the question of whether we may live furthermore in an EU with "more Europes" or whether or not more Europe, a further centralization towards the "United States of Europe" is needed (see Breuss, 2013b) which would fulfill the necessary condition for a monetary union ("one country, one money" instead of the present status of EMU with "one market, one money").

3.5 Saving the Eurozone and the Euro

Shortly after the outbreak of the Euro crisis, triggered by the Greek public debt crisis the break-up of the Euro zone stood at the brink. The no-bail-out clause of the Lisbon Treaty (Article 125 TFEU) was thought to be enough to avoid an insolvency of a Euro area Member State. The succession of crises (GFC, Great Recession) which led to the Euro crisis taught the opposite. But the EMU envisaged no rescue instruments and no procedure to bail-out a failing country. Step-by-step new rescue instruments were created, firstly, only on a bilateral basis (EFSF), later the ESM (see Figure 22.6). With these new instruments the Euro area partner countries could stabilize the debt crisis in Greece, Ireland and Portugal. Later Cyprus and Spain were supported in their banking crises (see the overview in Table 22.3). Greece is still at the brink of insolvency.

Table 22.3 Euro area rescue measures, 2010–2013

	Object	Time span	EFSM	EFSF	ESM	GLF	IMF	Bilateral	Bailout total (bn)
Greece 1	SD	5/2010–2/2015				52.9	28.3		81.2
Greece 2	SD	3/2012–3/2016		144.6			19.8		164.4
Greece 1+2			*50% haircut of PSI: 100.0*						245.6
Ireland	SD	11/2010–12/2013	22.5	17.7			22.5	4.8	67.5
Portugal	SD	5/2011–5/2014	26.0	26.0			26.0		78.0
Spain	Bank	12/2012–12/2013			41.4				41.4
Cyprus	Bank	5/2013–3/2016			9.0		1.0		10.0
	+ SD		*Laiki bank closed; Bank of Cyprus (BoC) – "haircut": shareholder capital written off; uninsured deposits above €100.000 lost*						
Total									**442.5**

Source: ESM Website: http://www.esm.europa.eu/.

Notes: SD = Sovereign default; PSI = Private Sector Involvement (banks and private financiers); EFSM = European Financial Stabilisation Mechanism, administered by the European Commission (EU budget: €60 bn); EFSF = European Financial Stability Facility (June 2010–June 2013; remains active in programmes for Portugal and Greece); ESM = European Stability Mechanism, inaugurated 8 October 2012 (since 1 July 2013 sole rescue instrument: €80 bn payed-in capital; lending capacity €500 bn; capital stock €700 bn); GLF = Greek Loan Facility – bilateral loans pooled by the European Commission.

The rescue operations started first for Greece, then followed by those for Ireland, Portugal, Cyprus and Spain, each under different targets, either to avoid sovereign default (Greece, Ireland and Portugal) or to rescue the banking system (Cyprus and Spain). The biggest bail-out was executed for Greece (€245.6 bn), followed by Portugal, Ireland, Spain and Cyprus (see Table 22.3). In the case of Greece, the second rescue package was mixed with a 50 percent haircut of PSIs. In the case of Cyprus for the first time the rescue operation changed from a pure "bail-out" to a "bail-in" with a cascade of "haircuts." The Cyprus case was then the model for the "bail-in" procedure foreseen in the case of the operation of the European Banking Union in case of future bank failures.

When the cost of debt financing became prohibitive (because of an interest burden above 7 percent for 10 years government bonds) some peripheral countries were cut off from the capital market and would need the support of its partners in the Euro zone. This was the case for Greece, Ireland, Portugal, Cyprus and Spain for their banks. After three years Ireland debarked from the rescue program of the Troika in December 2013, Portugal followed in May 2014. Spain's support for its banks ended in December 2013. Ireland was the first of the program countries which could come back to the capital market and place a government bond. Portugal followed in June 2014. Even Greece dived back on the bond market in April 2014, and Cyprus in June 2014.

Whereas the rescue programs were successful in stabilizing the economies of Ireland, Portugal and Spain, Greece[27] is still the problem country in the Euro area because it is hesitant in implementing the structural changes asked for by the Troika.[28]

The rescue operation for the PIIGS and three important political statements stopped the expectation that the Euro zone could break. Commissions President José Manuel Barroso (in November 2011) and German Chancellor Angela Merkel (in August 2012) declared to do whatever they could do to keep the Euro area in its present dimension of 19 Member States. These commitments and the most important message by ECB President Mario Draghi made more or less off-the-record in his speech at the Global Investment Conference in London, 26 July 2012 – "Within our mandate, the ECB is ready to do whatever it takes to preserve the euro … And believe me, it will be enough" – helped to reduce the probability of a break-up of the Euro zone. After Draghi's statement the ECB announced the program of Outright Monetary Transactions (OMT[29]). In order to fight "deflation" the ECB, on 1 March 2015 embarked upon a euro-style program of quantitative easing (QE). It will purchase assets each month amounting to €60 billion until September 2016 (in total €1.1 trillion).[30] Both actions were able to stabilize the upward trend in the spreads of sovereign bonds of the periphery countries. The interest rates of their bonds declined considerably since autumn 2012. And the euro revaluated since July 2012 up to May 2014 continuously by 13 percent.[31] The weak economic perspectives (with the fear of a "secular stagnation"[32]) due to the Ukraine–Russia conflict and the unresolved Greek debt crisis again weakened the euro.

4. Conclusions

Since 2007/08 the industrial world suffered from a sequence of crises: first the GFC 2008, followed by the Great Recession 2009 and – a specialty of Europe – the Euro crisis since 2010. Each crisis has a typical causal structure. The GFC was triggered by the housing bubble (subprime crisis) in connection with risky banking activity leading to a banking crisis in the US. The consequence was a Great Recession in the US and because of its spill-over to Europe also a considerable drop in GDP in Europe. The GFC and the Great Recession acted as asymmetric shocks to the Member States of the Euro area leading to the Euro crisis.

As was already forecast *ex ante* to the introduction of the Euro, countries which were not able to adjust by "internal devaluation" (because of the loss of the instrument of their own exchange rate changes) suffered the most. The Euro crisis was homemade and the outcome of a trinity of causes (debt, banking, macro-imbalances), which interacted in a vicious circle together.

The major lesson from the Euro crisis was that the asymmetric policy design of the EMU was not crisis-proven. Therefore a whole range of measures were implemented to make the Euro area fitter for future crises. The fiscal policy coordination was strengthened, new rescue instruments (ESM) were introduced, which did not exist before the crisis, and the banking sector should be organized by the European Banking Union with the target to break the vicious circle of bank bail-out and public debt accumulation.

Notes

1 Krugman (2009) named it so in contrast to the "Great Depression" in the 1930s.
2 Claessens and Kose (2013) offer a classification of financial crises.
3 Advocates of the low interest rates story as the trigger for the GFC (*Greenspan's overheating* during 2002 and 2005) are Taylor (2009) and Breuss (2011a).
4 For Shiller (2008) the crisis was principally about the unravelling of a bubble in US housing prices (*subprime crisis*) which peaked in approximately 2005–6. He called the real estate boom in an earlier book *irrational exuberance*.
5 Ball (2014) measures the damage of the Great Recession in terms of losses of potential output. The losses in potential output range from almost nothing in Australia and Switzerland to more than 30 percent in Greece (-35 percent), Hungary (-31 percent), and Ireland (-34 percent), Czech Republic and Spain -22 percent, Portugal -14 percent, US -5 percent, Austria -7 percent. During the GFC (2007–11) also the inequality of disposable income increased by 1 percentage point or more in most OECD countries (see OECD, 2014b). The hypothesis, however, that the increasing income/wealth inequality has caused the GFC (postulated e.g. by Stockhammer, 2011; Cynamom and Fazzari, 2014) can empirically not be confirmed (see Aiginger and Guger, 2013). Cingano (2014) finds in an econometric study for OECD countries that income inequality has a negative impact on economic growth.
6 Reinhart and Rogoff (2009) seek the similarities of the present crisis not only with those of the 1930s but over a period of eight centuries. For them "this time is not different."
7 See European Commission (2009a), OECD (2009a, 2009b), Breuss et al. (2009).
8 See Habermeier et al. (2013).
9 See Cour-Thimann and Winkler (2013).
10 However, in a report to the G-20, the WTO OMC (2014) states that the stock of restrictive trade measures introduced by G-20 economies since 2008 continues to rise despite the pledge to roll back any new protectionist measures that may have arisen.
11 In a post-mortem analysis the OECD (2014a) revealed the considerable forecasting errors across 2007–12 by 2½ percentage points. Also the European Commission (2009b: 8) documented the forecast failures in 2009.
12 See: http://ineteconomics.org/
13 PIIGS = Portugal, Ireland, Italy, Greece and Spain.
14 The Euro crisis convincingly confirms ex post findings of the ex ante shock-analysis by Bayoumi and Eichengreen (1994) who considered the PIIGS countries as not suitable as members of a monetary union.
15 However, the design failures of EMU were discussed already earlier to the Euro crisis but in the "nice weather" period up to 2008 there was no need to adjust the EMU governance (see James, 2012; Mourlon-Druol, 2014; and Sinn, 2014).
16 Via "Target2", the real-time gross settlement (RTGS) system owned and operated by the Eurosystem financial transactions – capital in and out flows between Euro area member states – are registered (TARGET stands for **T**rans-**E**uropean **A**utomated **R**eal-time **G**ross settlement **E**xpress **T**ransfer system; see: www.ecb.europa.eu/paym/t2/html/index.en.html). According to Sinn (2012) the Euro crisis has created huge disequilibria between capital creditors (e.g. Germany) and capital debtors (e.g. Greece).

17 Rating agencies believed (wrongly) that the "no-bail-out" clause of Article 125 TFEU will never be applied. It says that an EU Member State shall not be liable for the commitments (debts) of governments of other Member States.

18 In spring 2009 the European Commission forecasted for Greece for the year 2010 (each in percent of GDP): budget deficit -5.7 percent; public debt 108 percent; in autumn 2010 the forecasts were: budget deficit -9.6 percent, public debt 140.2 percent. Finally, in 2010 the realized figures were: budget deficit -11.1 percent, public debt 146 percent (see European Commission, 2015).

19 See Reinhart et al. (2011). "Financial repression" means reduction (deleveraging; see also IMF, 2014b) of debts via low interest rates. These low interest rates have asymmetric implications for savers and debtors. The latter are favored, the former are discriminated.

20 See the collection of arguments and counter-arguments of Reinhart-Rogoff's thesis in Wikipedia "Growth in a Time of Debt" (http://en.wikipedia.org/wiki/Growth_in_a_Time_of_Debt).

21 Based on model simulations of Oxford Economics (2012) several scenarios of a "Grexit" were presented for Greece and selected Euro area member states in Breuss (2012a: 92–3). Bootle (2012) even won the Wolfson Economics Prize 2012 for his study "Leaving the Euro: A Practical Guide". Further studies on this topic are surveyed in Breuss (2012a). After the parliamentary elections in Greece in January 2015 and after the building of a left-right coalition government, the discussion about a possible "Grexit" again got momentum.

22 For further details see the website of the European Commission (Economic and Financial Affairs): "The European Semester": http://ec.europa.eu/economy_finance/economic_governance/the_european_semester/index_en.htm

The *European semester* is one of the first key initiatives to emerge from a Task Force on economic governance set up at the request of the European Council in March 2010 and chaired by the President of the European Council, Herman Van Rompuy.

23 The first stock-taking in March 2014 revealed many shortfalls in reaching the targets (see European Commission, 2014).

24 The "Six-Pack" consists of 5 Regulations and 1 Directive and entered into force on 13 December 2011. A subgroup of 3 Regulations and 1 Directive concern the reform of the "SGP"; 2 new Regulations concern the macroeconomic surveillance under the new Macroeconomic Imbalance Procedure. See further details on the Commissions website: http://ec.europa.eu/economy_finance/articles/governance/2012-03-14_six_pack_en.htm

25 See more details on the Commission's website: http://ec.europa.eu/economy_finance/economic_governance/macroeconomic_imbalance_procedure/index_en.htm

26 The ESM – signed on 11 July 2011, renegotiated and signed again on 2 February 2012 by the heads of state or government of the Euro area Member States – is a permanent crisis resolution mechanism for the countries of the Euro area. It was established on 27 September 2012 and is located in Luxembourg; it has been operating since 8 October 2012. Since 13 July 2013, the ESM is the sole mechanism for responding to requests for financial assistance by euro area Member States. In order to make the ESM in conformity of EU law, Article 136 of the TFEU was amended by two lines (*"The member states whose currency is the euro may establish a stability mechanism to be activated if indispensable to safeguard the stability of the euro area as a whole. The granting of any required financial assistance under the mechanism will be made subject to strict conditionality."*). It was signed by 27 EU member states on 25 March 2011. See the website of the European Stability Mechanism: www.esm.europa.eu/

27 In an interview in June 2014, Poul Thomsen, head of the IMF's Greece team, saw only "ground for cautious optimism" (see: www.imf.org/external/pubs/ft/survey/so/2014/car060914a.htm)

28 The Troika is a team of experts from the ECB, the IMF (see factsheet "The IMF and Europe": www.imf.org/external/np/exr/facts/europe.htm) and the European Commission tasked to negotiate with problem countries of the Euro area to avoid their sovereign default. This group was created ad hoc by the Euro area Member States when the Greek crisis broke out in May 2010. The Troika was heavenly criticized by the European Parliament (see the Troika Report by the European Parliament, Rapporteur: Othmar Karas, Liem Hoang Ngoc: www.europarl.europa.eu/meps/en/4246/OTHMAR_KARAS_activities.html) because of its lack of democratic legitimacy and legal basis. The EP wants to finish the work of the Troika and sees the future of the Troika in the following three variants: (i) The IMF makes the task alone; (ii) The European Commission makes the job alone; or (iii) The ESM will be transferred into a European Monetary Fund (EMF). The new Greek government since January 2015 refuses even to cooperate with the Troika.

29 Since June 2013, the OMT programme is a legal case at the German *Federal Constitutional Court* in Karlsruhe (Bundesverfassungsgericht) because many German experts brought a complaint to the court. In a preliminary ruling as of 7 February 2014 the German Court of Justice came to the conclusion that the OMT programme has two legal caveats: (1) it is an infringement of Article 123 TFEU (although the ECB would buy government bonds only on the secondary market); and (2) it would intermingle monetary and fiscal policy by the ECB (its objective is only "price stability"). The Court pronounced the referral for a preliminary ruling to the Court of Justice of the European Union (ECJ). On 16 June 2015, the ECJ judged the OMT programme as conforming with the ECB mandate.

30 See the ECB announcement of the QE (or "Expanded asset purchase") programme on 22 January 2015: www.ecb.europa.eu/press/pr/date/2015/html/pr150122_1.en.html

31 Because of the already too strong Euro and the danger of a "deflation" in the Euro zone in light of the failure to reach its own targets of an inflation of 2 percent or near to it, on 5 June 2014 the ECB announced important monetary policy decisions (cut of the main refinancing rate to 0.15 percent; for the first time the deposit rate was set at -0.1 percent; conduct of three-month longer-term refinancing operations (LTROs)) in order to enhance the functioning of the monetary policy transmission mechanism and to curb credit supply (see ECB website: www.ecb.europa.eu/press/pr/date/2014/html/pr140605_2.en.html).

32 Recently, Summers (2013, 2014) came up with the pessimistic view of a "secular stagnation" in the context of the weak development of the industrial world. In Teulings and Baldwin (2014) several authors dealt with the explanation of this old notion invented by Alvin Hansen in 1938.

References

Aiginger, K. (2010), The Great Recession vs. The Great Depression: Stylized Facts on Siblings That Were Given Different Foster Parents, *Economics*, The Open-Access, Open-Assessment E-Journal, Vol. 4, No. 2010–18, May 25, 2010 (www.economics-ejournal.org/economics/journalarticles/2010–18).

Aiginger, K. and Guger, A. (2013), Stylized Facts on the Interaction between Income Distribution and the Great Recession, *Economics*, The Open-Access, Open-Assessment E-Journal, Discussion Paper, No. 2013–25, March 22, 2013 (www.economics-ejournal.org/economics/discussionpapers/2013–25).

Baciulis, M. (2013), Support for Financial Institutions Increases Government Deficits in 2012. Upward Impact of 0.4 pp GDP in the EU and 0.6pp in the Euro Area, *Statistics in Focus*, Eurostat. 10/2013, 22. April 2013.

Ball, L.M. (2014), Long-Term Damage from the Great Recession in OECD Countries, *NBER Working Paper*, No. 20185, May 2014.

Barroso, J.M.D. (2012), State of the Union 2012 Address. European Parliament, 12 September 2012.

Bayoumi, T. and Eichengreen, B. (1994), *One Money or Many? Analyzing the Prospects for Monetary Unification in Various Parts of the World*, Princeton Studies in International Finance, No. 76, September 1994.

Blanchard, O., Dell'Ariccia, G. and Mauro, P. (2010), Rethinking Macroeconomic Policy, *IMF Staff Discussion Note* 10/03.

Bootle, R. (2012), Leaving the Euro: A Practical Guide, Wolfson Economics Prize, 2012.

Breuss, F. (2011a), Global Financial Crisis as a Phenomenon of Stock Market Overshooting, *Empirica – Journal of European Economics*, Vol. 38, No. 1, February 2011: 131–152.

Breuss, F. (2011b), Downsizing the Euro Zone into an OCA or Entry into a Fiscal Transfer Union, *CESifo Forum*, Vol. 12, No. 4, Winter 2011: 5–12.

Breuss, F. (2012a), *EU-Mitgliedschaft Österreichs - Eine Evaluierung in Zeiten der Krise*, WIFO-Studie, Wien, Oktober 2012.

Breuss, F. (2012b), European Banking Union: Necessary, But Not Enough to Fix the Euro Crisis, *CESifo Forum*, Vol. 13, No. 4: 26–32.

Breuss, F. (2013a), Towards a New EMU, *WIFO Working Papers*, No. 447, March 2013 (published as Kindle eBook: www.amazon.com/Towards-New-EMU-Fritz-Breuss-ebook/dp/B00CBZBNLM).

Breuss, F. (2013b), Towards United States of Europe, in: *Visions for Economic Policy Coordination in Europe*, Federal Ministry of Economy, Family and Youth, Vienna, June 2013: 27–47.

Breuss, F. (2013c), Euro Crisis as a Chance for a Restart of the European Union, in: *European Economic Governance in an International Context*, Proceedings of the Global Jean Monnet Conference 2011, 24–25 November 2011, European Commission, Directorate-General for Education and Culture, Brussels, 2013: 168–180.

Breuss, F. (forthcoming), European Banking Union: The Last Building Block Towards a New EMU?, in: A. Bosco (ed.), *The Euro and the Struggle for the Creation of a New Global Currency. Problems and Perspectives in the Building of the Political, Financial and Economic Foundations of the European Federal Government*, Florence, forthcoming.

Breuss, F., Roeger, W. and in't Veld, J. (2015), *The Stabilising Properties of a European Banking Union in Case of Financial Shocks in the Euro Area*, European Economy – Economic Papers, No. 550, June 2015.

Breuss, F., Kaniovski, S. and Schratzenstaller, M. (2009), Macro-economic Effects of the Fiscal Stimulus Measures in Austria, *Austrian Economic Quarterly*, 4/2009 (Volume 14): 205–216.

Brunnermeier, M.K. and Sannikov, Y. (2014). A Macroeconomic Model with a Financial Sector, *The American Economic Review*, Vol. 104, No. 2, February 2014: 379–421.

Cingano, F. (2014), Trends in Income Inequality and its Impact on Economic Growth, OECD Social, Employment and Migration Working Papers, No. 163, Paris, 2014.

Claessens, St. and Kose, M.A. (2013), Financial Crises: Explanations, Types, and Implications, *IMF Working Paper*, WP/13/28, January 2013.

Cour-Thimann, Ph. and Winkler, B. (2013), The ECB's Non-Standard Monetary Policy Measures The Role of Institutional Factors and Financial Structure, *ECB Working Paper Series*, No. 1528, April 2013.

Cynamon, B.Z. and Fazzari, S.M. (2014), Inequality, the Great Recession, and Slow Recovery, Federal Reserve Bank of Saint Louis and Washington University in St. Louis, March 19, 2014 (http://papers.ssrn.com/sol3/papers.cfm?abstract_id=2205524).

De Grauwe, P. (2011), Managing a fragile Eurozone, *CESifo Forum*, Vol. 12, No. 2, Summer 2011: 44–45.

Eichengreen, B. and O'Rourke, K.H. (2012), A Tale of Two Depressions Redux, *VoxEU*, 6 March 2012 (updates of earlier articles in VoxEU, starting with, A Tale of Two Recessions, *VoxEU*, 6 April 2009; What Do the New Data Tell Us?, *VoxEU*, 8 March 2010) (www.voxeu.org/article/tale-two-depressions-redux).

European Commission (2008), EMU@10 - Successes and challenges after 10 years of Economic and Monetary Union, *European Economy*, No. 2, June 2008.

European Commission (2009a), The EU's Response to Support the Real Economy During the Economic Crisis: An Overview of Member States' Recovery Measures, Brussels: *European Economy, Occasional Papers*, 511, July 2009.

European Commission (2009b), *European Economic Forecast Autumn 2009*, Brussels: European Economy 10/2009.

European Commission (2010), *Europe 2020: A Strategy for Smart, Sustainable and Inclusive Growth*, Communication from the Commission, Brussels, COM (2010) 2020 final, 3.3.2020.

European Commission (2014), *Taking Stock of the Europe 2020 Strategy for Smart, Sustainable and Inclusive Growth*, Communication from the Commission to the European Parliament, the Council, the European Economic and Social Committee and the Committee of the Regions, corrected version, Brussels: COM(2014) 130 final/2, 19.3.2014.

European Commission (2015), *European Economic Forecast Winter 2015*, Brussels: European Economy 1/2015.

Financial Crisis Inquiry Commission (2011), *Crisis Inquiry Report*, Final Report of the National Commission on the Causes of the Financial and Economic Crisis in the United States, Official Government Edition, Washington, D.C., January 2011 (http://fcic-static.law.stanford.edu/cdn_media/fcic-reports/fcic_final_report_full.pdf).

German Council of Economic Experts (2012), *After the Euro Area Summit: Time to Implement Long-term Solutions*, Special Report, Wiesbaden: 30 July 2012.

Habermeier K. et al. (2013), *Unconventional Monetary Policies – Recent Experience and Prospects*, IMF, Washington, D.C: April 18, 2013.

IMF (2013), *Global Financial Stability Report: Old Risks, New Challenges*, Washington, D.C.: April 2013.

IMF (2014a), *Global Financial Stability Report: Moving from Liquidity to Growth-Driven Markets*, Washington, D.C.: April 2014.

IMF (2014b), *World Economic Outlook October 2014: Legacies, Clouds, Uncertainties*, International Monetary Fund, Washington, D.C.: October 2014.

IMF (2015), *World Economic Outlook: Update*, International Monetary Fund, Washington, D.C.: 19 January 2015.

James, H. (2012), Making the European Monetary Union, Bank for International Settlement, Basel, 2012.

Juncker, J.C., Tusk, D., Dijsselbloem, D., Draghi, M. and Schulz, M. (2015), *Completing Europe's Economic and Monetary Union*, Brussels: European Commission, 22 June 2015.

Kenen, P. (1969), The Theory of Optimum Currency Areas: An Eclectic View, in: R.A. Mundell and A.K. Swoboda (eds) (1969), *Monetary Problems of the International Economy*, The University of Chicago Press, 1969: 41–60.

Kollmann, R., Ratto, M., Roeger, W. and in't Veld, J. (2013), Fiscal Policy, Banks and the Financial Crisis, *Journal of Economic Dynamics and Control*, Vol. 37, No. 2, 387–403.

Krugman, P.A. (2009), The Great Recession versus the Great Depression, *The New York Times* (Online Edition), 20 March 2009.

Krugman, P.A. (2012), Revenge of the Optimum Currency Area, *The New York Times* (Online Edition), 24 June 2012.

Lo, A.W (2012), Reading about the Financial Crisis: A Twenty-One-Book Review, *Journal of Economic Literature*, Vol. 50, No 1, 151–178.

Mourlon-Druol, E. (2014), Don't Blame the Euro: Historical Reflections on the Roots of the Eurozone Crisis, *West European Politics*, Vol. 37, Issue 6, 1282–1296.

Mundell, R. (1961), A Theory of Optimum Currency Areas, *The American Economic Review*, Vol. 51, No. 4, September 1961: 657–665.

OECD (2009a), *Fiscal Packages Across OECD Countries: Overview and Country Details*, Paris, 2009.

OECD (2009b), *Policy Responses to the Economic Crisis: Investing in Innovation for Long-term Growth*, Paris, 2009.

OECD (2014a), *OECD Forecasts During and After the Financial Crisis: a Post Mortem*, OECD Economics Department Policy Note, No. 23, Paris, February 2014.

OECD (2014b), *Income Inequality Update: Rising Inequality: Youth and Poor Fall Further Behind*, Insights from the OECD Income Distribution Database, OECD: Directorate for Employment, Labor and Social Affairs Statistics Directorate, Paris, June 2014 (www.oecd.org/social/OECD2014-Income-Inequality-Update.pdf).

Oxford Economics (2012), Eurozone Breakup. Macroeconomic Implications using Oxford Economics' Global Macro Model, Oxford, June 2012 (update August 2012).

Reinhart, C., Kirkegaard, K. and Sbrancia, B. (2011), Financial Repression Redux, *Peterson Institute for International Economics*, June 2011 (http://mpra.ub.uni-muenchen.de/31641), MPRA Paper No. 31641.

Reinhart, C.M. and Rogoff, K.S. (2009), *This Time is Different: Eight Centuries of Financial Folly*, Princeton and Oxford: Princeton University Press.

Reinhard, C.M. and Rogoff, K.S. (2010), Growth in a Time of Debt, *The American Economic Review*, Vol. 100, No. 2, May 2010: 573–78.

Shiller, R.J. (2008), *The Subprime Solution: How Today's Global Financial Crisis Happened, and What to Do about It*, Princeton and Oxford: Princeton University Press.

Sinn, H.-W. (2012), *Die Target-Falle – Gefahren für unser Geld und unsere Kinder*, Carl Hanser Verlag, München, 2012.

Sinn, H.-W. (2014), *The Euro Trap – On Bursting Bubbles, Budgets, and Beliefs*, Oxford: Oxford University Press.

Stockhammer, E. (2011), Polarisierung der Einkommensverteilung als Ursache der Finanz- und Wirtschaftskrise, *Wirtschaft und Gesellschaft*, 2011, 37(3): 378–402 (http://econpapers.repec.org/article/clrwugarc/y_3a2011_3av_3a37i_3a3p_3a378.htm).

Summers, L. (2013), "*Remarks*" on the IMF Annual Research Conference, Washington, D.C., November 8th, 2013.

Summers, L. (2014), *Reflections on the 'New Secular Stagnation Hypothesis'*, in: Teulings, C., Baldwin, R. (eds.), *Secular Stagnation: Facts, Causes, and Cures*. A VoxEU.org ebook, London: Centre for Economic Policy Research (CEPR) (2014), 27–38.

Taylor, J.B. (2009), The Financial Crisis and the Policy Responses: An Empirical Analysis of What Went Wrong, *NBER, Working Paper*, No. 14631, January 2009.

Teulings, C. and Baldwin, R. (eds.) (2014), *Secular Stagnation: Facts, Causes, and Cures*, A VoxEU.org eBook, CEPR, London 2014.

WTO OMC (2014), Report on G-20 Trade Measures (Mid-May 2014 to Mid-October 2014), Geneva, 5 November 2014.

23

EXCEPTIONAL POLICIES FOR EXCEPTIONAL TIMES

The ECB's response to the rolling crises of the euro area

Lucrezia Reichlin and Huw Pill[1]

1. Introduction

This chapter provides an appraisal of European Central Bank (ECB) policy from the beginning of the financial crisis in the summer of 2007 to the summer of 2014.

We divide seven years of crises into three phases: (1) a banking crisis (2007–9), where the immediate issue was addressing liquidity difficulties in the financial sector; (2) a sovereign crisis (2010–12), where the central concerns were addressing (interrelated) solvency issues in public finances and bank balance sheets; and, finally, (3) an attempt to build a new, more workable framework for the euro area (2012 to date), starting with ECB President Mario Draghi's commitment to do 'whatever it takes' to sustain the euro (which took institutional form in the announcement of the ECB's outright monetary transactions (OMT) programme). We freeze our narrative in September 2014.

In each phase, the ECB faced a variety of challenges, which it met with various tools and varying degrees of success. As it fought the crises, the ECB expanded its functions beyond the traditional domain of monetary policy, eventually becoming the single banking supervisor for the euro area and taking a leading role in the creating and managing a new framework for macro prudential surveillance. In doing so, the ECB moved beyond the role that was originally assigned to it in the Maastricht Treaty: rather than an independent central bank assigned a single monetary policy instrument with a narrow mandate to maintain price stability, it evolved into an institution with a wider set of responsibilities many of which entailed making deeply political choices and interacting with a wider range of political actors.

During the first phase, the ECB was largely addressing liquidity problems. It acted to these problems promptly and aggressively. In this respect, the ECB proved successful in stabilising the financial sector, even if, as for the central banks of other major developed economies, it was unable to prevent a sharp macroeconomic downturn. Broadly speaking, the ECB delivered successfully on its core central banking tasks, while relying on other authorities to address underlying weakness in public and banking sector balance sheets that threatened solvency and sustainability in the medium term.

Unfortunately, the trust placed in other authorities proved misplaced. National fiscal authorities either could not, or would not, act to contain solvency problems in the fiscal and financial domains. The Maastricht framework did not provide the Union with area-wide 'federal' institutions that could have provided some risk-sharing mechanism. As predicted by some in the policy debate preceding the euro, this made it inadequate to face a large adverse shock such as the global financial crisis of 2007–8 (see Mourlon-Druol, 2014 for an account of the early discussion). The ECB was then called upon to act to address these solvency issues (which became entwined with, and to some extent indistinguishable from, liquidity concerns), even though they fell outside the traditional realm of central bank responsibilities. At this stage, the ECB's measures became less effective. Because sovereign and banking concerns had a national dimension, the failure to deal with them promptly and credibly led to a re-fragmentation of financial markets that both exacerbated the impact of the crisis itself (particularly in the stressed peripheral countries), but also impaired the ECB's attempts to stabilise the economy and prices.

The ECB's approach in this second phase of the crisis can be characterised as 'muddling through': enough was done to prevent a collapse of the financial system or break-up of the euro area, but the underlying problems – the solvency issues on public and bank balance sheets and the inadequacy of the institutional infrastructure to deal with them – were not really addressed. The ECB found itself in a dilemma: either stick to the old rules embodied in the Maastricht set-up (and risk financial and macroeconomic instability) or act in a pragmatic manner (and risk hitting the institutional and political constraints that Maastricht had set out to manage). Unsurprisingly, in real time and under the immediate pressure of market tension, the ECB adopted the latter strategy.

Looking ahead, at the heart of the matter is the issue of whether (and, if so, how) the ECB should manage legacy debt problems – which cannot simply be wished away – by taking fiscal and banking risk on to its own balance sheet.

On the one hand, the central bank balance sheet is a natural vehicle to warehouse a large stock of debt, which can then be reduced through time. There are many historical examples where the central bank has played the role of a 'sinking fund' in order to allow an economy to emerge from beneath an excessive debt burden.

On the other hand, in the context of Monetary Union, warehousing legacy debt has significant cross-country distributional effects since the legacy problems are of different magnitude in different euro area countries. There is an understandable reluctance on the part of those countries which would be net contributors to such a scheme to enter into large and potentially unlimited commitments without a credible institutional infrastructure to protect them from ill-discipline elsewhere. In this respect, the Maastricht Treaty framework has proved inadequate.

With Mr Draghi's pledge to do 'whatever it takes' to sustain the euro, we have entered a new phase, which centres on designing and implementing a new policy framework to supersede Maastricht. This new framework has several key elements: the ECB's OMT programme; the conduct of an asset quality review and stress test of all the major banks, as a first step towards the establishment of unified supervision at the ECB; and Mr Draghi's recent call for a framework to support a more appropriate 'policy mix' at the area-wide level, while building the political feasibility and economic effectiveness of further non-standard central bank actions via commitment by governments to (and monitoring of) reform.

Each of these elements can be seen as an attempt to build confidence that adjustment and reform will limit future exposures while facilitating the sharing of legacy burdens. This will be necessary to stabilise the euro area and create an environment more conducive to growth. Ultimately, restoring growth in the euro area is a precondition for achieving fiscal and financial sustainability.

As with any time consistency problem of this type, the key question is how to enforce commitment to longer-term adjustment while relieving the burden of legacy problems in the short run. The traditional answer to this question is to build economic institutions that underpin the credibility of reform and discipline over the medium term, and thereby give confidence that legacy problems can be addressed without creating moral hazard and/or threats to the credibility of the ECB in its pursuit of price stability. Mr Draghi's Jackson Hole initiative, complementing the creation of the banking union, should be seen in this light. At this stage, whether his efforts will be successful remains an open question.

2. Setting the scene – growing vulnerabilities ahead of the crisis

Before developing a narrative of the financial crisis from 2007, we outline a number of secular trends in the banking sector (focusing on the European experience) in the preceding decade, which played an important role in building the balance sheet vulnerabilities that eventually became important channels for the transmission of financial stress.

Over the course of the first decade of monetary union, European banks' dependence on wholesale funding rose. As bank credit growth increased rapidly during the mid-2000s, the ratio of loans to traditional deposits increased and banks made greater recourse to wholesale sources of funding (e.g., interbank deposits, etc.) (Giannone et al., 2012; Reichlin, 2014).

One aspect of the wholesale funding was the use of off-balance sheet vehicles to expand lending, which was associated with a growing role for securitisation and other structured products. While the bulk of such activity took place in the US, European banks also engaged and were, in some cases, purchasers of US-originated asset-backed securities.

These developments made bank funding more 'flighty' in nature than more traditional sources, such as retail deposits. Given the maturity and relationship-based nature of the corporate loan book in euro area banks, maturity transformation and liquidity risk faced by the banking system increased. Moreover, the accumulation of intra-banking sector leverage created systemic vulnerability: if one institution chose to shrink its balance sheet, the resulting withdrawal of wholesale funding puts pressure on others to do likewise (and so on). A self-sustaining spiral of forced deleveraging could ensue.

The first decade of monetary union saw a significant rise in cross-border exposures of banks. This had both: (1) a global dimension, reflecting flows across borders with the rest of the world (including London as an offshore financial centre for the euro area); and (2) an intra-euro area dimension, reflecting flows across borders within the euro area (e.g., financing from Germany to Spain). Although retail markets remained segmented as a consequence of national level supervision, the mid-2000s saw a large increase in cross-border bank wholesale funding, as savers in countries with slow growing economies (notably Germany) financed the higher growth of credit and demand in countries such as Spain and Ireland.

Behind this integration of European wholesale and financial markets was the progressive integration of the intra-euro area sovereign bond market and the resulting compression of sovereign spreads. This convergence has been interpreted as a consequence of the markets not pricing sovereign risk due to the implicit guarantee provided by the ECB (e.g., Ehrmann et al., 2011).

As a result of these developments, the euro area banking system became vulnerable. Exposure to external shocks, such as the consequences of the meltdown of the US subprime mortgage market from mid-2007 and subsequently the systemic effects of the failure of Lehman in September 2008, increased. Moreover, bank funding became more vulnerable to a run in the inter-bank market driven by non-domestic counterparts, both those resident outside the euro area but also those in other countries within the euro area (Colangelo et al., 2014). Hence the flight to safety took the form of a renationalisation of the inter-bank market and a fragmentation of the euro area financial system.

3. Phase 1: The banking/liquidity crisis

3.1 Narrative

In response to deteriorating bank balance sheets following the onset of the US subprime crisis and uncertainty as to which banks were most profoundly affected, adverse selection in the interbank market led to a hoarding of liquidity and to dislocations in the money market. The failure of Lehman Brothers in September 2008 intensified this adverse selection significantly: if an institutional as large as Lehman could fail, who was safe? Following Lehman's failure, the interbank market seized up altogether, both internationally and within the euro area (Heider et al., 2009).

One symptom of the panic then gripping financial markets was the substantial rise in money market interest rate spreads: spreads between secured and unsecured money market rates rose to unprecedented highs (see Figure 23.1), while interbank transactions volumes fell to low levels, especially at longer maturities. This was a global phenomenon: following the catalysts of subprime dislocations and Lehman's failure, the euro area was affected in largely the same manner as other jurisdictions such as the US or UK. Central banks were thus confronted with rising tensions and a seizing-up of the inter-bank money market. The ECB was in the vanguard in addressing these challenges.

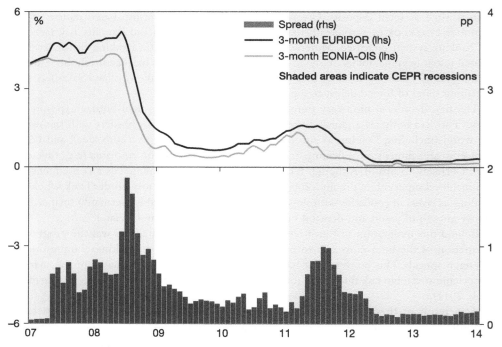

Figure 23.1 Spread between secured and unsecured money market rates

Source: Bloomberg.

Table 23.1 Timeline of events – Phase 1: The banking crisis

12 Sep 07	Money market funding problems prompt Northern Rock to ask the BoE for liquidity support
12 Dec 07	The ECB, Fed and SNB announce temporary reciprocal currency agreements (swap lines). The Fed will provide up to $20 billion and $4 billion to the ECB and SNB, respectively, for up to 6 months
17 Feb 08	Northern Rock is nationalised
28 Mar 08	ECB offers refinancing operations with longer maturities
2 Jul 08	ECB increases interest rates by 25bps to 4.25%
16 Sep 08	Lehman Brothers files for Chapter 11 bankruptcy protection
29 Sep 08	The ECB announces and conducts on the same day a special term refinancing operation with no pre set amount at variable rate
8 Oct 08	The ECB cuts refi rate by 50bps to 3.75% and reduces the corridor from 200bps to 100bps around the rate of the main refinancing operation
8 Oct 08	The ECB announces that the weekly main refinancing operation will be conducted through a fixed rate tender procedure with full allotment (FRFA)
15 Oct 08	The ECB announces a further expansion of the collateral framework
15 Oct 08	The ECB announces an enhancement of the provision of longer term refinancing with 1, 3 and 6 month operations
6 Nov 08	The ECB cuts the refi rate by 50bps to 3.25%
4 Dec 08	The ECB cuts the refi rate by 75bps to 2.50%
18 Dec 08	The ECB restores the corridor of standing facility rates to 200bps
15 Jan 09	The ECB cuts the refi rate by 50bps to 2.00%
15 Mar 09	The ECB cuts the refi rate by 50bps to 1.50%
2 Apr 09	The ECB cuts the refi rate by 25bps to 1.25%
7 May 09	The ECB cuts the refi rate by 25bps to 1.00%
7 May 09	The ECB announces that it will conduct one year longer term refinancing operations (LTROs) in June, September and December 2009, on FRFA basis
4 Jun 09	The ECB launches its Covered Bond Purchase Programme (CBPP) with a maximum amount of EUR60 billion
3 Dec 09	The ECB decides that its main refinancing operation will continue on FRFA basis for as long as needed
27 Jan 10	The ECB announces that it will discontinue the temporary swaps line

First and foremost, the ECB responded with the adoption of fixed rate/full allotment (FRFA) tender procedures in all its regular monetary policy operations (Table 23.1). This measure created a perfectly elastic supply of liquidity to bank counterparties at an interest rate determine by the ECB. By providing certainty on the availability of central bank liquidity (with regards to both quantity and price), this measure helped to restore confidence and stabilise the banking sector at a time of high stress.

Second, the ECB expanded its list of eligible collateral, to include securities (other than ABS) rated BBB or higher, while also further lengthening the average maturity of its outstanding operations (see Figure 23.2).

Third, over time the ECB increased the number and variety of Eurosystem longer-term operations. Innovations included: the introduction of a so-called 'maintenance period operation' (i.e. a repo operation at the start of the maintenance period that matures at the end of the maintenance period, with an implied maturity of around one month[2]); and the

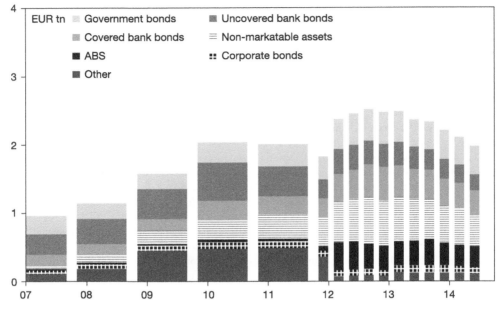

Figure 23.2 Collateral pledged at ECB monetary policy operations

Source: Bloomberg.

introduction of LTROs with six month maturity. The ECB also broadened its set of counterparties, notably to include the European Investment Bank (EIB).

Taken together, these measures considerably expanded the scope for central bank intermediation to substitute for a money market subject to severe disruption and which could no longer be relied upon to distribute liquidity efficiently across banks or serve its crucial payment function (Lenza et al., 2010). In so doing, the ECB maintained the circulation of payments and liquidity among banks – and thus avoided a more dramatic and costly dislocation in financial stability.

In parallel with these attempts to maintain inter-bank flows, the ECB also supported bank funding by undertaking (relatively small) purchases of bank covered bonds. The objective of these purchases was to revive market activity, rather than inject liquidity to the system. Moreover, in concert with other leading central banks, the ECB introduced operations to address the US dollar funding difficulties of its domestic counterparties against Eurosystem collateral, on the basis of financing via an FX swap agreed with the US Federal Reserve.

In sum, these actions resulted in a significant expansion of the ECB balance sheet from October 2008 (see Figure 23.3). But rather than an attempt to 'inject' liquidity into the euro money market, the balance sheet expansion was a by-product of a set of non-standard measures aimed at supporting the functioning of crucial segments of the financial market, thereby promoting effective monetary policy transmission and avoiding a costly financial collapse.

ECB actions in this period were governed by the so-called separation principle (Trichet, 2008), which dictated that its non-standard interventions in the money market were oriented to supporting market functioning, leaving the traditional interest rate instrument of monetary policy free to pursue the objective of price stability.

In this context, the ECB raised its policy rates by 25bp in July 2008 (see Figure 23.4), on the grounds that consumer price inflation was substantially above target and in order to

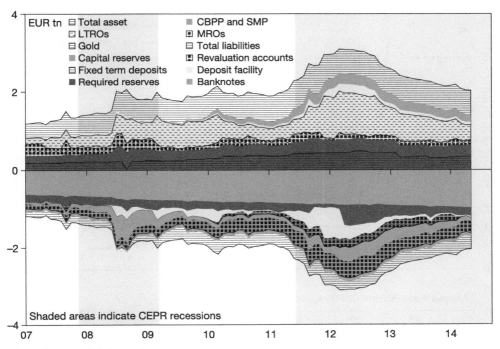

EUR tn
- ⊟ Total asset
- ⊟ LTROs
- ⊟ Gold
- ■ Capital reserves
- ⊟ Fixed term deposits
- ■ Required reserves
- ■ CBPP and SMP
- ▣ MROs
- ⊟ Total liabilities
- ▣ Revaluation accounts
- Deposit facility
- ■ Banknotes

Shaded areas indicate CEPR recessions

Figure 23.3 ECB balance sheet

Source: ECB, Haver Analytics, Goldman Sachs Global Investment Research.

pre-empt a self-fulfilling inflationary process that threatened to take hold via wage developments. With the benefit of hindsight, this decision suggests that the ECB was slow to recognise the weakening of the global economy that had started in the first half of 2008 and the underlying fragility of the financial system that triggered that weakening.

That said, both within and without the euro area, the ECB acted on the basis that conventional monetary policy should not be deflected from its primary goal of price stability, and that other measures would be taken to forestall a banking crisis. Clearly, in the case of Lehman, the ECB under-estimated the willingness of the US authorities to stand aside in the face of the failure of a core financial institution. As the euro area macroeconomic situation deteriorated sharply from Lehman's failure onwards, the rate hike was quickly reversed. Policy rates were cut in October, and progressively reduced from 4.25 per cent (for the rate on the main refinancing operation) to 1 per cent by the middle of 2009 (Figure 23.4).

3.2 Discussion

After Lehman's failure, the ECB – like the Federal Reserve and Bank of England – implemented non-standard policies that, as we have seen, led to the expansion of its balance sheet. But this outcome reflected standard central bank practice and orthodox economic thinking in the face of a liquidity problem. Given access to the 'printing press', central banks can provide liquidity at essentially zero cost and are thus uniquely well-placed to absorb liquidity risk. From a welfare perspective, central banks should absorb liquidity risk fully and at all times by satiating the private sector's demand for liquidity. This is an implication of both Friedman's rule for monetary policy and Bagehot's rule for containing financial crises.

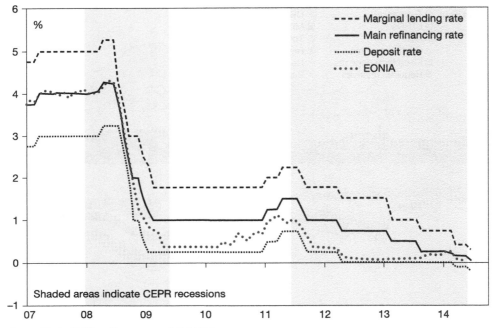

Figure 23.4 ECB policy rates and EONIA

Source: ECB.

Given the predominance of banks as a channel of financial intermediation in Europe, the ECB designed its policy so as to deal directly with banks and focused, in particular, on replacing the wholesale funding market which had come almost to a stop after the collapse of Lehman Brothers in the fall of 2008.

In this phase the ECB can be seen as having been very successful. As Tommaso Padoa-Schioppa correctly anticipated (Padoa-Schioppa, 2004) (and contrary to claims by some before the crisis), the Eurosystem proved to be sufficiently robust to be able to face an interbank run by providing emergency liquidity and adopting what he called a 'market operation approach' to its role as lender-of-last-resort (Reichlin, 2014).

The ECB did well also judging from the performance of the real economy and inflation developments. A recovery of economic activity started in the third quarter of 2009 (see the CEPR dating committee www.cepr.org) and HICP inflation returned to target by the end of the period (see Figures 23.5 and 23.6).

Among others, Lenza et al. (2010), Giannone et al. (2012), Peersman (2011) attempt to measure the macroeconomic impact of these non-standard policy measures. Based on a variety of counterfactual exercises, such papers conclude that the effectiveness of the ECB's actions was not constrained by the zero lower bound and that these measures were supportive of economic activity, largely by preventing a more discontinuous and dramatic curtailment of credit provision to the real economy.

As regards the level of interest rates over this period, Giannone et al. (2012, 2014) and Pill and Smets (2013) show that by the end of 2009 and until 2012 the actual path of 3-month Euribor was below the counterfactual one based on the historical ECB monetary policy rule. This indicates that, by its historical standard the ECB policy was very accommodative

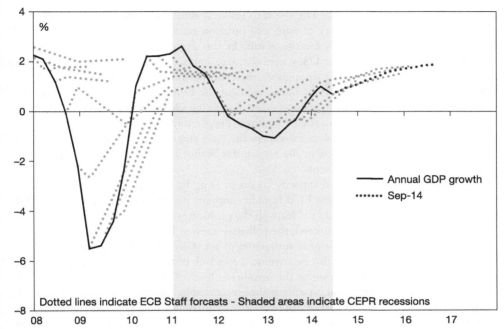

Figure 23.5   Euro area real GDP growth and ECB staff forecast of real GDP growth

Source: Eurostat, ECB.

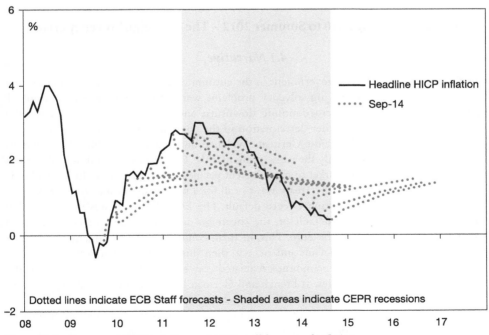

Figure 23.6   Euro area HICP inflation and ECB staff forecast of inflation

Source: Eurostat, ECB.

and, unlike what happened in the US, the zero lower bound constraint on the interest rate was very short lived. The recovery of euro area inflation rates to levels above 2 per cent by the end of this period accounts for this result. In this respect, the euro area experience contrasts with evidence from the US, where the zero lower bound appears to have been a binding constraint on rate setting throughout the crisis period (Stock and Watson, 2012).

However, the ECB's measures did not implement the fundamental changes (such as the restructuring of banks and their balance sheets, involving closures and recapitalisations as necessary) that may have been needed to address deeper underlying solvency problems in both public and private sector balance sheets in the euro area. But the ECB's measures were not intended to. Rather it was left to the responsible authorities (national governments and regulators) to address these concerns.

Where the state had the fiscal capacity to do so (e.g., in Germany), failing banks were rescued by state intervention (with ECB liquidity support merely smoothing the path). But in other cases, where fiscal capacity to clean-up the problem was inadequate, the fundamental problems were simply deferred. Indeed, the palliative created by the ECB's liquidity actions blunted the incentives for the national authorities to act (Giannone et al., 2011).

But such procrastination can also be attributed to a lack of tools (or lack of willingness to pool resources) for crisis resolution at the area-wide level. Where bank balance sheets are larger than GDP, inadequate fiscal capacity is almost inevitable, whatever the state of sovereign finances. This procrastination in the context of inadequate area-wide fiscal resources and institutions serves to explain why European banks started their necessary deleveraging process only in 2012 (see Figure 23.7), three years after the Lehman crisis and three years after the US banks that had been provided with prompt and conditional fiscal support via the TARP in 2009 (Reichlin, 2014).

4. Phase 2: Spring 2010 to Summer 2012 – The sovereign/solvency crisis

4.1 Narrative

The election of a new Greek government in the autumn of 2009 led to a restatement of the Greek fiscal position. Underlying solvency problems were laid bare. Concerns multiplied, especially as the broader macroeconomic downturn and implicit liabilities towards the financial sector threatened further deterioration in the context of the financial crisis.

Greek sovereign spreads against Germany widened and bidders at public debt auctions demanded greater concessions. By the early spring of 2010, Greece faced a funding strike: it was unable to raise funds on the market to meet current payments. This placed the ECB in a bind.

The natural implication of the Treaty was to call for a market solution to the Greek crisis which would have implied letting Greece default. The ECB, however, was understandably concerned that permitting a default on the sovereign debt of a euro area country could potentially trigger exit from the euro. This, in turn, could have led to contagion to other countries: if Greece were to default and/or exit, then this possibility would be entertained for other peripheral euro area economies. A related concern was financial contagion to the financial sector in core countries, as French and German banks had significant exposures to Greek sovereign debt.

But the ECB on its own was not well-equipped to address the solvency problem that threatened Greece. It had not been endowed with the necessary instruments and was subject to institutional constraints that were expressly designed to protect it from pressure to deliver quasi-fiscal support to address solvency problems.

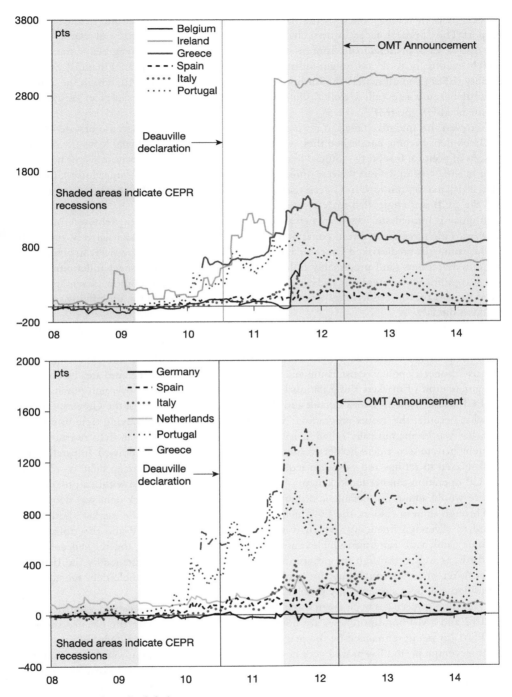

Figure 23.7 Bank credit default swaps

Source: Bloomberg.

The ECB therefore looked to the national governments to provide the necessary fiscal support. This approach faced its own challenges given the Treaty's 'no bail out' clause. But by late April a set of bilateral loans from other euro area countries had been agreed (a framework which eventually took a stronger institutional form in the European Financial Stability Facility (EFSF) and ultimately the European Stability Mechanism (ESM)), within the context of what became a so-called 'troika' adjustment programme under the auspices of (and also co-financed by) the IMF.

Yet even this initiative failed to restore market confidence, in part because private holders of Greek debt became concerned they were being subordinated by official loans (i.e., if – for reasons of political feasibility – official loans were to be made senior to private sector holdings, then in the event of default the remaining private holders would suffer larger losses). In early May 2010, market tensions in Greece reached fever pitch, cross-border contagion intensified and the ECB was compelled to act.

Imposing immediate losses on private holders of Greek sovereign debt was one way forward. This threatened severe contagion and financial disruption. Alternatively, the ECB could assume the credit risk in Greek sovereign debt by purchasing it aggressively in potentially unlimited amounts (and presumably holding it on the ECB balance sheet indefinitely). Yet this was politically contentious and would have violated Treaty prohibitions. Each approach faced its own practical difficulties – but either would have addressed the underlying solvency problem directly.

In the end, the ECB adopted a middle way between these two strategies. It announced the securities markets programme (SMP), which entailed making outright purchases of Greek (and other peripheral) sovereign debt (see Table 23.2). Ostensibly, the SMP was intended to maintain effective monetary policy transmission and market functioning across the euro area by avoiding a fragmentation of markets along national lines. But in practice these sovereign purchases by the ECB avoided a hard Greek default and allowed immediate funding of the Greek sovereign as (what became) the 'troika programme' was put in place (as well as buying time to prepare for what was euphemistically called 'private sector involvement' (PSI) in debt restructuring, whereby private sector debt holders voluntarily agreed to accept write-downs). In parallel, the ECB relaxed its ratings and valuation requirements for the use of sovereign debt as collateral in ECB operations, and reduced haircuts, justified on the basis that once within a programme Greece would adjust, not default, and therefore market pricing of Greek debt was wrong.

Through these measures, the ECB helped to take Greece 'out of the market', both with regard to sovereign financing (which was provided through the SMP and the troika programme) and bank funding (which came via ECB operations using the relaxed collateral standards, as well as through the provision of emergency liquidity assistance by the Bank of Greece). Yet since this 'muddling through' approach did not offer credible debt relief, it left the underlying debt sustainability problem to fester.

Over time, Greece has been given some debt relief: private holders accepted a restructuring in 2012 and SMP bond purchases are now maturing and rolling onto the balance sheet of the ESM (or being refinanced by the private sector as market access is slowly regained). But the intervening period has proved very costly for Greece, and contagion to other parts of the euro area has not been avoided. Both Ireland (in November 2010) and Portugal (in June 2011), in the face of their own macroeconomic and financial challenges, made their own requests for external official financial support and went into troika programmes.

Despite the severity of the ongoing sovereign crisis (see the dynamics of sovereign spreads described in Figure 23.8), in April 2011 the ECB increased its refi rate by 25bps to 1.25 per cent, and again in July to 1.5 per cent. These hikes reflected a belief that the peak of the

Table 23.2 Timeline of events – Phase 2: The sovereign crisis

10 May 10	The ECB resumes the temporary swaps line with the Fed
10 May 10	The ECB announces the creation of the Security Market Programme, for interventions in euro area public and private debt securities
10 May 10	The ECB announces that it will adopt FRFA in the regular 3 month longer term refinancing operations (LTRO) to be allotted on 26 May and 30 June
30 June 10	The ECB ends its Covered Bond Purchase Programme
28 July 10	The ECB announces stricter rules on collateral
28 Oct 10	EU leaders agree to strengthen the Stability and Growth Pact, and to establish a permanent crisis mechanism
21 Nov 10	Ireland seeks financial support
17 Dec 10	ECB and BoE agree to extend swaps lines
21 Dec 10	US dollar/euro swap lines prolonged
1 Jan 11	The European Banking Authority created
18 Mar 11	The European Banking Authority publishes details of the EU wide banking stress tests
6 Apr 11	Portugal requests activation of aid mechanism
7 Apr 11	The ECB raises refi rate by 25bps to 1.25%
9 Jun 11	The ECB announces that main refinancing operations will continue as FRFA for as long as necessary and at least until the end of the ninth maintenance period of 2011
29 Jun 11	US dollar/euro swap lines prolonged
13 July 11	The ECB increases refi rate by .25bps to 1.5%
25 Aug 11	Swap line with the Bank of England prolonged
15 Sep 11	Additional US dollar liquidity providing operations
6 Oct 11	2 one year LTROs conducted in October 2011 and December 2011, FRFA Second Covered Bond Purchase Programme for a maximum amount of EUR 40 billion
1 Nov 11	Mr Draghi becomes President of the ECB
3 Nov 11	The ECB cuts refi rate by 25bps to 1.25%
8 Dec 11	The ECB cuts refi rate by 25bps to 1.00%
8 Dec 11	Two 3 year LTROs, conducted as FRFA
8 Dec 11	Reserve ratio reduced from 2% to 1%
8 Dec 11	Increased collateral availability, accepting single A rated ABS
9 Feb 12	Eligibility criteria for additional credit claims for seven national central banks
28 Feb 12	Greek bonds no longer accepted as collateral for ECB refinancing operations
8 Mar 12	Greek bonds accepted as collateral, due to activation of the buy back scheme backed by the EFSF
7 Aug 11	Statement by Mr Trichet on Italy and Spain. ECB will actively implement its Securities Market Programme

crisis had passed and a normalisation of monetary policy could commence, with inflation already rising. At that juncture the ECB staff's macroeconomic projections were predicting a decline in GDP growth in 2011–12 (Figure 23.5) and an increase in inflation (Figure 23.6). It therefore appears that the weight given to the inflation outlook in driving policy decisions was (as in the 2008 episode) excessive: with the benefit of hindsight, these rate increases look premature.

As Greece, Ireland and Portugal entered troika programmes in 2010–11, questions arose about whether contagion would extend to the larger sovereign bond markets for Italy and Spain. Certainly, there were reasons for concern.

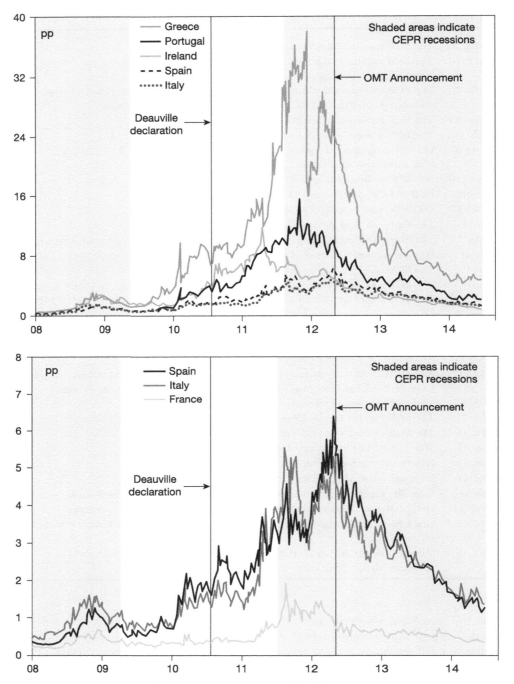

Figure 23.8 Sovereign spreads over 10-year German Bund yields

Source: Bloomberg.

Long-standing public finance challenges in Italy had been brought into sharp relief by the financial crisis and fiscal stresses elsewhere in the euro area. The political environment in mid-2011 was not conducive to taking difficult measures to arrest the slow erosion of market confidence, which was reflected in widening sovereign spreads (particularly from the spring of 2011). In Spain, the interaction between bank and sovereign balance sheets was at centre stage. Although Spain had entered the financial crisis with a relatively low level of public debt, the depth of the recession and the explicit and implicit public liabilities towards the financial sector (which had suffered as the credit-financed property boom in Spain collapsed) led to a rapid deterioration of the Spanish public finances (both in data and in perception).

A natural market concern in this context was whether the EFSF/ESM bailout mechanisms that had been used to support the smaller peripheral countries would be adequate to support large countries such as Spain or Italy. The magnitude of outstanding sovereign debt for these countries dwarfed the available funds. Despite the insistence of the European authorities that the losses that had been imposed on holders of Greek debt via PSI were a one-off, the fact of sovereign restructuring in the euro area had unnerved market participants. The rationale and legal basis for the ECB's actions – on the one hand, using the rhetoric of the Treaty regarding the avoidance of monetary financing while, on the other hand, acting to prevent a Greek sovereign default – created uncertainties as to how the ECB would deal with a broader sovereign crisis, and hence uncertainty about the future of the single currency itself. The ECB's approach also had controversial distributional consequences, transferring exposures to (and ultimately losses from) programme countries away from private sector balance sheets to the balance sheet of the public sector (see Figure 23.9).

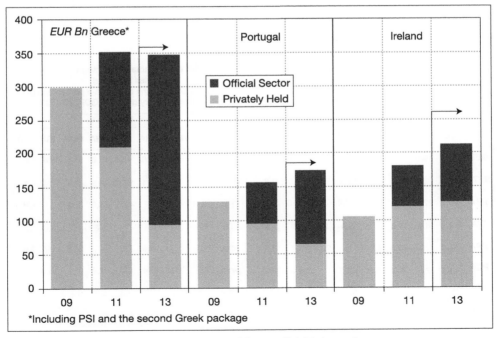

Figure 23.9 Warehousing peripheral sovereign debt on official balance sheets

Source: Goldman Sachs Global Investment Research.

These challenges were further compounded by the interactions between sovereign and bank balance sheets. As peripheral banks held large quantities of home country sovereign debt on their balance sheets, sovereign stresses weighed on attempts to stabilise and strengthen bank balance sheets that were anyway under pressure owing to the economic slowdown and the aftermath of excessive and ill-directed credit creation in the past (at least in Spain). Equally, because sovereigns had extended potentially large implicit guarantees to the banking sector by offering a fiscal backstop to preserve financial stability, weakness in bank balance sheets threatened to affect sovereign funding.

All of this was compounded by the newly perceived potential for euro exit. Faced with the possibility of a financial collapse owing to sovereign default and its impact on the banking sector, it was natural to assume that the affected country might re-introduce its own currency to provide liquidity to its financial system. Assets in vulnerable countries began to incorporate a 'redenomination' risk premium for fear of depreciation following euro exit. This risk premium pushed-up yields and bank funding costs, to the detriment of medium-term sustainability of sovereign and bank balance sheets as well as developments in the real economy, which in turn made exit more likely.

This vicious cycle, whereby rising redenomination risk became self-fulfilling, was an example of a multiple equilibria situation akin to developing countries' debt crises (Calvo, 1988 is the seminal discussion). In such circumstances, drawing a hard distinction between liquidity and solvency issues may not be possible (De Grauwe, 2012 was a forceful advocate of this point). The ECB was again faced with a dilemma: while it had proved comfortable in providing liquidity elastically to the banking sector in a classic lender-of-last-resort role during the early phases of the crisis, the fiscal solvency risks that had become manifest in Greece and the institutional constraints imposed by the Treaty complicated its assessment of how to deal with Italian and Spanish sovereign financing difficulties.

Another implication of the close relationship between banks and sovereigns and the emergence of redenomination risk was fragmentation of euro financial markets along national

Pre-Lehman, Euro interbank markets were highly integrated
(cross-border bank claims as a percentage of lending country quarterly GDP, 2008Q1)

	Lending to							
	GER	NETH	FRA	ITA	SPA	POR	IRE	GRE
GER		19.5	27.9	28.9	33.8	5.4	24.6	4.8
NETH	93.6		85.7	70.2	57.7	7.2	22.0	9.8
FRA	40.3	22.1		74.9	30.2	4.8	13.6	10.4
ITA	72.3	6.3	11.6		5.4	1.4	5.6	1.5
SPA	14.0	15.7	15.5	11.1		20.7	5.7	0.3
POR	11.5	7.9	9.8	8.3	49.5		9.5	11.2
IRE	78.0	29.6	44.3	80.2	54.4	7.5		14.7
GRE	2.0	1.2	1.8	0.5	0.2	0.1	0.5	

With the financial crisis, segmentation has emerged
(cross-border bank claims as a percentage of lending country quarterly GDP, 2013Q1)

	Lending to							
	GER	NETH	FRA	ITA	SPA	POR	IRE	GRE
GER		17.3	21.6	14.1	14.0	2.4	8.8	2.8
NETH	95.5		41.4	16.5	26.2	2.2	7.4	1.2
FRA	28.0	22.7		49.5	14.9	2.4	5.6	0.5
ITA	45.8	3.5	7.9		3.8	0.3	2.0	0.2
SPA	16.6	5.9	10.6	8.0		20.6	1.7	0.2
POR	2.4	16.0	10.6	6.3	42.4		13.3	12.7
IRE	2.6	3.6	8.9	1.3	5.9	0.7		0.2
GRE	4.7	1.2	2.1	0.7	0.5	0.0	0.8	

Figure 23.10 Fragmentation of euro financial markets

Source: BIS, Goldman Sachs Global Investment Research.

lines. Cross-border funding for banks dried-up because of fear of capital losses on exit and/ or crisis (see Figure 23.10).

Initially the ECB attempted to meet these challenges using the tools that had been employed for the small peripheral countries. In August 2011, ECB purchases of government bonds under the SMP extended to Italy and Spain. But this proved ineffective in halting the crisis for a number of reasons. First, in recognition of concerns in the core that ECB sovereign purchases constituted monetisation and undermined incentives for fiscal discipline and adjustment, the SMP actions were always characterised as limited and temporary, which undermined market confidence that the ECB was prepared to offer a full backstop. Second, also to ease sensitivities about the adverse incentives created for reform, the ECB had conditioned its provision of support to Italy via the SMP on certain policy commitments made by the government. But this led to a backlash against 'political interference from unelected technocrats' in Italy, which threatened the political feasibility of the support. This was compounded by comments from the Italian leadership that the conditionality would anyway be of no consequence. Third, concerns about subordination of private sector holders persisted.

As a result, sovereign tensions – and thus pressure on the banking system and fragmentation of euro markets – persisted. By late 2011 (as Mario Draghi replaced Jean-Claude Trichet as President of the ECB) the threat of a banking crisis loomed.

In response, Mr Draghi announced a set of longer-term refinancing operations with an exceptionally long 3-year maturity and FRFA tenders. In a similar manner to the shorter-term operations introduced by Mr Trichet following the failure of Lehman, these operations offered the ECB balance sheet as a central counterparty to conduct inter-bank transactions, but now at longer maturities more relevant to funding and not just liquidity management of banks. Moreover, through these operations the ECB used the banking system as a conduit for supporting the sovereign sector. Banks could engage in a 'carry trade' by borrowing at the ECB 3-year LTRO facility to buy domestic sovereign debt which (in the stressed peripheral countries) yielded much more. Not only did this improve the profitability and thus capital position of the banks, it also substantially eased the financing difficulties faced by Italy and Spain as foreign investors (from both within and outside the euro area) failed to roll their outstanding holdings for fear of exit, restructuring and crisis.

Because the ECB's role in these transactions largely consisted of intermediating cross-border flows of capital as the private euro financial markets fragmented, a rapid increase in so-called TARGET 2 balances emerged (see Figure 23.11).

Through these means, an immediate bank funding crisis in early 2012 was avoided. But – as with the money market operations conducted in late 2008 – these interventions left the fundamental issues unaddressed. In particular, purchases of sovereign debt by banks of the same country funded by 3-year LTRO borrowing from the ECB served to intensify the interconnectedness between bank and sovereign balance sheets that had been an underlying cause of tension.

4.2 Discussion

ECB policy during this phase was reactive rather than proactive. It enabled the financial system and sovereign funding to survive, but without creating good incentives for the necessary fundamental changes to be made.

Rather than choosing between the two solutions to solvency problems – either (1) strict 'monetary dominance', including the possibility of sovereign default, or (2) de facto

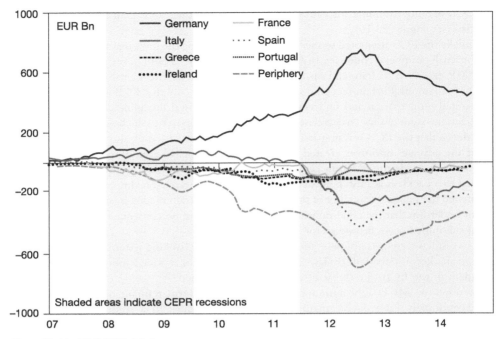

Figure 23.11 TARGET 2 balances

Source: National central banks.

monetisation by potentially unlimited purchases of troubled sovereign debt – the ECB opted for a middle way. But this strategy lacked credibility. It was tested by the market in the summer of 2011 when contagion spread to Italy and Spain.

The strategy failed not only because it lacked conceptual clarity but also because it was based on the miscalculation that provision of liquidity, fiscal austerity and an emphasis on supply side reforms would have led to the stabilisation of debt in Greece, Ireland and Portugal, especially in a context in which exchange rate devaluation could not be used in the adjustment.

Not addressing the problem of banks' recapitalisation in the early stage of the crisis also proved to be very costly. Cheap ECB funding allowed banks to continue to 'evergreen' their outstanding loan portfolios (including loans of questionable quality) rather than being forced to undergo the clean-up and strengthening of their balance sheets that the deleveraging process in the US (triggered by the TARP and Federal Reserve stress tests) had achieved. Figure 23.12 shows that in this period there was a collapse in loans to non-financial corporations which was more significant than that experienced in 2008–9 if we consider that the decline of industrial production in 2011–12 was more subdued (Colangelo et al., 2014; Reichlin, 2014). Figure 23.13 illustrates the weakness of lending by showing that, over this period, the growth of M3 was positive.

These were dark years for the euro area. Uncertainty about the repartition of responsibility between the different agencies – the central bank, the governments and the European federal authorities – led eventually, as we have seen, to a fragmentation of the financial markets, a credit crunch and a second recession.

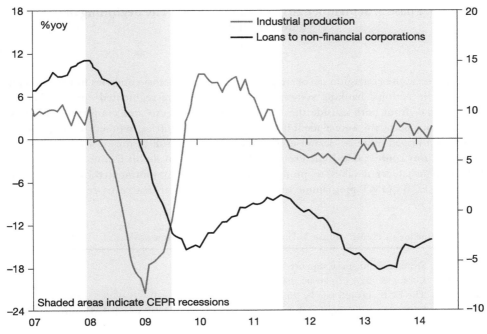

Figure 23.12   Industrial production and bank loans to non-financial corporations

Source: ECB.

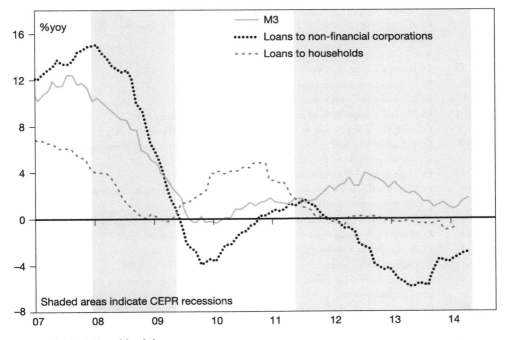

Figure 23.13   M3 and bank loans

Source: ECB.

5. Phase 3: September 2012 to August 2014 – The beginning of a new framework?

5.1 Narrative

As we have seen, the contagion of sovereign market tensions across countries interacted with already fragile national banking systems in a manner that re-segmented euro markets as foreign capital (from both outside the euro area and other euro area countries) withdrew. While solvency problems were evident in some peripheral countries, in others tensions appear to have been driven more by default concerns created as a result of roll-over risk.

It was in this context that ECB President Mario Draghi made his famous pledge in July 2012 to do 'whatever it takes' to preserve the euro. This commitment took institutional form in the ECB's OMT programme introduced in September that year (see Table 23.3).

Table 23.3 Timeline of events – Phase 3: The beginning of a new framework?

27 Jun 12	Spain seeks financial support
29 Jun 12	EU leaders agree to create the Banking Union and the SSM
5 Jul 12	The ECB cuts refi rate by 25bps to 0.75%
20 Jul 12	ECB stops accepting Greek bonds as collateral, as buy back scheme ends on 25 July 2012
20 Jul 12	Eurogroup grants financial assistance to Spain's banking sector
26 Jul 12	Mr Draghi pledges to do 'whatever it takes to preserve the euro'
6 Sep 12	ECB announces technical features of OMTs
19 Dec 12	ECB reinstates Greek bonds as collateral
21 Mar 13	ECB maintains the current level of Emergency Liquidity Assistance (ELA) until 25 March 2013
2 May 13	The ECB cuts refi rate by 25bps to 0.50%
28 Jun 13	ECB stops accepting Cypriot bonds as collateral
4 Jul 13	ECB introduces forward guidance
5 Jul 13	ECB reinstates Cypriot bonds as collateral
23 Nov 13	ECB starts comprehensive assessment ahead of supervisory role
16 Dec 13	Daniele Nouy appointed as Chair of the Supervisory Board
3 Feb 14	ECB collects the first set of data on comprehensive assessment. Stress tests will incorporate results of the AQR
25 Apr 14	ECB publishes SSM Framework regulation
5 Jun 14	ECB cuts refi rate by 10bps to 0.15%, bringing the interest rate on deposit facility to 0.10%, below zero for the first time
5 Jun 14	FRFA to continue as long as needed, and at least until December 2016
5 Jun 14	ECB suspends sterilisation of the liquidity injected under the SMP
5 Jun 14	ECB introduces a series of T LTROs
5 Jun 14	Intensification of preparatory work on outright purchases of ABS
17 Jun 14	ECB to continue one week US dollar liquidity providing operations after 31 July 2014 until further notice
17 Jul 14	ECB publishes disclosure process for comprehensive assessment
4 Sep 14	ECB cuts refi rate by 10bps to 0.05%
4 Sep 14	ECB announces the creation of the ASB Purchase Programme, to begin in October 2014
4 Sep 14	ECB announces a third covered bond purchase programme (CBPP3).

The OMT scheme foresaw the possibility of central bank purchases of the shorter-dated government debt of countries that entered European Stability Mechanism (ESM) programmes (and accepted the implied conditionality). This created the capacity for the ECB balance sheet to be used to warehouse the public debt of large peripheral countries in the face of roll over risk – just as had already been achieved for the small countries via the troika – while retaining the important element of conditionality to maintain incentives for fiscal discipline and contain moral hazard. In so doing, the ECB assumed the 'convertibility risk' that was associated with the potential exit of stressed countries from the euro area.

The introduction of the OMT has exerted a powerful effect on market sentiment, leading to a substantial narrowing of peripheral sovereign spreads over German yields (see Altavilla et al., 2014 for a quantitative assessment of the OMT on credit risk). In turn, the stabilisation of financial markets has created an environment conducive to the stabilisation of the real economy, while providing breathing space for the necessary underlying area-wide governance improvements and national structural reforms and fiscal consolidation to be implemented.

Crucially the OMT worked through expectational channels and the credibility of Mr Draghi's 'whatever it takes' announcement. The promise to underwrite sovereign debt has proved sufficient to re-coordinate private market participants on a 'good' equilibrium where debt rolls and sovereign credit risk premia remain contained. As a result, OMT purchases have never been made: the ECB has not bought one euro of peripheral sovereign debt since the OMT was announced in September 2012, and the larger peripheral countries (Italy and Spain) have not entered ESM programmes to activate the possibility of such purchases.

The substantial success of the OMT announcement was founded on using an 'off-balance sheet approach' to stabilise sovereign markets. In essence, Mr Draghi issued a put option on peripheral debt (albeit one with a vague strike price), rather than making outright purchases. This approach allowed him to navigate the dangerous waters between, on the one hand, understandable German concerns about the abuse of central bank financing stemming from the unique institutional set-up of the euro area and, on the other, market participants' concerns about the sustainability of peripheral fiscal positions in the face of both fundamental weaknesses in the public finances and roll over risk at a time of market tension.

But importantly this off-balance-sheet approach did not impose conditionality on the benefiting countries, which remained outside ESM programmes. Spain and Italy enjoyed substantial reductions in their financing costs as a result of the announcement of the OMT, but did not have to satisfy the conditions implied by participation in an ESM programme, comparable to those set for the small peripheral economies by the troika. Implementing the necessary macroeconomic adjustment was therefore a matter of trust.

To their credit, the Spanish authorities have pursued significant adjustment even without the imposition of explicit conditionality. But Italy's macroeconomic adjustment has been, at best, more hesitant than that in Spain. And with market pressure diminished by the OMT, it remains to be seen whether the promised institutional and economic restructuring of Italy will be delivered.

But it is not only at the national level that institutional and economic reform is required. As we have argued elsewhere, a fundamental weakness in the euro area construct remains the threat that a re-segmentation of financial markets will create an explosive dynamic. Rather than absorbing risk and helping to stabilise the system, the financial sector can become a magnifier and accelerant of centrifugal forces.

An important contributor to such financial segmentation is the emergence of the *Teufelskreis* (or 'diabolical loop') between sovereign and bank balance sheets: banking problems weaken sovereign balance sheets given the (often implicit) government guarantees provided to the financial sector, while banks typically hold a significant portfolio of domestic sovereign debt, such that a weakening of the sovereign balance sheet may raise concerns about the solvency of banks. Breaking this link and thereby establishing a 'level playing field' for euro area banks independent of their domicile and links to specific sovereigns is seen as an essential support for financial stability, better integrated markets and effective monetary policy transmission.

It was in this context that the June 2012 EU summit promised to create a 'banking union' with the goal of breaking the connection between sovereigns and banks. Indeed, the political pledges made at this summit were an important facilitator of Mr Draghi's 'whatever it takes' intervention and subsequent announcement of the OMT.

The European 'banking union' consists of several elements: a single supervisory mechanism (SSM) at the ECB; a single resolution mechanism (SRM) to deal with failing banks; more transparent and uniform application of state aid rules to government support for the banking sector; and the banking recovery and resolution directive (BRRD) to define when and how the authorities can intervene to support troubled banks. Other elements originally conceived at the time of the June 2012 announcement – notably a common area-wide deposit insurance scheme – appear, at least at this stage, stillborn (see Hellwig, 2014 for a critical appraisal).

A significant step in this context has been the announcement and then the implementation of a comprehensive review of the asset quality of the large banks under the supervision of the ECB. Only at this stage, in anticipation of this exercise, the euro area banks started a process of recapitalisation. Figure 23.7 shows that banks risk in Italy and Spain, as measured by CDS, started declining at this point (mid-2013).

But despite the improvement in financial market conditions, the macroeconomic situation remained stagnant and inflation commenced a persistent decline (Figures 23.5 and 23.6). The behaviour of longer-term interest rates in Germany reflects this decline in nominal growth rates (Figure 23.14). The ECB implemented a series of refi rate cuts (July 2012, May 2013, June 2014 and September 2014), introduced a negative rate on its deposit facility, launched new targeted LTROs and announced a purchase programme for ABS and covered bonds.

Moreover, in his August 2014 speech at Jackson Hole, Mr Draghi proposed initiatives to improve the institutional context for monetary policy: more emphasis on developing an appropriate monetary/fiscal policy mix at the area-wide level and greater commitment and European governance of structural reform.

5.2 Discussion

One way of characterising ECB policy in this most recent phase is as an attempt to find a balance between two extreme positions: one emphasising a strict interpretation of the 'no monetary financing' prohibition; and another calling on the ECB to act as a backstop in a debt crisis (De Grauwe, 2012; Krugman, 2014), disregarding moral hazard problems or concerns about the potential fiscal consequences of this action.

For example, the promise of potentially unlimited liquidity support subject to conditionality under the OMT can be seen as steering a middle way: recognition that a bad equilibrium resulting from self-fulfilling crisis is possible, but also containing moral hazard so as to avoid unsustainability and insolvency. In turn, this acts as a mechanism to manage a tradeoff between risks to price stability (stemming from the moral hazard and threat to central bank credibility) and risks to financial instability (stemming from destabilising self-fulfilling market dynamics).

Following the OMT, we have seen a further refinement in this direction. Mr Draghi's speech in June 2014 in London called for a euro area framework to coordinate and monitor

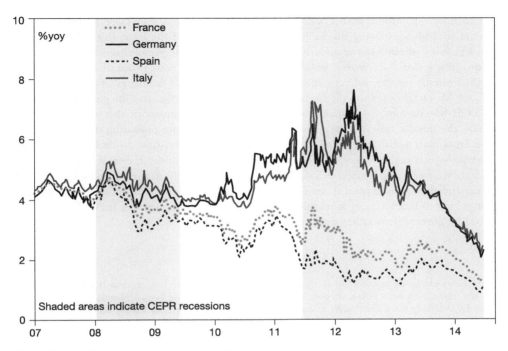

Figure 23.14 10-year government bond yields

Source: Bloomberg.

structural reforms. His Jackson Hole speech in August 2014 argued for greater coordination of monetary and fiscal policy to change the stance of fiscal policy at the euro area wide level. These initiatives can be seen as attempts to create a broader area-wide institutional set-up in the euro area, which overcomes some of the lacunae that the crisis identified in the Maastricht framework.

6. Concluding remarks

Our assessment is as follows.

The ECB was effective in the initial banking crisis of 2007–9, since it was largely called upon to address liquidity issues that fall squarely in the normal realm of central banking. But since the underlying, more fundamental solvency problems in sovereign and bank balance sheets were not addressed adequately by the responsible fiscal and regulatory authorities, in the subsequent euro area-specific crisis of 2010–12 the ECB was forced to act outside its natural domain and address solvency issues. Perhaps unsurprisingly, in this context it was found wanting.

In particular, the ECB attempted to pursue a middle path between two approaches. Fearing contagion and financial collapse, it was unwilling to enforce the 'monetary dominance' embodied in the Maastricht Treaty, which foresaw default as the solution to fiscal unsustainability. Yet understandably wary of a political backlash in creditor countries and naturally concerned about its own credibility, the ECB was equally unwilling to accept the risk of full 'fiscal dominance' and purchase the debt of troubled sovereigns in potentially unlimited amounts.

The resulting middle course was a pragmatic and perhaps inevitable response to the substantial challenges facing the ECB in the circumstances of the time. But it has failed to offer a genuine solution to the underlying solvency issues, while permitting (or even creating) a damaging set of dislocations, notably a fragmentation of euro financial markets, which weighed heavily on the real economy especially in the stressed countries of the periphery.

Since Mr Draghi's famous pledge to do 'whatever it takes' to sustain the euro in July 2012, the ECB has attempted to construct a new institutional framework that will allow it to manage the middle course more successfully. Although there are promising developments in some areas such as banking union, without a 'new bargain' on how to deal with the debt overhang which is the legacy of the crisis, the euro area is under threat. While the ECB's assumption of new responsibilities such as bank supervision and macroprudential surveillance has expanded its role beyond its original monetary domain, the creation of a new bargain upon which to build a more workable monetary union in the euro area inevitably relies on actions by governments rather than central bankers alone.

Notes

1 The views expressed in this chapter are those of the authors and do not necessarily reflect the views of the institutions with which they are currently or have in the past been affiliated.
2 See ECB (2012) for a description of monetary policy operations in the Eurosystem.

References

Altavilla, C., Giannone, D., and Lenza, M. (2014), The Financial and Macroeconomic Effects of OMT Announcements, *ECB Working Papers* 1707.

Calvo, G. (1988), Servicing the Public Debt: The Role of Expectations, *American Economic Review*, 78(4), 647–61.

Colangelo, A., Giannone, D., Lenza, M., Pill, H., and Reichlin, L. (2014), Cross-Border Transactions in the Euro Area and the Financial Crisis, unpublished.

De Grauwe, P. (2012), The Governance of a Fragile Eurozone, *Australian Economic Review*, 45(3), 255–68.

Ehrmann, M., Fratzscher, M., Gürkaynak, R.S., and Swanson, E.T. (2011), Convergence and Anchoring of Yield Curves in the Euro Area, *Review of Economics and Statistics*, 93(1), 350–64.

European Central Bank (2012), *The Implementation of Monetary Policy in the Euro Area*, Frankfurt: European Central Bank.

Giannone, D., Lenza, M., Pill, H., and Reichlin, L. (2010), Non-standard Monetary Policy Measures and Monetary Developments, *CEPR Discussion Paper* 8125.

Giannone, D., Lenza, M., Pill, H., and Reichlin, L. (2011), Monetary Policy and Financial Stability, in Claessens, S., Evanoff, D.D., Kaufman, G.G., and Kodres, L.E. (eds) *Macroprudential Regulatory Policies: The New Road to Financial Stability*? Singapore: World Scientific Publishing.

Giannone, D., Lenza, M., Pill, H., and Reichlin, L. (2012), The ECB and the Interbank Market, *Economic Journal*, 122(564), 467–86.

Giannone, D., Lenza, M., and Reichlin, L. (2012), Money, Credit, Monetary Policy and the Business Cycle in the Euro Area, *ECARES Working Paper* 12–008.

Giannone, D., Lenza, M., and Reichlin, L. (2014), Money, Credit, Monetary Policy and the Business Cycle in the Euro Area: What Has Changed Since the Crisis? unpublished.

Heider, F., Hoerova, M., and Holthausen, C. (2009), Liquidity Hoarding and Interbank Market Spreads: The Role of Counterparty Risk, *ECB Working Paper* 1126.

Hellwig, M. (2014), Yes Virginia, There is a European Banking Union! But It May Not Make Your, Wishes Come True, Max Plank Institute for Research on Collective Goods.

Krugman, P. (2014), Currency Regimes, Capital Flows and Crises, *IMF Economic Review*, 62(4), 470–93.

Lenza, M., Pill, H., and Reichlin, L. (2010), Monetary Policy in Exceptional Times, *Economic Policy*, 25(62), 295–339.

Mourlon-Druol, E. (2014), Don't Blame the Euro: Historical Reflections on the Roots of the Eurozone Crisis, *West European Politics*, 37(6), 1282–96.

Peersman, G. (2011), Macroeconomic Effects of Unconventional Monetary Policy in the Euro Area, *ECB Working Paper* 1397.

Pill, H. and Smets, F. (2013), Monetary Policy Frameworks after the Great Financial Crisis, in Braude, J., Eckstein, Z., Fischer, S., and Flug, K. (eds) *The Great Recession: Lessons for Central Bankers*, Cambridge, MA: MIT Press.

Reichlin, L. (2014), Monetary Policy and Banks in the Euro Area: The Tale of Two Crises, *Journal of Macroeconomics*, 39(PB), 387–400.

Stock, J.H. and Watson, M. (2012), Disentangling the Channels of the 2007–2009 Recession, *Brookings Papers on Economic Activity*, Spring 2012, 81–141.

Trichet, J.C. (2008), Speech delivered at the European Banker of the year 2007 award ceremony, Frankfurt, 30 September.

24

LIVING (DANGEROUSLY) WITHOUT A FISCAL UNION

Ashoka Mody[1]

"Now, here, you see, it takes all the running you can do to keep in the same place," said the [Red] Queen in Lewis Carroll's *Through the Looking Glass*.

1. Introduction

In 2008 and 2009, the specter of global economic catastrophe triggered an internationally-coordinated fiscal stimulus.[2] Virtually every government in the euro area joined to revive economic activity by either lowering tax rates or increasing public spending. This much-needed stimulus was reflected in larger fiscal deficits (Figure 24.1(a) displays the size and timing of the stimulus by the US and the euro area). Within the euro area, Ireland was an exception, as it was already dealing with its banking crisis.

In October 2009, the spectacular magnitude of the Greek fiscal deficit was revealed. The initial reaction was to treat it as a Greek problem, which would be addressed by Greek fiscal austerity. But Greece had an important cognitive effect: it served to emphasize the growing concern with rising public debt in the "advanced" economic world.

There was reason to be concerned. The public debt-to-GDP ratios rose in most advanced countries once the crisis started. And the debt ratios in several euro area economies were heading rapidly towards the 100 percent mark (Figure 24.2) – that threshold being significant because lowering the ratio to below 100 percent has historically presented important policy challenges (IMF, 2012).

The debt burden can be lowered either by raising inflation and GDP growth or by pursuing fiscal austerity. In 2010, the Americans continued a substantial fiscal stimulus to sustain their economic recovery. In contrast, virtually every country in the eurozone started tightening the fiscal belt – the important exception was Germany, where consolidation started a year later. Although the euro area's shift to austerity was prompted by Greece, it was reinforced during the course of 2010 by the perception that the global near-economic-disaster had been averted and further stimulus was unnecessary – and, as such, could no longer be politically sustained. Many economists warned that it was too early to declare victory, but the fears of a Greece-like economic collapse were invoked and spread rapidly across the eurozone, and beyond.

For three crucial years – between 2011 and 2013 – fiscal tightening caused a severe drag on the euro area's economic growth and thus nullified the intended goal of reducing public

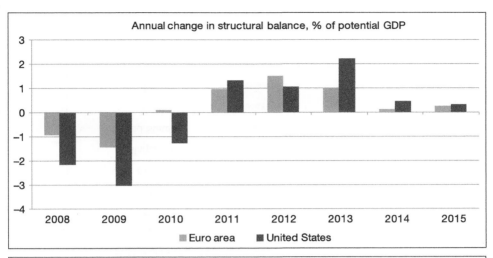

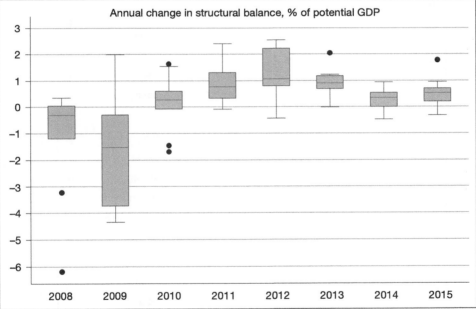

Figure 24.1 Fiscal consolidation (annual change in structural balance, % of potential GDP)

Source: IMF WEO 2014 (http://www.imf.org/external/ns/cs.aspx?id=28).

Note: The chart includes the following countries: Austria, Belgium, Finland, France, Germany, Ireland, Italy, Netherlands, Portugal, Spain.

debt burdens. The consequences were severe for three reasons. First, the eurozone's fiscal austerity came in the context of global austerity and economic weakness. Hence, the ability to grow by exporting to others was compromised. Second, European economies are heavily engaged in trade with each other (Figure 24.3); hence, as any one country slowed down, its weaker import demand hurt growth elsewhere. And, finally, while the US and the UK were able to partly offset the contractionary fiscal consolidation with aggressive monetary policy

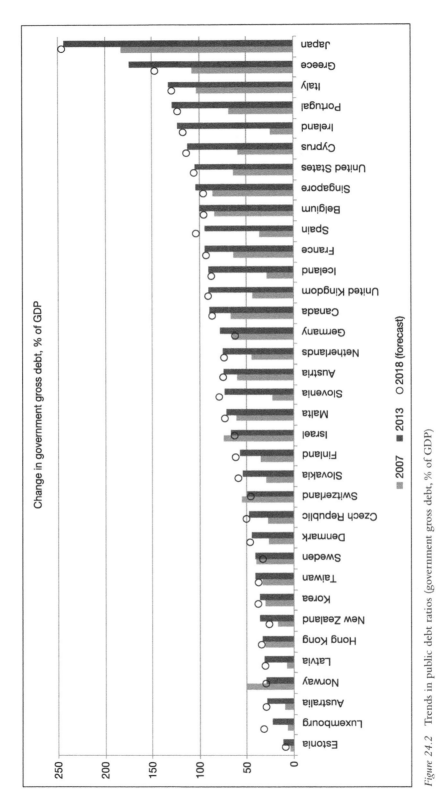

Figure 24.2 Trends in public debt ratios (government gross debt, % of GDP)

Source: IMF WEO 2014 (http://www.imf.org/external/ns/cs.aspx?id=28).

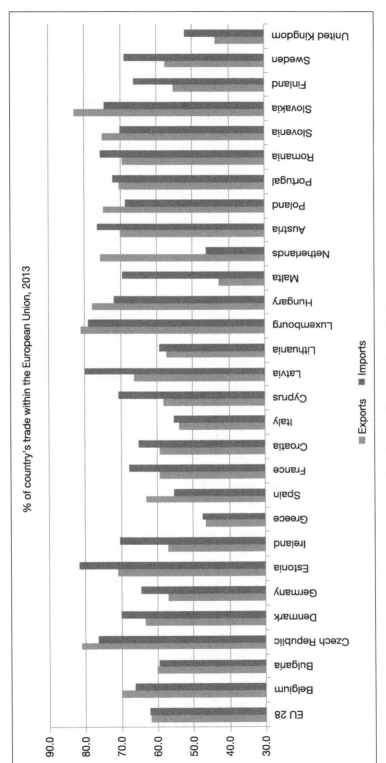

Figure 24.3 Intra-European trade (percentage of country's trade within the European Union, 2013)

Source: Eurostat (http://epp.eurostat.ec.europa.eu/portal/page/portal/statistics/search_database).

and efforts to rehabilitate their banking sectors, the eurozone's monetary policy was passive and banking sector problems were allowed to fester.[3]

Thus, the eurozone economies, especially those that experienced the greatest market stress, are in something of a trap. Slow growth and low inflation have kept their debt ratios rising or high. But precisely for that reason, they are expected to maintain fiscal austerity, which will dampen growth and inflation and keep debt ratios elevated.

Although prompted by Greece, the euro area's fiscal policy response to the crisis reflected the constraints imposed by the Maastricht Treaty. That political contract, which gave birth to the euro, did not prepare for the risk that a member state may experience deep fiscal distress. In principle, there was a provision. Because a member state was prohibited from repaying another's member state's debt obligations, one possibility was that private creditors would bear losses and thus relieve some of the distressed country's debt burden. But the framers of the Treaty viewed financial markets as fickle and untrustworthy and so created fiscal rules intended to ensure steadfast discipline. The subtext of the Treaty was that the rules would eliminate the likelihood of fiscal stress – and hence there would be no need for a financial safety net or for default on obligations to private creditors. But that finely balanced construction left no latitude for the possibility that a country may live beyond its means or circumstances may unexpectedly turn adverse.

In this sense, the euro was set up as a common currency of an incomplete monetary union. The sovereign member states of this union surrendered the exercise of independent monetary policy to the European Central Bank (ECB) without clear domestic alternatives to deal with economic distress. When faced with high unemployment risk at home, workers in Europe have traditionally not moved in significant numbers to other European nations with better employment prospects. And for fear of having to pay for the mistakes of others, the members of the monetary union were unwilling at Maastricht to contribute to a pool of sizeable centralized resources to alleviate acute pressures in member nations. Thus, monetary sovereignty was given up but fiscal responsibility remained firmly with the nation state.

This had profound implications for macroeconomic management. To maintain national fiscal insulation, member nations were required to wear a fiscal straightjacket overlaid on the monetary straightjacket of a common currency. Thus, precisely when fiscal policy was needed to dig an economy out of its economic troubles, the rules required the opposite.

Some had expected (hoped) that, as the crisis unfolded, the sense of European solidarity would foster greater tolerance for sharing the distress of other euro member states. However, that did not happen. Moreover, the fuzzy option of imposing losses on private creditors was taken off the table. The absence of any vent for the stress created an untenable situation. After much hesitation and delays, help came in the form of official loans. The legal requirement was that those receiving the assistance would repay the debt and, thus, bear the ultimate burden of their distress.

Thus, instead of initiating meaningful change, the crisis reinforced the national interests and preferences that had led to the eurozone's creation as an incomplete monetary union. Indeed, national fiscal discipline – austerity – was emphasized through several initiatives after 2010. And every effort towards sharing risks within a fiscal union was eventually discarded or has remained in limbo.

But the combination of official loans and fiscal austerity proved insufficient at critical points in the crisis. That led to a further improvisation. The repayment terms of official loans were eased. Once again, the strategy was to spread out the help in driblets, preventing a decisive resolution of the stress. Finally, with Germany remaining fiercely protective of its pocketbook, an uneasy alliance evolved between the German Chancellor, Angela Merkel, and the President of the ECB, first Jean-Claude Trichet and then his successor, Mario Draghi. This alliance now effectively governs eurozone macroeconomic policy. In deference to the ECB, Chancellor Merkel had to rein in her correct instinct that debt restructuring must be a necessary element of eurozone's fiscal adjustment. In turn, the ECB offered its deeper pockets as financial safety nets. As a consequence, the ECB has acquired an intrusive role in the fiscal management of member states.

The rest of this chapter is divided into two main parts. The next section documents the extraordinary austerity in the euro area after 2010. That austerity materially lowered economic growth, with the consequence that – for many countries – the challenge of reducing debt is greater today than in 2010. Continuation of an austerity-only policy promises continued anemic growth, low inflation, and high debt burdens, contributing to persistent financial vulnerabilities in the euro area. The other substantive section describes the evolution of the crisis management framework. Because debt restructuring remains anathema and a fiscal union is politically impossible, the financial safety net is a combination of financial assistance through the European Stability Mechanism (ESM), backstopped by the ECB's Outright Monetary Transactions (OMT) Program. The OMT is untested – and, given its economic, political, and legal weaknesses, it is best that it remains untested. In the meantime, a new Europhoria may cause imprudent lending and create new financial fragilities. By way of conclusion, the paper speculates on future scenarios.

2. Austerity

Before the onset of the crisis, eurozone countries were prone to somewhat greater austerity than other advanced economies. Specifically, they had a mildly stronger tendency to increase their primary budget surpluses – the fiscal balances that do not include interest payments – in response to higher debt ratios. But after 2010, the eurozone countries dramatically increased their response to higher debt. Indeed, while the eurozone aversion to debt went up, other advanced economies, on average, paid less attention to debt reduction.

The focus on debt reduction in the eurozone was not restricted to countries with higher debt ratios. Even the Netherlands, which had a modest debt ratio of around 75 percent of GDP, engaged in the same austerity drive as did the more heavily-indebted Italy.[4] In the euro area, austerity was a deeply ingrained instinct.

The fiscal rules crafted at Maastricht require that the budget deficit be less than 3 percent of GDP and the public debt ratio remain below 60 percent of GDP (or, if it is above, it should be declining to that level). Before the crisis, the benchmarks were flouted all the time and created a system of continuous game-playing and deception. Nevertheless, the countries did internalize a deficit reduction norm. Once the crisis started, that norm was geared up as the "creditor" countries made clear that they would not pay for the mistakes of others.

To be clear, austerity does eventually reduce the debt burden. But it does so at a cost. The cost can be especially high if the austerity is deep and persistent. Economic growth is reduced and inflation is dampened, both of which weaken the ability to repay debt. And because the debt burden remains elevated, the austerity continues, reinforcing the counterproductive cycle. Extended austerity can also cause long-term damage since workers' skills atrophy and the incentives to invest decline. These considerations are all the more serious in countries with high economic distress and low growth potential.

In two important papers, Henning Bohn (1995, 1998) proposed a framework to assess the deference accorded to debt reduction. This requires taking account of the country's output gap, the difference between its actual and potential output. When the output gap increases,

Table 24.1 The intensity of fiscal austerity: eurozone and non-eurozone advanced economies

	Euro Nations			Non-Euro Nations		
	Greenspan Put Era	Great Recession		Greenspan Put Era	Great Recession	
	(2002–7)	(2008–13)	(2011–15)	(2002–7)	(2008–13)	(2011–15)
Gross debt/GDP	0.06★★★	0.08★★	0.15★★★	0.04★	−0.00	0.04
	[4.78]	[3.48]	[7.15]	[2.06]	[−0.04]	[1.51]
Output gap	0.17★	0.28	0.30★	0.23★★★	0.27★★★	1.20★★
	[2.25]	[1.53]	[2.44]	[10.78]	[5.78]	[3.62]
Constant	−3.04★★	−7.40★★	−12.87★★★	−1.61★	−2.59	−4.48
	[−2.93]	[−3.64]	[−9.09]	[−2.02]	[−0.78]	[−1.77]
Observations	72	85	75	66	58	45
R-squared	0.11	0.15	0.41	0.25	0.11	0.52
Number of countries	13	15	15	12	11	9

Notes: Dependent variable: primary fiscal balance/GDP; t-statistics in brackets; ★★★ $p<0.01$, ★★ $p<0.05$, ★ $p<0.1$. The observation for Ireland in 2010 was dropped from regression for the period 2008–13 since an extraordinarily large deficit (−27.2 of GDP) was required for the banks' bailouts.

the economic strength generates more fiscal revenues and public spending on social safety nets declines: the primary surplus increases. Over and beyond this automatic tendency for temporary movements in the primary surplus, Bohn pointed out, the primary balance must rise to repay a rising debt-to-GDP ratio. A higher primary surplus in response to increased debt ensures that the country is "solvent," that it will eventually repay its debts.

Table 24.1 reports the regression estimates for a panel of advanced economies for the years before and after the Great Recession. The primary balance is regressed on the output gap in the same year and the public debt-to-GDP ratio at the end of the previous year. All data are from the International Monetary Fund's (IMF's) *World Economic Outlook*.[5] The econometric estimates correct for autocorrelation. While the results are influenced to some extent by the exclusion or inclusion of particular countries, the spirit of the results and the inferences drawn remain valid.

Consider first the period before the crisis. The years 2002–7 were economically buoyant, sometimes described as the Greenspan Put era, when many believed that monetary policy could contain prospective damage to the economy and financial markets. Even during those years, there was a tendency for the primary surplus to rise in response to higher debt. Figure 24.4 reports the "rolling" coefficients on the debt-to-GDP ratio (based in the regression specification in Table 24.1), with the coefficient plotted for the five-year period ending in that year. A ten percentage point increase in the debt ratio was accompanied by about a half percentage point increase in the primary surplus-to-GDP ratio. The countries in the euro area tended to be just slightly more responsive to a rise in the debt ratio. However, that minor difference was not statistically significant.

As noted above, the period after the crisis started had two policy phases. The coordinated stimulus was injected in 2009 and the world's major economies continued it in 2010. However, from 2011–15, the evidence is clear: the euro area responded with ever greater austerity as public debt increased. The euro area primary surplus response increased to 2 percent for a 10 percentage point increase in the public debt ratio in 2014, before falling in 2015.

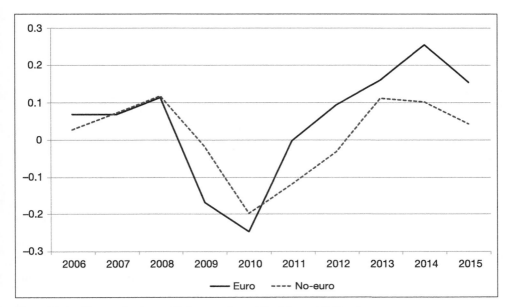

Figure 24.4 Changes in the coefficient on the public debt-to-GDP ratio

Note: The rolling regressions are estimated as in Table 24.1, and the coefficient on debt-to-GDP ratio is for the year in which the five-year sample ends.

Elsewhere in the advanced economies, the rise was considerably smaller, as if in recognition of the extraordinary times and the costs that austerity imposes when the economy is already stressed. To be sure, there were variations among the non-euro area countries. But where the fiscal stimulus was pulled back, as in the US in 2011 and (even earlier) in the UK, other stimulative policies (monetary policy and bank recapitalization) were pursued more aggressively to compensate.

Figure 24.5 explores the euro area response more closely. Controlling for the influence of the output gap, the figure shows the (partial) relationship between the primary surplus and public debt ratio during 2008–13. To compare the responses across countries with different debt ratios, the mean debt-to-GDP ratio for each country is set to zero. Notice that the proportionate increase in primary surplus to rising debt was the same in the Netherlands as in Italy. This was so even though the Dutch debt ratio (reported at the time at about 75 percent of GDP) was much lower than the Italian debt ratio (about 135 percent of GDP). In both cases, even as they implemented greater austerity, their debt ratios continued to rise. It is as if they were running faster but yet falling behind.

The extent to which the debt continues to rise despite an increase in the primary surplus is determined by the so-called "fiscal multiplier." The multiplier measures the contraction in growth due to the austerity. Today, the overwhelming evidence is that these multipliers are large especially in conditions of deep economic stress.

In October 2012, Olivier Blanchard and Daniel Leigh of the IMF published the finding that austerity had caused a significant reduction in the euro area's growth. The near instantaneous reaction of European authorities was to discredit that conclusion. The conclusion could not be right, they said, because austerity builds "confidence" in the sustainability of public finances and, thereby, stimulates investment and growth. Olli Rehn, Vice President

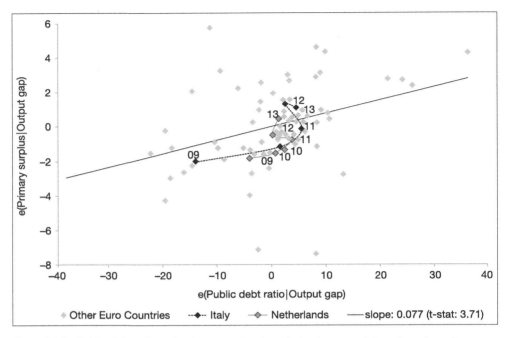

Figure 24.5 Public debt ratio and primary surplus (correlation between debt ratio and surplus, conditional on output gap, 2009–2013)

Source: IMF WEO 2014 (http://www.imf.org/external/ns/cs.aspx?id=28).

Note: Based on Table 1, column 2.

of the European Commission, in an open letter, complained that the IMF research had "not been helpful." Even more than the logic and evidence, he was concerned that the European institutional process would be undermined. By questioning the premise that austerity delivers, the IMF, he said, had worked to "erode the confidence that we have painstakingly built up over the past years in numerous late-night meetings."

But the empirical evidence was clear: any confidence-boosting effect was overwhelmed by the sharp contraction in incomes and demand. Blanchard and Leigh (2013a) published a more detailed analysis that confirmed their original findings. Several other studies also find that fiscal multipliers are high during recessions and, therefore, fiscal tightening will cause a sharp slowdown in growth (Auerbach and Gorodnichenko, 2012, Batini et al., 2012, and Baum et al., 2012). Riera-Crichton et al. (2014) go one step further. Because multipliers are large during recessions, fiscal stimulus can help, but tightening can cause particularly severe output loss. The central theme of these studies is that when the economy is weak, adjusting to that weakness through normal market mechanisms is compromised. Thus, efforts to revive employment through lower wage growth can hurt the ability of households to repay previously contracted debt; to meet their obligations, households save more, which reduces consumption demand and growth. Moreover, if the central bank has reduced interest rates to zero, its ability to provide stimulus is limited. For this reason, where fiscal spending is also cut back sharply, the decline in output can be large.

If, in addition, the fiscal tightening is attempted in a sustained drive, a simple arithmetic leads to persistently high (and rising) debt ratios (as Eyraud and Weber, 2013, demonstrate).

Growth never gets a chance to reduce the debt burden. And, beyond that arithmetic, there are deeper long-term consequences. Blanchard and Leigh (2013b) point out that persistent fiscal consolidation causes various "vicious cycles" to set in: higher long-term unemployment and a sharp fall in investment reduce the economy's growth capacity, causing debt ratios to remain elevated.

It is early to judge the long-term effects, but the evidence on the short-term consequences of fiscal austerity in the euro area is clear. The analysis reported here is a graphical presentation of the Blanchard and Leigh (2012 and 2013a) procedure. As they point out, growth projections have been steadily lowered: these are shown for the euro area, Italy, the Netherlands, and Greece (Figure 24.6a–6d). In April 2011, the expectation was that the economic slowdown would be modest and the GDP growth rate would bounce back. Not only did the short-term projections prove to be optimistic, but the longer-term growth outlook has also been gradually scaled down.

Blanchard and Leigh ask if the slowdown that was not anticipated could, in part, be explained by the pace of fiscal consolidation. In other words, could the failure to predict the severity of the growth slowdown in 2012 and 2013 be related to larger than anticipated consequences ("multipliers") of fiscal austerity? Figure 24.7 shows the relationship between fiscal consolidation from 2011 to 2013 and the "unexpected" slowdown during this period (the "unexpected" slowdown being measured as the difference between annual average growth rate anticipated in April 2011 over the years 2011–13 and the actual growth rate). The negative relationship confirms that the shortfall in growth was greater where fiscal consolidation was larger.

Notice that both Italy and the Netherlands fall on this regression line. In other words, both had about the same-sized fiscal multiplier. With both displaying the same tendency to respond to rising debt – albeit at very different ratios – they both sacrificed short-term growth to the same extent. In contrast, fiscal consolidation in the US was not as costly in terms of lost short-term growth. This was possibly because monetary policy was more aggressive and because the effort to heal banks came early in the crisis. The UK is also somewhat above the regression line, perhaps for the same reasons.

Some might argue that growth in the euro area was held back for reasons other than fiscal austerity. In particular, a sharp reversal occurred in capital flows that had been financing large current account deficits. The argument, thus, is that countries that had received large financial inflows before the onset of the crisis were suddenly required to repay the amounts due and had no choice but to reduce domestic spending.

Blanchard and Leigh (2013) examined this possibility and found that controling for the size of the pre-crisis current account deficit does not change the conclusion that fiscal auster-ity was amplified by a large fiscal multiplier. This is not a surprise. The outflow of private capital flows was compensated for by public capital inflows. Accominotti and Eichengreen (2013) find:

> In 2011 indeed, net official inflows to the GIIPS [Greece, Ireland, Italy, Portugal, and Spain] amounted to 12.4% of their collective GDP and more than com-pensated for net private outflows (8.3% of GDP). This explains how these countries could continue to run current account deficits, at least temporarily, despite the crisis.

Thus, in 2011, when the most intense phase of austerity started, the pressure was not from large capital outflows.

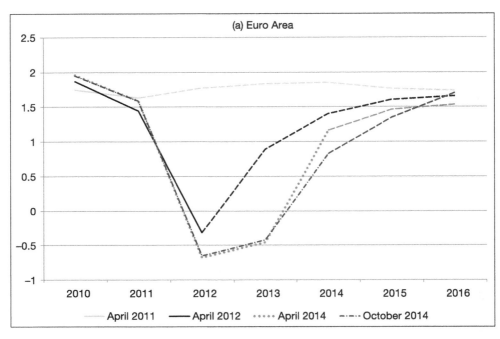

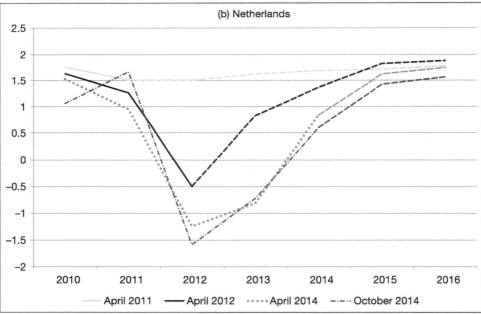

Figure 24.6 The changing growth outlook (Percentage annual GDP growth, actual outcomes and predictions for different vintages)

Source: IMF WEO 2011, 2012 and 2014 (http://www.imf.org/external/ns/cs.aspx?id=28).

Note: Dashed lines refer to projections at the time.

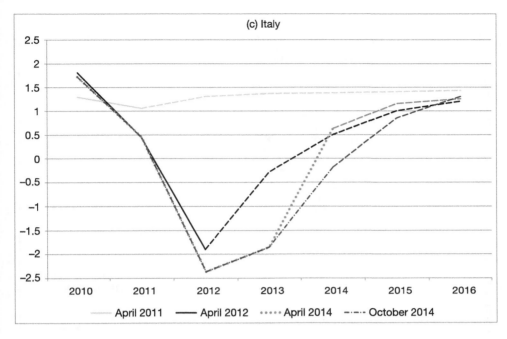

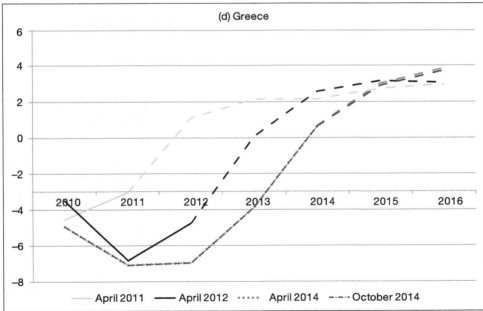

Figure 24.6 (Continued)

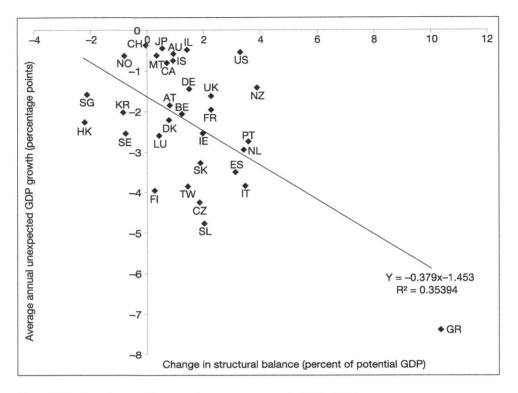

Figure 24.7 Actual consolidation and unexpected growth (2011–2013)

Source: IMF WEO 2011 and 2014 (http://www.imf.org/external/ns/cs.aspx?id=28).

Note: The average annual unexpected growth is calculated as the difference between the average annual realised growth between 2011 and 2013, as reported in the 2014 WEO data release ,and the average annual expected growth for the same period, as reported in the 2011 WEO data release.

The evidence is clear and the assessment is rather pessimistic. After the enormously costly austerity, the debt ratios have gone up in most euro area countries (Figure 24.8 reports the rise for the Netherlands and Italy). And just as growth has been lower than projected, the debt ratios have been higher than projected. The latest projections continue to suggest that the debt ratios will soon stabilize and decline; but these projections presume a further increase in the primary surplus, maintained over a longer period. Ghosh et al. (2013) warn that the presumption of persistent high primary surpluses runs counter to the history of the most indebted countries and therefore may not be politically viable. They find that "... while fiscal effort is generally increasing in the debt level, it eventually peters out as it becomes increasingly difficult to keep raising taxes or cutting non-interest expenditures."[6]

A further consequence of the single-minded focus on austerity is that private debt burdens have tended to remain high. Again, a comparison with the US is helpful. Households in the US have traditionally been more indebted relative to their incomes than euro area households (Figure 24.9). This arose from easier lending practices in the US but was sustained by the expectation of higher growth. Since the onset of the crisis, the average household debt ratio in the US has fallen substantially and is now approaching the ratio in the euro area, where it has remained unchanged.

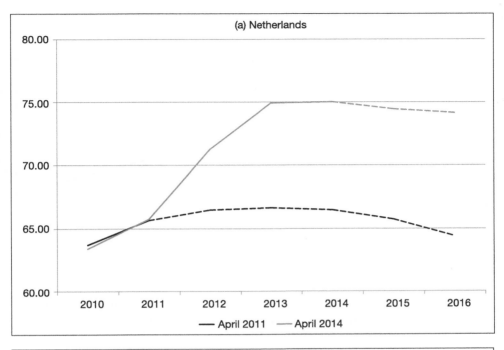

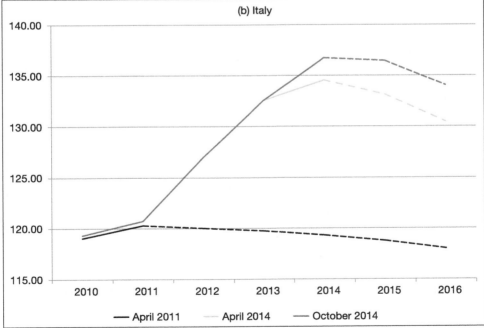

Figure 24.8 Evolution of debt–to–GDP outlook

Source: IMF WEO 2011 and 2014 (http://www.imf.org/external/ns/cs.aspx?id=28).

Note: Dashed lines refer to projections at the time.

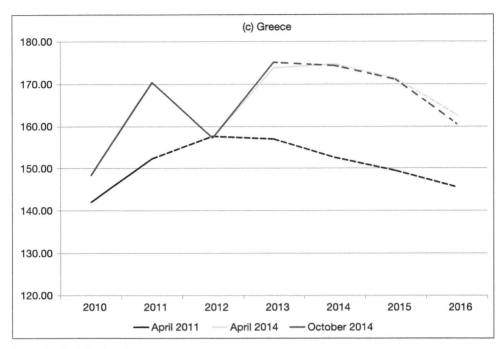

Figure 24.8 (Continued)

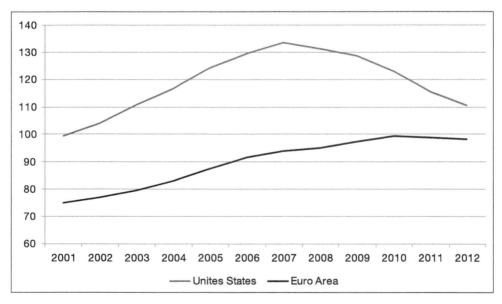

Figure 24.9 Household debt-to-income ratio

Source: Eurostat (http://epp.eurostat.ec.europa.eu/portal/page/portal/statistics/search_database).

Three factors have contributed to lowering the debt ratio in the US. First, the US has traditionally had greater tolerance for default: and some households were able to walk away from some of their debt obligations. Second, although extensive official relief for homeowners facing foreclosure did not materialize, a limited aid program helped ease the terms of unaffordable loans. And, third, greater economic stimulus helped raise disposable incomes. Hence, in the US, households now have lower per capita debt and higher per capita income, both contributing to lower debt-to-income ratios virtually across the entire country (Figure 24.10b).

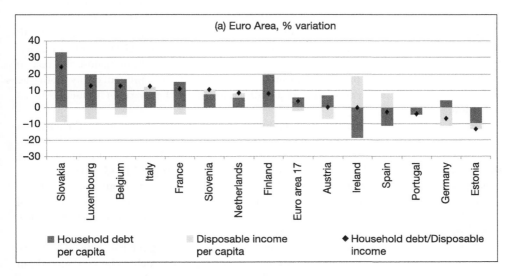

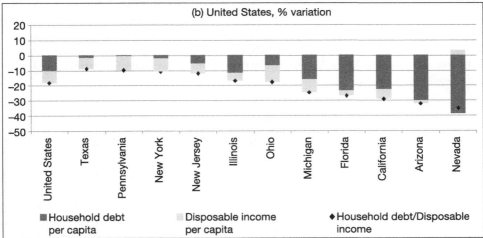

Figure 24.10a–b   Euro area and United States changes in household debt-to-disposable incomes, 2008–2012 (Percentage Change, 2012 over 2008)

Source: Eurostat (http://epp.eurostat.ec.europa.eu/portal/page/portal/statistics/search_database), Bureau of Economic Analysis (http://www.bea.gov/regional/index.htm) and Federal Reserve Bank of New York (http://newyorkfed.org/microeconomics/data.html).

In all these respects, the euro area lagged far behind. There was little direct relief to make a dent in mortgage debt; and due to the austerity-induced slowdown in growth, household disposable incomes stagnated or fell. Thus, while Irish and Spanish households worked to repay their debt obligations, their debt–income ratios rose in the initial phase of the crisis because disposable incomes fell. Even after the subsequent decline, the debt-to-disposable income ratios in 2012 were close to their 2008 levels (Figure 24.10a). In the Netherlands, households have taken on more debt even as their incomes have fallen.

Altogether, then, the eurozone crisis persisted in significant measure because of the single-minded focus on austerity. This focus on austerity comes from the German-inspired fiscal rules agreed to at Maastricht in 1992 and implemented with the framework of the Stability and Growth Pact (SGP) agreed to in 1997. While more refined rules were formulated during the course of the crisis, the requirement that fiscal deficits not exceed 3 percent of GDP remained unchanging and binding. This focal point was secured by the German-ECB alliance. For Germany, the limit on fiscal deficits was the presumed protection against the risk of paying the bills of other profligate governments. The ECB was influenced by both the traditional central bank aversion to fiscal indiscipline plus the German influence in its operation.

But, of course, the SGP rules were known to be economic nonsense. As Eichengreen (2003) noted, they bore no relationship to the goal of achieving debt sustainability. Moreover, they imposed a one-size-fits-all austerity in times of distress. The former President of the European Commission, Romano Prodi, described them as "stupid." Prodi was, of course, seeking discretionary authority for the Commission to make judgments appropriate to country and European economic conditions.[7] For some member nations, such loss of control to the Commission was, and is, unacceptable. Stupid though the rules may be, they are the only feasible equilibrium that balances national interests.

Thus, with weak monetary policy stimulus and delays in healing the banks, fiscal austerity was asked to shoulder the burden of controling the rise in public debt. The Netherlands, in particular, engaged in gratuitous austerity. The pressure to lower the public debt ratio was not acute. And with high household debt burdens, fiscal stimulus was needed to spur income growth, strengthen debt repayment capacity, and invigorate private spending. The one-size-fits-all fiscal policy, unmindful of the needs and capabilities of the country, added to the area-wide economic weakness. And the heavy trade traffic between the countries caused them to pull each other down.

3. Crisis management

Between Greece in October 2009 and ECB President Mario Draghi's "whatever it takes" speech in July 2012, ad hoc responses were used to prevent a meltdown. But born of compromises and self-imposed constraints, the structure retains economic, political, and legal fragilities.

A reliable Eurozone emergency management framework is not feasible because there are political limits to paying for the "mistakes" of others. Even the Werner Report, the first blueprint for the monetary union, emphasized that central fiscal resources were needed to deal with events of national economic distress. But such a fiscal union to accompany the monetary union was politically impossible. National fiscal insulation is required by the "no bailout" commitment in the Maastricht Treaty (Treaty of European Union) later incorporated in the current legal operational framework, the Lisbon Treaty (the Treaty on the Functioning of the European Union, the TFEU).

The Treaties do allow for – even encourage – imposing losses on private creditors. The ability to do so would simulate a fiscal union since it would provide relief to countries in distress. A reduction in debt repayment obligations is rightly perceived as – and in practice is – unfair. But it allows both borrowers and lenders to abandon a fractious relationship and begin afresh (see Mody, 2013, for a review of the relevant literature and Mian and Sufi, 2014 for a recent application of this principle). This ability to start again with reduced debt burdens is all the more important in conditions of weak economic growth. However, this option was also forsaken in the euro area, typically on the grounds of contagion – financial markets would panic causing indiscriminate damage.

This dual restraint – no fiscal union and no losses on private creditors – has three implications. First, as discussed extensively above, fiscal austerity is central to crisis management in the eurozone. Second, because this is an untenable basis for recovery from a crisis, rhetoric plays an unusually important role in the European policy process. Thus, with limited options for dealing with the real problems, the tendency is to delay action while cloaking the delays with high-minded projections of progress and sentiments of European solidarity. And when the limits to rhetoric run out, ad hoc technocratic solutions without political legitimacy are the outcome. Finally, the political economy of the crisis management has centered on Germany, the eurozone's presumptive paymaster and the ECB, the entity with virtually unlimited financing capability.

These themes are illustrated by Greece. The continuing effort to resolve the Greek crisis also created the precedents for the eurozone's crisis management framework.

That Greece needed help was clear by late 2009. However, German Chancellor Angela Merkel, facing regional elections, remained steadfastly resistant to a Greek bailout (Schneider and Slantchev, 2014). The rhetoric was that Greece was taking necessary corrective actions and a bailout would not be necessary. Every sign of good news was viewed as a turning point. In early March, 2010, after the Greek government was able to sell its bonds to private investors, albeit at an increased premium, the *Wall Street Journal* reported:

> The sale suggests that the European Union's strategy for dealing with the Greek crisis by relying on rhetoric instead of direct intervention is working. [. . .] policy makers are concerned that rescuing Greece too soon would damage the euro in the long run by encouraging other countries to flout deficit rules. Though the EU has signaled it would step in to save Greece from default if necessary and has drawn up plans to do so, officials insist that such a step will be taken only as a last resort.[8]

That was only the first of other critical junctures when rhetoric did not work. A large financial package for Greece was assembled in April and the assistance was delivered on May 10. The full package drew on the IMF's resources but was mainly funded by eurozone member states, each contributing according to its equity share in the ECB's capital. In July 2010, Christine Lagarde, who was France's finance minister at the time, recognized the damage due to those initial delays, "If we had been able to address it right from the start, say in February, I think we would have been able to prevent it from snowballing the way that it did."[9]

Greece was decisive. Along with the Greek bailout came a new financing facility – the European Financial Stability Facility (EFSF) – to lend to countries unable to borrow from private creditors and also a new crisis management team, the "troika" – the European Commission, the ECB, and the IMF. This basic structure would be used for the unfolding crises in Ireland, Portugal, and Spain.

Greece also defined the application of the eurozone's "no bailout" rules and asserted the primacy of fiscal austerity. The "no bailout" criterion required that any official assistance be in the form of loans to be repaid. The loans were initially justified under Article 122 of the TFEU, which allowed for emergency assistance when a member state was faced with circumstances under beyond its control. This argument was obviously not tenable in the Greek case – after all, the Greeks had lived beyond their means and willfully cooked the fiscal books for years. But that legal route had to do until a sounder structure was put in place.

Thus, Greece defined an important principle: loans would be provided to tide a country over its most stressful phase but because this did not reduce the country's debt burden, the loans would be accompanied by redoubled fiscal austerity. The "no bailout" principle was technically maintained because the loans were to be repaid.

The Greek rescue should have been used to forcefully establish the other implication of the "no bailout" requirement: enforce quick and substantial losses on private creditors. The closest historical analogy is a similar decision by the US Congress in the 1840s to not bailout US states, which were then not able to repay their private creditors. The decision had unpleasant consequences. Even the states that did not default saw their interest rates rise. Dutch and British bankers cried "foul" when the US federal government stood aside: they cut off the federal government's credit in 1842 and declared it a rogue debtor for not meeting its "implicit" obligations. But, as Henning and Kessler (2012, p. 12) write: "The fiscal sovereignty of states, the other side of the no bailout coin, was established."

But the idea that private creditors should bear the risks of lending was never taken seriously in European policy circles – and, hence, not taken seriously by markets. The problem grows out of an essential distrust of financial markets. The official view was stated well by the Delors Committee, whose report in March 1989 became the guiding document for the design of the incomplete monetary union. Prepared under the chairmanship of Jacques Delors, the President of the European Commission, the Committee's Report said that markets are unreliable:

> [. . .] market views about the creditworthiness of official borrowers tend to change abruptly and result in the closure of access to market financing. The constraints imposed by market forces might either be too slow and weak or too sudden and disruptive."[10]

Hence, the report concluded, it was essential that countries operate under fiscal restraint under the European Commission's surveillance.

The emphasis on centralized surveillance signaled that some was in charge and that it would be an embarrassment if the system failed. Thus, in the years before the crisis, it made sense for financial markets to assume that countries would be bailed out by other member states and private creditors would be paid in full. For this reason, the risk premia on sovereign bonds – relative to German sovereign bonds – were virtually zero in the months before the crisis began. In mid-2007, the Irish sovereign actually paid a lower interest rate than the German sovereign, and Greece paid virtually no premium.

In early 2010, even after it was clear that the Greek problems would not be solved merely by fiscal discipline, the restructuring of private debt remained taboo. Many commentators urged a prompt restructuring Greek public debt.[11] Among the clearest statements came from the Wall Street Journal on April 30:

> [Those] who dominate today's economic decision-making seem to believe that Greece merely has a liquidity problem that EU cash can solve. The unhappy reality is that Greece is busted and its political-economic model has reached a dead end.[12]

Having concluded that Greece was insolvent, the article went on to say:

> If a debt restructuring is inevitable, then it's far better to accept the pain now and get it over with. German and French banks would take losses, but those would be more bearable now that the world economy is recovering. If the banks do falter, then our guess is that European taxpayers would rather spend their money recapitalizing those banks instead of backstopping the retirement benefits of Greek civil servants.

Notice that this, coming from the well-known left-leaning financial newspaper, was not a cry for "burning bondholders" to ease the burden on the most beleaguered Greeks who would otherwise bear the burden. No, it was a simple economic calculation: when debt restructuring is needed, it is better to do so early rather than let the problem fester. Otherwise, all suffer.

On May 9, 2010, several Executive Directors on the IMF's Board protested when they gathered to approve the IMF's loan to Greece. Among them, the Indian Director, Arvind Virmani, submitted a stunningly prescient written statement:

> The scale of the fiscal reduction without any monetary policy offset is unprecedented. . . . (It) is a mammoth burden that the economy could hardly bear. Even if, arguably, the program is successfully implemented, it could trigger a deflationary spiral of falling prices, falling employment, and falling fiscal revenues that could eventually undermine the program itself. In this context, it is also necessary to ask if the magnitude of adjustment . . . is building in risk of program failure and consequent payment standstill. . . . There is concern that default/restructuring is inevitable.[13]

Susan Schadler, formerly a senior official in the IMF's European Department, later wrote that by lending to Greece without restructuring privately-held debt, the IMF had violated its own rules (Schadler, 2013). The IMF's staff had constructed "baselines" in which debt could be deemed sustainable. But the staff also felt obliged to report that the baseline was implausible. That should normally have prevented the IMF from proceeding.

But at this stage, the claim was that markets would irrationally spread havoc. Falling in with the European orthodoxy, the IMF's management used a dodge to finesse the institution's rules. The plea was that restructuring Greek debt would have "systemic consequences." In other words, financial markets would conclude that other sovereigns will rush to default on their debts, creating a contagious panic and global disruption. The specter of contagion loomed – and continues to loom – large.

A collective miasma of denial descended among decision makers, with steadfast opposition to debt restructuring between late 2009 and mid-2011. An IMF study (Cottarelli et al., 2010) made this a matter of principle: restructuring of advanced countries' public debt, that study said, was "unnecessary and undesirable." The premise was that the eurozone economies were institutionally strong and a quick resumption of growth would defang the debt crisis.

Some months later, in a brief – and much misunderstood – interlude, an opportunity was missed. At their Deauville summit on October 19, 2010, Chancellor Merkel and President Nicolas Sarkozy of France acknowledged the reality of unsustainable debts and agreed to a forward-looking debt restructuring process. They agreed that from 2013, distressed sovereigns who sought official financial assistance should also be required to negotiate a reduction in their debt repayment obligations to private creditors.

The Deauville proposal was met with instant fury, not least from euro area finance ministers and other officials assembled that same day in Luxembourg (Forelle et al., 2010). That gathering learned of the Merkel-Sarkozy proposal from the German Deputy Finance Minister Jörg Asmussen, who read from an email he received late in the afternoon. With no warning that this was coming, the ECB President Jean-Claude Trichet, yelled at the French delegation: "You are going to destroy the euro."

The drumbeat of criticism continued, and Deauville was quickly identified as the universal cause of many ills. Amazingly, George Papandreou, the Greek Prime Minister – whose nation was, for all intents and purposes, bankrupt – claimed that the German insistence on investors accepting losses was driving his nation to bankruptcy (Bastasin, 2012, p. 243). The IMF also pinned the blame for Greek woes on Deauville. In its July 2011 review of the Greek program, just days before the inevitability of Greek debt restructuring was officially acknowledged, it said (IMF, 2011a, pp. 32–3):

> [...] the very public debate on this issue [imposing losses on private creditors] has been a major problem for securing confidence around the [Greek] program.

The presumed evidence for a virulent Deauville effect is the market pressure experienced by distressed sovereigns in late 2010 and early 2011. The risk premia they paid increased rapidly. But was that rise due to Deauville? To answer that question, we cannot rely on the general increase in spreads; we must shine the spotlight on the days surrounding October 19, 2010.

When that is done, the impact of Deauville is, at best, modest (Mody, 2014a). A brief increase in Irish spreads (relative to trend in the days before the announcement) was followed by fall on the fourth and fifth days after the announcement. There was no noticeable change in Italian and Spanish spreads. Hence, there is no evidence of panic or contagion, the two charges against Deauville.

Risk spreads did rise in October and November 2010 – but the reason for that rise is clear. The strategy of using official loans to repay private debt did not change the debt burden of the distressed nation. However, private creditors who had yet to be repaid assumed that the official loans would be repaid first. In the other words, they assumed that they would be "junior" to the now substantial official debt. Chamley and Pinto (2011) pointed out that private creditors now faced a higher risk of an arbitrary and disorderly restructuring of their debt and would reasonably demand higher risk spreads. Steinkamp and Westermann (2014) and Mody (2014b) have since traced the rise in risk premia during this phase to the expansion of senior official debt. In contrast, Deauville had a comparatively minor effect.

Hence, if there was a villain, it was the strategy of outsized official loans alongside the expectation that the debt burden would brought down through fiscal austerity.

In the days that followed Deauville, Chancellor Merkel and her Finance Minister, Wolfgang Schäuble, continued to defend their position. At the European Council meeting on October 28, 2010, Merkel refused to back down when directly pressed by Trichet; and even Sarkozy tried to put Trichet in place (Bastasin, 2012, p. 240). At the G-20 summit in Seoul on November 11, Merkel said:

> Let me put it very simply: We cannot keep constantly explaining to our voters and our citizens why the taxpayer should bear the cost of certain risks and not those people who have earned a lot of money from taking those risks.[14]

The economic and political logic of this direct statement is compelling.

However, over the following months, Merkel was worn down in a series of meetings with Trichet, who seems to have persuaded her against the initiative (Bastasin, 2012, p. 243). The Deauville proposal was eventually abandoned. Merkel needed the ECB for extending the euro area financial safety net that the German taxpayer could not – would not – provide.

The characterization of Deauville as a Lehman-like moment for Europe has cast a pall over all discussion of sovereign debt restructuring, rare voices notwithstanding (Portes, 2011 and Buchheit et al., 2013). In early April 2011, Olli Rehn said that a Greek debt restructuring was "out of the question" (Souninen and Kirschbaum, 2011); a month later the ECB President, Jean-Claude Trichet, said "it was not on the cards" (Reuters, 2011b). On June 6, Lorenzo Bini Smaghi (2011), a member of the European Central Bank's Executive Board, devoted an entire speech to this subject. A "rational analysis" had led him to conclude that "Greece should be considered solvent and should be asked to service its debts."

The July 2011 troika review of the Greek "bailout" recognized that the Greek economy was deteriorating, but projected that Greece would resume growth in 2012 (IMF, 2011a). A customary "debt sustainability analysis" did show that things could go badly wrong and a text box clinically described the historical experience with debt restructuring. However, the "baseline" – the basis for the policy decision – showed that Greek public debt-to-GDP ratio would peak at that year's level of 170 percent and start falling smoothly thereafter.

By mid-2011, the favored strategy of austerity-cum-official financing had been applied also to Ireland and Portugal. Once again, official money was being used to pay private creditors. And risk spreads for Irish and Portuguese debt continued to spiral out of control because creditors who had not yet been repaid were being placed further back in the hierarchy of repayments. By early July, Irish sovereign debt carried a risk premium of 11 percent over the German sovereign (Figure 24.11). As the panic spread, Spain and Italy were also drawn into this maelstrom. Italian sovereign yields crossed the 6 percent mark on July 18, 2011.

Something had to give. Larry Summers (2011) – who had recently stepped down from his position in the US administration – was among those who called for more vigorous official action to deal with Europe's "dangerous new phase." Summers warned against imposing losses on private creditors, lest that cause a systemic crisis and, instead, proposed that the official loans be restructured. The specific proposal was to lower the interest rates on official loans to the level at which European authorities, using their collective credit, could borrow. The International Monetary Fund (IMF, 2011b) also called for more official support by purchasing sovereign debt on secondary markets and providing more resources to recapitalize banks. It was time, the IMF said, for European officials to show up with more money, and not just words.

The leaders of the euro area member countries met at an unscheduled summit on July 21 (Council of the European Union, 2011). They faced a dilemma: the continuing use of official funds to repay private creditors was reaching political limits but Greece was not ready to fend for itself. The solution was to finally abandon the fiction that Greece would fully repay its private creditors. Negotiations took months. An initially timid restructuring proposal was untenable. It took until February 2012 to negotiate the historically-large private debt restructuring – at which point, creditors would be paid only half their claims. Even so, Zettelmeyer et al. (2013) conclude, that the agreement left money on the table from the Greek perspective. Also, the generous treatment of the "holdouts" (those who refused to accept the reduced payments) created future risks for Greek taxpayers and will complicate restructurings elsewhere.

When the dust settled, Lee Buchheit, the veteran sovereign debt attorney who represented the Greek government, remarked: "I find it hard to imagine they will now man up to the

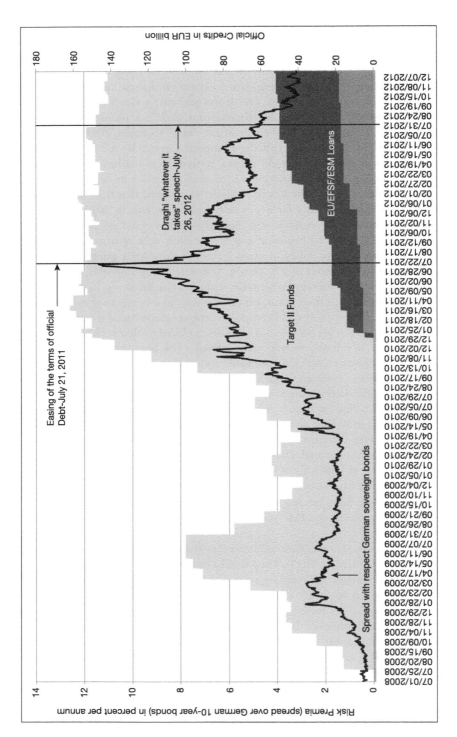

Figure 24.11 Ireland official credits and risk premia on sovereign bonds

Source: Datastream.

proposition that they delayed – at appalling cost to Greece, its creditors and its official sector sponsors – an essential debt restructuring" (Bases, 2012). It was only much later that the IMF offered its mea culpa (IMF, 2013). There has been no European recognition that delays in debt restructuring had, once again, inflicted great economic harm and inequity. Greece had borne an intolerable burden of austerity, which sent the economy into a tailspin and made the debt burden much greater. And while many creditors were paid with official funds (the creditors of arguably-insolvent Greek banks were repaid even in the final settlement), others were subjected to large losses, amounting to more than half their claims.

At the July 21, 2011 summit, the euro area leaders were anxious to emphasize that Greece was an exception and, going forward, debt restructuring was not eurozone policy. But a further problem arose. Even after the reducing the claims of private creditors, Greece would not be able to repay its official creditors on the terms agreed. Thus, the repayment terms on official debt also needed to be eased. Crucially, at that meeting, these easier terms were extended to Ireland and Portugal, whose interest rate was lowered from 5.5 to 3.5 percent and the repayment period extended from 7 to 15 years.

Thus, the need to forgive some of Greece's official debt triggered a pre-emptive restructuring of Irish and Portuguese official debt – and set an important new precedent. The message was that henceforth if sovereign debts were to become unsustainable, the official component would bear the first brunt of restructuring. Official debt – so long presumed to be "senior" – now became effectively "junior" to private debt, and a new approach to protecting private creditors was established.

The markets correctly read the signal – subsequently reinforced by continued rounds of forgiveness of Greek debt – that private creditors would be protected even if that required accepting reduced repayment of official debt. The response was immediate (Figure 24.11). Irish spreads started falling on July 18, the day the drumbeat of calls for official debt relief began. Franklin Templeton is thought to have started buying Irish sovereign debt around this date (Walsh, 2012), and Irish spreads were set on a strong downward course. Figure 24.11 shows a striking match between the decline in Irish spreads and the rise in official European credits, the credits most likely to be restructured if needed. Private creditors were right in interpreting that their risk had been lowered. In April 2013, the burden of official Irish debt was further lowered when concessions were made on the repayment of Ireland's Promissory Notes, providing more space for repaying private debt.

Thus, by late July 2011, the contours of euro area risk management were beginning to take shape. Austerity would do the hard work of restoring debt sustainability while official loans supported the distressed economies until they were able to return to fiscal health. Private creditors would be bailed out unless the circumstances were exceptional. Where that did not work, delayed relief would be provided on the repayment of official debt.

This framework required that official financial safety nets be strengthened. The EFSF, which had been the prime source of official funds, stood on shaky financial and legal grounds. In September 2012, the European Stability Mechanism (the ESM) was established. The ESM borrows from international markets (backed by repayment guarantees from member states); and it uses those funds to lend to euro area countries unable to access international markets.

The legality of official financing was not tested until July 2012, when Irish parliamentarian, Thomas Pringle, claimed before the Irish Supreme Court that the then-proposed ESM violated Article 125, the "no bailout" clause in TFEU. The Supreme Court referred the matter to the European Court of Justice (ECJ). In November 2012, the ECJ determined that the ESM did not violate Article 125 since it provided "financial assistance," which would be paid back with an "appropriate margin."[15] The ESM, in other words, was not making a prohibited fiscal transfer; instead, it was lending on the basis that the loans would be repaid. The fact that the repayment terms could be diluted over time was known to the ECJ but the dilution was not regarded as a fiscal transfer. The ECJ judgment stretched the interpretation of the TFEU – but any other finding at that critical moment in the crisis could have been destabilizing.

The task, however, was still incomplete. In the summer of 2012, spreads on Italian and Spanish bonds again began to levitate. That led to the last – and, arguably, the most decisive – feature of the crisis architecture.

On July 26, 2012, Mario Draghi, the President of the ECB, declared that the ECB would do "whatever it takes" to preserve the integrity and stability of the eurozone. He was extending a process that had been ongoing since the early phase of the crisis. The ECB had been providing a controversial life line to banks bordering on insolvency. In turn, the banks purchased government debt, supporting stressed sovereigns. On August 2, 2012, Draghi announced the Outright Monetary Transactions (OMT) Program to directly support the prices of euro area sovereign bonds by buying them in potentially "unlimited" quantities conditional on economic and fiscal reform efforts by the sovereign. And on September 7, the day after he announced more details about the program, Chancellor Merkel lent the program her support. Merkel's support was crucial since the OMT was fiercely – and publicly – opposed by Jens Weidmann, President of the Bundesbank and member of the ECB's Executive Board (see Mody, 2015 for details).

The ECB's deep pockets worked: the seemingly-uncontrollable rise of Spanish and Italian spreads was reversed, and the threat to the euro area was once again warded off. Merkel had made a political bargain. She could not ask more of the German taxpayer. The only way to create a secure financial safety net was through the ECB's "unlimited" financing prowess. But that raised the question: had the ECB acquired a fiscal authority? Had a fiscal union been created without a political agreement?

On January 14, 2014, the German Constitutional Court – relying to a large extent on the testimony of the Bundesbank – determined that the OMT was likely in contravention of the TFEU's Article 123 (which prevents the central bank from financing governments) and Article 125, which prohibits bailout. In Mody (2015), I have argued that the German Court's assessment had both legal and economic merit; the Court's decision to request the ECJ's opinion was also the right procedural step before reaching a final judgment. A year after the German Court's challenge to the OMT, the ECJ's Advocate General concluded that the challenge was largely without merit (European Court of Justice, 2015). This was confirmed by the ECJ in June 2015. A face-off between the German Court and the ECJ could have potentially important implications.

Some have viewed the OMT as the instrument by which the ECB performs its lender-of-last-resort function. That the euro area needs such a function is clear; the question is whether the OMT serves that purpose. As early as 1999, Christopher Sims pointed out that the lack of a lender-of-last-resort for its euro area sovereigns was a liability. But that gap was not accidental: it arose from the political contract in the Maastricht Treaty placing restrictions on ECB action. The problem is a simple one: if the ECB were to act as a lender-of-last resort to a particular sovereign, any losses resulting from that support would need to be shared by other sovereigns, as Sims noted more pointedly in a 2012 paper. Not only was there no agreement on sharing the losses – to the contrary, the political contract sought fiscal insulation from the fiscal problems of other member states.

Even viewed from a central banking tradition, the OMT is not a lender-of-last resort instrument. It is an IMF-style conditional lending program. The ECB promise is to support a sovereign's bond price conditional on that sovereign agreeing to an austerity program with the ESM. Former Bank of England historian Forrest Capie (2002) writes that a lender-of-last resort's function is "to provide the market with liquidity in times of need, and not to rescue individual institutions. Such rescues involve too much moral hazard." International institutions, such as the IMF, he says, "are invariably focused on one 'customer'– a country in difficulties – and so violate this rule of the lender-of-last-resort." Former senior officials of the IMF, Fischer (1999) and Rogoff (1999), emphasize that IMF-style lending must be accompanied by a clear and credible strategy for ensuring that private creditors share the burden. Bottom line: the distinction must be made between insolvency – which requires default (or centralized fiscal resources and Eurobonds) – and illiquidity, which requires a lender-of-last resort. The OMT conflates solvency and liquidity (Mody, 2015).

A final defense of the OMT invokes market irrationality. The ECB claimed that prices of similar securities varied widely across the euro area, and the OMT would help correct that distortion. However, the German Court correctly pointed out that it is not possible to distinguish market distortion from genuine differences in the riskiness of the securities.

Others have inferred market arbitrariness from the wild swings in risk spreads, which spiraled from near-zero pre-crisis levels to unmanageable heights during the crisis, only to fall back down again (De Grauwe and Ji, 2012). But these swings are as much the result of policy ambiguity as of market irrationality. The euro area authorities have sent mixed signals of their intent to enforce losses on private creditors. Before the crisis, the authorities welcomed the market's view that default would not be permitted, even though the policy said otherwise. Between 2008 and 2011, the market grew increasingly concerned that the authorities would not be able to deliver on their implicit bailout promise. This required a new, and more tangible, commitment to safeguard private creditors. On July 21, 2011, the new policy had signaled that official debt would take the first hit before private creditors bore losses. That promise proved insufficient to help Italy and Spain – and hence the ECB's "unlimited" promise was required a year later.

Once again the incentives are being created for private creditors to lend with abandon. The yields on sovereign bonds have fallen sharply. They are near-historic lows even for Italy and Spain even though the debt ratios of these sovereigns are historically high and still rising. Altogether, the current rescue efforts could well be sowing the seeds of a future build-up of debt. Buchheit and Gulati (2013) rightly warn that the sense of calm and confidence can quickly change. Speculators may "mercilessly" test the ECB's resolve to buy unlimited quantities of a distressed sovereign's bonds.

4. Looking ahead

In October 2013, euro area officials were in a quietly triumphal mood. The interest rates on sovereign bonds had fallen and the economy had stopped contracting. On October 9, five senior policymakers wrote in the *Wall Street Journal*: "Our approach to the crisis, which is based on an integrated approach by member states and European institutions, is beginning to deliver results" (Dijsselbloem et al., 2013). A month later, Draghi repeated the same upbeat message in a speech at Harvard University's Kennedy School (Draghi, 2013).

The achievements are clear. The eurozone has held together. Between 2010 and 2013, enhanced fiscal governance systems – the six-pack, fiscal compact, and two-pack – were established. Although some countries resented the pressure applied, all adhered broadly to the fiscal framework. In the matter of repaying debts, Greece was an exception; the other sovereigns have honored their obligations in a timely manner. The ESM and OMT financial safety nets are in place, and the interest rates that governments pay on their new borrowings are at, or near, historical lows. Although promise of economic growth in late 2013 proved elusive, today there is again a perception that growth is around the corner. If growth continues, the pressures will be released and a sense of normalcy could return.

But the legacy of the crisis years is deeply entrenched and will influence the fiscal and economic outlook. The public debt burdens are well above pre-crisis levels and private debt burdens are at or above pre-crisis levels. The fiscal belts are projected to remain tight everywhere – and may tighten further were the stress levels are highest. Collectively, the euro area fiscal position will continue to act as a break on renewed growth and inflation. That will perpetuate a tendency for financial fragility.

For this reason, the drumbeat of structural reforms to spur growth is not surprising. But the evidence in favor of this policy elixir is scant. German success with labor market reforms is often cited – and often by the German authorities. The so-called Hartz reforms, implemented during the years 2003–5, were contemporaneous with a revival of the German economy from several years in the doldrums. But the macroeconomic significance of the Hartz reforms remains inconclusive (Hertweck and Sigrist, 2012). Instead, as Dustmann et al. (2014) argue, the source of Germany's renewed economic strength must be sought in the years before the Hartz reforms. Over the 1990s, German industry and labor cooperated to harness and adapt traditional strengths. German manufacturing firms reinforced their innovation capabilities, made strategic moves to outsource from Emerging Europe, and renegotiated wage contracts.

Attributing German success to the Hartz reforms is misleading at best; more likely, it is downright wrong. Germany's historical manufacturing prowess and business-labor relationships cannot be easily replicated. The value of the Hartz reforms – if they had value – cannot be isolated from Germany's history and institutions. Thus, a superficial transplant of Hartz-like reforms will have little impact. Italy, for example, does no worse than Germany on the measurable labor market indicators: the real Italian problem lies with abysmal productivity performance (Hassan and Ottaviano, 2013).

The vent of world trade could also be elusive. Between 2003 and 2007, world trade grew at about 8 percent per year, and European nations rode that global tide of prosperity. After 2010, world trade has been growing at about 3 percent per year. And while projections continue to foresee a pickup, the shift to higher global trade growth is taking much longer than anticipated.

Through much of Europe, growth is also pulled down by weak private balance sheets. Households must lower their debt ratios and hence are reluctant to spend. Weak business profitability and economic outlook make businesses reluctant to invest. Public investment has been the most important casualty of the austerity drive.

If these legacies constrain growth, the challenges faced by the eurozone's austerity-only fiscal framework become serious. The new risk for countries in the eurozone periphery is a spiral of higher debt ratios and lower inflation, including entrenched deflation. Inflation rates have fallen sharply across the periphery. Moreover, inflation rates are lower – and for some countries considerably lower – in 2014 than had been expected in 2011. This unanticipated fall in inflation is strikingly correlated with the unanticipated rise in debt-to-GDP ratios (Figure 24.12). In other words, the factors pushing inflation down are related to those that are pushing debt ratios up. And there is no natural self-correcting process through which this tendency will be reversed, except in the medium-term when eventually the gain in international competitiveness will help a significant revival of exports and growth. Until that happens, the debt ratios will remain high, which will reinforce fiscal austerity and postpone economic recovery.

At this point, the Greek problems have become pathological. But it is also premature to declare victory elsewhere. With debt restructuring ruled out, the challenges brewing in Italy are particularly serious. The Italian economy is extraordinarily fragile and an Italian financial crisis could have far reaching effects on Europe and the world economy.

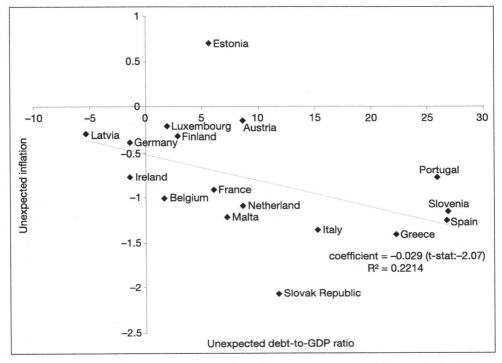

Figure 24.12 Debt-deflation dynamics: the relationship between unexpected changes in the debt-to-GDP ratio and unexpected changes in inflation

Source: IMF WEO April 2014 (http://www.imf.org/external/ns/cs.aspx?id=28).

A renewed crisis could challenge the integrity of the financial safety nets. So far, the ESM and the OMT have delivered a period of calm. Together, the insurance they provide may prove sufficient to deal with adversities. If, however, the legality of the OMT is successfully challenged – or its deployment proves politically contentious – a scaled-back alternative may prove insufficient. A market test of the OMT could prove unpleasant.

If a period of calm does descend, it would be wise to not waste it as in the heady first decade of the euro. The eurozone is still an incomplete monetary union that is ill-prepared for deep and persistent economic distress. While technocratic fixes have been found, they are unreliable because they have clear limits and lack political legitimacy. The same national interests that led to the creation of the incomplete monetary union have held back the creation of reliable safeguards against crises. Every effort to create anything resembling a fiscal union has been thwarted. Crudely-stated, countries were and remain unwilling to "pay" for the mistakes of others.

In addition, by closing the option of imposing losses on private creditors, the policy choices have been further narrowed. Despite a sensible German–French effort to incorporate an orderly debt restructuring process into the crisis management framework, the ECB push-back was successful. That left all the heavy-lifting to be done by a one-size-fits-all fiscal framework that targets the same numerical limits on deficits and debt across countries with very divergent levels of economic stress and growth potential. Instead of helping, such a straightjacket reinforces economic divergence across countries. The risks of continued anemic growth, social stress, and renewed instability are the direct consequence of the constraints within which the euro area countries operate.

In a recent paper, Reinhart et al. (2015) report on the mechanisms used in the past to reduce debt burdens. Three of their findings are especially relevant for the euro area. First, one in five instances of high debt end with a debt restructuring during peace times; the ratio is slightly higher for war-related debts. Second, the recent fall in nominal interest rates on government debt could – history warns – represent a refuge from an impending storm; the reprieve from the debt service burden could be short-lived. And, finally, what matters is the real interest rate. Where inflation rates are low, the real interest rate will be high even with low nominal rates. Resolution of debt burdens is virtually impossible in deflationary conditions.

The balance needs to be changed. A lighter emphasis on austerity needs to be accompanied by greater recourse to imposing losses on private creditors. Today, despite new proposals (Buchheit et al., 2013), the ambivalence towards debt restructuring continues alongside the generous regulatory risk treatment of sovereign debt. Where debt is unsustainable, wishing it away is not a wise policy. Deauville would have initiated a move away from reactive debt restructuring, when left with no other choice, to a proactive approach. It was a necessary first step to reestablishing a credible "no bailout" regime, crucial to the original intent and architecture of the euro area (Mody, 2013). Ultimately, it will be necessary to go further. Debt restructuring must occur through an automated system of contractually-determined contingent debt repayments that leaves little room for policy discretion (Mody 2014d).

The greater reliance on debt restructuring will require a careful, possibly painful, transition. In the short-run, the legacy debt – the debt inherited from the past excesses – will need to be dealt with. But steps towards a new balance will increase the incentives for lower debt ratios in the future. Markets will, undoubtedly, often get things wrong. But why would market discipline be worse than central surveillance, which has had interminable problems? Getting from here to there will be hard, but waiting will make it ever harder.

As the economics becomes harder, political risks will increase. With weak eurozone institutions, Germany and the ECB operate a *de facto* governing alliance. The German Chancellor gives the ECB political cover and the ECB provides the financial safety net. And while the alliance has prevented a euro area meltdown, its insulation from political accountability is weakening hard-won European solidarity. In January–February 2015, when the new Greek government came to power on the pledge that it would negotiate a lower burden of austerity, the German–ECB alliance once again ensured order. The ECB decided to remove the waiver on Greek sovereign debt and shifted funding of Greek banks to the Central Bank of Greece. This was interpreted by some as a not-so-veiled threat that the ECB would stop funding Greek banks – and thus accelerated the flight of deposits from the banks; the German authorities ensured that Greeks stayed broadly within their preferred framework of austerity alongside structural reforms. If by some luck, Greece and Europe grow again, all may be forgiven and forgotten. The greater likelihood is that national divisions and resentments will deepen.

The euro area has lived dangerously through this crisis without a fiscal union, and survived. How much longer will that remain true?

Notes

1 I am grateful especially to Giulio Mazzolini for collaboration and extensive discussions. For generous and helpful comments, I thank Kevin Cardiff, Ajai Chopra, Zsolt Darvas, Barry Eichengreen, Antonio Fatas, Peter Hall, Philip Lane, Karl Whelan, and Guntram Wolff.

2 The stimulus is measured as the change in the so-called "structural" fiscal balance. When a country faces economic distress, its fiscal balance naturally deteriorates since the tax obligations to the government decline and the government's spending on social safety nets increases. The "structural" balance nets out such automatic changes. Hence, the change in the structural balance measures the government's extra injection to stimulate economic recovery.

3 In May 2014, over five years after the US Federal Reserve had brought its policy rate to near zero and started the first of its three quantitative easing programs, and well after deflationary tendencies in the euro area were evident, the ECB was still publicly debating if it needed to do more. Through the crisis, the ECB provided virtually no stimulus but rather acted as a safety net against bank and sovereign insolvency (Mody, 2014c).

4 The debt-to-GDP ratios for the Netherlands were revised downwards to below 70 percent. Because the subsequent analysis uses earlier projections, for which revised figures are not available, all data on the Netherlands are based on the IMF's WEO Database through April 2014. Since this analysis relies on changes over time, the presumption is that the past and forecast changes would have been the same even with the revised series.

5 The eurozone countries in the sample are: Austria, Belgium, Finland, France, Germany, Greece, Ireland, Italy, Luxembourg, Portugal, and Spain. Slovenia is in the eurozone from 2007, the Slovak Republic from 2009, and Estonia from 2011. The non-eurozone countries include: Australia, Canada, Denmark, Japan, Korea, the Netherlands, New Zealand, Slovak Republic, Slovenia, Sweden, the United Kingdom, and the United States.

6 Ghosh et al. (2013, p. F5).

7 See Osoborn (2002), Richeter (2002), and Paterson (2003).

8 Mollenkamp and Bryan-Low (2010).

9 Schneider and Faiola (2010).

10 Delors (1989).

11 The list of these commentators is ably documented in the IMF's mea culpa that came three years too late. See IMF (2013, p. 29, footnote 17).

12 *Wall Street Journal* (2010).

13 *Wall Street Journal* (2013).

14 Spiegel and Oakley (2010).

15 European Court of Justice (2012).

References

Accominotti, O. and Eichengreen, B. (2013), The Mother of All Sudden Stops: Capital Flows and Reversals in Europe, 1919–1932, *BEHL Working Paper* 2013–07.

Auerbach, A.J. and Gorodnichenko, Y. (2012), Measuring the Output Responses to Fiscal Policy, *American Economic Journal: Economic Policy*, 4(2), 1–27.

Bases, D. (2012), The Governments' Man When Creditors Bay, *Reuters*, 23 May, available at www.reuters.com/article/2012/05/23/us-sovereign-buchheit-idUSBRE84M07N20120523.

Bastasin, C. (2012), *Saving Europe: How National Politics Nearly Destroyed the Euro*, Washington: Brookings Institution.

Batini, N., Callegari, G., and Melina, G. (2012), Successful Austerity in the United States, Europe and Japan, *IMF Working Paper* 12/190.

Baum, A., Poplawski-Ribeiro, M., and Weber, A. (2012), Fiscal Multipliers and the State of the Economy, *IMF Working Paper* 12/286.

Bini Smaghi, L. (2011), Private Sector Involvement: From (Good) Theory to (Bad) Practice, presented at the Reinventing Bretton Woods Committee, Berlin, 6 June 2011, available at www.ecb.europa.eu/press/key/date/2011/html/sp110606.en.html.

Blanchard, O. and Leigh, D. (2012), Are We Underestimating Short-Term Fiscal Multipliers? in International Monetary Fund, *World Economic Outlook: Coping with High Debt and Sluggish Growth*, Washington: International Monetary Fund.

Blanchard, O. and Leigh, D. (2013a), Growth Forecast Errors and Fiscal Multipliers, *IMF Working Paper* 13/1.

Blanchard, O. and Leigh, D. (2013b), Fiscal Consolidation: at What Speed?, *www.voxeu.org*, 3 May.

Bohn, H. (1995), The Sustainability of Budget Deficits in a Stochastic Economy, *Journal of Money, Credit, and Banking*, 27(1), 257–71.

Bohn, H. (1998), The Behavior of US Public Debt and Deficits, *Quarterly Journal of Economics*, 113(3), 949–63.

Buchheit, L.C. and Gulati, M. (2013), The Eurozone Debt Crisis: The Options Now, *Capital Markets Law Journal*, 8(1), 54–61.

Buchheit, L.C., Weder di Mauro, B., Gelpern, A., Gulati, M., Panizza, U., and Zettelmeyer, J. (2013), *Revisiting Sovereign Bankruptcy*, Washington: Brookings Institution.

Capie, F. (2002), Can there be an International Lender-of-Last-Resort? *International Finance*, 1(2), 311–25.

Chamley, C. and Pinto, B. (2011), Why Official Bailouts Tend Not to Work: An Example Motivated by Greece 2010, *The Economists' Voice* 8.1.

Cottarelli, C., Forni, L., Gottschalk, J., and Mauro, P. (2010), Default in Today's Advanced Economies: Unnecessary, Undesirable, and Unlikely, Fiscal Affairs Department, International Monetary Fund.

Council of the European Union (2011), Statement by the Heads of State or Government of the Euro Area and EU Institutions, available at www.consilium.europa.eu/uedocs/cms_data/docs/pressdata/en/ec/123978.pdf.

De Grauwe, P. and Ji, Y. (2012), Self-Fulfilling Crises in the Eurozone: An Empirical Test, *Journal of International Money and Finance*, 34(April), 15–36.

Delors, J. (1989), Economic and Monetary Union and Relaunching the Construction of Europe, in Committee for the Study of Economic and Monetary Union, *Report on Economic and Monetary Union in the European Community*, Luxembourg: Office of Official Publications of the European Communities.

Dijsselbloem, J., Rehn, O., Asmussen, J., Regling, K., and Hoyer, W. (2013), Europe's Crisis Response is Showing Results, *Wall Street Journal*, 9 October, available at www.wsj.com/articles/SB1000142405 2702304626104579123152208309932.

Draghi, M. (2013), Europe's pursuit of "a more perfect Union", presented at the Kennedy School of Government, Harvard University, 9 October, available at www.ecb.europa.eu/press/key/date/2013/html/sp131009_1.en.html.

Dustmann, C., Fitzenberger, B., Schönberg, U., and Spitz-Oener, A. (2014), From Sick Man of Europe to Economic Superstar: Germany's Resurgent Economy, *Journal of Economic Perspectives*, 28(1), 167–88.

Eichengreen, B. (2003), What to do with the Stability Pact?, *Intereconomics*, 38(1), 7–10.

European Court of Justice (2012), Judgment of the Court (Full Court): Thomas Pringle v Government of Ireland and The Attorney General, available at http://curia.europa.eu/juris/liste.jsf?num=C-370/12, 27 November.

European Court of Justice (2015), Advocate General's Opinion in Case C-62/14 Peter Gauweiler and Others v Deutscher Bundestag, Press Release No 2/15, 14 January.

Eyraud, L. and Weber, A. (2013), The Challenge of Debt Reduction during Fiscal Consolidation, *IMF Working Paper* 13/67.

Fischer, S. (1999), On the Need for an International Lender of Last Resort, *Journal of Economic Perspectives*, 13(4), 85–104.

Forelle, C., Gauthier-Villars, D., Blackstone, B., and Enrich, D. (2010), As Ireland Flails, Europe Lurches Across the Rubicon, *Wall Street Journal*, 27 December, available at http://online.wsj.com/news/articles/SB10001424052748703814804576035682984688312.

Ghosh, A.R., Kim, J.I., Mendoza, E., Ostry, J., and Qureshi, M.S. (2013), Fiscal Fatigue, Fiscal Space and Debt Sustainability in Advanced Economies, *Economic Journal*, 123(566), F4–F30.

Hassan, F. and Ottaviano, G. (2013), Productivity in Italy: The Great Unlearning, *www.voxeu.org*, 30 November.

Hertweck, M.S. and Sigrist, O. (2012), The Aggregate Effects of the Hartz Reforms in Germany, *SOEPpapers on Multidisciplinary Panel Data Research* 532.

Henning, C.R. and Kessler, M. (2012), Fiscal Federalism: US History for Architects of Europe's Fiscal Union, *PIIE Working Paper* 2012–1.

International Monetary Fund (2011a), Greece: Fourth Review under the Stand-By Arrangement and Request for Modification and Waiver of Applicability of Performance Criteria, *IMF Country Report* 11/175.

International Monetary Fund (2011b), IMF Executive Board Concludes Article IV Consultation on Euro Area Policies, *Public Information Notice* 11/91.

International Monetary Fund (2012), The Good, the Bad, and the Ugly: 100 Years of Dealing with Public Debt Overhangs, *World Economic Outlook*, October.

International Monetary Fund (2013), Greece: Ex Post Evaluation of Exceptional Access under the 2010 Stand-By Arrangement, *IMF Country Report* 13/156.

Mian, A. and Sufi, A. (2014), *House of Debt*, Chicago: University of Chicago Press.

Mody, A. (2013), Sovereign Debt and its Restructuring Framework in the Euro Area, *Oxford Review of Economic Policy*, 29(4), 715–44.

Mody, A. (2014a), The Ghost of Deauville, *www.voxeu.org*, 7 January.

Mody, A. (2014b), Europhoria, Once Again, available at www.bruegel.org/nc/blog/detail/article/1242-europhoria-once-again/.

Mody, A. (2014c), The ECB Can – and Must – Act, available at www.bruegel.org/nc/blog/detail/article/1323-the-ecb-must-and-can-act/.

Mody, A. (2014d), Making Argentina's Debt Debacle a Rarity – it is Time for Sovereign Cocos, available at www.bruegel.org/nc/blog/detail/article/1453-making-argentinas-debt-debacle-a-rarity/.

Mody, A. (2015), Did the German Court Do Europe a Favour?, *Capital Markets Law Journal*, 10(1), 6–22.

Mollenkamp, C. and Cassell Bryan-Low, C. (2010), Greece Leaps Crucial Hurdle with Debt Sale, *Wall Street Journal*, 5 March, available at http://online.wsj.com/news/articles/SB10001424052748703502804575101912171794390.

Paterson, L. (2003), Wanted: a Panacea for the Pact's Ills, *The Times (London)*, 21 July, p. 21.

Portes, R. (2011), Restructure Ireland's debt, *www.voxeu.org*, 26 April.

Reinhart, C., Reinhart, V., and Rogoff, K. (2015), Dealing with Debt, *Harvard KSG Faculty Research Working Paper* 15–009.

Reuters (2011), ECB's Trichet – Greek Restructuring "Not in the Cards", 5 May, available at www.reuters.com/article/2011/05/05/uk-ecb-bailouts-idUKTRE7443V120110505.

Riera-Crichton, D., Vegh, C.A., and Vuletin, G. (2014), Does it Matter Whether Government Spending is Increasing or Decreasing? *World Bank Policy Research Paper* 6993.

Rogoff, K. (1999), International Institutions for Reducing Global Financial Instability, *Journal of Economic Perspectives*, 13(4), 21–42.

Rogoff, K. (2002), Moral Hazard in IMF Loans: How Big a Concern, *Finance and Development*, 39(3).

Schadler, S. (2013), Unsustainable Debt and the Political Economy of Lending: Constraining the IMF's Role in Sovereign Debt Crises, *CIGI Paper* 19.

Schneider, C.J. and Slantchev, B.L. (2014), The Domestic Politics of International Cooperation during the European Debt Crisis, University of California, San Diego.

Schneider, H. and Faiola, A. (2010), Hesitation by Leaders Drove Costs of Europe's Crisis Higher, *Washington Post*, 16 June, available at www.washingtonpost.com/wp-dyn/content/article/2010/06/15/AR2010061505598.html?sid=ST2010061505700.

Sims, C. (1999), The Precarious Foundations of EMU, *DNB Staff Report* 34.

Sims, C. (2012), Gaps in the Institutional Structure of the Euro Area, *Banque de France Financial Stability Review* 16.

Spiegel, P. and Oakley, D. (2010), Irish Contagion Hits the Wider Eurozone, *Financial Times*, 11 November, available at www.ft.com/intl/cms/s/0/1d594dc6-edc4-11df-9612-00144feab49a.html?siteedition=uk#axzz3TVzg8lSm.

Souninen, S. and Kirschbaum, E. (2011), EU's Rehn Excludes Greek Debt Restructuring, Reuters, 9 April, available at www.reuters.com/article/2011/04/09/us-eurozone-greece-restructuring-idUSTRE7381IK20110409.

Steinkamp, S. and Westermann, F. (2014), The Role of Creditor Seniority in Europe's Sovereign Debt Crisis, *Economic Policy*, 29(79), 495–552.

Summers, L. (2011), Europe's Dangerous New Phase, *Reuters*, 18 July, available at http://blogs.reuters.com/lawrencesummers/2011/07/18/europes-dangerous-new-phase/.

Walsh, J. (2012), Franklin Templeton investment puts government debt in spotlight, *The Irish Examiner*, 4 September, available at www.irishexaminer.com/business/franklin-templeton-investment-puts-government-debt-in-spotlight-206349.html.

Wall Street Journal (2010), The Price of Greece, 30 April, available at www.wsj.com/articles/SB10001424052748704423504575212513003082840.

Wall Street Journal (2013), IMF Document Excerpts: Disagreements Revealed, 7 October, available at blogs.wsj.com/economics/2013/10/07/imf-document-excerpts-disagreements-revealed/?mod=WSJBlog.

Zettelmeyer, J., Trebesch, C., and Gulati, M. (2013), The Greek Debt Restructuring: An Autopsy, *Economic Policy*, 28(75), 513–63.

25

REFORMING THE ARCHITECTURE OF EMU

Ensuring stability in Europe

Jakob de Haan, Jeroen Hessel and Niels Gilbert

1. Introduction

During the 1990s, skeptics perceived plans for Economic and Monetary Union (EMU) as an ambitious project that would never fly, just like the emu, the large Australian bird.[1] Critics referred to the absence of political union (Feldstein, 1997) and heterogeneity among EMU countries due to which the euro area was not considered an optimal currency area (Bayoumi and Eichengreen, 1993; De Grauwe, 2012). It was argued that Europe fell far short of the United States, for example, in terms of labor mobility and fiscal integration (Gibson et al., 2014).

Still, as most European political leaders at the time were strongly committed to further European integration, EMU started in 1999. EMU was based on three mainstays. First, monetary policy was delegated to a strictly independent European Central Bank (ECB) with the primary objective of price stability. Second, fiscal policy remained a national responsibility, although fiscal policies had to comply with relatively strict rules. Third, except for trade and competition policies, macroeconomic and financial policies (such as banking supervision) were left to the responsibility of Member States.

As pointed out by Buti and Carnot (2012: 900), the rationale for the constraints on national fiscal policy was that "unsustainable fiscal dynamics in one country may eventually entail costs borne by all EMU participants. This could happen either *via* inflationary debt monetization or through large fiscal transfers between countries." By contrast, the potential spillover effects related to national economic policies were thought to be much smaller. This is why the Treaty contained no provisions in this area with the exception of the obligation for countries to "regard their economic policies as a matter of common concern and [. . .] coordinate them within the Council" (Article 121).

This original set-up of the monetary union appeared to function successfully in its first ten years, at least on the surface. In 2008, only months before the collapse of Lehman Brothers that marked the start of the global financial crisis, then-European Commissioner Almunia wrote: "A full decade after Europe's leaders took the decision to launch the euro, we have good reason to be proud of our single currency. The Economic and Monetary Union and the euro are a major success." (European Commission, 2008a: iii). However, in 2010 several important fault lines that had existed under the surface since the launch of the euro, notably weak public finances and persistent imbalances in some countries, unexpectedly became clearly visible in what is generally referred to as the euro crisis (Drudi et al., 2012).[2]

The euro crisis started in Greece. After several revisions of previously published deficit figures (even going back to the time of Greece's admission in the euro area) had been published it became clear that public finances in Greece were unsustainable. On May 10 2010, the ten-year yield spread between Greek and German government bonds reached about 1,000 basis points. Similar concerns arose in Ireland, Portugal and, later, Spain, and Italy. The interest spreads on government bonds of countries that came to be known as GIIPS did not only reflect increased credit risk, but also doubts about the sustainability of EMU.

A special feature of the crisis was what came to be known as the doom loop: the reinforcing relationship between the creditworthiness of sovereigns and banks. Concerns about the solvency of sovereigns fueled concerns about the solvency of banks, given their large holdings of government bonds. In turn, this further fueled concerns about the sovereigns' solvency, given the likelihood that they will have to bail out their relatively large banking systems.

Between 2010 and 2012, the ECB took several steps to combat the crisis. For instance, it continued the unlimited access to refinancing operations that started during the global financial crisis and decided to purchase public and private debt securities under the Securities Markets Programme (SMP), starting in May 2010. In December 2011, the ECB decided to conduct refinancing operations that significantly extended the horizon at which credit institutions could obtain liquidity from the Eurosystem. In particular, two three-year refinancing operations ("longer term refinancing operation," LTROs) were conducted in December 2011 and February 2012 providing banks with potentially unlimited amounts of three-year loans. At the same time, the ECB announced more generous rules regarding the type of collateral it would require. The LTROs are widely considered as having achieved their aims: they ensured that no bank would face a liquidity squeeze for the next three years and this allowed the inter-bank market to start functioning again.

In these years, European political leaders took several steps to enhance the governance of EMU. For instance, the Stability and Growth Pact (SGP) has been revised as part of a set of reforms known as the "Six-Pack," "Two-Pack," and the "Fiscal Compact," while the Macroeconomic Imbalance Procedure (MIP) has been introduced to prevent the emergence of maroeconomic imbalances (see section 3 for details). Despite these steps, financial market volatility remained, not least because progress on several important political issues, notably support to Greece, was extremely slow, leading to doubts about the commitment of European leaders to the euro.[3]

It was only after ECB President Draghi told an investment conference in London in July 2012 that: "Within our mandate, the ECB is ready to do whatever it takes to preserve the euro. And believe me, it will be enough" that bond spreads of GIIPS countries started to decline substantially.[4] To live up to those words, the ECB introduced the Outright Monetary Transactions (OMTs) program in September 2012.[5] With this instrument, the ECB made clear that scenarios involving the collapse of monetary union are out of the question. After European political leaders finally showed their commitment as well by agreeing on further support to Greece and the establishment of a banking union, financial markets calmed down.[6] Interest rate spreads between the core countries and the periphery, which had to that point reflected increased risk of a euro break-up, narrowed sharply in the second half of 2012 (see Figure 25.1). Whether this development will continue, arguably will also depend on how credible the improvements in the architecture of EMU will turn out to be.

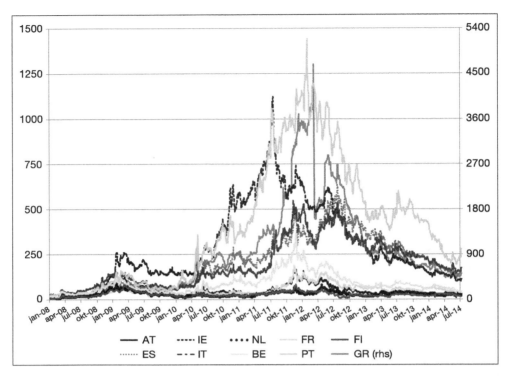

Figure 25.1 10-year government bond spreads against German bonds

Source: Thomson Datastream and authors' own calculations.

Even though the euro crisis as it unfolded was not fully foreseen even by the critics of EMU, it made some serious shortcomings in the architecture clearly visible.[7] Section 2 outlines what went wrong and why events unfolded so differently than expected. Section 3 discusses the improvements in the architecture of EMU. Even though substantial progress has been made, section 4 discusses how the current balance between policy coordination and risk sharing can eventually be improved.

2. Shortcomings in the architecture of EMU

The euro crisis was often primarily attributed to a lack of budgetary discipline, especially during its first stages. As hypothesized by Lane (2012), this probably reflects that the initial phase of the crisis was dominated by Greece, whose budgetary troubles could indeed be clearly attributed to a lack of budgetary discipline (and even deliberate statistical misreporting). Spain and Ireland, however, had stellar fiscal records when the crisis erupted before they too ran into budgetary problems. So a lack of budgetary discipline was not the only issue at play. Diverging financial cycles played a major role.[8] In several Member States, macroeconomic and financial imbalances built up in the years prior to the crisis and they were a major factor behind the deterioration of public finances. When the euro crisis erupted, problems were amplified by the fact that the architecture of EMU did not contain provisions for the resolution of a major sovereign debt crisis.

Financial factors played an important role in the crisis. Before the eruption of the global financial crisis in 2008, financial factors were largely missing from macroeconomic paradigms, such as the theory of optimum currency areas, and they also hardly figured in the Maastricht Treaty. Yet the start of EMU coincided with a period of very loose financial conditions. Many advanced economies experienced a strong growth of credit, house prices and the size of their financial sectors. Rapid financial integration induced a global surge in net and cross-border capital flows. The average size of foreign assets and liabilities in advanced economies increased from 70 percent of GDP in 1995 to over 210 percent of GDP in 2007. It even ran up to almost 300 percent of GDP in the euro area, as the euro further stimulated financial integration (Forbes, 2012). These financial factors amplified some of the vulnerabilities that already existed within EMU, and also created new ones that had not been anticipated (Lane, 2013; Obstfeld, 2013).

2.1 Non-compliance with the Stability and Growth Pact

Even though several academics had argued against the need to restrain national fiscal policies in a monetary union (cf. Buiter et al., 1993), the prevention of possible fiscal crises was a central preoccupation in the design of the single currency (Buti and Carnot, 2012). The SGP, adopted in 1997, defined the restrictions on national fiscal policy as provided in the Maastricht Treaty in greater detail. Under its "preventive arm" countries were required to achieve and maintain fiscal positions that are close to balance or in surplus, thereby ensuring sustainability while allowing room for cyclical stabilization without breaching the deficit limit of 3 percent of GDP. Under its "corrective arm" procedural steps to be followed once deficits were considered excessive were delineated in the so-called Excessive Deficit Procedure (EDP), specifying conditions and deadlines and the ultimate possibility of financial sanctions as foreseen by the Treaty.[9] The amendments of the SGP as introduced in 2005 brought more discretion and flexibility into the corrective arm, although the preventive arm became slightly more stringent (Amtenbrink and de Haan, 2006).

As we have shown elsewhere (de Haan et al., 2012, 2013), the major shortcoming of the SGP has been weak enforcement. There were no strong incentives for Member States to prevent other Member States from deviating from the objective to strive for a balanced budget in the medium term. Furthermore, Member States had no other means than peer pressure in the "preventive arm" of the SGP.

As a result, the preventive arm of the SGP was a dire failure. This is clearly illustrated in Figure 25.2, which is taken from Wierts (2006) and updated. Whereas EMU Member States submitted Stability Programs to the European Commission in which they outlined how they would reach a (cyclically adjusted) balanced budget, the budgetary adjustments that were implemented in practice were much less ambitious (Beetsma et al., 2009). Large countries, in particular, did not bring down their deficit sufficiently in economic good times (de Haan et al., 2004; Schuknecht et al., 2011). As a consequence, deficits exceeded the 3 percent threshold once the economic downturn set in 2000/2001. It then became clear that the "corrective arm" of the SGP was also weak. The European Council of Economics and Finance ministers (ECOFIN), was responsible for enforcing the rules. Based on a proposal of the European Commission, the ECOFIN had to decide whether an excessive deficit exists in a Member State, and if so which steps would then be taken. If a Member State did not take (sufficient) action to redress an excessive deficit, sanctions could be imposed. However, the ECOFIN would not automatically impose sanctions, as each step required a discretionary decision by the Council. The same ministers who were responsible for drafting national

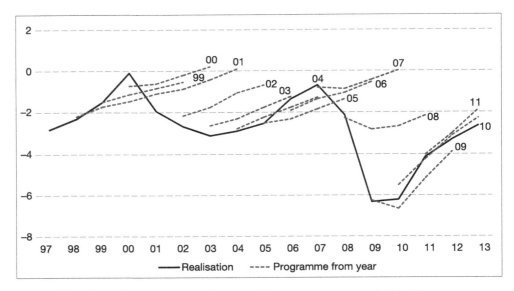

Figure 25.2 Weighted average Euro-12 budget deficit, plans vs outcome (% of GDP)

Source: EC and national stability plans of the respective countries Figure based on update of Wierts (2006).

budgets and who could therefore be accused of breaking the rules also had to decide whether one of their colleagues breached the same rules.

Financial markets did not discipline governments either, in contrast to the prediction of Buiter et al. (1993), as they hardy differentiated between sovereign bonds treating them all as (almost) risk-free (see Figure 25.1).[10] General risk aversion was very low before the crisis and financial markets apparently did not consider the no bail out clause as credible, expecting that the Union would renege on the no-bail out clause, if needed, to avert a financial crisis. When market discipline eventually came by the end of the decade, it took the form of a "sudden stop" (Buti and Carnot, 2012).

As a result of this combination of factors, at the outset of the worldwide financial crisis in 2008 budget deficits and government debts were higher than they would have been if the rules of the SGP had been adhered to (see Table 25.1, which is based on numbers from the European Commission Spring Forecast 2008, and thus provides a real time estimate of the budgetary situation).

Table 25.1 Budgetary starting situation in 2007 (% GDP)

	GR*	PT	FRA	ITA	EMU	GER	NL	IRL	SP
Budget balance	−6.4	−3.1	−2.7	−1.5	−0.7	0.3	0.2	0.1	1.9
Cyclically adj. budget balance	−7.1	−2.6	−2.6	−1.3	−0.8	−0.1	0.1	0	2.1
Government debt	105	68.3	63.9	104	66.2	64.9	45.3	25	36.1

Source: EC Spring Forecast 2008.

Note: *For Greece numbers from after the revision of budgetary aggregates in 2009 are reported. See Gilbert and Hessel (2013).

2.2 The role of the financial cycle

Although the euro crisis has some characteristics of a sovereign debt crisis, it was not only caused by unsustainable fiscal policies. In fact, at the outset of the global financial crisis nobody expected that European public finances would become a problem. The European Commission (2008b: 37) even stated that structural deficits were at "the lowest level on record since the early 1970s."

This begs the question *why* the economic downturn following the financial crisis could cause such a large swing in the budgetary position of Member States. This seems related to the fact that the nature and size of divergences in EMU were different than expected. In line with the theory of optimum currency areas, divergence is frequently measured as business cycle synchronization.[11] Yet, business cycles were very synchronized since the start of EMU, even during the crisis period (see Figure 25.3).

Instead, the divergences in the euro area were much more related to the financial cycle than to the normal business cycle. Characteristics of the financial cycle are that i) it is driven by growth in credit and house prices, ii) it has a much longer duration than business cycles: 16–20 years instead of up to 8 years, and iii) it has a wider amplitude while the correction of the financial cycle is often accompanied by a financial crisis (Drehmann et al., 2012; Borio, 2012a,b). As the financial cycle was largely neglected before the financial crisis, this may explain why these large and long lasting divergences in the euro area were not sufficiently recognized.

The upturn of the financial cycle in the decade before the global financial crisis was a worldwide phenomenon. Many advanced economies witnessed very rapid credit and house price growth (Borio, 2012b). Yet within the euro area, this financial cycle was asymmetric (see Figure 25.4, based on calculations in Comunale and Hessel, 2014). The upswing was strongest in a number of countries in the periphery, notably in Ireland, Spain and to a lesser extent Greece. In the run up to the financial crisis several countries had experienced strong credit booms, in part because joining the euro zone meant that their banks could raise funds from international sources in their own currency. Also, these countries were – at least

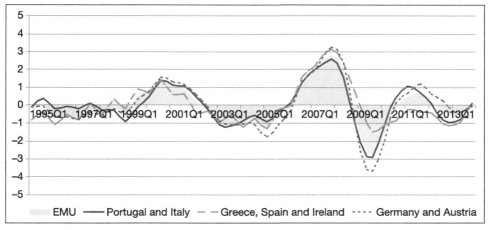

Figure 25.3 Business cycle fluctuations euro area highly synchronized

Source: Authors' calculations. Quarterly data for GDP filtered with HP-filter with λ =1600.

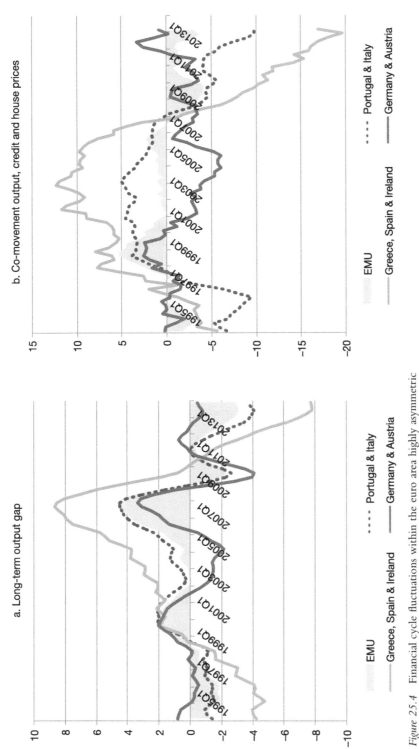

Figure 25.4 Financial cycle fluctuations within the euro area highly asymmetric

See Comunale and Hessel (2014). Inspired by Alessi and Detken (2009) and Drehmann et al. (2010). Calculated as quarterly GDP filtered with an HP-filter with λ = 100,000 (frequency of the financial cycle).

See Comunale and Hessel (2014). Inspired by Borio, Disyatat and Juselius (2013, 2014). Calculated as principal component of the output gap (HP-filter λ = 1600), real credit growth and real house price growth.

initially – experiencing a process of real convergence, while lower interest rates related to EMU-membership fueled consumption-related and property-related borrowing (Obstfeld, 2013). By contrast, the financial cycle was much more contained in Germany and Austria. This is partly because interest rates in these countries had already been low before EMU-membership. Germany was also recovering from a building boom induced by the reunification, while structural characteristics of the German housing market have likely also played a role. As a result, Germany is one of the very few advanced economies that managed to contain credit and house prices growth before the financial crisis (Hessel and Peeters, 2011).

The credit boom in some peripheral countries was fueled by capital inflows. When cross-border financial flows dried up, countries with the greatest reliance on external funding were disproportionately affected. This applies especially to Ireland and Spain, where the resulting decline in construction was a major shock to domestic economic activity, while abandoned projects and falling property prices indicated large prospective losses for banks that had made too many property-backed loans (Lane, 2012).

2.3 Diverging competitiveness

The credit boom fueled by capital inflows in much of Southern Europe facilitated another development that would come back to haunt EMU: diverging competitiveness positions. In the run up to the crisis, several countries saw their competitiveness deteriorate. Between 2001 and 2011 per unit labor costs in Greece rose by 33 percent, 31 percent in Italy, 27 percent in Spain and 20 percent in Ireland. By contrast, they grew by only 0.9 percent in Germany (Lin and Treichel, 2012), partly because the country needed to restore its price competitiveness after reunification. Although the large current account deficits of some countries signaled competitiveness problems, the deficits were relatively easy to finance as financial integration increased the availability of foreign funding (Obstfeld, 2013; Reis, 2013). In fact, capital inflows continued pushing up money and credit growth, which, in turn, increased inflation and caused competitiveness to deteriorate further (Gibson et al., 2014).[12] Growing current account deficits in the periphery were accompanied by increasing surpluses in core countries like Germany and the Netherlands.

As countries in the euro area no longer have the possibility to devalue their currency or to use national monetary policy, external imbalances can only be restored by improving competitiveness.[13] However, relative price adjustments without a change in the nominal exchange rate will be difficult when average euro area inflation is low; it will be a rather slow and painful route to rebalancing (Shambaugh, 2012), especially in the absence of further improvements in labor productivity.

The conventional wisdom before the crisis was that balance-of-payments of individual euro area countries would become as irrelevant as among regions within a country (Blanchard and Giavazzi, 2002). Yet the euro crisis has challenged the wisdom of this view (Merler and Pisani-Ferry, 2012). Still, it took a while before this was realized. In fact, the financing of national external positions in a supranational monetary union could be interpreted as proof of successful integration of capital markets and of real convergence within a monetary union. However, if capital inflows fuel investments that have little effect on future productivity growth (such as real estate) and delay adjustment to structural shocks they pose risks (Giavazzi and Spaventa, 2011).

This is not to say that competitiveness was not on the agenda of the EU. In 2000, the EU declared that it wanted to "become the most competitive and dynamic knowledge-based economy in the world." However, as argued by Wyplosz (2010), this so-called Lisbon strategy was a failure, as the mechanism of peer pressure on which it was based upon simply did not work (see also Kok, 2004). In addition, the recommendations were not always directly related to the emerging divergences described above (Fischer and Hobza, 2013). Therefore, the so-called MIP that was introduced aims to deal with monitoring competitiveness and where necessary redressing lack of competitiveness (see section 3.3).

When the financial crisis triggered a correction of these macro-financial imbalances, the budgetary impact was much larger than expected (Gilbert and Hessel, 2012, 2013). The average budget deficit in the euro area in 2009 was 5.2 percent of GDP larger than the European Commission had forecasted in March 2008, just months before the collapse of Lehman Brothers. The deterioration was even considerably larger in most of the countries in southern Europe, with the exception of Italy. In Portugal, Ireland, Greece and Spain, the budget deficit for 2009 increased by a staggering 11.2 percent of GDP on average.[14] Contrary to popular belief, these budgetary reversals can be mainly attributed to a large decline in public revenue, while the direct costs of financial sector bailouts played a more limited role in most countries.[15]

The worsening fiscal positions were caused by the turn of the financial cycle. Recent research shows that a turn of the financial cycle has a much larger negative impact on public finances than a turn of the normal business cycle (Borio, 2012b; Bénétrix and Lane, 2013). This is mostly due to their effect on government revenues (Eschenbach and Schuknecht, 2004; Dobrescu and Salman, 2011; Lendvai et al., 2011). Rising asset prices increase revenues in capital gains and transaction taxes. In addition, high wage growth increases income tax revenue, especially when the system is progressive. Finally, wealth effects stimulate domestic demand and thereby the revenues from indirect taxes. All these factors reverse when the financial cycle turns, resulting in a large budgetary deterioration.

This points to an important omission in the SGP, as the macroeconomic, financial, and fiscal risks associated with the expansion in external imbalances, credit growth, sectoral debt levels, and housing prices were not taken into account in assessing Member States' fiscal policies (Lane, 2012; Buti and Carnot, 2012).

2.4 No crisis instruments

When the upward revision of the Greek deficit drew attention to the fragility of public finances in Europe, market discipline returned with a vengeance. It had an on/off-nature: while spreads hardly reacted before the crisis, they reacted very strongly afterwards (Knot and Verkaart, 2013). Strikingly, bond spreads in the euro area reacted much stronger to the fiscal deterioration than in other advanced economies (De Grauwe and Yi, 2012, Dell'Erba et al., 2013). This was partly a rational reaction to specific vulnerabilities in the euro area, such as the lack of the nominal exchange rate to facilitate adjustment (Gilbert et al., 2013). But it is also related to the exceptionally high level of financial integration. While financial integration is often seen as a way to stabilize asymmetric shocks (Asdrubali et al., 1996), it also exposes countries to pro-cyclical capital flows (European Commission, 2008a). Highly integrated EMU countries are therefore more vulnerable to contagion than other advanced economies (Forbes, 2012), also because the euro may have increased the elasticity of capital flows (Lane, 2013).[16] Indeed, the share of foreign-owned government debt has a large upward effect on bond yields in EMU countries (Dell'Erba et al., 2013).

In such an environment, it was unfortunate that the architecture of EMU did not contain provisions for the resolution of a major sovereign debt crisis. No doubt, this contributed to the "makeshift and chaotic" character of the decision-making process to deal with the crisis (Buti and Carnot, 2012). Initially, the Member States had created the (temporary) European Financial Stability Facility (EFSF) to provide financial assistance to euro area Member States (Greece, Ireland, and Portugal[17]) within the framework of a macroeconomic adjustment program. In October 2010, it was decided to create a permanent rescue mechanism, the European Stability Mechanism (ESM), which entered into force on October 8 2012. In order to decouple weak banks from their national governments, it was agreed that, where necessary, banks could be recapitalised directly through this mechanism. The ESM is now the sole and permanent mechanism for responding to new requests for financial assistance by euro area Member States. It has a lending capacity of €500 billion.

Several authors have argued that lack of crisis instruments is problematic in view of the inherent instability in case of highly indebted sovereigns due to the lack of a lender of last resort for sovereign debt. As pointed out in section 1, the ECB is explicitly prohibited to purchase sovereign bonds in the primary market. According to Drudi et al. (2012: 893) this "prevents the ECB and Eurosystem central banks from becoming a kind of lender of last resort for governments and, more broadly, for any public sector bodies. It is precisely these limits which protect the integrity of the Eurosystem's balance sheet and thus preserve the independence and credibility of monetary policy in the eurozone." However, as pointed out by several authors (De Grauwe, 2011; Gros, 2012; Buiter and Rahbari, 2012), financing a high national public debt may become problematic in a supranational monetary union.[18] Here essentially the same mechanism is at work as in a bank run. If all depositors withdraw their money at the same time, the bank will not be able to liquidate immediately its loan portfolio. This is the main reason why central banks act as Lender of Last Resort (LoLR) for banks. Likewise, a solvent sovereign could be tripped into a fundamentally unwarranted payments default if the market were to adopt the "self-fulfilling fear equilibrium belief" that the government is not solvent (Buiter and Rahbari, 2012). As long as market confidence is high the government can pay interest payments, because its borrowing cost will be low. However, if market confidence is low the government may face a problem because the high-risk premium requested will make the debt service so expensive that it will not be able to find the necessary resources. Doubts about the ability of a government to service its debt could thus become self-fulfilling (Gros, 2012).

The implication of this analysis is that without a proper lender of last resort, bond yields in the euro area may display a higher risk of overshooting than yields in countries with their own currency. Yet, there is no consensus on the size and nature of this overshooting in the fast-growing literature on this topic.[19] According to De Haan et al. (2014), this in part reflects modeling uncertainty. While these authors do not find support for consistent and massive mispricing for the all countries in the periphery of the euro area, they do identify periods with misalignments for Greece, Portugal, and Ireland.

2.5 The doom loop

The funding problems of sovereigns were reinforced by a negative feedback loop with the banking sector. The banking system in the euro area is large.[20] Total assets of the banking system were equivalent to over 300 percent of euro-area GDP in 2007, compared with less than 100 percent in the United States (Shambaugh, 2012). The largest banks in the euro area are large in proportion to their home economies. Furthermore, most banks heavily invested in government bonds with a home bias which is particularly strong for banks of troubled sovereigns (Greece, Ireland, Italy, Portugal, and Spain).[21] In Spain, Portugal and Italy domestic banks owned around 25 percent of the outstanding stock of government debt (Pisani-Ferry, 2012). This is the basis for what came to be known as the "doom loop." Drawing on Acharya et al. (2012), the essence of the problem can be described as follows.[22] During the financial crisis, governments in several euro area countries engaged in large-scale, sometimes blanket, financial sector bailouts. Such bailouts require immediate issuance of additional debt by the sovereign causing an increase in the sovereign's credit risk. This has two possible consequences.

First, the government runs the risk that this debt overhang will affect the private sector. Households and corporations may anticipate that the high level of government debt will require higher taxes in the future, thereby diluting long-run returns on real-sector and human-capital investments. The resulting under-investment in the economy can cause economic growth to slow down, thereby further increasing the sovereign's credit risk. Second, the deterioration in the sovereign's creditworthiness may feedback adversely onto its financial sector through four channels (Mink and de Haan, 2013).[23] In the first place, the market value of the government debt on the balance sheet of the financial institutions reduces causing the financial sector's creditworthiness to decline. In the second place, higher sovereign risk reduces the value of collateral that financial institutions can use for funding purposes. In the third place, if sovereigns are downgraded by credit rating agencies this normally translates into lower ratings for banks located in the downgraded country. Finally, as the sovereign's creditworthiness declines, the value of the explicit and implicit government guarantees to the financial sector also declines, and this adversely impacts the financial sector's credit quality (Acharya et al., 2014; Obstfeld, 2013).

One of the consequences of financial institutions' exposure to impaired sovereign debt is that they may reduce their lending (Shambaugh, 2012). Popov and van Horen (forthcoming) provide evidence for this. Lower credit growth may further reduce economic growth, thereby reinforcing the doom loop.

During the course of the euro crisis the exposure of foreign banks on sovereign debt of the GIIPS reduced, whereas the exposure of domestic banks increased. Whereas, for instance, in December 2010 domestic banks held 67 percent of Greek sovereign debt, in June 2013 this percentage had risen to 99 (EBA, 2013).[24] This made the problem of the doom loop even more pressing. A proper banking union would break this deadly embrace between sovereigns and financial institutions (see section 3.4).

Due to the doom loop, funding problems on sovereign bond markets in the periphery went hand in hand with funding problems for banks in these countries. As a result, many countries in the periphery at some point experienced an outflow of capital which constituted a sudden stop in external financing (Merler and Pisani-Ferry, 2012). Most of the capital fled to so-called core countries that were considered a safe haven (see Figure 25.5). It made banks in vulnerable countries very dependent on ECB funding, which was also reflected in growing imbalances in the Target2 settlement system. Target2 liabilities (and assets) reached around 1,000 billion euro in the summer of 2012 (DNB, 2013). This financial fragmentation was at least partly driven by "unfounded fears on the reversibility of the euro" (Draghi, 2012).

3. The move towards a "genuine" monetary union

Over the last couple of years, important steps have been taken to repair the design flaws in EMU, under the guidance of blueprints by Van Rompuy (2012) and the European Commission (2012). Significant progress has been made in a relatively short time period. Fear that the euro crisis would spread further, thereby undermining the stability of the euro area and

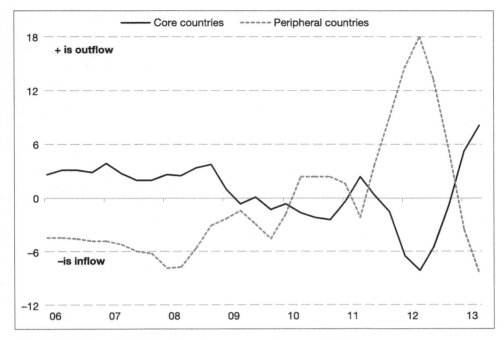

Figure 25.5 Net capital flows within the euro area, percentage of GDP

Source: IMF and DNB.

perhaps even the sustainability of the currency union, created the political willingness to take these steps.

3.1 Improved fiscal discipline[25]

In view of the compelling need for a reform of the fiscal policy governance framework, European policymakers have taken several steps, including the introduction of the "Six-Pack," "Two-Pack," and the Treaty on Stability, Coordination and Governance in the Economic and Monetary Union (TSCG).

The "Six-Pack," consisting of five Regulations and one Directive, hence its name, entered into force on December 13, 2011. It does not only cover fiscal policy surveillance, but also macroeconomic surveillance under the new MIP (see next section). In the fiscal field, the "Six-Pack" reinforces both the preventive and the corrective arm of the SGP. For instance, it defines quantitatively what a "significant deviation" from the medium term objective (MTO) or the adjustment path towards it means. Moreover, it enables that an EDP may be launched if a country does not meet the rule for the government debt ratio (i.e. the ratio is above 60 percent of GDP and does not diminish towards the Treaty reference value at a satisfactory pace). Financial sanctions are imposed in a gradual way, from the preventive arm to the latest stages of the EDP, and may eventually reach 0.5 percent of GDP. Most importantly, the "Six-Pack" introduces reverse qualified majority voting (RQMV) for decisions on most sanctions. RQMV implies that a recommendation or a proposal of the Commission is considered adopted by the Council unless a qualified majority of Member States votes against it, thereby bringing some automaticity in the procedure.

The "Two-Pack" added two more Regulations, entering into force on May 30 2013. Its main contribution lies in the preventive arm of the SGP: it obliges governments to submit their (draft) budgetary plan for the coming year to the European Commission. It allows the European Commission to check *beforehand* whether the budgetary plan is in line with its recommendations. If the Commission detects serious shortcomings, it can require a revision of the budget (EC, 2012b).

On January 1 2013, the Treaty on Stability, Coordination and Governance in the Economic and Monetary Union (TSCG) entered into force. The articles in Title III of the Treaty referring to fiscal policy are referred to as "Fiscal Compact". The two most important elements are a balanced budget rule, including an automatic correction mechanism, and a further strengthening of the excessive deficit procedure. The contracting parties commit to implementing in their national legislation a fiscal rule, which requires the general government structural budget balance to be in line with the country-specific MTO with a lower limit of a deficit of 0.5 percent of GDP (this limit is 1 percent if the government debt-to-GDP ratio is significantly below 60 percent and risks to long-term fiscal sustainability are low). The balanced budget rule must include a correction mechanism, which is automatically triggered in the event of significant deviations from the MTO or the adjustment path towards it. This balanced budget rule must be introduced in the national law of the countries concerned in a binding and permanent way, preferably at the constitutional level.

The "Fiscal Compact" also further strengthens the EDP of the SGP, in particular by increasing its automaticity if a euro area Member State is in breach of the deficit criterion. Most importantly, at each stage of the EDP euro area Member States will support the Commission's proposals or recommendations in the Council if a euro area Member State is in breach of the deficit criterion, unless a qualified majority of them is against it. Unfortunately, reverse qualified majority voting will not be applied following a breach of the debt criterion by a euro area Member State. As argued by De Haan et al. (2012), it seems that European policymakers still have to learn the lesson from the euro crisis that debt levels are more important than deficits when it comes to the sustainability of the currency union. Furthermore, as pointed out by the ECB (2012), for the new rules to work it is crucial that the Commission uses its increased influence by taking a rigorous approach when assessing fiscal deficits and avoids politically influenced decisions. One of the remaining weaknesses is that the new framework has become rather complicated. There are, for instance, still too many exceptional situations that can be taken into account when deciding on whether a deficit or debt-to-GDP ratio is excessive, or on whether a Member State has taken effective action.

3.2 Macroeconomic Imbalance Procedure

European policymakers have also enhanced the possibilities to monitor and prevent large macroeconomic and financial imbalances within the euro area. Particularly important is the introduction of the Macroeconomic Imbalance Procedure (MIP). The MIP is based on a continuous monitoring of a "scoreboard," consisting of a set of eleven indicators covering the major sources of macroeconomic imbalances. These include the current account balance, price competitiveness as measured by the change in the real effective exchange rate, as well as the growth of credit and house prices. For each indicator, thresholds have been defined to identify potential imbalances. According to the European Commission, the scoreboard and the thresholds are not applied mechanically, as the scoreboard is complemented by an economic interpretation. The aim of the scoreboard is to identify countries that warrant in-depth analysis in order to determine whether the potential imbalances identified in the early-warning system are benign or problematic. In analogy with the SGP, the MIP has a preventive arm and a corrective arm. Under the preventive arm policy recommendations can be issued by the Council to tackle imbalances early on. Under the corrective arm an Excessive Imbalance Procedure (EIP) may be opened for a Member State if it is deemed to experience excessive imbalances. In that case, the Member State concerned will have to submit a corrective action plan with a clear roadmap consisting of concrete policy measures and deadlines for implementing corrective action. Non-compliance with the Council recommendations may lead to financial sanctions that could eventually reach 0.2 percent of GDP. All decisions on sanctions are made in the Council via RQMV in order to increase automaticity.

In addition to the MIP, several other measures should reduce the risk of financial imbalances in the future. One is the establishment of the European Systemic Risk Board (ESRB), which may issue non-binding recommendations to Member States when risks to financial stability emerge. Another improvement is the (upcoming) introduction of macro-prudential policy frameworks in EMU Member States, including the possibility for European coordination. The Capital Requirements Regulation and Directive (CRR/CRDIV) allows national central banks (NCBs) to decide on the countercyclical capital buffer for banks. If necessary, the ECB Governing Council may overrule these decisions and decide on a stricter buffer.

Although these are important steps in the right direction, their effectiveness is not established yet, and will crucially depend on the actual implementation. Especially the MIP contains several potential weaknesses. First, the discretionary room of manoeuvre is relatively large. There are, for instance, no clear criteria to establish whether an imbalance exists and whether it is excessive or not. Second, the decision in the Council on the existence of an excessive imbalance is not made with RQMV. Third, there is a lot of discussion possible on the necessity and the effects of specific policy measures to contain the imbalances. Giavazzi and Spaventa (2010) point out that it is difficult to conceive of enforceable corrective actions. This increases the risk that recommendations are diluted in the Council. Furthermore, the approach is of much less use for prevention, as the recommendations in the preventive stage of the procedure are non-binding. Recommendations only start to become binding when imbalances are excessive, which means that they are already pretty large and difficult to reverse quickly.

3.3 Crisis mechanisms

As pointed out in section 2.2, backstop mechanisms have been set-up to provide financial assistance to Greece, Ireland, Portugal, Spain, and Cyprus. The most important tool to that effect is the ESM. However, the debate on whether enough has been done to ensure a robust crisis management system is not closed. Several observers have questioned whether sufficient funds are available. For instance, Lane (2012: 60) argues that "funding . . . was only enough to address the bailouts of Greece, Ireland, and Portugal—and thus not nearly sufficient to offer substantial support to Spain and/or Italy." Gilbert et al. (2013) argue that as an ESM-style rescue fund is inherently limited in size, it cannot by itself fully rule out contagion between EMU Member States. In the current set-up of the ESM (with only a small proportion of pre-funding), this is further amplified by the fact that one country's (additional) borrowing is another country's (additional) lending (Bijlsma and Vallée, 2012).

The ECB has also taken on an important role, by means of especially the announcement of the OMT programme. The ECB is capable of providing an effective backstop. However, this is probably not an optimal long-run solution as using OMTs comes with a number of negative side effects in the longer run. The function of lender of last resort could interfere with the ECB's monetary policy mandate and might create inflationary risks. In addition, ECB intervention also comes with risks specific for a central bank in a currency union. Whereas other central banks interact with a single government, after the adoption of the euro by Lithuania in 2015 the ECB interacts with nineteen. When the ECB buys government bonds this inevitably has distributional consequences. Should the ECB incur losses on its bond portfolio, those losses are transferred to its shareholders – i.e. the euro area Member States. The ECB thereby becomes a vehicle for fiscal transfers to countries benefiting from the purchases, for which it neither has the mandate nor the democratic legitimacy.[26]

3.4 Banking Union[27]

Until November 2014, national authorities were responsible for supervising the banking system and ensuring its stability. The crisis has made clear that this is not a viable arrangement. In line with the financial trilemma (Schoenmaker, 2011) a decentralized system of bank supervision and resolution is inadequate in an environment with a large banking sector and high interconnectedness among national banking systems as well as between banking systems and sovereigns (Obstfeld, 2013). Experience of the near failure of cross-border banks in Europe suggests that in times of crisis national authorities focus on preserving the national parts, while the integrated value of a bank is neglected. Furthermore, a banking union with a common safety can break the "doom loop" between national governments and banks (Gros and Schoenmaker, 2014).[28]

The European Council therefore decided in June 2012 for a European Banking Union, which involves three elements. First, under the so-called Single Supervisory Mechanism (SSM) micro-prudential supervision of banks has moved from national supervisors to the ECB since November 2014.[29] Also non-euro area Member States may participate in the SSM. By giving non-euro area Member States full membership and voting rights in the Supervisory Board – the body responsible for the preparation of decisions on supervisory matters – they are placed on an equal footing with euro area Member States. The role of the ECB Governing Council in the SSM is reduced to the possibility of accepting or rejecting the decisions of the Supervisory Board (Constâncio, 2013).

A crucial step towards the new supervisory regime was the large-scale health test of the top 130 banks in the euro area countries, which together account for some 85 percent of European bank assets. This so-called comprehensive assessment, consisting of an Asset Quality Review (AQR) and stress tests, aimed to reduce uncertainty on the state of bank balance sheets, which should increase confidence in the banking sector and encourage new lending. The comprehensive assessment should also ensure that the new banking union will not immediately be confronted with large losses from the pre-crisis period.[30]

Second, a Single Resolution Mechanism (SRM) has been introduced to deal with bank resolution, i.e. the orderly restructuring and/or liquidation of ailing financial institutions. A situation in which only supervision is delegated to the European level, but in which the resolution mechanism remains national could give rise to conflicts of interest. For example, supervisory decisions to withdraw the licence of a bank would be taken at a central level whereas the bill of such decisions would have to be footed at a national level. This would put tremendous pressure on the European supervisor not to pull the trigger but instead to exercise forbearance. The political agreement concluded in March 2014 about an SRM was therefore a major step. The SRM Regulation will be applicable from 2016, together with the bail-in provisions under the Bank Recovery and Resolution Directive (BRRD). Under this mechanism, losses are initially borne by shareholders and creditors. If necessary, temporary financing can be made available from the newly established Resolution Fund or – as the ultimate backstop – from public funds. The Resolution Fund composed of national compartments for a transitional phase of eight years is built up over time by contributions from the banking sector raised at the national level by the national resolution authorities to a funding level of 1 percent of covered deposits. Its target size of €55 billion would be enough to resolve all but the very largest banks in Europe (Gros, 2013). Resolution decisions will be prepared and monitored centrally by a Single Resolution Board (SRB).[31] The European Commission assesses the SRB's decision and can refer it to the Council if it wishes to depart materially from the Board's proposal.

According to Gros (2013), there are some weaknesses in the SRM, most importantly that there is as yet no explicit agreement on how to provide the SRF with a backstop. In the transition period, bridge financing will be available either from national sources, backed by bank levies, or from the ESM. The ECOFIN decided that a common backstop will be developed during the transition period. Such a backstop will facilitate borrowings by the SRF. The ECOFIN also decided that the banking sector ultimately will be liable for repayment by means of levies in all participating Member States. The backstop only will be fully operational (at the latest) after ten years. Another weakness is that it will take some time for the SRF to reach its target of €55 billion. But a long transition period was unavoidable as creditor countries were not willing to accept a mutualisation of the risks from the past (Gros, 2013).

Third, the introduction of a European deposit guarantee scheme. This has received a low priority as national schemes have been harmonized. However, Gros and Schoenmaker (2014: 537) argue for combining resolution and deposit guarantee at the European level as this

> allows for swift decision-making … By contrast, a myriad of national funds is difficult to activate during a crisis and may give rise to conflicts. Two separate European funds for deposit insurance and resolution may lead to inter-agency conflicts. Recognizing the interconnectedness, the functions of resolution and deposit insurance should be combined in Europe, as is done in the United States.

4. The road ahead

As discussed in detail above, in recent years all major weaknesses in the set-up of the EMU have been addressed in some way or the other, which is a major achievement. However, the effectiveness of the new arrangements is not established yet, and will crucially depend on the implementation in practice. Zooming out, two main facts stand out. First, by and large national sovereignty is preserved, especially in the most visible and politically sensitive areas. Despite improved policy coordination, fiscal and economic policies largely remain national prerogatives. Therefore imposing fiscal and especially macroeconomic discipline on reluctant sovereign states remains challenging. The loss of national sovereignty is larger in banking supervision, but national influence remains relatively large in bank resolution. Second, the introduction of the ESM, the OMTs, and the banking union has significantly increased the degree of risk sharing between EMU Member States, but in a relatively non-transparent and piecemeal way (see Table 25.2). Explicitly visible risk sharing via governments (ESM) remains relatively small, while there is a relatively large role for more implicit risk sharing

Table 25.2 Verdict EMU-variants

	Original set-up EMU		Enhanced EMU	Eurobonds (section 4.1)	No-bailout (section 4.2)
	Ex-ante	*Ex-post*			
Degree of coordination	−	−/−	+/−	+/+	+/−
• Fiscal policies	+/−	−	+	+/+	+/−
• Macroeconomic policies	−	−/−	+/−	+	+/−
• Banking regulation	−/−	−/−	+	+	+
⇒ *Political feasibility*			+/−	−	+/−
Degree of risk sharing	−/−	+	+	+	+/−
• Via governments (explicit)	−/−	+/−	+/−	+/+	+/−
• Via banking union (explicit)	−/−	−/−	+/−	+	+
• Other (implicit)	−/−	+/+	+	−/−	−/−
⇒ *Political feasibility*			+/−	−	+/−
Balance between degree of coordination and risk sharing	+	−/−	+/−	+/+	+/+
Economic desirability			+/−	+/+	+

Notes: −/− indicates a complete absence of risk sharing/policy coordination within EMU; +/+ indicates perfect risk sharing/full coordination. In the enhanced EMU both the degree of policy coordination and the degree of explicit risk sharing via the banking union have increased compared to the original set-up; but in both cases questions remain (see section 3). As a result, it is yet unclear to what extent the degree of implicit risk sharing (e.g. via the ECB) can be reduced. In the "Eurobonds" scenario as suggested in section 4.1, the balance between coordination and risk sharing is restored by strengthening coordination and by making risk sharing more explicit. The balance between risk sharing and coordination can also be restored by limiting risk sharing ("strengthening no bail-out"). This, however, requires a strong banking union and the possibility of liquidity support for governments (section 4.2). It is therefore not self-evident that in this scenario policy coordination can be reduced compared to the current status quo.

in case banks face problems (bail-in, Resolution Fund) and especially the ECB (VLTROs and OMTs).

In our view, this has two consequences. First, in the longer run the way risk sharing is organized can be improved. Especially, the currently large role of the ECB does not seem an optimal long-run solution. Second, an imbalance looms between the degree of risk sharing and the degree of national sovereignty (Weidmann, 2014). This is especially true if the current framework for policy coordination proves insufficiently effective, for instance, due to weak enforcement. If too much sovereignty is retained, this will also increase the risk of new budgetary, financial and economic imbalances and thereby the chance that risk sharing arrangements will be called upon. This in turn increases the risk that those risk sharing arrangements (like the ESM) turn out to be insufficient or turn out to have too large negative side effects. In this regard, EMU's current combination of a still relatively limited degree of policy coordination in combination with a significantly increased degree of risk sharing could be improved upon. Indeed, several authors claim that the current arrangements provide a half-build house, and that long-term solutions require either a move towards a full political union (Glienicker Gruppe, 2013), or a credible return to the no-bailout clause so that markets can discipline governments (Von Hagen, 2013; Mody, 2013).[32]

While we do not argue against intermediate solutions like the current arrangements, in our view further improvements are possible. It would in particular be beneficial to further optimize the balance between risk sharing and national sovereignty. Although many specific institutional settings are conceivable, this almost unavoidably requires a fundamental choice to move closer towards one of two broad solutions sketched in the literature. These are either a monetary union with a higher degree of (explicit) risk sharing and more curtailed sovereignty, or a union of the type referred to by Buiter and Rahbari (2011) as: "you break it, you own it," where insolvency of a sovereign is settled between the taxpayers of that sovereign and its creditors, without any permanent financial support from any other nation's taxpayers. In earlier work (De Haan et al., 2012, 2013, Gilbert et al., 2013) we have argued for Eurobonds, as this in our view is most desirable from a macroeconomic viewpoint. It is, however, highly politically sensitive. In the following, we will therefore also describe an alternative: a variant of the "you break it, you own it" Europe based on market discipline and a formal mechanism for debt restructuring.[33]

Yet, both alternatives will only become feasible after current vulnerabilities in the monetary union have been dealt with, in particular the high public debt overhang in many countries. Public debt now stands at 96 percent of GDP for the euro area as a whole, while five countries have debt levels above 120 percent of GDP. Such high levels of debt make Eurobonds costly, as they increase the risk of losses and may lead to a controversial "transfer union" (Gilbert et al., 2013). Likewise, these high debt levels make large-scale debt restructuring costly as well, as it may require unrealistically large write-offs and could lead to destabilizing contagion towards other Member States (Vihriälä and Weder di Mauro, 2014).

4.1 Eurobonds

Eurobonds are centrally issued, jointly guaranteed bonds for financing the euro area Member States' public debt. Eurobonds can protect individual Member States against contagion and speculation on financial markets in a more robust and fundamental way than emergency funds, by guaranteeing countries in fiscal difficulties access to market financing. This reduces the risk that liquidity problems turn into solvency problems via higher interest rates, as well as the risk that problems spread from one country to another (Boonstra, 2011; Gilbert et al., 2013).

Clearly, more explicit risk sharing and guaranteed access to finance have a flipside: countries face weaker incentives for keeping fiscal policies sustainable. This requires strict coordination of (fiscal) policy. In our view, Eurobonds can serve as an instrument to achieve this if countries can no longer enter the capital and money markets on their own initiative. All debt needs to be financed with centrally issued Eurobonds. In our proposal (De Haan et al., 2012; Gilbert et al., 2013) the sole issuer of Eurobonds is an independent Budgetary Authority, which is also in charge of the enforcement of the European fiscal rules. It thereby has exclusive authority over the granting of loans to Member States. As a general rule, access to Eurobonds will be limited to countries with debt levels below a "debt ceiling" of 60 percent of GDP (De Haan et al., 2012; Gilbert et al., 2013). Member States exceeding this ceiling should be placed in a form of receivership. They would be temporarily allowed to take on extra debt (not on their own, but via the Budgetary Authority) only if they set out a detailed budgetary adjustment program and stick to it. If the corrections proposed by the debtor nation were insufficient, the Authority would be able to impose corrections. Any country that failed to satisfy the requirements would be denied access to additional finance and would therefore have no choice but to immediately implement further austerity measures. In a system where Eurobonds would be the sole finance vehicle, such a sanction would be much more credible than anything that is currently imposed, because countries would have no access to finance except via the new Budgetary Authority, giving it maximum bargaining power.[34]

4.2 Minimizing the degree of risk sharing

The alternative approach of minimizing the degree of risk sharing within EMU and relying more on market discipline, requires a more credible commitment to the no-bailout clause and some form of explicit *ex-ante* debt restructuring mechanism for insolvent sovereigns within the euro area (Von Hagen, 2013; Mody, 2013; Buchheit et al., 2013). The proponents of this approach claim several advantages. First, it would reduce uncertainty as well as the cost of restructuring in case of clearly insolvent sovereigns (such as Greece). Second, it might enable a monetary union with significantly less policy coordination and hence constraints on national sovereignty (Mody, 2013).

In our view, the crisis has made it clear that eliminating all risk sharing within EMU is not feasible. A fully credible no-bailout is arguably not feasible in a highly financially integrated monetary union where Member States are vulnerable to contagion and self-fulfilling liquidity crises (see section 2.4). In such an environment, relying only on market discipline and debt restructuring may cause debt restructuring to occur too soon and too much.[35] This would unnecessarily increase risk premia, borrowing costs and welfare.

One reason for this is that while a debt restructuring mechanism might be beneficial when sovereigns are clearly insolvent, a distinction between illiquidity and insolvency is often impossible to make in practice: there is a grey area where debt sustainability cannot be established with certainty. While countries in a monetary union are more vulnerable to liquidity problems than countries having their own currency, it is less clear whether they are also more vulnerable to solvency problems. On the one hand, EMU countries lack monetary policy and the exchange rate to absorb shocks, which – ceteris paribus – implies lower debt sustainability (Sims, 2012; Buchheit et al., 2013). On the other hand, higher inflation cannot reduce debt in the long-run, as it will also affect nominal interest rates (Gross, 2012).[36] Therefore, the grey area may arguably be larger for EMU Member States than for other countries, making it harder to fully rely on market discipline and debt restructuring. It would make sovereign debt in the monetary union more explicitly risk-bearing than it other countries

The uncertainty surrounding debt sustainability would be reduced if EMU countries could agree on a clearly visible threshold above which debt restructuring becomes inevitable (Buchheit et al., 2013). Even then, the risk of self-fulfilling sovereign debt crises still requires the existence of liquidity support for governments (Buiter and Rahbari, 2011; Vihriälä and Weder di Mauro, 2014). A sufficiently large backstop therefore remains necessary.[37] Moreover, this also requires a certain degree of coordination of fiscal and macroeconomic policies, in order to prevent excessive reliance on liquidity support. Finally, as the possibility of debt restructuring will reinforce the doom loop between banks and sovereigns, a well-functioning banking union is needed as well. This could include risk weights and concentration limits of sovereign bond portfolios. In our view, it is therefore not so evident that a debt restructuring mechanism will significantly reduce the required degree of policy coordination in EMU compared to the current status quo.

Notes

1 Notably in the US, there was a lot of skepticism, summarized by Jonung and Drea (2009) as: "It can't happen. It's a bad idea. It won't last."
2 There are numerous papers on the crisis. Excellent overviews are provided by Shambough (2012) and Lane (2012). See also the collection of papers in Gibson et al. (2014).
3 According to Lane (2012: 60), "it may be fair to characterize Europe's efforts to address its sovereign debt problem as makeshift and chaotic, at least through the middle of 2012."

4 See www.ecb.europa.eu/press/key/date/2012/html/sp120726.en.html.

5 The ECB announced its intention to intervene on a large-scale in the event of disruptions in the bond markets of countries that duly implemented an adjustment programme. These interventions will not be aimed at a particular interest rate or spread level, but at countering expectations of a monetary union break-up that were reflected in interest rate movements. OMT interventions differ from the SMP: OMT interventions are in principle unlimited, do not enjoy privileged creditor status and are explicitly linked to sound policy. The conditionality attached to OMT interventions resolves coordination issues between the fiscal and monetary authorities. OMT interventions are sterilized.

6 See http://ec.europa.eu/economy_finance/assistance_eu_ms/greek_loan_facility/ for details.

7 Some of the shortcomings, such as fiscal rules and Europe-wide banking supervision, were discussed during the late 1980s and early 1990s, but Member States could not agree on solutions which implied further transfer of sovereignty. See James (2012) for a detailed discussion.

8 The academic debate about EMU focused instead on diverging business cycles. Some authors argued that countries in the euro area would become more similar over time, as monetary union increases trade intensity and business cycle synchronization (Frankel and Rose, 1998). Initial studies on the trade effect indicated that currency unions lead to large increase in international trade (Rose, 2000). Since then, estimates of the trade effect of EMU have become much smaller (see, e.g., Berger and Nitsch, 2008), while Inklaar et al. (2008) find that the trade effect on business cycle synchronization is smaller than previously reported.

9 For detailed discussions of the SGP, see Amtenbrink and de Haan (2003; 2006), Heipertz and Verdun (2010) and Schuknecht et al. (2011).

10 De Grauwe and Ji (2012) argue that in the 2000–8 period spreads were very close to zero even though underlying fundamentals different widely. The dramatic increase in the spreads since 2008 were, according to De Grauwe and Ji (2012), significantly larger than the changes in the underlying fundamentals.

11 This is also reflected in the original set-up of EMU. The balanced budget requirement in the Stability and Growth Pact would, for instance, enable countries to let automatic fiscal stabilizers work over the course of the (asymmetric) business cycle.

12 Furthermore, Fernández-Villaverde et al. (2013) argue that capital inflows reduced the pressure for reforms by relaxing the budget constraints that the countries in question faced.

13 Although some authors argued that EMU increased the need for labor market flexibility and therefore the incentives to undertake labor market reform (Bean, 1998; Gibson et al., 2014), empirical evidence does not suggest that EMU led to significant labor market reforms (Bednarek et al., 2010).

14 The situation in Greece differs in one important aspect from the situation in the other countries, as the deterioration of the (actual) deficit is partly driven by an upward revision of the deficit figures for previous years.

15 See Gilbert and Hessel (2013), who find that only in Ireland the direct costs associated with costs of financial sector bailouts played a serious role in the deterioration of public finances. These results are in line with the findings of Reinhart and Rogoff (2009) that financial crises usually lead to a large increase in government debt, caused primarily not by financial sector bailouts but by the deep and prolonged economic downturn.

16 According to Forbes (2012), another reason for the larger susceptibility to contagion is that euro area countries share the common institutional framework of the monetary union. It is therefore much more likely that decisions concerning one country will also affect the others.

17 See www.efsf.europa.eu/about/operations/index.htm for details.

18 It is important to point out that this problem may occur even if the government has a balanced budget. If the government is highly indebted, every year a part of the debt matures and requires refinancing.

19 See de Haan et al. (2014) for an overview of this literature.

20 Banks in the euro area heavily depend on the inter-bank money market for their funding and notably the non-domestic component of the inter-bank market has been particularly volatile during the crisis (Reichlin, 2014).

21 One of the main reasons for this is that the Capital Requirements Directive (CRD), allows for a 0% risk weight to be assigned to government bonds issued in domestic currency. Moreover, the CRD exempts government debt issued in domestic currency from the 25% limit on large exposures that applies to all other asset holdings (Popov and van Horen, forthcoming). This was exacerbated by the fact that these bonds could be used as collateral in ECB operations (Reichlin, 2014).

22 See Acharya et al. (2014) and Farhi and Tirole (2014) for formal analyses. See also Obstfeld (2013).

23 Mody and Sandri (2012) present evidence on the joint dynamics of sovereign spreads and measures of banks' financial health.

24 For the other GIIPS countries these percentages were as follows: Ireland from 66 to 84%, Italy from 66 to 84%, Portugal from 54 to 71% and for Spain from 78 to 89%. Source: EBA (2013).

25 This section heavily draws upon De Haan et al. (2012, 2013).

26 This is one of the reasons why support from OMTs is explicitly linked to the presence of an adjustment programme from the EFSF/ESM and to the requirement that the programme conditionality is fully respected. This reduces the financial risks for the ECB and ensures that the period of support is used to improve the underlying situation in the country concerned.

27 This section draws on Cavelaars et al. (2013).

28 Still, some further steps may be required to deal with this problem, notably with regard to the regulatory treatment of government bonds. According to Weidman (2014), "we need to end the preferential treatment afforded to sovereign debt. At present, sovereign bonds are treated by European regulators as being risk-free – an assumption that stands in contradiction both to the no bail out clause and to recent history. We should therefore put this regulatory fiction to rest. Hence, sovereign bonds should be adequately risk-weighted, and exposure to individual sovereign debt should be capped, as is already the case for private debt."

29 Whereas the ECB's direct supervisory responsibility focuses on the largest banks, the national supervisors will remain responsible for supervision of the smaller banks. However, the ECB will be "exclusively competent" regarding the supervision of all banks, setting the overall policy framework, guarding supervisory quality and consistency, and taking over supervision from national supervisors if it deems necessary.

30 The assessment found a capital shortfall of €25 billion at 25 banks. Twelve of the 25 banks have already covered their capital shortfall by increasing their capital by €15 billion in 2014. The comprehensive assessment also showed that a severe stress test scenario would deplete the banks' top-quality, loss-absorbing Common Equity Tier 1 (CET1) capital by about €263 billion. This would result in the banks' median CET1 ratio decreasing by 4 percentage points from 12.4 to 8.3 percent. Capital shortfalls should be covered within six months for those identified in the AQR or the baseline stress test scenario, and within nine months for those identified in the adverse stress test scenario. Shortfalls revealed by the AQR and the baseline stress test scenario may only be covered by Common Equity Tier 1 (CET1) capital instruments. The use of Additional Tier 1 (AT1) capital instruments to cover shortfalls arising from the adverse stress test scenario is limited, depending on the trigger point of conversion or write-down.

31 The Board will operate in two sessions: an executive one and a plenary one. In its executive session, the Board consists of the Chairman, the Vice Chair, the four permanent members and the relevant national authorities where the troubled bank is established. The executive session will adopt individual resolution decisions which involve the use of the Fund below a € 5 billion threshold. The plenary session will be competent to decide in individual resolution cases if the support of the Fund in a specific case is required above the € 5 billion threshold.

32 Regarding a political union: this idea stems from the fact that successful currencies have historically always been linked with successful nation states (Goodhart, 1998). Yet, as argued by Hoeksma and Schoenmaker (2011) and Van Riet (2014), the European Union is a supranational arrangement that already performs many tasks that traditionally were the prerogative of nation states. It therefore remains unclear how much more political integration would be necessary to keep the monetary union stable.

33 A larger role for debt restructuring in the euro area does not necessarily require a formal restructuring mechanism. Such a formal mechanism has both advantages and disadvantages. An advantage is that it may prevent restructuring from occurring too late, which could have high costs. This would be the case if uncertainty about restructuring leads to prolonged market turbulence, or if restructuring only occurs once bailouts have already moved most of the debt towards public authorities like the ESM, IMF or ECB. A disadvantage is that a formal mechanism may provides government with an easy way out of a high debt situation, possibly causing debt restructuring to occur too early. It could also increase moral hazard and reduce the prevention of high deficits. There is no consensus on which of these two effects dominates, although Buchheit et al. (2013) believe that the Greek restructuring was too little, too late. In any case, the relative importance of these two effects also depends on the specific shape of a restructuring mechanism.

34 This is also because the Budgetary Authority is able to refuse financing of *additional* debt without putting in doubt the (re)financing of the remaining debt stock. That decision therefore comes with much smaller financial stability risks than in the current practice, where refusal to grant extra financial support may induce remaining (private) creditors to run for the exit.

35 Interestingly, Flandreau et al. (1998) show that also in previous decades market discipline had the tendency to overshoot. The problem was especially severe in fixed exchange rate regimes, such as the period of the gold standard.

36 Gros (2012) reminds us that before the start of EMU, the monetary union was thought to increase debt sustainability in several countries, as it would reduce nominal interest rates thanks to more credible monetary policy and the absence of competitive devaluations.

37 Although it can be argued that the required size of the backstop may be smaller than the current backstops. This is especially the case when a debt restructuring mechanism is only introduced once public debts have been reduced below the 60% of GDP threshold. The banking union and the possibility of debt restructuring may also reduce the required amount of liquidity support.

References

Acharya, V.V., Drechsler, I. and Schnabl, P. (2012), A Tale of Two Overhangs: The Nexus of Financial Sector and Sovereign Credit risks. *Banque de France Financial Stability Review* No. 16, April 2012.

Acharya, V., Drechsler, I. and Schnabl, P. (2014), A Pyrrhic Victory? Bank Bailouts and Sovereign Credit Risk. *Journal of Finance*, 69 (6), 2689–2739.

Amtenbrink, F. and de Haan, J. (2003), Economic Governance in the European Union – Fiscal Policy Discipline versus Flexibility. *Common Market Law Review*, 40, 1075–1106.

Amtenbrink, F. and de Haan, J. (2006), Reforming the Stability and Growth Pact. *European Law Review*, 31 (3), 402–13.

Asdrubali, P., Sorensen, B. and Yosha, O. (1996), Channels of Interstate Risk Sharing. United States 1963–1990. *The Quarterly Journal of Economics*, 111 (4), 1081–1110.

Bayoumi, T. and Eichengreen, B. (1993), Shocking Aspects of European Monetary Unification. In: Torres, F. and Giavazzi, F. (eds), *Adjustment and Growth in the European Monetary Union* (Cambridge: Cambridge University Press).

Bean, C. (1998), The Interaction of Aggregate-Demand Policies and Labor Market Reform. *Swedish Economic Policy Review*, 5 (2), 353–82.

Bednarek, E., Jong-A-Pin, R. and de Haan, J. (2010), The European Economic and Monetary Union and Labour Market Reform. *European Union Politics*, 11 (1), 3–27.

Beetsma, R., Giuliodori, M. and Wierts, P. (2009), Planning to Cheat: EU Fiscal Policy in Real Time. *Economic Policy*, 24, 753–804.

Bénétrix, A. and Lane, P. (2013), Financial Cycles and Fiscal Cycles. *Journal of International Money and Finance*, 34, 164–76.

Berger, H. and Nitsch, V. (2008), Zooming Out: The Trade Effect of the Euro in Historical Perspective. *Journal of International Money and Finance*, 27 (8), 1244–60.

Bijlsma, M. and Valleé, S. (2012), The Creation of Euro Area Safety Nets. Bruegel Working Paper 2012/ 09.

Blanchard, O. and Giavazzi, F. (2002). Current Account Deficits in the Euro Area: The End of the Feldstein–Horioka Puzzle? *Brookings Papers on Economic Activity*, 33 (2), 147–86.

Boonstra, W.W. (2011), Can Eurobonds Solve EMU's Problems? *Rabobank Working Paper* August 2011.

Borio, C. (2012a), On Time, Stocks and Flows: Understanding the Global Macroeconomic Challenges. Lecture in the Munich Seminar Series, November 9, 2012.

Borio, C. (2012b), The Financial Cycle and Macroeconomics. What Have We Learnt? *BIS Working Paper* 395.

Buchheit, L., Gelpern, A. Gulati, M. Panizza, U. Weder di Mauro, B. and Zettelmeyer, J. (2013), Revisiting Sovereign Bankruptcy, Committee on International Economic Policy and Reform.

Buiter, W., Corsetti, G. and Roubini, N. (1993), 'Excessive Deficits': Sense and Nonsense in the Treaty of Maastricht. *Economic Policy*, 8 (16), 57–100.

Buiter, W. and Rahbari, E. (2011), The Future of the Euro Area: Fiscal union, Break-up or Blundering Towards a 'You Break It You Own It Europe'. Available at: https://ir.citi.com/Y8kIuwhlIFOQGH 08QG3xl9iCE1KOZrqX%2Bo7vaHSPZzPtMVMwXsgz4XdnuubbWUEp.

Buiter, W. and Rahbari, E. (2012), The European Central Bank as Lender of Last Resort for Sovereigns in the Eurozone. *Journal of Common Market Studies*, 50 (Annual Review), 6–35.

Buti, M. and Carnot, N. (2012), The EMU Debt Crisis: Early Lessons and Reforms. *Journal of Common Market Studies*, 50 (6), 899–911.

Cavelaars, P., de Haan, J. Hilbers, P. and Stellinga, B. (2013), Challenges for Financial Sector Supervision. *DNB Occasional Study* 11(6).

Constâncio, V. (2013), Towards the Banking Union. Speech at the 2nd FIN-FSA Conference on EU Regulation and Supervision, Banking and Supervision under Transformation organized by the Financial Supervisory Authority, Helsinki, 12 February 2013.

Comunale, M. and Hessel, J. (2014), Current Account Imbalances in the Euro Area: Competitiveness or Financial Cycle? *DNB Working Paper* 443.

De Grauwe, P. (2011), Governance of a Fragile Eurozone. *CEPS Working Document* 34. Available at: www.ceps.eu/book/governance-fragile-eurozone.

De Grauwe, P. (2012). Economics *of Monetary Union*, 9th ed. (Oxford: Oxford University Press).

De Grauwe, P. and Ji, Y. (2012), Mispricing of Sovereign Risk and Macroeconomic Stability in the Eurozone. *Journal of Common Market Studies*, 50 (6), 881–98.

de Haan, J., Gilbert, N.D., Hessel, J.P.C and Verkaart, S.A.M. (2012), Beyond the Fiscal Compact: How Well-Designed Eurobonds May Discipline Governments. *Zeitschrift für Staats- und Europawissenschaften (ZSE)* (Journal for Comparative Government and European Policy), 3, 323–37.

de Haan, J., Gilbert, N.D., Hessel, J.P.C and Verkaart, S.A.M.. (2013), How to Enforce Fiscal Discipline in EMU: A Proposal. *Swiss Journal of Economics and Statistics*, 149 (2), 205–17.

de Haan, J., Berger, H. and Jansen, D. (2004), Why Has the Stability and Growth Pact Failed? *International Finance*, 7 (2), 235–60.

de Haan, L., Hessel, J. and van den End, J.W. (2014), Are European Sovereign Bond Yields Fairly Priced? The Role of Modelling Uncertainty. *Journal of International Money and Finance*, 47, 239–67.

Dell'Erba, S., Hausmann, R. and Panizza, U. (2013), Debt Levels, Debt Composition, and Sovereign Spreads in Emerging and Advanced Economies. *Oxford Review of Economic Policy*, 29 (3), 518–47.

De Nederlandsche Bank (2013), Euro-area Imbalances have Declined, but Action Remains Necessary. *DNBulletin*, 21 November 2013, www.dnb.nl.

Dobrescu, G. and Salman, F. (2011), Fiscal Policy during Absorption Cycles. *IMF Working Paper* 11/41.

Draghi, M. (2012), Introductory statement to the press conference (with Q&A). Speech, Frankfurt am Main, 6 September.

Drehmann, M, Borio, C. and Tsatsaronis, K. (2012), Characterizing the Financial Cycle: Don't Lose Sight of the Medium Term! *BIS Working Paper* 380.

Drudi, F., Durré, A. and Mongelli, F.P. (2012), The Interplay of Economic Reforms and Monetary Policy: The Case of the Eurozone. *Journal of Common Market Studies*, 50 (6), 881–98.

Eschenbach, F. and Schuknecht, L. (2004), Budgetary Risks from Real Estate and Stock Markets. *Economic Policy*, 19, 313–46.

European Banking Authority (2013), EU-wide Transparency Exercise 2013 Summary Report.

European Central Bank (2012), A Fiscal Compact for a Stronger Economic and Monetary Union. *ECB Monthly Bulletin*, May 2012, 79–94.

European Commission (2008a), EMU@10. Successes and Challenges After Ten Years of Economic and Monetary Union. *European Economy* 2008/2.

European Commission (2008b), Public Finances in EMU2008. *European Economy* 4, 2008.

European Commission (2012a), A Blueprint for a Deep and Genuine Economic and Monetary union: Launching a European Debate. 28 November 2012.

European Commission (2012b), Six-pack? Two-pack? Fiscal compact? A Short Guide to the New EU Fiscal Governance, 14 March 2012.

Farhi, E. and Tirole, J. (2014), Deadly Embrace: Sovereign and Financial Balance Sheets Doom Loops. Mimeo.

Feldstein, M. (1997), EMU and International Conflict. *Foreign Affairs* 76, 60–73.

Fernández-Villaverde, J., Garicano, L. and Santos, T. (2013). Political Credit Cycles: The Case of the Eurozone. *Journal of Economic Perspectives*, 27 (3), 145–66.

Fischer, J. and Hobza, A. (2013), Balancing Imbalances: Integrated Surveillance and the Role of the MIP, paper presented at the 15th Workshop on Public Finance organized by Banca d'Italia in Perugia from 4 to 6 April 2013.

Flandreau, M., le Cacheux, J. and Zumer, F. (1998), Stability Without a Pact? Lessons from the European Gold Standard, 1880–1914, *CEPR Discussion Paper* 1872.

Forbes, C. (2012). The big "C": Identifying and Mitigating Contagion. *NBER Working Paper*, No. 18465.

Frankel, J.A. and Rose, A.K. (1998), The Endogeneity of the Optimum Currency Area Criteria. *The Economic Journal*, 108 (449), 1009–25.

Giavazzi, F. and Spaventa, L. (2010), The European Commission's proposals: Empty and useless. VOXEU. Available at: www.voxeu.org/article/european-commission-s-proposals-empty-and-useless.

Giavazzi, F. and Spaventa, L. (2011), Why the Current Account Matters in a Monetary Union. In: Beblavy, M., D. Cobham and L. Odor (eds), *The Euro Area and The Financial Crisis* (Cambridge: Cambridge University Press).

Gibson, H.D., Palivos, T. and Tavlas, G.S. (2014) (eds.), The Crisis in the Euro Area. Papers Presented at a Bank of Greece Conference. *Journal of Macroeconomics*, 39 (Part B), 233–460.

Gilbert, N. and Hessel, J. (2012), De Europese overheidsfinanciën tijdens de crisis, *Economisch Statistische Berichten*, 97, 166–69.

Gilbert, N. and Hessel, J. (2013), The Financial Cycle and the European Budgetary Reversal During the Crisis: Consequences for Surveillance, paper presented at the 15th Workshop on Public Finance organized by Banca d'Italia in Perugia from 4 to 6 April 2013.

Gilbert, N., Hessel, J. and Verkaart, S. (2013), Towards a Stable Monetary Union: What Role for Eurobonds? *DNB Working Paper* 379.

Glienicker Gruppe (2013), Aufbruch in die Euro-Union, available at www.glienickergruppe.eu.

Goodhart, C.A.E. (1998), The Two Concepts of Money: Implications for the Analysis of Optimal Currency Areas. *European Journal of Political Economy*, 14, 407–32.

Gros, D. (2012), On the Stability of Public Debt in a Monetary Union. *Journal of Common Market Studies*, 50 (Annual Review), 36–48.

Gros, D. (2013), The Bank Resolution Compromise: Incomplete, But Workable? *CEPS Commentary* 30.

Gros, D. and Schoenmaker, D. (2014), European Deposit Insurance and Resolution in the Banking Union. *Journal of Common Market Studies*, 52 (3), 529–46.

Heipertz, M. and Verdun, A. (2010), *Ruling Europe: The Politics of the Stability and Growth Pact* (Cambridge: Cambridge University Press).

Hessel, J. and Peeters, J. (2011), Housing Bubbles, the Leverage Cycle and the Role of Central Banking. *DNB Occasional Study* 2011/5.

Hoeksma, J. and Schoenmaker, D. (2011), The Sovereign Behind the Euro. *Duisenberg School of Finance Policy Paper* 15, September.

Inklaar, R., Jong-A-Pin, R. and de Haan, J. (2008), Trade and Business Cycle Synchronization in OECD Countries A Re-examination. *European Economic Review*, 52 (4), 646–66.

James, H. (2012), *Making the European Monetary Union* (Cambridge: Harvard University Press).

Jonung, L. and Drea, E. (2009), The Euro: It Can't Happen, It's a Bad Idea, It Won't Last. US Economists on the EMU, 1989 – 2002. *European Economy, Economic Papers*, 395.

Knot, K. and Verkaart, S. (2013), The European Debt Crisis and a Stable Design of EMU. In: Nowotny, E., P. Mooslechner and D. Ritzberger-Grünwald (eds), *A New Model for Balanced Growth and Convergence. Achieving Economic Sustainability in CESEE Countries* (Cheltenham: Edward Elgar).

Kok, W. (2004), *Facing the Challenge. The Lisbon Strategy for Growth and Employment.* Report from the high-level group chaired by Wim Kok, November 2004.

Lane, P.R. (2012), The European Sovereign Debt Crisis. *Journal of Economic Perspectives*, 26 (3), 49–68.

Lane, P.R. (2013), Capital Flows in the Euro Area. *European Economy Economic Papers*, 497.

Lendvai, J., Moulin, L. and Turrini, A. (2011), From CAB to CAAB? Correcting Indicators of Structural Fiscal Positions for Current Account Imbalances. *European Commission Economic Paper*, 442.

Lin, J.Y. and Treichel, V. (2012), The Crisis in the Euro Zone. Did the Euro Contribute to the Evolution of the Crisis? *World Bank Policy Research Working Paper*, 6127.

Mink, M. and de Haan, J. (2013), Contagion During the Greek Sovereign Debt Crisis. *Journal of International Money and Finance,* 34, 102–13.

Merler, S. and Pisani-Ferry, J. (2012), Sudden Stops in the Euro Area. *Bruegel Policy Contribution* 2012/6, March 2012.

Mody, A. (2013), A Schuman Compact for the Euro Area. Bruegel Essay and Lecture Series.

Mody, A. and Sandri, D. (2012), The Eurozone Crisis: How Banks and Sovereigns Came to Be Joined at the Hip. *Economic Policy*, 27, 199–230.

Obstfeld, M. (2013), Finance at Center Stage: Some Lessons of the Euro Crisis, *European Economy – Economic Papers* 493.

Popov, A., and van Horen, N. (forthcoming), Exporting Sovereign Stress: Evidence from Syndicated Bank Lending During the Euro Area Sovereign Debt Crisis. *Review of Finance*.

Reichlin, L. (2014), Monetary Policy and Banks in the Euro Area: The Tale of Two Crises. *Journal of Macroeconomics*, 39, 387–400.

Reinhart, C.M. and Rogoff, K.S. (2009), The Aftermath of Financial Crises. *NBER Working Paper*, No. 14656.

Reis, R. (2013), The Portuguese Slump and Crash and the Euro Crisis. *NBER Working Paper*, No. 19288.

Rose, A.K. (2000), One Money, One Market: The Effect of Common Currencies on Trade. *Economic Policy*, 15 (30), 7–45.

Shambaugh, J. (2012), The Euro's Three Crises. Brookings *Papers on Economic Activity,* Spring 2012, 157–231.

Schoenmaker, D. (2011), The Financial Trilemma. *Economics Letters*, 111, 57–9.

Schuknecht, L., Moutot, P. Rother, P. and Stark, J. (2011), The Stability and Growth Pact: Crisis and Reform. *ECB Occasional Paper*, 129.

Sims, C.A. (2012), Gaps in the Institutional Structure of the Euro Area. *Banque de France Financial Stability Review* No. 16, April 2012.

Van Riet, A. (2014), The Future of the Euro at 15, paper presented at the conference "In Search of European Political Union" 19–21 June 2014, Utrecht University. Available at: http://macrofinance. nipfp.org.in/PDF/12Pr_VanRiet_Rounding_the_corners_of_eurozone_trinity(2014–02–25)New% 20Delhi.pdf.

Van Rompuy, H. (2012), *Towards a Genuine Economic and Monetary Union.* Available at: http://ec.europa. eu/economy_finance/crisis/documents/131201_en.pdf.

Vihriälä, V. and Weder di Mauro, B. (2014), Orderly Debt Restructuring Rather Than Permanent Mutualisation Is the Way To Go. VOXEU, 2 April 2014. Available at: www.voxeu.org/article/ orderly-debt-reduction-rather-permanent-mutualisation-way-go.

Von Hagen, J. (2013), Governance of the Euro Area: Fiscal Union, Debt Union, Fiscal Freedom. Contribution at a seminar on the occasion of the farewell of Coen Teulings at the CPB. Available at: www.cpb.nl/sites/default/files/Contribution-Jurgen-von-Hagen-Coen-Teulings-farewell-25042013. pdf.

Wierts, P. (2006), Fiscal Rules and Fiscal Outcomes in EMU: Theory and Evidence. PhD thesis: University of Reading.

Weidmann, J. (2014), Monetary Union as a Stability Union. Speech at the Duitsland Instituut, Amsterdam, 7 April 2014.

Wyplosz, C. (2010), The Failure of the Lisbon Strategy. VOXEU, 12 January 2010. Available at: www. voxeu.org/article/failure-lisbon-strategy.

PART VII

Institutions

26

THE POLITICAL ECONOMY OF EUROPEAN INTEGRATION

Enrico Spolaore

1. Introduction and summary

The process of European integration is based on a time-honored strategy of partially integrating policy functions and institutions in a few areas – such as coal and steel, trade, or, later, a common currency – with the expectation that more integration will follow in other areas over time.

This strategy became the main approach to European institutional integration in the 1950s, after the collapse of a more ambitious attempt to create a defense and political community, which would have included a common army, a common budget, and common legislative and executive institutions – basically, a European federation. Faced with the failure to form a full political union directly, supporters of European integration pursued an alternative path of gradual and partial integration. The process took place mostly in technical and economic areas but with the expectation that deeper, more "political" integration would follow, in part as a result of the pressure from inefficiencies and crises associated with incomplete integration. From this perspective, incompleteness was not seen as a bug but, possibly, as a feature, as it was expected to lead to further integration down the road.

This gradualist strategy was mostly successful when applied to areas with large economies of scale and relatively low costs from heterogeneity of preferences and traits across different populations – for example, the creation of a common market. The approach, however, also led to the creation of dangerously incomplete and inefficient institutional settings. Most notably, the euro was introduced in the absence of other institutions historically associated with a successful monetary union, resulting in a "half-built house" (Bergsten 2012). A widespread rationalization of the imperfections and shortcomings of European institutions was based on the expectation that the problems associated with previous steps could always be fixed by more integration: commercial integration and monetary integration would in due course be followed by more institutional and political integration, such as a banking union, a fiscal union, or even a fully-fledged political union, in what has been described as a "chain-reaction" towards an "ever-closer union."

A fundamental problem with this chain-reaction approach is that it underestimates the costs and constraints associated with heterogeneity of traits and preferences over public goods and policies in populations with diverse societal structures, cultures, and identities. In fact, the trade-off between benefits from integration and heterogeneity costs is at the center of a vast and growing literature on the political economy of integration (and disintegration). An analysis of the implications of such trade-off can shed insights on the successes and limits of the actual process of European integration, as well as on the theories that have been developed over the decades to understand the objectives and strategies behind the European project.

This chapter provides a discussion of the process of European institutional integration from a political economy perspective, linking the long-standing political debate on the nature of European integration to the more recent economic literature on political borders.[1]

The rest of this chapter is organized in three parts. Section 2 briefly discusses a few key concepts on the political economy of integration and their implications for the European project, with an emphasis on the basic trade-off between economies of scale and scope associated with larger political unions and the costs from sharing public goods and policies among more heterogeneous populations. Section 3 covers the two main political theories of European integration, intergovernmentalism and functionalism, and argues that both theories capture important aspects of European integration, but neither approach provides a complete and realistic interpretation of this complex process. Finally, the actual process of European institutional integration, from its beginnings after the Second World War to the current crisis, is critically discussed in Section 4. Section 5 concludes.

2. The political economy of institutional integration: A fundamental trade-off and its implications for Europe

A useful starting point to study the political economy of institutional integration is the fundamental trade-off between *economies of scale* and *heterogeneity costs*.[2] When larger and diverse groups form common institutions and pool public functions and policies – a common legal and judicial framework, a common currency, fiscal policies, defense and security – and so on, they can benefit from economies of scale in the provision of public goods, which are non-rival in consumption and therefore cheaper on a per-capita basis when the costs are spread over a larger population. Larger jurisdictions may also allow governments to internalize externalities over a broader area, and to provide insurance against shocks, such as natural disasters or regional economic crises.

Larger and more diverse jurisdictions, however, tend to face higher heterogeneity costs stemming from different political, economic and cultural traits and conflicting preferences over public goods and policies. The relations between various measures of heterogeneity (ethnic and linguistic fractionalization and polarization, measures of genetic and linguistic distance, and other measures of historical and cultural diversity) and a series of political outcomes (provision of public goods, quality of government, redistribution, conflict within and across states) have been documented in a vast and growing empirical literature, including for instance Alesina et al. (2003), Alesina and La Ferrara (2005), Montalvo and Reynal-Querol (2005), Esteban, Mayoral and Ray (2012), Desmet, Ortuño-Ortín and Wacziarg (2012), Spolaore and Wacziarg (2012), and Arbatli, Ashraf and Galor (2013). This empirical literature is still in its infancy, and there are numerous open questions about the definitions and methods to measure the effects of heterogeneity on different outcomes.[3] Nonetheless, a general finding is that more heterogeneous populations typically face higher political costs in the provision of public goods and a higher likelihood of civil conflict.

In principle, heterogeneity can also be a source of benefits as well as of costs for societies. In communities where agents have diverse preferences and characteristics, individuals and groups can benefit by specializing in the production of different goods and services, while also learning new ideas from each other. Benefits from heterogeneity, however, are mostly about interactions over *rival* goods, which cannot be consumed simultaneously by several people. In fact, *low* heterogeneity may lead to conflict if different individuals and groups share very similar preferences over the *same* rival goods, such as specific territories and resources (Spolaore and Wacziarg 2012). The opposite relation holds for diverse preferences over *non-rival* goods – such as a common government, legal system, and public policies – which must be shared by all within a given political jurisdiction, whether they like them or not. In the area of public goods, therefore, different preferences mean higher political costs and a higher likelihood of domestic conflict. In sum, heterogeneity of traits and preferences is mostly beneficial when different individuals and groups interact about rival goods but costly when the interaction is about non-rival goods. Consequently, heterogeneity of preferences over public goods is a major limit to the integration of institutions that provide common policies to large and diverse populations.

Up to a point, the trade-off between economies of scale and heterogeneity of preferences can be addressed through decentralization at different layers of administration. Public goods with higher heterogeneity and lower economies of scale can be more efficiently provided at lower administrative levels (e.g., municipal and regional governments), while public functions with higher economies of scale and externalities, relative to heterogeneity costs, can be centralized at increasingly higher levels.[4] These ideas are partly reflected in the legal documents at the basis of European integration. For instance, the Maastricht Treaty of 1992, which reorganized and redefined European institutions, specified the following "principle of subsidiarity" (Article 3b):

> In areas which do not fall within its exclusive competence, the Community shall take action, in accordance with the principle of subsidiarity, only if and in so far as the objectives of the proposed action cannot be sufficiently achieved by the Member States and can therefore, by reason of the scale or effects of the proposed action, be better achieved by the Community.[5]

Nonetheless, the creation of layers of distinct and overlapping jurisdictions, each organized around a subset of public functions and policies with different economies of scale and heterogeneity costs, faces limitations and challenges both in terms of economic efficiency and political stability. A key issue for disentangling different functions at different levels is that the provision of public goods comes not only with significant economies of scale, but also with *economies of scope*. It is usually more efficient to provide several public goods together, rather than through separate authorities. A particularly important kind of "economies of scope" is associated with the exercise of fundamental *sovereignty* and monopoly of *legitimate coercion*, which is a prerequisite for the provision of a vast range of public goods and policies. In fact, even when different public goods are decentralized at lower administrative layers, modern federal systems tend to centralize sovereignty – which can be defined as the residual power to take fundamental decisions over domestic and foreign relations for a state or federation, after all other specific rights and powers have been assigned to various layers of authorities. In practice, the centralization of sovereignty is often achieved through the pooling of the means on which the ultimate monopoly of legitimate coercion depends, including explicit military power. Consequently, the formation of a sovereign polity usually goes hand-in-hand with the integration of defense and security under one authority, which exercises the ultimate monopoly of coercion within a territory. In turn, such power of coercion can be used to collect resources and finance a broader set of public goods, on which different groups and individuals may have different preferences. Therefore, ultimate political integration – the formation of a sovereign state or federation – has historically been associated with the pooling of defense, security and foreign policy – public functions with very high economies of scale and scope but also very high heterogeneity costs across large and diverse populations. It is not clear how the European "principle of subsidiarity" would apply to the fundamental issue of centralizing sovereign power and control over means of coercion.

Over the centuries, the formation of large and heterogeneous states, federations and empires has taken place as the result of actions by non-democratic rulers (Leviathans) interested in maximizing their own rents while ignoring the preferences of large part of their subjects, and/or in response to significant external security threats.[6] In contrast, there are very few historical examples – if any – of consensual formation of sovereign states or federations by large and diverse populations under democratic and peaceful conditions.

In this respect, the history of European institutional integration so far has been no exception. A founding document of the process of European integration is the Schumann declaration of 1950, which defined the pooling of coal and steel production as "the first concrete foundation of a European federation indispensable to the preservation of peace." Nonetheless, no European federation was formed. In 1952 the six founders of the European Steel and Coal Community signed a treaty for the establishment of a European Defense Community and a European Political Community, which would have included a common army, a common budget, and common legislative and executive institutions – basically, a European federation. The project was abandoned, however, after the treaty failed to be ratified in the French parliament. Instead, the supporters of European integration focused on the creation of a European common market, established with the Treaty of Rome in 1957. The Treaty of Rome no longer mentioned a European federation, but stated the vaguer objective of laying the "foundations of an ever-closer union among the peoples of Europe."

Consistently, with the analysis of this section, those earlier successes of European integration took place in areas, such as commercial integration, where economies of scale are very high, while heterogeneity costs are relatively low and partially offset by benefits from diversity. In contrast, failure occurred in areas, such as defense and security, with the highest political costs from heterogeneity. The subsequent history of European institutional integration stems from the lessons (both learned and not learned) of those early successes and failures, as we will see in the rest of this chapter.

3. Political theories of European integration: Intergovernmentalism vs. functionalism

Europe's political economy is notoriously complex and controversial. Over the decades, scholars and commentators have emphasized different motivations, strategies and interactions among the several actors involved in the process of European integration, from national governments and voters to supranational technocrats and domestic interest groups.

A traditional distinction in the political literature on European integration is between the "intergovernmentalist" view and the "functionalist" view.[7] The two views differ in their answers to two basic questions: what are the objectives of European integration, and who is in charge?

Intergovernmentalists believe that the European project is in the hands of national governments who pursue domestic interests, mostly in the economic area. For instance, Moravcsik (1993, 1998, 2012), a leading proponent of this theory, argues that national governments have built European institutions to pursue the economic interests of their domestic constituencies, and views the euro as an economically-motivated project, mainly reflecting the interests of German exporters and other powerful economic agents. This line of analysis is part of a broader political economy literature stressing the connections between domestic economic interests and national attitudes and policies towards European integration (for example, Frieden 2002).[8]

From an intergovernmentalist perspective, the European Union is just a particularly complex international organization of sovereign states. European supranational institutions, such as the European Commission and the European Court of Justice, are only instruments and commitment devices that nation states have built and use in order to pursue their own objectives, while their national governments retain all fundamental power about key decisions.

Functionalists, in contrast, believe that supranational institutions are distinct from national governments, and fully in charge of specific functions – hence the term "functionalism."[9] In their view, "supranational actors" such as Jean Monnet (head of the European Coal and Steel Community in the 1950s) or Jacques Delors (head of the European Commission in the 1980s and early 1990s) played an autonomous role and provided impetus to the process, independently of national governments' more parochial interests.

Perhaps even more important is the functionalists' different emphasis on the long-term objectives and dynamics of European integration. The process of functional integration, while starting within specific and relatively narrow economic functions (coal and steel, trade), is expected to move to broader and more "political" areas. In the long run, economic integration is expected to lead to political integration – either to a fully-fledged sovereign federation ("the United States of Europe") or to a "post-modern" political community in which traditional sovereign states have become much less powerful or even obsolete.[10]

From a functionalist perspective, building partial and incomplete institutions is not a shortcoming, but a natural feature of a dynamic process, whereas crises and problems associated with previous integration can be solved through further integration. The creation of the euro can then be seen as the ultimate example of functionalist integration. From this perspective, commercial integration and capital mobility could be maintained within Europe only by forming a monetary union, which, in turn, might be sustained in the long run only through further institutional integration: a banking union, a fiscal union, possibly full political unification.

Both the intergovernmentalist view and the functionalist view capture important aspects of European integration. However, neither view provides a complete, realistic and satisfying interpretation of this complex process.[11]

Intergovernmentalists are fundamentally correct when they stress the central role of national governments and national interests in the actual process of European integration. The history of the European Union (and of its predecessor, the European Community) shows that Europe's supranational institutions – such as the European Commission or the European Court of Justice – cannot move far against the fundamental interests of national governments. Supranational institutions and procedures, while playing an important role in the daily functioning of Europe, "could not work for a week in the absence of the will to cooperate of the member states, especially the largest ones – Germany and France above all" (Gilbert 2012, p. 3).

Moreover, by emphasizing and analyzing the interactions between national governments and domestic economic interests, this line of research provides useful insights on the details of the political economy of European integration.[12]

Intergovernmentalist analyses, however, with their sharp focus on domestic economic interests, can miss the central role of long-term political goals and strategies that have historically determined the process of European integration. At its roots, the European project is motivated by broader political considerations. Since its very beginnings, right after the Second World War, the paramount goal of the European project has been to build, through gradual integration, a political and institutional system that would prevent the tragedies of the first half of the twentieth century, when independent and unconstrained nation states had pursued unilateral and costly protectionist policies during the Great Depression and engaged in two enormously destructive wars. Even though economic interests have certainly played an important role in the actual process of European integration, the overall design and strategy would not be comprehensible without considering its long-term political and strategic motivations.

Insofar as it emphasizes the ultimate political goals of the process and its dynamic aspect, functionalism is much closer to capture the political and ideological framework and strategy behind much of the European construction, from the earlier steps by Jean Monnet and his followers in the 1950s to the new impetus provided by Jacques Delors and his collaborators in the 1980s and 1990s. Nevertheless, the functionalist interpretation is not fully adequate to capture the actual process of European integration either. A problem with the theory is that it tends to overestimate the role and powers of supranational agents and institutions – in this dimension, as already mentioned, the intergovernmentalist view is much more realistic.[13]

The overestimation of supranational actors is a symptom of a deeper issue with the functionalist view, stemming in part from its dual nature, as a *positive* description of the ideology and goals of the supporters of European integration, but also as a *normative* theory of how European integration should actually proceed. While the functionalist analysis is a very useful description of the political objectives of European integration, it is also an involuntary mirror of its problems and limits. As a normative strategy of integration, the functionalist approach tends to *underestimate* the obstacles and limitations that would eventually affect a dynamic process of gradual integration towards an "ever-closer" union.

As highlighted in the previous section, in order to understand the political economy of European integration it is crucial to consider the implications of the fundamental trade-off between benefits from integration and heterogeneity costs. A central problem with the functionalist strategy of European integration, based on gradual integration of specific functions, has indeed been the lack of a realistic assessment of the *increasing costs and constraints* imposed by heterogeneity of preferences over the provision of public goods and policies when populations have different traits, cultures and identities.

As we already mentioned in Section 2, successful integration is more likely to take off in areas such as commercial integration, where heterogeneity costs are relatively low and partly offset by the benefits from diversity. As integration proceeds to other areas, heterogeneity costs continue to increase and become politically prohibitive. The functionalist approach does not anticipate that heterogeneity costs and constraints will eventually become binding and may stop the process for good. Followers of this approach are therefore prone to setting up incomplete and inefficient arrangements, relying on the overoptimistic expectation that such inefficiencies can always be addressed at a later stage through additional integration.

Hence, as we will see in more detail in the next section, the functionalist perspective can provide a useful interpretation of the earlier successes of European integration, but its optimistic implications are not a good guidance to the problems and limitations that the process is bound to meet as functional integration moves from lower heterogeneity areas to higher heterogeneity areas.

4. The actual process of European integration: Successes and limits

The history of European institutional integration started with an early success (the formation of a coal and steel community, proposed with the Schuman declaration in 1950 and established with the Treaty of Paris in 1951), and a dramatic failure (the collapse of the defense and political community in 1952, discussed in Section 2). Those two different experiences motivated the subsequent strategy of European integration. The fathers of European institutions came to believe that the creation of an ambitious federal structure with major political functions faced insurmountable political obstacles, at least in the shorter run. Instead, they hoped to proceed towards increasing political integration through a gradualist and dynamic strategy, basically along the functionalist lines described in the previous section. Specific functions could be delegated to supranational institutions in relatively narrow areas, mostly technical and economic (coal and steel, common market, later a common currency), but with the expectation that this would lead to more institutional integration in other areas over time. In other words, Monnet and his followers shared the functionalist view that partial integration would gradually lead to an ever-closer union over time, by creating pressure for more functional integration.

The strategy was partly motivated by the hope that, in the long run, national politicians, voters and interest groups would learn about the benefits of integration, and would therefore demand broader and deeper integration in more areas. Even more important was the expectation that different European populations and policy-makers, by learning to interact and cooperate in economic and institutional matters, would gradually converge in values, norms, and preferences. Over time, this would lead to an "endogenous" reduction in what we have called heterogeneity costs, therefore facilitating further integration in more sensitive and political areas.

These optimistic expectations have been fulfilled only in part. There is no doubt that the European project has greatly expanded from its early beginnings, dramatically growing both in member countries – from the initial six to twenty-eight – and in the extent of functions involved – from a European Coal and Steel Community (ECSC) to a European Economic Community (EEC) to a European Union (EU) including an economic and monetary union (EMU).

It is however much less clear whether European policy-makers and populations have converged in values and preferences over public goods and policies, along the lines expected by the supporters of European integration. In principle, cultural traits and preferences can indeed change and adapt in response to economic and political changes.[14] There is little evidence, however, that the kind of economic and political cooperation associated with the building of European institutions is bringing about a significant convergence in national preferences, characteristics, and behaviors or the formation of a unitary "European identity."[15]

Nevertheless, the builders of European institutions did not rely only on positive mechanisms, such as an increasing demand for integration due to learning and convergence of preferences. Monnet and his followers also expected that partial integration might lead to further integration, paradoxically, because of its own shortcomings and limits – its own "incompleteness." This was clearly explained by one of Monnet's collaborators (Ball 1994, p. 10):

> There was a well-conceived method in this apparent madness. All of us working
> with Jean Monnet well understood how irrational it was to carve a limited

economic sector out of the jurisdiction of national governments and subject that sector to the sovereign control of supranational institutions. Yet, with his usual perspicacity, Monnet recognized that the very irrationality of this scheme might provide the pressure to achieve exactly what he wanted - the triggering of a chain-reaction. The awkwardness and complexity resulting from the singling out of coal and steel would drive member governments to accept the idea of pooling other production as well.

More recently, the functionalist argument that partial steps in integration would create need and pressure for further integration, in a sort of "chain-reaction," was explicitly echoed by Tommaso Padoa-Schioppa (2004, p. 14), a close collaborator of Jacques Delors and a key architect of the euro:

> [T]he road toward the single currency looks like a chain-reaction in which each step resolved a preexisting contradiction and generated a new one that in turn required a further step forward. The steps were the start of the EMS [European monetary system] (1979), the re-launching of the single market (1985), the decision to accelerate the liberalization of capital movements (1986), the launching of the project of monetary union (1988), the agreement of Maastricht (1992), and the final adoption of the euro (1998).

In fact, the EMU was seen by its creators not in purely economic and technical terms, but, in Monnet's tradition, as "a further step—and as a prerequisite for yet other steps—in the political unification of Europe" (Padoa-Schioppa 2004, p. 6).[16] The same idea was stressed by the first President of the European Central Bank, Wim Duisenberg, according to whom EMU was a "stepping stone on the way to a united Europe."[17] And this stepping-stone role could be played in spite of (or even *as a consequence of*) its institutional shortcomings. In the functionalist tradition, the fact that EMU lacked institutions historically associated with a successful monetary union – such as a fully-fledged lender of last resort, a banking union, a fiscal union, and so on – could be rationalized as part of a dynamic path that, in the longer term, would necessarily lead to a political union. For instance, in 1991 German Chancellor Helmut Kohl said: "It is absurd to expect in the long run that you can maintain economic and monetary union without political union."[18] In Monnet's chain-reaction tradition, Kohl's statement was not meant as a damning assessment of the long-term viability of EMU, but as an optimistic prediction that, eventually, political union would "have to" follow economic and monetary union.

The current crisis in the Euro Area certainly confirms the risks and inefficiencies associated with incomplete institutional integration. Up to a point, recent events have also confirmed that such inefficiencies and crises can create the pressure for more institutional integration – for example, in banking supervision. It is indeed possible (but far from guaranteed) that Europeans will come out of their economic, financial and political crisis with stronger and more deeply integrated institutions. Nonetheless, the crisis has also illustrated the very high costs, dangers, and limitations associated with the chain-reaction method of partial integration.[19]

As we have seen, a fundamental problem with the functionalist chain-reaction approach – both as a theory of European integration and as a policy strategy – is that it underestimates the heterogeneity costs and constraints involved when political integration is attempted among populations with different preferences, cultures, and identities.

Successful integration is more likely to take off in areas such as trade, where heterogeneity costs across populations are relatively low, and partly offset by the benefits from diversity. As integration proceeds to other areas, after low-hanging fruits are picked, steeper hetero-geneity costs are encountered. At some point, such costs may become politically prohibitive, and stop the process, or even lead to a collapse of the whole system. The risks are particularly high if the previous steps towards more integration have not been taken with the broad democratic consensus of all populations involved.[20]

Consequently, successes in areas with lower heterogeneity costs (such as commercial integration) do not necessarily imply further successes in integrating more "political" areas with higher heterogeneity costs (such as fiscal policies or defense). Therefore, the functionalist approach to European integration is really based on a misconception: the expec-tation that *economic* integration will lead to *political* integration. While political unification historically has been used to foster economic integration within a unified domestic market, the opposite does not typically hold. On the contrary, economic integration reached through international cooperation is a *substitute* rather than a *complement* of political integration. If countries can manage to lower barriers to trade among themselves without full political integration, they will face lower incentives to form a political union with a unified domestic market, because such union would generate smaller additional gains from trade. In fact, both theoretical considerations and empirical evidence suggest that international economic integration is associated not with political integration but with political *dis*integration (Alesina and Spolaore 1997, 2003; Alesina, Spolaore, and Wacziarg 2000).

In sum, the method of gradual and partial integration can be successful when applied to areas with lower heterogeneity costs and higher economies of scale, but there is no guarantee that it can lead to further integration in areas with much higher heterogeneity costs, or that those costs would endogenously decrease as a consequence of integration.

The formation of a common market, as already mentioned, is an excellent instance of the appropriate and effective use of partial integration. Overall, the reduction of barriers to economic exchanges was in the general interest of European populations, even though specific sectors within each country benefited from protectionism. As it has often been noted (e.g., Eichengreen 2006), institutional integration in different areas allowed "linkages" between issues and credible side-payments. For example, Europe's Common Agricultural Policy (CAP) – originally introduced in 1962 and amounting to a substantial share of the European institutions' budget – can be explained as part of a deal between France and Germany, whereby German taxpayers subsidized French farmers and German exporters gained access to the French market.

The creation of a common European legal framework and common supranational institutions has provided national governments with a credible "commitment technology," going beyond the institutional framework of traditional international organizations. For example, in a landmark case in the early 1960s,[21] the European Court of Justice decided directly in favor of a Dutch importer of German chemical products that had objected to a tariff charged by the Netherlands in violation of article 12 of the Treaty of Rome. In fact, in this and other cases the European Court of Justice went beyond the legal provisions that had been formally agreed with the Treaty of Rome, and, according to some scholars, brought Europe close to a federal legal system (Weiler 1991; Krasner 1999). These novel legal doctrines, however, were established not in conflict with national governments, but exactly in order to enforce norms consistent with national goals, such as trade liberalization. Therefore, the expansion of powers of the European Court of Justice illustrates the success of the strategy of supranational institutional integration insofar as it is directed towards areas with relatively low heterogeneity cost and high economies of scale and externalities. In contrast, supranational integration and centralization have been met with increasingly binding constraints when attempting to move to more sensitive and political areas. For instance, in recent years Germany's Constitutional Court has elaborated the legal theory of *conditional* acceptance of the supremacy of European norms, which can be accepted only insofar as they are consistent with "fundamental German rights." In an important ruling on the Lisbon Treaty in 2009,[22] the German Constitutional Court explicitly called the national states "the masters of the treaties," and "therefore must see to it that there are no uncontrolled, independent centralization dynamics" within the EU.[23]

In spite of all its limitations, many supporters of the European project believe that economic integration has benefited Europeans not only directly – through gains from trade – but also indirectly, by reducing the risk of a European conflict. The hypothesis that international trade reduces the risk of war has a long pedigree, going back at least to Montesquieu and Kant, and is part of the broader theory of "liberal peace" brought in by democracy, trade, and international organizations (e.g., Oneal and Russett 1999). Recent empirical studies (Martin, Mayer and Thoenig 2008 and 2010) cast doubt on a positive relation between multilateral openness (globalization) and peace. On the contrary, the ability to trade with third parties reduces the costs of going to war between pairs of countries. *Bilateral* trade, however, by increasing the opportunity cost of war between two countries, lowers the likelihood of conflict between them, even when controlling for the degree of historical, linguistic and religious similarity between their populations (Spolaore and Wacziarg 2012). These studies suggest that regional trade agreements between "old enemies" – such as the formation of a European common market – have probably decreased the risk of conflict among European countries after the Second World War. An open question is whether European integration has played a major or only a minor role in securing peace in Europe, when compared to other factors, such as the role of the United States and NATO.

5. Conclusions

This chapter has discussed the political economy of European integration in light of the implications of the fundamental trade-off between benefits from integration and political costs associated with heterogeneous preferences over public goods and policies.

High heterogeneity costs have so far prevented Europeans from forming a full political union. Attempts to integrate sensitive political functions – such as defense and foreign policy – have not been successful. Instead, Europeans have adopted a gradual strategy of pooling and delegating functions and policies to supranational institutions in a relatively limited set of areas, mostly economic, while maintaining other prerogatives at the national or sub-national level. In spite of supranational rhetoric, ultimate sovereign control and the monopoly of the legitimate use of coercion have firmly remained in the hands of national governments.

This strategy has provided significant benefits to Europeans when appropriately implemented in areas with relatively low heterogeneity costs and high economies of scale and scope. However, serious problems and crises have their roots in the expectation that incomplete and partial integration could always be overcome with further integration, in a "chain-reaction" towards an "ever-closer union." The euro, with its institutional incompleteness and shortcomings, is a child of this strategy.

A more realistic political economy analysis naturally suggests a different, more effective strategy, whereby if any further steps are taken towards European integration, they should be taken only when they are economically beneficial and politically stable on their own merits, and openly and democratically supported by the populations involved.

Notes

1 The chapter heavily builds on Spolaore (2013). General discussions of the economic approach to political borders and integration are provided in Alesina and Spolaore (2003) and Spolaore (2006, 2014). For overviews of the large literature on European institutional integration by political scientists and political economists, see for example Gilpin (2001, chapter 13), Eichengreen and Frieden (2001), Eichengreen (2006 and 2012), and Sadeh and Verdun (2009). Recent historical studies of the process of European integration include Gilbert (2012), Ludlow (2006), James (2012), and Mourlon-Druol (2012).
2 Alesina and Spolaore (1997, 2003) and Spolaore (2006, 2014).
3 In particular, an important question is the extent to which ethnic and cultural divisions are endogenous, and respond to political and institutional change - an issue on which we will return in section 4.
4 These issues are at the center of the large literature on fiscal federalism – e.g., Oates, 1999; for a discussion from a political economy perspective see Alesina and Spolaore, 2003, chapters 2, 9 and 12.
5 www.eurotreaties.com/maastrichtec.pdf.
6 For a classic analysis of federalism from this perspective, see Riker (1964). Conflict and political borders are studied in Alesina and Spolaore (2005, 2006) and Spolaore (2012). For a discussion of the attempts to integrate defense and security in Europe see Spolaore (2013, pp. 128–131).
7 We only focus on these two views here because, historically, they have been the most influential in the study of European integration by political economists. Of course there exist many other political theories and interpretations of European integration – for example, social constructivism, which investigates how identities such as "European citizenship" have been "socially constructed" through the use of norms and language (see for example Rosamond, 2003) – a theme connected to the endogenous formation of a European identity, on which we briefly touch below (see also the discussion in Spolaore 2013).
8 The intergovernmentalist view of European integration is sometime qualified as "liberal" intergovernmentalism to distinguish it from "realist" approaches that also emphasize the central role of nation states, but stress power and military interests rather than domestic economic goals achieved through international cooperation (e.g., Garrett 1993 and Gilpin 2001).
9 The leading functionalist theorist of European integration was Haas (1958, 1964). The view of Haas and his followers is sometime labeled as "neo-functionalist," to distinguish it from Mitrany's pre-existing theory of international integration (Mitrany 1975). A critical reconsideration of functionalism was provided by Haas (1975). For more recent analyses from a functionalist perspective see for instance Pierson (1996), Sandholtz and Stone Sweet (1998), and Stone Sweet (2000).
10 For an early critical discussion from a political perspective see Hoffman (1966).
11 Recent historical studies, such as Gilbert (2012), Ludlow (2006), James (2012), and Mourlon-Druol (2012), have also moved away from a stark dichotomy between functionalist and intergovernmentalist perspectives, while embracing more complex and nuanced interpretations of the actual process of European integration.
12 For example, see Frieden (1998, p. 33) for prescient insights on the political economy of European integration and the euro.
13 For a more extensive discussion of this point, see Spolaore (2013, pp. 136–138).
14 For example, see Fearon (2006) for a discussion of the political literature on how ethnic and linguistic divisions and their relevance can be affected by political and institutional changes. Bisin and Verdier (2010), Spolaore and Wacziarg (2013) and Spolaore (2014) provide discussions of the growing economic literature on culture and economic outcomes.
15 Analyses of the political economy of "nation-building" are provided in Alesina and Spolaore (2003, pp. 76–78) and Alesina and Reich (2013).
16 For detailed historical analyses of the negotiations and decisions leading to EMU see Dyson and Featherstone (1999) and James (2012).
17 Quoted in Van Overtveldt (2011, p. 63).

18 Quoted in Marsh (2011, p. 301).
19 For a more detailed discussion of these issues see Spolaore (2013, pp. 138–139). An interesting diagnosis along partially similar lines is provided by Mody (2013). For an empirical analysis see Guiso, Sapienza and Zingales (2014), who find that the 1992 Maastricht Treaty, the 2004 enlargement and the 2010 Eurozone crisis seem to have reduced pro-Europe sentiment among European citizens, even though most Europeans still support the common currency. These authors conclude that "Europe seems trapped in catch-22: there is no desire to go backward, no interest in going forward, but it is economically unsustainable to stay still."
20 For a discussion of the so-called democratic deficit in European institutions see Alesina and Spolaore (2003, chapter 12).
21 *Van Gend en Loos* v *Nederlandse Administratie der Belastingen* (26/62)
22 *BVerfG, 2 BvE 2/08* of June 6, 2009
23 Quoted in *Der Spiegel*, 2009.

References

Alesina, A., Devleeschauwer, A., Easterly, W., Kurlat, S. and Wacziarg, R. (2003), Fractionalization, *Journal of Economic Growth*, 8(2), 155–94.
Alesina, A. and La Ferrara, E. (2005), Ethnic Diversity and Economic Performance, *Journal of Economic Literature*, 43(3), 762–800.
Alesina, A. and Reich, B. (2013), Nation Building, *NBER Working Paper* 18839.
Alesina, A. and Spolaore, E. (1997), On the Number and Size of Nations, *Quarterly Journal of Economics*, 112(4), 1027–56.
Alesina, A. and Spolaore, E. (2003), *The Size of Nations*, Cambridge, MA: MIT Press.
Alesina, A. and Spolaore, E. (2005), War, Peace, and the Size of Countries, *Journal of Public Economics*, 89(7), 1333–54.
Alesina, A. and Spolaore, E. (2006), Conflict, Defense Spending, and the Number of Nations, *European Economic Review*, 50(1), 91–120.
Alesina, A. and Spolaore, E. and Wacziarg, R. (2000), Economic Integration and Political Disintegration, *American Economic Review*, 90(5), 1276–96.
Arbatli, E., Ashraf, Q. and Galor, O. (2013), The Nature of Civil Conflict, *Brown University Working Papers* 2013–15.
Ball, G. W. (1994), Foreword, in Duchêne, F., *Jean Monnet. The First Statesman of Interdependence*, New York: Norton.
Bergsten, C. F. (2012), Why the Euro Will Survive: Completing the Continent's Half-Built House, *Foreign Affairs*, September/October.
Bisin, A. and Verdier, T. (2010), The Economics of Cultural Transmission and Socialization, in Benhabib, J., Bisin, A., and Jackson, M. (eds), *Handbook of Social Economics*, Amsterdam: Elsevier.
Der Spiegel (2009), Germany's Lisbon Treaty Ruling: Brussels Put Firmly in the Back Seat, July 6, available at www.spiegel.de/international/germany/germany-s-lisbon-treaty-ruling-brussels-put-firmly-in-the-back-seat-a-634506.html.
Desmet, K., Ortuño-Ortín, I. and Wacziarg, R. (2012), The Political Economy of Linguistic Cleavages, *Journal of Development Economics*, 97(2), 322–38.
Desmet, K., Ortuño-Ortín, I. and Weber, S. (2009), Linguistic Diversity and Redistribution, *Journal of the European Economic Association*, 7(6), 1291–318.
Dyson, K. and Featherstone, K. (1999), *The Road to Maastricht. Negotiating Economic and Monetary Union*, Oxford: Oxford University Press.
Eichengreen, B. (2006), European Integration, in Weingast, B. R. and Wittman, D. A. (eds), *Oxford Handbook of Political Economy*, Oxford: Oxford University Press.
Eichengreen, B. (2012), European Monetary Integration with Benefit of Hindsight, *Journal of Common Market Studies*, 50(S1), 123–36.
Eichengreen, B. and Frieden, J. A. (2001), The Political Economy of European Monetary Unification: An Analytical Introduction, in Eichengreen, B. and Frieden, J. (eds), *The Political Economy of European Monetary Unification*, Boulder: Westview Press.
Esteban, J., Mayoral, L. and Ray, D. (2012), Ethnicity and Conflict: An Empirical Study, *American Economic Review*, 102(4), 1310–42.

Fearon, J. (2006), Ethnic Mobilization and Ethnic Violence, in Weingast, B. R. and Wittman, D. A. (eds), *Oxford Handbook of Political Economy*, Oxford: Oxford University Press.

Frieden, J. A. (1998), The Euro: Who Wins? Who Loses? *Foreign Policy*, 112, 24–40.

Frieden, J. A. (2002), Real Sources of European Currency Policy: Sectoral Interests and European Monetary Integration, *International Organization*, 56(4), 831–60.

Garrett, G. (1993), The Politics of Maastricht, *Economics and Politics*, 5(2), 105–23.

Gilpin, R. (2001), *Global Political Economy: Understanding the International Economic Order*, Princeton: Princeton University Press.

Gilbert, M. (2012), *European Integration. A Concise History*, Lanham: Rowman Littlefield.

Guiso, L., Sapienza, P. and Zingales, L. (2014), Monnet's Error?, EIEF, Northwestern and Chicago Booth School.

James, H. (2012), *Making the European Monetary Union*, Cambridge (MA): Harvard University Press.

Haas, E. B. (1958), *The Uniting of Europe: Political, Social, and Economic Forces, 1950–1957*, London: Stevens.

Haas, E. B. (1964), *Beyond the Nation State*, Stanford: Stanford University Press.

Haas, E. B. (1975), *The Obsolence of Regional Integration Theory*, Institute of International Studies, University of California.

Krasner, S. D. (1999), *Sovereignty. Organized Hypocrisy*, Princeton: Princeton University Press.

Ludlow, N. P. (2006), *The European Community and the Crises of the 1960s: Negotiating the Gaulist Challenge*, London: Routledge.

Martin, P., Mayer, T. and Thoenig, M. (2008), Make Trade Not War?, *Review of Economic Studies*, 75(3), 865–900.

Martin, P., Mayer, T. and Thoenig, M. (2010), The Geography of Conflicts and Free Trade Agreements, *CEPR Discussion Papers* 7740.

Mitrany, D. (1970), *The Functional Theory of Politics*, New York: St. Martin's Press.

Mody, A. (2013), A Schuman Compact for the Euro Area, Bruegel Essay and Lecture Series.

Montalvo, J. G. and Reynal-Querol, M. (2005), Ethnic Polarization, Potential Conflict and Civil Wars, *American Economic Review*, 95(3), 796–816.

Moravcsik, A. (1993), Preferences and Power in the European Community: A Liberal Intergovernmentalist Approach, *Journal of Common Market Studies*, 31(4), 473–524.

Moravcsik, A. (1998), *The Choice for Europe. Social Purpose and State Power from Messina to Maastricht*, Ithaca: Cornell University Press.

Moravcsik, A. (2012), Europe After the Crisis, *Foreign Affairs*, May/June.

Marsh, D. (2011), *The Euro. The Battle for the New Global Currency*, New Haven: Yale University Press.

Mourlon-Druol, E. (2012), *A Europe Made of Money. The Emergence of the European Monetary System*, Ithaca: Cornell University Press.

Oates, W. E. (1999), An Essay on Fiscal Federalism, *Journal of Economic Literature* 37, 1120–49.

Oneal, J. R. and B. M. Russett (1999), The Kantian Peace: The Pacific Benefits of Democracy, Interdependence, and International Organizations, *World Politics* 52(1), 1–37.

Padoa-Schioppa, T. (2004), *The Euro and Its Central Bank. Getting United After the Union*, Cambridge (MA): MIT Press.

Pierson, P. (1996), The Path to European Integration: a Historical Institutionalist Analysis, *Comparative Political Studies*, 29, 123–63.

Riker, W. (1964), *Federalism*, New York: Little Brown.

Rosamond, B. (2003), New Theories of European Integration, in Cini, M. (ed.), *European Union Politics*, Oxford: Oxford University Press.

Sadeh, T. and Verdun, A. (2009), Explaining Europe's Monetary Union: A Survey of the Literature, *International Studies Review*, 11, 277–301.

Sandholtz, W. and Stone Sweet, A. (eds) (1998), *European Integration and Supranational Governance*, Oxford: Oxford University Press.

Spolaore, E. (2006), National Borders and the Size of Nations, in Weingast, B. R. and Wittman, D. A. (eds), *Oxford Handbook of Political Economy*, Oxford: Oxford University Press.

Spolaore, E. (2012), National Borders, Conflict and Peace, in Garfinkel, M. R. and Skaperdas, S. (eds), *Oxford Handbook of the Economics of Peace and Conflict*, Oxford: Oxford University Press.

Spolaore, E. (2013), What is European Integration Really About? A Political Guide for Economists, *Journal of Economic Perspectives*, 27(3), 125–44.

Spolaore, E. (ed.) (2014), *Culture and Economic Growth*, Cheltenham: Edward Elgar.

Spolaore, E. and Wacziarg, R. (2012), War and Relatedness, Tufts and UCLA Anderson School.

Spolaore, E. and Wacziarg, R. (2013), How Deep Are the Roots of Economic Development?, *Journal of Economic Literature*, 51(2), 1–45.

Stone Sweet, A. (2000), *Governing with Judges: Constitutional Politics in Europe*, Oxford: Oxford University Press.

Van Overtveldt, J. (2011), *The End of the Euro*, Chicago: Agate Publishing.

Weiler, J. H. H. (1991), The Transformation of Europe, *Yale Law Journal*, 100, 2403–83.

27

EFFICIENCY, PROPORTIONALITY AND MEMBER STATES' POWER IN THE EU COUNCIL OF MINISTERS[1]

Nikolaos Antonakakis, Harald Badinger and Wolf Heinrich Reuter

1. Introduction

The power of EU member states in the Council is a recurring topic in debates of EU treaty reforms and has been extensively studied.[2] And while the relevance of power indices is still subject to debate in the literature,[3] anecdotal evidence suggest that they have played a non-negligible role in the political bargaining process preceding the treaties of Nice and Lisbon. Moreover, Kauppi and Widgren (2007) find that voting power explains almost 90 percent of the variance in budget shares for the EU member states between 1976 and 2001.

This chapter provides a comprehensive reassessment of the consequences of treaty changes and (EC) EU enlargements on EU member states' power, the EU's capability to act (efficiency), and the proportionality of the voting mechanism, focusing on the EU Council of Ministers.

Unlike previous studies, which mainly focus on a treaty-to-treaty comparison (see, for instance Le Breton et al., 2012; Baldwin et al., 2002; Hosli, 1995), we start from the original six EC member states (treaties of Rome) and consider each regime shift (treaty change or enlargement) until the Treaty of Lisbon that came into force in 2009, account for changes in the voting procedures as of 2014 and consider the effects of possible EU enlargements by Turkey as well as further candidate countries (Iceland, Macedonia, Montenegro). Finally, we also examine the implications of more recently introduced enforcement mechanisms under the revised Stability and Growth Pact such as reversed qualified majority voting.

2. Member states' power, efficiency, and proportionality

In the following, we define the measures of power, efficiency, and proportionality that will be calculated for the EU Council of Ministers over the period 1958–2014 (2017). We focus on the Banzhaf (1965) and Shapley-Shubik (1954) indices, which are still the most widely used measures of power.[4]

2.1 Power indices: A probabilistic statement

Throughout we assume a "yes/no" voting system, where an assembly N of n different players may vote either "yes" or "no" under certain rules that determine under which conditions a proposal is adopted. In a weighted voting system each player is assigned a specific number of votes. A group of players (actors) voting with "yes" is called coalition. A particular voting outcome is referred to as S. The number of yes-votes is given by $\|S\|$.

Straffin (1977) focuses on the distributional assumptions regarding actors' voting behavior. More recently, Paterson (2005) gives an alternative probabilistic interpretation of power indices, focusing on the probability distribution of voting polls, i.e., the number of actors in favor of the proposal (0 to n). Following Paterson (2005), we define the power of an actor as *expected* decisiveness (δ_i) of his or her vote for a given distribution of the voting polls:

$$\delta_i = \sum_{s=0}^{n} d_i(s)\, p(s). \tag{1}$$

Decisiveness $d_i(s)$ of player i in a particular poll $(0 \leq s \leq n)$ is the share of combinations (coalitions), that are $\pm$ swing votes for player i. In formal terms, consider the outcome sets S_s with exactly s players in favor of the proposal. Moreover, define $S_i^* = S\{i\}$ if $i \in S$ and $S_i^* = S \cup \{i\}$ if $i \notin S$. Then

$$d_i(s) = \frac{1}{\binom{n}{s}} \sum_{S \subseteq S_s} |v(S) - v(S_i^*)|. \tag{2}$$

Note that decisiveness (d_i) depends only on the parameters of the voting game, not on any probabilistic aspects, and is thus identical under the Banzhaf (1965) and Shapley-Shubik (1954) approach. It holds that the decisiveness d_i is the sum of the positive decisiveness (d_i^+) and negative decisiveness (d_i^-):

$$d_i = d_i^+ + d_i^-, \tag{3}$$

where $d_i^+ = \frac{1}{\binom{n}{s}} \sum_{S \subseteq S_s} [v(S) - v(S - \{i\})]$ and $d_i^- = \frac{1}{\binom{n}{s}} \sum_{S \subseteq S_s} [v(S + \{i\}) - v(S)]$.

The voting poll distribution is described by the density function $p(s)$, $s = 0, \ldots, n$, which assigns a probability of there being s votes in favor (and $n - s$ against it). The Banzhaf index *(BFI)* assumes that the voting polls have a binomial distribution, with probability ½, i.e.,

$$p_{BFI^d}(s) = \frac{\binom{n}{s}}{\sum_{s=0}^{n} \binom{n}{s}} = \binom{n}{s}\frac{1}{2^n}, s = 0, \ldots, n. \tag{4}$$

Hence, the Banzhaf approach assigns a probability close to zero to voting polls close to zero "yes"-votes or unanimity.

The Shapley-Shubik index *(SSI)* assumes that all voting polls are equally likely and have a uniform distribution over the interval 0 to n, , i.e.,

$$p_{SSI}(s) = \frac{1}{(n+1)}, s = 0, \ldots, n. \tag{5}$$

Hence, in terms of voting polls, the two indices can be defined as (Paterson, 2005):

$$\delta_{BFI^a, i} = \sum_{s=0}^{n} d_i(s) p_{BFI^a}(s), \text{ and} \tag{6}$$

$$\delta_{SSI, i} = \sum_{s=0}^{n} d_i(s) p_{SSI}(s). \tag{7}$$

The two indices can be additively decomposed into a positive swing balance (δ_i^+) and a negative swing balance (δ_i^-), both under the Banzhaf and Shapley-Shubik assumptions: $\delta_i = \delta_i^+ + \delta_i^-$, with $\delta_i^+ = \sum_{s=0}^{n} d_i^+(s) p(s)$ and $\delta_i^- = \sum_{s=0}^{n} d_i^-(s) p(s)$.

The approach by Paterson (2005) is closely related to the one by Straffin (1977), which focuses on the distribution of voting behavior over all voting constellations, given by $p'(S) = p'(s)$, where $s = \|S\|$. Given the assumptions of the SSI and the BFI, we have

$$p'_{SSI}(S) = \frac{1}{(n+1)} \frac{1}{\binom{n}{s}} = \frac{(n-s)! \, s!}{(n+1) \, n!} = \frac{(n-s)! \, s!}{(n+1)!}, \tag{8}$$

$$p'_{BFI^a}(S) = \frac{1}{2^n} \tag{9}$$

and the power indices can also be written equivalently as

$$\delta_{SSI, i} = \sum_{S \subseteq N} |\, v(S) - v(S_i^*)\,| \, p'_s(S), \tag{10}$$

$$\delta_{BFI^a, i} = \sum_{S \subseteq N} |\, v(S) - v(S_i^*)\,| \, p'_{BFI^a}(S). \tag{11}$$

Intuitively, the two (normalized) indices measure a country's power as a fraction of 1 (100 percent), accounting for the "rules of the game," though under different probabilistic assumptions regarding voting behavior (voting polls).

A voting body's capability to act (efficiency, E), also referred to as "passage probability" can generally be defined as the probability of a coalition being a winning coalition:

$$E = \sum_{S \subseteq N} v(S) p'(S). \tag{12}$$

Using the distributional assumptions of the Banzhaf approach, the Coleman (1971) measure is obtained.

$$E_{BFI} = \sum_{S \subseteq N} v(S) p'_{BFI^a}(S) = \sum_{S \subseteq N} \frac{v(S)}{2^n}. \tag{13}$$

Paterson (2005) also suggests a Shapley–Shubik analog of efficiency, which is given by

$$E_{SSI} = \sum_{S \subseteq N} v(S) p'_{SSI}(S) = \sum_{S \subseteq N} v(S) \frac{(n-s)! \, s!}{(n+1)!}. \tag{14}$$

2.2 The overall proportionality of a voting system

Apart from the individual power of single actors, a question of interest in this context relates to the proportionality of a voting system. A natural approach is to compare countries' normalized power indices with their population shares. A summary measure of the differences between countries' voting power and their population share, referred to as power gradient (*PG*), has been suggested by Paterson (1998) and Paterson and Silárszky (1999).

Arranging the players in ascending order of countries' population shares (p_i), the power gradient, based on the normalized power index (*PI*), is defined as

$$PG_{PI} = \frac{\sum_{i=1}^{n} p_i (1 - 2i + (I_i + I_{i-1})n)}{-n + \sum_{i=1}^{n} p_i (2i - 1)} \tag{15}$$

where p_i is the population share of country i and I_i is the cumulative sum of the respective power index up to country i. It is equal to zero, when all players have equal power, and it is equal to 1 if the countries' (normalized) power indices are equal to their population shares.

3. Power, efficiency, and proportionality: Results for the EU council of ministers

Summing up the discussion in Section 2, the Banzhaf index (*BFI*) and Shapley-Shubik index (*SSI*) will be considered as measures of country's power. Relating to the EU Council of Ministers as a whole, we calculate the efficiency in terms of Coleman's capability to act (E_{BFI}) and the Shapley-Shubik analog (E_{SSI}) and the proportionality of the voting system, i.e., the power gradient implied by each (country-specific) power index.

3.1 Voting rules in the EU council of ministers

The indices will be calculated for all regimes (countries' voting weights and majority rules) in place since the establishment of the European Communities by the treaties of Rome in 1957 (in force 1958) until the latest revision through the Treaty of Lisbon in 2009. Table 27.1 gives an overview of the regimes in place.

Until the reform through the Treaty of Lisbon, a qualified majority weighted voting regime has been in place in the EU Council of Ministers. Thereby, each member state is assigned a certain number of votes and a certain threshold (around 70 percent) is required for the passage of a proposal (see the third column of Table 27.1).

The weighting of votes will be abolished as of March 2017 due to the Treaty of Lisbon and replaced by a double majority system. Then each vote has the same weight ("one country, one vote") and a qualified majority will require 55 percent of the EU member states (comprising at least 15 member states) of the Council representing 65 percent of the population of the EU. A blocking minority requires i) either 13 members or ii) the votes of at least four Council members (Art. 16 para 4 TEU) altogether representing more than 35 percent of the population of the EU. According to Article 3 para 2 of the Protocol on Transitional Provisions of the Treaty of Lisbon (Protocol No 36) a transitional rule applies between November 1 2014 and March 31 2017. Within this period of time upon request by one member state the former procedure shall be applied (255 out of 345 weighted votes).

Another issue that has to be taken into account in the calculation is the so-called demographic clause that took effect as of November 1 2004 and shall be perpetuated until

Table 27.1 Voting rules in the EU Council of Ministers, 1958–2017 (and beyond)

Regime	Time period	Rules	Further legal provisions
EC6	1958–1972	QMV, 12 of 17 (70.6%)	Luxemburg compromise, 1966–1987
EC9	1973–1980	QMV, 41 of 58 (70.7%)	Luxemburg compromise, 1966–1987
EC10	1981–1985	QMV, 45 of 63 (71.4%)	Luxemburg compromise, 1966–1987
EC12	1986–1994	QMV, 54 of 76 (71.1%)	Luxemburg compromise, 1966–1987
EU15	1995–04/2004	QMV, 62 of 87 (71.3%)	Ioannina compromise I, 1995–4/2004
EU25	05/2004–10/2004	QMV, 88 of 124 (71.0%)	–
EU25	11/2004–2006	QMV, 232 of 321 (72.3%)	Demographic clause, 11/2004–4/2017
EU27/28	2007–10/2014	QMV, 255 of 345 (73.9%)	Demographic clause 11/2004–4/2017
EU28	11/2014–3/2017	QMV/DMV (transition)	Ioannina compromise II, 11/2014–3/2017
EU28	4/2017–	DMV	Ioannina compromise III, 4/2017–

Notes: *QMV* . . . (weighted) qualified majority voting, *DMV* . . . double majority voting (55% of member states, 65% of population).

April 1 2017. According to Article 12 para 1(b) of the Treaty of Athens (later on inserted into Article 205 TEC) the following rule applies: If a decision was adopted by a qualified majority it shall be verified upon request of one member of the Council whether the qualified majority is representing at least 62 percent of the total population of the EU. If this threshold turns out not to have been met, the decision shall not be adopted.

As can be seen from the overview in Table 27.1, regime shifts took place either through enlargements of the EC (EU) or treaty revisions. Detailed information on the country-specific number of votes in each of the regimes is given in the Appendix.

The results for the regime under the Lisbon Treaty will be given for the EU27 as well as for the EU28, including Croatia which joined the EU in 2013 (before the Lisbon Treaty will come into force). In addition we will consider the consequences of possible further EU enlargements by the four remaining candidate countries (Iceland, Macedonia, Montenegro, and Turkey), based on the double majority voting procedure and the population projections for 2020.

In the calculation of the power indices, it will be assumed throughout that all EU member states participate in the voting and vote either in favor or against a proposal, i.e., there are no abstentions. We regard this as the most relevant and representative case, since it is reasonable to assume that countries will make full use of their voting power, in particular when important issues are at stake.

Obviously, the complex and multifaceted procedure of EU legislation comprises more than qualified majority voting in the Council of Ministers, which limits the generality of our results. First, the EU Council of Ministers usually adopts legislative proposals by the EU Commission (or the High Representative of the Union for Foreign Affairs and Security Policy) in co-decision with the European parliament. With the Treaty of Lisbon, co-decision with the Parliament has become the "ordinary legislative procedure" and thus the norm for most policy areas. It is based on the principle of parity and means that neither institution (European Parliament or Council) may adopt legislation without the other's assent. Hence, by focusing on voting power in the Council, the (equally strong) role of the European Parliament is not considered.

Second, while Article 16 of the Treaty on European Union stipulates that the Council shall act by a qualified majority except where the Treaties provide otherwise and qualified majority voting has been extended steadily since the Single European Act in 1987, there are still matters requiring an unanimous vote, in particular in the intergovernmental "second pillar" (foreign and security policy) and "third pillar" (police and judicial cooperation) of the Treaty on European Union. Moreover, in (exceptional) cases, where the Council does not act on a proposal by the Commission or the High Representative, different (higher) thresholds than those stated in Table 27.1 apply under the qualified majority requirement (Article 238 TFEU). On the other hand, there are also important policy areas where the qualified majority requirements are less stringent than the ones in Table 27.1, namely under the excessive deficit procedure, where a reversed qualified majority voting procedure has been recently introduced for the adoption of enforcement measures. This case will be considered in Section 3.

Finally, due to the so-called "culture of consensus" in the Council, proposals typically only reach the voting stage if most of the initial conflicts between countries have already been resolved (Heisenberg, 2005). However, while formal voting power cannot explain the inter-action between all relevant "players" and describe the political negotiations preceding the actual voting, it is certainly an influential determinant of EU member states' bargaining power at all stages of preparing and taking decisions (through so-called "shadow voting").

Hence, notwithstanding the complexity of the process of EU legislation, the "standard qualified majority voting procedure" summarized in Table 27.1 can be reasonably regarded as maybe its single most important element, and as the predominant and most representative case for the part of EU legislation taking place in the EU Council of Ministers.

3.2 Basic results

In the following we report the basic results from the calculation of the power measures defined in Section 2 from Rome to Lisbon. We then turn to alternative voting rules introduced during the sovereign debt crisis such as the revised Stability and Growth Pact.

3.2.1. Country-specific results

Table 27.2 shows the (normalized) Banzhaf indices for EU member states under various regimes since the treaties of Rome. Given the high similarity of the Shapley-Shubik index for individual member states, the corresponding results are omitted for the sake of brevity.

For the transitional regime during the period 11/2014–3/2017, during which both regimes will be in place (QMV and DMV), results for the EU27 are given for the DMV regime only, since the power indices under qualified majority voting are the same as those for the EU27 in the period 2007–10/2014. Results for the period as of 2014 are also reported for the EU28 including Croatia (under DMV using the population project-ions for 2015). Finally, we also consider the effects of the potential EU enlargements by the candidate countries (Iceland, Macedonia, Montenegro and Turkey) using population pro-jections for 2020.

Obviously, with each EC (EU) accession the power of the incumbent member states was reduced as evident from the downward trend in member states' power indices. Clearly, the largest power is held by the large EU member states. However, the power indices of Germany (7.78 percent, EU27 QMV), France (7.78 percent), Italy (7.78 percent), the UK (7.78 percent) and Spain (7.42 percent), are well below their population shares (16.62 percent, 12.85 percent, 11.94 percent, 12.27 percent and 8.98 percent, respectively) as shown in

Table 27.2 Evolution of EU Member States' power from 1958–2017, normalized Banzhaf Index (in %)

	EC6	EC9	EC10	EC12	EU15	EU25	EU25	EU27, QMV	EU27, DMV	EU28, DMV	EU32, DMV
	1958–72	1973–80	1981–85	1986–94	1995–4/2004	5/2004–10/04	11/2004–06	2007–10/14	11/2014–3/17	11/2014–	(2020)
Belgium	14.29	9.15	8.20	6.66	5.87	4.14	3.91	3.68	2.94	2.73	2.38
France	23.81	16.72	15.77	12.87	11.16	7.60	8.57	7.78	8.40	9.47	7.91
Germany	23.81	16.72	15.77	12.87	11.16	7.60	8.57	7.78	10.24	11.61	9.20
Italy	23.81	16.72	15.77	12.87	11.16	7.60	8.57	7.78	7.91	8.87	7.40
Luxembourg	0.00	1.58	4.10	1.80	2.26	1.69	1.32	1.25	1.90	1.40	1.35
Netherlands	14.29	9.15	8.20	6.66	5.87	4.14	4.23	3.97	3.49	3.44	2.90
Denmark		6.62	4.10	4.59	3.59	2.52	2.31	2.18	2.40	2.03	1.83
Ireland		6.62	4.10	4.59	3.59	2.52	2.31	2.18	2.30	1.90	1.75
Untd. Kingdom		16.72	15.77	12.87	11.16	7.60	8.57	7.78	8.16	9.18	7.75
Greece			8.20	6.66	5.87	4.14	3.91	3.68	2.96	2.75	2.38
Portugal				6.66	5.87	4.14	3.91	3.68	2.89	2.66	2.30
Spain				10.89	9.24	6.36	8.13	7.42	6.24	6.81	6.02
Austria					4.79	3.38	3.27	3.09	2.67	2.38	2.10
Finland					3.59	2.52	2.31	2.18	2.38	2.01	1.82
Sweden					4.79	3.38	3.27	3.09	2.79	2.54	2.24
Cyprus						1.69	1.32	1.25	1.93	1.44	1.37
Cz. Republic						4.14	3.91	3.68	2.89	2.66	2.31
Estonia						2.52	1.32	1.25	1.98	1.50	1.42
Hungary						4.14	3.91	3.68	2.82	2.57	2.23
Latvia						2.52	1.32	1.25	2.06	1.60	1.49
Lithuania						2.52	2.31	2.18	2.17	1.74	1.59
Malta						1.69	0.99	0.94	1.89	1.38	1.33

(Continued)

Table 27.2 (Continued)

	EC6	EC9	EC10	EC12	EU15	EU25	EU25	EU27, QMV	EU27, DMV	EU28, DMV	EU32, DMV
	1958–72	1973–80	1981–85	1986–94	1995–4/2004	5/2004–10/04	11/2004–06	2007–10/14	11/2014–3/17	11/2014–	(2020)
Poland						6.36	8.13	7.42	5.69	5.61	5.26
Slovakia						2.52	2.31	2.18	2.38	2.02	1.82
Slovenia						2.52	1.32	1.25	2.05	1.59	1.49
Bulgaria								3.09	2.56	2.25	1.96
Romania								4.26	3.91	3.99	3.25
Croatia										1.87	1.70
Iceland											1.32
Turkey											9.27
Macedonia											1.48
Montenegro											1.35

Notes: for an overview of the regimes, see Table 27.1 EU28 and EU32 (DMV) calculated with population projections for 2015 and 2020 respectively.

Table 27.3. The largest disproportionality (relative to the population share) is shown for Germany. These qualitative results also hold up for the *SSI*.

As a mirror image, the smaller member states show more than proportional power indices: e.g., the power indices of Malta (0.94 percent, EU27 QMV), Cyprus (1.25 percent) and Estonia (1.25 percent) are much larger than their respective population shares (0.08 percent, 0.16 percent and 0.27 percent, respectively). But also medium sized countries such as Belgium, Netherlands, Denmark, Ireland, Greece, Portugal, Austria, Finland, and Sweden have power indices which are well above their population shares.

Regarding the evolution of the relative positions of the incumbent member states, we can see that the positions of the large players (Germany, France, Italy, and the UK) remained virtually unchanged over the period 1973–10/2004. This also evident from the fact that Germany, France, Italy, and the UK held the same number of votes throughout that period.

With the introduction of the double majority voting system through the Treaty of Lisbon, we observe a reduction (though no elimination) of the disproportionality in the weighted QMV system in place up to 2014 (2017). For instance, the power index of Germany increases from 7.78 percent to 11.61 percent, though it is still under its population share. On average, large EU countries gain relatively more in terms of power from the DMV system than small countries: This move towards proportionality will also be reflected in the results for the power gradients below.

While the EU-accession of Croatia had quantitatively only minor consequences, Turkey would – in case of its EU-accession – appear as one of the most powerful players in the Council with a power index of 9.27 percent, which is almost identical to that of Germany.

3.2.2 Results for the EU council of ministers as a whole

Having considered the power of EU member states, we now turn to the results for the EU Council of Ministers as a whole. Table 27.3 gives an overview of the evolution of the EU's

Table 27.3 The EU Council of Ministers: efficiency and proportionality, 1958–2017

Regime	Period	Efficiency (%)		Power gradients (%)	
		E_{BFI}	E_{SSI}	PG_{BFI}	PG_{SSI}
EC6	1958–72	21.88	35.00	44.81	41.99
EC9	1973–80	14.65	32.30	44.69	53.44
EC10	1981–85	13.67	32.14	46.32	58.74
EC12	1986–94	9.81	31.03	43.87	49.02
EU15	1995–4/2004	7.78	31.03	42.32	46.53
EU25	5/2004–10/04	3.49	30.49	37.11	42.95
EU25	11/2004–2006	3.59	29.19	48.87	55.35
EU27	2007–10/14	2.03	27.50	47.19	55.47
EU27, DMV	11/2014–3/17	16.62	37.80	50.96	77.25
EU28, DMV	11/2014–	15.73	36.79	63.20	87.14
EU32, DMV	2020	16.96	37.93	59.35	84.07

Notes: E_{BFI} ... Coleman measure of capability to act, E_{SSI} ... capability to act (Shapley-Shubik analog), PG_{BFI} ... Power gradient based on Banzhaf Index, PG_{SSI} ... Power gradient based on Shapley-Shubik Index efficiency defined by E_{BFI} (Coleman's measure of capability to act, see equation (13)) and E_{SSI} (the Shapley-Shubik analog, see equation (14)) and the proportionality in terms of the power gradient PG (see equation (15)) for the BFI and SSI.

As can be seen from Table 27.3, the EU's capability to act (in the Council of Ministers) declined over time in terms of both efficiency measures E_{BFI} and E_{SSI}, mainly as a result of the EC (EU) enlargements. This is also illustrated in Figure 27.1. The downward trend is much more pronounced for the Coleman measure that relies on the Banzhaf assumptions: According to E_{BFI}, the passage probability of a vote reached a minimum of 2 percent under the Nice Treaty for the EU27 (and the transitional period from 2014–17 under the Lisbon Treaty). In contrast, the Shapley-Shubik analog (E_{SSI}) suggests a different picture, as the index E_{SSI} has only slight decreased since the treaties of Rome until 2014 (2017) to a value of 27.5 percent. This highlights the relevance of the distributional assumptions regarding voting behavior for the quantification of the EU's capability to act.

Both efficiency indices show an increase with the shift from qualified majority to double majority voting that will come fully into force in 2017 (and co-exist with weighted qualified majority voting for the period 11/2014–3/17). Efficiency in terms of the E_{BFI} index increases to a value of 15.7 percent under DMV for the EU28, whereas its Shapley-Shubik analog even increases to 36.8 percent. Notably, this points to a passage probability that is higher than under the treaties of Rome for the original six member states.

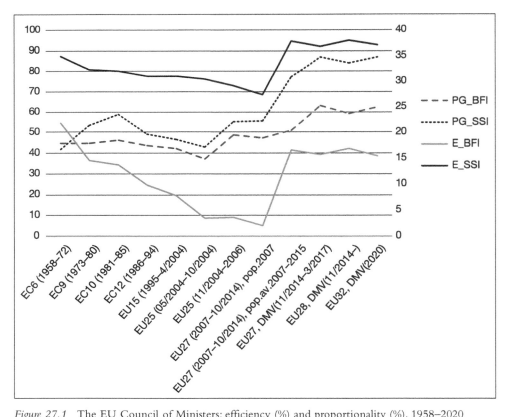

Figure 27.1 The EU Council of Ministers: efficiency (%) and proportionality (%), 1958–2020

Under the DMV system, further accessions by Turkey (and other candidate countries) would only slightly reduce efficiency but would have no sizeable effect on the EU's capability to act. It is also interesting to note that the switch to the double majority system and the increase in efficiency goes hand in hand with a strong move towards proportionally. The power gradients remained fairly flat util 2014 (2017) and increased towards proportionality thereafter.

The sharpest increase in proportionality is shown by the power gradient based on the *SSI* (as also apparent from the country-specific results) which is closest to proportionality with a value of 50.96 under the current regime, EU27, 2007–10/2014 and 87.22 under the potential enlargement to the EU32 in 2020.

Summing up, the conclusions regarding efficiency (and also) proportionality are rather different under the Banzhaf and the Shapley-Shubik approach. The latter indicates a much more efficient and more proportional voting system. From a supranational perspective this is the most relevant result. Hence it will be of particular interest in future research to judge the plausibility of the distributional assumptions underlying the Banzhaf and Shapley-Shubik approach, and to explore the changes in efficiency (and proportionality) against variations in the distributional assumptions, both in general terms and with respect to the EU Council of Ministers.

3.3 EU governance reform during the sovereign debt crisis

As a consequence of the euro area sovereign debt crises several reforms, most notably the so-called "Six-Pack" and "Two-Pack" regulations, have been implemented at the European level. Tables 27.4 and 27.5 summarize the increasing complexity in EU decision-making that has come with these reforms. On December 13 2011, the revised Stability and Growth Pact

Table 27.4 Enforcement mechanisms under the revised stability and growth pact

Enforcement measures underpinning the SGP in the euro area

Trigger of the sanction	Sanction	Adoption
Council decision establishing failure to take action in response to a Council recommendation under Art. 121(4).	Interest-bearing deposit (as a rule 0.2% of GDP)	Reversed Qualified Majority Voting
Council decision based on Art.126(6) of the Treaty (i.e. existence of an excessive deficit), only if the member states had already lodged an interest-bearing deposit (i.e. in case of non-compliance with the preventive arm provisions) or in case of particularly serious non-compliance with the rules	Non-interest-bearing deposit (as a rule 0.2% of GDP)	Reversed Qualified Majority Voting
Council decision based on Art.126(8) of the Treaty (i.e. non-effective action in response to the recommendation to correct the excessive deficit under Art. 126(7))	Fine (as a rule 0.2% of GDP)	Reversed Qualified Majority Voting
Council decision based on Art.126(11) of the Treaty (i.e. non-effective action in response to the notice to correct the excessive deficit under Art. 126(9))	Fine (0.2% of GDP + variable component)	Qualified Majority Voting

Notes: See press release, MEMO/11/898.

(SGP) came into force with a new set of rules for economic and fiscal surveillance. The so-called "Six-Pack" is made up of five regulations and one directive proposed by the European Commission and approved by all 27 member states and the European Parliament in October 2011 (Regulation (EU) 1173/2011 to 1177/2011 and Council Directive 2011/85/EU). It comprises an early warning mechanism related to measures of public finance (and macroeconomic imbalances), triggering Council recommendations to take corrective actions, and is backed up by enforcement measures in case of non-compliance under the so-called excessive deficit (imbalances) procedure.

Of particular interest in the present context are the changes related to the enforcement measures, for which a reversed qualified majority voting procedure has been introduced in order "to take all the relevant decisions leading up to sanctions. This semi-automatic decision-making procedure makes it very difficult for member states to form a blocking majority" (European Union, 2011).

In case of a persistent failure to respect the rules of the pact, the Commission will draft a recommendation to the member state to take corrective action, which is adopted by the Council through a reversed qualified majority voting procedure, i.e., unless a qualified majority of member states votes against it.

For euro area member states, the recommendation will be backed by an enforcement mechanism (based on Article 136 of the Treaty) in the form of an interest-bearing deposit amounting to 0.2 percent of GDP, which can also be converted into a fine. These enforcement measures are also adopted by reversed qualified majority voting. In case the member state concerned faces a notice under Article 126(9), the financial sanction will be adopted by qualified majority voting as foreseen by the Treaty. Table 27.5 gives an overview of the enforcement measures underpinning the SGP and the voting procedures.

Most of the "Six-Pack" reforms are based on the Lisbon Treaty and therefore perpetuate the clear distinction between euro area and non-euro area countries. In particular, regulation

Table 27.5 Increasingly complex decision-making

Six-Pack item	Regulation/ Directive No.	Six-Pack Regulation	Applies to	Voting rule
1	1175/2011	Improving budgetary positions and economic policies	EU27 (with minor exceptions which only apply to euro area+ERM2)	1
2	1177/2011	Improving the excessive deficit procedure	EU27, ECB surveillance only applies to euro area+ERM2 countries	N/A
3	2011/85/EU (Directive)	Budgetary frameworks requirements	EU27, the UK does not have to abide by Articles 5 to 7 (concerning numerical fiscal rules)	N/A
4	1176/2011	Macroeconomic Imbalances	EU27	2
5	1173/2011	Enforcing euro area budgetary surveillance	Euro area	2
6	1174/2011	Correcting excessive imbalances	Euro area	3

Two-Pack item	Regulation No.	Two-Pack Regulation		
1	385/2011	Surveillance for member states with financial stability difficulties	Euro area	3
2		Common provisions for draft budgetary plans and excessive deficit correction	Euro area in general (with minor exceptions for members who are subject to macroeconomic adjustment programmes or already subject to an excessive deficit procedure)	3
		Agreement		
		Fiscal Compact (TSCG)	EU25 (the UK, the Czech Republic and Croatia did not ratify it yet)	4
		European Stability Mechanism (ESM) Treaty	Euro Area	5

Notes: voting rules: 1 = QMV, excluding the member state concerned (only euro-area countries vote on euro-area members), Council can reject Commission recommendation by simple majority. 2 = QMV, excluding the member state concerned. 3 = QMV of euro-area countries, excluding the member state concerned. 4 = Reversed QMV (euro-area countries). 5 = QMV or mutual agreement by the Board of Directors and the Board of Governors.

1175/2011 on the strengthening of the surveillance of budgetary positions applies to the EU27, but the associated sanctions refer to the euro area. Regulation 1176/2011 on the prevention and correction of macroeconomic imbalances also applies to the whole EU. However, the alert mechanism, which is part of the regulation, is, in accordance with Article 121(3) of the TFEU, discussed in the eurogroup for the euro area countries. Finally, the enforcement mechanism to correct excessive macroeconomic imbalances adopted as part of the "Six-Pack" is exclusively addressed to euro area countries (Regulation 1174/2011). For the most part, the regulations require QMV by the Council to adopt a European Commission recommendation. For euro area countries, only euro area countries vote. But as shown in Table 27.6 for some regulations more complex voting schemes have been implemented.

Summing up, five main different voting regimes can arise from these new regulations, which will be considered quantitatively in the following:

- The usual qualified majority vote including all 27 member states (EU27),
- QMV with all 27 countries, excluding the member state concerned,
- Qualified majority vote including only the 17 euro area countries,
- QMV with only euro area countries, but excluding the member state concerned,
- Reversed QMV (RQMV) with only euro area countries (excluding the member state concerned).

Table 27.6 Thresholds and total votes under different QMV regimes

	EU27 QMV		Euro Area QMV		Euro Area RQMV	
	Acceptance Threshold	*Total Votes*	*Acceptance Threshold*	*Total Votes*	*Acceptance Threshold*	*Total Votes*
All	255	345	157	213	57	213
Excluding FR/DE/IT/UK	233	316	136	184		
Excluding ES/PL	235	318	137	186		
Excluding NL	245	332	148	200		
Excluding RO	244	331				
Excluding BE/CZ/GR/HU/PT	246	333	148	201		
Excluding AT/BG/SE	247	335	150	203		
Excluding DK/IE/FI/LT/SK	250	338	152	206		
Excluding CY/EE/SI/LU/LV	252	341	154	209		
Excluding MT	253	342	155	210		

Notes: Country results are grouped by voting weights in QMV, but always only excluded from each set separately.

The voting weights and threshold percentages stay the same as before. The respective absolute thresholds for majorities and total vote counts change though and are presented in Table 27.6. Thereby, countries with identical number of votes (see Table A1 in the Appendix) are grouped together in the respective rows, whereas the figures under voting without the member state concerned exclude only one of these countries at a time.

Qualified Majority Voting in the EU27 and the Euro Area

We apply these changed thresholds and voting rules using the power measures introduced above. Table 27.7 gives an overview of the efficiency and proportionality of the EU Council of Ministers under the various QMV regimes.

Irrespective of the underlying set of countries (EU27 or euro area) the exclusion of a country increases the efficiency of the scheme relying on the Banzhaf measure (E_{BFI}) and decreases for the Shapley-Shubik analog (E_{SSI}). This is another case in point where the two indices differ regarding their implications for efficiency. Although the power gradients are only comparable within each set of countries (EU27 and euro area) in Table 27.7, we see that proportionality increases for most of the indices when medium sized countries are excluded, but decreases when small or big countries are not allowed to vote.

Reversed Qualified Majority Voting in the economic governance package

One characteristic of the economic governance package is the use of a particular voting system that is referred to as reversed qualified majority voting. Under this voting procedure a Commission recommendation is deemed to be adopted unless the Council decides by qualified majority to reject the recommendation within a given deadline that starts to run from the adoption of such a recommendation by the Commission. The current rules for the calculation of a qualified majority are set out in Article 3 of Protocol (No. 36) on transitional provisions.[5]

Table 27.7 Efficiency and proportionality under different QMV regimes

Regime	Efficiency (%)		Power gradients (%)	
	E_{BFI}	E_{SSI}	PG_{BFI}	PG_{SSI}
EU27 QMV				
All	2.03	27.50	47.19	55.47
Excluding FR/DE/IT/UK	2.32	22.53	45.81	54.75
Excluding ES/PL	2.28	21.41	45.59	54.62
Excluding NL	2.37	22.28	47.66	55.32
Excluding RO	2.42	22.97	48.08	55.91
Excluding BE/CZ/GR/HU/PT	2.32	21.66	48.05	56.00
Excluding AT/BG/SE	2.36	22.56	47.52	55.62
Excluding DK/IE/FI/LT/SK	2.19	20.52	47.28	55.43
Excluding CY/EE/SI/LU/LV	2.15	20.79	46.93	55.09
Excluding MT	2.08	20.09	47.21	55.53
Only euro area countries QMV				
All	6.25	93.67	49.93	58.46
Excluding FR/DE/IT	6.90	89.64	47.55	54.16
Excluding ES	7.26	91.31	49.05	54.48
Excluding NL	6.89	89.78	50.47	57.98
Excluding BE/GR/PT	7.13	91.19	51.44	59.86
Excluding AT	6.80	89.68	50.69	59.55
Excluding IE/FI/SK	6.71	89.28	51.34	60.19
Excluding CY/EE/SI/LU	6.61	89.34	50.40	60.52
Excluding MT	6.37	88.29	50.08	59.94

Notes: country results are grouped by voting weights in QMV, but always only excluded separately. There is a small difference in the power gradients between the countries within one group, because population numbers differ.

Under RQMV, if the Council decides to vote on the Commission recommendation, the weighted votes of member states as laid down by the Treaties will remain unchanged. Hence, the "acceptance threshold" becomes a "prevention threshold" and the "acceptance threshold" under RQMV is equal to the total number of votes minus the number of votes required for preventing the proposal plus one vote.

The implied efficiency of the Council of Ministers as a whole under the old regime (QMV) and the new regime (RQMV) amounts to 6.25 percent and 93.75 percent in terms of E_{BFI} respectively, and to 93.67 percent and 99.79 percent in terms of E_{SSI} respectively.[6] Hence, as expected, the capability to act sees a tremendous increase, as far more acceptance coalitions are possible with the much lower threshold; to put it differently, much less blocking coalitions are possible. At the same time, the country-specific power to prevent proposals shrinks drastically due to the much higher threshold requirement under the reversed QMV regime. The overall efficiency of the Council increases dramatically both in terms of E_{BFI} and E_{SSI}. Hence, our quantitative results confirm that the introduction of the RQMV mechanisms achieves the Commissions' declared goal to introduce a "semi-automatic decision-making procedure [that] makes it very difficult for member states to form a blocking majority" (European Union, 2011).

4. Conclusion

This chapter provides a comprehensive reassessment of the consequences of past treaty changes and previous and upcoming (EC) EU enlargements for its member states' power, the EU's capability to act (efficiency), and the overall proportionality of the voting mechanism in the EU Council of Ministers. We employ the most widely used measures of power, such as the Banzhaf (1965) and Shapley-Shubik (1954) indices. Regarding efficiency (the capability to act), we use Coleman's (1971) measures, which are based on the assumptions underlying the Banzhaf approach, and Shapley-Shubik analogs more recently introduced by Paterson (2005). The overall proportionality of the voting system is also judged in terms of the power gradient (Paterson, 1998). Moreover, we also judge the implications of more recently introduced enforcement mechanisms under the revised Stability and Growth Pact such as reversed qualified majority voting.

Our results show in quantitative terms, how the accession of new member states over time has diluted voting power of the incumbents and led to a reduction in the EU's capability to act, which has been resurrected by the introduction of the double majority voting system in the Lisbon Treaty.

There are large differences between the Banzhaf and Shapley-Shubik approaches when it comes to measuring the EU's capability to act. Hence, further theoretical and empirical research on the validity of the assumptions underlying the two approaches seems warranted.

We also highlight the increasing complexity and variety of voting rules in the EU and quantify the large increase in efficiency implied by the introduction of the reversed qualified majority voting procedure in the area of economic governance.

Notes

1 Financial support by the Oesterreichische Nationalbank (Anniversary Fund, project number: 14028) is gratefully acknowledged.
2 See, e.g., Widgren (2009) for a survey of the literature.
3 See, e.g., Garret and Tsebelis (1999) for a critical review of power indices.
4 In Antonakakis et al. (2014) we also provide detailed (country-specific) results for of a number of alternative measures (Johnston, Deegan-Packel, Holler-Packel, Inclusiveness index, Colman power to prevent or initiate action) and assess the relevance of additional rules of the game (such as the Luxemburg compromise, the Ioannina compromise, and the Demographic Clause).
5 Different rules will apply from November 1 2014 (see Article 16(4) TEU and Article 238(2) and (3) TFEU).
6 Notice that the country-specific power measures such as the Banzhaf or Shapley-Shubik indices are not changed numerically under the RQMV regime (with the same countries and weights), the only change being that the interpretation becomes different: positive swings of a country making the coalition winning in the sense that a Commission proposal can be successfully blocked.

References

Antonakakis, N., Badinger, H., and Reuter, W. (2014), From Rome to Lisbon and beyond: member states' power, efficiency, and proportionality in the EU Council of Ministers, *WU Department of Economics Working Paper*, No. 175.

Baldwin, R.E., Francois, J.F., and Portes, R. (2002), The costs and benefits of eastern enlargement: the impact on the EU and central Europe, *Economic Policy*, 12(24), 125–76.

Banzhaf, J.F. (1965), Weighted voting doesn't work: a mathematical analysis, *Rutgers Law Review*, 19, 317–43.

Coleman, J.S. (1971), Control of collectives and the power of a collectivity to act, in: Lieberman, B. (ed.), *Social Choice*, New York: Gordon and Breach.

European Union (2011), EU Economic Governance 'Six-Pack - State of Play, Memo/11/627, Brussels, Belgium.

Heisenberg, D. (2005), The institution of consensus in the European Union: formal versus informal decision-making in the council, *European Journal of Political Research*, 44, 65–90.

Hosli, M.O. (1995), The balance between small and large: effects of a double-majority system on voting power in the European Union, *International Studies Quarterly*, 39(3), 351–70.

Kauppi, H. and Widgren, M., (2007), Voting rules and budget allocation in the enlarged EU, *European Journal of Political Economy*, 23(3), 693–706.

Le Breton, M., Montero, M., and Zaporozhets, V. (2012), Voting power in the EU council of ministers and fair decision-making in distributive politics, *Mathematical Social Sciences*, 63(2), 159–73.

Paterson, I. (1998), Vote weighting in the European Union – confronting the dilemma of dilution. *East European Series*, No. 54, Institute for Advanced Studies, Vienna.

Paterson, I. and Silárszky, P. (1999), Redesigning the institution of the Council of Ministers in advance of EU Enlargement – issues and options, *Journal of Institutional Innovation, Development, and Transition* (IB Review), 3, 43–54.

Paterson, I. (2005), A lesser known probabilistic approach to the Shapley-Shubik index and useful related voting measures. Paper presented at the EPCS, Durham, March 31–April 3, 2005.

Shapley, L. S. and Shubik, M. (1954), A method for evaluating the distribution of power in a committee system, *The American Political Science Review*, 48(3), 787–92.

Straffin, P.D. (1977), Homogeneity, independence, and power indices, *Public Choice*, 30(1), 107–18.

Widgren, M. (2009), The impact of council voting rules on EU decision-making, *CESifo Economic Studies*, 55(1), 30–56.

Appendix

Voting Weights and Power Indices of EU Member States, 1958–2020

Table A1 Voting weights under qualified majority voting, 1958–2014

	EC6	EC9	EC10	EC12	EU15	EU25	EU25	EU27
	1958–72	1973–80	1981–85	1986–94	1995–4/2004	05/2004–10/2004	11/2004–2006	2007–10/2014
Belgium	2	5	5	5	5	5	12	12
France	4	10	10	10	10	10	29	29
Germany	4	10	10	10	10	10	29	29
Italy	4	10	10	10	10	10	29	29
Luxembourg	1	2	2	2	2	2	4	4
Netherlands	2	5	5	5	5	5	13	13
Denmark	–	3	3	3	3	3	7	7
Ireland	–	3	3	3	3	3	7	7
Un. Kingdom	–	10	10	10	10	10	29	29
Greece	–	–	5	5	5	5	12	12
Portugal	–	–	–	5	5	5	12	12
Spain	–	–	–	8	8	8	27	27

(Continued)

Table A1 (Continued)

	EC6	EC9	EC10	EC12	EU15	EU25	EU25	EU27
	1958–72	1973–80	1981–85	1986–94	1995–4/2004	05/2004–10/2004	11/2004–2006	2007–10/2014
Austria	–	–	–	–	4	4	10	10
Finland	–	–	–	–	3	3	7	7
Sweden	–	–	–	–	4	4	10	10
Cyprus	–	–	–	–	–	2	4	4
Cz. Republic	–	–	–	–	–	5	12	12
Estonia	–	–	–	–	–	3	4	4
Hungary	–	–	–	–	–	5	12	12
Latvia	–	–	–	–	–	3	4	4
Lithuania	–	–	–	–	–	3	7	7
Malta	–	–	–	–	–	2	3	3
Poland	–	–	–	–	–	8	27	27
Slovakia	–	–	–	–	–	3	7	7
Slovenia	–	–	–	–	–	3	4	4
Bulgaria								10
Romania								14
Total	17	58	63	76	87	124	321	345
Majority rules	QMV	QMV	QMV	QMV	QMV	QMV	QMV	QMV, DMV
Treshold	12	41	45	54	62	88	232	255
%	70.6	70.7	71.4	71.1	71.3	71.0	2.3	73.9

Notes: QMV ... qualified majority voting, DMV ... double majority voting (55% of MS, 65% of population). After the transitional period from 11/2014–03/2017, weighted voting will be replaced by double majority voting.

28

MEASURING EUROPEAN ECONOMIC AND INSTITUTIONAL INTEGRATION

Helge Berger and Volker Nitsch

1. Introduction

A quantitative assessment of the level of integration among geographic units (such as regions, states or countries) is of interest to a wide range of audiences. Policy-makers, for instance, may want to identify barriers to cross-regional interaction. José Manuel Barroso (2009, p. 28), the then President of the European Commission, provides an illustrative example; in the political guidelines for his second term as the head of the Commission he notes: "I intend to launch a major analysis of the 'missing links' in the internal market, to find out why it has not delivered on its full potential and thereby to identify new sources of growth and social cohesion." Five years later, but still along similar lines, the European Commission (2013, p. 4) argues: "Today, during the crisis, it is more necessary than ever to address where the single market does not yet function as it should to the benefits of citizens and businesses."

For economists, the measurement of integration is of particular importance when quantifying the gains from exchange. Any reasonable assessment of the consequences of a removal of barriers to trade requires measures (observed or constructed) that allow a comparison of different states of integration. As a result, empirical findings may be sensitive to the exact definition of measures of integration. Rodriguez and Rodrik (2001), for instance, highlight the relevance of measurement issues in an article which has become an instant classic; in a critical review of empirical analyses of the effect of trade openness on economic growth, they illustrate the difficulties in quantifying a country's openness to trade.

In this chapter, we review the process of European integration in the post-Second World War period and discuss issues related to the measurement of economic and institutional integration. Starting from the observation that the quantitative assessment of the level of integration is a non-trivial task, in Section 2 we highlight the challenges involved in the quantification from a European perspective. In Section 3, we review a selection of available indicators of European integration in more detail. A brief summary concludes the chapter.

2. Challenges

European integration has always been a process involving periodic stops and leaps. Measures towards further integration were taken and implemented at irregular intervals. The underlying decisions were often driven by hard-to-build political consensus and shaped by circumstances. As a consequence, integration has followed a path not necessarily aiming at gradual improvement and not always following economic logic. Examples include the discussions of monetary union, which was first proposed in the late 1960s but not implemented until the late 1990s, and the formation of a banking union only in response to the euro area crisis some ten years later.[1]

In view of these nonlinear developments, it may be particularly useful to summarize and document the progress of European integration with a single quantitative indicator. In the European context, however, the quantitative assessment of the level of integration is further complicated by two features: the various qualitative dimensions of integration and the geographic expansion of the integration area. We will discuss each of these features in turn.

2.1 Dimensions of integration

Empirical analyses that aim to analyze the effects of institutional integration have often used the simplest possible measure, a plain binary dummy variable that differentiates between participants and non-participants of a particular integration scheme. Based on this indicator variable, the level of integration can then be assessed by examining relevant economic data (such as, for instance, cross-border trade or pair-wise differentials in the price level). However, while this approach may work well in a setting with only one single integration scheme, it becomes increasingly problematic when the integration measures taken differ across arrangements and/or over time.

To address these issues, various extensions have been proposed in the literature. An obvious solution is to replace the single integration dummy with separate dummies for different integration arrangements; see, for example, Frankel's (1997) analysis of regional trading blocs for an application of this procedure which comes at the cost of limited generalizability.[2] Baier, Bergstrand and Feng (2014) provide a more general approach. Instead of differentiating between individual arrangements, they analyze different types of economic integration arrangements. Specifically, they distinguish between one-way preferential trade agreements, two-way preferential trade agreements, free trade agreements, customs unions, common markets, and economic unions. However, there may be still considerable heterogeneity in the coverage of issues even within a single type of economic integration arrangements, such as free trade agreements, as emphasized by Horn, Mavroidis and Sapir (2010) and Kohl (2013), among others. To highlight and capture these differences, they examine in detail the policy areas that are covered by individual agreements and code the content of these agreements. Kohl (2013), for instance, reviews 296 free trade agreements and finds that almost all agreements contain provisions on export and import restrictions, anti-dumping measures and customs administration, while environmental issues are covered in less than one-third of the sample and labor policies are regulated in just one out of six agreements.

While a quantification of the level of integration based on categorical variables is already difficult for integration initiatives pursued along a single dimension (such as trade liberalization), it can be close to impossible to capture the effects of wider forms of integration which occasionally span a wide range of policy domains. European integration provides a notable example. A hard-to-predict historical process during which a core of neighboring countries with a long shared political, social, and economic history agrees to deepen their integration is difficult to model based on (ordered-)categorical variables alone. However, even continuous measures are unlikely to capture the full extent of European integration. For instance, a non-categorical indicator of trade integration, such as within-area trade intensity, may be appropriate to illustrate the effects of a gradual removal of formal and informal barriers to trade, but fails to capture other, potentially more relevant, areas of integration, such as a harmonization of structural, fiscal, and monetary policies.

2.2 Geographic expansion

For a proper assessment of the effects of preferential integration (where a selection of partners is treated favorably relative to others who stay outside), it is essential to define a benchmark area, where none of the analyzed integration measures are taken, to which developments in the integration area can then be compared. Ideally, this benchmark area shares with the integration area as many other characteristics as possible to avoid potential misspecifications, such as omitted variables bias. The proper selection of the control group is critical, given that observed differences in the patterns of development across areas may be explained by many factors other than integration, and it may be difficult (if not impossible) to control for all these factors in an econometric model.[3]

In the case of European integration, a natural starting point for the selection of a comparison group of countries may be other European countries that did not participate in the (institutional) process of European integration. However, such countries are rare. A number of countries joined the European Union along the way towards further integration; the number of member countries of the European Union increased from six founding members in 1957 to 28 member countries in 2014. Other countries participated indirectly in European integration; examples include the establishment of the European Economic Area which allow member states of the European Free Trade Area to participate in the European Union's internal market in 1994 and the bilateral agreements between the European Union and Switzerland. In sum, the variation in the geographic expansion of the integration area, with a gradual enlargement of the European Union and a corresponding decrease in the number of countries which did not participate in the process of integration, makes a long-run comparison difficult.

3. Selected measures

Despite these conceptual challenges, there have been a number of attempts to quantify the level of European integration. Before we discuss a selection of measures in more detail, it may be useful to provide a taxonomy of the various approaches. While integration indicators can probably be organized along many dimensions, two features seem to be particularly relevant. A first possible categorization differentiates between de jure and de facto measures.[4] De jure measures of integration refer to legal arrangements, such as Kohl's (2013) analysis of the content of trade agreements; de facto measures, in contrast, determine the level of integration based on actual data, such as trade flows adjusted for country characteristics as a measure of trade liberalization. While both measures can be expected to be correlated (at least in the long term), there are often sizable differences. For instance, the European Commission typically reports considerable delays in the implementation of integration measures related to the single market legislation by individual member countries.[5] Another reasonable categorization groups indicators into single measures and composite indices. Single measures explore one specific aspect of integration (and often draw on a single statistic), such as cross-border migration as a fraction of a country's total population; summary measures, in contrast, provide an aggregation of various indicators (occasionally even comprising information from many different areas). Table 28.1 provides a tabulation of selected individual measures of economic and institutional integration.

Table 28.1 A classification of integration measures

	Single Indicator	*Summary Index*
De jure	Integration agreement membership classification	Integration index covering different stages of integration
De facto	Trade openness (ratio), cross-border activities adjusted for country pair characteristics ('gravity estimates')	Principal components analysis, Single Market Indicator

3.1 Trade

Many attempts to quantify the extent of European integration focus on one particular aspect of cross-border activities, trade. This focus seems to be motivated, among other things, by the European Union's initial emphasis on trade integration, with the completion of a customs union on 1 July 1968; early analyses of European integration therefore examine specifically, almost by definition, the progress in this area.[6] Another plausible rationale for the particularly strong interest in trade is that, both conceptually and practically, integration schemes tend to start with a removal of barriers to trade. The European Union may then provide a reasonable example for studying the measurement of the effects of integration. Finally, data on cross-border trade transactions are readily available, allowing a relatively easy, straight-forward assessment of the de facto level of integration.[7]

The analysis of trade integration further benefits from the fact that the methodological challenges seem to be manageable. A de jure analysis may focus on legal barriers to trade, such as the level of tariffs. When most of the easily identifiable restrictions have been formally removed, however, probably more complex measures have to be constructed. For a de facto analysis, actual patters of trade can be analyzed which are often compared to some relevant benchmark. For instance, an obvious measure is the ratio of trade within the integration area (that is, exports, imports or the aggregate of both) to the total external trade of the respective member countries. An alternative indicator is a measure of trade intensity, calculated as the ratio of the intra-area trade share to the share of world trade with the integration area, where index values above one indicate that trade within the integration area is larger than expected given the importance of the area in world trade.

Still, the most prominent and by now widely-used empirical approach to assessing biases in empirical patterns of trade, including possible deviations from the benchmark level due to institutional integration, is the application of the gravity model of trade. Building on the analogy of Newton's law of universal gravitation, the gravity equation states that the volume of trade between any pair of countries is directly proportional to the (product of the) size of these countries and the distance between them. Since this framework is, even in its simplest form, extremely successful empirically, it provides a reasonable counterfactual to which actual cross-border trade within an integration scheme can be compared. Specifically, a binary dummy variable is typically added to the gravity equation to capture any measurable differences in the patterns of trade within and outside the integration area.

Numerous studies have applied variants of the gravity model to analyze the trade effects of European integration. Often, the results turn out to be somewhat weak, with statistically significant but moderate effects; see, for instance, Frankel (1997). However, as interests have gradually shifted away from the estimation of simple integration effects, early estimates of the trade effect of European integration, such as Frankel's results, are hardly any more comparable with more recent findings from gravity estimates.[8] For one thing, the estimation of the gravity model has become much more sophisticated over the last few years. For instance, standard practices involve the derivation and estimation of theory-consistent specifications of the gravity equation.[9] Baldwin (2006) provides an extensive discussion of potential pitfalls in the estimation of gravity models; see also De Benedictis and Taglioni (2011) for some interesting (historical) background on the gravity approach. Head and Mayer (2015) carefully analyze best-practice methods in the application of gravity equations.

Another extension is to supplement the estimation of simple (time-invariant) average effects with more flexible approaches in which integration effects are allowed to vary over time. These approaches not only highlight the speed of adjustment in patterns of trade after the implementation of liberalization measures; they also allow identifying possible anticipation effects. In practice, time-varying integration effects are often identified by estimating cross-section equations for individual years. Alternatively, pooled estimation may be applied to panel data, thereby jointly estimating year-specific integration effects. For European integration, it has become commonplace to focus on individual (and clearly identifiable) steps towards further integration (such as the Single Market initiative or the introduction of the euro) and then to estimate separate effects.

With a greater availability of micro data sets in recent years (containing information on patterns of trade at finely disaggregated industry level, at the firm-level, or even at the level of the individual trade transaction), there has also been a growing interest in new dimensions of trade integration. An obvious starting point is to simply replicate analyses examining aggregate trade for separate industries or product groups and then aiming to explain observed differences in trade integration. Flam and Nordström (2003), for instance, find particularly strong effects of the euro for differentiated products (relative to homogeneous or standardized products). Later studies focus on the effects of integration on the number of firms active in international trade, the number of traded product varieties, or the number of markets served (in short, the extensive margins) and differentiate these effects from a plain extension of an already existing trade relationship (that is, the intensive margin); see, among others, Nitsch and Pisu (2008).

3.2 Foreign direct investment

In principle, it seems reasonable to augment the results on trade integration with evidence on foreign direct investment, potentially even applying similar techniques of analysis. In practice, however, there are various reasons why this exercise is more complicated than the analysis of patterns in trade. An obvious issue is the broad variety of motives for foreign direct investment. Motivations for firms to acquire foreign assets range from using a foreign location's comparative advantage and exercising control to decisions primarily determined by financial considerations such as taxation, exchange rate movements and/or stock market developments. Depending on the motives, it may also be useful to examine different measures of foreign direct investment. Specifically, capital account data may mainly reflect financial considerations and valuation issues, while production (and other real economy) motives are perhaps best captured by analyzing firm-level data on the number, employment and sales of foreign affiliates. At a more technical level, integration measures may also be affected by the decision whether investment stocks or flows are analyzed – for example, stocks and flows vary in their sensitivity to fluctuations in the exchange rate, flows are occasionally heavily influenced by a few large transactions (so-called, megadeals), and both variables will influence each other as existing foreign direct investment can make additional investment more or less likely.

In view of these difficulties, there are fewer studies available which aim to assess the level of integration in foreign direct investment. Reviewing the literature on the effects of the euro on foreign direct investment, Baldwin, DiNino, Fontagné, De Santis and Taglioni (2008) and Flam (2009) provide more extensive discussions of the issues involved in the analysis of cross-border investment patterns.

3.3 Capital

While the analysis of foreign direct investment may be easily extended to other types of capital flows, a broader range of analytic approaches is typically applied to assess financial market integration. The diversity of available indicators is probably best illustrated by the European Central Bank's regularly published statistical indicators of integration in the euro area financial markets. Among other things, these price and quantity-based indicators cover the money market, the government and corporate bond markets, the equity market, the banking sector as well as the market infrastructure. Examples of indicators include the cross-country standard deviation of interbank lending rates (money markets), the share of cross-border holdings of debt securities (bond markets), the dispersion in equity returns (equity markets), the foreign affiliates' share of total loans (banking) and the share of debit transactions processed in Single Euro Payments Area (SEPA) format (infrastructure).[10]

In view of the various features of financial integration, some indicators explicitly seek to reduce the dimensionality of the data. The European Central Bank, for instance, has recently constructed a composite measure, the Synthetic Indicator of Financial Integration (SYNFINT), by aggregating selected indicators. The composite measure is computed as a weighted average where the weights reflect the average relative size of each market segment in terms of outstanding amounts.[11]

Another useful empirical methodology to identify and describe common features of a set of economic variables is principal components analysis (PCA) which converts a vector of possibly correlated variables into a smaller number of new, linearly uncorrelated variables (components) such that the first principal component accounts for most of the observed variability in the data. Volosovych (2011, 2013) provides an application of this method for financial market integration, analyzing monthly sovereign bond data for the period from 1875 to 2009 to track integration in financial and physical asset markets and explore potential determinants of its long-run dynamics.[12]

The level of financial integration can also be assessed by analyzing macroeconomic data from national accounts. Feldstein and Horioka (1980) examine domestic saving and investment rates and find that both rates are highly correlated both within and between OECD countries; they interpret this finding as evidence of low capital mobility.[13] More specifically, when capital is mobile, countries should be able to borrow and lend abroad, without being constrained by domestic saving decisions. Choudhry, Jayasekera and Kling (2014) provide an application of this approach for the European Union. The approach has also recently been used to evaluate the degree of risk sharing in the euro area compared to other currency areas such as the United States; see, for example, Furceri and Zdzienicka (2013).

3.4 Prices

An alternative approach to the exploration of cross-border flows and interactions (relative to some benchmark) is the analysis of discrepancies in consumer, wholesale or producer prices across locations. Implicitly, it is hypothesized that large price differentials between geographic localities could only exist because of bilateral barriers to trade, where the existence of information and transaction costs hinder arbitrage transactions to exploit price differentials.

The use of prices to analyze market integration offers some notable advantages. For one thing, there is, in principle, very detailed price information available. At an extreme, scanner price data register the exact product or service as well as the time and location of individual purchases. Consequently, price differentials can be computed at a deeply disaggregated level; for instance, since the variation in prices between locations within a given country can often be easily computed, intra-national price differentials may serve as a reasonable benchmark when assessing the level of cross-border integration. Moreover, for some goods (and commodities), price information has been collected for centuries, allowing a long-term analysis of integration by economic historians.

However, there are also disadvantages. Most notably, a major challenge is often the compilation of comparable price statistics since scanner price data are not always readily available. In particular, raw price level data (in absolute terms) are rarely published by official sources; statistical offices typically release price level indices (relative to some base year). Also, prices have to refer to identical products such that, for instance, quality differences do not affect the results. In addition, aggregation issues, taxation, the exchange rate and various specifics of the data collection (such as timing and the outlet from which the price data are obtained) may be relevant.

Where adequate data can be collected, an obvious approach to assessing the degree of price level integration is to analyze absolute price differences. This analysis can be applied to individual products and services within a single industry. In the European context, for instance, probably the most heavily analyzed market is automobiles; see, among others, Flam (1992) and Goldberg and Verboven (2001, 2004). Alternatively, the analysis may cover a diverse set of items, potentially reflecting the full range of consumer expenditures, as with Engel and Rogers (2004). In a similar fashion, it is possible to vary the level of geographic detail that is involved in the compilation of the integration indicator. In its simplest form, the measure merely highlights the price level at a specific location (e.g., defined as an index relative to the mean of the integration area). However, the indicator could also focus more explicitly on relative price pairs between locations (e.g., defined as the maximum price differential within the integration area), or it captures the average price dispersion within the area (e.g., defined as the mean squared error of relative prices). Exploring the evolution of such measures over time then allows drawing conclusions about the convergence or divergence of prices. Baldwin et al. (2008) provide a useful survey; see also Anderson and van Wincoop (2004).

3.5 Composite indicators

Few attempts have been made to construct indicators which cover simultaneously a broad range of policy domains and, thereby, allow assessing the European experience of a deepening of integration along multiple dimensions and over a long period. In the following, we discuss four selected composite indicators in more detail, each putting particular emphasis on a specific aspect of European integration.[14]

Mongelli, Dorrucci and Agur (2005) focus strongly on the institutional features of integration.[15] Following Balassa (1961), they distinguish between five main stages of regional integration, free trade area, customs union, common market, economic union, and total economic integration. For each of these stages, they assign scores between 0 and 25, according to the degree of integration achieved. Summing up the scores at each point in time, they construct an overall index ranging between 0 and 100. This procedure has various advantageous features, apart from covering different areas of integration. For one thing, the measure can, in principle, be constructed on a daily basis. Indeed, Mongelli et al. (2005) report a monthly indicator based on the actual implementation of integration measures. Also, the measure quantifies the degree of integration for individual countries. Still, a major disadvantage of this methodology is the arbitrary nature of assigning scores based on the individual assessment of the researcher.

Berger and Nitsch (2008) construct an index of European integration based on measures of de facto integration. Similar to Mongelli et al. (2005), they define sub-indicators which apply to different episodes of integration and then sum up these index values to obtain the aggregate indicator. Instead of distinguishing between formal stages of integration, however, they focus on three separate phases of integration: the removal of quantitative restrictions on trade in the 1950s, the phase-out of tariffs in the 1960s, and the completion of the Single Market. For each of these episodes, they identify a variable which summarizes the key element of the integration process, based on the actual progress that is made by a country in a given year. These variables are scaled from 0 (no liberalization) to 10 (full liberalization), such that the overall index ranges from 0 to 30. Reassuringly, the results on the integration performance of European countries do not differ substantially from the findings in Mongelli et al. (2005).

Another composite indicator of the European Union's de facto integration is the Single Market Scoreboard (formerly labeled the Internal Market Index) that is compiled and published by the European Commission.[16] This indicator focuses exclusively on the implementation of Single Market policies. Accordingly, the index value for each country is scaled to be 100 in 1992, when the internal market entered into force. This methodology allows tracking integration trends over time, but is not particularly helpful for cross-country comparisons. While the construction of the index has been revised several times, its key feature is the combination of various sub-indicators which are meant to measure the "core business" of the internal market; these sub-indicators include, among other things, the value of published public procurement (in % of GDP), telecommunication costs, electricity prices, gas prices and postal tariffs. A principal components analysis is then applied to compute the index.

König and Ohr (2013) basically follow a similar approach. In line with the Internal Market Index, they apply a principal components analysis to assess the degree of Single Market integration. However, borrowing from the literature on the measurement of "globalization" (see Dreher, Gaston and Martens [2008] for a good introduction), they explore a broader range of indicators, analyzing 25 different variables. Specifically, they define four dimensions of European integration and group the variables accordingly; the dimensions are the Single Market, homogeneity, symmetry and conformity.[17]

4. Summary

The measurement of economic and institutional integration has become the subject of a growing literature. There is considerable interest in all aspects of economic integration – from trade to financial markets – and researchers have been deploying a variety of approaches, including the analysis of economic transactions or price data. Other approaches are documenting the de jure and de facto integration of markets and their institutional underpinnings in the form of indicators.

At the global level, researchers are often interested in the assessment of the level of integration. At the regional level, there is considerable interest in the measurement of the progress of integration – not least by those institutions and policy-makers who are charged with fostering these processes (such as, for example, the European Commission and the Asian Development Bank).[18] Within regions, the academic literature has focused primarily on border effects and the question of whether different degrees of institutional or economic integration affect them. European integration, with its long history of stops and leaps, from trade to currency and banking union, has drawn particular attention in this regard.

This chapter discussed issues related to the measurement of economic and institutional integration. A selection of available indicators was reviewed, with a special focus on European integration.

Notes

1 It is interesting to note that most of the variation in the process of European integration occurred over time, with periods of rapid progress and episodes of stagnation ('Eurosclerosis'). There has been much less variation, in contrast, in the depth of integration. Integration measures have been rarely scaled back, except for some minor corrections (especially in the field of monetary integration).

2 At an extreme, a separate dummy variable is defined for each single integration arrangement.

3 The argument is related to the synthetic control method applied in case studies; see, for example, Abadie, Diamond and Hainmueller (2010).

4 Alternatively, the categories could be labeled institutional and actual measures.

5 In view of possible discrepancies between legal measures of integration and their actual implementation, the European Commission provides a Single Market Scoreboard. Specifically, the European Commission notes on its website:

> The Single Market is based on a large body of EU law, accompanied by national transposition measures. However, it is essential to ensure that the Single Market does not exist only on paper but also in reality for citizens and businesses who want to work, travel, shop, invest or do business across borders. This requires effective governance of the Single Market by the European Commission and by the EU and EEA Member States, as well as effective implementation "on the ground", in the Member States. This scoreboard aims to give an overview of the practical management of the Single Market.

See http://ec.europa.eu/internal_market/scoreboard/index_en.htm.

6 The customs union had been completed one and a half years earlier than planned in the 1957 Treaty of Rome. For a more detailed documentation, see http://ec.europa.eu/taxation_customs/40customs/index_en.htm.

7 The analysis has become more complicated, however, with the establishment of the Single Market, which had been accompanied by the compilation of separate statistics for the trading of goods between member states (Intrastat) and for the trading of goods with countries outside the union (Extrastat); see the Council Regulation (EEC) No 3330/91 of 7 November 1991 on the statistics relating to the trading of goods between Member States available at http://eur-lex.europa.eu/legal-content/EN/TXT/?uri=CELEX:31991R3330.

8 Analyzing the European Union's external trade policies, De Benedictis and Salvatici (2011) provide an extensive discussion of current issues in the application of the gravity equation, including a meta-analysis by Cipollina and Pietrovito (2011) to reconcile the variation in estimation results from various studies.

9 Theory-consistent specifications, for instance, highlight the fact that all bilateral patterns of trade are determined simultaneously such that bilateral frictions alone are inadequate to deal with this N-body problem where for each country the distance from all others matters (typically captured by adding

"multilateral resistance" terms to the gravity equation). Another recent modification is the use of estimation techniques that properly take into account the discrete choice features of trade observations by allowing for zero trade, with Poisson pseudo-maximum likelihood estimation being a prominent example.

10 After the first release of the indicators in September 2005, the European Central Bank (ECB) has gradually extended work on the measurement of financial integration in the euro area. The indicators are updated and published biannually on the ECB's website at www.ecb.europa.eu/stats/finint/html/index.en.html; the ECB also publishes a yearly report on "Financial Integration in Europe."

11 To our knowledge, the index values have not been officially published yet. For more details, see www.ecb.europa.eu/press/pr/date/2014/html/pr140428.en.html.

12 Volosovych (2011, 2013) also provides a discussion and critique of alternative measures of financial market integration, such as cross-market correlations.

13 Obstfeld and Rogoff (2001) argue that the Feldstein-Horioka finding is one of the six major puzzles in international macroeconomics.

14 An alternative but similarly encompassing approach is to analyze survey-based data on sentiments towards integration; see, for example, Guiso, Sapienza and Zingales (2014).

15 Dorrucci, Ioannou, Mongelli and Terzio (2015) provide an update.

16 Detailed results are available online at http://ec.europa.eu/internal_market/score/index_en.htm. For technical details, see http://ec.europa.eu/internal_market/score/docs/score11/im-index-2002_en.pdf.

17 For more details, see König (2014) and www.eu-index.uni-goettingen.de/?lang=en.

18 See, for instance, http://aric.adb.org/integrationindicators.

References

Abadie, A., Diamond, A., and Hainmueller, J. (2010), Synthetic Control Methods for Comparative Case Studies: Estimating the Effect of California's Tobacco Control Program, *Journal of the American Statistical Association*, 105(490), 493–505.

Anderson, J.E. and van Wincoop, E. (2004), Trade Costs, *Journal of Economic Literature*, 42(3), 691–751.

Baier, S.L., Bergstrand, J.H., and Feng, M. (2014), Economic Integration Agreements and the Margins of International Trade, *Journal of International Economics*, 93(2), 339–50.

Balassa, B. (1961), *The Theory of Economic Integration*, Homewood, IL: Irwin.

Baldwin, R. (2006), The Euro's Trade Effects, *European Central Bank Working Paper* #594.

Baldwin, R., DiNino, V., Fontagné, L., De Santis, R.A., and Taglioni, D. (2008), Study on the Impact of the Euro on Trade and Foreign Direct Investment, *European Economy Economic Papers* #321.

Barroso, J.M. (2009), *Political Guidelines for the Next Commission*, available at http://ec.europa.eu/commission_2010–2014/president/pdf/press_20090903_en.pdf.

Berger, H. and Nitsch, V. (2008), Zooming Out: The Trade Effect of the Euro in Historical Perspective, *Journal of International Money and Finance*, 27(8), 1244–60.

Choudhry, T., Jayasekera, R., and Kling, G. (2014), The Global Financial Crisis and the European Single Market: The End of Integration?, *Journal of International Money and Finance*, 49(Part B), 191–6.

Cipollina, M. and Pietrovito, F. (2011), Trade Impact of EU Preferential Policies: A Meta-Analysis of the Literature, in De Benedictis, L. and Salvatici, L. (eds) *The Trade Impact of European Union Preferential Policies*, Heidelberg: Springer.

De Benedictis, L. and Salvatici, L. (eds) (2011), *The Trade Impact of European Union Preferential Policies*, Heidelberg: Springer.

De Benedictis, L. and Taglioni, D. (2011), The Gravity Model in International Trade, in De Benedictis, L. and Salvatici, L. (eds) *The Trade Impact of European Union Preferential Policies*, Heidelberg: Springer.

Dorrucci, E., Ioannou, D., Mongelli, F.P., and Terzio, A. (2015), The Four Unions 'PIE' on the Monetary Union 'CHERRY': A New Index of European Institutional Integration, *ECB Occasional Paper Series* No. 160.

Dreher, A., Gaston, N., and Martens, P. (2008), *Measuring Globalization: Gauging Its Consequences*, Heidelberg: Springer.

Engel, C. and Rogers, J.H. (2004), European Product Market Integration after the Euro, *Economic Policy*, 19(39), 347–84.

European Commission (2013), *The European Union Explained: Internal Market*, Brussels: European Commission.

Feldstein, M. and Horioka, C. (1980), Domestic Saving and International Capital Flows, *Economic Journal*, 90(358), 314–29.

Flam, H. (1992), Product Markets and 1992: Full Integration, Large Gains?, *Journal of Economic Perspectives*, 6(4), 7–30.

Flam, H. and Nordström, H. (2003), Trade Volume Effects of the Euro: Aggregate and Sector Estimates, *IIES Seminar Paper* No. 746.

Flam, H. (2009), The Impact of the Euro on International Trade and Investment: A Survey of Theoretical and Empirical Evidence, Swedish Institute for European Policy Studies.

Frankel, J.A. (1997), *Regional Trading Blocs in the World Economic System*, Washington, DC: Institute for International Economics.

Furceri, D. and Zdzienicka, A. (2013), The Euro Area Crisis: Need for a Supranational Fiscal Risk Sharing Mechanism? *IMF Working Paper* 13/198.

Goldberg, P.K. and Verboven, F. (2001), The Evolution of Price Dispersion in the European Car Market, *Review of Economic Studies*, 68(4), 811–48.

Goldberg, P.K. and Verboven, F. (2004), Cross-Country Price Dispersion and the Euro, *Economic Policy*, 19(40), 484–521.

Guiso, L., Sapienza, P., and Zingales, L. (2014), Monnet's Error?, Einaudi Institute for Economics and Finance, Northwestern University and University of Chicago.

Head, K. and Mayer, T. (2015), Gravity Equations: Workhorse, Toolkit, and Cookbook in Helpman, E., Rogoff, K., and Gopinath, G. (eds) *Handbook of International Economics*, Amsterdam: Elsevier.

Horn, H., Mavroidis, P.C., and Sapir, A. (2010), Beyond the WTO? An Anatomy of EU and US Preferential Trade Agreements, *The World Economy*, 33(11), 1565–88.

Kohl, T. (2013), I Just Read 296 Trade Agreements, *UNU-CRIS Working Paper* W-2013/9.

König, J. (2014), Measuring European Integration, Göttingen University.

König, J. and Ohr, R. (2013), Different Efforts in European Economic Integration: Implications of the EU Index, *Journal of Common Market Studies*, 51(6), 1074–90.

Mongelli, F.P., Dorrucci, E., and Agur, I. (2005), What Does European Institutional Integration Tell Us About Trade Integration? *ECB Occasional Paper Series* No. 40.

Nitsch, V. and Pisu, M. (2008), Scalpel, Please! Dissecting the Euro's Effect on Trade, ETH Zürich and National Bank of Belgium.

Obstfeld, M. and Rogoff, K. (2001), The Six Major Puzzles in International Macroeconomics: Is There a Common Cause?, in Bernanke, B.S. and Rogoff, K. (eds) *NBER Macroeconomics Annual: 2000*, Cambridge, MA: MIT Press.

Rodriguez, F. and Rodrik, D. (2001), Trade Policy and Economic Growth: A Skeptic's Guide to the Cross-National Evidence, in Bernanke, B.S. and Rogoff, K. (eds) *NBER Macroeconomics Annual: 2000*, Cambridge, MA: MIT Press.

Volosovych, V. (2011), Measuring Financial Market Integration over the Long Run: Is there a U-Shape? *Journal of International Money and Finance*, 30(7), 1535–61.

Volosovych, V. (2013), Learning about Financial Market Integration from Principle Components Analysis, *CESifo Economic Studies*, 59(2), 360–91.

29

THE DYNAMICS OF EUROPEAN ECONOMIC INTEGRATION

A legal perspective

Erich Vranes[1]

1. Introduction

European integration is a process of economic and political regional transformation of unprecedented dynamism. It is clear that the EU, and its predecessors (ECSC, EEC, EC[2]), are at the centre of this dynamic. From the perspective of political science, there are several rivalling theories striving to explain why economic and political integration has been moving forward on a quasi-automatic basis[3] in the EU, and why it has spilt over to neighbouring countries, several of which have over the years joined the EU, the latter having been functioning as an economic and political centre of gravity since its very beginnings. From a legal viewpoint, there are likewise many features that can be cited as an explanation for this dynamic economic integration, and the political transformation of Europe that ensued from it, ranging from factors such as the specific institutional structures of the former Community and the EU, the rules establishing the internal market, the EU's far-reaching internal and external competences and many more.

Usually, however, lawyers refer to the fundamental principles underlying the formal and substantive constitution of the EU as reasons for this quasi-automatic economic and political integration and transformation process.[4] As regards relevant formal principles, these comprise the direct effect of EU law, its supremacy, and − ostensibly a technicality − the preliminary reference procedure, which has taken a 'veritably prodigious' development during the initial years of the EEC's existence.[5] Furthermore, regarding the formal-institutional aspects that have accelerated the integration project, lawyers commonly refer to the specific powers of the former Community's and today's Union's institutions that have utterly distinguished them from any existing international organization. On the other hand, there are the substantive principles, such as that of mutual recognition, which serve as fundaments of the internal market and, just as the formal principles, have been defined and further developed by the ECJ in its case law. By having been ingeniously coupled with the aforementioned formal principles and the specific powers of the Community's and Union's institutions, these substantive principles have made EU integration a self-sustaining transformation process that is spurred by overlapping political, economic and individual interests.

It has also been said that the formal principles that where developed by the ECJ in the early 1960s constitute the defining characteristics of EU law[6] and have 'transcended anything that has happened since' in the 'inexorable dynamism of enhanced supranationalism' in the EU integration project.[7] In the words of historians, the last half-century in Europe can hardly be appreciated without understanding the role of law and the judiciary.[8] In this particular regard, it has been pointed out by one of the drafters of the EEC Treaty, *Pierre Pescatore*, that the European integration project is channelled by a very small number of legal rules, namely the aforementioned formal and substantive principles, in particular.[9] For reasons of space restraint, and in line with this view, which probably is shared by virtually any EU lawyer, this contribution will place its focus first on the relevant formal principles of EU law; it will then briefly address the specific powers of the EU institutions, and will finally explain the most important substantive principles underlying the internal market.

2. The formal constitution: Direct effect, supremacy, and preliminary references

2.1 Background

The political expectations after the Second World War were famously expressed by *Winston Churchill* in 1946, when he claimed that '[w]e must build a kind of United States of Europe [...] The first step in the re-creation of the European family must be a partnership between France and Germany [...] The structure of the United States of Europe will be such as to make the material strength of a single State less important. Small nations will count as much as large ones [...].'[10]

Building on *Churchill's* vision, the *Schuman Plan*, developed by *Jean Monnet* in April and May 1950 and presented by *Robert Schuman* on 9 May 1950, proposed

> that action be taken immediately on one limited but decisive point. [The French Government] proposes that Franco-German production of coal and steel as a whole be placed under a common High Authority, within the framework of an organization open to the participation of the other countries of Europe. The pooling of coal and steel production should immediately provide for the setting up of common foundations for economic development as a first step in the federation of Europe [...] In this way, there will be realised simply and speedily that fusion of interest which is indispensable to the establishment of a common economic system; it may be the leaven from which may grow a wider and deeper community [...].[11]

Although *Monnet* avoided the term 'supranationality', he made it very clear, as head of the diplomatic conference drafting the ECSC treaty, that the integration project was not to be based on any conventional type of international organization or cooperation.[12]

While the *Schuman Plan's* implications for the Community and EU institutions will be discussed below, it should be recalled – as regards the background for understanding the legal, political and economic impacts of the *formal* principles of Community and EU law – that enthusiasm for supranational and federalist views of Europe rapidly declined during the 1950s. Therefore, the EEC treaty – which later on became the EC treaty and then today's Treaty on the Functioning of the EU (TFEU) – bore more features of classic intergovernmental co-operation than the ECSC treaty. Crucially, however, although the majority of governments appeared to be opposed to supranational characteristics of, and a constitutional basis for, the EEC, during the negotiations on the EEC treaty, the *groupe de rédaction*, consisting of a small number of jurists, together with the help of some politicians and diplomats were able to discretely insert some ambiguous clauses into the EEC treaty that allowed both an understanding of the treaty in terms of classic international law (and traditional intergovern-mentalism) and a constitutional reading. The relevant provisions were in particular those dealing with infringement proceedings (to be brought by the Commission or Member States against a Member State failing to carry out its obligations under the treaty; Articles 169–171 EEC treaty), the preliminary reference procedure (Article 177 EEC treaty, to be discussed below), secondary law (Article 189 EEC treaty, expressly attributing direct effect to regulations), the concept of a community of law ('*Rechtsgemeinschaft*' as opposed to a classic international organization, Article 164 EEC treaty), and the liability of the EEC (Article 215 EEC treaty).

It is telling, for example, that the *groupe de rédaction* consciously relegated the concept of 'EU laws', as regards terminology, to 'regulations' so as to make their direct effect – and the analogy with state laws – less conspicuous for the Member States.[13] A further example for discretely introducing quasi-constitutional concepts in the treaty is the fact that the EEC's liability was modelled on domestic constitutional law as opposed to the international responsibility of international organizations.[14] It is equally revealing that the legal report on the new EEC treaty for the Luxembourg House of Representatives stated that:

> In reality, the new Communities are more pragmatic than legal; they are based on principles, but above all on the individuals to whom they are entrusted and who, to the extent permitted by the political and economic conditions, will make of them what they want them to be.[15]

It was this possibility of a constitutional reading which eventually enabled the legal and judicial transformation of Europe through the ECJ's development, above all, of the formal principles of direct effect and supremacy.[16]

2.2 The van Gend *ruling: The introduction of direct effect*

As has been shown by legal historians, from the very first case that was brought before the ECJ when the ECSC had entered into force, the legal service of the High Authority (the predecessor of the Commission) tried to convince the ECJ to develop a teleological interpretation of the EEC treaty taking full account of its aforementioned quasi-constitutional, federal potential. Initially the legal service did not achieve a decisive breakthrough.[17] When the EEC came into existence in 1958, the legal service, led by *Michel Gaudet* and backed by *Walter Hallstein* as Commission President, began to perceive of the potential direct effect and primacy of the EEC treaty within the national legal orders as the main means for making EEC law and the rules meant to establish the common market more effective. Moreover, according to the legal service's view, these rules should uniformly be interpreted by the ECJ, making EEC law a 'genuine *droit communautaire*'. The potential means for the latter aim consisted in the preliminary reference procedure.[18]

Already in 1963, the Commission was able to secure the aspired victory and to convince the ECJ of its understanding of the treaty in the ground-breaking *van Gend* case.[19] This case, dealing with the EEC prohibition on Member States to increase tariffs, raised the fundamental question of direct effect of EEC law, namely whether this provision could be invoked by individuals against a Member State before national courts. Moreover, in this case the ECJ also had to deal with the systemic preliminary question as to whether the route chosen by the litigants in this case, namely the preliminary reference procedure, could lawfully be used by individuals, although questions as to whether a Member State has violated EEC law apparently ought to be addressed, upon legal action by the Commission or other Member States, in infringement proceedings against the Member State in question.

The momentousness of the first question becomes clear when one considers how international law ordinarily deals with the issue of direct effect. International law leaves it to the *national* constitutional law of any given State to decide whether or not it attributes direct effect to norms of international law, thereby empowering its national courts and/or authorities to apply norms of international law in concrete cases and, possibly, its individuals to invoke such norms within a State. Hence, pursuant to the interplay between traditional international law and national constitutional law, individuals hold those rights which accrue to them under national law and those rights, stemming from international law, which have deliberately been declared by a State to exert direct effect in the domestic legal order (or which have explicitly been transformed by a State into national law, the exact techniques of transformation depending on the constitutional law of any individual State).[20]

In the *van Gend* ruling, the ECJ reversed these principles of international and national constitutional law, thereby revolutionizing[21] international relations and the interplay of international law and national law in the Community: according to the ECJ, the EEC treaty, 'is more than an agreement which merely creates mutual obligations between the contracting states'. Relying on interpretative arguments such as the treaty's preamble, the sovereign rights that had been transferred on the Community institutions, their effects on citizens, the existence of the European Parliament and the preliminary reference procedure, the ECJ concluded that the Community constitutes

> a *new legal order of international law* [...] the subjects of which comprise not only Member States but also their nationals. *Independently of the legislation of Member States*, Community law therefore not only imposes obligations on individuals but is also intended to confer upon them rights' which they can invoke before national courts as against the Member States.[22]

In the concrete case, the ECJ held that the relevant norm of Community law contained a clear and unconditional prohibition, which did not depend on any further implementing measures by the Community or its Member States. Furthermore, the ECJ found that the aforementioned alternative procedural avenue of infringement proceedings (to be started by the Commission or Member States) does not mean that individuals cannot invoke the directive effect of such norms against a Member State before its national courts. Conspicuously, the ECJ reasoned that 'the vigilance of individuals concerned to protect their rights amounts to an *effective supervision* in addition to' infringement proceedings.[23]

2.3 Direct effect: The economic and legal consequences

Practically and economically speaking, the impact of the doctrine of direct effect is tremendous, as any individual in the EU has become a potential plaintiff who can invoke Community (today: Union) law against every Member State. In other words, the *van Gend* judgment has created a virtually infinite number of 'private attorney generals' who can take action against any EU Member State that violates its EU obligations by invoking the rights they derive from EU law. This vast 'enforcement pull' arguably constitutes the most effective enforcement model not only due to the sheer number of potential legal actions, but also since very real economic, political and social interests of the individual and private enterprises, which are protected by EU law, are utilized to promote the public interest of ensuring Member State compliance with their obligations under EU law.[24]

Legally speaking, the weaknesses of the *public* enforcement of EU law, through infringement proceedings by the Commission against Members States, have been more than made up for by this model of *private* enforcement: whereas the Commission and Member States may hesitate to take legal action against another Member State when disputes might have political consequences or when 'small violations' are at issue,[25] individuals and private enterprises typically will not have such concerns. Moreover, the legal empowerment of individuals through direct effect overcomes the problem that the Commission has limited resources for investigating alleged infringements of EU law. Finally, the fact that, due to direct effect, the final rulings in domestic proceedings between individuals and Member States are rendered by national courts has made the enforcement of such judgments highly effective: as has been emphasized by *Weiler,* it is virtually impossible for Western democracies to disregard the rulings of their own domestic courts.[26]

In its subsequent jurisprudence, the ECJ has expanded the doctrine of direct effect in several ways. On the one hand, it has loosened the conditions which it had defined for direct effect in *van Gend*, where it had required that norms, in order to be capable of exercising such effect, must be precise and unconditional prohibitions that do not depend on further implementing measures by the Community or its Member States: according to the ECJ's expansive approach, even a norm granting discretion to Member States (such as Article 36 TFEU, which allows Member States to plead e.g. public health concerns as a justification for restricting the free movement of goods) can be invoked directly against Member States in national proceedings.[27] The same holds true for treaty provisions that require implementing measures by the EU or its Member States.[28] This approach has led to the result that for a norm to be directly effective it is sufficient that a national court – with the possible assistance of the ECJ in the preliminary reference procedure – is able to apply a provision of EU law in the case at hand.[29] The underlying 'judicial activism' of the ECJ has been explained as a reaction to the 'legislative sclerosis' that had resulted from the 1966 Luxembourg Compromise, which will be discussed below and which enabled each Member State to veto the adoption of secondary law and thereby impair the progress of integration: the need to (unceasingly) wait for legislative action by the Member States within in the Council was to a considerable extent overcome by the ECJ's reaction of declaring an ever increasing number of treaty norms to be directly effective in Member States.[30]

Furthermore, the ECJ extended the concept of direct effect to other legal instruments, namely decisions,[31] general principles,[32] most international agreements,[33] and directives which have not been implemented into national law in due time or which have been implemented incorrectly.[34] The ECJ also requires national administrative authorities to take account of the direct effect of EU law[35] (even though administrative authorities appear to rarely comply with this duty[36]) and obliges all national courts and authorities to interpret national law in line with EU law, which incurs a practically important 'indirect effect' of EU law.[37]

The ECJ's doctrine of direct effect has also served as the first essential building block for the constitutionalization of Community and Union law, which has large-scale consequences regarding the balance of powers on the levels of EU law and national law, and in the interaction of these planes. As these effects result in particular from the interplay between direct effect and two further constitutional building blocks, namely supremacy and the preliminary reference system, it is to these that we will turn in the next two sections.

2.4 The supremacy of EU law

The direct effect of Community and Union law has always been meant to make relevant norms decisively more effective, in particular those dealing with the internal market. It is obvious that a true common market requires a legal 'level playing-field', which necessitates that EU law applies equally in all Member States. This of course requires that the Member States cannot invoke national law against EU law. In other words: EU law must take precedence over national law, in principle. Although this issue was not openly addressed in the *van Gend* judgment, establishing the primacy of Community law vis à vis national law was the 'logical' next step that was to be expected of the ECJ.

The occasion for addressing this question presented itself almost immediately after *van Gend* in the 1964 *Costa/ENEL* case. In this case, which involved a conflict between an EEC treaty provision and an Italian act of parliament, the Italian Constitutional Court had already ruled that the Italian norm, which was later in time and arguably more specific, prevailed over Community law. This decision was perceived as a vital danger for the EEC project,[38] which the ECJ tried to avert by holding that 'the integration into the laws of each Member State of provisions which derive from the Community, and more generally the terms and spirit of the Treaty, make it impossible for the states, as a corollary, to accord precedence to a unilateral and subsequent measure over a legal system accepted by them on the basis of reciprocity. Such a measure cannot therefore be inconsistent with that legal system. The executive force of Community law cannot vary from one State to another in deference to subsequent laws, without jeopardizing the attainment of the objectives of the Treaty [...].'[39]

Hence, by adopting a teleological interpretation focusing on the uniformity and effectiveness of Community law, the ECJ concluded that Community norms enjoy supremacy vis à vis national law, even if national law is later in time or more special. By distinguishing Community law from 'normal' international law and by developing the principle of supremacy, the ECJ has managed to overcome two practically highly important weaknesses of international law: its lack of internal primacy and uniform application in national legal orders.[40]

As has become clear in later cases, the ECJ's doctrine of supremacy is particularly far-reaching, the Court claiming that any piece of EU law (even secondary and tertiary law such as 'minor' Commission regulations) takes precedence over any conflicting rules of national law, be they rules of constitutional rank or human rights.[41] It does not come as a surprise that Member State courts have not fully accepted this claim of supremacy, in particular as regards (fundamental principles of) national constitutional law. This resistance, expressed in several landmark rulings by national supreme courts, has not only prompted the ECJ to develop a comprehensive EU human rights jurisprudence, which is meant to mitigate the consequences of the far-reaching doctrine of supremacy.[42] It has also acted as a catalyst in the debates leading to the EU Charter of Fundamental Rights and the (failed) attempt of setting into force the Treaty Establishing a Constitution for Europe.

2.5 Direct effect, supremacy, and preliminary references

The extensive consequences of the principles of direct effect and supremacy cannot fully be understood, unless one also takes into account their interlinkages with the preliminary reference procedure. According to this procedural device, domestic courts may – and courts of last instance must in principle – refer questions on the interpretation of EU law to the

ECJ, whose answers are to be taken into account by the national courts, which also render the final judgments in such proceedings.[43]

Originally, this procedure was meant to enable the ECJ to promote a uniform application of EU law throughout the Union. It was not conceived, by the drafters of the EEC treaty, that it could be used by individuals to sue Member States for transgressions of EU law. In plain contrast, after the *van Gend* ruling, the preliminary reference system has developed into the 'infringement procedure of the European citizen'.[44] Its ties with the doctrines of direct effect and supremacy have been particularly well described by *Weiler*: direct effect makes EU law the 'law of the land' in every Member State; supremacy makes it the 'higher law of the land'.[45] The fact that this higher law can be invoked as a shield against national law before all national courts makes it so effective in concrete proceedings, but also, more generally, in furthering integration. Nonetheless, as pointed out by *Weiler*, national judges will often perceive EU law as 'foreign law' and may also hesitate to convict their own State. These are two further aspects where the preliminary reference procedure comes in as a 'remedy': as regards the first problem, preliminary rulings of the ECJ help national courts become familiarized with this supranational type of 'foreign law', in that they do not really have 'to grapple with hermeneutic uncertainty'. As regards the second problem, the ECJ's interpretation is *de facto* binding for the domestic courts of all Member States, so a single domestic court 'is not alone' when it enforces EU law against its own government.[46]

2.6 Implications, transformation and constitutionalization

In sum, due to the doctrine of direct effect, EU institutions can reach the individual directly, without the intermediary of the Member States.[47] Moreover, supreme EU law is directly infused into national proceedings.[48] Due to the judicial coupling of direct effect and supremacy, individuals can force EU Member States to change national law, thereby promoting the progress of legal, economic and political transformation.

In addition, given the interaction between direct effect, supremacy and the preliminary reference procedure, a uniform interpretation of this 'higher law of the land' is ensured, which is not only essential for the common market, but has also helped to create a community of law, which has brought the EU construct closer to *Monnet's* and *Hallstein's* vision of founding a new kind of political organization that has very little in common with traditional international organizations and is much closer to a federalized system.[49] Hence, the ECJ's jurisprudence, in using the constitutional potential of the EEC treaty, has considerably contributed to the creation of a *sui generis* legal order that is 'coherent, effective and significantly more influential in the national legal systems' than public international law.[50]

However, these legal developments have not only spurred economic integration. They have also incurred fundamental constitutional and political transformations: on the one hand, the role of courts has been strengthened at the expense of the national executive and legislature,[51] and national courts have acquired a double role, in that they have functionally also become EU courts, when they are required to apply EU law and declare conflicting national law inapplicable.[52] At the same time, the armoury of individuals willing to take action against Member States has been remarkably enriched, by making them subjects of the supranational legal order, entitled to invoke EU rights invested with legal primacy over national law.[53]

It has, therefore, often been asked why the Member States have accepted these judicially developed legal principles, which are at the source of these transformations. One possible explanation is provided by *Weiler's* 'equilibrium theory', according to which the Member States did not feel threatened by the supranational features of EU law, at least as long as they were able to control the legislative process at the supranational level through their individual veto, a veto that was guaranteed by the Luxembourg Accords until the mid-1980s at least.[54] It has also been presumed that the apparent technicalities of direct effect, supremacy and preliminary references have made their constitutional effects lack saliency in the political realm. Another explanation is that a fundamental renegotiation of the EEC treaty would have been politically unthinkable in the 1960s and 1970s and that the original Member States came to implicitly accept these principles, which, moreover, were explicitly confirmed, as part of the *acquis communautaire*, in the successive rounds of accessions of new Member States.[55] Furthermore, it may have been an 'incentive' for Member State governments that, by having been empowered to enact directly effective law that takes precedence over national law, they have been enabled to escape the constraints of national parliaments on many occasions.[56] National courts, on the other hand, may have accepted direct effect and supremacy, as they possibly have been perceived as ensuing from a convincing interpretation in line with the teleology of the original EEC treaty; additionally, it should not be overlooked that (lower) national courts have seen their powers substantially increased through these formal principles of Community and Union law, in that they, having received the competence to declare national law inapplicable, have become 'negative legislators' even in Member States where such a role is in principle reserved to constitutional or supreme courts.[57]

3. The specific powers of the EU institutions

3.1 Supranational versus intergovernmental structures and dynamics

As indicated above, the Community has been, and the EU is, characterised by an institutional structure that has set them clearly apart from any international organization. At the same time, the EU institutions, and their balance of powers, do not correspond to traditional nation state concepts. This specific institutional framework has its origin in the 1950 *Schuman Plan* (and arguably also in the professional experiences of its principal author, *Jean Monnet*[58]), which regarded the High Authority as the crucial organ of the ECSC. Necessary compromises in the ECSC treaty negotiations eventually led to a four-pillar structure, in which the High Authority held considerable administrative powers to apply relatively clear-cut treaty rules, which were balanced by the competences of the other three institutions.[59]

Although the ECSC agreement was used as a model for the 1957 EEC treaty,[60] the latter's drafters were bound by a compromise decision taken at political level, which was to become a defining characteristic of the Community's and Union's institutional structure: thus, the principal decision-making powers were initially vested in the Council (the European Parliament having acquired broader decision-making powers only later on), but the right to legislative initiative[61] lay with the Commission, whose proposals could only be amended by a unanimous vote in the Council.[62] Since, by contrast with the ECSC agreement, the EEC treaty, to a considerable extent, merely contained general principles and objectives, and provided procedures for rendering them more precise and operative,[63] the original institutional concept of the Community was described as the Commission in principle occupying the driving seat.[64]

While during the first years of its existence, the EEC was perceived as a 'pragmatic economic community under construction' with an undecided political dimension and open-ended political objectives that appeared acceptable for all political currents,[65] tensions soon arose, when, according to the treaty, the EEC Council was to move to majority voting in 1966. French President *de Gaulle* regarding the possibility of being outvoted as a threat to the Member States' role as the 'Masters of the Treaty', France resorted to its ominous empty chair policy of failing to participate in Council meetings for six months, thereby triggering a constitutional crisis that could only be resolved through the 1966 Luxembourg Accords. Pursuant to this compromise, which in essence is an 'agreement to disagree', the Member States decided that 'where, in the case of decisions which may be taken by a majority vote on a proposal from the Commission, very important interests of one or more partners are at stake, the Members of the Council will endeavour, within a reasonable time, to reach solutions which can be adopted by all the Members [...]'. The Accords noted also 'that there is a divergence of views on what should be done in the event of a failure to reach complete agreement'. As the Accords concluded that 'this divergence does not prevent the Community's work being resumed in accordance with the normal procedure',[66] the immediate crisis was overcome, but the Community's decision-making capacity continued to be severely hampered well into the 1980s, since the Council would consistently strive for unanimity due to the threat of the veto of a Member State pleading 'vital' national interests.[67]

The impacts of the Luxembourg Accords have been significant and manifold. On the one hand, they were a major cause of the aforementioned legislative sclerosis of the Community, which lasted until the adoption of the Single European Act (SEA) in the 1980s (on the SEA see Section 3.2). On the other hand, the possibility for each Member State to unilaterally veto the enactment of secondary law by the Council has arguably made the principles of direct effect and supremacy tolerable for the Member States, thus safeguarding essential elements of the supranational character of the Community – elements which were consistently further developed by the ECJ, as has been indicated in the text above. Moreover, the impairment of the Community's legislative capacity has arguably been a major factor for the ECJ's introduction of the constitutional principle of mutual recognition (on this principle, see Section 4 below).

While the Luxembourg Accords, which have never been formally repealed,[68] have represented an important intergovernmentalist counterweight against the supranational dynamism of the Community, they are not the only means through which the Member States have been able to re-increase their *intergovernmental* influence on European integration. While the Luxembourg Compromise has permitted them to invoke essential national interests to block supranational legislation, they have been able to more subtly, but effectively, influence integration by other institutional devices: thus, the Coreper (*Comité des représentants permanents*), established at the very first Council meeting in 1958 and consisting of national diplomats, is highly influential in the preparation of Council meetings and decisions, the Coreper's members acting both as state agents and supranational actors.[69] Another instrument is the Comitology system, introduced in the 1960s and substantially extended and revised several times, which enables the Member States to control the Commission, when the latter enacts implementing measures.[70] Furthermore, the European Council, which emanated from informal meetings of the heads of state in the 1960s and was institutionalized in 1974, has become ever more influential in the shaping of the general political strategies and evolution of the EU: it has always been closely involved in the EU's external relations, treaty amendments, EU accessions, institutional issues and other questions of fundamental political nature.[71]

3.2 The SEA: Legislative ability to act regained

In 1985, a White Paper on the internal market was presented by the Commission, enumerating 279 legislative measures to be adopted so as to complete the internal market until 1992.[72] This paper took a technocratic approach to the common market goal that appeared acceptable to all Member States, making it possible for them to agree on *majority voting* in the 1986 SEA revising the EEC treaty. Importantly, majority voting also applied under a new clause giving the Community the power to harmonize Member State laws, where such measures had 'as their object the establishment and functioning of the internal market' (Article 100a EEC Treaty, now Article 114 TFEU).[73] This central provision had the effect that practically all decision-making then functioned under the majority principle, effectively reviving the Community and allowing it to regain a legislative dynamic that had been stifled with the Luxembourg Accords.[74]

This return to majority voting has been regarded as virtually as fundamental a transformation as the *van Gend* ruling: while direct effect, supremacy and preliminary references have made it possible for individuals and courts to push on integration on the occasion of concrete cases, the SEA has greatly accelerated the dynamism of this process, as individual Member States could now be outvoted, having to accept the enactment of general rules that are likewise directly applicable, taking precedence over their national law.[75]

4. The material constitution: Principles of internal market law

Central to this dynamic is the internal market which is the focus of EU legislation and the rights that are invoked by individuals on the basis of direct effect, supremacy, and preliminary references. Hence, it is the internal market, to which we will turn now.

The goal of the internal market has always been the essential driving force in EU integration, economically just as politically. Legally speaking, it has been the 'logic' of a relatively small number of landmark ECJ rulings concerning substantive EU law, which – through their interaction with the formal principles and the passing of EU legislation that has been described above – have untied the vast integrative potential of the fundamental freedoms that form the basis of the internal market. These seminal judgments on substantive internal market law – in particular *Dassonville, Cassis, Keck* and some more recent rulings – have all concerned the free movement of goods. Since they have served as a conceptual model, which the ECJ has at least in part transposed to the other freedoms,[76] and for reasons of space, this section essentially focuses on these classic verdicts in the free movement of goods as examples *par excellence* of the EU's market-based integration dynamic.

A first important case, that preceded the leading cases and set the tone in this field, was *Statistical Levy*, which concerned an Italian charge levied on imported and exported products in order to finance statistical inquiries on transborder movements of goods. The Court held that even a non-discriminatory

> pecuniary charge, however small [. . .] which is imposed unilaterally on domestic or foreign goods by reason of the fact that they cross a frontier, and which is not a customs duty in the strict sense constitutes a charge having equivalent effect [. . .], even if it is not imposed for the benefit of the state, is not discriminatory or protective in effect and if the product on which the charge is imposed is not in competition with any domestic product.[77]

This strict approach, according to which *any non-discriminatory obstacles* to trade are to be removed, has lastingly influenced the ECJ's foundational case law in this field, as it has been extended, from pecuniary border measures, to qualitative internal regulations in *Dassonville*, one of the ECJ's most important decisions: pursuant to this ruling on what is Article 34 TFEU today, 'all trade rules enacted by the Member States which are capable of hindering, directly or indirectly, actually or potentially, intra-Community trade are to be considered as measures having an effect equivalent to quantitative restrictions'.[78] In later judgments, the ECJ has extended this formula from trade regulations to any state measures.[79] Originally, such restrictions could be justified under a limited number of exceptions only.[80]

For many years, this landmark judgment has been read as implying that the internal market relies on the principle of removing any Member State *obstacles* to trade, thus going well beyond a mere prohibition on discriminatory domestic regulation.[81] It has allowed the ECJ to scrutinize even non-discriminatory product-related and non-product-related measures[82] as to their necessity and proportionality, virtually inviting legal action by private businesses, whenever they saw their economic freedom impeded.[83] It has, however, been submitted that this judicial approach of establishing analogous judicial scrutiny regimes for charges having an effect equivalent to tariffs (*Statistical Levy*) and for domestic regulations (*Dassonville*) was misconceived: customs duties, and charges having an equivalent effect, typically are presumed to be protectionist or discriminatory.[84] This sweeping presumption cannot simply be transposed to internal qualitative regulations dealing with matters such as health or safety standards of products, as such domestic regulations are not necessarily protectionist *per se* and may have non-discriminatory impacts on imported and domestic products. Hence, a more appropriate approach would have been to treat EU rules on domestic regulation in analogy with EU rules on *internal* taxation, which are not obstacle-based, but according to which only Member State measures with differential effects on imported products (which cannot be justified on non-economic grounds) are illegal.[85]

Although the *Dassonville* approach can rightly be criticized on the aforementioned grounds, it needs to be recognized that it has promoted market integration by inciting private business to challenge perceived impediments to trade. It has also contributed to market integration by greatly extending the Community's harmonization competence, which as mentioned above, has functioned on the basis of majority voting after the SEA (Article 100a EEC Treaty, now Article 114 TFEU[86]) and is applicable, in particular, whenever a Member State measure is justified as being necessary for non-economic concerns under Article 36 TFEU (or under mandatory requirements as defined in the *Cassis* case,[87] to which we will turn now).

In *Cassis*, the second ground-breaking case, the ECJ reconfirmed that Article 34 prohibits non-discriminatory obstacles to trade (subject to justification under Article 36), but it also recognized a new unwritten category of non-exhaustive legitimate 'mandatory requirements' that can be invoked by Member States to justify national regulation that impedes trade, thereby correcting the conceptual incongruity between the exceedingly broad reading of the *prima facie* prohibition in Article 34 in *Dassonville*, on the one hand, and the narrow, exhaustive list of grounds for justification in Article 36, on the other hand. Furthermore, in *Cassis* the ECJ introduced the principle of mutual recognition, according to which a product, which has lawfully been produced and marketed in one Member State, is allowed to circulate freely in all Member States (unless State restrictions can be justified under Article 36 or mandatory requirements recognised by the ECJ).

As the principle of mutual recognition also applies when no relevant harmonizing legisla-tion exists, *Cassis* has clearly promoted integration.[88] Besides, this jurisprudence also caused the Commission to fundamentally reconsider its legislative approach in the 1980s: under its so-called 'new approach to harmonization', it in particular decided henceforth to concentrate its legislative harmonization efforts on tackling domestic technical and qualitative regulations that impair trade, but can be justified under Article 36 or the mandatory requirements intro-duced by the ECJ in *Cassis*.[89] Furthermore, the Community has required its Member States, since the 1980s, to communicate to the Commission and the other Members States any draft technical regulations that one of them intends to enact, the Commission being entitled to proactively adopt or propose harmonizing secondary law on the supranational level.[90] Under the 'new approach', the EU restricts itself to defining essential health and safety requirements, which are then specified, in detail, by private standardization organizations, so that policy goals are harmonized, while the regulatory means remain flexible.[91] Such specifications are not legally binding *per se*, but create a presumption that compliant products are in conformity with the aforementioned essential requirements, obliging any Member State to admit such goods to its market, unless it can reverse this presumption. This new approach, which greatly benefitted from the SEA-based return to majority voting and was reformed in 2008, has perceptibly accelerated legislation.[92]

Whereas the *Cassis* principle of mutual recognition represents an important basic component of the 'new approach' in the legislative field, the *Cassis* ruling did not fully resolve another dilemma that dates back to *Dassonville:* as mentioned above, the judicial recognition, in *Cassis*, of the category of 'mandatory requirements' mitigated the broad reading of Article 34 in *Dassonville,* enabling the Member States to invoke additional, non-economic grounds for justifying restrictions of trade. However, every Member State nonetheless remained under a duty to constantly show that its regulatory measures pursuing legitimate goals were least trade-restrictive, even when they were non-discriminatory, whenever it was sued by private persons or enterprises.

This is where the third leading case comes into play. Since the *Dassonville* formula was used, in conjunction with direct effect and the supremacy of EU law, ever more frequently by private businesses to question even non-discriminatory state regulations, the ECJ declared in its 1993 *Keck* ruling, that 'the Court considers it necessary to re-examine and clarify its case law on this matter'. Explicitly overruling its constant jurisprudence, the ECJ found that

> contrary to what has previously been decided, the application to products from other Member States of national provisions restricting or prohibiting certain selling arrangements is not such as to hinder directly or indirectly, actually or potentially, trade between Member States within the meaning of the *Dassonville* judgment [. . .], so long as those provisions apply to all relevant traders operating within the national territory and so long as they affect in the same manner, in law and in fact, the marketing of domestic products and of those from other Member States.[93]

Hence, in *Keck* the ECJ has expressly restricted its far-reaching *Dassonville* formula, which had arguably stretched the prohibition in Article 34 TFEU to the maximum,[94] thereby restoring considerable regulatory autonomy to the Member States. Likewise, by limiting the reach of Article 34 TFEU, the harmonization competence of the EU (which is also triggered when a domestic regulation comes under Article 34, even if it 'survives' scrutiny under Article 36 or the 'mandatory requirements), was curtailed.[95]

This judicial turnaround has provoked a sustained intense academic discussion, which cannot fully be restated here.[96] One principal reason for this controversy has been the debatable adequacy of the concept of 'selling arrangements', which was central to *Keck*. It is to be noted, however, that the ECJ has also held in *Keck* that provided that the aforementioned conditions are fulfilled (i.e. equal treatment of all traders and of products imported from other Member States), 'the application of such rules to the sale of products from another Member State meeting the requirements laid down by that State is not by nature such as to prevent their *access to the market* or to impede *access* any more than it impedes the access of domestic products. Such rules therefore fall outside the scope of [Article 34 TFEU]'.[97] In later cases such as *Gourmet* and *Mickelsson*, the ECJ has arguably clarified and reconfirmed that its new approach to determining the ambit of Article 34 hinges on the concept of market access.[98]

Even though the concept of 'market access' may not have acquired an unambiguous meaning so far,[99] the ECJ's judicial tendency seems to have become clearer: accordingly, rules that are non-discriminatory, that do not impose product requirements and do not significantly impair market access, arguably may not come under Article 34 TFEU anymore. Hence, national measures of this type would not need to be justified by the Member States, which are not, therefore, required to design such measures to be least restrictive of trade.[100] Consequently, although several details are still uncertain, the Member States have regained considerable regulatory freedom through the *Keck* and post-*Keck* case law.

In sum, while *Dassonville* has represented a distinctly liberalist approach, that – in conjunction with direct effect, supremacy and preliminary rulings – has incited many individuals to challenge even Member State rules whose specific impact on trade may have been doubtful, the court's re-orientation in *Keck* and post-*Keck* has arguably been attempting to steer this dynamism into more appropriate channels that are genuinely conducive to transborder market integration.

5. Concluding remarks

Even after more than sixty years of progress achieved within the EU integration project, it is still correct to observe that, in legal terms, this process relies on the – originally wholly unusual – interplay between a small number of formal and substantive principles and some quite special powers of the EU institutions.[101] Also, for more than sixty years, *Jean Monnet's* prediction has proved true that institutions, which have been successfully put into operation, will remain in existence for decades. However, although the successes of the integration project have been numerous, unique and of genuinely transformative impact in Europe, former objectives having become a truly common reality,[102] it should not be forgotten that some elements of this interplay, and its interaction with national law and politics, may at times be fragile and should not be taken for granted.

Notes

1 The author wishes to thank *Mag.ᵃ Martina Almhofer, LL.M. (WU), B.Sc. (WU)* for her valuable research assistance.
2 The European Community of Coal and Steel (ECSC) was in force from 1952 until 2002; the European Economic Community (EEC) entered into force in 1958. The EEC was renamed European Community (EC), when the EU came into force in 1993. Until 2009, the EU constituted the common roof for three 'pillars', the first pillar comprising the EC, the ECSC and Euratom, the second pillar comprising the EU's Common Foreign Security Policy, and the third pillar comprising Justice and Home Affairs (Police and Judicial Cooperation in Criminal Matters after 1999). With the entry into force of the Lisbon Treaty in 2009, the EU has become the legal successor to the EC. When this contribution uses the term 'Community', it refers to the EEC or EC, respectively.
3 See e.g. Stone Sweet, (2011) 122 ff, at 133; Craig, (2011) 13, at 14 ff; Barnard, (2013) 13 ff.
4 These issues have been explained in two truly seminal papers, which have shaped the field and constitute inevitable conceptual guidelines: see, on the one hand, Weiler, (1991) 2402; and, on the other hand, Weiler, (2002) 201.
5 See Pescatore, (1981) 159, at 173.
6 de Witte, (2011) 323 ff.
7 Weiler, (1991) 2402, at 2410 ff.
8 Davies and Rasmussen, (2012) 305 ff, at 310.
9 Pescatore, (1981) 159, at 177–178.

10 *Winston Churchill*, speech delivered at the University of Zurich, 19 September 1946, available at the website of the Council of Europe (www.coe.int/t/dgal/dit/ilcd/archives/selection/churchill/ZurichSpeech_en.asp), last visited 22 July 2014.

11 Schuman Declaration, presented by French foreign minister Robert Schuman on 9 May 1950, available at the website of the EU (http://europa.eu/about-eu/basic-information/symbols/europe-day/schuman-declaration/index_en.htm), last visited 22 July 2014.

12 See the memoirs of *Monnet*: Monnet, (1988) 367 ff and 403 ff.

13 Pescatore, (1981) 159, at 171.

14 Pescatore, (1981) 159, at 175; on this see also Boerger-de Smedt, (2012), 339, at 347 ff.

15 Cited in Boerger-de Smedt, (2012), 339, at 355.

16 Boerger-de Smedt, (2012), 339, at 339 ff; Rasmussen, (2014) 136, at 141 ff and *passim*.

17 Rasmussen, (2014), 136, at 140 ff.

18 See the archive-based historic study by Rasmussen, (2014), 136, at 146–156 (quotation at 152–153).

19 ECJ, judgment of 5 February 1963, *NV Algemene Transport- en Expeditie Onderneming van Gend & Loos v Netherlands Inland Revenue Administration*, Case 26/62, [1963] European Court Reports, 1; the number of analyses of this judgment is legion; for recent contributions cf e.g. *Joseph H.H. Weiler*, Revisiting Van Gend, in Court of Justice of the European Union (ed.), 50th Anniversary of the Judgment in Van Gend en Loos. 1963–2013 (2013) 11 ff; *Marise Cremona*, The Judgment – Framing the Argument, in Court of Justice of the European Union (ed.), 50th Anniversary of the Judgment in Van Gend en Loos. 1963–2013 (2013) 23 ff; see also the other contributions in the aforementioned volume.

20 See e.g. Meng, (1995) 1063; Mayer, Van Gend en Loos, (2010) 16 ff; Weiler, (1991) 2402, 2413 ff.

21 The question as to what extent this judicial move amounts to a legal revolution – although it is regarded as such by most lawyers – is disputed; cf e.g. *Weiler*, who has spoken of a legal revolution in his earlier writings, but now designates the ECJ's ruling as an audacious interpretation based on solid legal hermeneutics (Weiler, Van Gend en Loos, (2014) 94, at 95); see also Rasmussen, (2014), 136.

22 ECJ, judgment of 5 February 1963, *NV Algemene Transport- en Expeditie Onderneming van Gend & Loos v Netherlands Inland Revenue Administration*, Case 26/62, [1963] European Court Reports, 1.

23 ECJ, judgment of 5 February 1963, *NV Algemene Transport- en Expeditie Onderneming van Gend & Loos v Netherlands Inland Revenue Administration*, Case 26/62, [1963] European Court Reports, 1.

24 *Joseph H.H. Weiler*, Van Gend en Loos: The individual as subject and object and the dilemma of European legitimacy, 12 I-CON (2014) 94, at 94 ff; *Paul Craig* and *Grainne de Burca*, EU Law (5th edition, 2011) 186.

25 It should be mentioned, however, that the Commission has committed itself – as part of the strategy to 'complete' the internal market – to improve enforcement inter alia by giving priority to cases which have severe impact on individuals, cf EU Commission, Communication from the Commission – A Europe of Results – Applying Community Law, COM(2007) 502 final.

26 On all of this cf Weiler, (1991) 2402, 2421.

27 ECJ, judgment of 19 December 1968, Case 13/68, *SpA Salgoil* [1968] ECR 453; ECJ, judgment of 4 December 1974, Case 41/74, *Van Duyn* [1974] ECR 1337; on this see also Craig and de Burca, (2011) 186 ff; de Witte, (2011) 323 ff.

28 ECJ, judgment of 21 June 1974, Case 2/74, *Reyners* [1974] ECR 631, paras 15 ff.

29 de Witte, (2011) 323, 329 ff.

30 Cf Craig and de Burca, (2011) 188; Weiler, (1991) 2402, 2423–2424 and *passim*.

31 ECJ, judgment of 6 October 1970, *Franz Grad* [1970] ECR 825, paras 2 ff.

32 See e.g. ECJ, judgment of 26 April 2005, Case C-376/02 *Stichting*, [2005] ECR I-3445, para 32.

33 For an overview cf e.g. *Thomas Oppermann et al*, Europarecht (6th edition, 2014) 620–621.

34 On all of this see de Witte, (2011) 323, at 333 ff; Streinz, (2012) 170 ff, 185, 153 with further references.

35 ECJ, judgment of 22 June 1989, Case 103/88, *Costanzo* [1989] ECR 1839, paras 28 ff.

36 de Witte, (2011) 323, 329 ff.

37 Cf e.g. Wulf-Henning Roth, (2010) 393, at 398 ff; *Gänswein*, (2009) with extensive further references.

38 See Rasmussen, (2010) 69 ff.

39 ECJ, judgment of 15 July 1964, Case 6/64, *Costa/ENEL*, [1964] ECR 585.

40 Rasmussen, (2010) 69, 72–73; de Witte, (2011) 323, 340 ff.

41 ECJ, judgment of 17 December 1970, C-11/70, *Internationale Handelsgesellschaft*, [1970] ECR 1125, paras 3 ff.

42 These barriers to integration are analysed in the country-specific contributions in von Bogdandy et al., (eds) (2008); see also Griller et al, (2011).

43 See Article 234 TFEU; for an in-depth study of the preliminary reference procedure see e.g. Schima, (2004) with comprehensive further references; see also Middeke, (2014) 222 ff.

44 Pescatore, (1981) 159, at 173 ('développement judiciare proprement prodigieux').

45 Weiler, (1991) 2402, at 2413 ff.

46 Weiler, Van Gend en Loos, (2014) 94, at 97.

47 Weiler, (1991) 2402 ff.

48 Halberstam, (2010) 26, at 28 ff.

49 See Monnet, (1988) 367 ff; see also Pernice, (2010) 47 ff.

50 Davies and Rasmussen, (2012) 305, at 305.

51 Hofmann, (2010) 60 ff.

52 Pernice, (1998) 325 ff; Halberstam, (2010) 26, at 28 ff.

53 Weiler, Van Gend en Loos, (2014) 94, at 96 ff.

54 The equlibrium theory was introduced by Weiler, (1991) 2402, 2428; on the Luxembourg Accords see Section 3.A. below.

55 Rasmussen, (2014) 136, at 160 ff.

56 Weiler, (1991) 2402, 2430 and *passim*.

57 Weiler, (1991) 2402, 2423 ff and 2430 ff.

58 *Monnet* had *inter alia* served in executive task forces with special powers during the First and Second World War, as deputy secretary general of the League of Nations and as head of the French post-Second World War Planning Commissariat (Commissariat général du Plan). The task forces, in particular, arguably have had supranational features, cf Monnet, (1988).

59 The Commission's powers were balanced by consultative and restricted decision-making competences vested in the Council, consultative and supervisory powers of the Assembly composed of delegates of national parliaments, and the competences of the Court, which was mandated to ensure the rule of law in the interpretation and application of the EEC treaty (cf Articles 7 ff ECSC treaty; on this see also Boerger-de Smedt, (2012), 339, at 340 ff; Pescatore, (1981) 159; Craig, (2011) 41, at 41 ff; Craig and de Burca, (1998) 9 ff).

60 Pescatore, (1981) 159, at 165.

61 On this 'monopoly' of the Commission cf e.g. Gellermann, (2012) 2473, paras 6–9 with further references.

62 Pescatore, (1981) 159, at 169–170.

63 Beutler et al., (1993) 1 ff; Bast, (2009) 495; Boerger-de Smedt, (2012), 339, at 347, 350.

64 Craig, (2011) 41, at 43 ff.

65 As to this characterization cf Rasmussen, (2010) 69 ff.

66 Extraordinary Session of the Council, Luxembourg, 17–18 and 28–29 January 1966, Bulletin of the European Communities, March 1966, 3–66, pp. 5–11 (text available at www.eurotreaties.com/lux-embourg.pdf).

67 Borchardt, (2010) 165 ff.

68 Borchardt, (2010) 166.

69 See Craig, (2011) 41, at 45–46.

70 Cf Article 291 TFEU and Regulation 182/2011; on comitology and the regulation see e.g. Streinz, (2012) 204 ff; Craig, (2008) 123 ff; Gellermann, (2012) 2468, paras 15 ff with further references.

71 Craig, (2011) 41, at 50; Pechstein, (2012) 153 ff with further references.

72 Cf e.g. Barnard, (2013) 633–634.

73 Article 100a EEC treaty (introduced by Article 18 of the SEA).

74 Weiler, (1991) 2402, 2453 ff; Rasmussen, (2014) 136, at 160 ff; Craig and de Burca, (1998) 19 ff.

75 Weiler, (1991) 2402, 2462.

76 On this see e.g. the (critical) comments by Streinz, (2012) 304 ff with further references; Barnard, (2013) 24–25.

77 ECJ, judgment of 1 July 1969, *Statistical Levy*, [1969] ECR 193, para 9.

78 ECJ, judgment of 11 July 1974, *Dassonville*, [1974] ECR 837, para 5; on all of this, cf the seminal study by Weiler, (2002) 201, at 205 ff; see also Eilmansberger et al., (2012) 31 ff.

79 See e.g. Fenger and Schonberg, (2010) 171, at 172.

80 These legitimate aims can be found in Article 36 TFEU today. This exhaustive list has been extended by the ECJ in its *Cassis* jurisprudence (see below).

81 On these issues cf also Vranes, (2010) 953, at 955 ff.

82 See Rosas, (2010) 433 ff.

83 This was noted even by the ECJ in its *Keck* ruling (ECJ, judgment of 24 November 1993, *Keck* [1993] ECR I-6097, para 14); on this decision see in the following text below.

84 Cf Weiler, (2002) 201, at 207; see also Pauwelyn, (2005), 131 ff; Vranes, (2010) 953, at 958; Winter, (2001) 71, at 79 ff; Matsushita, Schoenbaum and Mavroidis, (2006) 269 ff.

85 Cf Weiler, (2002) 201, at 207 ff, who also compares EU law to the law of the GATT, which is in stark contrast to the ECJ's approach; on the GATT/WTO context see also Vranes, (2010) 953, at 955 ff.

86 On Article 100a see already Section 3.2 above.

87 See Weiler, (2002) 201, at 216; Craig and de Burca, (2011) 684 ff; Kingreen, (2011) 681 ff, at paras 210 ff with extensive further references.

88 On this and the following see also Craig and de Burca, (2011) 684 ff.

89 See Communication from the Commission concerning the consequences of the judgment given by the Court of Justice on 20 February 1979 in Case 120/78 ('Cassis de Dijon') 3 October 1980, [1980] OJ C256/2, at 3.

90 Directive 98/34 of 22 June 1998, [1998] OJ L 204/37; pursuant to this directive, the Member States are to communicate to the Commission any draft technical regulation, which notifies it to the other Member States. Comments made by them or the Commission have to be taken into account by the Member intending to enact the technical regulation. The adoption of such regulations must be postponed for three to six months, if the Commission or any Member State takes the view that they may create obstacles to trade, and for twelve months, if the Commission announces its intention of adopting or proposing harmonising secondary law (cf Articles 7–9 of Directive 98/34).

91 Cf Pelkmans, (1987) 249, at 257.

92 For an early detailed analysis see Pelkmans, (1987) 249 ff; for an overview cf Craig and de Burca, (2011) 581–600; Barnard, (2013) 666 ff with further references.

93 ECJ, judgment of 24 November 1993, *Keck* [1993] ECR I-6097, paras 14–15.

94 Cf also Fenger and Schonberg, (2010) 171, at 172.

95 See Joseph H.H. Weiler, (2002) 201, at 227–228.

96 Cf e.g. the detailed account in Barnard, (2013) 125 ff with further references; Schroeder, (2012) 509 ff, paras 41 ff with further references.

97 ECJ, judgment of 24 November 1993, *Keck* [1993] ECR I-6097, para 17. The focus on 'selling arrangements' has also been criticized e.g. by Weiler, (2002) 201, at 228; Rosas, (2010) 433 ff.

98 ECJ, judgment of 8 March 2001, *Gourmet* [2001] ECR I-1795, paras 18 ff; ECJ, judgment of 4 June 2009, Case C-142/05, *Mickelsson* [2009] ECR I-4273, paras 24 ff.

99 Bernard, (2010) 456, at 462–463; Cf also Fenger and Schonberg, (2010) 171, at 185 ff; Barnard, (2013) 21 ff, 105 ff *et passim*, all with further references.

100 This reading of the ECJ's rulings is also proposed e.g. by Craig and de Burca, (2011) 662 ff with further references; on these issues see also the detailed analysis by Kingreen, (2011) 681 ff, at paras 51 ff with extensive further references.

101 Cf Pescatore, (1981) 159, at 177–178, as cited already above in Section 1.

102 Constantinesco, (2010) 97 ff.

References

Barnard, C., (2013), *The Substantive Law of the EU: The Four Freedoms*, 4th ed., Oxford: Oxford University Press.

Bast, J. (2009), Handlungsformen und Rechtsschutz, in von Bogdandy, A. and Bast, J. (eds), *Europäisches Verfassungsrecht: theoretische und dogmatische Grundzüge*, 2nd ed., Berlin: Springer-Verlag, 495.

Bernard, N. (2010), On the Art of Not Mixing One's Drinks: Dassonville and Cassis de Dijon Revisited, in Azoulai, L. and Maduro, M. (eds), *The Past and Future of EU Law*, Oxford: Hart Publishing, 456.

Boerger-de Smedt, A. (2012), Negotiating the Foundations of European Law, 1950–57, *Contemporary European History*, 21, 339.

Borchardt, K.-D. (2010), *Die rechtlichen Grundlagen der Europäischen Union*, 4th ed., Vienna: Facultas. WUV.

Churchill, W. (1946), speech delivered at the University of Zurich, 19 September 1946, available at the website of the Council of Europe (www.coe.int/t/dgal/dit/ilcd/archives/selection/churchill/ZurichSpeech_en.asp), last visited 22 July 2014.

Constantinesco,V. (2010), 'Plus vite, plus haut, plus fort!': quelques réflexions sur l'intégration européenne, in Koch, H. et al. (eds), *Europe. The New Legal Realism. Essays in Honour of Hjalte Rasmussen*, Copenhagen: Djøf Publishing, 97.

Craig, P. and de Burca, G. (1998), *EU Law: Text, Cases, and Materials*, 2nd ed., Oxford: Oxford University Press.

Craig, P. and de Burca, G. (2011), *EU Law: Text, Cases, and Materials*, 5th ed., Oxford: Oxford University Press.

Craig, P. (2011), Institutions, Power, and Institutional Balance, in Craig, P. and de Burca, G. (eds), *The Evolution of EU Law*, 2nd ed., Oxford: Oxford University Press, 41.

Craig, P. (2011), Integration, Democracy, and Legitimacy, in Craig, P. and de Burca, G. (eds), *The Evolution of EU Law*, 2nd ed., Oxford: Oxford University Press, 13.

Craig, P. (2008), The European Parliament under the Lisbon Treaty, in Griller, S. and Ziller, J. (eds), *The Lisbon Treaty*, Vienna: Springer, 123.

Cremona, M. (2013), The Judgment – Framing the Argument, in Tizzano, A. et al. (eds), *Court of Justice of the European Union 50th Anniversary of the Judgment in Van Gend en Loos. 1963–2013*, Luxembourg: Office des publications de l'Union européenne, 23.

Davies, B. and Rasmussen, M. (2012), Towards a New History of European Law, *Contemporary European History*, 21, 305.

De Witte, B. (2011) Direct Effect, Primacy, and the Nature of the Legal Order, in Craig, P. and de Burca, G. (eds), *The Evolution of EU Law*, 2nd ed, Oxford: Oxford University Press, 323.

Eilmansberger, T., Herzig, G, Jaeger, T., Thyri, P. (2012), *Materielles Europarecht*, 3rd ed., Vienna: LexisNexis.

Fenger, N. and Schonberg, S. (2010), Market Access, Restrictions on the Use of Lawfully Marketed Products and Article 34 TFEU, in Koch, H., Hagel-Sørensen, K., Haltern, U. and Weiler J.H.H. (eds), *Europe. The New Legal Realism. Essays in Honour of Hjalte Rasmussen*, Copenhagen: Djøf Publishing, 171.

Gänswein, O. (2009), *Der Grundsatz der unionsrechtskonformen Auslegung nationalen Rechts*, Frankfurt: Peter Lang.

Gellermann, M. (2012), Commentary on Article 291 and Article 293, in Streinz, R. (ed.), *EUV/AEUV*, 2nd ed., Munich: C.H. Beck.

Griller, S., Keiler, S., Kröll, T., Lienbacher, G., Vranes, E. (2011), *National Constitutional Law and European Integration*, Brussels - Strasbourg: European Parliament.

Halberstam, D. (2010), Pluralism in Marbury and Van Gend, in Azoulai, L. and Maduro, M. (eds), *The Past and Future of EU Law*, Oxford: Hart Publishing, 26.

Hofmann, H. C. H. (2010), Conflicts and Integration, in Azoulai, L. and Maduro, M. (eds), *The Past and Future of EU Law*, Oxford: Hart Publishing, 60.

Kingreen, T. (2011), Commentary on Articles 34–36, in Calliess, C. and Ruffert, M. (eds), *EUV/AEUV. Kommentar*, 4th ed., Munich: C.H. Beck.

Matsushita, M., Schoenbaum, T. J. and Mavroidis, P. C. (2006), *The World Trade Organization*, 2nd ed., Oxford: Oxford University Press, 269.

Mayer, F.C. (2010), Van Gend en Loos: The Foundations of a Community of Law, in Azoulai, L. and Maduro, M. (eds), *The Past and Future of EU Law*, Oxford: Hart Publishing, 16.

Meng, W. (1995), Gedanken zur unmittelbaren Anwendbarkeit von WTO-Recht, in Beyerlin, U. (ed.), *Recht zwischen Umbruch und Bewährung. Festschrift für Rudolf Bernhardt*, Berlin: Springer, 1063.

Middeke, A. (2014), Das Vorabentscheidungsverfahren, in Rengeling, H.-W. et al. (eds), *Handbuch des Rechtsschutzes in der Europäischen Union*, 3rd ed., Munich: C.H. Beck, 222.

Monnet, J. (1988), *Erinnerungen Eines Europäers*, Baden-Baden: Nomos.

Oppermann, T., Classen, C.D. and Nettesheim, M. (2014), *Europarecht*, 6th ed., Munich: C.H. Beck.

Pauwelyn, J., Rien ne Va Plus? Distinguishing Domestic Regulation from Market Access in GATT and GATS, *Duke Law School Legal Studies Research Paper Series*, Research Paper No. 85, October 2005.

Pechstein, M. (2012), Commentary on Article 15, in Streinz, R. (ed.), *EUV/AEUV*, 2nd ed., Munich: C.H. Beck.

Pelkmans, J. (1987), The New Approach to Technical Harmonization and Standardization, *Journal of Common Market Studies*, 25 (3), 249.

Pernice, I. (1998), Commentary on Article 23, in Dreier, H.H. *Grundgesetz-Kommentar, Volume 2*, Tübingen: Mohr Siebeck, 325.

Pernice, I. (2010), Costa v ENEL and Simmenthal, in Azoulai, L. and Maduro, M. (eds), *The Past and Future of EU Law*, Oxford: Hart Publishing, 47.

Pescatore, P. (1981), Les travaux du 'groupe juridique' dans la négociation des traités de Rome, *Studia Diplomatica*, 34, 159.

Rasmussen, M. (2010), From Costa/ENEL to the Treaties of Rome, in Azoulai, L. and Maduro, M. (eds), *The Past and Future of EU Law*, Oxford: Hart Publishing, 69.

Rasmussen, M. (2014), Revolutionizing European Law: A History of the Van Gend en Loos Judgment, *International Journal of Constitutional Law*, 12 (1), 136.

Rosas, A. (2010), Life after Dassonville and Cassis, in Azoulai, L. and Maduro, M. (eds), *The Past and Future of EU Law*, Oxford: Hart Publishing, 433.

Roth, W.-H. (2010), Die richtlinienkonforme Auslegung, in Riesenhuber, K. (ed.), *Europäische Methodenlehre*, 2nd ed., Berlin, Boston: De Gruyter, 393.

Schima, B. (2004), *Das Vorabentscheidungsverfahren vor dem EuGH*, 2nd ed., Vienna: Manz.

Schroeder, W. (2012), Commentary on Article 34, in Streinz, R. (ed), *EUV/AEUV*, 2nd ed., Munich: C.H. Beck.

Stone Sweet, A., (2011) The European Court of Justice, in Craig, P. and de Burca, G. (eds), *The Evolution of EU Law*, 2nd ed., Oxford: Oxford University Press, 122.

Streinz, R. (2012), *Europarecht*, 9th ed., Heidelberg: C.F. Müller.

Von Bogdandy, A., Cruz Villalón, P., Huber, P.M (eds) (2008), *Handbuch Ius Publicum Europaeum, volume 2*, Heidelberg: C.F. Müller.

Vranes, E. (2009), The WTO and Regulatory Freedom, *Journal of International Economic Law*, 12 (4), 953.

Weiler, J.H.H. (2001), Epilogue: Towards a Common Law of International Trade, in Weiler, J.H.H. (ed.), *The EU, the WTO, and NAFTA*, Oxford: Oxford University Press, 201.

Weiler, J.H.H. (2013), Revisiting Van Gend, in Tizzano, A. et al. (eds), *Court of Justice of the European Union 50th Anniversary of the Judgment in Van Gend en Loos. 1963–2013*, Luxembourg: Office des publications de l'Union européenne, 11.

Weiler, J.H.H. (1991), The Transformation of Europe, *The Yale Law Journal*, 100 (8), 2402.

Weiler, J.H.H. (2014), Van Gend en Loos: The Individual as Subject and Object and the Dilemma of European Legitimacy, *International Journal of Constitutional Law*, 12 (1), 1294.

Winter, G. (2001), Welthandelsrecht und Umweltschutz, in Dolde, K.-P. (ed.), *Umweltrecht im Wandel*, Berlin: Schmidt, 71.

Other Materials

EU Commission, Communication from the Commission – A Europe of Results – Applying Community Law, COM(2007) 502 final.

EU Commission, Communication from the Commission concerning the consequences of the judgment given by the Court of Justice on 20 February 1979 in Case 120/78 ('Cassis de Dijon') 3 October 1980, [1980] OJ C256/2.

Extraordinary Session of the Council, Luxembourg, 17–18 and 28–29 January 1966, Bulletin of the European Communities, March 1966, 3–66, pp. 5–11 (text available at www.eurotreaties.com/luxembourg.pdf).

Schuman Declaration, presented by French foreign minister Robert Schuman on 9 May 1950, available at the website of the EU (http://europa.eu/about-eu/basic-information/symbols/europe-day/schuman-declaration/index_en.htm), last visited 22 July 2014.

Cases in chronological order

ECJ, judgment of 5 February 1963, Case 26/62, *NV Algemene Transport- en Expeditie Onderneming van Gend & Loos v Netherlands Inland Revenue Administration* [1963] ECR 1.

ECJ, judgment of 15 July 1964, Case 6/64, *Costa/ENEL* [1964] ECR 585.

ECJ, judgment of 19 December 1968, Case 13/68, *SpA Salgoil* [1968] ECR 453.

ECJ, judgment of 1 July 1969, Case 24/68, *Statistical Levy* [1969] ECR 193.

ECJ, judgment of 6 October 1970, Case 9/70, *Franz Grad* [1970] ECR 825.

ECJ, judgment of 17 December 1970, Case 11/70, *Internationale Handelsgesellschaft* [1970] ECR 1125.

ECJ, judgment of 21 June 1974, Case 2/74, *Reyners* [1974] ECR 631.

ECJ, judgment of 11 July 1974, Case 8/74, *Dassonville* [1974] ECR 837.

ECJ, judgment of 4 December 1974, Case 41/74, *Van Duyn* [1974] ECR 1337.

ECJ, judgment of 22 June 1989, Case 103/88, *Costanzo* [1989] ECR 1839.

ECJ, judgment of 24 November 1993, Case C-267/91, *Keck* [1993] ECR I-6097.

ECJ, judgment of 8 March 2001, Case C-405/98, *Gourmet* [2001] ECR I-1795.

ECJ, judgment of 26 April 2005, Case C-376/02, *Stichting* [2005] ECR I-3445.

ECJ, judgment of 4 June 2009, Case C-142/05, *Mickelsson* [2009] ECR I-4273.

INDEX

Page numbers in italic refer to figures and tables

absorptive capacity 261, 263
"acceptance threshold" (RQMV) 463
accession countries *see* enlargement
accession dummy variable 191, 194
accountability 129
Acharya, V.V. 418
Action Programme (1962) 41–2
ad valorem tariff equivalents (AVEs) 226–7
Africa 212, 240, 247
African, Caribbean and Pacific Group (ACP)
    238–49; BRICS 245; EC trade 241; EPAs
    212; EU oversight 247; EU summits 238;
    Georgetown Agreement (1975) 240; migration
    246
African Regional Economic Communities
    (RECs) 246
African Union 247
agency autonomy 208
"Agenda 2010" (Germany) 291
agricultural subsidies 274, 276, 277
agriculture 210–11, 271–2, 275–6, 277, 278
    see also Common Agricultural Policy (CAP)
Agur, I. 474
Ahearne, A. G 73
aid 242, 247–8, 256, 261
AK model of investment 10
Albuquerque, R. 74
allocation of capital 71–2, 87
allocative inefficiency 61n9
Almunia, Joaquín 49, 408
AMADEUS data (BvD) 77–8
anchor currencies 85
Anderson, J. E. 225
Angeloni, I. 95
Anglophone countries 240
Anglo-Saxon countries 39, 287, 290
Annual Economic Report (CEC, 1980) 45–6

annual policy cycle *see* European Semester
Anti-Counterfeiting Trade Agreement (ACTA,
    2012) 208–9
anti-Europe movements 342
anti-Western sentiment 242
'Application' dummy variable 191
arbitrage 297
Aristotle 23
Arkolakis, C. 174, 177, 180, 183, 230
Armington model 174, 183, 230
Asian crisis (1997) 94
Asia-Pacific Economic Cooperation (APEC) 215
Asmussen, Jörg 396
Asset Backed Securities (ABS) 326
asset quality review (AQR) 150, 322, 324, 326,
    372, 422 *see also* stress tests
asset sales 121
association status 240
asymmetric adjustment processes 126
asymmetric countries 304
asymmetric information 158, 164, 284
asymmetric shocks 108–9, 111, 113, 114, 416
austerity 123–4, 126, 381–92, 404
austerity-cum-official financing (2011) 397
Austria 163, 338, 415
autarky 182

Bacchetta, P. 87
Badinger, H. 7, 11
Bagehot, Walter 24, 357
Baier, S. L. 8, 188, 190, 468
bail-ins 150, 326, 343
bail-outs 71, 111, 339, 343
balance of payments 14–16, 40, 41, 415
Balassa, B. 4, 10, 209, 474
Baldwin, R. 235, 472
Ball, G. W. 441–2

Balladur, Edouard 32, 47
bank failures 35, 323, 343 *see also* Lehman Brothers
bank funding 353–4, 367
bank lending channel 135, 137–8
Bank Lending Survey (BLS) 134–6, 140, 141
bank loans 368, *369*
Bank of England 89
bank recapitalization 146, 150, 316, 324, 368, 417
Bank Recovery and Resolution Directive
    (BRRD) 321, 322, 372, 423
bank rescue programs 343–4
bank resolution 104, 108, 115, 322–3, 422–3
bankers' bonuses 292
Banking Advisory Committee (EC) 315
banking assets/GDP 417
banking crisis (2007–09) 339, 351, 355
banking crisis (2011) 367
banking fragmentation 104
banking supervision: central banks 35; fiscal
    indiscipline 103; larger/smaller banks 115;
    national frameworks 315, 324; and sovereignty
    106; SSM 325, 422–3
Banking Supervisory Committee 315
Banking Union: asset quality review (AQR) 150;
    financial integration 321–3; and monetary
    union 106; political imperatives 324–5;
    sovereigns-banks links 372; supervisory
    authorities 103, 115, 422–3
banks: bail outs 71, 339; borrowing short/lending
    long 120; BRRD rescue rules 321; capital
    requirements 321; credit default swaps
    (2008–14) *361*; credit growth (2000s) 353;
    cross-border balance sheets 84; cross-border
    exposures 316–17, 353; cross-border funding
    367; ECB supporting 356; gross assets and
    liabilities *84*; holding sovereign debt 120, 150,
    324, 366–7, 371–2, 417–18; loan portfolios 368;
    ownership 316, 325; regulatory systems 315; US
    subprime mortgage crisis (2007) 354 *see also*
    asset quality review (AQR); domestic banks;
    stress tests
Banzhaf index (BFI) 452, *455–6*
Banzhaf, J. F. 450
Barre Memorandum (1969) 42–3
Barre, Raymond 25, 28, 33, 43
Barroso, José Manuel 345, 467
Bartelsman, E. J. 152
Basic Food Law Regulation 279
Bayoumi, T. 8–9
BBB rated securities 355
Becker, S. O. 259, 260–1, 263–4, 266
Beetsma, R. M. W. J. 148, 149, 152, 153
Belaisch, A. 315
Belgium 34, 75, 163, 165, 240, 290
Bénassy-Quéré, A. 90, 95
Berden, K. 225, 227
Berger, H. 474

Bergsten, C. F. 95
Bergstrand, J. H. 188, 190, 468
Berlin Wall 48
Bernanke, B. S. 132
Bernard, A. B. 174
Besedeš, T. 189, 191
beta convergence 314
Beugelsdijk, M. 259
Beveridgean countries 287
big push theory of development 264–6
bilateral investment treaties (BITs) 234
bilateral trade 215–16, 444
binary dummy variables 468, 470
Bini Smaghi, Lorenzo 397
Bishop, G. 153
Bismarckian system 287
Blanchard, Olivier 383, 384, 385
"blood diamonds" 242
"blue" bonds 153
Bohn, Henning 381
Boldrin, M. 259
Bolkestein Report (2001) 300
Boltho, A. 11
Bonn Summit (1978) 46
booms and busts 119–20, 121–3, 124
Boonstra, W. W. 153
border controls 58
Bradford, D. F. 302
Brandt, Willy 28, 43
Brazil 216
Breinlich, H. 65
Brennan, G. 303
Bretton Woods system 27, 88
Breuss, F. 7, 342
Brexit 185–6
Briand Plan (1930) 4
BRICS group 245
broad credit channel variable 135
"Brouwer report" 315
Brueckner, J. K. 306
Bruinshoofd, W. A. 153
Bryce's law 114
Buchanan, J. 303
Buchheit, L. C. 397–9, 401
Bucovetsky, S. 303, 304
Budgetary Authority proposal 425
budgetary discipline 145, 151, 410
budgets: balances *107*; centralizing 130; draft
    plans 147, 149; stabilizing features 120–1, 124;
    surveillance framework 148 *see also* deficits;
    European Semester; Stability and Growth Pact
    (SGP)
Buiter, W. 425
Bulgaria 75
Bundesbank 31
bureaucratic integration 129
Bureau van Dijk (BvD) 77–8

Burnside, C. 261
business cycles 144, 413
Buti, M. 408

Cambridge Economic Policy Group model
    (CEPG) 15–16
Cameroon 243
Campos, N. F. 11
Canada 163, 165, 228
Canova, F. 259
capability to act (Coleman) 452, 458, 464
Capie, Forrest 400
capital allocation 71–2, 87
capital flows 35, 74, 75–6, 415, 472 *see also*
    financial integration; Foreign Direct
    Investment (FDI)
capital markets 26, 70, 304, 345
capital mobility 46, 64–5, 303–4
Capital Requirements Directive (CRD IV) 321,
    421
Capital Requirements Regulation (CRR) 421
capital-skill complementarities 261–3
capital tax rates 303
capital thresholds 322 *see also* stress tests
capitalism 119
Cappelen, A. 259
Caribbean 244, 247
CARICOM 246
CARIFORUM – EU EPA 244
Carnot, N. 408
'carry trade' 367
Cassis case (ECJ, 1979) 487, 488–9
Castellacci, F. 259
Cecchini report (1988) 58
Celtic Tiger economy 13–14
Central Africa 240, 243
central banks: countercyclical capital buffers 421;
    Emergency Lending Assistance (ELA) 103;
    intermediation 355–6; lender of last resort 93,
    120; liquidity 357; monetary union 33
central rates 31, 45
centralization 114–15, 153–4, 165, 394, 437
ceteris paribus scenario 235
CFA franc 240
chain-reaction approaches 435, 442
Chamley, C. 396
chemicals 226
Cheptea, A. 66
China 90, *210*, 213, 216, 242
Chinn, M. 91
Chiṭu, L. 88–9
Choudhry, T. 472
Churchill, Winston 479
Cipollina, M. 228
civil wars 25
Claessens, S. 153
classical tax competition models 303

clearing mechanisms 297
Cohen, B. J. 82, 93
Cohesion Fund (CF) 65, 255, 256
cohesion policies 256
"Colbertist" tradition 39
Cold War 241–2
Coleman, J. S. 452, 458, 464
collateral 355–6
colonial legacies 239–41
Comitology system 486
commercial integration 438, 440
commitment technologies 443
Committee of Presidents of Committee (Werner)
    28
Committee of Wise Men (Lamfalussy) 312
commodity tax competition 304–5
Common Agricultural Policy (CAP) 269–80;
    agricultural prices 271; background 269–70,
    443; budget 278; coupled support 276, 277;
    direct farm payments *275*; expenditure *274*;
    Parliament "co-decision powers" 278; reforms
    272–4, 276–8; tariffs 271; trade-diverting effects
    210–11 *see also* agriculture; food
Common Commercial Policy (CCP) 208, 209
common consolidated corporate tax base
    (CCCTB) 300
common debt instruments *see* Eurobonds
common economic policies 41
common market 5, 40, 191, 194, 195–6, 438, 443
"Common methodology for state aid evaluation"
    SWD (2014) 259
common resolution authority 108
common supervision 103, 106 *see also* Banking
    Union
Community Charter of the Fundamental Social
    Rights of Workers 288
Community law 483
Community Mechanism for Short-term Monetary
    Assistance (1970) 43
competition 58–63, 66
competitiveness 338, 415–16
composite indicators 473–4
comprehensive economic and trade agreement
    (CETA) 228
comprehensive trade agreements 231, 236
Computable general equilibrium (CGE) 173, 174
"conditionality" (Lomé III, 1985) 242
conflicts 444
constitutional laws 480–1
construction 415
consumer consumption 70–1, 72, 73
consumer surpluses 57
contagion 159, 362, 416
Continental Welfare States 287
convergence criteria 48, 105, 106
'Convergence of medium-term economic policy'
    (Barre Memorandum, 1969) 43

convergence patterns 259
convergence of preferences 441
Convergence Programs 144
convergence regressions 12–13
co-ordinated stimuli (2009–10) 382
Corcos, G. 174
Coreper (*Comité des représentants permanents*) 486
Coronation Theory 105–8
corporate bonds 71, 314
corporate taxation 299–300, 305, 306
corrective arms: MIP 421; SGP 411
corruption 74
Costa/ENEL case (ECJ, 1964) 483
Costinot, A. 174, 175, 181, 183–4, 185
costs, international currencies 92–3
Cotonou Agreement (2000) 238, 242–3
Council of Ministers 208, 452–4, 457–9, 485, 486
countercyclical borrowing and lending 70 *see also* Foreign Direct Investment (FDI)
countercyclical capital buffers 421
counterfactual impact evaluations 258–9
counterfactual scenarios 173, 182
"coupled support" (CAP) 276, 277
Cournot-Nash competitors 57, 58, 61
Covered Bonds 326
credibility problems 162 *see also* "no-bail out" clause (TFEU Article 125)
credit boom 415
credit channel of monetary policy theory 132–40
credit frictions 140
credit institutions 321–2
credit rating agencies 334, 418
credit supply 133, 135
crisis instruments 417
crisis management 104, 392–401, 403, 421–2
crisis/non-crisis countries 112–13
Croatia 75, 457
cross-border funding 316–17, 353, 367
cross-border intermediation 73
cross-border monetary experimentation 24
cross-border profit shifting activities 305
cross-border shopping 305, 306
cross-border trade 297–8
"culture of consensus" (EC) 454
currencies *see* euro; international currencies; pound sterling; US dollar
currency invoicing 87
currency union 9, 23–4, 34
current account balances 25–6, 27, 125–6, 415
customs union 5, 56, 57, 212
cyclical downturn (2001–05) 159
cyclically-adjusted balances 144
Cyprus 75, 108, 345

dairy quotas 278
Dalgaard, C.-J. 261
dall'Erba, S. 263

Darwinian competition arguments 66
Dassonville case (ECJ, 1974) 487–8, 490
Deauville summit (2010) 35, 395–7
debt brake 34, 151
debt burdens 352, 376–7, 385, 388, 393, 402
debt ceilings 425
debt criteria (Maastricht Treaty) 34–5
debt-deflation dynamics *403*
debt financing 345
debt ratios 381, 384–5, 388, 391–2
debt reduction 121, 126, 376, 381, 404
debt relief 362, 393
debt restructuring: ambivalence 404; crisis management 403; delays 399; PSI 362; reward for misbehavior 112; sovereign insolvency 425, 426; speed of resolution 395
debt rules 161–2
debt servicing 35
debt shifting 305
debt sustainability 392, 395, 397, 426
debtor countries 35, 126–7
debt-to-GDP ratios 376, 382, *389–90*
decentralized fiscal discipline 115
decision-making processes 104, 161, 417, 485
de facto integration 469–70, 474
defense and security 437
deficit bias problem 159
deficit rules 34–5, 160, 161–2, 381
deficits: euro area 381, *412*; European Council limits 151; fiscal framework 145; monitoring 147; negative spillover 158–9; size (2009) 416; Stability Programs 411, *412*; stop-go cycle 25 *see also* Excessive Deficit Procedure (EDP)
deflation 124, 127, 341
de Gaulle, Charles 485–6
De Grauwe, P. 23, 104, 153
de Groot, H.L.F. 259
De Gucht, Karel 220
De Haan, J. 417, 420
de jure integration indicators 469–70
de Larosière, Jacques 317
Del Gatto, M. 174
d'Elia, A. 147, 149
Delors Committee (1989) 27, 32–3, 34, 47–8, 105, 394
Delors, Jacques 27, 32, 47, 439, 440
Delpla, J. 153
demographic clause (Treaty of Athens) 452–3
de Mooij, R. 259
Demyanyk, Y. 73
Denmark 30, 162, 290, 292, 300
"denomination rents" (Swoboda) 92
deposit insurance 315
deregulation 285, 291
De Santis, R. A. 472
destination principle of taxation 296–7
Deutsche Mark zone 44

developing countries 242
development finance 70, 71, 241
Devereux, M. 86, 87
Devereux, M. P. 295, 306
DG Development and Cooperation (DEVCO) 239
DG II (DG Ecfin) 38, 47
Dillon trade negotiations (GATT, 1960–2) 209
DiNino, V. 472
direct effect doctrine 480–1, 482, 484
direct foreign exchange *86*
direct ownership 77
direct payments (CAP) 274, *275*
direct taxation 292, 299–302
discretionary monetary policies 164n19
disposable incomes 392
distressed sovereigns 395
divergence indicators (EMS) 31, 32
divergent macroeconomic movements 122
diverging competitiveness 83, 415–16
diversification finance 70, 71
doctrine of supremacy (ECJ) 483
Doha Round trade negotiations 205, 211–12, 221
Dollar, D. 261
domestic banks 92, 150, 315, 418 *see also* banks
donor–recipient relationships 244–5
doom loop 120, 150, 324, 366–7, 371–2, 417–18
Dorrucci, E. 474
dose-response functions 265–6
'Dossier préparatoire au mandat de Hanovre sur la construction monétaire européenne' (DG II 1988) 47
"double coincidence of wants" 86n6
double-dip recessions 127, 341
double majority voting (DMV) 452, 457, 459
Draghi, Mario: alliance with Angela Merkel 380–1; peripheral debt 371; refinancing operations 367; reforming euro area 23; 'whatever it takes' pledge 317, 345, 352, 370, 372, 400, 409
droit communautaire 480
Drudi, F. 417
Duisenberg, Wim 105, 442
Dullien, S. 166
duration of trade 189
Dustmann, C. 402
dynamic economies of scale 62

East African Community (EAC) 243
Easterly, W. 261
Eastern African EPAs 243
Eastern European countries 71, 181–2, 182–3, 275–6, 306
Eaton, J. 173, 174
Eaton-Kortum model 173, 174
Economic Community of West African States (ECOWAS) 240
economic growth *see* growth

economic integration 467–75; chronology 5; degrees of 4; deregulation 291; effects 56, 468–9; functionalist approaches 443; labor and social policies 285; legal developments 484; political character 42; tax competition 305; trade 6–9, 189; transportation costs 305 *see also* integration
Economic Integration Agreements Database (Baier and Bergstrand) 188, 190
Economic and Monetary Community of West African States (UEMOA) 240
Economic and Monetary Union (EMU): 10-year review 49; background 43, 48, 408–10; competitiveness 334–5; design flaws 22; euro crisis 410–18; governance 334, 342–4; policy coordination 424; political unification 442; reforms 418–23; risk sharing 423–6; sovereign debt crisis 49; Stage Three 48
Economic Partnership Agreements (EPAs) 212, 243–4
economic policy coordination 28, 342 *see also* European Semester
economic union 42, 49, 191
economies of scale 61–2, 436, 437
economies of scope 437
Ederveen, S. 259
Edison, H. J. 73
education 261
Edwards, J. 303
EEC/EU (independent) Africa link 240
EEC treaty *see* Treaty of Rome (1957)
efficiency 61, 452, 457–9, 464 *see also* growth; production efficiency
Egger, P. H. 230, 231, 259, 260–1, 263–4, 266, 304, 305, 306
Eggert, W. 305
Eichengreen, B. 8–9, 11, 88–9, 89, 90, 91, 94, 95, 392
Eijffinger, S.C.W. 259
Elsig, M. 208
emergency funds *see* European Stabilisation Mechanism (ESM)
Emergency Lending Assistance (ELA) 103
emigrants/immigrants ratios 109, *110*
Emminger, Otmar 31
"Empire of the Mark" (*Le Monde*) 32
employment *109*, 286–7, *290*, 291
"EMU@10" report (CEC, 2008) 49, 342
endogeneity problem 263
enforcement: EU law 481–2; moral hazards 72; SGP 459–61
Engel, C. 473
engrenage 46
enlargement 5–6, 190, 194, 196–7, *198*, 245
"entrapment" (Kirshner) 88
environment, the 276
EONIA 314, *358*

EPL rigidity index *287*
equalization mechanism (Germany) 154
'equilibrium theory' (Weiler) 484
equity market integration 65
equity returns 314
Estonia 71, 75
ethnic identification 73
EU–15 7–8, 66–7, 189–90
EU–27 74, 339, 462
EU–28 90, 339, 341
EU–ACP Cooperation Agreement (2000) 243
EU–ACP Joint Parliamentary Assembly 239, 247
EU–ACP relationships 242–9
EU–Canada CETA 228
EU–CARICOM EPA 243
EU–CARIFORUM EPA 213n29, 243, 244
EU–Central Africa EPA 213n29
EU–ECOWAS EPA 243
EU–EFTA free-trade area 209
EU–Gulf Cooperation Council 213n29
'EU in effect' dummy variable 194
EU laws: enforcement 482; as 'foreign law' 484;
    formal principles 478–9; primacy 483, 485
EU–Mercosur relations 213n29, 247
EU–Mexico FTA 213
EU-Pacific islands engagement 247
'EU pair' dummy variable 191, 195
EUREPO 314
EURIBOR 314
euro: 10-year review 49; anchor currency 85;
    bank note design 23; creation of the name 34;
    diversification currency 83; economically-
    motivated project 439; financial markets 366–7;
    foreign-exchange reserves 91; international
    currency 82–95; international debt securities
    85; liquidity 83; long term yields 314; and
    member countries 104, 123; monetary union
    380; as a store-of-value 83; strength against US
    dollar 104; unit-of-account function 85
euro area: austerity 381–92; competitiveness 338;
    crisis (2008) 315–23; current account *123*;
    deficits 381, *412*; design failures 121; domestic
    banks 315; double-dip recession (2012–14) 341;
    external asymmetric shocks 336; financial cycle
    413; fiscal governance 103, 401; fiscal tightening
    (2010) 376–7; fiscal transfers 166; fragmentation
    315–16; GDP 339–41, *359*; governance reforms
    160–1; growth 95, *386*; inflation *359*, 360;
    lending conditions 317, *319*; net capital flows
    419; new framework 351; periphery banking
    339; political union 95; public debt 341, 382;
    QMV regimes 462; reference interest rates 314;
    risk management 399; sovereignty 116; stock
    market capitalization 313, *314*; summit (July
    2011) 397, 399; supervision 106
euro crisis: budget discipline 410; causes 336–9;
    definition 334; economic impact 339–41;

governance reforms 160–1; institutional
    integration 442; intergovernmentalism 342;
    reforms 50; as a sovereign debt crisis 413;
    unequal distribution 341
euro debt crisis 291–2
Eurobonds 153, 324–5, 425
"Europe à la carte" structure 343–4
European Banking Authority (EBA) 317
European Central Bank (ECB) 351–74;
    accountability 129; analysis and research 49;
    balance sheet 356, *357*; banking crisis 355–6;
    buying bonds 326, 362; financing capability
    393, 400; fiscal/monetary dominance 373;
    fiscal transfers 422; and Germany 392, 404;
    integration indicators 472; lender of last resort
    124–5, 128, 366, 400, 417; liquidity 128, 140;
    'middle way' policies 362, 367–8, 372, 373–4;
    "no bail-out clause" 143; non-standard
    interventions 357; policy rates 132, 356–7, *358*;
    public debts backstop 104; quantitative easing
    327; recapitalizing banks 368; refinancing
    operations 367, 409; refi rate cuts 372; sovereign
    debt crisis 128; supervision 321–2, 325–6, 422;
    TARGET imbalances 104; warehousing public
    debt 371
European Coal and Steal Community (ECSC) 4,
    296–7, 485
European Cohesion Policy 266
European Commission (EC) 38–50; Action
    Programme (1962) 41–2; agency autonomy
    208; agricultural objectives 271; budgetary
    plans 420; democratic legitimacy 129; economic
    thought 38–40; EMS proposals (1982) 45; 'fiscal
    capacity' proposals (2012) 166; harmonization
    488–9; integration processes (1990) 48;
    legislative initiatives 485; parallel currency
    strategy 45; political union 128–9; reforms
    (2012) 114; stability bonds 153; trade
    negotiations 208 *see also* High Authority
European Council 35, 49, 161, 166, 454, 486
European Council of Economics and Finance
    ministers (ECOFIN) 30, 159, 161, 411–12, 423
European Court of Justice (ECJ) 400, 443–4,
    480–4, 487–8
European Currency Unit (ECU) 32, 44, 83
European Defense Community 438
European deposit guarantee scheme 423
European Development Fund (2014–20) 238
European Development Fund (EDF) 239, 240,
    247
European Economic Area (EEA) 8, 56
European Economic Community (EEC) 4–6, 10,
    485
European Employment Strategy 288–9
European External Action Service 91
European Financial Stabilisation Mechanism
    (EFSM) 145

European Financial Stability Facility (EFSF):
adequacy 365; creation 111, 145, 417; rescue
instruments 344–5; supervision of SSM 321;
'troika' adjustment programme 362, 393
European Food Safety Authority (EFSA) 279
European Free Trade Association (EFTA) 5–6, 8,
206, 209, 209–10
European Insurance and Occupational Pensions
Authority (EIOPA) 317, 321
European integration *see* integration
European integration index (Berger and Nitsch)
474
European Investment Bank (EIB) 356
European Monetary Cooperation Fund 27
European Monetary Fund 32, 47
European Monetary Institute 34
European Monetary System (EMS) 30–2, 44–6
European Parliament 208–9, 246, 278, 453
European Payments Union (EPU) 4, 8
European Political Community 438
European project 440
European Regional Development Fund (ERDF)
255, 256, *257–8*
European Reserve Fund 41, 43
European Securities and Markets Authority
(ESMA) 317
European Semester 149, 161, 342–3, *343*
European Social Charter (1961) 288
European Social Fund (ESF) 255, 256, *257–8*
European Stability Mechanism (ESM): banking
union 324; financial assistance 146, 399–400;
lending instruments 146; recapitalizing banks
167, 417; rescues 344–5; resources 124, 365,
421; transfers 111–12; 'troika' adjustment
programme 362
European Steel and Coal Community 438
European System of Central Banks (ESCB)
33, 48
European Systemic Risk Board (ESRB) 321, 421
European Union (EU): enlargement 5–6, 190,
194, 196–7, *198*, 245; FTA 214–15; geopolitical
and geo-economic interests 247; global trader
206–7; institutional framework 485; national
interaction 147–8; pre-accession agreements
197–200; regionalism 214–15; status of
organization 439; trade agenda 245; trade
policy actor 207–9; upgrading to common
market 195–6; US Summit (2011) 220; US
trade negotiations (2013–) 220–1; world GDP
89–90, *221*
European Union supervisory authorities (ESAs)
317
eurosceptics 17, 246
eurosclerosis 289, 290, 468n1
Eurosystem 358
Eurozone *see* euro area
Everything But Arms (EBA) 213

Excessive Deficit Procedure (EDP) 144, 159, 161,
411, 420 *see also* deficits
Excessive Imbalance Procedure (EIP) 161, 421
exchange efficiency 297
exchange rate mechanism (ERM) 44
exchange rates 27, 113
exogenous fiscal shocks 152
"exorbitant privilege" (Giscard d'Estaing) 92, 93
'export-platform' FDI 14
exports 7, 87, 271, 297
external asymmetric shocks 336
external imbalances 415

factor mobility 63–5
Fagerberg, J. 259
farm payments 274, 275–6 *see also* Common
Agricultural Policy (CAP)
farming 270, 271, 275
Federal Reserve System for Europe 27
Federal Reserve (US) 94
federal states 114
federalism 438, 441, 479
Feenstra, R. 224
Felbermayr, G. 225, 230, 231, 235
Feldstein, Martin 24, 472
Feng, M. 468
Fichtner, F. 166
Fiji 244
financial assistance (ESM) 146, 399–400
financial crisis (2007–08): credit channels 139–40;
ECB supervisory role 35; 'exorbitant duty' 93;
financial factors 411; origins 24–6; US dollar
dependence 84; US dollar swaps 94; welfare
policies 291–2
Financial Crisis Inquiry Commission (2011) 331–2
financial cycles 413–15, 416
financial fragmentation 316–17, 366–7
financial frictions 140
financial integration 70, 71–2, 73, 416, 472 *see also*
capital flows
financial inter-linkages 150
financial intermediation 73, 358
financial markets 313–15, 353, 412
financial regulation 89 *see also* Single Supervisory
Mechanism (SSM)
Financial Services Action Plan (FSAP) 70, 312
financial shocks 114
financial stability 71, 88, 91
firewalls 317n12
fiscal austerity 377, *382*, 385, 393, 394
fiscal capacity 166, 360
Fiscal Compact (TSCG) 108n11, 115, 147, 409,
420
fiscal consolidation *377*, 385
fiscal coordination 144, 385
fiscal councils 162–5
fiscal deficits (1975–95) 157–8

fiscal discipline 34, 115, 419–20, 423
fiscal federalism 295
fiscal frameworks: crisis management 403; EMU
 143–5; integration 150–2; national reforms
 161–2; public debt 153; SGP reforms 145–50;
 tax-transfer systems 153–4
fiscal indiscipline 103, 106, 112
fiscal multipliers 383, 384, 385
fiscal responsibility 380
fiscal rules 158, 159–60, 380, 381, 392
fiscal stimuli 383
fiscal surveillance *see* Two-Pack directives (2013)
fiscal tightening 376–7, 380, 384–5
fiscal transfer schemes 165, 166
fiscal union: debt guarantees 165–6; euro area 167,
 393; federal approach 106; fiscal transfer system
 166; insurance 166; monetary union 392, 403;
 private creditors 393; redistribution 166; risk
 sharing 380; structure 129–30
fiscal watchdogs 163 *see also* fiscal councils
Fischler, Franz 276–7
Fisher, I. 121
fixed exchange rates 25, 27, 46
fixed rate/full allotment (FRFA) 355
Flam, H. 472, 473
Flandreau, M. 88–9
flexibility-oriented reforms 291
Fons-Rosen, C. 72
Fontagné, L. 472
food: exports 272; prices 270, 277; safety 270, 276,
 279 *see also* Common Agricultural Policy (CAP)
forced bail-ins (BRRD) 325
foreign affairs 91
foreign currencies 87, 104
Foreign Direct Investment (FDI): Celtic Tiger
 economy 14; corporate taxation 305; EU–US
 224; flows 74–7; integration 471–2; Lisbon
 Treaty (2009) 208; measurement 77–8;
 productivity 72; Single Market Program 64;
 by source region *78*
foreign-exchange reserves 85, 91
foreign shocks 92
formal principles, EU laws 478–9
Forouheshfar, Y. 95
Forslid, R. 65
fortress Europe 182–3 *see also* protectionism
France: agriculture 270, 271; deficits 25, 159;
 economic traditions 39; empty chair policy
 485–6; EMS initiative 45; government
 bond yields *373*; pay harmonization 289;
 post-colonial protectionism 240–1; Snake 30;
 trade with US 223
Francois, J. 229–30, 231
Francophone countries 240
Frankel, J. A. 11, 91, 190, 468
free movement: capital 46, 55, 64–5; goods 55;
 labor 55, 63–4; services 55

free trade agreements (FTA) 185, 212, 468
Free Trade Association of the Americas (FTAA)
 215
French franc 31–2, 41
Friberg, R. 87
frictions 140, 176
Friedman's rule 357
fringe trade relationships 200–2
functional integration 439–43
Furceri, D. 152

G20 meetings: euro area representation 91;
 London (2009) 212; Seoul (2010) 396
Gali, J. 144
GAMS 173
Garcia Bercero, Ignacio 234
Gasiorek, M. 16
Gaskell, S. 17
GATT 209–11
Gaudet, Michel 480
GDP: densely populated regions 13; euro area
 339–41, *359*; geography *13*; Great Recession
 (2009) 332, 339–41, *340*; monetary policy 132,
 139–40; Objective 1 funds 261; post-accession
 differences *12*; public debt ratios 381; Single
 Market 66; total trade exposure 11
GEMPACK 173
General Agreement for Tariffs and Trade (GATT)
 209
general equilibrium models 230
Generalized System of Preferences (GSP)
 212–13
Genscher, Hans-Dietrich 24, 32, 47
geographic expansion 196–7, *198*, 469
geopolitical approaches 85, 88, 247
Georgetown Agreement (1975) 240
German Constitutional Court 124–5, 127–8, 400,
 444
German–ECB alliance 392, 404
Germany: agriculture 270–1; attitude to colonial
 possessions 240; competitiveness 338; debt brake
 rule 115, 151; economic traditions 39; EMS
 initiative 45; EMU 29; equalization mechanism
 154; euro masterplan theories 25; excessive
 deficit procedures 159; financial cycle 415; fiscal
 councils 162; fiscal tightening (2011) 376;
 government bond yields *373*; Hartz reforms
 292; labor market reforms 402; paymaster euro
 area 393; role in monetary union 24–5, 34;
 social market economy 39; trade with US 222,
 223; unification 48; yield curve 314 *see also* West
 Germany
Gertler, M. 132
Ghosh, A. R. 388
Giannone, D. 358
Giavazzi, F. 421
Gibbons, S. 306

GIIPS countries 75–7, 409–10, 418 *see also* PIIGS countries
Gilbert, N. 421
Giovannini Group 312–13
Giscard d'Estaing, Valéry 30, 44, 92
Global Europe strategy (2006) 213
global financial crisis (GFC, 2008/09) 331–2, 333, 352, 411, 412
global free trade pact 215
global merchandise trade 206–7
global trade policy regime 205
Goldberg, L. S. 87, 88
Goldberg, P. K. 473
Gomes, Patrick Ignatius 244, 246
Gopinath, G. 87
Gorter, J. 259
Gourinchas, P.-O. 93
Gourmet case (ECJ, 2001) 490
'gouvernement économique' proposal 48
governance reforms 164, 459–62
government bonds 314, 334, *335*, 367 *see also* doom loop
government debt crises (2010–12) 160
governments: acting in self-interest 303; agriculture *272*; bankruptcy 158–9; direct taxation as a subsidiary prerogative 292; disciplining 412; fiscal councils 164–5; informational asymmetries 157–8; primacy of EU law 485; quality/absorptive capacity 263
gradual integration strategies 435, 440
grain production quotas 273–4
gravity coefficient 231
gravity model (Badinger and Breuss) 7–8
Great Depression 333
Great Recession (2009) 74, 75–7, 212, 332–3, 339, 382
Greece: bail-outs 345, 393, 393–4; bank lending 72; competitiveness 415; consumer consumption 72; crisis management 112; debt purchases 362; debt-to-GDP ratio *390*, 397; debt write-offs 150; deficit revision (2010) 145, 409, 416; deficits 160, 339; euro crisis 334; funding strike (2010) 360; Grexit 341; growth *387*; impact of EU membership 11; inequality/employment levels 290; institutional failure 261; interest rates 122; new government (2009) 360; new government (2015) 404; official debt 399; private debt holders 362, 397; public debt crisis 337; regional development 65; solvency 394–5, 397; sovereign spreads 360, *361*; troika programmes (2010–11) 362, 363, 397
Greenspan Put era (2002–07) 382
Grevena (Greece) 264
Grexit 341
Griever, W. L. 73
Gropp, R. 14
Gros, D. 423

groupe de rédaction 479–80
groupthink 104
growth: austerity 388; constraints 402; debt reduction 385, 393; euro area (2013) 401–2; fiscal multiplier 383–4; outlook (2010–16) *386*–7; Single Market 66; Structural Funds transfers 264 *see also* production efficiency
growth regressions 11
GSP programme 212–13
Guillain, R. 263
Gulati, M. 397, 401

Hague Summit (1969) 44
Hallands län (Sweden) 264
Hallstein, Walter 42, 480, 484
Hamilton, A. 23
Hammond, G. 151
Hanover European Summit (1988) 47
Harberger, A. 10
harmonization: corporate taxation 299, 300; direct taxation 299–302; government bonds yields 334; indirect taxation 296–9; Member State laws 487; pay non-discrimination 289; tax rates 307; welfare schemes 291
Harrison, G. 10
Hartz reforms (2003–05) 292, 402
hazard of trade *192, 193,* 203
Head, K. 181, 228, 231
health and safety 288
"health check" reform (CAP) 278
hegemonic stability 93–4
Helleiner, E. 85
Hellwig, C. 153
Henning, C. R. 394
Hess, W. 189
heterogeneity costs 165, 436–8, 443 *see also* integration
heterogeneous populations 436–7
HICP inflation *359*
High Authority 480, 485 *see also* European Commission
"holdouts" private creditors 397
home bias 73
home currency debt 92
Honohan, Patrick 22
Horioka, C. 472
"horizontal spillovers" 72
Horn, H. 61, 468
"hot money" volatile capital flows 75
House of Lords report (2014) 50
household debt 402 *see also* mortgages
household debt-to-disposable incomes *391*
household debt-to-income ratio 388, *390*
household disposable incomes 392
household loans 137–8
human capital 261–3
Hungary 163, 165

iceberg type frictions 176
idiosyncratic shocks 151–2
ifo Institute 230
illiquidity 401
Ilzkovitz, F. 10
IMF 27, 339, 383–4, 395, 400–1
immigration 17
imperfect markets 284
implicit guarantees 366
import quotas 60–1
import tariffs 225, 271
imports 17, 272, 297
'impossible triangle' 46
income diversification 70–1
income levels 11, *286*, 293
income shocks 70
India 216
indirect foreign exchange *86*
indirect taxation 296–9
industrial locations 13
industrial restructuring 63
inequality 290
inflation 35, 86, 122, *359*, 360
Information Exchange System (VIES) 298
insolvency 400, 401
institutional integration 442, 467–75
institutional quality 74, 261, 304
instrumental approaches 85, 88
insurance mechanisms 151–2, 166
integrated market, differential rates of regional growth 65
integration: functionalism 439–43; geographic expansion 469; gradualist strategies 435, 440; heterogeneity costs 436; history 4–6; index 11; internal market 39, 46; scale effects *62*; social policy framework 294; tax competition 296; trade barriers 210; trade duration 202–3; trade relationships 200, 209 *see also* economic integration; measures of integration
intellectual property rights 229
interbank market 104, 354
interest rates: 3-month Euribor 358–9; ECB imposed 122; Maastricht debt criteria 35; new loans to corporations *320*; PIIGS 334; reference 314; sovereign bonds 104, 401; spreads core-periphery countries 409–10 *see also* spreads
Interest and Royalty Directive (2003/49/EC) 300
intergovernmental cooperation 479
intergovernmentalism 342, 438–9, 439–40
intermediate goods 183–4
internal/external trade 57–8, 210
internal market 39, 46, 486–7
Internal Market Index 474
internal market law 487–90
internal revaluations 126–7
international competitiveness 285

international currencies 82–95; approaches 85, 87–8; benefits 92; costs 92–3; euro 83–5, 89–93; functions 82–3, 86, 87; market shares *83–4*; stability 93–5; theories 85–9
international debt 85, 92
international law 480, 481
international lender of last resort 93
international stability 93–5
international tax rates 305
international trade 7, 188–9, 444
interstate commerce (US) 293
intervention requirements, EMS 31
intra-Community marginal band 29
intra-European trade 8, 296–7, 377, *379*
investments 385, 418
investor protection 74
investor-state dispute settlement (ISDS) 234–5
Ireland: asymmetric external shocks 334; austerity-cum-official financing 397; credit boom 160, 415; deficits 339; economic growth 13–14; FDI 14, 65, 75; fiscal discipline 108; single interest rate 122; Snake 30; sovereign bonds risk 397, *398*; sovereign spreads 399; troika programmes 363
Issing, Otmar 34, 105
Italian Constitutional Court 483
Italy: adequacy of bailout 365; asymmetric external shocks 334; austerity 381; banks owning government debt 417–18; competitiveness 415; debt-to-GDP outlook *389*; ECB purchasing government bonds (2011) 367; fiscal multiplier 385; government bond yields *373*; growth outlook (2010–16) *387*; inequality/employment levels 290; Maastricht debt criteria 35; OMT effect on financing costs 371; political environment (2011) 365; productivity 402; trust-territory Somaliland 240

Japan 89, *210*, 213
Jayasekera, R. 472
Jenkins, Roy 30, 33, 44
Jensen, J.B. 174
job creation 261
Joint Supervisory Teams (ECB) 325–6
jointly-guaranteed debt 153, 165–6
'judicial activism' (ECJ) 482
Juncker, Jean-Claude 70, 238
junior debt "red" bonds 153

Kalemli-Ozcan, S. 72, 74, 77
Kanbur, R. 304, 305
Kang, J.-K. 73
Kashyap, A. K. 138
Kawai, M. 89
Keck case (ECJ, 1993) 487, 489
Keen, M. 303, 304, 305
Kenen, P. 336

Kennedy trade negotiations (GATT, 1962–7) 209
Kessler, M. 394
Keuschnigg, C. 304
Keynes, John Maynard 28, 121
Keynesian Concerted Action Plan (1978) 39
Keynesianism 39
Kirk, Ron 220
Kirshner, J. 85, 88, 91
Kleven, H. C. 303
Kling, G. 472
Knapp, Georg Friedrich 23
Knudsen, A. C. 271
Kohl, Helmut 34, 47, 442
Kohl, T. 468, 469
König, J. 474
Korea 213
Korsun, V. 74
Kortum, S. 173, 174
Kostial, K. 14
Krugman, P. 65, 82, 85, 173, 174
Kwan, C. H. 94

labor costs 122, 126–7, 338
labor markets 16, 233, 289–90
labor mobility 63–4, 108–9, 113, 293, 303–4
    see also migration
labor and social policies 284–94
labor taxation 304
Labour Party (UK) 16
Lagarde, Chistine 393
Lambsdorff, Otto Graf 31
Lamfalussy, Alexandre 34, 312
Landais, C. 303
Lane, P. R. 410, 421
language barriers 63, 67
Latin America 239
Latin Monetary Union (1865) 24
Le Gallo, J. 263
Le Monde 32
Le, V. P. M. 17
"leaderless" currency system 93
legacy assets doctrine 315–16, 324
legacy debts 404
legal terminology 480
legislative initiatives 485
legislative sclerosis 482, 486
legitimate coercion 437–8
Lehman Brothers 333, 354
Leibenstein, Harvey 61n9
Leigh, Daniel 383, 384, 385
lenders 138, 146
lenders of last resort 89, 124–5, 128, 339, 400–1, 417
lending standards 134–5, 137–8
Lenza, M. 358
"liberal peace" 444
liberalization 16, 26, 46, 230

limited integration scenarios 230
liquidity 89, 90, 93, 357
liquidity constraints 140
liquidity crisis 123
liquidity discounts 92
liquidity management currency 83
liquidity premium 92
liquidity risk 353, 357
Lisbon strategy 415–16 *see also* Treaty of Lisbon (2009)
Lithuania 73
Li, Y. 86–7
Ljungman, G. 149
loan demand, VAR model 135
Lockwood, B. 306
Lomé III (1985) 242
Lomé IV (1990) 242
Lomé Convention (1975) 212, 240, 241
London G20 summit (2009) 212
long-term economic objectives 42
"longer term refinancing operation," (LTROs) 356, 409
Loretz, S. 295
Lucas critique 46
Ludlow, P. 271
Luttini, E. 72
Luxembourg 34–5, 292, 480
Luxembourg Compromise (1966) 482, 486

M3, and bank loans 368, *369*
Maastricht Treaty (1992): background 32–6; chronology 5; euro area 105; fiscal rules 381, 392; monetary union 48; no-bailout clause 36; process 46–8; risk-sharing 352; subsidiarity 437
MacDougall, Sir Donald 44
macroeconomic adjustment program 146, 417
Macroeconomic Imbalance Procedure (MIP) 49, 128–9, 161, 409, 416, 419, 420–1
macroeconomic policies 39–40, 121
macro-imbalances crisis 337–9, *338*
MacSharry Reforms 274
Maddaloni, A. 140
Maggiori, M. 88
'maintenance period operation' (ECB) 355
maize prices 277n11
majority voting 486, 487
malfunctioning currency unions 25
Malta 75
Mann, Thomas 48
manufacturing sector tariffs 225, *226*
Marjolin, Robert 39, 41
market access 58–9, 226, 228, 490
market barriers 285, 289
market-based approaches 85, 87, 278
market confidence 367, 417
market discipline 416, 426
market distortions 284, 299

market integration 65, 473
market irrationality 401
market operation approaches 358 *see also* lenders of last resort
market segmentations 153
Marshall Plan 4
'Masters of the Treaty' 486
mathematical models 173
Matsui, A. 86–7
Matsuyama, K. 86
maturity transformation 353
Mavroidis, P. C. 216, 468
Mavromatis, K. 153
Mayer, M. 181
Mayer, T. 228, 231
means-of-exchange currency function 86
measures of integration: background 467–8; capital 472; classification 469–70; composite indicators 473–4; FDI 471–2; prices 473; trade 470–1 *see also* integration
medium-term budgetary framework (MTBF) 148–9
medium-term objectives (MTO) 147
mega-regional agreements 205
Melitz, M. J. 63, 173
Melitz model 173–4
Member States: harmonizing laws 487; as the 'Masters of the Treaty' 486; reaction to EU law 484–5; secondary law 486; secondary laws 482
Memorandum (Balladur, January 1988) 47
Memorandum (Genscher, February 1988) 47
Mergers Directive (90/434/EEC) 300
Merkel, Angela 35, 345, 380–1, 393, 395, 396, 400
Merkel-Sarkozy proposal (2010) 395–7
Mickelsson case (ECJ, 2009) 490
micro data sets 471
Midelfart-Knarvik, K. H. 259
Mieszkowski, P. 302
migration 64, 109, *110*, 113, 242 *see also* labor mobility
military forces 91
"minimal balance" deficit norm 144
minimum tax burden 299
Mintz, J. 304
Mion, G. 174
"mixed" agreements 239
mobile capital 302–3
mobility of tax bases 304, 307
Mody, A. 396
Moesen, W. 153
monetarists 48
'*Monetary capacity*' (SEA) 47
monetary channels 132–3
Monetary Committee (Treaty of Rome) 40
monetary cooperation 28

'Monetary and Financial Cooperation in the European Economic Community' (CEC, 1963) 42
monetary integration 22, 44, 46
monetary policy: credit channel 132–40; Friedman's rule 357; 'impossible triangle' 46; loss of control 92; price stability 357; risk-taking 138; shocks 87, 133, 135, 137, 139–40; sovereignty 108; supervision 315, 326; transmission 139–40, 141
monetary policy interest rates 132, 139, 140, 356–7, *358*
monetary power fragmentation 93–4
monetary rates 133, 138–9
monetary sovereignty 380
monetary union: 10-year review 408; banking union 106; booms and busts 122; capital market liberalization 26; deficit bias of fiscal policy 158; Delors Report 33, 105; EMU 48–9; exchange rate depreciation 113; German role 24–5, 34; interest rates 334; OCA theory 112; simplifying politics 26; sovereignty 106, 114; stalling (1970s) 44; third stage of common market (1966–9) 42; Werner Report (1970) 29
monetary vs. fiscal dominance concept 105
money 23–4
money markets 314, 354, 356
Mongelli, F. P. 474
Monnet, Jean 22, 28, 439, 440, 441–2, 479, 484
"Monsieur 3.0" (Theo Waigel) 34
moral hazard problem 72, 112, 146, 152, 165
Moravcsik, A. 438–9
Moreno-Cruz, J. 189, 191
mortgages 65, 392 *see also* household debt
most-favored nations (MFN) 6, 185, 212, 213
multilateral surveillance 159
multilateralism 215–16, 235–6, 444
multinational firms (MNEs) 223–4, 300, 305
multiple lending instruments (ESM) 146
multipolar systems 95
Mundell, R. 95, 336
mutual recognition principle 488–9

Nahuis, R. 259
Napoleon III 24
Nash-equilibrium 303
national administrative authorities 482
national central banks (NCBs) *see* central banks
national champion banks 314–15, 325
"national compartment" (SRF) 150
national constitutional law 481
national courts 484, 485
national debt 129, 165–6 *see also* sovereign debt
national economic boundaries 293
national external positions 415
national laws 483, 485
national moneys 23–4

national sovereignty: common resolution authority 108; economic objectives 44; EMU 423; foreign affairs 91; monetary union 106, 114; risk sharing 424; TTIP 234–5

national welfare 177–80 *see also* welfare

natural barriers 226

"negative lists," sovereignty 234

"negotiated" currencies 88

Neighborhood Policy 247

neoclassical growth model 72

net capital flows, euro area *419*

net trade 272–3

Netherlands: agriculture 271; austerity 381, 392; debt-to-GDP *389*; fiscal councils 162; fiscal multiplier 385; flexibility-oriented reforms 291; growth *386*; MTBF 148

network externalities 86

Neumark Report (1963) 297, 299

'new approach to harmonization' (EC) 488

new economic geography models 13

New Economic Governance (EMU) 342–4

new framework (2012–14) 370–2

new macroeconomics 333

'new quantitative trade models' (NQTMs) 173–86

'new trade theory' model (Krugman) 174

New Transatlantic Agenda (1995) 220

New World Economic Order 241

Nicomachean Ethics (Aristotle) 23

Nitsch, V. 189, 191, 474

"no bail-out" clause (TFEU Article 125): credibility 162; defaults 36; ESM violating 399–400; EU leaders ignoring 160; fiscal framework 143; Greece 362, 394; market discipline 426; overruling 343; rating agencies 334; restoring 167 *see also* Lisbon Treaty (2009)

nominal rate of assistance (NRA) 271, *272*, 277 *see also* agriculture

nominal stability 90–1

non-agricultural goods 206, 209

non-categorical indicators 469

non-crisis countries 112–13

non-democratic rulers 438

non-discriminatory obstacles to trade 487–8

non-European regional communities 248

non-exhaustive legitimate 'mandatory requirements' 488

non-financial corporations 368, *369*

'non-institutional' development (EMS) 45

non-reciprocal PTAs 212

non-standard interventions 356, 357, 358

non-tariff barriers (NTBs) 5, 16, 185–6, 226, 229

non-tariff measures (NTMs) 225–8, 229–30, 235

non-uniform indirect taxes 296

norms 444, 482

North-Atlantic Treaty Organization (NATO) 215

Northern countries 112, 122, 125–6, 181–2, 182–3, 264

NUTS3 recipient regions 266

Oates, W. E. 114, 295, 302

Obama, Barack 220

Objective 1 funding 259–66 *see also* regional policy

Obstfeld, M. 71

OECD 74, 77–8, 163, 225

off-balance sheet approaches 353, 371

official money 362, 397, 399

offshoring 304

Ohr, R. 474

Ohsawa model 304, 306

oilseeds production quotas 273–4

'One Market, One Money' (CEC, 1990) 48

Oort, Conrad 30

"open method of coordination" 288

Optimum Currency Area (OCA) 22, 104, 105–6, 108–14, 336

Ordnungspolitik economic policy 39

Organization for European Economic Cooperation (OEEC) 4

origin principle 297

"original sin" problem 92

Ottaviano, G. I. P. 63, 174, 185

output gap 381–2

Outright Monetary Transactions (OMT): Banking Union 324; IMF-style lending 400, 401; market testing 403; negative side effects 421–2; public debts backstop 104; 'whatever it takes' declaration 370–1, 400

outsourcing 304

Overman, H. G. 259, 306

overvalued currencies 93

Pacific EPA 244

Pacific Islands Forum (PIF) 246

Padoa-Schioppa, Tommaso 45, 358, 442

Papaioannou, E. 92

Papandreou, George 396

Pape, Elisabeth 238

Papua New Guinea (PNG) 244

parallel currency strategy 45, 48

Parchet, R. 306

Parent Subsidiary Directive (2003/123/EC) 300

"passage probability" 451

Paterson, I. 450, 451, 452

payment systems 314 *see also* TARGET2

Peersman, G. 358

pensions 64

peripheral banks 317, *318*, 366

peripheral countries 415

peripheral sovereign spreads 317, *318*, 371

Perotti, R. 144

Persson, M. 17, 189

Pessoa, J. P. 185
Peydró, J.-L. 140
Pfaffermayr, M. 306
Philippon, T. 153
PIIGS countries 334, 337, 338, 341, 345 *see also* GIIPS countries
Pill, H. 358
Pinto, B. 396
Pisani-Ferry, J. 261
Pittaluga, G. B. 87
Plato 129
Pöhl, Karl Otto 33, 47–8
Poland 71
policy cycles 149, 161, 342, *343*
policy interest rates 132, 139, 140, 356–7, *358*
policy processes 393
policy regime switch theory (Sargent) 105
political costs 129, 436–7
political dialogues 241, 242, 248
political economy 393, 435–44
political groups 271, 276, 341–2
political integration 129, 443
political union 95, 128–9, 443
Pompidou, George 28
Popov, A. 418
Portes, R. 86, 92
portfolio-choice model 87, 95
portfolio holdings 73
Portugal 75, 160, 339–41, 363, 397, 417–18
"positive lists," sovereignty 234
post-Cold War 242, 245
post-colonial era 239–41, 248
post-Cotonou negotiation process 238–9
post-Second World War: economic integration 4; policy objectives 288; urban–rural income gap 271
pound sterling 27, 88–9
poverty 272, 287
poverty-trap theory of development 264–6
power gradient (PG) 452
power indices 450–7
pre-accession agreements 191, 197–9
precautionary principle 226
pre-crisis regulatory systems 315
preferential integration 469
preferential trade agreements (PTAs) 212–13, 241
preliminary reference procedure 483–4
"prevention threshold" (RQMV) 462–3
preventive arms: MIP 421; SGP 411
price differentials 473
price stability 48, 357
price support 274
primary surpluses 383, *384*, 388
principal-agent framework 208
principal components analysis (PCA) 472
Pringle, Thomas 399

private creditors 362, 393–6, 397, 399, 401, 404
private debt burdens 388, *390*
private enforcement 482
private sector debt reduction 121
Private Sector Involvement (PSI) 35, 362
privileged subsidies 242
procedural rules 161
pro-cyclical capital flows 416
Prodi, Romano 35, 392
product variety 62–3
production efficiency 285, 288, 297 *see also* efficiency; growth
production quotas 273
productivity 66, 337
program evaluation 259
proportionality 457–9
protectionism: agriculture 270, 271; European project 440; Great Recession 212; NTBs 226–8; UK 16; US 182–3; world import tariffs 184
Prusa, T. J. 189
public debt: fiscal indiscipline 103; fiscal union 165–6; and growth 341
public debt crisis, 337
public debt ratios 144, *378*, 380, 381, 383–4
public debt-to-GDP ratio 382–3
public enforcement 482
public finance report (1977) 44
public finances 292, 383–4
public institutions *see* institutional quality
pyramid of trade preferences 213, *214*

Quad group of countries 211
qualified majority voting (QMV) 452–4, 462, *462, 463, 465–6*
quantitative easing (QE) 94, 327, 345
quantitative restrictions 487
quasi-constitutional treaty concepts 480

race to the bottom tax rates 296, 303
Rahbari, E. 425
rate-cut-cum-base-broadening reforms 300
rating agencies 334, 418
receiverships 425
"red" bonds 153
redenomination risk premium 317, *320*, 366
redistribution 154, 166, 292–3
Redoano, M. 306
referendums 14
refi rate cuts 372 *see also* interest rates
refinancing operations 409
regime change theory 106
regional communities 248
Regional Comprehensive Economic Partnership (RCEP) 205
regional development 65
regional funding *264*

regional policy 255–66; correcting imbalances 256; funding programs *257–8*; growth effects 258–9; research studies 259 *see also* Objective 1 funding
regional trade agreements (RTAs) 6, 205, 212–13, 215–16
regional transfers 264
regionalism 215
regression discontinuity design 259
regression estimates 382
regulations 285, 292–3
regulatory powers, ECB 35
Rehn, Olli 383–4, 397
Reinhart, C. M. 341, 404
Reinhart, V. 404
reserve currencies 27
resolution costs ("waterfall") 323
Resolution Fund 423
retail banking 314–15, 353
revenue maximizing governments 304
Reversed Qualified Majority Voting (RQMV) 419, 420, 421, 462–4
Rey, H. 86
Ribi, E. 304
risk aversion 412
risk of conflict 444
risk premiums 317, 394, 396, 397
risk sharing 70, 73, 316, 423–6
risk-taking 138
robust statistical models 183–5
Rodriguez, F. 467
Rodriguez-Clare, A. 174, 175, 181, 183–4, 185
Rodrik, D. 467
Roederer-Rynning, C. 278
Rogers, J. H. 473
Rogoff, K. 341, 404
Romer, D. 11
Ruding Report (1992) 299–300
Rueff, Jacques 22
rulebook (European Council) 321
Russia 213

Saez, E. 303
Sala-i-Martin, X. 259
Salvaticci, L. 228
Sampson, T. 185
sanctions 161
sanitary and phytosanitary measures (SPS) 226, 229
Sapir, A. 4, 8, 209, 214, 215, 216, 288, 468
Sargent, T. 22–3, 105
Sarkozy, Nicolas 35, 395
savings 71, 87, 121
Scandinavian welfare model 286–7, 290
scanner price data 473
Schadler, Susan 395
Schäuble, Wolfgang 396
Schiller, Karl 29
Schmidt, Helmut 30, 31, 44

Schoenmaker, D. 423
Schuldenbremse (debt brake) 34, 151
Schuman Plan (1950) 438, 479, 485
Schumpeterian argument 66
Schwarz, Hans Peter 34
search models 86–7
Second World War 4
secondary laws 482, 483, 486
Securities Markets Programme (SMP) 362, 367, 409
securitization 353
Seghezza, E. 87
Segre Report (1966) 312
seigniorage 92
self-fulfilling liquidity crises 123
'selling arrangements' concept 489
senior debt 153, 396
separation principle 356
Services Directive (2009) 55
Shapley-Shubik index (SSI) 450, 452
Shi, S. 86
short-term assistance (Barre Memorandum) 28
short-term interest rates 334
Silárszky, P. 452
Sims, Christopher 400
single currency proposal (Delors) 33
Single European Act 1986 (SEA) 5, 46–7, 486, 487
Single European Market (SEM) 297, 299
single farm payments (SFP) 276
Single Market 10, 66, 297
Single Market Act I and II 56
Single Market Program 55–66, 255
Single Market Scoreboard 474
Single Resolution Board (SRB) 150, 322
Single Resolution Fund (SRF) 150, 321, 323
Single Resolution Mechanism (SRM) 150, 321, 322–3, 325, 372, 422
Single Rulebook, bank resolution 322
Single Supervisory Mechanism (SSM) 115, 150, 321–2, 324–6, 372, 422
Sinn, H.-W. 307, 342
Six-Pack directives (2011) 106, 146–7, 342, 409, 419, 460–1
slack 61
Slovenia 163
Small Island Development States (SIDS) 246
Smets, F. 358
Smith, A. 63
"Snake" exchange rate agreement 30, 44
social expenditure 286
social insurance 304
social market economies 39
social-policy convergence 291
solvency crisis (2010–12) 360–9
Sørensen, B. E. 72, 73, 74
South Africa 245

Southern African Development Community (SADC) 244
Southern African EPAs 243
Southern European countries: bad equilibrium 125–6; effect of booms 122; EU transfers 264; fiscal consolidation 112; trade gains 181–2; US protectionism 183; Welfare State models 287
sovereign bond markets 353, 371, 418
sovereign debt: banks' exposure 120, 150, 324, 366–7, 371–2, 417–18; ECB as guarantor 128; underwriting 371 *see also* national debt
Sovereign Debt Crisis (2010–12): bank lending 72; and the euro crisis 413; flaws in the EMU 49; OCA theory 108, 113; timeline 351, 360–9, 363
sovereign default risks 334, *335*, 366
sovereign insolvency 425, 426
sovereign polity 437
sovereign risk 72, 418
sovereign spreads 360, *361*, *364*
sovereign stress 139–40
sovereign tensions 367
sovereignty *see* national sovereignty
Spain: asymmetric external shocks 334; bank rescues 321n14, 339; credit boom 415; doom loop 417–18; FDI inflows 75; financial crisis 365; fiscal discipline 108; government bonds 367, *373*; inequality and employment 290; interest rates 122; OMT 371; unsustainable booms 160
spatial econometric methods 304, 306
Spaventa, L. 421
special consumer taxes (excise duties) 299
Special Drawing Rights (SDR) 27, 83
speculative short future contracts 317, *320*
spending reductions 129
spreads: 10-year government bond rates 124, *125*; core-periphery countries 409–10; money market rates 354 *see also* interest rates
STABEX (Stabilization of Export Earnings) 241
Stability and Growth Pact (SGP): 2005 revision 106, 145; 2011–12 reforms 114, 146–7, 409; background 144; corrective arm 411; economic nonsense 392; and Fiscal Compact 115, 420; fiscal indiscipline 103; preventive arm 144, 411; public debts 113; Regulation 1466/97 144; Regulation 1467/97 145; surveillance framework 148; suspension 35
stability oriented policies 105
Stability Pact 34, 35, 159
Stability Programs 144, 411
stabilization: budgets 120–1, 124; OMT 371
State Theory of Money (Knapp) 23
states: formation 438; legitimacy 129; rescue programs 343–4
Statistical Levy case (ECJ, 1969) 487
statistical misreporting 162

statistical models: NQTM 173–4; robustness 183–5; trade gains 180–2
Stein, J. C. 138
Steinkamp, S. 396
stock market capitalization 313, *314*
Stoltenberg, Gerhard 47
store-of-value function, currencies 86, 87
Straathof, B. 58
Straffin, P. D. 450, 451
Strange, S. 88
strategic complements: tax rates 303; VAT rates 306
strategic interaction, tax rates 306
strategic orientation 247, 248
strategic substitutes, tax rates 303
Stresa conference (1958) 270
stress tests 322, 324, 422 *see also* asset quality review (AQR); banks
"strict conditionality" criterion (ESM) 146
Structural and Cohesion Funds (SCF) 255, *257–8*
structural creditors 4
Structural Funds Program 65, 259, 263, 266
Stufenplan (Tietmeyer) 28
Stulz R. M. 73
substitutability of currencies 94–5
successful integration 443
sugar quotas 278
Summers, Larry 397
summit meetings 104
supervision *see* banking supervision
supply-side-oriented approaches 39, 45–6
supranational actors, overestimation 440
supranational institutions, and national governments 439
supranational views of Europe 479
supremacy: ECJ 483; European norms 444
surveillance 49, 50
sustainable debt 392, 395, 397, 426
Sweden 87, 163, 165
Switzerland 34, 306
Swoboda, A. 85, 92
symmetric macroeconomic policies 125–7
synthetic counterfactuals methods 11
Synthetic Indicator of Financial Integration (SYNFINT) 472
SYSMIN (System for Stabilisation of Export Revenues in Minerals) 241
systemic financial crises 160, 167

Taglioni, D. 472
TARGET imbalances 104
TARGET2 314, 334n16, 367, *368*
tariffs: agriculture 271; Brexit 185–6; EU–US 225, *226*, 230–1; MFN partners 213; reduction 209; statistical models 176–7; TTIP 231; welfare 182, 184

tax competition 295–307; capital taxes 303; empirical evidence 305–6; harmonization 300; mobile capital 302–3; models 303; outcomes 295–6; theory 302–5

tax-and-subsidy programs 292–3

taxation: centralization 153–4; coordination 295, 307; destination principle 296–7; EC powers 129; harmonization 296–302; income stabilization 293; labor mobility 303; origin principle 297; policies 297, 300; rates 303–7; reaction functions 303

Taylor, A. M. 71

technical barriers to trade (TBT) 226, 229

teleological interpretations 480, 483

Templeton, Franklin 399

10-year government bond yields *373*

terms-of-trade 56–7

tertiary laws 483

Teufelskreis see doom loop

3-month Euribor 358–9

Tiebout, C. 302

Tietmeyer, Hans 28

Tille, C. 87

time-inconsistency problems 159, 164

timing assumptions 195

Tinbergen Committee (1953) 296, 297

Tokyo Round trade negotiations (1973–8) 209

"too-big-to-fail" problem (TBTF) 339

"top" currencies 88

'Towards a Genuine Economic and Monetary Union' (EC, 2012) 49

trade 173–86; contribution to welfare 180; creation 10, 56–8; defense measures 212; distortions 274; economic integration 6–9; EU–ACP relations 242, 248; EU membership 8; gains 180–2, 183–4; global trading 206–7; invoicing 87; manufactures 66–7; non-agricultural goods 206; non-discriminatory obstacles 487; product composition *207*

trade agreements *9*, 228, 231

trade barriers 209, 210

trade concentration index (UNCTAD) *111*

trade costs: currency union 9; economic integration 6–7, 189, 200–2; eliminating 56–7; EU–US 224–5, 230–1; multilateral agreements 235; new economic geography models 13; removing 59–60

trade disputes 215–16

trade diversion 56–8

trade duration 190, 191, *192*, 202–3

trade effects *9*, 58, 231

trade integration 10, 177–80, 443, 468–9, 470–1

trade liberalization 6, 9–10, 63, 212

trade negotiations 208, 228–9, 238–9

trade policies 173, 207–15

Trade Policy Committee (TPC) 208

trade relationships 189, 192–4, 200–3

Trade in Services Agreement (TISA) 216

trading partners 206–7, 213–14

transaction costs 85–6, 92

Transatlantic Economic Council (2007) 220

Transatlantic Economic Partnership (1998) 220

Trans-Atlantic Free Trade Area (TAFTA) 215

transatlantic trade 223–4

Transatlantic Trade and Investment Partnership (TTIP): market access 228; mega-regional agreements 205; negotiations 221; objective 220; regulatory issues 229; sovereignty 234–5; third country effects 235–6; trade effects 231 *see also* United States (US)

transfer intensity, and growth 265–6

transfer pricing 305

transfers 111–12, 293

Trans-Pacific Partnership (TPP) 205

Treaty of Athens (2003) 452–3

Treaty on the European Union (TEU): Article 3 295; Article 16 453–4

Treaty on the Functioning of the European Union (TFEU): Article 34 489–90; Article 122 394; Article 125 *see* "no-bail out" clause (TFEU Article 125); Article 127(6) 321; Article 149 288; Article 151 288; Article 153 288; supranational characteristics 479

Treaty of Lisbon (2009) 49, 208, 278 *see also* "no bail-out" clause (TFEU Article 125)

Treaty of Nice (2001) 208, 276

Treaty of Rome (1957): agriculture 270; basic economic principles 41; CCP 208, 209; colonial possessions 240; common market 40–1, 438; direct effect 481; direct effect of law 480–1; *droit communautaire* 480; European Commission 38; formation of EEC 4–5, 55; *groupe de rédaction* 479–80; pay harmonization 289; regional policy 256

Treaty on Stability, Coordination and Governance (TSCG) 108n11, 147–8, 149, 420

Trebesch, C. 397

Trichet, Jean-Claude 23, 35–6, 381, 396–7

Triffin dilemma 94

Triffin, Robert 26, 40, 41

troika programmes 345, 362, 363, 393, 397

Tulkens, H. 304

Turkey 457, 459

Two-Pack directives (2013) 106, 147, 149, 409, 420, *461*

UEMOA (Economic and Monetary Community of West African States) 240

UN COMTRADE database 188, 189–90

UN Millennium Development Goals 242

unanimous voting 454, 486

unconstrained discretionary fiscal policies 157–8

under-investment 418

unemployment 289–90, 341, 385
unemployment insurance 166, 286–7
unipolar systems 93, 95
United Kingdom (UK): Brexit impact on welfare
  16–17, 185–6; colonies 212, 240; Delors
  Committee 33; devaluation (1967) 27;
  economic traditions 39; fiscal councils 163;
  fiscal stimuli 383; House of Lords report (2014)
  50; implications of EU membership 14–18;
  rate-cut-cum-base-broadening reforms 300;
  Snake 30; trade with US 222; and US as
  economic power 88; welfare gains 17–18
United States of Europe 4, 479
United States (US): 19th century financial
  regulation 89; academic influences 39; Asian
  crisis (1997) 94; bailout US states (1840s) 394;
  and Britain as economic power 88; debt ratios
  391; equity investments 73; EU FDI 224; EU
  trade 222–4; "exorbitant privilege" (Giscard
  d'Estaing) 93; FDI in EU 224; fiscal councils
  163; fiscal stimuli 376, 383; geopolitical interests
  247; global financial crisis (2008) 91; household
  debt-to-disposable incomes *391*; interstate
  commerce 293; labor mobility 293; liquidity
  premium 92; market access 228–9; MFN
  partner 213; monetary hegemony 31; post-War
  of Independence policies 22–3; private debt
  burdens 388; protectionism 182–3; recovery
  (2009/10) 341; share of world GDP 90, *221*;
  social policy 286; structural creditor 4; subprime
  mortgage crisis (2007) 334, 353, 354; tariffs
  225–8; trade policy measures *210*; trade with
  EU 222–4; unemployment (2016) 341 *see also*
  Transatlantic Trade and Investment Partnership
  (TTIP)
unit-of-account currency functions 85
unprotected free trade relations 244
unsustainable debts 395
urban-rural income gap 271
Uruguay Round Agreement on Agriculture
  (URAA 1992) 274
Uruguay Round trade negotiations (1986–94)
  209, 211
US dollar 27, 84, 88–9, 91, 356

Van den Tempel Report (1970) 299
van Gend case (1963) 480–1, 482
Van Grasstek, C. 211
van Horen, N. 418
Van Reenen, J. 185
van Rompuy, Herman 49, 418
van Wincoop, E. 73, 87, 225
variables 190–1, 195
VAT 297, 298–9, 306
Vaubel, R. 114
vector autoregressive model (VAR) 135, 137, 139
vehicle currencies 86

Venables, A. J. 13, 63, 65
Verboven, F. 473
Verdict EMU-variants *424*
Verspagen, B. 259
"vertical spillovers" 72
Villegas-Sanchez, C. 74
Viner, Jacob 56, 235
Virmani, Arvind 395
volatility 75, 94–5
Volosovych, V. 72, 73, 472
von Ehrlich, M. 259, 260–1, 263–4, 266
von Hagen, J. 151
von Weizsäcker, J. 153
voting systems 450–4
voting weights 465–6

wages 64, 337
Waigel, Theo 34, 144
Wall Street Journal 393, 394–5
warehousing peripheral sovereign debt *365*
Warnock, F. E. 73, 92
Warnock, V. C. 92
Wassenaar agreement (1982) 291
weak governance 104
Wei, S.-J. 74
Weidmann, Jens 400
Weiler, J. H. H. 482, 484
welfare 70, 180, 182, 184, 200
welfare effects: Brexit 16–17, 185–6; customs
  union 56–7; factor mobility *64*; trade costs
  59–60; TTIP 231–3; UK entry into EEC
  14–16
welfare gains 16, 17–18, 73
welfare of savers 71
Welfare States 285–7, 290–3
welfare-triangle gains 10
Werner, Pierre 44
Werner Report (1970) 27–30, 43–4, 392
West Africa 240, 243
West Germany 8, 27, 270–1 *see also* Germany
Westermann, F. 396
Western countries: trade gains 181–2; US
  protectionism 182–3
'whatever it takes' pledge (Draghi, 2012) 317, 345,
  352, 370, 371, 400, 409
Wierts, P. 411
Wilander, F. 87
Wildasin, D. E. 303
Wilson, J. D. 302, 303, 304
Winner, H. 305, 306
'with-without' accession comparisons 11
Wolf, Martin 49
working conditions 288, 289
World Input-Output Database (WIOD) 181
World Monetary Conference (1867) 24
world trade 221, 402
World Trade Organization (WTO) 205, 215–16

Wu, Y. 74
Wu, Y.-T. 73
Wyplosz, C. 163, 416

X-inefficiency (Leibenstein) 61n10

Yaoundé Convention (1963) 212, 240
Yosha, O. 73

"you break it, you own it" union
425

Zdzienicka, A. 152
Zettelmeyer, J. 397
Zhu, Y. 73
Zodrow, G. R. 302
Zoellick, Robert 235

For Product Safety Concerns and Information please contact our EU
representative GPSR@taylorandfrancis.com Taylor & Francis Verlag GmbH,
Kaufingerstraße 24, 80331 München, Germany

Printed and bound by CPI Group (UK) Ltd, Croydon, CR0 4YY
08/05/2025
01864347-0005